CONTRACT LAW:
CASES AND MATERIALS

REFERENCE

AUSTRALIA
Law Book Co.
Sydney

CANADA AND USA
Carswell
Toronto

HONG KONG
Sweet & Maxwell Asia

NEW ZEALAND
Brookers
Wellington

SINGAPORE and MALAYSIA
Sweet & Maxwell Asia
Singapore and Kuala Lumpur

CONTRACT LAW: CASES AND MATERIALS

FIRST EDITION

By

GEOFFREY SAMUEL

LONDON
SWEET & MAXWELL
2007

First edition 2007

Published in 2007 by
Sweet & Maxwell Limited of 100 Avenue Road,
http://www.sweetandmaxwell.co.uk
Typeset by LBJ Typesetting Ltd of Kingsclere
Printed and bound in Great Britain by
Ashford Colour Press Ltd, Gosport, Hants.

No natural forests were destroyed to make this product;
only farmed timber was used and re-planted.

British Library Cataloguing in Publication Data

A CIP catalogue record for this book
is available from the British Library

ISBN 978-1-84703-216-4

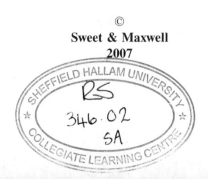

ABBREVIATIONS

AC	Appeal cases (Third Series)
AJCL	American Journal of Comparative Law
All ER	All England Law Reports (Butterworths & Co)
App Cas	Appeal Cases (Second Series)
BGB	Bürgerliches Gesetzbuch (German Civil Code)
C	Code of Justinian
CA	Court of Appeal
CC	Code civil (French Civil Code)
Ch	Chancery Division (Third Series)
Ch D	Chancery Division (Second Series)
CLJ	Cambridge Law Journal
CLP	Current Legal Problems
CLR	Commonwealth Law Reports
C&MT	G Samuel, *Cases and Materials on Torts* (Law Matters, 2006)
CUP	Cambridge University Press
D	Dalloz (also Digest of Justinian)
EHRR	European Human Rights Reports
ER	English Reports
FLR	Family Law Reports
G	Institutes of Gaius
HL	House of Lords
ICLQ	International and Comparative Law Quarterly
IECL	International Encyclopedia of Comparative Law
J	Institutes of Justinian/Justice (High Court)
JCL	The Journal of Comparative Law
JCP	Jurisclasseur périodique (La Semaine Juridique)
KB	King's Bench (Third Series)
LC	Lord Chancellor
LJ	Lord Justice (Court of Appeal)
LJCP	Law Journal Common Pleas
LJ Ex	Law Journal Exchequer
LJQB	Law Journal Queen's Bench
Ll Rep	Lloyd's List Law Reports
LQR	Law Quarterly Review
LR. . .CP	Common Pleas Cases (First Series)
LR. . .Eq	Equity Cases (First Series)
LR. . .Ex	Exchequer Cases (First Series)
LR. . .HL	English and Irish Appeals (First Series)
LR. . .QB	Queen's Bench Cases (First Series)

LS	Legal Studies
LT	Law Times Reports
MLR	Modern Law Review
NILQ	Northern Ireland Legal Quarterly
OJLS	Oxford Journal of Legal Studies
OUP	Oxford University Press
P	Probate Division (Third Series)
PC	Privy Council
PECL	Principles of European Contract Law
PETL	Principles of European Tort Law
PL	Public Law
QB	Queen's Bench (Third Series)
QBD	Queen's Bench (Second Series)
UC&TO	G Samuel, *Understanding Contractual and Tortious Obligations* (Law Matters, 2005)
WLR	Weekly Law Reports
ZEuP	Zeitschrift für Europäisches Privatrecht

DEDICATION

This casebook on contract is dedicated to Colin Turpin, Emeritus Reader in Law, University of Cambridge, whose lectures on Roman and on English contract law stimulated my career-long interest in the comparative law of obligations

PREFACE

This cases and materials book on contract follows the same pattern, and has the same didactic aims and objectives, as my *Cases and Materials on Torts* published last year by LawMatters. That is to say it is deliberately very modest in its size and is designed to act as bridge between lectures and library (or Internet) research. It is not designed as a portable library comprehensive enough to guarantee in itself success in university contract exams. This modesty of size means that the reader will find in this collection reference to only a tiny fraction of the vast amount of material published, since Roman times, on the notion and function of contract. This said, the book will, it is hoped, provide a solid conceptual and functional overview of contract through the words of some of those who have fashioned this most central of legal subjects.

As with the tort book, two specific characteristics might be associated with this casebook. The first is the European and comparative orientation. In fact contract as a notion can really be understood only if its civilian roots are fully appreciated, for most commentators accept that a general theory of contract was imported into the common law from Continental learning and practice. This Continental dimension has been re-stimulated with the publication of the *Principles of European Contract Law*, and this tentative EU code will be used not just to give the present casebook some of its structure but equally as an alternative model of contract thinking. The second characteristic is an emphasis on legal method. It is no doubt tempting to think that knowledge of contract law is about absorbing a detailed model of rules and applying this model to factual situations in a syllogistic way. The judgments extracted in this book ought to indicate that matters are far more complex. Different methodological approaches often produce different solutions, with the result that knowledge of contract law is in part a knowledge of differing methodological schemes. This, of course, is what helps make contract, still largely based on precedent, such a rewarding topic (and one with a rich history).

Many thanks to my Sorbonne colleague and friend Pierre Legrand for providing me, directly and indirectly, with a number of the ideas, questions and problems to be found in the chapters that follow. A week teaching with Steve Smith and his colleagues at the University of McGill was equally invaluable, and Steve's challenging ideas provoked much reflection. Many thanks also to Jeremy Stein for his support in respect of these casebooks and to the Sweet and Maxwell editorial team. And then of course there is my wife, Jennifer, who this year had to endure my computer (as well as me) as a summer holiday companion in France. I much appreciate her enormous and loving support.

Geoffrey Samuel
Kent Law School
July 2007

ACKNOWLEDGMENTS

Grateful acknowledgement is made to the following authors and publishers for permission to quote from their works:

Atias, Christian: *Épistémologie juridique* (Presses Universitaires de France, 1985), p.129 (translation Geoffrey Samuel). © PUF, 1985

Collins, Hugh: *The Law of Contract* (4th edn, Butterworths, 2003), pp.1, 9, 18. Reproduced by permission of Cambridge University Press.

Dworkin, Ronald: *Law's Empire* (Fontana, 1986), p.229. Reprinted by permission of the publisher from LAW'S EMPIRE by Ronald Dworkin, Cambridge, Mass.: The Belknap Press of Harvard University Press, Copyright © 1986 by Ronald Dworkin

Giliker, Paula: "Unifying European Contract Law: Identifying a European Pre-contractual Obligation to Inform" in John Bell and Claire Kilpatrick (eds), *Cambridge Yearbook on European Legal Studies 2004–5* (Hart Publishing, 2006), pp.135, 154, 155–6

Gordley, J: "Contract in Pre-commercial Societies and in Western History" in *International Encyclopedia of Comparative Law*, Vol.VII, Ch.2. Reproduced by permission of BRILL NV

Heil v Hedges [1951] 1 T.L.R. 512, KBD. © The Times/NI Syndication

Jolowicz, HF: *Lectures on Jurisprudence* (The Athlone Press, 1963), pp.379–380. Reproduced by kind permission of Continuum International Publishing Group

Jones, Gareth H and Schlechtriem, Peter: "Breach of Contract" in *International Encyclopedia of Comparative Law*, Vol.VII, Ch.15. Reproduced by permission of BRILL NV

Kahn-Freund, O: "Introduction". From: *The Institutions of Private Law and Their Social Functions*, Karl Renner, © 1949, Routledge & Kegan Paul, pp.5–6, 28, 39. Reproduced by permission of Taylor & Francis Books UK.

Turpin, Colin: "Public Contracts" in *International Encyclopedia of Comparative Law*, Vol.VII, Ch.4. Reproduced by permission of BRILL NV

Van Caenegem, RC: "History of European Civil Procedure" in *International Encyclopedia of Comparative Law*, Vol.XVI, Ch.2. Reproduced by permission of BRILL NV

Von Mehren, AT: "A General View of Contract" in *International Encyclopedia of Comparative Law*, Vol.VII, Ch.1. Reproduced by permission of BRILL NV

Waddams, Stephen: *Dimensions of Private Law: Categories and Concepts in Anglo-American Legal Reasoning* (Cambridge University Press, 2003), pp.165, 225–226

Weir, Tony: "Complex Liabilities" in *International Encyclopedia of Comparative Law*, Vol.XI, Ch.12, p.5. Reproduced by permission of BRILL NV

Wightman, John: *Contract: A Critical Commentary* (Pluto Press, 1996), p.37

Grateful acknowledgement is also made to The Incorporated Council of Law Reporting for England and Wales and LexisNexis Butterworths for permission to quote from a number of their works.

While every care has been taken to establish and acknowledge copyright, and contact the copyright owners, the publishers tender their apologies for any accidental infringement. They would be pleased to come to a suitable arrangement with the rightful owners in each case.

CONTENTS

TABLE OF CASES

TABLE OF STATUES

1 General introduction

The purpose of this first chapter is to set out the background characteristics to the law of contract and to try to give a definition to the term. Given its long history, which goes back to Roman law, it is tempting to think that fashioning a suitable definition would pose relatively few problems; yet the exercise is not as easy as it might at first seem. Certainly one can appeal to broad propositions such as legally enforceable agreements or promises. But the case law soon suggests that the idea is more complex. Much depends upon the scheme of analysis adopted, and thus it will probably be useful to think in terms of both a conceptual (what is a contract?) and a functional (what does contract law do?) definition. What cannot be denied is that contract is a central area to both the ancient and the modern law of Europe. It is one of the first legal domains to attract translational codification.

1.1 Definitional considerations

It might be useful to begin with some attempts at defining the law of contract. As will be seen, the subject seemingly forms part of a greater whole, and thus this whole will need to be considered as well.

1.1.1 Some preliminary definitions

In this first subsection some general definitions will be given. If nothing else, they may help to orientate the newcomer to this area of the law.

Civil Code of Québec (official translation)

"**1378.** A contract is an agreement of wills by which one or several persons obligate themselves to one or several other persons to perform a prestation."

Academy of European Private Lawyers European Contract Code

"*Article 1: Notion*

1. A contract is the agreement of two or more parties to establish, regulate, alter or extinguish a legal relationship between the said parties. It can also produce obligations or other effects on only one of the parties.

1

> 2. Except as provided for in the following provisions, a contract can also be created by concluding acts or omissions, following a previous statement of intent or according to custom or good faith."

NOTE

The above definitions are from the civil law (Continental) legal tradition. The following extracts are taken from English law sources.

Aris v Orchard (1861) 30 L.J. Exch. 21, Exch

> **Wilde B.:** ". . . There can be no contract until there is a final and mutual assent; an agreement of the minds of the parties, upon the same terms. When that assent has taken place, and no matter what may have taken place before, there is a contract; and a cause of action on that contract then and there arises . . ."

Preston v Luck (1884) 27 Ch. D. 497, Ch D

> **Kay J.:** ". . . A contract means consensus ad idem. Lord Westbury, than whom very few people had greater command of language, puts it thus in the case of *Chinnock v Marchioness of Ely* (4 D. J. & S. 638, 643): "An agreement is the result of the mutual assent of two parties to certain terms, and if it be clear that there is no *consensus*, what may have been written or said becomes immaterial." If I may respectfully say so, I concur in every word of that definition, and think it as good a definition of contract as I know of . . ."

NOTE

It may be that these definitions are too abstract; as we shall see, English contract law is based more on promise rather than agreement (see **4.1**). Perhaps contract should be defined in terms of its formal requirements, as the next extract indicates.

Rose and Frank Co v JR Crompton and Bros Ltd **[1923] 2 K.B. 261, CA**

> **Atkin L.J.:** ". . . To create a contract there must be a common intention of the parties to enter into legal obligations, mutually communicated expressly or impliedly. Such an intention ordinarily will be inferred when parties enter into an agreement which in other respects conforms to the rules of law as to the formation of contracts. It may be negatived impliedly by the nature of the agreed promise or promises, as in the case of offer and acceptance of hospitality, or of some agreements made in the course of family life between members of a family as in *Balfour v Balfour* ([1919] 2 K.B. 571) . . ."

NOTE

Nevertheless, there has been an attempt to codify a definition of contract in English law.

Contract Code (drawn up on behalf of the Law Commission)

"1 Definition of contract

A contract is an agreement between two or more persons which the law recognises as creating, altering or extinguishing legal rights and duties.

2 Agreements which are contracts

Every agreement is a contract except where—

  (a) the terms of the agreement are too uncertain,
  (b) the persons making the agreement do not intend to be legally bound by it, or
  (c) the agreement lacks the necessary formal characteristics."

1.1.2 Contract and the law of obligations

As is evident from the above extracts, the "whole" of which contract forms a part is the law of obligations.

Percy v Church of Scotland **[2006] 2 A.C. 28 HL(S)**

Lord Hope: ". . . 109. According to Stair's classification, the law of contract belongs to the law of obligations. An obligation is a legal tie, whereby the debtor may be obliged to pay or perform something by his own consent and engagement: Stair, *Institutions of the Law of Scotland*, I.1.22. As *Gloag on Contract* (2nd edn. (1929), p.8 puts it, a contract is an agreement constituted by an offer and an acceptance which creates, or is intended to create, a legal obligation between the parties to it. The agreement must, as Gloag accepts later on the same page, be concerned with matters of which the courts will take cognisance. An agreement for purely social purposes is not capable of being enforced by any legal process. As a general rule, where the agreement is with a voluntary association such as a church, some patrimonial interest must be involved before a court will accept that it has jurisdiction to enforce it. Where there is such an interest, the court will provide a legal remedy . . ."

NOTES

  1. This piece of judgment is of course referring to Scots law, but a similar analysis has been applied to English law.

  2. In *The Halley* (1867), Sir Robert Phillimore said that an "Obligatio is (according to the admirable definition in the Institutes) 'vinculum juris quo necessitate astringimur alicujus rei solvendæ;' it is 'lien de droit,' as the French say" (at p.15). This idea of a "legal chain" (*vinculum juris*) is a fundamental metaphor in the civil law for a contractual obligation.

Moschi v Lep Air Services Ltd [1973] A.C. 331, HL

Lord Diplock: "The law of contract is part of the law of obligations. The English law of obligations is about their sources and the remedies which the court can grant to the obligee for a failure by the obligor to perform his obligation voluntarily. Obligations which are performed voluntarily require no intervention by a court of law. They do not give rise to any cause of action.

English law is thus concerned with contracts as a source of obligations. The basic principle which the law of contract seeks to enforce is that a person who makes a promise to another ought to keep his promise. This basic principle is subject to an historical exception that English law does not give the promisee a remedy for the failure by a promisor to perform his promise unless either the promise was made in a particular form, e.g., under seal, or the promisee in return promises to do something for the promisor which he would not otherwise be obliged to do, i.e., gives consideration for the promise . . .

Each promise that a promisor makes to a promisee by entering into a contract with him creates an obligation to perform it owed by the promisor as obligor to the promisee as obligee. If he does not do so voluntarily there are two kinds of remedies which the court can grant to the promisee. It can compel the obligor to pay to the obligee a sum of money to compensate him for the loss that he has sustained as a result of the obligee's failure to perform his obligation. This is the remedy at common law in damages for breach of contract. But there are some kinds of obligation which the court is able to compel the obligor actually to perform. In some cases . . . a remedy to compel performance by a decree of specific performance or by injunction is also available. It was formerly obtainable only in a *court of* equity . . . But, since a court of common law could make and enforce orders for payment of a sum of money, where the obligation was itself an obligation to pay a sum of money, even a court of common law could compel the obligor to perform it . . ."

NOTES

1. *Law of obligations*. Lord Diplock does not directly define the law of contract but he goes far in setting it within its conceptual and institutional context. First, he states that contract is part of the law of obligations. This will make little sense to anyone who has not studied Roman law, since the idea of a law of obligations is one of the great inheritances from Rome. The Romans recognised two basic kinds of legal relations or, to use today's language, legal rights: there were the legal relations between person and thing which formed the foundation of the law of property, and which were in later civil law called rights *in rem*; and there were relations between person and person, or rights in personam. Very generally one can describe this distinction as one between "owning" and "owing", the law of obligations regulating the situations when one person must pay money or transfer property to another or carry out a service.

2. *Promise*. A second noteworthy point is that Lord Diplock states that the law of contract is about enforceable *promises*. This is noteworthy because in the legal systems based on Roman law (the civil law tradition) a contract is founded upon *agreement* rather than promise. Does this distinction matter? Arguably it does, because it helps explain several key aspects of English contract law, two of which are the requirement of consideration and the absence of any general theory of mistake. Consideration attaches to a promise and not to an agreement, and differentiates those promises that will be enforceable at common law (as opposed to equity) from those that are not (but see below). If contract were to be based upon a meeting of two minds (agreement) then logically a mistake would act as an obstacle to the agreement, for the minds cannot meet. If, however, it is based on promise, it does not necessarily follow that a mistake will act as an obstacle to the formation of a contract. It may affect the validity, but it is still feasible to say that a promise can be objectively valid even if made under a mistake. See further **4.1**.

3. *Promise under seal*. A third observation made by Lord Diplock is that a promise, even without consideration, will be legally enforceable if made under seal. This is a form that goes back to the very early days of the common law and was a hangover from the old writ of covenant. Promises under seal have in form been abolished by statute and replaced by a written, signed and witnessed deed procedure (Law of Property (Miscellaneous Provisions) Act 1989, s.1).

4. *Remedies (1): debt and damages*. Another important point noted by Lord Diplock is the distinction between two types of remedy at common law to enforce a contract. At common law (as opposed to equity), a contracting party can bring an action (claim) to compel the other party to perform his promise under a contract where that promise is one to pay a specific sum of money. This is a claim in debt and is descended from the old writ of debt (one of the earliest writs) (see **11.2**). Another, quite different, remedy at common law is an action for compensation—an action for damages—brought by a contracting party who has suffered damage resulting from the other party's breach of promise (see **11.3**). As we shall see, debt and damages are very different claims (see **Chapter 11**).

5. *Remedies (2): equitable remedies*. Debt and damages are remedies that issued out of the common law courts. The Court of Chancery fashioned, in addition, a range of other remedies relevant to contract. The one mentioned by Lord Diplock is specific performance in equity, whereby the Lord Chancellor could force a contractor to perform his promise; thus equity can, for example, compel a seller to convey to a buyer the property that forms the subject-matter of a contract of sale, but only if damages would be an inadequate remedy (which it always is where land is the object of the sale) (see 12.1). Other important equitable remedies are injunction, rescission, rectification and account of profits (see **Chapters 11–12**).

5

1.1.3 Contract in the civil law

Given that the whole notion of contract comes from Roman law, it might be valuable to look in more detail at how Roman and later civil lawyers defined a contract.

René-Marie Rampelberg, *Repères romains pour le droit européen des contrats* (LGDJ, 2005), pp.25, 26 (translation Geoffrey Samuel)

"The notion itself of 'contract' was of little interest to the Romans, who focused for much of their time on the specific types of transaction. These arose out of set forms, out of the handing over of a thing or out of an entry into an account book or, again, they were purely consensual. However their approach, which evolved over time, was very rich and coherent . . .

The term *contractum*, formed out of *contrahere*, 'to contract' in the general sense of the word (an illness), was not at first a technical term. Legally, *contrahere* meant to assume a liability, even a non-contractual one . . .

However in the first century AD, Sextus Pedius, known only through Paul and Ulpian (D.2.14.1.3), formally expressed the idea that to undertake an obligation implied an agreement between the parties, a *conventio*. Thus there is no contract, be it verbis or *litteris*, which does not have an agreement, the expression of the consent of the parties . . . Pedius asserted that even the *actum* of the *stipulatio* would be valueless in the absence of consent."

NOTE

It has to be stressed that the Romans never developed a general theory of contract. They thought in terms only of a law of contracts. Nevertheless they recognised that the word *contractum* meant an obligation between two people giving rise to an obligation on both sides (D.50.16.19). Their major contribution, as the next extract indicates, consisted not just in recognising the importance of *contractum* and *convention*.

Digest of Roman Law* Book 44, Title 7 *(De obligationis et actionibus)

"**1. GAIUS**. Obligations arise out of contract (*ex contractu*), out of wrongs (*ex maleficio*) or from some special legal connection (*ius*) arising out of various causes. 1. Obligations *ex contractu* are contracted by the transfer of a thing (*re*), by words or by consent. . . .

2. GAIUS. Consent (*consensus*) makes obligations in purchase and sale, letting and hiring, partnership, mandate. 1. Accordingly, we say that an obligation is contracted by consent in these forms of contract because neither words nor writing in any special form is required, but it is sufficient for those who conduct negotiations to agree. . . . 3. Likewise in these contracts one person is obligated to another with regard to this, that one person with respect to the other ought to perform in accordance with fairness and equity.

> **3. PAUL**. The substance of obligations does not consist in making some tangible thing (*corpus*) or servitude ours, but in binding another person to give, to do or to perform something for us. . . ."

NOTE

In addition to *convention* (agreement), one finds the expressions *consensus* (consent) and *ex contractu* (the idea of an obligation arising out of contract). These three elements—that is to say contract (as a category), *conventio* and *consensus*—provided the building blocks for the later, post 11th-century civil lawyers gradually to construct a general theory of contract. At first this development was hampered by a clear statement in the Roman sources (which were rediscovered in Italy in the 11th century and treated as absolute authority by the medieval jurists) that "no obligation arose out of a bare pact" (D.2.14.7.4). This was taken to mean, by the medieval Roman law specialists, that *conventio* and *consensus* were not enough in themselves to create a binding contractual obligation; there had to be some "clothing", that is to say a *causa*, which meant a transactional foundation (sale, hire, stipulation, etc.) (D.2.14.7.4).

René-Marie Rampelberg, *Repères romains pour le droit européen des contrats* (LGDJ, 2005), 68 (translation Geoffrey Samuel)

> "In France the *Parlements* [courts] of the second half of the 16th century fully recognised the obligation born out of simple consent and very quickly this was followed by doctrine [academic writing]. Dumoulin asserted that 'from a bare pact an action is born' and that the coming together of consent sufficed to gives rise to the agreement. In 1608, Loysel, in his *Institutes coutumières*, said that all contracts are obligatory as a result of the simple effect of the promise, even a non solemn one. The principle was fully triumphant in the 17th and 18th centuries with Domat and Pothier . . ."

NOTE

Just how the later jurists overcame the technicalities to be found in the Roman sources is explained in the next extract.

Reinhard Zimmermann, 'Roman Law and the Harmonisation of Private Law in Europe' in A. Hartkamp *et al.* (eds), *Towards a European Civil Code* (3rd edn, Kluwer/Ara Aequi Libri, 2004), pp.28–29 (footnotes omitted)

> "The *Corpus Juris* . . . presented, in this as in many other areas, a somewhat patchy picture, marked by haphazard distinctions and internal inconsistencies. However a trend had become apparent, that was to set the tone for the ever-increasing erosion, and ultimate abandonment, of the principle *ex nudo pacto non oritur action* [from a bare pact no action arises]. This development was propelled, in the first place, by the Canon lawyers who had charitably, as could be expected

of them, taken pity on the poor and naked pacts; and thus we find in the Decretals of Pope Gregory IX a sentence which was to have far-reaching consequences: *pacta quantumcunque nuda servanda sunt*—the direct root of our expression *pacta sunt servanda* [agreements must be kept]. But international commercial practice also played its role in the development; and many an author took his inspiration from the supposedly Germanic concept of good faith on which Tacitus had mused without much appreciation. Thereafter, from the 17th century onwards, the Natural lawyers made it their business to fashion a single dress pattern for all pacts. The binding nature of all agreements was, for them, an essential tool for the regulation of human affairs; all the more so since even God would be acting against his nature were he not to keep his word. At the same time the lawyers of the *usus modernus* finally overcame, for all practical purposes, the dogma of the non-actionablity of the naked pact . . .”

NOTE

The direct authority of Roman law was to be ended in France with the coming into force of the French *Code civil*.

Code civil (1804)

“**Art 1101**. A contract is an agreement by which one or more persons obligate themselves toward one or more others to give, to do or not to do something.

Art 1102. A contract is synallagmatic or bilateral when the contracting parties obligate themselves reciprocally toward each other.

Art 1103. It is unilateral when one or more persons are obligated toward one or more others without there being an engagement on the part of the latter.

Art 1104. It is commutative when each one of the parties engages to give or to do a thing which is regarded as the equivalent to what is given to or done for him.
  When the equivalent consists of the chance of gain or loss for each one of the parties according to an uncertain event, the contract is aleatory.

Art 1105. A gratuitous contract (*contrat à titre gratuit*) is one in which one of the parties procures for the other a purely gratuitous advantage.

Art 1106. A contract for valuable consideration (à titre onereux) is one which obliges each one of the parties to give or to do something.

Art 1107. Contracts, whether they have a name of their own or not, are subject to general rules, which are the subject of the present Title.
  Particular rules for certain contracts are established under the Titles relating to each of them; and the particular rules for commercial transactions are established by the laws relating to commerce.

Art 1108. Four conditions are essential for the validity of an agreement:

The consent of the party who binds himself;
His capacity to contract;
An object certain which forms the subject-matter of the engagement;
A licit *cause* in the obligation

. . .

Art 1134. Agreements legally made take the place of legislation for those who make them.

They may be revoked only be mutual consent or for causes which the law authorizes.

They must be performed in good faith."

NOTE

The French Civil Code represents the culmination of the history of contractual obligations, from the Roman law of contracts to a general theory of contract based on agreement (*convention*) and consent (*consensus*). Indeed this general theory looks even precocious for its time (although the idea is to be found in Domat, a 17th-century jurist); contract, says art.1134, is a form of private legislation, although some later codes specifically or implicitly rejected this contract as legislation thesis. Some of the less abstract Roman characteristics have, however, not completely disappeared from this code of 1804: thus *causa* remains a requirement (art.1108) and, as will be indicated later, actual types of contract (named contracts) still remain an essential characteristic of the modern codes.

Principles of European contract law

"*Article 2:101* Conditions for the conclusion of a contract

(1) A contract is concluded if

    (a) the parties intend to be legally bound, and
    (b) they reach a sufficient agreement without any further requirement.

(2) A contract need not be concluded or evidenced in writing nor is it subject to any other requirement as to form. The contract may be proved by any means, including witnesses.

Article 2:102 Intention

The intention of a party to be legally bound by contract is to be determined from the party's statements or conduct as they were reasonably understood by the other party.

9

Article 2:103 Sufficient agreement

(1) There is sufficient agreement if the terms:

   (a) have been sufficiently defined by the parties so that the contract can be enforced, or

   (b) can be determined under these Principles.

(2) However, if one of the parties refuses to conclude a contract unless the parties have agreed on some specific matter, there is no contract unless agreement on that matter has been reached.

   . . .

Article 2:211 Contracts not concluded through offer and acceptance

The rules in this section apply with appropriate adaptions even though the process of conclusion of a contract cannot be analysed into offer and acceptance."

NOTE

The PECL continue to be based upon the theory of *conventio* and *consensus*.

1.1.4 Contract in the common law

When one turns to the common law, one can find similar definition ideas about contract.

Ditcham v Worrall (1880) 5 C.P.D. 410, CPD Div C

Lord Coleridge C.J.: ". . . In order to ground an action, the promise must be mutual; it must be an agreement, an *aggregatio mentium*, to the same terms at the same time; the promise of each being the consideration for the promise of the other. So that here there must have been an actual present fresh promise to marry one another on the day when, having promised years ago, the woman is asked to fix the day on which the promise is to be fulfilled, and fixes it accordingly. Pothier, again, says that for a binding contract there must be consent of contracting parties, capacity to contract, *a thing certain* to form the subject of the contract, and that the contract must be legal. So that the *thing certain* here was, I must presume, not the day which was uncertain before, which it was important to render certain, and which was rendered certain by the contract, but the marriage itself which had been already certain, as far as promises could make it so, for many years past . . ."

Foster v Wheeler **(1887) 36 Ch. D. 695, Ch D**

Kekewich J.: ". . . Definitions of 'contract' are to be found in the text-books, and I have consulted several of them, including an American one, that of Mr *Parsons*. They are all founded on, and many of them simply adopt, the definition given by *Pothier* in part I, ch 1, sec 1, of his work on Contracts. This is his definition, which I take from the English translation of Mr *WD Evans*: 'An agreement by which two parties reciprocally promise and engage, or one of them singly promises and engages to the other to give some particular thing, or to do or abstain from doing some particular act.' Mr *Pollock's* definition in his work on the same subject slightly differs from this, and is, in my opinion, more complete and more accurate. He defines a contract, or rather an agreement, to be 'an act in the law whereby two or more persons declare their consent as to any act or thing to be done or forborne by some or one of those persons for the use of the others or other of them;' and in commenting on this definition he explains what is intended by an act in the law, saying that it must be on the face of the matter capable of having legal effect and concerned with duties and rights which can be dealt with by a Court of Justice . . ."

NOTE

Care must, however, be taken before assuming that the English definition of contract is simply taken from Pothier. In fact, as we shall see, the history of the contract in the common law turns out to be very different from the history of contract in the civil law tradition.

K. Zweigert and H. Kötz, *An Introduction to Comparative Law* (2nd edn, OUP, 1992), p.353 (translation T Weir)

"The essence and function of the obligational contract has received much more thoughtful attention in the Common Law and in the Scandinavian systems . . . than in other legal families. For the Common Law the essence of contract lies not in the simple fact of agreement but in the 'promise' expressed by the parties in the contract. Thus the American Restatement (Second) of Contracts (1981) has the following definition in § 1: 'A contract is a promise or a set of promises for the breach of which the law gives a remedy, or the performance of which the law in some way recognises as a duty.' ROSCOE POUND found in the Common Law seven theories which attempt to explain why contractual promises are enforceable: (1) a will-theory, that the legal order is implementing the promisor's intention to be bound; (2) a theory that genuine intentions must carry some external guarantee; (3) the theory that breach of promise is delictual in character; (4) the theory that promises are binding only if some counterprestation is provided . . . ; (5) the theory of the sanctity of promises: promises are enforced because they are intrinsically sacrosanct; (6) the theory that reliance on promises must have some legal backing; (7) the theory that promises are enforceable only if they are part of a 'bargain'. POUND himself clearly inclines to the sixth of these theories and rejects the 'moribund requirement of consideration'. Whatever the value of these different theories may be, one certainly comes closer to the essence and function of contract if one sees its legal enforceability as based on 'promise rather than on 'agreement', as is the view in Continental systems . . .""

NOTES AND QUESTIONS

1. This excellent paragraph (which does not appear in the third edition of the book) from two German comparative lawyers is valuable not just in the way it summarises all the main theories of contract in common law doctrine, but also in the distinction it identifies between promise and agreement. This distinction will be considered in detail below (**1.3**). With regard to the various theories outlined above, it might be useful to test them against the cases extracted in the pages and chapters that follow. Is it valuable to think in terms of a single theory, or do all of the theories set out above have some relevance?

2. One theory worth emphasising immediately is number (3) in the extract above. The idea that a breach of contract is "delictual" in character offers several important insights into English contract law. First, the theory certainly reflects an historical truism: the action for breach of promise can be traced back through the action of *assumpsit* to the old writ of trespass, which is the foundational writ for our law of torts (delicts). Failing to do what one had promised to do was eventually actionable as a "trespass" (see Weir (1992) 66 *Tulane Law Review* 1615, at 1638–9). Secondly, breach of contract (i.e. breach of promise) is a cause of action in itself; in terms of actionability, then, all that needs to be shown is damage, breach and causation in order to succeed in a claim for damages. This contrasts with the law of tort where there is no such general notion of a "breach of tortious obligation". In order to succeed a claimant must establish a specific tort, such as trespass, nuisance, defamation or negligence.

3. Thirdly, the frontier between breach of contract and tort is not a clear and precise one, in as much as many breaches of contract can also be torts. Thus where the breach of contract consists in failing to take care (Supply of Goods and Services Act 1982, s.13) (below, at p.381) such a breach might equally amount to a tort (*Henderson v Merrett Syndicates Ltd* (1995)). In addition, the tort of negligence can "fill the gaps" in the law of contract, and so where there is a relationship "close to contract" this relationship might be enough in itself to establish a duty of care in tort (*Hedley Byrne & Co v Heller & Partners Ltd* (1964) (below, at p.234); *White v Jones* (1995)). When considering the domain of contract, one has to include within this domain aspects of the law of tort (see, e.g., *The Albazero* (1977)).

1.1.5 Functional definitions of contract

The difference between a formal and a functional definition is that the latter puts the emphasis on what contract *does*. As the next extract indicates, this approach to contract started to replace the older, often civilian-orientated, formal definitions during the 20th century.

A.T. von Mehren, "A General View of Contract" in International Encyclopedia of Comparative Law, Vol.VII, Ch.1 (footnotes omitted)

"21 . . . In the nineteenth and early twentieth centuries, both adherents of the principle of private autonomy and adherents of the planning principle commonly explained the enforcement of contracts from the perspective of the individual parties in terms of a will theory. Contracts were thought to result from the orders or commands by which individuals regulated their own affairs . . .

25 . . . Towards the end of the last century [i.e. the 19th century], the foregoing explanations of contract enforcement began to be complemented or replaced by explanations in terms of economic purpose and social function. Adherents of the principle of private autonomy are now less prone to describe contract as a manifestation of will and more prone to speak of it as a means by which a society without pervasive central planning can elicit and discipline the myriad of discrete decisions required to allocate and distribute resources . . .

. . . Legal obligations are no longer said to exist simply because they are subjectively assumed, but because of the social and economic consequences that these obligations carry with them . . .

In part, this change in the explanation given for contract enforcement represents the revival of the idea that one cannot talk about what the law is without discussing the purpose which it is designed to serve . . ."

QUESTION

What do you think this purpose is?

Hugh Collins, *The Law of Contract* (4th edn, Butterworths, 2003), pp.1, 9, 18

"The law of contract states the fundamental legal rules governing market transactions. In most societies markets serve as the principal mechanism for the production and distribution of wealth. This part of the law reveals some of the basic organising principles of their economic arrangements. It describes the elementary regulation of such key economic institutions as sale of goods, employment relations, arrangements for credit, and the provision of professional services. Individuals enter these market transactions for a variety of motives. The

13

law of contract supports these practices by making transactions legally enforceable, but at the same time it places restraints on conduct, shapes the types of
obligations which can be created, and limits the extent to which the parties may
enforce their agreement by means of self-help or coercion from legal institutions
. . .

How, therefore, should we conceive the law of contract today? It comprises those
rules, standards and doctrines which serve to channel, control, and regulate the
social practices which we can loosely describe as market transactions . . .

. . . An interpretation of these legal ground-rules setting standards of behaviour
during market transactions provides a representation of the scheme of distributive
justice embedded in the market order. A fresh interpretation of those legal
standards,. . . can claim in a sense to amount to a reconstruction of the market
order itself. By altering our system of thought, thereby facilitating a new
understanding of the economic sphere of social life, we can restate the legal
doctrines, which in turn will serve to consolidate this new vision of the market
order and its favoured distributive outcomes . . ."

QUESTIONS

1. Do you think that the 17th century jurist Domat, who (re)stated many of the
   fundamental principles of contract, thought that he was stating "the fundamental legal rules governing market transactions"?

2. Is Collins' idea of the "market transaction" really much of an advance on the
   old Roman view of contracts arising from different *causae*?

3. To what extent should contract rules reflect economic ideas? Should all judges
   have training in economics?

1.1.6 Policy and functionalism in contract

One way in which social and economic fact can make itself felt in legal reasoning in
contract cases is through recourse to policy arguments. However, the question that
needs to be asked is whether the gap between formal rules and functionalism is really
bridged by recourse to policy.

Barclays Bank v O'Brien **[1992] 3 W.L.R. 593, CA; [1994] 1 A.C. 180, HL**

(For facts, see p.297.)

Scott L.J. (Court of Appeal): ". . . These authorities seem to me to leave the
developing law, if not at the crossroads, at least at the junction of two diverging
roads . . . The choice between the two roads cannot, in my opinion, be made

simply by reference to binding authority. Binding authority can be found to justify either. The choice should, I think, be a matter of policy. Ought the law to treat married women who provide security for their husband's debts, and others in an analogous position, as requiring special protection? The position of married women today, both generally and vis-à-vis their husbands is very different from what it was . . . But . . . in the culturally and ethnically mixed community in which we live, the degree of emancipation of women is uneven."

Lord Browne-Wilkinson (House of Lords): ". . . On the other hand, it is important to keep a sense of balance in approaching these cases. It is easy to allow sympathy for the wife who is threatened with the loss of her home at the suit of a rich bank to obscure an important public interest viz, the need to ensure that the wealth currently tied up in the matrimonial home does not become economically sterile. If the rights secured to wives by the law renders vulnerable loans granted on the security of matrimonial homes, institutions will be unwilling to accept such security, thereby reducing the flow of loan capital to business enterprises. It is therefore essential that a law designed to protect the vulnerable does not render the matrimonial home unacceptable as security to financial institutions."

QUESTION

Should contract law be about *rights* rather than *policy*?

1.1.7 Contract and interests

Another way of approaching contract from a functional position is to look at the interests it protects. This becomes particularly attractive if one subscribes to the theory that legal "rights" are nothing more than legally protected "interests".

Beswick v Beswick **[1966] Ch. 538, CA**

(For facts, see p.23.)

Lord Denning M.R.: ". . . The general rule undoubtedly is that 'no third person can sue, or be sued, on a contract to which he is not a party'; but at bottom that is only a rule of procedure. It goes to the form of remedy, not to the underlying right. Where a contract is made for the benefit of a third person who has a legitimate interest to enforce it, it can be enforced by the third party in the name of the contracting party or jointly with him or, if he refuses to join, by adding him as a defendant. In that sense, and it is a very real sense, the third person has a right arising by way of contract. He has an interest which will be protected by law . . . It is different when a third person has no legitimate interest, as when . . . he is seeking to rely, not on any right given to him by the contract, but on an exemption clause . . ."

15

QUESTIONS

1. Imagine (i) that this statement by Lord Denning is good law (but see the House of Lords decision in *Beswick*, below at p.23, and cf. the Contracts (Rights of Third Parties) Act 1999, at p.392), and (ii) that in *Goodwill v British Pregnancy Advisory Service* (1996) (read in the law report, or in C&MT, p.33) the man who had had the vasectomy had had it done under a contract with a private clinic (rather than an NHS one). Would you allow the woman claimant to sue the clinic in contract?

2. Does contract protect expectation interests? (Cf. *Ruxley Electronics v Forsyth* **(1996)**, below at p.442.)

Blackpool & Fylde Aero Club Ltd v Blackpool BC **[1990] 1 W.L.R. 1195, CA**

(For facts, see p.177.)

Bingham L.J.: ". . . [I]f he submits a conforming tender before the deadline he is entitled, not as a matter of mere expectation but of contractual right, to be sure that his tender will after the deadline be opened and considered . . . Had the club, before tendering, inquired of the council whether it could rely on any timely and conforming tender being considered along with others, I feel quite sure that the answer would have been 'of course'. The law would, I think, be defective if it did not give effect to that."

QUESTION

Is the interest in this case (see p.177) very different from the claimant's interest in *Goodwill* (C&MT, p.33)?

1.2 Historical considerations

One of the differences between the civil and the common law is that common lawyers have not, since the 11th century, thought in terms of a category of contract. In the civil law the idea of a contractual obligation is to be found in the Roman materials which acted as the basis for Continental legal thought. There has always, in other words, been a law of contract(s). But in England, lawyers, before the 19th century, thought largely in terms of forms of action.

J. Gordley, "Contract in Pre-commercial Societies and in Western History" in *International Encyclopedia of Comparative Law,* **Vol.VII, Ch.2 (footnotes omitted)**

"22. *Roman jurists and English judges.*—Much of the story will concern the interaction between Roman law and English common law. The ancient Roman jurists and the medieval and early modern English judges had one characteristic in common. They were intensely practical. They were not interested in theoretical consistency but in arriving at sound results.

One difference, however, was that the Roman jurists were not judges. They gave learned and highly prestigious opinions but did not decide actual cases. . . . The judges were primarily concerned with doing justice to the parties before them. Stating the law was secondary. Many points that the Romans would pursue through endless hypotheticals could be left unsettled.

Another difference was that the Roman jurists addressed questions of substantive law without enmeshing them in questions of procedure. The English judges did not, in part because originally Common Law courts were not courts of general jurisdiction but heard only those cases brought before them by the King's writ. To receive a remedy the plaintiff had to fit his case within one of the forms of action on which he could bring a writ. Common Law became organised around writs rather than around types of obligations such as contract or tort. Thus even in the late 18th century, English judges did not think in terms of a law of contract. They thought in terms of forms of action such as *assumpsit* and covenant.

Beginning in the late 18th century, this traditional structure changed dramatically. English law ceased to be the exclusive concern of judges and barristers. Beginning with *Blackstone*, it became a university subject . . . The first treatise on contract law, written by *Powell* in 1790, was followed by a stream of others.

Moreover, the forms of action were abolished by statute. Supposedly, English judges still gave the plaintiff a remedy only when the traditional forms of action would have entitled him to receive one. But the treatise writers and eventually the judges came to think in terms of a law of contract rather than of covenant and *assumpsit*. They tried to give this law an intellectual coherence that it has previously lacked. They did so, in part, by trying to sharpen the statement of English law they found in the cases. They did so also by borrowing ideas from continental lawbooks, either to clarify a traditional rule or to solve a problem that the Common Law judges had not addressed. . . . By the end of the 19th century . . . the Common Law had acquired a new doctrinal structure largely by borrowing from the continent . . ."

NOTES

1. See also the extracts in **11.1.2**.

2. By the end of the 19th century England had a substantive law of contract. However, it is also important to appreciate that the old system of forms of action, rigid in many ways, was also flexible in that it allowed judges to develop utilitarian reasoning techniques, as the next extract indicates.

Michael Lobban, *The Common Law and English Jurisprudence 1760–1850* **(OUP, 1991), pp.68, 69, 70, 77, 78–9**

"In common law theory, the lawful claim of a right depended on the correct following of procedures from the outset, and in theory, the first step in the process was the obtaining of an original writ, to secure the defendant's appearance in court . . . In essence . . . the writ was a demand to 'do justice', a justice undefined. By the eighteenth century, the original writ was in practice insignificant and usually fictitious . . . However, it remained the theoretical grounding of any case.

More importantly, the plaintiff had to choose the correct form of action and make the claim conformable to the writ. In theory, the common law had a remedy for every conceivable wrong, and it was a maxim that there was no right without a remedy. In practice, however, remedies were constrained by the forms of action available. By the eighteenth century, the commonest forms of action were trespass and case, the former alleging direct injuries, the latter consequential harms . . . Not every wrong . . . had a remedy: there were *damna sine injuria* for which the law gave no redress if the plaintiff could not find the legal remedy which ascribed particular guilt and responsibility to the chosen defendant . . .

The system . . . depended upon precise claims and counterclaims by the parties . . . There had to be a clear foundation for a verdict; and it was a cardinal rule that a jury could not find anything contrary to the record, nor could it find anything not set out upon the record. In its finding, the jury was not guided by an abstract rule, but by the case presented to it.

. . . According to the theory, rules came later, inferred from cases and principles, and rules and decisions could be influenced by all manner of 'sources of law', provided that the law obeyed its own forms. The pleas did not decide the law, but only defined the fact at dispute, leaving the court to rule whether the wrong was illegal, from all manner of sources. This view of the common law explains how the courts could function by taking as their sources of law such questions as policy or expedience, as well as precedent and past rules. In a sense, the courts could make utilitarian adjudications in cases, acting flexibly with a view to particular justice, since the question to be decided had already been well-defined . . . The law was no abstract set of defined guides and rules: it was a flexible system of adjudication responding to society's problems. The science of pleading had two functions: first, it defined the point to be adjudicated; and second, it produced a legal point that could act as a precedent. As we shall see, the first was more important than the second, for the second was not a *rule* but evidence of what judges had done in the past, and hence one reason why judges should adjudicate in like manner again."

NOTE

This dichotomy between form and reasoning flexibility is of the utmost importance in understanding how the English law of contract functions in the courts. This point will be developed in the next chapter.

18

1.3 Domain of contract

It is one thing to say that contract is about enforceable promises or agreements, but another thing to say just what sets of facts fall within the category of contract. What makes this factual exercise even more difficult is that certain facts which may not display an enforceable contact may nevertheless generate a remedy. For example, the statement made in *Hopkins v Tanqueray* (1854) (see p.141) was deemed not to be a contractual promise, but this does not mean that such a statement will never attract a remedy in equity or in tort (see **5.2**). Contract thus has to be placed within its conceptual and its empirical contexts.

1.3.1 General considerations

The conceptual context concerns the boundaries between the law of contract and other areas of law such as tort, restitution, property and public law. Equity is particularly difficult in this respect in that it is both an independent foundational subject and a body of rules much of which is integrated into other areas such as property and contract. One focal point where this independence and integration meet is remedies: equity often acts within contract via the granting of, say, specific performance or rescission (see **Chapter 12**). The empirical context involves facts that strictly fall outside contract and yet may be subject to rules that are often taught in contract courses. The following extract gives a general overview.

Bernard Rudden, "The Domain of Contract" in D. Harris and D. Tallon (eds), *Contract Law Today: Anglo-French Comparisons* (OUP, 1989), pp.81, 89 (footnotes omitted)

"19. It is deceptively easy to describe the heartland of contract, but its frontiers are very hard to map save by the use of a priori assumptions. There are numerous reasons for this difficulty. One is the fact that the law of delict may occasionally stray beyond its primary function of compensating losses caused by actions in order to protect expectations. The testamentary beneficiary cheated of his legacy by an erasure of the will (D.9.2.41pr.) or by the testator's lawyers may compel the tortfeasor to provide the expected benefit. (And perhaps a similar function is performed by systems which order him to cover the victim's 'loss of a chance'.) Similarly, notions of restitution may lead the law to insist that a person enriched should pay for it. The overlap of both these categories with that of contract is the subject of many exhaustive and perceptive studies, and it seems unnecessary to rehearse the details of the lawsuits and their commentaries yet again.

The laws of tort and of restitution flourish where there is no relevant contract at all. They may also, however, operate 'paracontractually' where the particular contract fails either *in limine* or at some later stage. Further, there are some cases where, since different categories produce exactly the same result as would a contract, it does not matter to a Common lawyer what label is given to the situation. Atiyah suggests the example of someone who boards a bus consciously and deliberately intending not to pay. Whether we call the fare damages for trespass to the bus, restitution for the ride, or the price in a contract (consent to which is not merely fictional but blatantly false), the result is the same: he has to pay . . .”

NOTE

Professor Rudden goes on to describe two domain areas of difficulty: pre-contractual and post-contractual situations. These areas will be considered in more detail in **Chapter 8** and in subsequent parts of the book. But it might be useful at this preliminary stage to indicate some of the main focal points of difficulty with respect to the boundaries between contract and other areas of the law.

1.3.2 Contract and tort

The frontier between contract and tort is of major importance for several reasons. The same set of facts may disclose both a contractual and a tortious obligation. A set of facts may seemingly disclose an absence of an enforceable contractual obligation (for example in a pre- or a post-contractual situation) but the existence of a tort (see *Hedley Byrne v Heller & Partners* (1964), below at p.234). A recent example of this latter situation is to be found in the next extract.

Lennon v Commissioner of Police of the Metropolis **[2004] 1 W.L.R. 2594, CA**

This was an action for damages by a police officer against the defendant's force which had handled the arrangements for the claimant's transfer from the defendant's force to another force. The officer who arranged the transfer (Mrs Bewley) had assured the claimant that his entitlement to a housing allowance would not be affected if he took time off before the move. Accordingly the claimant took time off; but it transpired that the unpaid leave did constitute a break in his service and the claimant thus lost the valuable housing allowance. A claim in negligence was upheld by the Court of Appeal (Ward, Mummery and Rix L.JJ.).

> **Mummery L.J.:** "1. The issue in this appeal is whether a duty of care was owed in respect of pure economic loss flowing from a failure to give advice. The parties were in a non-contractual relationship akin to that of employment. The claimant contended that he suffered financial loss as the result of a breach of duty to give him advice; that the duty situation arose from an express voluntary assumption of responsibility for handling specific transfer arrangements and continued entitlement to service allowances after transfer; and that he relied upon the defendant to perform, with due care and skill, the responsibility which was undertaken.

2. The claimant is a serving police officer pursuing a complaint of continuing economic loss against the Commissioner of Police of the Metropolis (the Commissioner). The case rests on the vicarious liability of the Commissioner for the handling of the arrangements for the transfer of the claimant to another force and for the failure of the Commissioner's staff to give advice to the claimant about the preservation of his housing allowance entitlement . . .

6. . . . He was unable to sue the Commissioner for breach of contract, as a member of a police force does not have a contract of employment: at common law he acts as an officer of the Crown and as a public servant who carries out his duties by virtue of his office as a constable . . .

24. [Counsel for the defendant's] main criticism was that the judge's decision broke new ground and that it involved a radical departure from the existing law. I do not agree. No new category of duty situation is created by the decision. The particular facts found by the judge bring the case within the *Hedley Byrne* principle, as applied in later decisions of the highest authority. It is now well established that liability in tort for pure economic loss can arise from the negligent carrying out of a task undertaken pursuant to an express voluntary assumption of responsibility, on which the claimant has relied. In those circumstances it is unnecessary for the court to consider specifically whether it would be fair, just or reasonable to impose a duty of care. The test laid down for the existence of a duty has already been passed by judicial decisions admitting such cases to the category of recognised duty situations: see *Henderson's* case [1995] 2 AC 145, 181D, per Lord Goff . . .

28. In my judgment, Mrs Bewley expressly assumed responsibility in a particular transaction, namely the transfer of Mr Lennon from the MPS to the RUC, for giving advice to Mr Lennon in relation to a particular type of loss, namely the loss of the housing allowance, which he had expressly raised with her. Although she was not a professional person or a professional adviser, she occupied a managerial position in the MPS. She had, or had access to, special complex knowledge concerning the effect of transfers on service allowances of that kind. She led Mr Lennon to believe that he could leave it to her and rely on her to be responsible for handling the arrangements. She did not tell him, as she could easily have done if the matter was outside her area of responsibility, to seek advice elsewhere, such as the Police Federation. Those features of the case were sufficient to attract the duty to give him advice in respect of the very type of loss about which he had expressed his concern to her and which he actually suffered as a result of her failure to advise him of the implications of completing the Form No 8485 by inserting 11 January 1999 as his leaving date . . ."

NOTES

1. This case is based on the precedent of *Hedley Byrne v Heller & Partners* (1964), which can be found in C&MT, p 115, and below at p.234. One might note that the *Hedley Byrne* case was one "close to contract", in as much as the

relationship between claimant and defendant would have been contractual but for the absence of consideration. In the *Lennon* case the relationship (employment) was very close to contract (see para.6 of Mummery L.J.'s judgment) and thus is an almost perfect example of tort playing a "contractual" role.

2. *Hedley Byrne* established that a person suffering loss as a result of another's misstatement could sue if two conditions were fulfilled: there had to be an *undertaking* by the defendant to apply its skill; and there had to be a *reliance* by the claimant on the statement and the skill. These two conditions were clearly fulfilled in *Lennon*. However, there is a general presumption in the tort of negligence that a person suffering pure economic loss cannot sue in negligence because normally there is no duty of care (or, put another way, the economic interest is not strongly protected in the tort of negligence) (C&MT, pp.137–141; UC&TO, pp.111–114). There are, of course, exceptions (*Hedley Byrne* being one), but this so-called economic loss rule does not apply in contract. In other words, the economic interest is strongly protected in contract. And it must be remembered that in any contract of service there is an implied promise that the person supplying the service will take care (Supply of Goods and Services Act 1982, s.13).

QUESTIONS

1. What if there is no actual reliance by the claimant and no actual statement. Is a claim in tort bound to fail? (See *White v Jones* (1995) (C&MT, p.260).

2. What if a third party encourages another person not to perform her contractual obligation? (Cf. *OBG Ltd v Allan* (2007).)

3. What is the difference between a contractual and a tortious fact situation?

Tony Weir, "Complex Liabilities" in *International Encyclopedia of Comparative Law,* Vol.XI, Ch.12, p.5

6. ". . . Human good, for which the law exists, depends on the maintenance and development of human goods—life, health, property and wealth, *inter alia*. To ensure their maintenance we have the law of tort, and to promote their development we have the law of contract. Contract is productive, tort law protective. In other words, tortfeasors are typically liable for making things worse, contractors for not making them better. The distinction can be obscured by saying that the man who makes things worse is also not making it better, or even that damage to a thing is simply damage to the expectation that it would continue undamaged, but in general there is a perceptible difference between the complaint that things are worse than they were and the complaint that things are not as good as they should have been. Because contractors are typically employed or retained by those who want to benefit from them, the typical contractual claim

is in respect of the non-provision of the contemplated benefit. This may, indeed, take a physical form—one's chickens die because the electricity fails—but typically it takes an economic form—one is simply worse off by reason of the non-performance of the promise to make one better off . . . Accordingly, it is characteristic of contractual claims to be brought in respect of economic harm while it is characteristic of tort claims to be concerned with physical harm . . ."

QUESTION

Did the clinic in *Goodwill v British Pregnancy Advisory Service* (1996) (read in the law report, or in C&MT, p.33) undertake to make things better?

1.3.3 Contract and property

In Roman law there was a very sharp distinction between obligation (contract) and property relations (UC&TO, pp.3–4). For example, contract could not in itself transfer the ownership in a thing sold; there had to be a separate conveyance of the thing. Modern civilians talk in terms of a fundamental distinction between real rights (*jura in rem*) and personal rights (*jura in personam*). In English law the distinction is much more ambiguous.

Beswick v Beswick **[1966] Ch. 538, CA; [1968] A.C. 58, HL**

Lord Guest (House of Lords): My Lords, by agreement, dated March 14, 1962, the late Peter Beswick assigned to Joseph Beswick his business as coal merchant in consideration of Joseph employing Peter as a consultant for the remainder of his life at a weekly salary of £6.10s.0d. For the like consideration Joseph, in the event of Peter's death, agreed to pay his widow an annuity charged on the business at the rate of £5 per week. Peter Beswick died on November 3, 1963, and the respondent is the administratrix of his estate. She claims in these proceedings personally and as administratrix of her late husband against Joseph Beswick the appellant for specific performance of the agreement and for payment of the annuity . . ."

Lord Denning M.R. (Court of Appeal): ". . . Section 56(1) of the Law of Property Act 1925 says that:

'A person may take an immediate or other interest in land or other property, or the benefit of any condition, right of entry, covenant or agreement over or respecting land or other property, although he may not be named as a party to the conveyance or other instrument and by section 205(1)(xx) "Property" includes any thing in action, and any interest in real or personal property.'

Apply that section to this case. The promise of the nephew to pay the widow £5 a week was a 'thing in action': for the simple reason that it could be enforced by action, namely, an action by the contracting party. This section says, as clearly as can be, that the widow can take the benefit of the agreement, although she is not named as a party to it. Seeing that she is to take the benefit of it, she must be able to sue for it, if not by herself alone, at least jointly with the contracting party. Otherwise the section is made of no effect. *Ubi jus, ibi remedium*. If there was, therefore, any doubt as to her ability to sue at common law or equity, that doubt is removed by this section. I adhere, therefore, to the view which I expressed on this section in *Smith and Snipes Hall Farm v River Douglas Catchment Board* and *Drive Yourself Hire Co (London) Ltd v Strutt*: and I am fortified by the judgment which Danckwerts L.J. is about to deliver . . .." (See also p.15.)

Danckwerts L.J. (Court of Appeal): ". . . The definition of 'property' in section 205(1)(xx) 'includes any thing in action, and any interest in real or personal property'. The section replaces section 5 of the Real Property Act 1845 and applies to personal as well as real property. The Act of 1845 only applied to real property, and presumably there was some intelligible object in the extension. The new section obviously cannot be confined to covenants running with the land. Why should the section not be taken to mean what it says? There really is no ambiguity. The section says that 'A person may take . . . the benefit of . . . any agreement over or respecting land or other property, although he may not be named as a party to the conveyance or other instrument'. The section seems to have come as a shock to conventional lawyers who could not believe their eyes, but the section does say that a person not a party can take the benefit of a contract. Faced with the unexpected and unfamiliar there has been a tendency to take a timorous view of the provisions of this section . . .."

Lord Guest (House of Lords): ". . . It may be that the draftsman in incorporating the wide definition of 'property' into section 56 had overlooked the result which it would have on the effect of this section by extending it beyond its predecessor. I am constrained to hold that if section 56 is to replace the previous law in section 5 of the Act of 1845, this can only be done by limiting the word 'property' in section 56 to real property and thereby excluding the wide definition of 'property' contained in section 205(1)(xx). The result is that the respondent has, in my view, no right to sue on the agreement of 14th March 1962 in her individual capacity . . .."

NOTES

1. This case, although now to some extent rendered obsolete by statute (Contracts (Rights of Third Parties) Act 1999 (below, p.392), remains of interest conceptually in as much as it shows: (a) the importance of the law of remedies in contract; (b) the role of equitable principles in contract; (c) the difficulty of discerning the boundary between property and contract (debt being a form of property); and (d) the willingness of the judges to abandon on

occasions both logic and a strict literal approach to statutory interpretation (cf. Danckwerts L.J.).

2. In the civil law systems the law of property is governed by the Roman model, which basically subdivided property into three sub-categories: (i) ownership; (ii) possession; and (iii) rights in another's property. However, the common law is different, as Professor Lawson has pointed out:

"[T]he Common Law systems differ radically from the Civil Law. Thus, although the distinction between real and personal rights is perfectly well understood by Common Law lawyers, its various applications are thought of as belonging not to property law but to the law of remedies, including the law of insolvency; and the much discussed question whether the beneficiary of a trust has a real or only a personal right is of little more than academic significance. Moreover, such personal claims arising out of contracts as debts are, along with industrial property such as patents, treated as property under the generic term of choses in action. Again, the relativity of most titles to things, and the frequent co-existence of interests in them, make it unprofitable to pay much attention to ownership . . ." (Lawson, "Structural Variations in Property Law: Comparative Conclusion", IECL, Vol.VI, Ch. 2, Pt. VIII, para.274.)

QUESTIONS

1. Is the House of Lords' decision in *Beswick* an example of the courts ignoring the actual words of a statute?

2. Are obligations property? If so, can one own a debt?

3. Are all rights forms of property?

4. From a law of actions viewpoint, did the plaintiff succeed in her debt claim? (Cf. **12.1.2.**)

5. In a sale of goods contract, is it the contract that acts as the means of conveying ownership in the goods from seller to buyer? (See next extract.)

Sale of Goods Act 1979 (c 54)

"**16. Goods must be ascertained**
 Subject to section (20A) below where there is a contract for the sale of unascertained goods no property in the goods is transferred to the buyer unless and until the goods are ascertained.
17. Property passes when intended to pass
 (1) Where there is a contract for the sale of specific or ascertained goods the property in them is transferred to the buyer at such time as the parties to the contract intend it to be transferred. . . .

25

18. Rules for ascertaining intention

Unless a different intention appears, the following are rules for ascertaining the intention of the parties as to the time at which the property in the goods is to pass to the buyer.

Rule 1.—Where there is an unconditional contract for the sale of specific goods in a deliverable state the property in the goods passes to the buyer when the contract is made, and it is immaterial whether the time of payment or the time of delivery, or both, be postponed. . . .

20. Passing of risk

(1) Unless otherwise agreed, the goods remain at the seller's risk until the property in them is transferred to the buyer, but when the property in them is transferred to the buyer the goods are at the buyer's risk whether delivery has been made or not.

. . .

(4) In the case where the buyer deals as a consumer [. . .] subsections (1) to (3) above must be ignored and the goods remain at the seller's risk until they are delivered to the consumer."

PROBLEMS

1. Basil bids for a valuable 1960s' plastic nodding duck on an Internet auction site and is the winner. However, the seller, Esin, informs Basil that she has given the duck to her friend, Simon. Can Basil sue Esin for damages in the tort of conversion? Can Basil sue Simon for damages?

2. Nicholas states in a classified advert in a newspaper that he has a job lot of valuable 1970s' furry dice and is offering them individually for sale at £20 each. Paula contracts with Nicholas to buy 12 of the dice; but before they can be delivered to Paula, the warehouse in which Nicholas stores the whole job lot is destroyed by fire. Can Paula sue Nicholas for damages? (Cf. *Re Goldcorp Exchange Ltd* (1995).)

NOTE

The Sale of Goods Act involves moveable property. When the subject matter of a sale is land the rules are quite different, as the next extract indicates.

F.H. Lawson and Bernard Rudden, *The Law of Property* (3rd edn, OUP, 2002), pp.53–4, 59

"The modes of transferring property vary with the different kinds of thing transferred. Moreover, sometimes the actual transfer is and sometimes is not preceded by preliminaries which are almost as important as the transfer itself. Gifts rarely need preliminaries—you do not look a gift horse in the mouth. But the actual transfer of land on a sale is almost always preceded by a contract, and the contract preceded by enquiries about the property itself and about the seller's title therein. On the other hand, when goods are bought for cash in a shop, contract and transfer are rolled into one, there are usually no negotiations, there is nothing in writing, and there is certainly no investigation of title. The acquisition of shares and other securities lies somewhere between the two; the transfer is preceded by a contract but there is nothing like the same ritual as in the purchase of land . . .

To be valid the full contract of sale [of land] must be in writing signed by or on behalf of both parties. It will, of course, contain a promise by the seller to convey his interest in the specific property and by the buyer to pay the agreed price. At that stage the buyer is not formally and for all purposes the owner of the land because there has been neither deed nor registration. Yet as *between seller and buyer* this contract has an effect similar to the default status enacted for the sale of goods—the land at once belongs to the buyer, the money does not yet belong to the seller. This result is attained because historically, disputes concerning land contracts came most frequently before the Chancery which was prepared, at the request of the buyer and on tender of the price, to order the seller to carry out the formalities necessary to make the buyer owner *erga omnes*, that is to execute the appropriate deed and yield possession (sellers who refused were jailed). In effect, the court regarded the buyer as already the owner of the land and would protect that entitlement against the seller, his creditors, any donee, and any other buyer who knew or ought to know of the contract . . ."

NOTES

1. The above extract is of interest to the private lawyer for a number of reasons. First it indicates an important distinction between common law and equity (to be discussed further on in this chapter). A contract for the sale of land does not pass title to the land at common law; there has to be a separate conveyance. However, because the Court of Chancery is prepared to award the remedy of specific performance (see **12.1**), and because equity considers what can be done as done, the signing of the contract passes an *equitable* title to the buyer. Between contract and conveyance there exist in effect two owners of the same land: the seller is the owner in law, while the buyer is the owner in equity. The contract, in other words, passes title in equity but not at common law.

2. Secondly, the extract indicates the important role of legal remedies in English law. The buyer of land becomes the equitable owner as a result of the existence of the equitable remedy of specific performance; it is a right created indirectly through the remedy, by ricochet so to speak. This is why one French comparative lawyer (R. David), when writing about the common law, described it as a system in which "remedies precede rights".

3. Thirdly, one should note that with respect to contracts for the sale of land, the contract, to be enforceable, must be in writing (Law of Property (Mis-

cellaneous Provisions) Act 1989, s.2) (see p.213). This is a formality that does not normally apply in contract; according to the general theory of contract, a promise given orally, if supported by consideration and seriously intended, is normally sufficient to create an enforceable contract.

QUESTIONS

1. Why do common lawyers treat land differently from moveable property?

2. Imagine that, with regard to goods, the contract of sale did not pass property in the goods: what advantages would this have? How would a conveyance of title be achieved? (Clue: how is title passed when one person gives goods to another as a birthday present?)

3. Is it a *function* of contract to transfer titles in property? If so, should all gifts be classed as contracts? What about a declaration by Tony that he holds a house on trust for Basil?

4. Consider the following:

   (a) Sue lends a book to her hall of residence neighbour Elsbeth for the weekend; on Monday Sue finds the book on the table in the communal kitchen. Can Sue retake the book?
   (b) Sue lends a loaf of bread to Elsbeth; on Monday she finds the loaf unused on the table in the communal kitchen. Can she retake the loaf?
   (c) Sue lends £5 to Elsbeth for the weekend; on Monday she finds the same £5 on the floor of the kitchen (she recognises it from a distinctive ink stain). Can Sue retake the £5?

1.3.4 Contract and bailment

Beswick involved debts as a form of property. However, tangible moveable things also impact upon the law of obligations, as the next extract indicates.

> **Building and Civil Engineering Holidays Scheme Management Ltd v Post Office [1966] 1 Q.B. 247, CA**
>
> **Lord Denning M.R.:** ". . . At common law, bailment is often associated with a contract, but this is not always the case, see *R v McDonald, Meux v Great Eastern Railway*. An action against a bailee can often be put, not as an action in contract, nor in tort, but as an action on its own, *sui generic*, arising out of the possession had by the bailee of the goods, see Winfield on the *Province of the Law of Tort*, p.100, Fifoot's *History of the Common Law*, p.24, *Midland Silicones v Scrutton*. The incidents of this cause of action are not to be found by looking at the old books on detinue and trover. We have outlived those forms of action, together with trespass and case, see *Letang v Cooper*. Suffice it to say at the present day that if goods, which have been delivered to a bailee, are lost or damaged whilst in his

custody he is liable to the person damnified (who may be the owner or the bailor) unless the bailee proves that the loss or damage is not due to any fault on his part, see *Coldman v Hill*, per Scrutton L.J. . . .

At common law in a case of bailment, the general principle is *restitutio in integrum*, which means that the party damnified is entitled to such a sum of money as will put him in as good a position as if the goods had not been lost or damaged. This is subject, however, to the qualification that the damages must not be too remote, that is, they must be such damages as flow directly and in the usual course of things from the loss or damage, see *The Argentino*. If the party damnified suffers damage of a special kind, he is entitled to recover it, subject to the qualification that the damages must not exceed such damages as would be produced in the ordinary course of things by the act complained of, see *Cory v Thames Ironworks*. When goods are lost or damaged in transit, the damage ordinarily produced is, in the case of loss, the cost of replacement; or in the case of damage, the cost of repair. That is the amount which, in the absence of contract, the bailor can recover. He cannot recover indirect or consequential damages (such as loss of profits on a business) because those can only be recovered in cases on contracts proper, where notice of special circumstances is brought home, see *British Columbia Saw-Mill Co v Nettleship* . . .

NOTES

1. See also *Morris v CW Martin & Co* (1966) (at p.113) and UC&TO, p.14.

2. Bailment is of particular importance in contract domain questions, because there are many contracts that involve the transfer of possession in a chattel (moveable thing). Thus contracts to transport goods, to clean clothes and to hire vehicles will bring into play rules of bailment. Some of these rules may of course be modified by the contract (thus obligations can modify property rights), but any clause that tries to do so runs the risk of being declared void if the owner is a consumer (see **8.4.6**). In commercial contracts, however, the courts are likely to give effect to the insurance position, and international conventions may regulate certain transport contracts. One might note that the remedies of bailment are to be found in the law of tort (see Torts (Interference with Goods) Act 1977). When contract, tort and bailment rules intermix the result can be very complicated: see e.g. *The Albazero* (1977).

1.3.5 **Contract and restitution**

Until quite recently much of what is now called the law of restitution was to be found within the law of contract (UC&TO, pp.165–72). Just as a number of damages actions could not be accommodated within contract—and thus had to be placed in a category called "tort"—so there existed a number of debt claims that could not be properly classed within contract. The next extract explains this situation.

United Australia Ltd v Barclays Bank Ltd **[1941] A.C. 1, HL**

Lord Atkin: ". . . The story starts with the action of debt which was not necessarily based upon the existence of a contract, for it covered claims to recover sums due to customary dues, penalties for breaches of by-laws, and the like. The action of debt had its drawbacks, the chief being that the defendant could wage his law. There followed the application of the action on the case of assumpsit to debt. 'The defendant being indebted then promised.' At first there must be an express promise; then the Courts implied a promise from an executory contract: *Slade's* case. *Slade's* case was not a claim in *indebitatus assumpsit*, but the principle was applied, and it became unnecessary to prove an express promise in those cases. Then the action was allowed in respect of cases where there was no contract, executory or otherwise, as in the cases where debt would have lain for customary fees and the like; and by a final and somewhat forced application to cases where the defendant had received money of the plaintiff to which he was not entitled. These included cases where the plaintiff had intentionally paid money to the defendant, e.g. claims for money paid on a consideration that wholly failed and money paid under a mistake: cases where the plaintiff had been deceived into paying money, cases where money had been extorted from the plaintiff by threats or duress of goods. They also included cases where money had not been paid by the plaintiff at all but had been received from third persons, as where the defendant had received fees under colour of holding an office which in fact was held by the plaintiff: and finally cases like the present where the defendant had been wrongfully in possession of the plaintiff's goods, had sold them and was in possession of the proceeds. Now to find a basis for the actions in any actual contract whether express or to be implied from the conduct of the parties was in many of the instances given obviously impossible. The cheat or the blackmailer does not promise to repay to the person he has wronged the money which he has unlawfully taken: nor does the thief promise to repay the owner of the goods stolen the money which he has gained from selling the goods. Nevertheless, if a man so wronged was to recover the money in the hands of the wrongdoer, and it was obviously just that he should be able to do so, it was necessary to create a fictitious contract: for there was no action possible other than debt or assumpsit on the one side and action for damages for tort on the other. The action of *indebitatus assumpsit* for money had and received to the use of the plaintiff in the cases I have enumerated was therefore supported by the imputation by the Court to the defendant of a promise to repay . . ."

NOTES

1. There are three main types of non-contractual debt claim: (i) an action for money had and received (see e.g. *Rowland v Divall* (1923), below at p.340); (ii) an action for money paid (see e.g. *Brook's Wharf & Bull Wharf Ltd v Goodman Brothers* (1937)); and (iii) an action on a *quantum meruit* (see e.g. *Sumpter v Hedges* (1898), below at p.484). Until quite recently these claims in quasi-contract were placed within the domain of contract on the ground that

their normative basis was an implied contract. Thanks to academic pressure, this implied contract theory has now been abandoned and replaced by the normative principle of unjust enrichment, which has had the effect of removing the claims from the domain of contract and placing them, along with a number of equitable claims and tort cases, in the independent category of restitution (see **6.6.1**). This development in one sense brings the English model closer to that of Europe, for both the category of quasi-contract and the principle of unjust enrichment are Roman in origin. However, in English law the category of restitution is not purely an "obligations" category since it contains cases that belong within the law of property (rights *in rem*) rather than in the category dealing with rights *in personam* (obligations) (see **12.8**).

2. This new category of restitution means that a number of areas normally regarded as being within the domain of contract are now strictly outside the domain, as the next extract explains (and see further **6.6.1**).

Whittaker v Campbell [1984] Q.B. 318, QBD

Robert Goff L.J.: ". . . [T]here is, in our opinion, no general principle of law that fraud vitiates consent. Let us consider this proposition first with reference to the law of contract. In English law every valid contract presupposes an offer by one party which has been accepted by the offeree. Plainly there can be no such acceptance unless offer and acceptance correspond, so the offer can only be accepted by the offeree, the acceptance must relate to the same subject matter as the offer and must also be, in all material respects, in the same terms as the offer. But the test whether there has been correspondence between offer and acceptance is not subjective but objective. If there is objective agreement, there may be a binding contract, even if in his mind one party or another has not consented to it, a principle recently affirmed by the Court of Appeal in *Centrovincial Estates plc v Merchant Investors Assurance Co Ltd* (1983) *The Times*, 8 March. Furthermore putting on one side such matters as the ancient doctrine of *non est factum* and relief from mistake in equity, there is no principle of English law that any contract may be 'avoided', i.e., not come into existence, by reason simply of a mistake, whether a mistake of one or both parties. The question is simply whether objective agreement has been reached and, if so, on what terms. If objective agreement has been reached, in the sense we have described, then the parties will be bound, unless on a true construction the agreement was subject to a condition precedent, express or implied, failure of which has in the event prevented a contract from coming into existence.

What is the effect of fraud? Fraud is, in relation to a contract, a fraudulent misrepresentation by one party which induces the other to enter into a contract or apparent contract with the representor. Apart from the innocent party's right to recover damages for the tort of deceit, the effect of the fraud is simply to give the innocent party the right, subject to certain limits, to rescind the contract. These

31

rights are similar to (though not identical with) the rights of a party who has been induced to enter into a contract by an innocent, as opposed to a fraudulent, misrepresentation, though there the right to recover damages derives from statute, and the limits to rescission are somewhat more severe. It is plain, however, that in this context fraud does not 'vitiate consent', any more than an innocent misrepresentation 'vitiates consent'. Looked at realistically, a misrepresentation, whether fraudulent or innocent, induces a party to enter into a contract in circumstances where it may be unjust that the representor should be permitted to retain the benefit (the chose in action) so acquired by him. The remedy of rescission, by which the unjust enrichment of the representor is prevented, though for historical and practical reasons treated in books on the law of contract, is a straightforward remedy in restitution subject to limits which are characteristic of that branch of the law.

The effect of rescission of a contract induced by a misrepresentation is that property in goods transferred under it may be revested in the transferor (the misrepresentee). But this may not be possible if the goods have been transferred to a third party, for the intervention of third party rights may preclude rescission. In such a case, especially if the misrepresentor has disappeared from the scene or is a man of straw so that damages are an ineffective remedy, the misrepresentee's only practical course may be to seek to establish that there never was any contract (i.e., that the supposed contract was 'void'), so that he never parted with the property in the goods and can claim the goods or their value from the third party. To succeed in such a claim, he has generally to show that there was no objective agreement between him and the representor. For that purpose, however, the misrepresentation (fraudulent or innocent) is simply the origin of a set of circumstances in which it may be shown that there was no objective agreement, eg, that the offer was, objectively speaking, made to one person and (perhaps as a result of fraud), objectively speaking, accepted by another. Again, it cannot be said that fraud 'vitiates consent'; fraud was merely the occasion for an apparent contract which was, in law, no contract at all . . ."

NOTE

This is an important piece of judgment for the comparative contract lawyer because it illustrates an important difference between the common law and Continental models of contract. In civil law, mistake, fraud and duress are obstacles to agreement itself and thus may, in theory, prevent the formation of a contract. This is not true of English law. On rare occasions a mistake may be serious enough to prevent the formation of a contract, but normally mistake, fraud and duress are matters for equity (or at least once were) rather than the common law (although equity has now lost interest in mistake as a result of a recent decision of the Court of Appeal: *The Great Peace* (2003), p.255). As Goff L.J. explains, the common law takes an objective view of a promise; equity, however, takes the view that where a justified form of enrichment has become unjustified thanks to fraud or duress then it will intervene to prevent this unjust enrichment. Indeed this is why equity once intervened when mistake threatened to turn a contract into a means of unjustified enrichment (*Solle v Butcher* (1950); cf. *The Great Peace* (2003), below at p.255).

1.3.6 Contract and equity

Contract is one area of English law that cannot be understood without a solid appreciation of the distinction, and interrelation, between law and equity.

The First Report of the Judicature Commission 1869

"This distinction [between law and equity] led to the establishment of two systems of Judicature, organized in different ways, and administering justice on different and sometimes opposite principles using different methods of procedure, and applying different remedies. Large classes of rights, altogether ignored by the Courts of Common Law, were protected and enforced by the Court of Chancery, and recourse was had to the same Court for the purpose of obtaining a more adequate protection against the violation of Common Law rights than the Courts of Common Law were prepared to afford. The Common Law Courts were confined by their system of procedure in most actions,—not brought for recovering the possession of land,—to giving judgment for debt or damages, a remedy which has been found to be totally insufficient for the adjustment of the complicated disputes of modern society. The procedure at Common Law was founded on the trial by jury, and was framed on the supposition that every issue of fact was capable of being tried in that way; but experience has shown that supposition to be erroneous . . ."

NOTES

1. *Law and equity*. Law and equity have been fused since 1875, but only at the level of procedure (see now Supreme Court Act 1981, s.49). Accordingly, the distinction emerges at several important points within the law of contract. Perhaps the area of greatest importance is remedies (see below and **Chapter 12**), but the equitable doctrine of estoppel is of particular importance in some situations where consideration is wanting (see **4.6.3**). Relief against penalty clauses is another key area of equitable intervention (see **7.3.2**).

2. *Remedies*. The two main remedies at common law, as the above extract indicates, are actions for debt and actions for damages (see **Chapter 11**). Equity, however, offers a series of non-monetary remedies in the area of contract law: injunction, specific performance, rescission and rectification (see **Chapter 12**). What is important about these equitable remedies, besides being non-monetary, is that they act as vehicles for importing into contract law principles of equity. An example of a situation clearly calling for equitable intervention is provided by the next case.

Credit Lyonnais Bank Nederland v Burch **[1997] 1 All E.R. 144, CA**

Millett L.J.: ". . . Mr Pelosi provided the bank with an unlimited all moneys guarantee given by Miss Burch at his request. She was a junior employee of the company employed at a modest wage. She was not a director of the company or shareholder in it. Her guarantee was supported by a second charge on her home, a small flat of suitably modest value, which was valued at £100,000 and was subject to a mortgage of £30,000. She understood that the guarantee and charge were unlimited in time and amount, but she had not taken independent legal advice.

No court of equity could allow such a transaction to stand. The facts which I have recited are sufficient to entitle Miss Burch to have the transaction set aside as against Mr Pelosi and the company. Every one of those facts was known to the bank when it accepted the security. The bank must accordingly be taken to have had notice of Miss Burch's equity, and must submit to the transaction being set aside against it also.

An eighteenth century Lord Chancellor would have contented himself with saying as much. It is an extreme case. The transaction was not merely to the manifest disadvantage of Miss Burch; it was one which, in the traditional phrase, 'shocks the conscience of the court'. . . . The transaction gives rise to grave suspicion. It cries aloud for an explanation . . ."

(Nourse and Swinton Thomas L.JJ. delivered concurring opinions.)

NOTES

1. The contract of mortgage was perfectly valid at common law. However, because of the circumstances surrounding its formation—the undue influence exercised by an employer on a junior employee—the contract could be rescinded in equity (see *Barclays Bank v O'Brien* (1994), at p.297). Of course it was not the bank that actually exercised the undue influence, but it knew (or should have known) of its existence and thus was in breach of an equitable duty owed to the employee in failing to advise her to seek independent advice before signing the contract.

2. Equity is also prepared to rescind a contract where there has been misrepresentation (see *Redgrave v Hurd* (1881), at p.240) or duress. When equity does use its remedy of rescission the contract becomes *voidable*: that is to say the contract is not deemed never to have existed (it is not *void*), though where the rescission is said to be *ab initio* the effect may be similar (see **5.1**).

1.3.7 Contract and crime

The overlap between contract and crime is at the factual level considerable, since failing to pay for goods and services can amount not just to a breach of contract but also to an offence. Thus in *DPP v Ray* (1974), a customer who rushed out of a restaurant without paying, and having consumed the meal, was held to be guilty of a crime. There are, however, some criminal cases which are directly relevant to contract rules, as the next extract indicates.

Fisher v Bell [1961] 1 Q.B. 394, QBD

Lord Parker C.J.: ". . . The sole question is whether the exhibition of that knife in the window with the ticket constituted an offer for sale within the statute. I think that most lay people would be inclined to the view (as, indeed, I was myself when I first read these papers), that if a knife were displayed in a window like that with a price attached to it, it was nonsense to say that was not offering it for sale. The knife is there inviting people to buy it, and in ordinary language it is for sale; but any statute must be looked at in the light of the general law of the country, for Parliament must be taken to know the general law. It is clear that, according to the ordinary law of contract, the display of an article with a price on it in a shop window is merely an invitation to treat. It is in no sense an offer for sale the acceptance of which constitutes a contract. That is clearly the general law of the country . . .

In those circumstances I, for my part, though I confess reluctantly, am driven to the conclusion that no offence was here committed . . ."

(Ashworth and Elwes JJ. delivered concurring opinions.)

QUESTIONS

1. Do you think that the courts would interpret a criminal law statute in this same way today?

2. Is this an example of axiomatic (deductive) reasoning? (Cf. 2.5.)

NOTES

1. See also *Pharmaceutical Society of GB v Boots* (1953) (at p.152).

2. Some breaches of contract can be crimes, as we have mentioned. But it may be that, for example, poor goods or bad workmanship could result in criminal proceedings.

Consumer Protection Act 1987 (c 43)

"10. The general safety requirement
(1) A person shall be guilty of an offence if he—

(a) supplies any consumer goods which fail to comply with the general safety requirement;
(b) offers or agrees to supply any such goods; or
(c) exposes or possesses any such goods for supply."

Trade Union and Labour Relations (Consolidation) Act 1992 (c 52)

"**240. Breach of contract involving injury to persons or property**
(1) A person commits an offence who wilfully and maliciously breaks a contract of service or hiring, knowing or having reasonable cause to believe that the probable consequences of his so doing, either alone or in combination with others, will be—

(a) to endanger human life or cause serious bodily injury, or
(b) to expose valuable property, whether real or personal, to destruction or serious injury."

1.3.8 Contract and public law

In French law the distinction between public and private law is fundamental, and the distinction extends to the law of contract in as much as administrative contracts are distinguished from ordinary private contracts (UC&TO, pp.14–15). The position in France is explained in the next extract.

Jean Brèthe de la Gressaye, "Droit administratif et droit privé" in *Études offertes à Georges Ripert*, LGDJ, 1950, Vol.I, p.304 (translation Bernard Rudden and Geoffrey Samuel)

"2. . . . Contracts intended for the supply of goods and services to the Administration, and not the ones by which it furnishes to consumers public services, are called 'administrative contracts'. The principal ones are: public works transactions, supply of goods and services transactions, public service concessions.

These administrative contracts are distinguished from private law contracts, which the administration can also conclude following the ordinary law, by some special rules of form (tendering, for example) and above all by some rules of substance which seriously deviate from contractual law principles.

In private law there is equality between the contractual parties. They are bound by the contract, neither of them can unilaterally modify it during performance, and if one of them has to complain of non-performance by the other of his undertaking, he can obtain rescission of the contract and damages only by going to court.

In administrative contracts there is not equality between the supplier or business entity and the administration because the latter enjoys certain prerogatives. It has the right to modify unilaterally the conditions of the transaction or the concession, if the needs of the service require it, subject to indemnifying the co-contractor for any damage that might be caused in upsetting the financial equilibrium of the contract (theory of unforeseen circumstances (*imprévision*)).

And if the supplier, business or concessionaire fails to fulfil exactly his undertakings, the administration itself has the power to impose sanctions on him: fines, rescission, supervision or sequestration. Here again the privilege of pre-emption comes into play: the administration uses self-help without having to go to court.

The reason for these privileges is that the administrative contract brings into play on the one side the public service interest and on the other side a private interest. This is what justifies the inequality between the parties and the superiority of the administration . . ."

QUESTION

Is the public/private distinction still of relevance in the 21st century, especially given the regime of EU law? (Cf. Joerges (1998) 18 L.S. 146.)

NOTES

1. This position in France is interesting to contrast with the position in England. Common lawyers make no formal distinction between public and private law, and thus public bodies are bound by the ordinary law of contract (see, e.g., *Blackpool & Fylde Aero Club v Blackpool BC* (1990), at p.177). Why the difference? The most obvious reason is a difference of political ideology: the French political and social model lays much greater emphasis on the role of the state in all aspects of French life. Yet the seeds of the legal difference are to be found in Roman law. Not only did the Romans formulate the grand distinction between public and private law (D.1.1.1.2), but they also recognised that the *fiscus* (imperial treasury) enjoyed an unequal power relationship with the private subject (D.49.14.28). This whole issue of a power difference with respect to the *fiscus* was then developed into a theory by the medieval Roman lawyers (J-L. Mestre, *Introduction historique au droit administratif français* (PUF, 1985), p.156).

2. However, "inequality" between parties, while not formalised in any public/private distinction in English law, is not absent at the level of economic and (or) political reality, and so the question arises as to how the law of contract tackles such inequalities. The response to this question, until relatively recently, is probably to say "not well" (see, e.g., *Galbraith v Mitchenall Estates Ltd* (1965)). But of course inequality is by no means confined to the dichotomy between the administration on the one hand and private parties on the other. Indeed, some commercial entities are more powerful, economically, than some public bodies. Legislation now exists that can be used to curb some abuses of economic power, and administrative law (judicial review) is available to control abuses of power by the administration. However, the problem with judicial review is that it cannot be used to obtain damages; if a party damaged by such a public authority abuse wishes to obtain compensation from the courts, it must establish a cause of action in contract or tort, or perhaps under the Human Rights Act 1998.

3. One might note how "administrative" contract type cases are handled in English law: see, e.g., *Blackpool & Fylde* (1990) (at p.177); *Davis Contractors Ltd v Fareham UDC* (1956) (at p.426); *Staffs Area Health Authority v South Staffs Waterworks Co* (1978) (at p.428).

4. Nevertheless, the public/private divide is not completely irrelevant, as the next extract illustrates.

Roy v Kensington & Chelsea Family Practitioner Committee **[1992] 1 A.C. 624, HL**

A doctor brought, *inter alia*, an action in debt against his Family Practitioner Committee (FPC) for breach of contract. The FPC sought to have the claim struck out as an abuse of process, on the basis that the relationship between a doctor and the FPC was a matter only of public law and that the sole remedy available to the doctor was an action for judicial review. The House of Lords (Lords Bridge, Emslie, Griffiths, Oliver and Lowry) refused to strike out the claim.

Lord Bridge: ". . . I do not think the issue in the appeal turns on whether the doctor provides services pursuant to a contract with the family practitioner committee. I doubt if he does and am content to assume that there is no contract. Nevertheless, the terms which govern the obligations of the doctor on the one hand, as to the services he is to provide, and of the family practitioner committee on the other hand, as to the payments which it is required to make to the doctor, are all prescribed in the relevant legislation and it seems to me that the statutory terms are just as effective as they would be if they were contractual to confer upon the doctor an enforceable right in private law to receive the remuneration to which the terms entitle him. It must follow, in my view, that in any case of dispute the doctor is entitled to claim and recover in an action commenced by writ the amount of remuneration which he is able to prove as being due to him. Whatever remuneration he is entitled to under the statement is remuneration he has duly earned by the services he has rendered. The circumstance that the quantum of that remuneration, in the case of a particular dispute, is affected by a discretionary decision made by the committee cannot deny the doctor his private law right of recovery or subject him to the constraints which the necessity to seek judicial review would impose upon that right . . ."

Lord Lowry: ". . . An important point is that the court clearly has jurisdiction to entertain the doctor's action . . . It is concerned with a private law right, it involves a question which could in some circumstances give rise to a dispute of fact and one object of the plaintiff is to obtain an order for the payment (not by way of damages) of an ascertained or ascertainable sum of money. If it is wrong to allow such a claim to be litigated by action, what is to be said of other disputed claims for remuneration? I think it is right to consider the whole spectrum of claims which a doctor might make against the committee. The existence of any dispute as to entitlement means that he will be alleging a breach of his private law rights through a failure by the committee to perform their public duty. If the committee's argument prevails, the doctor must in all these cases go by judicial review, even when the facts are not clear. I scarcely think that this can be the right answer . . .

Although he seeks to enforce performance of a public law duty . . . his private law rights dominate the proceedings . . ."

QUESTIONS

1. Is this an example of a non-contractual debt claim? If so, what is the cause of action which motivates the claim? Is it restitution (unjust enrichment), or public law?

2. Is the House of Lords acting "as if" there was a contractual relationship between the parties?

NOTE

At the level of form there may be no distinction between administrative and private contracts in English law. But at the level of substance, government contracts can be seen as something of a discrete area, as the next extract suggests.

Colin Turpin, "Public Contracts" in *International Encyclopedia of Comparative Law, Vol. VII, Ch.4*

8. *Placing of public contracts.*—In every national legal system there are rules which regulate the placing of contracts by public authorities. These rules govern such matters as publicity for projected contract awards, the mode of selection of the contractor, establishment of the contract price, and formalities attending the award of the contract. Matters of these kinds may be regulated in great detail, or again may be governed only by a few broad principles which leave a considerable discretion to the public authorities concerned. Moreover the rules in question may be instantly recognisable as legal rules, having been enacted by bodies with legislative competence or declared in authoritative judicial decisions, or on the other hand may be mere directions of an administrative character which—although binding upon those authorities to whom they are addressed—are not obligatory upon other persons. A study of public contracts must take account of the rules governing the placing of contracts by public authorities, whether or not such rules are acknowledged to have the same legal status as other rules of a particular national legal system . . .

NOTES

1. See, e.g., *Blackpool and Fylde Aero Club v Blackpool BC* (1990) (at p.177).

2. *Blackpool* is important for another reason as well. The claimant in the case, instead of using private law, might have been able to bring an action for judicial review (although this would not have permitted it to claim damages). Accordingly, the public/private law divide can also be important at the level of remedies. If the contractor is a "public authority", it may be possible to seek the quashing of a decision or, indeed, damages under the Human Rights Act 1998. Sometimes a "private" body will be treated as a 'public authority': see *R. (Beer) v Hampshire Farmers' Markets Ltd* (2004).

QUESTION

What if a contract endows a commercial corporation with a discretionary power over its co-contractor: should the exercise of such a power be subject to the test of reasonableness as in judicial review? (Cf. Daintith (2005) 68 M.L.R. 554.)

1.4 Contract and the European ddimension

Contract has, by definition, a close connection with continental Europe, as we have seen in terms of contract's history and definition. However, the relationship between contract and continental Europe extends beyond this historical and definitional aspect. First there is European Union law, which impacts upon English contract law in a direct way through Directives. Secondly, there is the proposal to harmonise the contract law of all the Member States through codification. This project is, in terms of an actual text, well underway—indeed there is now in existence a code of general contract law called the *Principles of European Contract Law* (PECL). Thirdly, there is the European Convention for the Protection of Human Rights and Fundamental Freedoms, incorporated into English law by the Human Rights Act 1998. Contract law is by no means immune from human rights questions. Lastly, developments in contract law in the civil law systems, while not of any direct relevance to English law, have a certain indirect influence as a result of both academic doctrine and a judicial interest in Continental ideas.

1.4.1 European Union law

There are a number of important EU Directives that impact directly or indirectly on UK contract law. For example, there are the Directives on defective products (25 July 1985, 85/374/EEC: L 210/29), on unfair terms in consumer contracts (5 April 1993, 93/13/EEC: L 95/29), on electronic commerce (8 June 2000, 2000/31/EC), on product safety (3 December 2001, 2001/95/EC), and on contracts negotiated away from business premises (20 December 1985, 85/577/EEC). Many of these Directives have been transposed into English law through secondary legislation (statutory instruments), one of the most prominent being the Unfair Terms in Consumer Contracts Regulations 1999 (see p.416). The general impact of EU law on English contract law is in many ways simply one of new legislative texts transposing Directives. However, some of these texts may contain concepts that are civilian rather than common law in origin, and this can give rise to doctrinal debate. One such concept relevant to contract law is good faith, which has its origins in Roman law and is to be found in all of the Continental codes; the common law, in contrast, is traditionally said never to have adopted such a general notion. Good faith will be discussed in **Chapter 3**.

1.4.2 **Codification**

A more ambitious project is the harmonisation of the contract law of all the EU Member States through codification. Two contract codes already exist: these are the UNIDROIT Principles for International Commercial Contracts (UNIDROIT) and the *Principles of European Contract Law* (PECL).

Arthur S. Hartkamp, "Principles of Contract Law" in A. Hartkamp *et al.* (eds), *Towards a European Civil Code* (3rd edn, Kluwer/Ara Aequi Libri, 2004), pp.128–31 (footnotes omitted)

"The UNIDROIT Principles are not meant to become binding law. It would be unrealistic to hope for a codification of the general part of contract on a world scale. . . . On a European scale the idea of such a codification, be it only of contract law, is less unrealistic but still not very probable, strange though this may seem taking into account the official goals of an internal market unhampered by national economic or legal barriers. . . . What then are the functions that the Principles [of European contract law] are meant to achieve? Those functions could be the following:

1. Since codification of private law, be it on a world or a European scale, is fragmentary, it is important to dispose of a general set of principles from which inspiration may be derived by national and international courts to interpret the provisions of the existing uniform law, to fill the gaps which it presents and to offer a background, however informal, for new law to be created . . .

2. The Principles may serve as a model law that could inspire legislators who strive for law reform . . .

3. The Principles (and their accompanying comments) may serve to enlighten parties negotiating a contract in order to identify the problems to be resolved in their contract and, possibly, to find suitable rules to settle them. Parties may even decide to incorporate the Principles in part or as a whole in their contract . . .

4. Parties to an international contract could choose the Principles as the law applicable to their contract . . .

5. The Principles will certainly have an important scholarly and educational value. Concerning the European legal scene, they will encourage the

41

emerging trend to find the common denominator of the different private law systems in Europe in order to construct a new *ius commune Europae*. Moreover, the Principles will make it more attractive to introduce in law schools new curricula teaching European side by side with the national laws of their respective countries of residence. In the long run, this seems to be the most promising way to attain such a new ius commune.

6. Finally, the principles will, by the sheer fact of their existence, prove that a reasonable compromise between the various legal systems of Europe and beyond, can be reached. It seems probable that this will add weight to the voices of those who advocate the preparation of a European Civil Code . . ."

NOTES AND QUESTIONS

1. The PECL will certainly be employed in this present casebook for some of the reasons outlined above. In particular they will give a structural overview of contract (a sort of map of the law), and of course they will act as a vehicle for bringing in the European dimension (although it should be stressed that these Principles do *not* represent English law). Yet one of the purposes of this casebook is to encourage the student to ask the following question: Can an area of law really be summed up in a set of axiomatic principles? Jurists from the civil law tradition tend to answer this question positively, for this is a tradition where scientific reductionism in law has been a major intellectual feature since the 16th century (see P. Stein, *Roman Law in European History* (Cambridge University Press, 1999)). Law is a rational and scientific discipline where every category is a sub-category of a higher category (but cf. Legrand (1998) 18 L.S. 216). Common lawyers were never much attracted by such an approach, save perhaps during the 19th century and early 20th century (see Hedley (1999) 50 N.I.L.Q. 283). And one reason for this is that there were few faculties of law teaching the common law in England and Wales before the 20th century (judges are not interested in rationalising the law: see Lord Macmillan in *Read v J Lyons & Co* (1947), at 175). However, these methodological points will be developed in the next chapter.

2. In compiling these transnational codes, do you think that the members of the various drafting commissions start off from practical commercial problems or from the provisions in their own national codes? Do you think, in other words, that some of the members have their own codes open beneath the table (so to speak) when trying to agree on a transnational provision?

3. Tony Weir has described the idea of a European Civil Code as "demented". Do you agree? Other writers are equally sceptical, as the next extract indicates.

Pierre Legrand, "A Diabolical Idea" in A. Hartkamp *et al.* (eds), *Towards a European Civil Code* (3rd edn, Kluwer/Ara Aequi Libri, 2004), pp.266–267 (footnotes omitted)

"The European Community represents a particular articulation of universality which is almost entirely market-orientated and economistic, emphasising trade and investment and the economies of production and distribution. In this spirit, the prevailing concern is for the systematic unification of all that is perceived to be calculable and controllable. A symptom of this ethically deficient globalism, or uncreditable cosmopolitanism, is the proposal in favour of a European Civil Code. The paradox, however, is that such universalisation depends on the promotion of a perspective of the whole which is totally oblivious of the historical fact that legal traditions reveal moral preferences which are culturally embedded and which, on that account, are incompatible and incommensurable, that is, *incommisicible*. In other words, the European Community's agenda in favour of uniformisation rests on the effective denial of sites of contestation within itself. The common-law experience, although it belongs to the universality that is sought, is not allowed to shape the universalisation process; it is, thus, simultaneously empowered and disempowered. In suggesting the adoption of a European Civil Code, civilians foster a modality of experience which is uniquely theirs . . . Why, then, should the common law be made to think of law as a science? Why should common-law lawyers have to learn to think like civilians when both legal traditions are inherently valid and legitimate? . . . At this juncture, a civilian may test his own capacity for thinking otherwise: if he were entrusted with the codification of the common law, would it ever occur to him to proceed *alphabetically*? Why not? After all, as Bernard Rudden wryly observes, 'the alphabet is virtually the only instrument of intellectual order of which the common law makes use' . . ."

NOTES

1. Professor Legrand, a leading and original comparative lawyer, is of the view that the essence of a legal system is not to be found in its surface rules but in its deep cultural elements and mentality (see (1996) 16 L.S. 232). What are the epistemological (theory of knowledge) foundations of a legal system? That is to say, what are its deep reasoning and mental structures? When one takes this approach, Pierre Legrand argues that there is a fundamental cultural and mentality difference between the civil law and the common law traditions which acts as a major obstacle to harmonisation projects (see also his two leading articles on this topic: (1996) 45 I.C.L.Q. 52; (1997) 60 M.L.R. 44). Of course one can fashion a code—it has been done with UNIDROIT and the PECL. But, as Legrand indicates in the extract above, this simply amounts to legal imperialism. Tony Weir associates law with language and argues that just as one cannot forge a new common language out of all the existing European languages, so one cannot forge a trans-cultural civil code ([1998] ZEuP 564).

2. Other writers, of course, disagree. They take the view that there is an aspect to law that transcends cultural boundaries, and they point to the influence of

Roman law in Europe from the late Middle Ages onwards (see e.g. Zimmerman (1996) 112 L.Q.R. 576). What is at issue is largely a paradigm debate: is a legal system simply the product of the culture in which it has developed (cultural paradigm), or is there a 'scientific' dimension to law and legal knowledge that, like mathematics, transcends any particular culture (nature paradigm)? The difficulty with this debate is that there is no way in which one side can actually prove the other side to be wrong; neither theory, in other words, can be falsified. Whatever the answer, one is left with some transnational codes of contract (especially UNIDROIT and PECL), and this book will use these codes as one means of connecting English contract law with more general European thinking in this area. But comparison does not imply convergence.

1.4.3 Human rights

In addition to EU law, the European Convention for the Protection of Human Rights and Fundamental Freedoms has now been directly incorporated into UK law by the Human Rights Act 1998. This does not mean that the case law of the European Court of Human Rights has direct application (see Human Rights Act 1998, s.2(1)), but the incorporation does have implications for commercial law, as the following extract indicate.

> ### *Mousaka Inc v Golden Seagull Maritime Inc* [2002] 1 W.L.R. 395, QBD
>
> **David Steel J.:** "1. The tentacles of the Human Rights Act 1998 reach into some unexpected places. The Commercial Court, even when exercising its supervisory role as regards arbitration, is not immune. A corporate body is a person with rights protected by the Act and thus, for instance, can invoke article 6 where it may be the victim of action incompatible with its right to a fair trial. The particular issue that arises on the present application is whether a judge, in refusing to give permission to appeal to the High Court from an arbitration award, has a duty to state his reasons in full for that refusal . . ."

NOTE

These "tentacles" have now reached into the substance of commercial law and the law of contract.

> ### *Wilson v First County Trust Ltd (No. 2)* [2004] 1 A.C. 816, HL
>
> This was in its origin a claim for the return of a car that had been pawned for a loan of £5,000 by the claimant with the defendants. The claimant asserted that the contract of loan was unenforceable on grounds described by Lord Nicholls: 'The

agreement was a regulated agreement for the purposes of section 8 of the Consumer Credit Act 1974. A regulated agreement is not properly executed unless the document signed contains all the prescribed terms: section 61(1)(a). One of the prescribed terms is the "amount of the credit": see the Consumer Credit (Agreements) Regulations 1983 (SI 1983/1553), regulation 6 and Schedule 6, para 2. The consequence of failure to state all the prescribed terms of the agreement is that the court is precluded, by section 127(3), from enforcing the agreement. In the absence of enforcement by the court the agreement is altogether unenforceable: section 65(1).' The County Court judge held that the agreement was unenforceable because it did not contain details of a 'document fee' added to the loan. On an appeal, the Court of Appeal expressed concern that s 127(3) of the Consumer Credit Act 1974 infringed art 6(1) of the European Convention on Human Rights and art 1 of the First Protocol to the Convention. After an adjourned hearing, the court ([2002] QB 74) 'made a declaration, pursuant to section 4 of the Human Rights Act, that section 127(3), in so far as it prevents the court from making an enforcement order under section 65 of the Consumer Credit Act unless a document containing all the prescribed terms of the agreement has been signed by the debtor, is incompatible with the rights guaranteed to the creditor by article 6(1) of the Convention and article 1 of the First Protocol to the Convention'. The Secretary of State (but not the defendants) appealed in respect of this declaration and the House of Lords (Lords Nicholls, Scott, Hobhouse, Hope and Rodger) allowed the appeal.

Lord Nicholls: ". . . **61** The Human Rights Act 1998 requires the court to exercise a new role in respect of primary legislation. This new role is fundamentally different from interpreting and applying legislation. The courts are now required to evaluate the effect of primary legislation in terms of Convention rights and, where appropriate, make a formal declaration of incompatibility. In carrying out this evaluation the court has to compare the effect of the legislation with the Convention right. If the legislation impinges upon a Convention right the court must then compare the policy objective of the legislation with the policy objective which under the Convention may justify a prima facie infringement of the Convention right. When making these two comparisons the court will look primarily at the legislation, but not exclusively so. Convention rights are concerned with practicalities. When identifying the practical effect of an impugned statutory provision the court may need to look outside the statute in order to see the complete picture, as already instanced in the present case regarding the possible availability of a restitutionary remedy. As to the objective of the statute, at one level this will be coincident with its effect. At this level, the object of section 127(3) is to prevent an enforcement order being made when the circumstances specified in that provision apply. But that is not the relevant level for Convention purposes. What is relevant is the underlying social purpose sought to be achieved by the statutory provision. Frequently that purpose will be self-evident, but this will not always be so . . .

45

72 Undoubtedly, as illustrated by the facts of the present case, section 127(3) may be drastic, even harsh, in its adverse consequences for a lender. He loses all his rights under the agreement, including his rights to any security which has been lodged. Conversely, the borrower acquires what can only be described as a windfall. He keeps the money and recovers his security. These consequences apply just as much where the lender was acting in good faith throughout and the error was due to a mistaken reading of the complex statutory requirements as in cases of deliberate non-compliance. These consequences also apply where, as in the present case, the borrower suffered no prejudice as a result of the non-compliance as they do where the borrower was misled. Parliament was painting here with a broad brush.

73 The unattractive feature of this approach is that it will sometimes involve punishing the blameless pour encourager les autres. On its face, *considered in the context of one particular case*, a sanction having this effect is difficult to justify. The Moneylenders Act 1927 adopted a similarly severe approach. Infringement of statutory requirements rendered the loan and any security unenforceable. So did the Hire Purchase Act 1965, although to a lesser extent. This approach was roundly condemned in the Crowther report (Report of the Committee on Consumer Credit, under the presidency of Lord Crowther, March 1971) (Cmnd 4596), vol. 1, p.311, para.6.11.4:

'It offends every notion of justice or fairness that because of some technical slip which in no way prejudices him, a borrower, having received a substantial sum of money, should be entitled to retain or spend it without any obligation to repay a single penny.'

74 Despite this criticism I have no difficulty in accepting that in suitable instances it is open to Parliament, when Parliament considers the public interest so requires, to decide that compliance with certain formalities is an essential prerequisite to enforcement of certain types of agreements. This course is open to Parliament even though this will sometimes yield a seemingly unreasonable result in a particular case. Considered overall, this course may well be a proportionate response in practice to a perceived social problem. Parliament may consider the response should be a uniform solution across the board. A tailor-made response, fitting the facts of each case as decided in an application to the court, may not be appropriate. This may be considered an insufficient incentive and insufficient deterrent. And it may fail to protect consumers adequately. Persons most in need of protection are perhaps the least likely to participate in court proceedings. They may well let proceedings go by default: see, in relation to money lending agreements, the Crowther report, p.236, para. 6.1.19.

75 Nor do I have any difficulty in accepting that money lending transactions as a class give rise to significant social problems. Bargaining power lies with the lender, and the social evils flowing from this are notorious. The activities of some lenders have long given the business of money lending a bad reputation. Nor, becoming more specific, do I have any difficulty in accepting, in principle, that Parliament may properly make compliance with the formalities required by the Consumer Credit Act regarding 'prescribed terms' an essential prerequisite to enforcement. In principle that course must be open to Parliament. It must be open to Parliament to decide that, severe though this sanction may be, it is an appropriate way of protecting consumers as a matter of social policy. In making its decision in the present case Parliament had the benefit of experience gained over many years in the working of the Moneylenders Act 1927 and the hire purchase legislation, and also the views of the Crowther committee. Further, it must be open to Parliament so to decide even though the lender's inability to enforce an agreement will not assist a borrower who consents to the enforcement of the agreement in ignorance of the true legal position . . ."

Lord Rodger: ". . . **181** It is well recognised . . . that Convention rights are to be seen as an expression of fundamental principles rather than as a set of mere rules. In applying the principles the courts must balance competing interests. . . . Therefore, when deciding whether the order sought by one private party would infringe a Convention right of the other, a court must balance the interests of both parties. If the court finds that the order would infringe the Convention right of the party against whom it would be made, this can only be because the court has concluded that his interests are to be preferred to any competing interests of the party seeking the order. In particular, the court must have concluded that the Convention right of the party resisting the order is to be preferred to the other party's common law or statutory right to obtain it . . ."

(For further extract, see p.114.)

QUESTIONS

1. Ought the protection of *human* rights really to be extended to companies?

2. Ought companies to have the right to vote? Is not their exclusion from the constitutional scene, in a market economy, a breach of their human rights?

3. Could it be said that in charging such a high rate of interest plus a 'document fee', the lending company was in breach of its obligation of good faith? (Cf. *Director General of Fair Trading v First National Bank* (2002) (at p.131).)

1.4.4 European comparative law

A third way in which English contract law can be influenced by European Union ideas is through comparative law, using this expression here simply to mean influences from the contract law of other EU Member States. We have already seen how contract itself was largely an import from the civil law (and see Simpson (1975) 91 L.Q.R. 247), but in more recent years senior judges have become, once again, more sensitive to European ideas. Perhaps this influence should not be exaggerated, as the next extract possibly indicates, but at least the judges are aware that some of our EU partners might do things differently.

Shogun Finance Ltd v Hudson [2004] 1 A.C. 919, HL

(For facts, see p.265.)

Lord Millett (dissenting): ". . . **84** We cannot leave the law as it is. It is neither fair nor principled, and not all the authorities from which it is derived can be reconciled; some, at least, must be overruled if it is to be extricated from the present quagmire. If the law is to be rationalised and placed on a proper footing, the formulation which I have proposed has the merit of according with the recommendations made in the Twelfth Report of the Law Reform Committee on the Transfer of Title to Chattels (Cmnd 2958) and in *Anson's Law of Contract*, 28th ed, p.332. It would also bring English law into line with the law both in the United States and in Germany. The law of the United States has not stood still. Section 2–403 of the Uniform Commercial Code, 14th ed, p.117 provides by subsection (1):

> 'A person with voidable title has power to transfer a good title to a good faith purchaser for value. When goods have been delivered under a transaction of purchase the purchaser has such power even though—(a) the transferor was deceived as to the identity of the purchaser . . . '

Any restriction of the rule to face-to-face transactions has disappeared. In the Official Comment on the section, p.118, reference is made to 'the long-standing policy of civil protection of buyers from persons guilty of such trick or fraud'. This seems to me to be a policy which accords with good sense and justice and one which we ought to adopt for ourselves. I agree with the view of Professor Atiyah, *An Introduction to the Law of Contract*, 5th ed (1995), p 86 that 'a person who hands goods over to a stranger in return for a cheque is obviously taking a major risk, and it does not seem fair that he should be able to shift the burden of this risk on to the innocent third party'.

85 Under German law, too, the innocent third party obtains a good title, though this is a consequence of the law of property rather than the law of contract. Article 932 of the German Civil Code provides that a purchaser acting in good faith acquires title where he obtains possession from a seller who has no title. The purchaser is not in good faith if he knew, or by reason of gross negligence did not know, that the goods did not belong to the seller. Thus, under German law, whether or not A obtained title from B, he is able to pass a good title to D.

86 German law reaches this conclusion by admitting a far wider exception to the nemo dat quod non habet rule than we accept, and this enables it to dispense with the need to decide the contractual effect of mistaken identity (and the meaning of 'identity' in this context) or to conduct a fruitless inquiry into the

> identity of the intended counterparty. Our inability to admit such an exception compels us to adopt a different analysis, but it would be unfortunate if our conclusion proved to be different. Quite apart from anything else, it would make the contemplated harmonisation of the general principles of European contract law very difficult to achieve."

NOTE

Lord Millett might also have mentioned CC art. 2279. In French law, unlike Roman and German law, the contract acts as the means of passing title in goods (and see also the Sale of Goods Act, ss.16–18, above at p.25). However, French law avoids the problem of the innocent third party who acquires goods from someone who turns out not to have good title, because of a defective contract, by having a provision that states that in the case of movables, possession is equivalent to title. English law, which has no such general provision, ends up, as Lord Millett indicates, by leaving innocent purchasers unprotected (see also *Ingram v Little* (1961)).

2 Theory and method

There is a considerable literature, especially from academics writing within the common law tradition, devoted to the theory and philosophy of contract (see, in particular, S. Smith, *Contract Theory* (OUP, 2004)). Much of this literature seeks an answer to the question as to why agreements, or promises, should be enforceable at law. However, as was suggested in the last chapter, there is also a large body of literature devoted to the function of contract. Just how important this literature is for the student following a contract course will depend upon the preference of those teaching the subject. But one feature of contract, compared to many other legal subjects, is its structural coherence, which in turn brings with it a set of often interconnected rules. Thus a course on contract, unlike say one on tort, is usually tempted to focus much of its time on these rules. One need only look at the civil codes of Europe: contract can take up more than two hundred or so articles, while tort (delict) may have only half a dozen. There are not many rules to learn in tort, and as a result policy issues, factual situations and general aims and objectives tend to be more prominent as elements of knowledge. In truth, as this chapter will attempt to indicate, policy issues and methodological approaches are just as relevant for contract, but they can get hidden behind formal rules such as offer and acceptance, implied terms, interpretation of clauses and non-performance. How judges reason in contract cases can, in short, be as important as how they reason in less rule-governed subjects.

With respect to the philosophy of contract, there tends to be two dominant approaches. There are moral based theories and there are functional theories. Like many theories, none is completely satisfactory; nor are they all that original, the moral theories, for example, being largely based on the idea that one should keep one's word or agreements (*pacta sunt servanda*, above at p.8). Many contemporary functional theories fall into one of three broad approaches: there are market capitalism approaches, business efficacy approaches, and economics and law approaches. It would be an exaggeration to say that some of these theories say more about those proposing them than about contract, but the point remains that the relationship between philosophy/theory and contract is extremely elusive, as some of the extracts below will suggest. It may, therefore, be better to spend time looking at the reasoning methods of judges and contract lawyers, comparing approaches between the civil and the common law.

2.1 Problem of theory

One of the main difficulties with respect to fashioning a theory of contract is that the history of the subject offers only limited help, as the following extract indicates.

James Gordley, *The Philosophical Origins of Modern Contract Doctrine* **(OUP, 1991), pp.1–2, 4, 6 (footnotes omitted)**

"The origin of [the] common doctrinal structure [of contract] is, at present, something of a mystery. Supposedly, the common law developed through the decisions of English courts. The civil law was based on the Roman texts of the *Corpus iuris civilis* of the Emperor Justinian, which was in force in most parts of continental Europe before civil codes were enacted nearly everywhere in the late eighteenth and nineteenth centuries. Nevertheless, one cannot find the doctrinal structure . . . in either the English court decisions before the nineteenth century or in the Roman texts. Before the nineteenth century, English law was organized not by general concepts of property, tort, and contract, but by 'forms of action' such as trespass and assumpsit. The Roman law of the *Corpus iuris* contains many particular rules, a few general maxims, but hardly any systematic doctrine . . .

The gap that lies between these larger doctrines and concepts and the Roman texts or English case law has been recognized only in this century. Among continental legal historians the recognition came only after 1900 when, with the enactment of the German Civil Code, the Roman texts ceased to be in force. Before that time, scholars tended to miss the difference between saying that a Roman text could be cited to illustrate a particular doctrine and saying that the ancient Romans themselves had formulated that doctrine. The English legal historian Maitland did see this difference. He knew that the judges who created the English forms of action did not have 'the great elementary conceptions, ownership, possession, contract, tort and the like', distinctly in mind. He concluded that these conceptions had somehow evolved from the English forms of action, although he acknowledged that the history of how they evolved had yet to be written . . .

[The] account of the origin of modern legal doctrine will seem odd to those who are used to economic explanations of legal change. None of the changes we shall consider had much economic significance. What did change was the way contract law was understood . . .

It is not fanciful . . . to identify the late scholastics as the builders of a doctrinal system that, after various modifications, is still with us . . .

It is, however, a surprising story. Its most surprising feature is that doctrines which, in modified form, now govern most of the world were founded on philosophical ideas that fell from favour centuries ago . . ."

NOTE

There is a gap not just between doctrinal structure and positive contract law, but, as the next extract indicates, between contract and reality as well.

John Wightman, *Contract: A Critical Commentary* (Pluto Press, 1996), p.37

"How important is contract law in reality? This question matters because the claim for the central place occupied by the law of contract in legal education turns in part on the notion that contract law is somehow important in the real world. Some law teachers point out the pervasive nature of the practice of contracting by demonstrating to students how many contracts they make unwittingly each day. The thousands of reported cases—which as students soon learn are a fraction of those litigated—provide evidence in the form of situations where contract law has become embroiled. The textbook's confident generalisation of legal principle and how it applies to the facts can result in the impression that those principles are applied in the sort of situations in which they are applied in the books. The tacit understanding (which the text does not discourage) is that a breach of contract will be followed by reparation in the form indicated by the rules, backed by legal threat or actual legal action if necessary. As we shall see, this picture is simply wrong . . ."

NOTES

1. See also the extract from Mulcahy and Tillotson (at p.81).

2. History and business reality seem of little help when it comes to explaining the nature and function of the modern law of contract. It may be that the theorists are too busy focusing on the doctrinal structure of contract, and on the remedy of damages, and not on the statistically most important remedy used to enforce contractual obligations.

Tony Weir, "Non-Performance of a Contractual Obligation and its Consequences in English Law" in L. Vacca (ed.), *Il contratto inadempiuto: Realtà e tradizione del diritto contrattuale europeo* (G Giappichelli, 1998), pp.71, at p.72 (footnotes omitted)

"The critical matter is, what did the defendant promise to do and under what conditions? Here the principal distinction, as it seems to me, is between promises to pay money and all other promises, and I am glad to see that the distinction is taken in both the Lando principles and those from Unidroit. Of course all other promises are not the same, and much may turn on whether the promise is to do a service or transfer a thing (and when it is a thing, the law in England is vastly different depending on whether it is land or a chattel); but money promises are really *very* distinctive, and this is true even if other promises tend to collapse, on breach, into monetary obligations by way of damages. Though one would never suppose it from the books, the money promise is the commonest of all promises, and the one most commonly unperformed. Consumers are always presented as victims; the truer view is that they are people who don't pay for what they've got. Whatever academics say or might like to think, courts are principally collectors of *debts*, not extractors of *damages*. The money promise dominates the whole banking, insurance and bond market; it is the promise most commonly assigned; and under our very eyes it is becoming abstract, as is shown by demand guarantees and confirmed credits, as well as by negotiable instruments which have to be monetary.

. . . But the damages remedy is fundamentally different from the enforcement remedy of claiming a debt, since the latter does not involve exciting matters like harm, causation, mitigation, contributory negligence, remoteness, quantum and other topics which delight the heart and mind of the scholar and judge. And perhaps this audience will find it of interest that in medieval times there were quite different formulae for actions to claim a specific sum and for actions in respect of other promises, namely debt and *covenant* respectively: not all the distinctions drawn by our ancestors were stupid . . ."

NOTE

The remedy of debt is thus central to the law of contract (and its history in England), and perhaps holds the key to contract's importance in the modern world. See further extracts in **11.2**.

QUESTIONS

1. If reality is the order of the day, would it not be better for law schools to have courses entitled "Debt" rather than "Contract" (plus another course entitled "Damages")?

2. Many contract theorists ask: why are contracts enforceable? But is this the right question? Should one perhaps be asking: why should one pay one's debts? Are there situations when a debtor should be relieved from a legal obligation to pay?

3. Given the difficulty of propounding a theory that links contract with commercial and social reality, or even fully explains its history or its purpose, should one adopt an anti-theory approach?

Tony Weir, "Contracts in Rome and England" (1992) 66 *Tulane Law Review* 1615, at 1616 (footnotes omitted)

"We have no theory to propound, neither of the institution of contract nor of its historical development. Contract, like tort, and rather more so than obligation, is a construct, an institution, not a natural system such as a cat or a stone, and unlike Jeremy Bentham and all too many of his ilk, we are not persuaded of the merits of propounding a single theory for the explanation, much less for the determination or delimitation, of such a construct or institution. It is not by reason of any entelechy in the notion of contract that it covers what it now does, or ever did. Like history itself, we are not opposed to casuistry. It is possible for us, like Hamlet, to tell a hawk from a handsaw, and to do so without a complete theory of aerial predators or an exhaustive inventory of the carpenter's toolbox; furthermore, we can effect such telling without having a theory of telling, though the current fad of epistemology might lead one to doubt that (given a theory of doubting). Nor, though we shall talk of developments, shall we suppose that they occurred in response to any rule or even as instances of any trend . . .”

QUESTIONS

1. Is Weir in truth propounding a theory?

2. What is the difference between a “theory”, a “construct” and an “institution”?

3. If contract is a “construct”, what is being “constructed”: a set of rules (the rules of the law of contract), or a set of facts (a factual situation deemed as contractual)?

2.2 Practical importance of theory

What has been said so far might give the impression that theory is largely irrelevant or unhelpful to the understanding of contract as a practical law subject. However, such a conclusion would amount to a misunderstanding of the role of theory. Of course much depends upon what is meant by “theory” in this context, since it is a term that masks as much as it reveals. Simply to propound a “theory” is often to advance a whole bundle of conscious and unconscious positions operating at what might be termed different levels of abstraction. And so behind every theory there are associated reasoning methods (e.g. induction or deduction), schemes of intelligibility (e.g. structuralism or functionalism), paradigms (holism or individualism) and knowledge orientations (synchronic or diachronic) (see Samuel (2007) 2 J.C.L. 1).

For example, in the last extract in **2.1** above, Tony Weir asserts that he has no theory. In truth, if one reads all his important contributions to private law, one will find in these writings all manner of reasoning methods, schemes of intelligibility, paradigms and epistemological (and ideological) orientations, and the fact that he is disdainful of all of this does not make his position any less theoretically informed. He is propounding a theory in as much as his anti-theory stance is hiding his own ideological and economic opinions with respect to the role and place of law and of contract. Equally judges have ideologies and economic beliefs, and these inform decisions as much as any objective rules of contract (see, e.g., Sir George Jessel, below at p.117). When one looks at contract over the last couple of centuries, it soon becomes clear that these ideological and economic beliefs have changed; and as a result, contract, and the assumptions behind contract, have equally changed.

P.S. Atiyah, *The Rise and Fall of Freedom of Contract* (OUP, 1979), pp.398, 400, 402, 404

"The period 1770–1870 saw the emergence of general principles of contract law closely associated with the development of the free market and the ideals of the political economists. The period saw the shift in emphasis from property law to contract; and within the realm of contract it saw the shift from particular relationships, or particular types of contract, to general principles of contract, and the shift from executed to executory contracts. The first requirement of the lawyers in this new age was for a new kind of literature. They needed books which treated contract law as a whole, which enunciated general principles of contract law, and illustrated the application of these general principles to the solution of particular problems. The existing literature lacked the necessary generality, it emphasized procedure rather than substance, and it also lacked simple clarity let alone literary grace . . .

There seems no doubt that all this generality, this attempt to state the law in terms of abstract principle, fitted well with the new political economy. It was a law suited to the free market, in which the subject matter of the contract was immaterial. During the course of this century, that is between 1770 and 1870, this general law of contract did very largely create a body of rules applicable to all contracts alike . . .

This emphasis on contract law as the law of the market was, in England at least, well established by 1870, although in America it may have been a later development. One of its principal characteristics was its abstractness, its lack of particularity, its attempt to treat all contracts as being of the same general character . . . The emphasis on the fixed rules of contract law, the emphasis on the abstract nature of these rules and of their applicability to all people and all subject-matter alike, has been treated as part of the very nature of certain and predictable rules as opposed to more flexible, but more unpredictable discretionary justice. The rule of the market place is thus equated with the Rule of Law itself . . .

In general terms, this equation of general principles of contract law with the free market economy led to an emphasis on the framework within which individuals bargained with each other, and a retreat from interest in substantive justice or fairness. The model of contract theory which implicitly underlay the classical law of contract—for such we may now call it—was thus the model of the market . . .

The Court's function in all this is to ensure procedural fair play: the Court is the umpire to be appealed to when a foul is alleged, but the Court has no substantive function beyond this. It is not the Court's business to ensure that the bargain is fair, or to see that one party does not take undue advantage of another, or impose unreasonable terms by virtue of superior bargaining position. Any superiority in bargaining power is itself a matter for the market to rectify . . . It is the task of the parties to fix their liabilities themselves . . ."

QUESTION

How can one actually prove any association between the development of contract and the development of the free market? If the basic "construct" of contract comes from an era well before 1770–1870 (Roman law, Domat, Pothier), is not the connection one of *post hoc ergo propter hoc*?

NOTES

1. This classical model attitude has found its greatest expression, as the above extract suggests, in the principle of freedom of contract: see **3.2**. Note, in particular, the comment of Sir George Jessel (at p.117).

2. This idea of a "classical" model of contract has now become accepted wisdom amongst a great many common law contract lawyers. As a "construct" (*pace* Weir), it does seem to be an historical truism, in that before the 19th century, as many writers have pointed out, there was not much of a law of contract as such, only a series of forms of action. Moreover, as the next extract indicates, there seems in the 20th century to have been a retreat from this classical model (and see also *Lloyds Bank v Bundy* (1975), at p.72).

> **K. Zweigert and H. Kötz, *An Introduction to Comparative Law* (3rd edn, OUP, 1998), p.331 (translation T. Weir)**
>
> "The phrase 'inequality of bargaining power' raises a question much discussed by contract theorists: modern conditions being what they are, is it still right to treat contract as a central pillar of the legal system? Should it not be limited *ex lege* wherever the parties to a contract are unequal in bargaining power, where 'parity of contract' is disturbed and the weaker party needs protection? Is it not time to replace or supplement the principle of freedom of contract by a principle of 'contractual justice'?
>
> The way contracts are made today makes the question unavoidable, for as everyone knows, their terms are very rarely negotiated in any real sense. Often this is because one party has so much more economic clout than the other and can dictate the terms on which he will do business. In many markets, such as housing and employment, demand is so great and supply so short that the applicant has really no chance of exercising his freedom of contract and having any effect on the terms of the deal. In many other cases one party blindly accepts whatever terms are offered without any negotiations at all because he lacks business experience or bargaining skill or much interest in getting favourable terms.
>
> All legal systems have reacted to this situation in one way or another, for everyone recognizes that devices such as competition law are needed to constrain the free play of economic forces, for otherwise economic dominance will result

and be abused. Accordingly when there is no real competition and one person badly needs a resource controlled by another, the law may entitle the former and require the latter to enter into a contract for its supply, often on terms laid down by a state authority or approved by them for fairness, as in the case of provision of utilities or transport. Many other contracts, such as contracts of employment, domestic lettings, insurance contracts, and consumer credit bargains, are subject to a thicket of rules which give some protection to the weaker party. These 'regulated' contracts now seem to lead a kind of life of their own outside the pale of general contract law, thereby shrinking the area over which the flag of freedom of contract can flutter. But even the terms of 'unregulated' contracts are subject to supervision: courts in most countries now have a general power to invalidate contract terms which are 'unconscionable' or 'unfair' or which cause 'a significant imbalance between the rights and duties of the parties in a manner contrary to the dictates of good faith' . . . To what is this development due? Many observers say that it is now quite fanciful to think that the adult individual is a responsible person concerned for his advancement and capable of foreseeing and evaluating the consequences of his actions, and that the task of the law of contract today should be to ensure 'contractual justice': contract must become a device for co-operation and fairness by increasing the protection of the weaker party and obliging both parties to look out for the interests of the other . . ."

PROBLEM

Ian, an expert on fine art, enters a charity shop and discovers a very rare drawing, which he believes to be by Poussin, on sale for £30. Ian pays this price and, subsequently, resells the drawing at an auction house for £1 million. The charity shop discovers what has happened and contacts Ian, claiming that the original contract of sale for £30 was in bad faith and against contractual justice. Ought the charity shop to be able to claim part, if not all, of the resale profit made by Ian? What if the seller was not a charity shop but a private person selling off stuff at a car boot sale, and Ian was an amateur fine arts expert?

QUESTIONS

1. Do you think that English law is attracted by this idea of a contractor having to take account of his co-contractor's interests? Might it depend upon the type of contract?

2. If an adult is to be treated as not a "responsible person", does this imply that he should be treated like a child? Might it not depend upon the adult in question—the rocket scientist and stock broker being treated differently by the law of contract than the manual worker with no educational qualifications?

2.3 Contract and fact

One of the important roles of theory is to explain the relationship between contract and the reality in which it functions. Yet this is, not surprisingly, complex and operates at a variety of different levels. There are the everyday facts that make up the contract cases found in the law reports. How does the law actually relate to these facts? At a more general level one can identify types of factual situations: for example, the sociologist recognises differences between sale transactions, employment situations, family co-operative ventures and so on. The sociologist, together with the economist, might even talk of different status groups, such as consumers, suppliers and manufacturers, and public bodies. How does the law of contract relate to these typical fact situations and status groups? At an even more general level of social reality there are notions such as culture, beliefs, economies, political institutions and the like. How does contract relate to these aspects of society? This section will not provide a comprehensive response to these questions, but it will try to indicate some of the broader formal ways contract as a law subject responds to differences in factual and social reality.

2.3.1 Contract and transaction

Tony Weir might be disdainful of theory, but one of his important contributions to our understanding of the subject (besides his stressing of the important role of debt) is his insistence that there is a gulf between a general theory of contract and the factual transactions and relations to which contract applies.

Tony Weir, "Contracts in Rome and England" (1992) 66 *Tulane Law Review* **1615, at 1638–1640 (footnotes omitted)**

"The civilian emphasis on the different kinds of contract rather puzzles the English lawyer, for he assumes that contract consists only of the general part and is strongly disinclined to pay much attention to the nature of the transaction in question. In complete contrast to his attitude to torts, his approach to contract is abstract and unitary. The reason is that whereas the law of torts developed (as did the Roman law of contracts) under different forms of action—trespass, case, trover and so on—the English law of contract since the early seventeenth century had really only one form of action—*assumpsit* . . . A student asked to specify what kind of contract he has in mind will sooner think of replying 'bilateral' than 'sale' or 'employment' or 'carriage'.

This abstraction is distractingly unrealistic. Before entering law school the student knows better than to offer a 'premium' to the bus-conductor, or pay 'freight' when he (as opposed to his baggage) travels by air . . . Yet three weeks in a contract course makes him forget what every layman knows, namely that these different designations are given to the money you pay, depending on what you pay it for.

59

Instead of realizing that such distinctions would not be made if they did not matter, he is induced to give the same name, 'consideration,' not only to whatever it is one is paying for but also to the money one pays for it. It is as if medical students had a first-year course entitled 'Disease,' and consequently came to believe that diseases were all much of a muchness and that when it was a question of remedies, it did not really matter whether it was a case of nephritis or schizophrenia.

Now of course the lawyer in practice knows that it really does matter what the transaction is, because different rules do apply to different transactions . . ."

NOTE

Accordingly there are, for example, different statutory regimes depending upon whether the contract is one of sale of goods (Sale of Goods Act 1979), hire of goods (Supply of Goods and Services Act 1982), marine insurance (Marine Insurance Act 1906), partnership (Partnership Act 1890), hire-purchase (Hire-Purchase Act 1964; Consumer Credit Act 1974), carriage of goods by road (Carriage of Goods by Road Act 1965), carriage of goods by sea (Carriage of Goods by Sea Acts 1971 and 1992) and so on. The whole of this article by Tony Weir will repay reading.

2.3.2 Supply of goods and supply of service contracts

One important transactional distinction to be found within the law of contracts is the distinction between a contract to supply a thing and a contract to supply a service. The focal point of the first type of contract is the thing, whereas in the second type of contract it is the personal acts of the contractor. To what extent is this difference reflected in the general law of contract?

Sale of Goods Act 1979 (c. 54)

"14. Implied terms about quality or fitness

(1) Except as provided by this section and section 15 below and subject to any other enactment, there is no implied term about the quality or fitness for any particular purpose of goods supplied under a contract of sale.

(2) Where the seller sells goods in the course of a business, there is an implied term that the goods supplied under the contract are of satisfactory quality;

(2A) For the purposes of this Act, goods are of satisfactory quality if they meet the standard that a reasonable person would regard as satisfactory, taking account of any description of the goods, the price (if relevant) and all the other relevant circumstances. . . .

(3) Where the seller sells goods in the course of a business and the buyer, expressly or by implication, makes known—

(a) to the seller . . .
(b) . . . any particular purpose for which the goods are being bought,

there is an implied term that the goods supplied under the contract are reasonably fit for that purpose, whether or not that is a purpose for which such goods are commonly supplied, except where the circumstances show that the buyer does not rely, or that it is unreasonable for him to rely, on the skill or judgment of the seller . . ."

QUESTION

A shop stocking cans of cola, manufactured by a well-known corporation, sells a can to a consumer, who becomes very ill as a result of a decomposed snail that had somehow got into the can during the manufacturing and canning process. There were no means by which the seller could possibly know if any of the cans that he sold were contaminated. Can the consumer nevertheless sue the seller for damages for breach of contract?

Frost v Aylesbury Dairy Co Ltd [1905] 1 K.B. 608, CA

Collins M.R.: "This is an appeal by the defendants in an action in which the plaintiff sued to recover expenses to which he was put by the illness and death of his wife, caused, as he alleged, by typhoid fever of which the infection was caught from milk supplied by the defendants. The jury found that the milk was the cause of the fever, and gave a verdict for the plaintiff, for whom judgment was entered. The first point taken is whether in point of law, on the facts as ascertained, there can be any liability on the defendants even if it is admitted that the milk was the cause of the fever, and on this it is contended for the defendants that there was no actionable wrong on their part. The point is whether the circumstances under which the milk was bought bring the case within the provisions of s 14, sub-s 1, [see now s.14(3) of the 1979 Act] of the Sale of Goods Act 1893 . . . Considering the matter by steps, it appears that there was no specific evidence as to the inception of the relation of buyer and seller, because, as a matter of fact, people do not, when they want a milk supply, enter into an elaborate negotiation with the vendor of the milk. We begin the discussion with the practice followed in the dealing between two parties. The fact of the supply of the article involves a contract. That contract is for the supply of food, for no one would question that the milk was bought as an article of consumption . . . [M]ilk was supplied for a purpose known to the sellers under circumstances which showed that the buyer relied on the sellers' skill or knowledge, and that the goods were of a description which it was in the course of the sellers' business to supply. The point mainly pressed upon us on behalf of the defendants was that the buyer could not be said to rely on the skill or judgment of the sellers in a case in which no amount of skill or judgment would enable them to find out the defect in the milk supplied. That amounts to a contention that a seller of goods cannot be answerable for a latent defect in them unless upon a special contract to that effect. That argument is not employed for the first time, for it was used before the Sale of Goods Act 1893, which consolidated and crystallised the law, which seems to me to be just the same under the statute as it was under the common law. The matter was specifically dealt with in the considered judgment of the Court of Appeal in *Randall v Newson*, where it was held that on the sale of an article for a specific purpose there is a warranty by the vendor that it is reasonably fit for the purpose, and that there is no exception as to latent undiscoverable defects. That was the case of a defective pole for a carriage, and the view of the Court is expressed thus: 'If the subject-matter be an article or commodity to be used for a particular purpose, the thing offered or delivered must answer that description, that is to say, it must be that article or commodity, and reasonably fit for the particular purpose. The governing principle, therefore, is that the thing offered and delivered under a contract of purchase and sale must answer the description of it which is contained in words in the contract, or which would be so contained if the contract were accurately drawn out. And if that be the governing principle, there is no place in it for the suggested limitation.' The suggested limitation was that the principle applied only to such defects as could be discovered by reasonable care and skill. The judgment continues:

'If the article or commodity offered or delivered does not in fact answer the description of it in the contract, it does not do so more or less because the defect in it is patent, or latent, or discoverable.'

That appears to me to be a conclusive authority on that part of the case raised on behalf of the defendants. I may, however, refer also to a matter that was dealt with in the judgment of this Court in *Preist v Last*, that a good deal of difficulty and some confusion may arise as to whether an article is sold for a particular purpose where it is capable of being used for a number of purposes. Where the thing dealt with carries in its description a limitation to a particular purpose the difficulty does not arise. In this case we begin with the purchase of milk, a commodity which carries with it a special limitation to the purpose of food. It is obvious that the obligation of the seller of food must stand in a different position from that of the seller of an article that may or may not, according to the special circumstances of the case, be used for a particular object. All the difficulty is gone when once we get in the description of the article itself the purpose for which it is to be used. That principle was applied in the case to which I have referred, which was that of the purchase of a hot-water bottle, a description which carries with it the purpose for which the article is bought. The same principle applies in this case, where it is clear that the milk was bought for a special purpose, and sold by persons who claimed and received the confidence of the purchaser in the special skill and knowledge asserted by the sellers. It seems to me to be clear that there is no legal difficulty in upholding this verdict, and that the appeal should be dismissed."

(Mathew and Cozens-Hardy L.JJ. were of the same opinion.)

NOTES

1. The sellers of the milk in this case were trying to argue that they were not in breach of contract because they themselves had committed no wrong. How were they to know the milk was infected? The court decided, however, that the promise attached not to their behaviour but to the thing (milk) itself. Either the milk was fit, or it was not. If it was not, there was a breach of s.14 of the Sale of Goods Act 1893 (now 1979).

2. The Sale of Goods Act has been considerably amended since this case: see now the Sale of Goods Act 1979. One should note, also, how the Act is dependent upon the existence of a general law of contract, which of course has not been officially codified.

QUESTIONS

1. A doctor, treating a patient under a private contract (and not the NHS) for a particular disease, fails to cure the disease, despite using her best professional skills. Can the patient sue the doctor for damages for breach of contract? (Cf. the Supply of Goods and Services Act 1982, s.13, below at p.381.)

2. A private clinic advertises that it will carry out vasectomies for a certain price, and that those who avail themselves of the clinic's services can have "full confidence in the service provided". A client has a vasectomy, but it proves ineffective and the client's partner becomes pregnant. Assuming that no negligence can be attributed either to the clinic itself or to any of its employees, can (i) the client, or (ii) the client's partner sue the clinic for breach of contract?

Thake v Maurice [1986] Q.B. 644, CA

This was a successful action for damages founded in contract and tort against a surgeon for failing to warn a married couple that a vasectomy does not always render a man permanently sterile. One question that arose for discussion in the case was the level of duty: was the defendant under a strict contractual duty to render Mr Thake permanently sterile, or only under a duty to use care and skill? In the Court of Appeal Kerr L.J. thought that it was a strict duty, but the majority (Neill and Norse L.JJ.) thought that it was a duty to take care.

Kerr L.J. (dissenting in part): ". . . The judge reached the conclusion that in the unusual circumstances of this case the plaintiffs had established that the revival of Mr Thake's fertility gave rise to a breach of the contract concluded between the defendant and the plaintiffs . . .

On this issue I have reached the same conclusion as the judge. Having regard to everything that passed between the defendant and the plaintiffs at the meeting, coupled with the absence of any warning that Mr Thake might somehow again become fertile after two successful sperm tests, it seems to me that the plaintiffs could not reasonably have concluded anything other than that his agreement to perform the operation meant that, subject to two successful sperm tests, he had undertaken to render Mr Thake permanently sterile. In my view this follows from an objective analysis of the undisputed evidence of what passed between the parties, and it was also what the plaintiffs understood and intended to be the effect of the contract with the defendant.

The considerations which lead me to this conclusion can be summarised as follows. First, we are here dealing with something in the nature of an amputation, not treatment of an injury or disease with inevitably uncertain results. The nature of the operation was the removal of parts of the channels through which sperm had to pass to the outside in such a way that the channels could not reunite. This was vividly demonstrated to the plaintiffs by the defendant pulling apart his arms and fists and turning back his wrists, as well as by a sketch. The defendant repeatedly and carefully explained that the effect of the operation was final, as the plaintiffs said again and again in their evidence, subject only to a remote possibility of surgical reversal, and that was the only warning which the defendant impressed on them. Subject to this and the two sperm tests of which the plaintiffs were told, designed to make sure that the operation had in fact been successful, I cannot see that one can place any interpretation on what the defendant said and did other than that he undertook to render Mr Thake permanently sterile by means of the operation. Nor can I see anything in the transcripts of the evidence which leads to any other conclusion, and the defendant himself agreed that in the context of the discussion as a whole, the word 'irreversible' would have been understood by the plaintiffs as meaning 'irreversible by God or man'. On the evidence in this case the position is quite different, in my view, from what was in the mind of Lord Denning MR in *Greaves & Co (Contractors) Ltd v Baynham Meikle & Partners* [1975] 1 WLR 1095, 1100, when he said: 'The surgeon does not warrant that he will cure the patient.' That was said in the context of treatment or an operation designed to cure, not in the context of anything in the nature of an amputation. The facts of the present case are obviously extremely unusual, but I do not see why the judge's and my conclusion on these unusual facts should be viewed by surgeons with alarm, as mentioned by the judge. If the defendant had given his usual warning, the objective analysis of what he conveyed would have been quite different . . .

Accordingly, I would uphold the judge's conclusion that the plaintiffs succeed in their claim that the revival of Mr Thake's fertility gave rise to a breach of contract on the part of the defendant . . ."

Neill L.J.: "I have had the advantage of reading in draft the judgment of Kerr LJ and . . . I regret to say, however, that I am unable to agree with his conclusion as to the claim in contract . . .

I accept that there may be cases where, because of the claims made by a surgeon or physician for his method of treatment, the court is driven to the conclusion that the result of the treatment is guaranteed or warranted. But in the present case I do not regard the statements made by the defendant as to the effect of his treatment as passing beyond the realm of expectation and assumption. It seems to me that what he said was spoken partly by way of warning and partly by way of what is sometimes called 'therapeutic reassurance'. Both the plaintiffs and the defendant expected that sterility would be the result of the operation and the defendant appreciated that that was the plaintiffs' expectation. This does not mean, however, that a reasonable person would have understood the defendant to be giving a binding promise that the operation would achieve its purpose or that the defendant was going further than to give an assurance that he expected and believed that it would have the desired result. Furthermore, I do not consider that a reasonable person would have expected a responsible medical man to be intending to give a guarantee. Medicine, though a highly skilled profession, is not, and is not generally regarded as being, an exact science. The reasonable man would have expected the defendant to exercise all the proper skill and care of a surgeon in that speciality; he would not in my view have expected the defendant to give a guarantee of 100 per cent success . . ."

Nourse L.J.: ". . . The contract contained an implied warranty that, in carrying out the operation, the defendant would exercise the ordinary skill and care of a competent surgeon. It did not contain an implied warranty that, come what may, the objective would be achieved: see *Greaves & Co (Contractors) Ltd v Baynham Meikle & Partners* [1975] 1 WLR 1095, 1100, per Lord Denning MR . . .

Lord Denning thought, and I respectfully agree with him, that a professional man is not usually regarded as warranting that he will achieve the desired result. Indeed, it seems that that would not fit well with the universal warranty of reasonable care and skill, which tends to affirm the inexactness of the science which is professed. I do not intend to go beyond the case of a doctor. Of all sciences medicine is one of the least exact. In my view a doctor cannot be objectively regarded as guaranteeing the success of any operation or treatment unless he says as much in clear and unequivocal terms. The defendant did not do that in the present case . . ."

NOTES

1. If a service provided by a contractor turns out to be defective, why is it that the law does not take the same approach as it does when goods prove

defective? There are several responses. First, although at first sight it might seem harsh to make the seller strictly liable for the condition of the goods, it has to be remembered that the seller can probably in turn claim damages or an indemnity for breach of s.14 of the Sale of Goods Act 1979 under the contract of sale he has with his supplier of the goods (manufacturer or wholesaler).

2. Secondly, the difference is one of focus. In a contract of sale the focal point of the contract is the product or thing sold (*res*), whereas in a contract of service the focal point is the behaviour and skill of the other contractor (*persona*). English contract law has long distinguished (for better or worse) between people and things. Thus, for example, if a coach company loses a passenger's suitcase, it will be strictly liable (see *Houghland v RR Low (Luxury Coaches) Ltd* (1962)); but if it causes personal injury to the passenger himself, fault must be proved (*Readhead v Midland Railway Co* (1869), at p.377).

3. Thirdly, the strict liability might be justified as a matter of economic policy. The seller is the one who profits from his mark-up on the goods, and so he should be the one who takes the risk (see *Hyman v Nye* (1881), at p.376). Services are different because the paradigm example has traditionally been the doctor: she never promises to cure the patient, only to use her best professional skill (but *cf. Thake v Maurice*, above). None of this is to say that this economic policy with respect to the difference between goods and services always makes sense. Note that s.14 of the Sale of Goods Act 1979 and s.13 of the Supply of Goods and Services Act 1982 apply only to professional sellers ("in the course of a business").

2.3.3 Short-term and long-term contracts

A general theory of contract which covers sale, employment, hire, carriage and so on has no means of formally distinguishing between the substance of the relationships in question. All contracts are contracts and a contract is a single set of rules. However, doctrine has increasingly recognised an important distinction between instantaneous and relational contracts.

John Bell, "The Effect of Changes in Circumstances on Long-term Contracts" in D. Harris and D. Tallon (eds), *Contract Law Today* (OUP, 1989), p.195, at pp.195, 197, 198 (footnotes omitted)

"**1.** . . . The notion of a 'long-term contract' is a sociological, not a legal, category, but one which none the less creates specific legal problems. Such a contract may be contrasted with a discrete, one-off contract, where performance is more or less instantaneous, and there need be no prior or subsequent dealings between the parties. The notions of 'long-term' contractual relationships and 'discrete contracts' are not rigidly demarcated categories, but represent ends of a spectrum along which contractual relationships may fall . . .

5. The problems posed by long-term consensual relationships are not new. Classically, the law has provided for them by establishing special regimes which have, to a greater or lesser extent, removed such relationships from the application of ordinary contract-law principles. The contract of marriage, for instance is governed by rules of a status kind from which the parties cannot escape by private agreement, and by rules on property governing the ownership and occupation of the matrimonial home. The relationships of landlord and tenant, and employer and employee are increasingly regulated by similar rules of a status kind, governing the right to enter into and remain in such a relationship, and governing its terms. Company law and the special rules on partnership also show the willingness of the law to provide special regimes for recurrent forms of long-term relationship. Whether one classifies such relationships as 'special contracts' or 'non-contractual relationships', it remains important to note that the ordinary rules of contract law may well not be the way in which many long-term relationships are handled by English (and French) law.

6. The problem of long-term *contracts* is thus in many ways a residual area of the law. It concerns relationships which are, on the one hand, either too novel to have acquired specialized regimes, such as franchising, or are too diverse to be capable of being organized into a specialized regime, or, on the other hand, have proved to be adequately handled by the creation of *de facto* specialized regimes by the trade without the need for State intervention, e.g. construction and engineering contracts, or charterparties . . .

7. Long-term relationships give rise to problems which are different from one-off, instantaneous contracts, such as the purchase of petrol from a motorway garage. The planning and specificity of the obligations undertaken by the parties, which are the hallmark of the latter, become more difficult because of the added complexities and uncertainties which are involved in long-term relationships. Given limited information and the bounded rationality of the parties, planning as to the duration, price, or other terms of a long-term contract becomes more difficult. It will be harder for each of the parties to make an adequate judgment about what is going to be a rational course of action several years hence—what will be their requirements, how will their businesses operate, or what kind of alternative opportunities will be available? Equally, in many cases, it will not be possible to foresee or calculate adequately the impact of external market and other forces and circumstances. What may start out as a perfectly sensible bargain may turn out to be unexpectedly onerous because of changed economic, supply, political, or technological conditions . . . In such circumstances, it may be appropriate, as Macneil and others have argued, to treat such relational contracts as different, both economically and legally, from other types of contract . . ."

NOTES AND QUESTIONS

1. As Professor Bell indicates, long-term contracts give rise to special problems. First, the circumstances that were in play when the contract was signed could well, as the years go by, change. For example, a long-term contract to supply a product such as water or gas for a fixed price could well become the victim of inflation or sudden changed global conditions. Should the supplier be forced to continue to supply at what might have become a totally unrealistic price? What about the construction contract where a constructor, having stipulated a total price, finds that there is a sudden and unforeseeable shortage of materials and labour? (Cf. *Staffs Area Health Authority v South Staffs Waterworks Co* (1978), at p.428; *Davis Contractors Ltd v Fareham UDC* (1956), at p.426.)

2. Secondly, the interests in play in long-term relationships may well prove different from those in instantaneous contracts. A contract to buy a newspaper is hardly likely to generate the same party interests as a long-term employment contract. The seller and buyer of a newspaper or can of paint need not concern themselves too much with the general welfare of the person with whom they are dealing. But can the same be said of the employer–employee relationship? Or what about the family solicitor who has been retained by the same family over many years? (Cf. *White v Jones* (1995).)

3. Thirdly, if the law of contract does wish to differentiate between instantaneous and relational contracts, how should it do this? What contractual concepts can be employed to give expression to the distinction? A further problem is distinguishing between the instantaneous and the relational contract: a well-known, high-street chain-store places orders for goods with a particular manufacturer over many years—is this a long series of instantaneous contracts, or a long-term relational contract? (Cf. *Baird Textiles Holdings Ltd v Marks & Spencer plc* (2001), at p.207.)

FURTHER NOTE

Note how some long-term relationships transform themselves from mere *contractual* relationships to situations of *status*. The distinction between contract and status goes back to Roman law: the latter notion formed part of the law of persons, while the former was part of the law of things. Status was a category that attached to the person (*persona*) and fixed his or her position in society. In ancient and in some more contemporary societies status was (and remains) a means of distinguishing between different groups of people, and perhaps of granting fewer rights to some groups than to others (e.g. to slaves, or to Jewish people in Nazi Europe). The distinctions between citizens and aliens and between minors and adults are typical modern examples of status, and sometimes this can lead to unacceptable discrimination (see, e.g. *A v Secretary of State for the Home Department* (2005)).

FURTHER QUESTION

With regard to the relationship between status and contract, Sir Henry Maine famously remarked in 1861 that "we may say that the movement of the progressive societies has hitherto been a movement *from Status to Contract*". Is Professor Bell suggesting that we are now moving back from contract to status relationships?

H.F. Jolowicz, *Lectures on Jurisprudence* (The Athlone Press, 1963), pp.379–380 (footnotes omitted)

"Now Maine regarded the movement 'from status to contract' as definitely a progress, and this view could scarcely be challenged when he wrote; for it was part of the prevailing philosophy to regard freedom of will as the ultimate aim of the law and indeed to consider government as an evil to be reduced within the strictest possible limits of what was required for the delimitation of the spheres of competing wills. But it must not be forgotten that Maine was careful to limit his generalisation to the past—he said 'hitherto'—and it has been observed that recently there has been a move in the opposite direction. Freedom of contract has been severely limited by social legislation, such as the rule against an employer's contracting out of liability to one employee for the negligence of another in common employment with him; and the innumerable restrictions on hours and conditions of labour by Factory Acts, Shop Acts and the like.

But legislative interference with freedom of contract is not the only thing to be considered here Though the individual workman still makes his contract of employment himself, in a huge number of cases the conditions of his employment are in fact settled for him by agreements made between the employers and the Trade Unions. The theory of the law may be that a man only becomes a boiler-maker or a coal-miner if he wishes and can freely negotiate the terms of his employment, but in fact there is not much choice for the boy of merely ordinary capacity born in a mining village. He has to make a contract of employment with the mine-owner and his duties are determined by his birth and by the *de facto* necessity of entering a Trade Union. Though the pretence of freedom of contract may be maintained, in truth the conditions of his working life are attributable at least as much to status as to contract . . ."

NOTES AND QUESTIONS

1. Professor Jolowicz was writing nearly half a century ago, when there were still operational coalmines and mining villages. Can you think of a contemporary analogy to replace his coalmining example?

2. Freedom of contract has become even more restricted since Professor Jolowicz's time. In particular the legislator, often as a result of Brussels Directives, has intervened to protect consumers by modifying, sometimes quite dramatically, the ordinary rules of contract (see **8.4**). Can one talk of "consumer" being a status category?

2.3.4 Human and non-human contractors

Whether one is talking about short- or long-term contracts, a contract is about a legal relation between two "persons". It is described by civil lawyers as a *vinculum juris* (legal chain) binding the two parties. However, in emphasising the relationship it is easy to forget about the notion of a "person" itself. If one looks at the names of the parties in the contract cases mentioned in this book, it soon becomes evident that "person" covers more than just humans; it includes corporations, public as well as private, and these corporations are treated as if they are humans. But how is a non-human contractor to perform its contract, if not through humans?

Tesco Supermarkets Ltd v Nattrass **[1972] A.C. 153, HL**

Lord Reid: ". . . I must start by considering the nature of the personality which by a fiction the law attributes to a corporation. A living person has a mind which can have knowledge or intention or be negligent and he has hands to carry out his intentions. A corporation has none of these: it must act through living persons, though not always one or the same person. Then the person who acts is not speaking or acting for the company. He is acting as the company and his mind which directs his acts is the mind of the company. There is no question of the company being vicariously liable. He is not acting as a servant, representative, agent or delegate. He is an embodiment of the company or, one could say, he hears and speaks through the persona of the company, within his appropriate sphere, and his mind is the mind of the company. If it is a guilty mind then that guilt is the guilt of the company. It must be a question of law whether, once the facts have been ascertained, a person in doing particular things is to be regarded as the company or merely as the company's servant or agent. In that case any liability of the company can only be a statutory or vicarious liability . . ."

QUESTION

What if a mere servant (employee) or an agent of the company does an act which is at odds with the company's contractual obligation to another?

Photo Production Ltd v Securicor Transport Ltd **[1980] A.C. 827, HL**

(For full facts, see p.406.)

Lord Wilberforce: "My Lords, this appeal arises from the destruction by fire of the respondents' factory involving loss and damage agreed to amount to £615,000. The question is whether the appellant is liable to the respondents for this sum . . .

The duty of Securicor was, as stated, to provide a service. There must be implied an obligation to use due care in selecting their patrolmen, to take care of the keys and, I would think, to operate the service with due and proper regard to the safety and security of the premises. The breach of duty committed by Securicor lay in a failure to discharge this latter obligation. Alternatively it could be put upon a vicarious responsibility for the wrongful act of Musgrove—viz, starting a fire on the premises: Securicor would be responsible for this upon the principle stated in *Morris v C W Martin Sons Ltd* [1966] 1 QB 716, 739 . . ."

Lord Diplock: ". . . My Lords, it is characteristic of commercial contracts, nearly all of which today are entered into not by natural legal persons, but by fictitious ones, i.e. companies, that the parties promise to one another that some thing will be done; for instance, that property and possession of goods will be transferred, that goods will be carried by ship from one port to another, that a building will be constructed in accordance with agreed plans, that services of a particular kind will be provided. Such a contract is the source of primary legal obligations upon each party to it to procure that whatever he has promised will be done is done. (I leave aside arbitration clauses which do not come into operation until a party to the contract claims that a primary obligation has not been observed.)

Where what is promised will be done involves the doing of a physical act, performance of the promise necessitates procuring a natural person to do it; but the legal relationship between the promisor and the natural person by whom the act is done, whether it is that of master and servant, or principal and agent, or of parties to an independent subcontract, is generally irrelevant. If that person fails to do it in the manner in which the promisor has promised to procure it to be done, as, for instance, with reasonable skill and care, the promisor has failed to fulfil his own primary obligation. This is to be distinguished from 'vicarious liability'—a legal concept which does depend upon the existence of a particular legal relationship between the natural person by whom a tortious act was done and the person sought to be made vicariously liable for it. In the interests of clarity the expression should, in my view, be confined to liability for tort . . ."

Lord Salmon: ". . . No one has suggested that Securicor could have foreseen or avoided by due diligence the act or default which caused the damage or that Securicor had been negligent in employing or supervising Musgrove.

The contract between the two parties provided that Securicor should supply a patrol service at Photo Production's factory by four visits a night for seven nights a week and two visits every Saturday afternoon and four day visits every Sunday. The contract provided that for this service, Securicor should be paid £8 15 a week. There can be no doubt that but for the clause in the contract which I have recited, Securicor would have been liable for the damage which was caused by their servant, Musgrove, whilst indubitably acting in the course of his employment: *Morris v C W Martin Sons Ltd* [1966] 1 QB 716 . . ."

NOTES

1. What the defendants (Securicor) were trying to argue in this case was that the act of their employee was not part of the contractual nexus. It was outside the scope of the employee's function and did not thus form a 'contractual' act that could be attributed to Securicor. But, as the judgments suggest, Securicor itself had promised to provide a service and, but for the exclusion clause (see

below at p.406), would in principle be liable when this promise was breached by the deliberate act of Securicor's employee.

2. The foundations of corporate personality are to be found in Roman law: see P. Duff, *Personality in Roman Private Law* (CUP, 1938).

2.3.5 Equality and inequality of bargaining power

One of the effects of treating corporations as legal persons capable of contracting, is that such persons can find themselves in economically superior positions when it comes to contracting with human persons. And given (i) that all the major European systems of contract law have long subscribed to the principle of freedom of contract (see **3.2**), and (ii) that there has traditionally been an assumption of equality between contractors, this superior position has often meant that companies can dictate the terms of the contract to human consumers (see Lord Denning M.R., at p.119). What if a company inserts into a contract, using small print and complex language, that it is not to be liable even if it is in breach of its contractual obligations? What if a company—or indeed anyone—is able to use its dominant economic position, or to exploit circumstances of severe shortage, to impose what many might see as an outrageously high price? What if a contractor takes advantage of another's inexperience or old age? Can and should the law of contract take into account inequalities of bargaining position?

Lloyds Bank Ltd v Bundy **[1975] Q.B. 326, CA**

This was an action for rescission in equity of a contract of mortgage. Mr Bundy, the elderly owner of a farm, had mortgaged the property to Lloyd's Bank, which for many years had been both his and his son's bankers, as security for a loan on behalf of his son's business. When the son's business got into further difficulties, the son and the assistant bank manager went out to the farm in order to increase the overdraft and the charge on the farm. It seemed, however, that the assistant manager took with him the charge forms already filled out. Moreover, he neither left the forms with the elderly man for detailed reading before signing nor advised him to seek independent advice before signing. The son's business nevertheless failed and the bank sought possession of the farm. The Court of Appeal (Lord Denning M.R., Sir Eric Sachs and Cairns L.J.) decided that the contract should be set aside, the majority (Sir Eric Sachs and Cairns L.J.) holding that there was a fiduciary relationship between the bank and Mr Bundy and that there was undue influence.

Lord Denning M.R.: ". . . Now let me say at once that in the vast majority of cases a customer who signs a bank guarantee or a charge cannot get out of it. No bargain will be upset which is the result of the ordinary interplay of forces. There are many hard cases which are caught by this rule. Take the case of a poor man who is homeless. He agrees to pay a high rent to a landlord just to get a roof over his head. The common law will not interfere. It is left to Parliament. Next take the case of a borrower in urgent need of money. He borrows it from the bank at high interest and it is guaranteed by a friend. The guarantor gives his bond and gets nothing in return. The common law will not interfere. Parliament has intervened to prevent moneylenders charging excessive interest. But it has never interfered with banks. Yet there are exceptions to this general rule. There are cases in our books in which the courts will set aside a contract, or a transfer of property, when the parties have not met on equal terms—when the one is so strong in bargaining power and the other so weak—that, as a matter of common fairness, it is not right that the strong should be allowed to push the weak to the wall. Hitherto those exceptional cases have been treated each as a separate category in itself. But I think the time has come when we should seek to find a principle to unite them. I put on one side contracts or transactions which are voidable for fraud or misrepresentation or mistake. All those are governed by settled principles. I go only to those where there has been inequality of bargaining power, such as to merit the intervention of the court.

The categories

The first category is that of 'duress of goods.' A typical case is when a man is in a strong bargaining position by being in possession of the goods of another by virtue of a legal right, such as by way of pawn or pledge or taken in distress. The owner is in a weak position because he is in urgent need of the goods. The stronger demands of the weaker more than is justly due: and he pays it in order to get the goods. Such a transaction is voidable . . .

[The] second category is said to extend to all cases where an unfair advantage has been gained by an unconscientious use of power by a stronger party against a weaker . . .

The third category is that of 'undue influence' usually so called . . .

The fourth category is that of 'undue pressure.' The most apposite of that is *Williams v Bayley* (1866) LR 1 HL 200, where a son forged his father's name to a promissory note and, by means of it, raised money from the bank of which they were both customers. The bank said to the father, in effect: 'Take your choice— give us security for your son's debt. If you do take that on yourself, then it will all go smoothly: if you do not, we shall be bound to exercise pressure.' Thereupon the father charged his property to the bank with payment of the note. The House of Lords held that the charge was invalid because of undue pressure exerted by the bank . . .

The fifth category is that of salvage agreements. When a vessel is in danger of sinking and seeks help, the rescuer is in a strong bargaining position. The vessel in distress is in urgent need. The parties cannot be truly said to be on equal terms. The Court of Admiralty have always recognised that fact . . .

The general principles

Gathering all together, I would suggest that through all these instances there runs a single thread. They rest on 'inequality of bargaining power.' By virtue of it, the English law gives relief to one who, without independent advice, enters into a contract upon terms which are very unfair or transfers property for a consideration which is grossly inadequate, when his bargaining power is grievously impaired by reason of his own needs or desires, or by his own ignorance or infirmity, coupled with undue influences or pressures brought to bear on him by or for the benefit of the other. When I use the word 'undue' I do not mean to suggest that the principle depends on proof of any wrongdoing. The one who stipulates for an unfair advantage may be moved solely by his own self-interest, unconscious of the distress he is bringing to the other. I have also avoided any reference to the will of the one being 'dominated' or 'overcome' by the other. One who is in extreme need may knowingly consent to a most improvident bargain, solely to relieve the straits in which he finds himself. Again, I do not mean to suggest that every transaction is saved by independent advice. But the absence of it may be fatal. With these explanations, I hope this principle will be found to reconcile the cases. . . ."

Sir Eric Sachs: ". . . In my judgment . . . a breach by the bank of their duty to take fiduciary care has, upon the evidence, as a whole been so affirmatively established that this court can and should make an order setting aside the guarantee and the charge of December 17, 1969 . . ."

QUESTIONS

1. Do you think this case had an effect upon the procedures used by the banks in granting mortgages and the like?

2. How would you qualify Lord Denning's reasoning: as inductive, or deductive? Do you think Lord Denning's description of the facts at the beginning of his judgment provides a clue as to how he will decide the case? (Cf. below, at **2.5.**)

NOTES

1. The majority's reluctance to follow Lord Denning's reasoning based on the induction of a principle of inequality of bargaining power subsequently proved to be wise: the House of Lords some years later was to hold that there was no such principle known to English law (*Photo Production Ltd v Securicor* (1980), at p.406). In fact the principle was to prove largely unnecessary because (i) Parliament subsequently intervened with legislation controlling the validity of exclusion clauses imposed in situations of inequality (followed by further legislation as a result of an EU Directive) (see **8.4**), and (ii) undue influence and equitable rescission, developed in *Bundy*, were to prove relatively fruitful tools (see **6.3**). See also *Credit Lyonnais Bank Nederland v Burch* (1997) (at p.34).

2. Equity is also prepared to intervene in situations where one party puts into a contract a term known as a penalty clause: see **7.3.2** and **8.5**.

2.3.6 Commercial and non-commercial promises

We have seen that many contracts fall into one of a range of transactional categories such as sale, hire, carriage, employment and so on. However, a general theory of contract attaches not to categories but to abstract promises, and this means that in theory almost any promise might attract legal proceedings. Such promises made in a commercial or professional context could well be actionable (although there are exceptions: see **4.7**), yet should this be true of promises made between family members or between friends? One person does a service for his brother, the latter promising to do the same for him sometime: should this promise be actionable in a court of law?

Jones v Padavatton **[1969] 1 W.L.R. 328, CA**

This was an action by a mother for repossession of a house in which her daughter was living. Some years earlier the mother had offered to pay maintenance and fees if her daughter would go to England and study for the Bar. The daughter went to England but discovered that the maintenance was much less than she anticipated because the mother was thinking in terms of West Indian dollars while the daughter assumed that the sum would be US dollars. Nevertheless the daughter accepted the payments without objection, and subsequently the mother agreed to buy a house in which her daughter could live, rent from letting off other rooms to provide the maintenance money. Some five years after the original offer, the daughter still not having completed her Bar studies, the mother brought the action for possession; the daughter resisted the action by claiming that there was a binding contract between her and her mother. The Court of Appeal (Danckwerts, Fenton Atkinson and Salmon L.JJ.) held that the mother was entitled to repossession.

> **Danckwerts L.J.:** ". . . There is no doubt that this case is a most difficult one, but I have reached a conclusion that the present case is one of those family arrangements which depend on the good faith of the promises which are made and are not intended to be rigid, binding agreements. *Balfour v Balfour* was a case of husband and wife, but there is no doubt that the same principles apply to dealings between other relations, such as father and son and daughter and mother. This, indeed, seems to me a compelling case. Mrs Jones and her daughter seem to have been on very good terms before 1967. The mother was arranging for a career for her daughter which she hoped would lead to success. This involved a visit to England in conditions which could not be wholly foreseen. What was required was an arrangement which was to be financed by the mother, and was such as would be adaptable to circumstances, as it in fact was. The operation about the house was, in my view, not a completely fresh arrangement,

but an adaptation of the mother's financial assistance to her daughter due to the situation which was found to exist in England. It was not a stiff contractual operation any more than the original arrangement.

In the result, of course, on this view, the daughter cannot resist her mother's rights as the owner of the house to the possession of which the mother is entitled."

Salmon L.J.: "I agree with the conclusion at which my Lord has arrived, but I have reached it by a different route . . .

Did the parties intend the arrangement to be legally binding? This question has to be solved by applying what is sometimes (although perhaps unfortunately) called an objective test. The court has to consider what the parties said and wrote in the light of all the surrounding circumstances, and then decide whether the true inference is that the ordinary man and women, speaking or writing thus in such circumstances, would have intended to create a legally binding agreement . . ."

Fenton Atkinson L.J.: ". . . If the test were the giving of consideration by the daughter, the answer would be simple. She gave up well-paid work and good living accommodation, and removed herself and her son to England, where she began her studies in November 1962. But the giving of consideration by the daughter cannot decide the question whether the parties intended to make a binding contract . . . I do not think that the lack of formality and precision in expressing the arrangement is necessarily an indication that no contract was intended having regard to what the court knows of the parties and their relationship. The problem is, in my view, a difficult one, because though one would tend to regard a promise by a parent to pay an allowance to a child during a course of study as no more than a family arrangement, on the facts of this case this particular daughter undoubtedly gave up a great deal on the strength of the mother's promise . . .

. . . The whole arrangement was, in my view, far too vague and uncertain to be itself enforceable as a contract; but at no stage did the daughter bring into the discussions her alleged legal right to £42 per month until her studies were completed, and how that right was to be affected by the new arrangement . . .

At the time when the first arrangement was made, mother and daughter were, and always had been, to use the daughter's own words, 'very close.' I am satisfied that neither party at that time intended to enter into a legally binding contract, either then or later when the house was bought. The daughter was prepared to trust her mother to honour her promise of support, just as the mother no doubt trusted her daughter to study for the Bar with diligence, and to get through her examinations as early as she could."

NOTES AND QUESTIONS

1. The judges are not starting out from an abstract set of rules concerning contract formation—the "law" so to speak—but from within a particular

factual situation, and as a result it is by no means clear whether or not there existed a 'contract'. Salmon LJ clearly thought that there was one at one point because of what the daughter had given up, but there is sympathy with the mother's position as well. A judge once described judging as 'an educated reflex to the facts'. Does *Jones* support this description?

2. What if a mother agrees to give her daughter a lift to work every day, provided that the daughter makes a contribution to the cost of the petrol? If the daughter never actually pays, can the mother sue in debt?

Albert v Motor Insurers' Bureau [1972] A.C. 301, HL

Lord Cross: ". . . If I get into a taxi and ask the driver to drive me to Victoria Station it is extremely unlikely that either of us directs his mind to the question whether we are entering into a contract. We enter into a contract not because we form any intention to enter into one but because if our minds were directed to the point we should as reasonable people both agree that we were in fact entering into one. When one passes from the field of transactions of an obviously business character between strangers to arrangements between friends or acquaintances for the payment by the passenger of a contribution towards expenses the fact that the arrangement is not made purely as a matter of business and that if the anticipated payment is not made it would probably never enter into the head of the driver to sue for it disposes one to say that there is no contract, but in fact the answer to the question 'contract' or 'no contract' does not depend on the likelihood of an action being brought to enforce it in case of default.

Suppose that when one of Quirk's fellow workers got into touch with him and asked him whether he could travel in his car to Tilbury and back next day an 'officious bystander' had asked: 'Will you be paying anything for your transport?' the prospective passenger would have answered at once: 'Of course I will pay.' If the 'officious bystander' had gone on to ask Quirk whether, if he was not paid, he would sue the man in the county court, Quirk might well have answered in the words used by the driver in *Connell's* case [1969] 2 QB 494: 'Not bloody likely.' But the fact that if default was made Quirk would not have started legal proceedings but would have resorted to extra-judicial remedies does not mean that an action could not in theory have been brought to recover payment for the carriage. If one imagines such proceedings being brought a plea on the part of the passenger that he never meant to enter into a contract would have received short shrift and so, too, would a plea that the contract was void for uncertainty because no precise sum was mentioned. If the evidence did not establish a regular charge for the Tilbury trip the judge would have fixed the appropriate sum . . ."

QUESTION

What would Lord Cross have made of the facts of *Jones v Padavatton* (1969) (at p.75)?

NOTES

1. The other Law Lords in this case did not think that there necessarily would have been a contract in situations where a passenger agrees to pay a contribution. But as with *Jones v Padavatton* (1969) (at p.75), so much depends upon the actual facts. The rules of contract are not necessarily that helpful, in that in both *Jones* and the car passenger situations there may well be most of the elements for a binding contract (offer, acceptance and consideration), and as a result the outcome has to depend upon the so-called 'intention to create legal relations' (see **4.7**). See further *Esso Petroleum Ltd v Commissioners of Custom and Excise* (1976) (below p.203).

2. One favourite tool used by judges is the 'officious bystander'. He or she appears quite frequently as a means of justifying a decision on difficult facts. This extract from *Albert* should, then, serve equally as an example of reasoning methods in contract cases (see below **2.5**).

2.4 Interdisciplinary approaches

We have already seen examples in the doctrine of how theoretical approaches to contract make use of other disciplines. James Gordley uses history and philosophy (p.52), while Patrick Atiyah uses history and economics (p.56). Sociological investigations have equally been employed to inform us about how business people view contract law (see Mulcahy and Tillotson, *Contract Law in Perspective* (4th edn, Cavendish, 2004), pp.45–7). Whether these interdisciplinary approaches have that much influence on the judges is an interesting question. Moreover, actually establishing cause and connection between a system of legal concepts and norms and other knowledge disciplines is more difficult than one might believe (correlation is not the same as causation). But interdisciplinary approaches cannot be ignored, since it would be idle to think that somehow legal knowledge is "pure" and divorced from other forms of knowledge. In fact, as we shall see, legal reasoning probably cannot be understood without considerable (if unconscious) input from social science theorists and methodologists. The student, also, needs to develop a critical approach towards law if anything interesting is to be said beyond the exercise of simply trying to apply rules. What is more, the comparative lawyer has to step outside the paradigms used by lawyers if anything useful is to be said using comparative methodology. However, this section (and to an extent the next section on methodology) will provide only a brief introduction to the interdisciplinary approaches to contract law.

2.4.1 Contract and economics

Probably the most important discipline to impact on contract studies in more recent years is the law and economics movement.

Prof Dr M.W. Hesselink and Dr G.J.P. de Vries, *Principles of European Contract Law* **(Kluwer, 2001), pp.80–81 (footnotes omitted)**

"1. Economic Analysis of Contract Law

The economic analysis of contract law is based on the assumption that contracts are an important economic institution, because they allow the exchange of goods and services, which, in turn, allows an efficient allocation of these goods and services. Contract law is an equally important institution. The main purpose of contract law, according to legal economists, is to facilitate efficient exchange and to repair market failures.

2. Efficiency

Suppose A owns a bicycle that he values at 50 Euro and B values the same bicycle at 100 Euro. If they decide to exchange the bike against a specific price between 50 and 100 Euro, say 75 Euro, not only are both parties better off, but also society as a whole (wealth maximisation), assuming that no third parties are harmed (no externalities). Legal economists call a transaction efficient when it makes at least one person better off and nobody worse off (Pareto efficiency) or, in a more sophisticated version, if the winners could fully compensate the losers and still be better off (Kaldor-Hicks efficiency, cost--benefit analysis). The (utilitarian) assumption on which the economic theory of contract law is based is that efficiency is good, and that therefore the main function of contract law should be to facilitate efficient exchange by making efficient contracts enforceable and by encouraging parties (incentives) to conclude efficient transactions.

3. Market Failures

Clearly, legal economists have great confidence in the operation of the market, and in freedom of contract, which is essential to a well-functioning market. However, they also recognise that freedom of contract sometimes exists only in a nominal sense, e.g. because a party does not possess enough information to evaluate properly whether a certain transaction will make her better off, or because a party is under pressure to conclude a contract which she knows will not make her better off. Scholars in law & economics regard such problems, from an economic perspective, as market failures. Therefore, although the basic assumption in the economic theory of contract law is that it should make people's promises enforceable, thus helping them to make their commitments credible, in the case of market failures enforceability may have to be limited. Thus, in the economic theory of contract law, another function of contract law is to correct market failures.

4. Criticism

According to its proponents, law & economics can provide a 'neutral' and 'scientific' basis to the law. However, the result of economic analysis very much depends on what economic theory one starts with. Clearly, the prevalent economic theory of contract law (and indeed the prevalent economic theory of law in general) is based on a series of assumptions that, plausible as they may be to many or even most of us, are neither inevitable nor irrefutable. Different choices are possible. Indeed, the economic analysis of law has been contested by several legal theorists and other legal scholars, sometimes very strongly. They reject the economic theory of law because it is based on an economic view (liberal-capitalist) which they do not share, because it depends on unrealistic abstractions (man as a rational wealth maximiser) and because it disregards (or treats as 'irrational') important values (e.g. altruistic and distributional values). Others take a more moderate view. They regard the economic analysis of law as a useful tool which provides an insight into the way rules of contract law may affect the behaviour of the contracting parties, although they are aware that it begs a number of important questions . . ."

NOTES

1. This extract is not the last word (or for that matter even the first word) on the law and economics school, but it is a brief and elegant summary of the main thesis. A more detailed coverage can be found in Beale, Bishop and Furmston, *Contract Cases and Materials* (4th edn Butterworths, 2001), pp.77–84. These authors of this casebook fall into the category of those who "take a more moderate view", and thus the coverage is full and measured but not uncritical.

2. Whatever one's view on the relationship between law and economics, there is no doubt that the two disciplines have been interconnected in a mutually dependent way since Roman times. One only has to read *The Institutes of Gaius* (published around AD160) to appreciate how law, money and wealth are interconnected as a system. And it is not just concepts such as ownership (*dominium*) and intangible property (*res incorporales*) that are so integrated into economic thinking; the organisation of law into a coherent system—Gaius' great contribution—is equally part of the integration in that, as Gaius appreciated, the legal system itself can create property, that is to say wealth. Thus if one returns to the extract from *Beswick v Beswick* (1966) (at p.23), the "property" in issue was not a physical asset that one could touch; it was an intangible "thing"—a debt—created by the law itself. Debts are as much assets as a bag of diamonds under the bed. For an excellent historical perspective on law and economic theory, see J.W. Jones, *Historical Introduction to the Theory of Law* (OUP, 1940), pp.235–69.

3. One of the leading exponents of the law and economics school is Richard Posner. He has written: "I have tried to develop a moral theory that goes

beyond classical utilitarianism and holds that the criterion for judging whether acts and institutions are just or good is whether they maximize the wealth of society. This approach allows a reconciliation among utility, liberty, and even equality as competing ethical principles. The approach seems to have played an important role in the growth of the common law, which is not surprising when the limitations of common law as a means of redistributing, as distinct from creating, wealth are taken into account" (R. Posner, *The Economics of Justice* (Harvard University Press, 1983), p.115).

2.4.2 Contract and sociology

Sociological, or empirical, research work on contract law is of considerable importance to anyone wishing to understand how contract is actually used in social and commercial practice.

Linda Mulcahy and John Tillotson, *Contract Law in Perspective* (4th edn, Cavendish Publishing, 2004), p.51

"There is no doubt at all as to the importance of empirical work on contracts for anyone interested in the relationship between business transactions, contract and contract law. These studies indicate that business policy and practice often operate to marginalise the role of the formal law of contract in everyday business transactions. To the extent that business transactions operate 'outside' contract, this amounts to a rejection by the business community of legal doctrine. Does this matter? According to Macaulay's evidence, it would seem that it does not, unless you are a lawyer who is losing fees. None of the business people that Macaulay interviewed appeared to be losing sleep over their non-contractual relations. However, another view is that it would be dangerous to 'write off' contract as a business device on the strength of the empirical studies conducted. Rather, it could be argued that greater efforts should be made to make the law relevant to the business community. After all, the basic function of contract has long been identified as facilitating business exchanges.

What becomes clear from the analysis . . . is that the theories underpinning the law of contract are in a state of flux . . ."

QUESTION

Judges often use an "officious bystander" from the business world, or indeed "commercial reality", to justify a conclusion reached in a judgment (see, e.g., Bingham L.J. in *Blackpool & Fylde* (1990), at p.177). Does the above extract suggest that such bystanders are mythical creations that might have little connection with commercial reality?

NOTE

Just what amounts to a sociological approach to law has been well articulated by Professor Cotterrell. He has written:

> "The numerous approaches to legal analysis which can be categorised as sociological in the broadest sense are unified only by their deliberate self-distancing from the professional viewpoint of the lawyer. It is implicit in the aim of empirical legal theory that law is always viewed 'from the outside,' from the perspective of an observer of legal institutions, doctrine and behaviour, rather than that of a participant, although participants' perceptions may be taken into account as data for the observer . . . Behind such an objective usually stands the motive of adopting an epistemological standpoint from which a radical critique of and challenging to lawyers' professional conceptions of law becomes possible" (R. Cotterrell, "The Sociological Concept of Law" (1983) 10 *Journal of Law and Society* 241 at pp.242, 243).

2.4.3 **Contract and moral philosophy**

The relationship between a law of contract and morality has a long history. Indeed in civilian legal history, a key step, as we have seen, in the movement from a law of contracts based on empirical transactions to a law of contract based on abstract agreement, was the work of the canon lawyers (see **1.1.3**). *Pacta sunt servanda* was as much a moral as a legal principle. Nevertheless, the relationship between law and morality, at the level of legal theory at least, has for long been a contentious one.

P.S. Atiyah, *Promises, Morals and Law* (OUP, 1981), p.2

"With isolated and minor exceptions, most of this literature [by philosophers on promising] has, in recent years, proceeded in total disregard of the law. Just as the lawyer tends to think of the philosopher as an airy theorist having little contact with reality, so the philosopher tends to see the law as technical and abstruse, having little contact with morality. It was not always thus. Until Bentham and Austin wrought their work in setting apart legal and moral obligations, discussions of the nature and limits of promissory liability treated the two as though they were inextricably interwoven. In the works of the seventeenth-century Natural Lawyers, for example, positive law, natural law, and the moral law are all treated together in such a way as to suggest that it would be impossible to understand at least the latter two in isolation from each other. And even in the writings of moralists and philosophers in the British tradition, such as Hume and Paley, there is a much greater awareness of, and reference to, the law as itself of profound relevance to the moral issues involved in the subject of promises. With the common lawyers, too, particularly in the early formative period of the development of modern contract law, there are signs that lawyers tended to fashion the law of contracts broadly in accord with what they took to be moral principles. They tended to create the law in the image of morality as they understood it. No doubt, as the Natural Lawyers made explicit, positive law did sometimes diverge from morality. But in its central doctrines and ideas, law and morality were largely congruent."

NOTE

It is easy enough to think that when the law enforces a promise it is giving expression to the moral principle of *pacta sunt servanda* (agreements must be kept). But one difficulty is always the clear promise made and relied on by another that the law decides not to enforce (see e.g. *Jones v Padavatton* (1969), at p.75). Does this not expose a fundamental flaw in the relationship between law and morality? Perhaps, but this has not stopped theorists from asserting that the basis of the law of contract is the moral obligation that promises must be kept (see e.g. C. Fried, *Contract as Promise* (Harvard University Press, 1981)). Yet whatever the value of these ideas as theories, the relationship between contract and morality cannot be dismissed at the European level. French lawyers, as the extract from Paula Giliker will indicate (see p.434), prefer a moral underpinning to contract law rather than an economic one. Contractual solidarity means that each party to the contract must have a certain regard for the interests of the other party. This thesis of contractual "solidarity" has been dismissed by the House of Lords (see *Walford v Miles* (1992), at p.174).

2.4.4 Contract and politics

The relationship between law and politics is another delicate and contentious area. It is contentious, of course, because law aims (ideologically of course) to be above and independent of politics in the practical sense, but as the next short extract indicates, history and theory can present a different picture.

Walter Ullmann, *The Growth of Papal Government in the Middle Ages* (2nd edn, Methuen, 1962), pp.367, 368

"Every system of law is the product of those forces that created the society to which the law is to apply. Law reflects the ideology of any organised community of men . . . The 'rediscovery' of Roman law concerned not the law, which was being studied in any case, but its underlying ideas. Without the familiarity with Roman law its ideological wealth would not have been grasped: and the realization of ideological opulence exhibited in Roman law, led to the unparalleled intensification of Roman law scholarship from now onwards. What is of further interest to us is that the Justinianean codification was considered a guidebook for the imperial-laical government. The study of Roman law, therefore, provided the supply of technical and jurisprudential concepts . . ."

NOTE

The relationship between contract and political theory is a very long and rich one in Western politico-legal thought, for the idea that society itself is founded on a social contract between *populus* and *princes* was at the basis of much political theorising from after the nominalist revolution, associated with the late medieval philosophers, right up to the 19th century (when the existence of such contracts was shown to be a myth). The theory even has an echo in Roman law (D.1.4.1pr), and has certainly not completely disappeared from contemporary political theorising. As the next extract shows, contract was once seen as a source of natural (human) rights.

J.W. Jones, *Historical Introduction to the Theory of Law* (OUP, 1940), pp.109–110 (footnotes omitted)

"*Social contract*. But there was a still wider field open to contract, conceived as an institution of the law of Nature. In the form of a *pactum unionis* it could be used to supply political theorists with both an explanation and a justification of the existence of the State itself; in the form of a *pactum subiectionis* it could be made to provide some sort of legal basis for the resistance to the pretensions of a ruling prince. Being an implied and not express contract, its terms were to be formulated by reference to its purpose and thus in different hands it could be brought to yield very different results. For Hobbes the original contract involved the surrender of all powers except possibly the liberty of self-defence and self-preservation, while to Locke its only purpose seemed to be that 'preservation of property' so long as 'property' was understood to include 'life, liberty and estate'. Each new form of oppression engendered a new form of natural right. Through the concept of social contract vague generalizations about the natural freedom and equality of men became concrete in specific demands against governments, for the maxim *Princeps legibus solutus* had no place in the law of Nature. Thus out of the ancient idea of a law of Nature was born the peculiarly modern notion of the rights of man."

NOTE

The influence of contract on political thinking and ideology seems evident enough, but the influence of politics and ideology on contract is a different matter since contract as a formal institution has a long history going back to Roman law. Perhaps the classical analysis set out in the next extract remains the most useful starting point, in that it seems to show respect both to the history of legal thought and legal institutions, and to their political and ideological possibilities in terms of their social functions.

O. Kahn-Freund, "Introduction" in Karl Renner, *The Institutions of Private Law and Their Social Functions* (Routledge & Kegan Paul, 1949), pp.5–6, 28, 39

"A simple photographic picture of a given society at a given stage of its development will fail to reveal the manner in which legal concepts and institutions are used and grouped for economic and social purposes. Society must always be viewed as a process, a dialectical process. Hence it is, as it were, a cinematographic picture which the sociologist has to envisage. Only thus will he discern the laws which determine the grouping and re-grouping of legal institutions, the sequence of uses to which they are put and of arrangements into which they enter. Society handles the institutions of law much in the same way as a child handles his bricks. It uses the same bricks all the time—or for a long time,—to-day to build a manor house, to-morrow to build a factory, and the day after to build a railway station. The number of bricks is limited: the manor house may have to be pulled down to make way for the factory. But—this is Renner's positivist axiom—the bricks remain the same. The law provides the bricks. What society makes of them, is none of the lawyer's business. The legal institution is a rigid abstract, a congeries of crystallised imperatives, and, owing to its very rigidity and abstract nature, a 'fetish' in the Marxist sense, like the 'commodity' concept of the economist . . . The discrepancy between the normative content of the law (which is static) and its economic and social function (which is dynamic) is the key to its dialectical development . . .

Of these complementary institutions [to the institution of property] the contract of employment was the first to appear on the scene, and it has remained the principal actor in the drama. The contract itself is, like all legal institutions, a blank without intrinsic social significance, and adaptable to an infinite number of social objectives. In industrial capitalism, however, it is also 'blank' in a more poignant sense. Whatever the law may say, from a sociological point of view this is a 'contract' without contractual content. It is a command under the guise of an agreement. The employer, by exercising his power to command, fills in the blank, and that power vests in him by virtue of his *dominium*, his ownership in the means of production. . . . As simple commodity production gave way to manufacture, and manufacture to factory production, ownership became a *dominium* over persons . . .

. . . The monopolist and his client are parties to a 'contract'. A passenger who takes a railway ticket 'accepts' the terms 'offered' by the company. A householder 'contracts' with the local authority or public utility company which supplies him with gas, water, or electricity. The law cannot admit that these acts are acts of submission, that these relations are power relations, it must 'construe' them as agreements, it must press into the form of a contract what has no contractual substance whatsoever. Conditions by which a monopolist excludes or limits his legal liabilities are 'deemed' to have been freely accepted, if 'reasonable notice'

> was given by the other party, eg by the magic formula 'for conditions see back' on a ticket. The customer has 'assented' even if he is blind or illiterate (*Thompson v LMS* [1930] 1 KB 41) . . . To-day a large part, if not the majority, of commercial contracts derive their substance from terms and conditions laid down by trade associations or similar bodies . . . As long as private monopolies exist, relations of sub-ordination must be hidden behind the veil of a legal norm which signifies co-ordination . . ."

NOTES AND QUESTIONS

1. This impressive piece by one of the 20th century's leading comparative lawyers nevertheless must be accompanied, if not by a number of criticisms, then by some qualifying remarks. The first and most obvious remark is that the law has moved on from when this piece was written. The courts were to decide that gas, water and electricity are not actually supplied under a contractual relationship but pursuant to a statutory duty (see now *Norweb Plc v Dixon* (1995), at p.211). Legislation was then introduced to limit the use of conditions in consumer and standard form contracts (see **8.4**). Kahn-Freund himself was to be (almost single-handedly) one of the founders of labour law in England as an area independent of the law of obligations, and in consequence the employment contract (as we have seen, at p.69) has become an area governed largely by statute.

2. Nevertheless one can reflect, after reading the cases in this casebook, on whether the last of the paragraphs in the extract above still has some force. Is the relationship between consumer and supplier still one of subordination? Cannot railway company officials fine customers travelling on a train with a technically inappropriate ticket? Cannot banks impose large penalties on those who inadvertently slip into overdraft? Are not these relations of subordination? And what about employees: is there not much talk these days about the manager's "right" to manage? How easily can workers paid poor wages go on strike? Is it not as easy to dismiss employees today as it was over half a century ago?

3. Another criticism that might be directed at the Kahn-Freund/Renner analysis is that it focuses too much upon abstract legal institutions like ownership (*dominium*) and contract. What about the political biases of the judges themselves? On this point see J.A.G. Griffith, *The Politics of the Judiciary* (5th edn Fontana, 1997). However, might this kind of bias not be one that attaches to the reasoning and methods of the judges rather than to institutions such as contract?

4. A further criticism that might be levelled at this kind of analysis, especially the child's bricks metaphor, is that it is too civilian in its thinking and as a result fails to take account of cultural differences between legal traditions (see the extract from Pierre Legrand, at p.43). However, in terms of the social function of property and contract in capitalist economic systems, can the force of the

Kahn-Freund/Renner argument be easily deflected by references to the cultural paradigm? In fact Kahn-Freund himself goes some way in addressing this issue: 'To what extent', he asks (at p.8), "is Renner's analysis without validity for a capitalist society whose legal system differs from any Continental system as fundamentally as does the English common law?"

5. Some regard the late Sir Otto Kahn-Freund as one of the greatest UK-based legal academics of the 20th century. An essay on his career, written by Mark Freedland, has recently been published: see J. Beatson and R. Zimmermann (eds), *Jurists Uprooted* (OUP, 2004), pp.299–323 (the whole book will repay reading).

2.5 Contract and method

In moving from theory to method one is seemingly moving from an abstract to a more concrete level of legal knowledge and practice. Academics can theorise about contract, and about its relationship with other disciplines, but judges have to solve contract cases and give reasons for their decisions. Yet the gap between theory and method is not as clear-cut as it might at first seem. Methods are not conducted in an intellectual vacuum but are embedded in various frameworks (e.g. logical, interpretative, functional, structural, dialectical), these frameworks themselves being embedded in networks of categories and concepts (e.g. the category of contract and its concepts such as consideration). In turn the categories and concepts are embedded in knowledge assumptions (e.g. that law as a body of knowledge consists of rules), and in turn these knowledge assumptions are embedded in what a philosopher of science has called "paradigms" (loosely meaning world view). Theories themselves are often fashioned from elements operating at all of these different levels (thus, for example, the legal theorist Ronald Dworkin has fashioned a theory around the method of interpretation—see below at p.101—while the American Realists developed their view of law around functionalism—see below at p.97).

Does any of this really matter to the contract law student? To a large extent it does, in that the student will, for example, come across dissenting judgments, and this raises the question of why two judges in the same case might come to different conclusions. Moreover, if a student is to adopt a critical approach to cases, then he or she must be able to dissect a judgment so as to be able to identify the elements which have led a judge to arrive at a particular conclusion. One assumption, of course, is that judges in contract cases are directed towards their decisions by a "law of contract", and thus it is this body of knowledge that will in the end determine the outcome of any dispute. Indeed, a lawyer who adheres to the "paradigm" that the law of contract consists of precise rules induced out of precedents which then can be applied deductively, so as automatically to produce the solution, might be puzzled by all the talk of method, knowledge assumptions, paradigms and the like. But, as the extracts in this section will indicate, few adhere to this logic paradigm today (although this is not to say that it is irrelevant).

2.5.1 Introduction: the judges' view of method

Perhaps the safest starting point is that of the judges themselves. How do they view their role in terms of method?

Derby & Co v Weldon (No.5) [1989] 1 W.L.R. 1244, Ch D

Vinelott J.: ". . . The function of a judge of first instance is to find the relevant facts and, with the assistance of counsel, to ascertain the law as set out in any relevant statutory provisions and in principles to be derived from the decisions of the House of Lords and the Court of Appeal, and to draw the appropriate legal consequences. It is not open to the judge in performing this primary function to consider, far less express an opinion, as to the correctness of a decision of the Court of Appeal or the House of Lords except in those rare cases where he is faced with conflicting decisions of the Court of Appeal and must choose which to follow. That does not rest solely upon the feelings of deference and respect which a judge of first instance will naturally and properly approach a decision of the Court of Appeal or the House of Lords. An opinion which the judge may entertain as to the correctness or otherwise of, for instance, the interpretation of a decision of the House of Lords by the Court of Appeal, is simply irrelevant to his primary duty which is to ascertain the statutory provisions and the principles stated in decisions that are binding on him which govern the case before him . . ."

NOTE AND QUESTION

So, the role of the judge, at least a first instance judge (and the law student?), is to:

(a) find the relevant facts;

(b) ascertain the law (which will be found either in a statute, or in principles derived from precedent); and

(c) apply the law and "draw the appropriate consequences".

Is this not, then, merely a scientific exercise?

2.5.2 Legal reasoning as logic

By "science" is meant rational reasoning, and rational reasoning has been described by one French law professor as "inferring a proposition from its connection with other propositions already established or, conversely, in demonstrating a given proposition in searching the propositions which can logically justify it" (J-L. Bergel). In other words, it is a matter of logic.

Kevin Gray and Susan Gray, "The Rhetoric of Reality" in J. Getzler (ed.), *Rationalizing Property, Equity and Trusts* **(Butterworths, 2003), p.204, at p.208 (footnotes omitted)**

"There is much to be said for the view that . . . law comprises an axiomatic system of rules in which legal outcomes emerge as the sweet distillation of an invincible logical process. As Lord Devlin once pointed out, 'no system of law can be workable if it has not got logic at the root of it'. Logic, with all its frailty, is still the essential operating system of the human condition—our ultimate operational resource. Logic is commonly seen as providing a universal standard by which it can be judged whether a particular conclusion has been correctly derived from its supposed premises. Indeed, the very universality of the logical process goes far towards ensuring both our freedom from the exercise of arbitrary will and a measure of equality in the enforcement of the law—in short, towards guaranteeing that we have a government of laws and not of men . . . Logical systems tend, furthermore, to satisfy that component of the 'moral emotion of justice' which causes humans to desire that 'the proposition by which conduct is evaluated be taken as the consequence of some larger, more general, proposition' (Max Radin)."

NOTES

1. Lord Goff has written: "When I was a student there appeared to exist some judges who saw the law almost as a deductive science, a matter of finding the relevant authorities and applying them to the facts of the particular case" ("The Search for Principle", in W. Swadling and Gareth Jones (eds), *The Search for Principle* (OUP, 1999), at p.326).

2. The identification of legal reasoning with logic is a general European phenomenon, although it has a stronger foundation in the civil law world than in the common law for several reasons. First, there is a tradition of law as science in the civil law that goes back to the 16th-century French law professors (see P. Stein, *Roman Law in European History* (CUP, 1999), pp.79–82). Secondly, the reduction of private law to codes of abstract rules continues, to some extent, to encourage the idea of law as a set of "axioms". Thirdly, unlike Continental Europe, there was no university tradition of law in England before the 19th century, and thus no corps of law professors dedicated to turning law into a science.

QUESTION

What is meant by "axiom" in this context?

Kevin Gray and Susan Gray, "The Rhetoric of Reality" in J. Getzler (ed.), _Rationalizing Property, Equity and Trusts_ (Butterworths, 2003), p.204, at pp.208–209 (footnotes omitted)

"The essence of an axiomatic structure is, of course, that 'axioms' (or 'fixed postulates') enjoy a fundamental and autonomous status within the scheme. An axiomatic proposition is a raw _datum_ whose validity is assumed, never proved. One can no more seek to go _behind_ an axiom than one may question why, in a game of chess, the knight or the bishop moves in the peculiar ways these pieces do. It is irrelevant that the axiom in question is morally neutral or indifferent and that no evil of any kind would ensue from a denial of its validity. Axioms are simply immune from rational challenge. To knock at an axiom is to want to play a different game; and to alter an axiom is already to have begun a different game . . ."

NOTES

1. Kevin and Susan Gray are writing about land law, but their comments are equally applicable to an area of law like contract which can easily be given the appearance of an "axiomatic" structure in the form of a code (see the PECL and UNIDROIT).

2. Perhaps a good example of reasoning by deductive or syllogistic logic is to be found in the case of _Fisher v Bell_ (1961) (at p.35):

   (a) Major premise (axiomatic rule): goods displayed in a shop window do not constitute an "offer" but an "invitation to treat".

   (b) Minor premise (facts): the defendant displayed a (prohibited) article in his shop window.

   (c) Conclusion: this display did not amount to an "offer" and thus the defendant could not be convicted of the offence of "offering for sale" a prohibited article.

3. This same kind of reasoning can be applied to someone injured in a supermarket by a defective product, as the next extract (from a French case) illustrates.

Paris 14.12.1961; JCP.1962.II.12547 (_Soc. des Eaux de Vittel c. Dehen & Soc. Supermag-Rennes_) (translation Bernard Rudden)

THE COURT:—"Considering that . . . Mme Dehen, having made several purchases including a bottle of beer and a bottle of 'Vittel-Delices' in the self-service store at the Rennes Supermag, went to the check-out to pay; that an employee took from the basket supplied by the store the goods Mme Dehen had placed therein; that she, while waiting for her bill to be rung up, transferred them to her own bag; that then the bottle of 'Vittel-Delices', having knocked lightly against the bottle of beer that was there, exploded, and that either a splinter or the stopper injured her right eye . . . Considering that . . . Mme Dehen filed suit against the Supermag and [the manufacturer] . . . on the basis both of art 1382. 1383 and 1384 civ. c [the tort provisions] and of art 1641ff [sale] . . . Considering however that Mme Dehen's action against the Supermag is receivable but the latter's liability can be envisaged only as contractual; Considering in fact that in dealing with a purchase in a self-service store the sale is concluded, even if the price is not due until the check-out, from the moment the customer, having selected from a shelf an article offered for sale with a price tag which the customer accepts, puts the article in the basket . . ."

(The supermarket brought a *pourvoi en cassation*: "But whereas after having correctly observed that the liability of the Société Supermag with regard to the victim could only be contractual . . . " (Cass.civ. 20.10.1964; DS.1965.62))

NOTES

1. The importance of logic (in theory) in French law is revealed by the very style of the court judgment: it is set out in the form of a syllogism. In this particular case the complex syllogism is as follows:

   (a) Major premise (1) (axiomatic rule): goods on a supermarket shelf constitute a contractual offer.
   (b) Major premise (2) (axiomatic rule): a contractual obligation is formed when the offer is accepted.
   (c) Major premise (3) (axiomatic rule): an offer is accepted by a customer in a supermarket when he or she puts the product in the basket supplied by the supermarket.
   (d) Major premise (4) (axiomatic rule): goods sold under a contract must be free from hidden defects.
   (e) Minor premise (facts): the claimant (Madame Dehen) was injured when a product she had taken from the shelf and put into her supermarket basket exploded, before the price had been registered on the till, injuring her.
   (f) Conclusion: the supermarket was liable to her for failing to fulfil its contractual obligation (which came into being when she put the goods in her supplied basket) to supply her with goods free from hidden defects.

2. This logic may look impressive but it immediately gives rise to other logical problems. Given that ownership in goods, as we have seen (cf **1.3.3**), normally passes when the contract is made, Madame Dehen must have become the owner of the bottle of water the moment she put it in her basket. But say she changed her mind a few minutes later? Presumably she could not put the water back on the shelf without getting the specific assent of the supermarket to annul the contract.

3. This is, perhaps, the reason why English law has a different logical structure. Thus in England the syllogism would be as follows:

(a) Major premise (1) (axiomatic rule): goods on a supermarket shelf are not contractual offers but only invitations to treat.

(b) Major premise (2) (axiomatic rule): it is the customer in a supermarket who makes the offer, which is accepted when the price is registered on the supermarket till (see *Pharmaceutical Society of GB v Boots* (1953), at p.152).

(c) Major premise (3) (axiomatic rule): goods sold in the course of a business must be reasonably fit for their purpose and of satisfactory quality (Sale of Goods Act 1979, s.14).

(d) Minor premise (facts): the claimant (Madame Dehen) was injured when a product she had taken from the shelf and put into her supermarket basket exploded, before the price had been registered on the till, injuring her.

(e) Conclusion: the supermarket could not be liable to her under the Sale of Goods Act 1979.

QUESTION

The supermarket in England might not be liable to Mme Dehen in contract, but could she sue anyone in tort? (Cf. C&MT, pp.158–163.)

2.5.3 **Limits of logic**

It is important to note that logic is simply a *means*, not an *end* so to speak. It is a bare form and everything will depend upon the premises adopted, as the next extract illustrates.

Harbour Assurance Co v Kansa General International Insurance Co Ltd **[1993] QB 701, CA**

This was a claim for a declaration that an arbitration clause contained in an insurance contract void for illegality was also void. The Court of Appeal (Ralph Gibson, Leggatt and Hoffmann L.JJ.) held that the arbitration clause was not affected in this case by the illegality of the contract.

Hoffmann L.J.: ". . . Mr Longmore's argument is extremely simple. He says that the question raised on the pleadings is whether the retrocession agreement was void *ab initio*. The arbitration clause formed part of the retrocession agreement. Therefore the issue must involve the validity of the arbitration clause itself.

Mr Longmore calls this logic. I call it over-simplification. The flaw in the logic, as it seems to me, lies in the ambiguity of the proposition that the arbitration clause 'formed part' of the retrocession agreement. In one sense of course it did. It was clause 12 of a longer document which also dealt with the substantive rights and duties of the parties. But parties can include more than one agreement in a single document. They may say in express words that two separate agreements are intended. Or the question of whether the document amounts to one agreement or two may have to be answered by reference to the kind of provisions it contains . . . There is no single concept of 'forming part' which will provide the answer in every case . . ."

NOTES AND QUESTIONS

1. The syllogism is reliable only in certain situations, and it is easy to fall into error. Given that natural language is also a system in itself (in addition to law as an 'axiomatic' system), there are a number of dangers when it is used to give expression to other knowledge systems:

   (a) Major premise: a mouse eats cheese;
   (b) Minor premise: a mouse is a word of one syllable;
   (c) Conclusion: therefore words of one syllable eat cheese.

   In particular the words employed must keep their same signification in the major and minor premises. If they do not then the conclusion can be absurd, as the example indicates.

2. Care must also be taken not to confuse genus and species (sometimes referred to as a category mistake):

   (a) Major premise: cats eat meat;
   (b) Minor premise: cats are animals;
   (c) Conclusion: therefore animals eat meat.

   This conclusion might not be quite as absurd as words eating cheese, but it is equally wrong in as much as it does not accord with reality. Not all animals eat meat.

3. In addition there is the problem of the missing premise (*tertium non datur*):

   (a) Major premise: smoking causes lung cancer;
   (b) Minor premise: Socrates died of lung cancer;
   (c) Conclusion: therefore Socrates was a smoker.

   The missing premise is that lung cancer has causes other than smoking.

4. *Harbour Assurance* illustrates how the syllogism can prove particularly weak in law, in as much as the structure or model is subject to little external restraint

and thus proves a "moveable goal post". Intellectual systems can, in short, contain uncertainties and ambiguities. Does *Harbour Assurance* indicate that logic is simply a form of argumentation? Or does it indicate that legal reasoning should never be seen as a matter of logic as such, but a matter of what premise is to be adopted?

2.5.4 Induction

Before one looks at the alternatives to logical reasoning, something must be said about reasoning by induction given that it is used in conjunction with reasoning by deduction. If deduction is going from the general (principles, axioms) to the particular (facts), induction is often said to be the reverse. It is a matter of going from the particular to the general. For a good example of this type of method, see Lord Denning in *Lloyds Bank v Bundy* (1975) (above, p.72) and Lord Diplock in *Home Office v Dorset Yacht Co* (1970) (C&MT, p.31).

2.5.5 Reasoning by analogy (casuistic reasoning)

Logical, or axiomatic, reasoning is not the only type of formal reasoning recognised by philosophers and epistemologists, as the next extract indicates.

> **Albert R. Jonsen and Stephen Toulmin,** *The Abuse of Casuistry* **(University of California Press, 1988), pp.19, 34–35**
>
> ". . . On the one hand, for some 2,500 years there have always been those who regarded ethics as a topic for *theoretical* discussion: a kind of 'moral geometry' that makes particular ethical perceptions more intelligible by showing how they exemplify rules or laws that are both *more general* and also capable of being known with *greater certainty*. This first view treats ethics as a science, which gives a coherent and systematic account of human conduct of a kind that our unsystematized moral perceptions can only hint at.
>
> On the other hand, from the very beginning there have been other thinkers who challenged the adequacy of this first approach. Aristotle, for instance, questioned whether moral understanding lends itself to scientific systematization at all . . . Far from being based on general abstract principles that can at one and the same time be universal, invariable, and known with certainty (he argued), ethics deals with a multitude of particular concrete situations, which are themselves so variable that they resist all attempts to generalize about them in universal terms. In short, Aristotle declared, ethics is not and cannot be a science. Instead, it is a field of experience that calls for a recognition of significant particulars and for informed prudence: for what he called *phronesis*, or 'practical wisdom.'. . .

Theoretical arguments are structured in ways that free them from any dependence on the circumstances of their presentation and ensure them a *validity* of a kind that is not affected by the practical context of use. In formal arguments particular conclusions are deduced from ('entailed by') the initial axioms or universal principles that are the apex of the argument. So the truth or certainty that attaches to those axioms *flows downward* to the specific instances to be proved . . .

In the language of formal logic, the axioms are *major premises*, the facts that specify the present instance are *minor premises*, and the conclusion to be 'proved' is deduced (follows *necessarily*) from the initial premises.

Practical arguments, by contrast, involve a wider range of factors than formal deductions and are read with an eye to their occasion of use. Instead of aiming at strict entailments, they draw on the outcomes of previous experience, carrying over the procedures used to resolve earlier problems and reapplying them in new problematic situations. Practical arguments depend for their power on how closely the *present* circumstances resemble those of the earlier *precedent* cases for which this particular type of argument was originally devised. So, in practical arguments, the truths and certitudes established in the precedent cases *pass sideways*, so as to provide 'resolutions' of later problems . . ."

NOTES

1. The two authors are of course discussing ethics rather than law, but it should be evident that their words apply equally to law as to ethics (in fact Stephen Toulmin was a philosopher who took much interest in how lawyers reason). The distinction between axiomatic and practical (casuistic) reasoning is said to be one of the distinctions that separates the Continental (civil) law tradition from the common law. English law is known for its system of precedents, whereas the civil law is known for its "axiomatic" codes. For a discussion of the development of legal science in German law, see F. Wieacker, *A History of Private Law in Europe* (OUP, 1995; trans T. Weir), especially pp.239–256, 292–319, 341–353. See also P. Stein, *Roman Law in European History* (CUP, 1999), pp.79–82, 119–123.

2. This axiomatic approach to law can be compared with comments to be found in English judgments. Thus: ". . . the common law of England has not always developed on strictly logical lines, and where logic leads down a path that is beset with practical difficulties the courts have not been frightened to turn aside and seek the pragmatic solution that will best serve the needs of society" (Griffiths L.J. in *Ex p. King* (1984), at 903). A more pertinent example is given in the next extract.

Lister v Hesley Hall Ltd [2002] 1 A.C. 215, HL

Lord Steyn: ". . . 16. It is not necessary to embark on a detailed examination of the development of the modern principle of vicarious liability. But it is necessary to face up to the way in which the law of vicarious liability sometimes may embrace intentional wrongdoing by an employee. If one mechanically applies *Salmond's* test, the result might at first glance be thought to be that a bank is not liable to a customer where a bank employee defrauds a customer by giving him only half the foreign exchange which he paid for, the employee pocketing the difference. A preoccupation with conceptualistic reasoning may lead to the absurd conclusion that there can only be vicarious liability if the bank carries on business in defrauding its customers. Ideas divorced from reality have never held much attraction for judges steeped in the tradition that their task is to deliver principled but practical justice. How the courts set the law on a sensible course is a matter to which I now turn . . ."

NOTE

This idea of "practical justice" has been used with increasing frequency since it was deployed by Lord Goff in *White v Jones* (1995) (C&MT, p.260). Admittedly most of the cases where it occurs are tort, although *White v Jones* does have a contractual dimension; but casuistic or practical reasoning can be found in contract cases, as the next extract indicates.

The Eurymedon [1975] A.C. 154, PC

Lord Wilberforce: ". . . If the choice, and the antithesis, is between a gratuitous promise and a promise for consideration, as it must be, in the absence of a *tertium quid*, there can be little doubt which, in commercial reality, this is . . . English law, having committed itself to a rather technical and schematic doctrine of contract, in application takes a practical approach, often at the cost of forcing the facts to fit uneasily into the marked slots of offer, acceptance and consideration . . ."

NOTES

1. See also *Blackpool & Fylde Aero Club v Blackpool BC* (1990) (at p.177). In these cases, despite the axiomatic ("schematic") nature of contract law (a model of abstract rules divorced from facts), judges often justify their conclusions by reference to the businessman or commercial practice.

2. A good example of an argument based on analogy (put by counsel for the claimant) can be found in *Goodwill v British Pregnancy Advisory Service* (1996) (C&MT, p.33). The analogy was, of course, rejected by the Court of Appeal.

2.5.6 Dialectical reasoning

Another form of reasoning is dialectical reasoning, which to some extent can be said to fall midway between deductive and casuistic reasoning. A dialectical approach to reasoning with respect to an object or phenomenon is one that sees such an object or phenomenon as consisting of two contradictory parts. Thus, to give a simple example, the human emotion might be seen as consisting of a dichotomy between love and hate or good and evil. Karl Marx applied this form of reasoning to society: capitalist societies consisted of a struggle between two interest groups, capital and labour.

A dialectical approach can be found operating within legal logic: "No premise can be admitted without admitting at the same time the opposite premise, so much so that no conclusion can be accepted without accepting at the same time the opposite conclusion and without having made a choice between two possible conclusions" (J-L. Bergel, *Théorie générale du droit* (4th edn Dalloz, 2004), p.295). Is a knife displayed for sale in a shop window an "offer" (conclusion: contract) or an "invitation to treat" (conclusion: no contract)? The reasoning process in *Fisher v Bell* (1961) (above, at p.35) thus gets reduced to a dialectical tension between offer and invitation to treat: there is simply a choice between two categories in tension one with the other. The same technique can be found in many rights cases, in that one right often has to be balanced against another right (for instance, freedom of the press versus privacy): see Lord Rodger in *Wilson v First County Trust Ltd (No.2)* (2004) (above, at p.47).

Dialectical reasoning can also be important in the analysis of precedents. Sometimes there are cases that at first sight appear to contradict (compare, for example, *Donoghue v Stevenson* (1932) (C&MT, p.112) with *Lockett v Charles* (1938) (p.398)). The contraction can be solved by the dialectical process of putting the facts side by side and comparing them in detail; differences should then emerge, thus solving the contradiction (café versus restaurant, friendship versus marriage, etc.). This is an approach that was developed to a high level of sophistication by the medieval philosophers and jurists; they used the dialectical method to solve contradictions to be found in the authoritative texts (the Bible, the Corpus of Roman law): see M. Bellomo, *The Common Legal Past of Europe 1000–1800* (The Catholic University of America Press, 1995; trans. L.G. Cochrane), p.181.

2.5.7 Functional reasoning

A very different reasoning method is functionalism. This approach has already been discussed and illustrated in **Chapter 1**, and one manifestation of this kind of reasoning is to be found in policy arguments (see e.g. *Barclays Bank v O'Brien* (1992, CA), at p.14). The essence of functional reasoning is that it puts the emphasis on the *purpose* of the rule or contractual concept and uses this purpose to justify the conclusion arrived at by the judge. See generally **1.1.5–1.1.6**; and UC&TO, pp.86–87.

2.5.8 Interpretative (or hermeneutical) reasoning

Another form of reasoning to be found in law—indeed some would say the main form of reasoning—is interpretation or hermeneutics. The structure of this form of reasoning is not one of downward flowing reasoning (deduction) or sideways reasoning (analogy) (cf. Jonsen and Toulmin, at p.94), or, indeed, reasoning based upon the existence of an internal contradiction (dialectics). The essence of hermeneutical reasoning is to give *meaning* or *significance* to a sign (normally a text or a word) by reference to some deeper reference point (for example the intention of the author or legislator). What does this sign *mean*? This method of reasoning, then, treats the object to be interpreted as a mere signifier, a carrier of some hidden sense or meaning.

Hermeneutical reasoning was again developed by the medieval philosophers, theologians and jurists whose mission was to explain the meaning of texts such as those to be found in the Bible and in the Roman laws. Thus, just as theologians sought to reveal the hidden meanings behind the Word of God as presented in the texts in the Bible, so the Glossators struggled to explain the expressions and concepts of Roman law as found in the *Corpus Juris Civilis*. The methods that they employed were dialectical reasoning (in respect of apparent contradictions in the texts) and explanatory glosses next to the various texts explaining their significance.

Given that many commercial contracts are reduced to writing—indeed, often to long and complex documents full, as one might expect, of technical legal terms—interpretation has an important role in many contract cases. The extracts below give a flavour of this interpretation reasoning.

Genossenschaftsbank v Burnhope [1995] 1 W.L.R. 1580, HL

A clause in an insurance contract included the words "theft . . . or false pretences, committed by persons present on the premises". In this case the fraud had not involved any human person being on the premises.

Lord Steyn (dissenting): ". . . The word persons in a notice in a cinema that 'No persons under 18 years may be admitted' can only refer to natural persons. That is generally speaking the obvious meaning of the word. But it is not the ordinary meaning of the word in a contractual stipulation in a commercial contract. Thus the *Oxford English Dictionary* in both the first and second editions gives this meaning (s.v. 'person'): 'IV. *Law,*. A human being (*natural person*) or body corporate or corporation (*artificial person*), having rights and duties recognized by the law.' Moreover, section 61 of the Law of Property Act 1925 provides that in all contracts, unless the context otherwise requires, 'person' includes a corporation. That was a statutory provision declaratory of the common law. The question is not whether the parties had in mind section 61: it operates ipso jure unless the context displaces it. The result is that in a commercial contract the prima facie meaning of the word 'person' includes a company.

The question is whether the prima facie meaning of the word is displaced by the context of this policy. It can only be displaced in one of two ways. First, it may be displaced if the prima facie meaning turns counter to the commercial purpose, objectively ascertained, of the clause or policy. Neither Hobhouse J nor any members of the Court of Appeal was sure what the purpose of the provision is.

Neither leading counsel could help on this point. There is no discoverable single purpose which could serve to displace the prima facie meaning of 'persons.' . . .

Secondly, a prima facie meaning may have to yield to contrary indications in the contract. Only one such indication has been put forward. It is said that the words 'persons *present* on the premises' are sufficient to displace the prima facie meaning. I disagree. The concept of presence is not inconsistent with the word 'persons' including a company. The company was present at the bank's premises through its innocent agent, Mr Towers, who was duly authorised by the company to receive the securities. And the same would have been the case if Mr Towers had been a messenger who was duly authorised to receive the securities . . ."

Lord Hoffmann: ". . . The crime of theft can be committed by a company because, in principle, companies are subject to the criminal law and it is possible to imply rules for determining whose acts and states of mind are for this purpose to count as acts of the company. It is however a non sequitur to argue that because a company can be guilty of theft, therefore a company must be included in the persons who can be present on the premises within the meaning of this clause. The former involves the interpretation of a rule of criminal law, the latter a question of the construction of this clause. It is to my mind clear from the terms of this clause taken as a whole, with its references to 'burglary, robbery or hold-up,' 'mysterious unexplainable disappearance' and 'damaged, destroyed or misplaced' that the parties had in mind physical people and things and not abstractions. So the presumption in section 61 of the Law of Property Act 1925 is rebutted.

I do not think that it helps to produce examples of where the difference between theft by a person on the premises and a person off the premises is narrow and arbitrary. The clause deliberately uses a physical boundary line of delimit liability. If Mr Smith had gone round and collected the securities himself, there would clearly have been a theft by a person on the premises. If he had parked outside on a double yellow line and called up on his car telephone to ask an employee of the bank to bring them out to him, there would equally clearly have been no theft by a person on the premises. I agree with my noble and learned friend, Lord Lloyd of Berwick, that the obvious case which the parties intended to exclude was theft by electronic means employed from a remote location. But in order to achieve this, the parties have drawn a line on the map which can have fairly arbitrary consequences . . ."

NOTES

1. It is not untypical of insurance contract cases that the solution can depend simply on the interpretation of a single word (see also *Young v Sun Alliance Insurance* (1977), at p.349).

2. Other cases involving interpretation of contractual documents are: *Schuler v Wickman Machine Tool Sales Ltd* (1974) (p.327); *Staffs Area Health Authority v South Staffs Waterworks Co* (1978) (p.428).

QUESTION

When interpreting a contract, are the courts to be guided by the dictionary or by what the parties themselves meant by a word or phrase?

ICS v West Bromwich Building Society **[1998] 1 W.L.R. 896, HL**

(See also p.355.)

Lord Hoffmann: ". . . Finally, on this part of the case, I must make some comments upon the judgment of the Court of Appeal. Leggatt LJ said that his construction was 'the natural and ordinary meaning of the words used.' I do not think that the concept of natural and ordinary meaning is very helpful when, on any view, the words have not been used in a natural and ordinary way. In a case like this, the court is inevitably engaged in choosing between competing unnatural meanings. Secondly, Leggatt LJ said that the judge's construction was not an 'available meaning' of the words. If this means that judges cannot, short of rectification, decide that the parties must have made mistakes of meaning or syntax, I respectfully think he was wrong. The proposition is not, I would suggest, borne out by his citation from *Through the Looking-Glass*. Alice and Humpty-Dumpty were agreed that the word 'glory' did not mean 'a nice knock-down argument.' Anyone with a dictionary could see that. Humpty-Dumpty's point was that 'a nice knock-down argument' was what *he* meant by using the word 'glory.' He very fairly acknowledged that Alice, as a reasonable young woman, could not have realised this until he told her, but once he had told her, or if, without being expressly told, she could have inferred it from the background, she would have had no difficulty in understanding what he meant . . ."

NOTE

1. The reference to Humpty-Dumpty was not new. In *Liversidge v Anderson* (1942) Lord Atkin said (at 245): "I know of only one authority which might justify the suggested method of construction: 'When I use a word,' Humpty Dumpty said in rather a scornful tone, 'it means just what I choose it to mean, neither more nor less.' 'The question is,' said Alice, 'whether you can make words mean so many different things.' 'The question is,' said Humpty Dumpty, 'which is to be master—that's all.'" (*Through the Looking Glass*, c. vi.).

2. The relationship between law and literature goes well beyond the odd judicial reference to well-known authors and quotes. One leading legal philosopher has developed a whole theory of law around the process of interpretation in literature.

Ronald Dworkin, *Law's Empire* **(Fontana, 1986), p.229**

". . . We can find an even more fruitful comparison between literature and law . . . by constructing an artificial genre of literature that we might call the chain novel.

In this enterprise a group of novelists writes a novel *seriatim*; each novelist in the chain interprets the chapters he has been given in order to write a new chapter, which is then added to what the next novelist receives, and so on. Each has the job of writing his chapter so as to make the novel being constructed the best it can be, and the complexity of this task models the complexity of deciding a hard case under law as integrity . . . In our example . . . the novelists are expected to take their responsibilities of continuity . . . seriously; they aim jointly to create, so far as they can, a single unified novel that is the best it can be.

He may find, not that no single interpretation fits the bulk of the text, but that more than one does. The second dimension of interpretation then requires him to judge which of these eligible readings makes the work in progress best, all things considered. At this point his more substantive aesthetic judgments, about the importance or insight or realism or beauty of different ideas the novel might be taken to express, come into play . . ."

NOTES AND QUESTIONS

1. This extract may appear at first sight to be taking us well beyond the boundary of a contract law course. Yet it ought to be borne in mind that contract is one of the few areas left that is based almost entirely, at least in its foundational principles, on precedents. Accordingly it is worth reflecting upon the activity of judges and their methods within this subject area. Have the foundational principles of contract been developed by the judges over the last two centuries in the way suggested by Dworkin? Or have judges simply focused on a precise area, say the nature of an "offer" or the notion of "consideration", and fashioned their judgment with reference only to this precise rule or concept and to the actual facts in question? Are there any cases in which judges have taken a view of the whole of the law of contract (and beyond) before arriving at their decision in a particular case? These questions might usefully be borne in mind as one reads the mass of contract cases in the chapters that follow and in the law reports.

2. Dworkin is inviting one to think that the judges focus exclusively on texts. But what about facts?

Christian Atias, *Épistémologie juridique* **(Presses Universitaires de France, 1985), p.129 (footnotes omitted) (translation Geoffrey Samuel)**

". . . The reflections of jurists on the relationship between fact and law can also be brought to bear on the way in which the law ought to take in fact. Several difficulties are to be faced here. The first concerns an intellectual activity of primary importance, categorisation. Here it is a matter of trying to understand the reasoning which allows the translation of fact circumstances into legal conditions. Without this work of selection, of comparison, of making distinctions, the lawyer will be weaponless. And yet he has at his disposal no real tools to verify the quality of his work. Certainly the distinction between the presupposition and the legal effect of the rule is rational and shows him the way to go. The fact remains however that the actual reasoning of the lawyer is probably rather different. In the first place, the jurist can hardly study the facts without seeing them through a pre-categorisation. In the second place, the incessant coming-and-going from fact to law which permits him progressively to arrive at the best categorisation available is evidently not independent of the opinion that he has on the just solution in the case. In the third place, the function of the categorisation is not to describe reality, but to subject it to the most appropriate legal regime. In order to know if a wild rabbit is a chattel or real property, it is not necessary to get stuck into issues about whether it has greater or lesser mobility. Consequently, the difficulty of the work of categorisation consists in finding the balance between the consideration of fact and the objective to be promoted in law."

NOTES

1. See also the extracts from Peter Birks and Stephen Waddams in C&MT, pp.255–7; and Kevin Gray and Susan Gray, "The Rhetoric of Reality", in J. Getzler (ed.), *Rationalizing Property, Equity and Trusts* (Butterworths, 2003), p.204, at p.223.

2. Whether the construction and categorisation of facts is actually an interpretative (hermeneutical) exercise is an interesting question. Some certainly think that it is, and that is why the hermeneutical method is one of the respectable methodological schemes to be found in sociology. However, there is another school of thought that sees the perception of facts as something different; between the immediate perception of facts and their categorisation in law there is a "vision of the world" mental process that is not entirely neutral (P. Amselek, in P. Amselek (ed.), *Interprétation et droit* (Bruylant, 1995), at p.24). This point is illustrated by *Lazenby Garages v Wright* (1976) (below, at p.537).

3. *Lazenby Garages v Wright* (1976) looks at first sight like a straightforward interpretation of a contractual damages rule. But the key to the actual conclusion reached by Lord Denning is to be found in his construction of the factual situation: a second-hand car is a *unique* object, while a new car is a *generic* object. Being a unique object, the agreed contract price and the actual resale price attached to this specific car; and as the latter was more than the former, the seller "obviously" suffered no loss. Had the car been categorised as a generic object then the whole damage picture would change: the price would attach not to the individual car but to the sale figures of this *class* of car as a whole. Thus the seller would have "lost" the profit on the sale of one of

these cars. The defendant's lawyer and the claimant's lawyer were, in effect, presenting to the court two different "realities".

2.5.9 Axiological reasoning

Axiological reasoning is different yet again from the other forms of reasoning in that it emphasises social and moral values. It is often said that legal rules are to be distinguished from moral rules, but this does not mean that axiological considerations do not re-enter by the back door, so to speak, via judicial reasoning.

Kevin Gray and Susan Gray, "The Rhetoric of Reality" in J. Getzler (ed.), *Rationalizing Property, Equity and Trusts* (Butterworths, 2003), p.204, at pp.229–30 (footnotes omitted)

". . . [T]he processes of legal reasoning include a rather broader range of cognitive activity than that encompassed by formal or analytic systems of logic. Deeply entrenched, for instance, in the philosophy of the American Realists was the perception that juristic reasoning 'is not merely thought; it is argumentation' (Nathan Isaacs). Indeed a more recent school of 'rhetorical reasoning', associated mainly but not exclusively with the civilian tradition, holds that the intellectual enterprise of law is not deductive, but dialogic; not formal, but contextual; not axiomatic, but interactive and reflective . . .

It follows that what is at work here is not logic of axioms and deductions, but rather a 'logic of attitudes'. The *axiomatic* has given way to the *axiological* (in the sense of a pervasive concern with the values which underpin legal phenomena). Thus the truly formative premises of the law are often those unwritten principles which command the assent of an 'interpretative audience' of knowledgeable participants in the particular juristic enterprise concerned . . . It also has strong links with an older common law tradition in which the 'common erudition', 'common learning' or *communis opinion* of the practising profession was regarded as an independent source of law . . ."

NOTES

1. On the relationship between legal reasoning and legal argumentation, see also C&MT, pp.38–40; UC&TO, pp.84–91.

2. Axiological reasoning is often associated with the hard case: "But problems arise when hard cases have to be decided and those decisions justified. What if no valid norm seems to govern the case? Which norm has to be chosen? What if a norm which tendentially governs the case leads to undesirable consequences? How must a norm be interpreted in order to obtain the best possible result? It is clear that all these questions take us to the domain of axiology, morality, or politics and yet legal justification is not expected to question the very system of law nor the ideology of adjudication embodied

therein, ie the postulate that legal decisions have to be grounded on legally relevant sources, a postulate that embodies the rule of law ideal . . . " (Bengoetxea, *The Legal Reasoning of the European Court of Justice* (OUP, 1993), p.146).

3. A good example of axiological reasoning is to be found in Lord Steyn's judgment in *McFarlane v Tayside Health Board* (2000), extracted in C&MT, at p.45. Sometimes this axiological reasoning can be combined with functional (policy) reasoning: see e.g. Lord Steyn in *Smith New Court Securities Ltd v Scrimgeour Vickers Ltd* (1997), extracted in C&MT, at pp.288–9.

QUESTION

Should a person who deliberately fails to perform his contractual obligation(s) pay more by way of damages than a person who negligently fails to perform? (Cf. *Smith New Court Securities Ltd v Scrimgeour Vickers Ltd* (1997), at p.233.)

2.5.10 **Methodology: concluding overview**

The reasoning methods employed by judges to solve contract problems are varied. Logic no doubt has its role, but functional (policy), interpretative and moral reasoning also have an important place. Judgments should be studied in order to identify the reasoning scheme(s) employed on the path towards the solution. In fact, more often than not, judges use a variety of schemes, mixing, for example, policy with moral reasoning (see Lord Steyn, C&MT, pp.288–9) or logic with interpretation and perhaps analogy. As the next extract indicates, the way judges reason, even in what might appear to be clear-cut "rule" subjects like contract, is at best complex.

Stephen Waddams, *Dimensions of Private Law: Categories and Concepts in Anglo-American Legal Reasoning* (CUP, 2003), pp.225–226

"Legal reasoning, as we have seen, has been a complex process, neither illogical in the sense of unreasoned or badly reasoned, nor reducible to any form of logic recognized outside the law. The concepts of contract, wrongdoing, and unjust enrichment have, at the point of their operation (that is, in the context of particular legal issues), often worked concurrently and cumulatively. They have been mutually complementary in the sense that each has supplemented and filled out the meaning of the others. At higher levels of generality the same complementarity may be observed in the relations between obligations and property, and between private right and public policy. Two consequences follow on these complexities: it has not been possible to explain Anglo-American private law in terms of any single concept, nor has any map, scheme, or diagram proved satisfactory in which the concepts are separated from each other, as on a two-dimensional plane. The idea of mapping cannot entirely be discarded, and it owes its attraction partly to the fact that it is understood in many different ways, some of which are essential to the organization of thought. But insofar as it implies a separation of legal concepts from each other, or the assignment of each legal issue to one concept alone, it is apt to distort an understanding of the past, and consequently also of the present . . ."

NOTES

1. See also the extracts from Peter Birks and Stephen Waddams in C&MT, pp.255–7. One might study, in addition, the extract from Tony Weir set out in C&MT, at p.39.

2. Further interesting examples of types of reasoning, policy, etc can be found in case extracts elsewhere in this book: see e.g. *The Chikuma* (1981) (at p.346).

3. For an in-depth discussion of Professor Waddam's book, see Samuel (2005) 55 *University of Toronto Law Journal* 271.

QUESTION

The (Draft) Restitution (Mistakes of Law) Bill (Law Com. No.227) has a paragraph which reads as follows: "A view of the law may be regarded for the purpsoes of this section as having been settled at any time notwithstanding that it was not held unanimously or had not been the subject of a decision by a court or tribunal" (para.3(2)). Where might one find a "settled view" of the law of contract? Is such a "settled view" one based on rules or how the courts might react to a given set of facts? Read the case of *Blackpool & Fylde Aero Club v Blackpool BC* (1990) (p.177) and try to form a "settled view" of the rules regarding the formation of tendering contracts? Might a "settled view" of apsects of the law of contract be found simply in what business people do?

3 General provisions

Both the PECL and UNIDROIT open with a chapter on general provisions. This is sensible since there are a number of matters that need to be examined before one can descend into the actual provisions dealing with the formation, interpretation and effects of a contract. There are, however, some matters that the two codes do not cover, in particular the classification of contracts (which is covered in the French civil code). Equally there are other matters which are covered but will not be discussed in this chapter because of questions of space, relevance and importance.

3.1 Classification of contracts

We saw in the last chapter that the idea of a general theory of contract must be treated with some caution. Empirically speaking, there are many different types of transactions and relationships; and although all involve a contract, it is important to distinguish between these transactions. The sale of an onion is very different from the hire of a ship, just as this latter contract (a charterparty) has little in common with a contract of employment (see Tony Weir extract, at p.59). Many of these differences function at the level of fact rather than law, and so, for example, there is no formal legal distinction between an instantaneous and a long-term contract (see **2.3.3**). However, in the civil law codes formal distinctions are made between certain different types of contract (see UC&TO, pp.26–27). Accordingly, in the French *Code civil*, in addition to the articles devoted to the general theory of contract, there are articles dealing with the specific contracts of sale, hire, partnership and other contracts inherited from Roman law. Some of the more recent codes have recognised certain kinds of special contracts unknown to the Romans, such as insurance and banking. In addition to these special contracts, the French *Code civil* makes some important distinctions at the level of general theory itself, the distinction between a unilateral and bilateral contract being one of the most important.

English law also distinguishes certain specific contracts from general contract theory in as much as it has special legislative rules covering, for example, sale of goods, partnership, marine insurance, carriage of goods and so on (see UC&TO, pp.27–30). Not all of these special contracts will be formally identified in this section, but some of the main ones will, where the differences need to be appreciated at the level of a general theory of contract.

3.1.1 Bilateral and unilateral contracts

One important distinction to be made at the level of general theory itself is the difference, set out in the French *Code civil*, between a unilateral and bilateral contract.

See *Code civil*, arts 1102–1103 (above, at p.8). The relevance of this French provision for English law is set out in the next extract.

United Dominions Trust Ltd v Eagle Aircraft Services Ltd [1968] 1 W.L.R. 74, CA

Diplock L.J.: ". . . [T]he present appeal does turn on the difference in legal character between contracts which are synallagmatic (a term which I prefer to bilateral, for there may be more than two parties), and contracts which are not syllagmatic but only unilateral, an expression which, like synallagmatic, I have borrowed from French law (Code Civil, art 1102 and art 1103). Under contracts of the former kind, each party undertakes to the other party to do or to refrain from doing something, and, in the event of his failure to perform his undertaking, the law provides the other party with a remedy. The remedy of the other party may be limited to recovering monetary compensation for any loss which he has sustained as a result of the failure, without relieving him from his own obligation to do that which he himself has undertaken to do and has not yet done, or to continue to refrain from doing that which he himself has undertaken to refrain from doing. It may, in addition, entitle him, if he so elects, to be released from any further obligation to do or to refrain from doing anything . . . The mutual obligations of parties to a synallagmatic contract may be subject to conditions precedent, that is to say, they may not arise until a described event has occurred; but the event must not be one which one party can prevent from occurring, for if it is, it leaves that party free to decide whether or not he will enter into any obligations to the other party at all. The obligations under the contract lack that mutuality which is an essential characteristic of a synallagmatic contract . . ."

NOTE

The synallagmatic or bilateral contract needs to be distinguished from the unilateral.

United Dominions Trust Ltd v Eagle Aircraft Services Ltd [1968] 1 W.L.R. 74, CA

Diplock L.J.: ". . . Under contracts which are only unilateral—which I have elsewhere described as 'if' contracts—one party, whom I will call 'the promisor', undertakes to do or to refrain from doing something on his part if another party, 'the promisee', does or refrains from doing something, but the promisee does not himself undertake to do or to refrain from doing that thing. The commonest contracts of this kind in English law are options for good consideration to buy or to sell or to grant or take a lease, competitions for prizes, and such contracts as that discussed in *Carlill v Carbolic Smoke Ball Co* [1893] 1 QB 256. A unilateral contract does not give rise to any immediate obligation on the part of either party to do or to refrain from doing anything except possibly an obligation on the part of the promisor to refrain from putting it out of his power to perform his undertaking in the future. This apart, a unilateral contract may never give rise to any obligation on the part of the promisor; it will only do so on the occurrence of the event specified in the contract, viz, the doing (or refraining from doing) by the promisee of a particular thing. It never gives rise, however, to any obligation on the promisee to bring about the event by doing or refraining from doing that particular thing. Indeed, a unilateral contract of itself never gives rise to any obligation on the promisee to do or to refrain from doing anything. In its simplest form (e.g., 'If you pay the entrance fee and win the race, I will pay you £100'), no obligations on the part of the promisee result from it at all. But in its more complex and more usual form, as in an option, the promisor's undertaking may be to enter into a synallagmatic contract with the promisee on the occurrence of the event specified in the unilateral contract, and in that case the event so specified must be, or at least include, the communication by the promisee to the promisor of the promisee's acceptance of his obligations under the synallagmatic contract. By entering into the subsequent synallagmatic contract on the occurrence of the specified event, the promisor discharges his obligation under the unilateral contract and accepts new obligations under the synallagmatic contract. Any obligations of the promisee arise, not out of the unilateral contract, but out of the subsequent synallagmatic contract into which he was not obliged to enter but has chosen to do so.

Two consequences follow from this. The first is that there is no room for any inquiry whether any act done by the promisee in purported performance of a unilateral contract amounts to a breach of warranty or a breach of condition on his part, for he is under no obligation to do or to refrain from doing any act at all. The second is that, as respects the promisor, the initial inquiry is whether the event, which under the unilateral contract gives rise to obligations on the part of the promisor, has occurred. To that inquiry the answer can only be a simple 'Yes' or 'No' . . ."

QUESTIONS

1. French law does not have a requirement of consideration. Are there not therefore important differences between the French notion of a bilateral contract and the English notion? (Cf. **4.6.**)

2. At what point in a unilateral contract is the contractual offer accepted?

3. Is the contract that a vendor of a house makes with an estate agent a unilateral or a bilateral contract? (Cf. *Luxor (Eastbourne) Ltd v Cooper* (1941).)

PROBLEM

Pierre advertises in his local newspaper that he will pay £10 to anyone who returns his lost cat "Tibbins". Horatia finds Tibbins, whose collar contains Pierre's address, and returns her to Pierre, who says nothing about the reward. The next day Horatia sees, for the first time, the reward advert in the paper: can she claim the £10? What if Horatia, after seeing the advert and then finding Tibbins, carelessly loses the cat while taking her to Pierre's house: can Pierre sue Horatia for the value of the cat?

3.1.2 Specific contracts: introduction

In civilian legal systems contracts are classed as named or unnamed. The origin of this distinction is to be found in Roman law.

***Digest of Roman Law*, Book 2, Title 14 (*De pactis*)**

"**7. ULPIAN**. With regard to law of nations (*ius gentium*) agreements, some give rise to actions (*actiones*), some to defences (*exceptions*). 1. Those that give rise to actions are not known under the term agreement, but in their own contract names: that is to say, sale, hire, partnership, loan, deposit and other similar contracts. 2. Even if the matter cannot be classified under one of these contracts, yet a sufficient ground (*causa*) exists, Aristo's nice relpy to Celsus says there is an obligation. So that I gave you a thing on the basis that you were to give me another thing or that you were to do something: this will be a *synallagma* and gives rise to a civil obligation. . . . 4. But if no ground (*causa*) exists with regard to the agreement, then no obligation can exist; a bare agreement (*nudum pactum*) gives rise to no obligation, but to an *exceptio* . . ."

NOTES

1. The modern Continental codes have largely adopted these Roman specific contracts of sale, hire, partnership, loan, deposit and other similar contracts: see e.g. *Code civil*, art. 1107 (above, at p.8).

2. One distinction between civil and common law contractual thinking is to be found "in the fact that the civilian systems construct contract law in starting out from the list of 'named' contracts, the unnamed contract playing only a marginal role . . . [T]he civilian jurists practically never work within the general category of contract; in particular they never worry about knowing if a new agreement can or cannot be considered as a contract. Indeed, when faced with a new form of agreement, they deal with it either by combining existing agreements or adapting a quite different one" (R-M. Rampelberg, *Repères romains pour le droit européen des contrats* (LGDJ, 2005), p.35).

3. Professor Rampelberg continues by saying that the common lawyers, on the other hand, "are not familiar with types of contractual agreement" and from "the very moment an agreement has a patrimonial content, the English judge has to determine if there is a contract in starting out from the general notion of unnamed contract, the only category on which he can base himself, but one maginalised by the civilians on the continent." The professor thus warns that "when the civilians wish to convince the common lawyers to abandon the requirement of consideration they run the risk of doing away with the one authentic unifying element . . . in exchange for a mutilated general notion of contract" (*op. cit.*, p.35). For Professor Rampelberg, then, the foundation of contract in the civil law is the named transaction which acts as the *causa*; in the common law it is consideration which acts as the causa, operating within

the general category of contract (see **4.6**). To do away with consideration would therefore be to do way with an English form of *causa*, in turn breaking a link with Roman law. This is an interesting thesis, but it is nevertheless dangerous to try to link English law with Roman law, especially through ideas like *causa*. The notion of *causa* attaches to the transaction, while consideration attaches to the promise. What they share, of course, is a similar functional role; legal systems need to distinguish the enforceable promise or agreement from the unenforceable.

3.1.3 **Sale of goods**

Nevertheless, specific contracts do have something of a role in English law. One of the most important of these specific contracts is the sale of goods transaction.

Ashington Piggeries Ltd v Christopher Hill Ltd **[1972] A.C. 441, HL**

Lord Diplock: ". . . My Lords, the claim in each of these appeals is for damages for breach of a contract for the sale of goods. It will, therefore, be necessary to relate them to the relevant statutory provisions of the Sale of Goods Act 1893. In the form in which the Bill was originally drafted by Sir MacKenzie Chalmers that Act was intended to state the common law rules relating to the sale of goods as they had been developed by judicial decision up to 1889. Although a number of amendments were made in committee during the passage of the Bill through Parliament, they did not alter the essential character of the Act as expository of the common law of England at the date at which it was passed. But the exposition contained in the Act is only partial. It does not seek to codify the general law of contract of England or of Scotland. It assumes the existence as a basic principle of the English law of contract that, subject to any limitations imposed by statute or by common law rules of public policy, parties to contracts have freedom of choice not only as to what each will mutually promise to do but also as to what each is willing to accept as the consequences of the performance or non-performance of those promises so far as those consequences affect any other party to the contract . . . The provisions of the Act are in the main confined to statements of what promises are to be implied on the part of the buyer and the seller in respect of matters upon which the contract is silent, and statements of the consequences of performance or non-performance of promises, whether expressed or implied, where the contract does not state what those consequences are to be. Even a code whose content is so limited must proceed by classifying promises, both those which are expressed and those to be implied; the circumstances which give rise to implied promises, and how they are to be performed and the consequences of performing each class of promise or of failing to perform it. Because of the source of the rules stated in the Sale of Goods Act 1893 the classification adopted is by reference to the promises made in relatively simple types of contracts for the sale of goods which were commonly made in the nineteenth century and had been the subject of judicial decision before 1893. But although the language in which the rules are expressed is appropriate to these simple types of contracts, it has to be applied today to promises made in much more complicated contracts which cannot be readily allotted to any single class of contract which appears to be primarily envisaged by a particular section or subsection of the code. Unless the Sale of Goods Act 1893 is to be allowed to fossilise the law and to restrict the freedom of choice of parties to contracts for the sale of goods to make agreements which take account of advances in technology and changes in the way in which business is carried on today, the provisions set out in the various sections and subsections of the code ought not to be construed so narrowly as to force upon parties to contracts for the sale of goods promises and consequences different from what they must reasonably have intended. They should be treated rather as illustrations of the application to simple types of contract of general principles for ascertaining the common intention of the parties as to their mutual promises and their consequences which ought to be applied by analogy in cases arising out of contracts which do not appear to have been within the immediate contemplation of the draftsman of the Act in 1893.

In each of the instant appeals the dispute is as to what the seller promised to the buyer by the words which he used in the contract itself and by his conduct in the course of the negotiations which led up to the contract. What he promised is determined by ascertaining what his words and conduct would have led the buyer reasonably to believe that he was promising. That is what is meant in the English law of contract by the common intention of the parties. The test is impersonal. It does not depend upon what the seller himself thought he was promising, if the words and conduct by which he communicated his intention to the seller would have led a reasonable man in the position of the buyer to a different belief as to the promise; nor does it depend upon the actual belief of the buyer himself as to what the seller's promise was, unless that belief would have been shared by a reasonable man in the position of the buyer. The result of the application of this test to the words themselves used in the contract is 'the construction of the contract'. So far as the reasonable belief of the buyer as to what the seller's promise was, would have been influenced by any conduct of the seller before the contract was made, any implication as to the nature of his promise falls to be determined by applying to his conduct the general principles for ascertaining the common intention of parties to a contract for the sale of goods which underlie the relevant provisions of the Sale of Goods Act 1893 . . .

A contract for the sale of goods is one whereby the property in goods which have been physically identified is transferred from the seller to the buyer (see: ss 1(1) and 16). But a contract may be made for the sale of unascertained goods before the actual goods in which the property is to be transferred are physically identified and agreed upon. At the time of making such a contract the kind of goods which are its subject-matter can only be identified verbally and/or by reference to a sample . . ."

NOTES AND QUESTIONS

1. The Sale of Goods Act has been amended over the last century, and a consolidated version of 1979 has now replaced the Act of 1893. Compare s.14 of the original 1893 Act with the fully amended s.14 now to be found in the 1979 Act: do you think this section has lost its original code-like quality?

2. Lord Diplock talks about the classification of promises into those that are express and those that are implied. If it is statute that implies some promises, is it true to say that such promises (terms) have been agreed by the parties? Are they not simply rules imposed upon those entering certain kinds of transactions? To what extent ought parties, today, to be able to exclude implied terms? (Cf. **8.4.**)

3. Is Lord Diplock reinforcing the thesis that English contract law is based upon promise rather than agreement? (Cf. **4.1.**)

4. Goods are not just bought and sold, but also hired. With respect to implied terms as to description, fitness and quality, these are now analogous to those implied into sale contracts: see Supply of Goods and Services Act 1982, ss.8–9. In a contract of service where the service also involves the transfer of property (ownership) in goods (e.g. a contract to service a car in which the garage replaces some car parts), the implied terms as to description and quality are equally analogous to those found in ss.13–14 of the 1979 Act: see Supply of Goods and Services Act 1982, ss.1, 3–4.

3.1.4 Bailment contracts

The distinction between a contractual relationship and a bailment relationship has already been identified (see **1.3.4**). However, because so many commercial and consumer contracts involve a bailment, and because the bailment relationship imposes its own duties in addition to any contractual ones, this type of contract needs special mention once again.

Morris v CW Martin & Sons Ltd **[1966] 1 Q.B. 716, CA**

The owner of a mink stole brought an action against a firm of cleaners for its value. She had sent it to Beder, a furrier, for cleaning; Beder, with the owner's consent, sent it to the defendants for the actual cleaning. The defendants' employee, who was supposed to clean the fur, stole it instead. The trial judge held the defendants not liable, but an appeal to the Court of Appeal (Lord Denning M.R., Diplock L.J. and Salmon L.J.) was allowed.

Lord Denning M.R.: ". . . Once a man has taken charge of goods as a bailee for reward, it is his duty to take reasonable care to keep them safe: and he cannot escape that duty by delegating it to his servant. If the goods are lost or damaged,

> whilst they are in his possession, he is liable unless he can show—and the burden is on him to show—that the loss or damage occurred without any neglect or default or misconduct of himself or of any of the servants to whom he delegated his duty . . . The bailee, to excuse himself, must show that the loss was without any fault on his part or on the part of his servants. If he shows that he took due care to employ trustworthy servants, and that he and his servants exercised all diligence, and yet the goods were stolen, he will be excused: but not otherwise. Take a case where a cleaner hands a fur to one of his servants for cleaning, and it is stolen. If the master can prove that thieves came in from outside and stole it without the fault of any of his servants, the master is not liable. But if it appears that the servant to whom he entrusted it was negligent in leaving the door unlocked—or collaborated with the thieves—or stole the fur himself, then the master is liable. . . ."

NOTE

See also the extracts from Diplock L.J. which can be found in C&MT, p.23, and from Lord Denning in the *Post Office* case (above, p.28).

3.1.5 **Credit and security contracts**

Lenders of money normally require security for their loans, and such security is often provided by a mortgage on the borrower's real property. Mortgage contracts do not normally form part of contract law because they are covered in detail in land law courses. One question that does arise, however, is with respect to chattel mortgages. Can one mortgage one's car in security for a loan? The answer to this question is "yes" in theory but "no" in practice, because the law virtually made such chattel mortgages impossible. The commercial world then developed the hire-purchase contract, which can be seen as a sort of contract for "sale" where the seller retains title (ownership) in the goods until the final instalment is paid. Such contracts were recognised as avoiding the Factors Act 1889, s.9, which gave protection to third parties who bought goods from anyone who bought from a person who had bought or agreed to buy, by giving the third party good title to the goods (thus depriving the original seller of his security) (*Helby v Matthews* (1895)). These kinds of contract are now regulated by statute: Consumer Credit Act 1974. This statute lays down a number of formalities to which a contract of credit and security must conform. Failure to conform can make the contract unenforceable.

Wilson v First County Trust Ltd (No.2) **[2004] 1 A.C. 816, HL**

(For facts and further extracts, see p.44.)

> **Lord Nicholls:** ". . . **28** . . . Before turning to these articles I should outline the salient provisions of the Consumer Credit Act 1974. Subject to exemptions, a

regulated agreement is an agreement between an individual debtor and another person by which the latter provides the former with a cash loan or other financial accommodation not exceeding a specified amount. Currently the amount is £25,000. Section 61(1) sets out conditions which must be satisfied if a regulated agreement is to be treated as properly executed. One of these conditions, in paragraph (a), is that the agreement must be in a prescribed form containing all the prescribed terms. The prescribed terms are the amount of the credit or the credit limit, rate of interest (in some cases), how the borrower is to discharge his obligations, and any power the creditor may have to vary what is payable: Consumer Credit (Agreements) Regulations 1983, Schedule 6. The consequence of improper execution is that the agreement is not enforceable against the debtor save by an order of the court: section 65(1). Section 127(1) provides what is to happen on an application for an enforcement order under section 65. The court 'shall dismiss' the application if, but only if, the court considers it just to do so having regard to the prejudice caused to any person by the contravention in question and the degree of culpability for it. The court may reduce the amount payable by the debtor so as to compensate him for prejudice suffered as a result of the contravention, or impose conditions, or suspend the operation of any term of the order or make consequential changes in the agreement or security.

29 The court's powers under section 127(1) are subject to significant qualification in two types of cases. The first type is where section 61(1)(a), regarding signing of agreements, is not complied with. In such cases the court 'shall not make' an enforcement order unless a document, whether or not in the prescribed form, containing all the prescribed terms, was signed by the debtor: section 127(3). Thus, signature of a document containing all the prescribed terms is an essential prerequisite to the court's power to make an enforcement order. The second type of case concerns failure to comply with the duty to supply a copy of an executed or unexecuted agreement pursuant to sections 62 and 63, or failure to comply with the duty to give notice of cancellation rights in accordance with section 64(1). Here again, subject to one exception regarding sections 62 and 63, section 127(4) precludes the court from making an enforcement order.

30 These restrictions on enforcement of a regulated agreement cannot be sidestepped by recourse to a pledge or other form of security furnished in support of the debtor's obligations under the agreement. The security is not enforceable to a greater extent than the loan: section 113. Where an application for an enforcement order is dismissed, except on technical grounds only, or the court makes a declaration under section 142 that the agreement is not enforceable, any security provided in relation to a regulated agreement 'shall be treated as never having effect': section 106(a). Property lodged with the creditor by way of security has to be returned by him 'forthwith'.

31 These restrictions on enforcement of a regulated agreement are for the protection of borrowers. They do not deprive a regulated agreement of all legal effect. They do not render a regulated agreement void. A regulated agreement is enforceable by the debtor against the creditor. It seems, for instance, that a borrower may insist on making further drawdowns under a regulated agreement even though the agreement is unenforceable against him. Further, section 173(3) expressly permits consensual enforcement against a borrower. A borrower may consent to the sale of a security or to judgment. Moreover, the creditor is entitled to retain any security lodged until either an application for an enforcement order is dismissed or the court makes a declaration under section 142 that the agreement is not enforceable. That is the effect of sections 113(3) and 106 . . ."

NOTES

1. See also *Wilson v Robertsons (London) Ltd* (2006).

2. Consumer credit agreements (including of course hire-purchase) often give rise to property as well as contract and tort problems (see, e.g., *Shogun Finance v Hudson* (2004), at p.265).

3.1.6 **Insurance contracts**

Insurance contracts are special because they impose upon both parties a positive duty of disclosure.

Agnew v Länsförsäkringsbolagens AB **[2001] 1 A.C. 223, HL**

Lord Millett: ". . . English law draws a clear distinction between misrepresentation and non-disclosure. There are, of course, exceptional cases where in the particular circumstances silence amounts to a positive statement. Apart from these, however, there is normally no duty to disclose information which is material to the other party's decision whether or not to enter into the contract. English law knows no general obligation of good faith in pre-contractual negotiations. In this respect it differs from civilian systems. There is, however, an exception in the case of contracts where in the nature of the case knowledge of the relevant facts is in the exclusive possession of one of the parties. Such contracts are described as contracts 'of the utmost good faith.' The party who is in possession of the relevant facts must make full disclosure of them to the other party. If he does not, the other party may have the contract set aside ab initio. Contracts of insurance (which for this purpose includes reinsurance) are the paradigm example of such contracts. The insured is bound to make a fair presentation of the risk to the insurer. If he does not, the insurer may avoid the contract. This is so whether the insurer is able to prove a positive misstatement of the facts or merely a failure to state them fairly.

QUESTIONS

1. A father wishes to obtain insurance cover for his car so that his sons can drive it. The proposal form submitted to the insurance company states that the

father has a provisional driving licence, when in fact he has no licence at all. Do you think that this would amount to a breach of the duty to disclose, permitting the insurance company to rescind the contract? Would it make any difference to your answer if (a) the misstatement was not due to any dishonesty on the father's part, and/or (b) the father had no intention of ever using the car himself? (Cf. *Magee v Pennine Insurance Co* (1969).)

2. A person seeking fire insurance cover for his home fails to disclose that he has a criminal conviction for armed robbery. Should the insurance company be able to rescind the fire policy? (Cf. *Woolcott v Sun Alliance and London Insurance Co* (1978).)

3.2 Freedom of contract

The principle of freedom of contract is regarded as one of the fundamental principles of Western contract law:

Principles of European Contract Law

"Article 1:102 Freedom of contract

(1) Parties are free to enter into a contract and to determine its contents, subject to the requirements of good faith and fair dealing, and the mandatory rules established by these Principles.
(2) The parties may exclude the application of any of the Principles or derogate from or vary their effects, except as otherwise provided by these Principles."

NOTES

1. See also UNIDROIT, arts 1.1 and 1.5.

2. The principle of freedom of contract is one that has in many ways dominated the whole notion of contract, to some extent since Roman times. But during the 19th century it was elevated into an axiom, and it continued to exert an extraordinary influence right into the second half of the 20th century. Even today, as the extracts above confirm, it remains a fundamental principle of contract law, although in many ways it has been brought under control not just by statute but, in some civilian systems at least, by the re-emphasis of other fundamental contractual principles, such as good faith and reasonableness in contracting. The principle of freedom of contract had its greatest impact in the area of exclusion clauses (cf. **8.4**), but it pervades other topics as well. The classical expression of freedom of contract is to be found first in the *Code civil*, art. 1134 (above, at p.9) and in the following extract.

Printing and Numerical Registering Co v Sampson **(1875) L.R. 19 Eq. 462, Ch**

Sir George Jessel: ". . . If there is one thing more than another which public policy requires, it is that men of full age and competent understanding shall have the utmost liberty of contracting and that their contracts, when entered into freely and voluntarily, shall be held sacred and shall be enforced by courts of justice . . ."

NOTES AND QUESTIONS

1. "I think, if we held this action to be maintainable, we should violate a most important principle of law, that parties to contracts are to be allowed to regulate their contracts and liabilities themselves; and that the Court will only give effect to the intention of the parties as it is expressed by the contract" (Erle J. in *Gott v Gandy* (1853), at 3). Is contract a form of private legislation?

2. "[T]he defendants are at liberty to make any contract they please, and where the question is, what were the terms of the bailment so made? the reasonableness of the terms is an irrelevant inquiry, the parties being at liberty to choose their own terms . . ." (Erle C.J. in *Van Toll v SE Ry* (1862), at 244). Ought parties to a contract to have the right to make an unreasonable contract? How might one judge reasonableness in this context?

Manchester, Sheffield & Lincolnshire Railway Co v Brown **(1883) 8 App. Cas. 703, HL**

Lord Bramwell: ". . . For here is a contract made by a fishmonger and a carrier of fish who know their business, and whether it is just and reasonable is to be settled by me who am neither fishmonger nor carrier, nor with any knowledge of their business . . .

. . . But, for my own part, I am prepared to hold that unless some evidence is given to shew that a contract voluntarily entered into by two parties is unjust and unreasonable, it ought to be taken that that contract is a just and a reasonable one, the burden of proof being upon the man who says that it is unjust and unreasonable. First of all, its justice and reasonableness are prima facie proved against him by his being a party to it; and if he means to say that what he agreed to is unjust and unreasonable, he must shew that it is so . . . It seems to me perfectly idle, and I cannot understand how it could have been supposed necessary, that it should be referred to a judge to say whether an agreement between carriers, of whose business he knows nothing, and fishmongers, of whose business he equally knows nothing, is reasonable or not. If it is a question it is one of fact; and evidence should be given to shew that the fishmonger and carrier did not understand their business but made an unjust and unreasonable contract. However, so it is, and I repeat that I am for my own part prepared to hold, not that an agreement between two people which has been voluntarily entered into by them cannot be unreasonable, but that the fact that it has been voluntarily entered into by them is the strongest possible proof that it is a reasonable agreement, and that I should require the strongest possible evidence, or something more even than a possibility, to shew me that that was an unreasonable agreement . . .

Now just let me ask this question—'Just and reasonable'—Is it just? If it is not, it is unjust. Is it unjust? Will any human being say that this man has been unjustly treated? Well, but justice alone is not sufficient; you must not only be just, but you must be reasonable, which, by the way, rather imports that you may be one without the other. I should think that that was an extremely difficult thing. However, if it is just, is it reasonable? Why its very justice shews its reasonableness."

QUESTION

What would Lord Bramwell have made of *Ruxley Electronics v Forsyth* (1996) (see p.442)?

NOTE

The principle was reaffirmed, with respect to commercial contracts at any rate, by the House of Lords in *Photo Production v Securicor* (1980) (p.406). And see also *Watford Electronics Ltd v Sanderson CFL Ltd* (2001), *per* Chadwick L.J. (below, at p.409). These cases involved a limitation of liability clause, and a brief history of some of the problems caused by the principle in relation to these clauses is given in the next extract.

George Mitchell (Chesterhall) Ltd v Finney Lock Seeds Ltd [1983] Q.B. 284, CA

(For facts and further extracts, see p.421.)

Lord Denning M.R.: ". . . None of you nowadays will remember the trouble we had—when I was called to the Bar—with exemption clauses. They were printed in small print on the back of tickets and order forms and invoices. They were contained in catalogues or timetables. They were held to be binding on any person who took them without objection. No one ever did object. He never read them or knew what was in them. No matter how unreasonable they were, he was bound. All this was done in the name of 'freedom of contract.' But the freedom was all on the side of the big concern which had the use of the printing press. No freedom for the little man who took the ticket or order form or invoice. The big concern said, 'Take it or leave it.' The little man had no option but to take it. The big concern could and did exempt itself from liability in its own interest without regard to the little man. It got away with it time after time. When the courts said to the big concern, 'You must put it in clear words,' the big concern had no hesitation in doing so. It knew well that the little man would never read the exemption clauses or understand them.

It was a bleak winter for our law of contract. It is illustrated by two cases, *Thompson v London, Midland and Scottish Railway Co* [1930] 1 KB 41 (in which there was exemption from liability, not on the ticket, but only in small print at the back of the timetable, and the company were held not liable) and *L'Estrange v F Graucob Ltd* [1934] 2 KB 394 (in which there was complete exemption in small print at the bottom of the order form, and the company were held not liable).

The secret weapon

Faced with this abuse of power—by the strong against the weak—by the use of the small print of the conditions—the judges did what they could to put a curb upon it. They still had before them the idol, 'freedom of contract.' They still knelt down and worshipped it, but they concealed under their cloaks a secret weapon. They used it to stab the idol in the back. This weapon was called 'the true construction of the contract.' They used it with great skill and ingenuity. They used it so as to depart from the natural meaning of the words of the exemption clause and to put upon them a strained and unnatural construction. In case after case, they said that the words were not strong enough to give the big concern exemption from liability; or that in the circumstances the big concern was not entitled to rely on the exemption clause. If a ship deviated from the contractual voyage, the owner could not rely on the exemption clause. If a warehouseman stored the goods in the wrong warehouse, he could not pray in aid the limitation clause. If the seller supplied goods different in kind from those contracted for, he could not rely on any exemption from liability. If a shipowner delivered goods to a person without production of the bill of lading, he could not escape responsibility by reference to an exemption clause. In short, whenever the wide words—in their natural meaning—would give rise to an unreasonable result, the judges either rejected them as repugnant to the main purpose of the contract, or else cut them down to size in order to produce a reasonable result . . . But when the clause was itself reasonable and gave rise to a reasonable result, the judges upheld it; at any rate, when the clause did not exclude liability entirely but only limited it to a reasonable amount. So where goods were deposited in a cloakroom or sent to a laundry for cleaning, it was quite reasonable for the company to limit their liability to a reasonable amount, having regard to the small charge made for the service . . .

Fundamental breach

No doubt has ever been cast thus far by anyone. But doubts arose when in this court—in *Karsales (Harrow) Ltd v Wallis* [1956] 1 WLR. 936—we ventured to suggest that if the big concern was guilty of a breach which went to the 'very root' of the contract—sometimes called a 'fundamental breach'—or at other times a 'total failure' of its obligations—then it could not rely on the printed clause to exempt itself from liability . . . But we did make a mistake—in the eyes of some—

120

in elevating it—by inference—into a 'rule of law.' That was too rude an interference with the idol of 'freedom of contract.' We ought to have used the secret weapon. We ought to have said that in each case, on the 'true construction of the contract' in that case, the exemption clause did not avail the party where he was guilty of a fundamental breach or a breach going to the root. That is the lesson to be learnt from the 'indigestible' speeches in *Suisse Atlantique Société d'Armement Maritime SA v NV Rotterdamsche Kolen Centrale* [1967] 1 AC 361. They were all obiter dicta. The House were dealing with an agreed damages clause and not an exemption clause and the point had never been argued in the courts below at all. It is noteworthy that the House did not overrule a single decision of the Court of Appeal. Lord Wilberforce, at p 433, appears to have approved them. At any rate, he cast no doubt upon the actual decision in any case.

The change in climate

In 1969 there was a change in climate. Out of winter into spring. It came with the Law Commission's *Exemption Clauses In Contracts, First Report: Amendments to the Sale of Goods Act 1893* (Law Com No 24, HC 403) which was implemented in the Supply of Goods (Implied Terms) Act 1973. In 1975 there was a further change. Out of spring into summer. It came with the Law Commission's Exemption Clauses, Second Report (Law Com No 69, HC 605) which was implemented by the Unfair Contract Terms Act 1977. No longer was the big concern able to impose whatever terms and conditions it liked in a printed form—no matter how unreasonable they might be. These reports showed most convincingly that the courts could and should only enforce them if they were fair and reasonable in themselves and it was fair and reasonable to allow the big concern to rely on them. So the idol of 'freedom of contract' was shattered. In cases of personal injury or death, it was not permissible to exclude or restrict liability at all. In consumer contracts any exemption clause was subject to the test of reasonableness . . ."

NOTE

Freedom of contract has given way, in short, to the principle of consumer protection (see generally **8.4**). However, just as English law was abandoning the "fundamental breach" rule mentioned by Lord Denning, French law seemed to be moving towards adopting it: see Cass.com. 22.10.1996 (*Banchereau v Chronopost*) D.1997.121 note Sériaux.

3.3 Good faith: general considerations

Another principle to be found at the forefront of the two international contract codes is that of good faith:

Principles of European Contract Law

Article 1:201 Good Faith and Fair Dealing

(1) Each party must act in accordance with good faith and fair dealing.
(2) The parties may not exclude or limit this duty.

Article 1:202 Duty to Co-operate

Each party owes to the other a duty to co-operate in order to give full effect to the contract.

NOTES

1. See also UNIDROIT, art. 1.7.

2. In addition to the idea of consumer protection, the notion of good faith is proving a means of intruding upon the domain of freedom of contract. However, unlike consumer protection, good faith (*bona fides*) is almost as old as the notion of contract itself. The principle comes from Roman law, where it was described as "equitable dealing in the highest degree" (D.16.3.31pr). The difficulty with regard to the principle in Roman law is not just with respect to defining exactly what it meant in practice. The difficulty is that other Roman texts declare that according to natural law, one is free to take advantage of another in contract (D.4.4.16.4; D.19.2.22.3). How are the two ideas to be reconciled? This question sums up, perhaps, the ambiguity of good faith in the face of freedom of contract and party autonomy.

3. In truth, although the expression *bona fides* comes from Roman law, its sense is more modern and, according to Elisabeth Zoller, is reflected in the idea of a society based on faith and fidelity (feudal and Christian medieval Europe). As she points out, contemporary Europe is "no longer constructed on faith but on interest" (Zoller, "Bonne foi", in D. Alland and S. Rials, *Dictionnaire de la culture juridique* (PUF, 2003), p.143, at p.144), and this is a point developed by Gunther Teubner (discussed below, at p.124).

4. Whatever the situation in Roman law, two points must be made at the outset. First, the principle is very much one associated with the civilian law of contract and not English law (on which see **3.4**). It is traditionally said that English law formally recognises no such a principle. Secondly, even in the civil law the history of the principle has been chequered. As the next extract indicates, good faith as an active concept is undergoing something of a metamorphosis.

122

Prof Dr M.W. Hesselink and Dr G.J.P. de Vries, *Principles of European Contract Law* (Kluwer, 2001), pp.54–55 (footnotes omitted)

"In many European legal systems the good faith principle has developed over the last century into a means by which the courts have imposed solidarity (altruism) in limitation of autonomy, both within contract law and outside. Indeed, the duty of good faith is frequently defined as the duty to take the other party's interests into account. Many of the typical applications of good faith (*Fallgruppen*) which were developed by legal doctrine translate aspects of a duty to take the other party's interests into account (altruism): duty of care, duty of loyalty, duty to co-operate, duty to inform, *venire contra factum proprium non valet* (similar to estoppel), proportionality. At first sight, therefore, it seems that good faith is the intrinsically altruist concept that imposes solidarity and counterbalances party autonomy.

However ... good faith, as it developed in European legal systems like the German and the Dutch, ... is best conceived as a means to compensate for a formalist approach towards rules and rights ... In contract law most of the anti-formalism judicial activism was aimed at limiting the absolute (ie formal) application of the rule *pacta sunt servanda*, which, of course, is closely related to party autonomy. Therefore, today in Europe most of the 'content of the good faith norm' consists of social, altruist norms . . ."

NOTES

1. The notion of "contractual solidarity" is proving influential in France and some other civilian jurisdictions (see the extract from Paula Giliker, at p.434). One motivating norm is that of good faith. The point to be noted, however, is that although the principle is to be found in the *Code civil* (CC art. 1134), it did not play an active role in contract law until more recent times, and this indicates that its effect is as much one of prevailing theory as universal positive duty. In other words, good faith can be treated:

   (a) as a "negative" duty (good faith is assumed unless actual bad faith is proved);
   (b) as a passive duty (allowing the courts to develop certain principles such as change of circumstances); or
   (c) as a positive duty (placing active duties to act on contracting parties).

   It should not be assumed, therefore, that good faith means the same thing in all civil law systems.

2. Indeed, this point is effectively made by Gunther Teubner, who emphasises the importance of the economic and social environment in which good faith functions ((1998) 61 M.L.R. 11). According to Teubner, "the procedural dimension of good faith is profoundly influenced by the difference of production regimes" (at 30), which would involve the courts in each system

having to determine for themselves "the legitimate interest of the other party to the contract" (at 31). And thus, instead of being a unifying principle, good faith "would indeed result in widely divergent rules in different countries, even in contradictory decisions in apparently equal cases" (at 31). So much for European harmonisation via the PECL.

3. Nevertheless, if one is looking for some general statement about the role of good faith in civilian contract law, the observation of Teubner is probably as good as it gets. He writes: "Historically, *bona fides* had been contract law's recourse to social morality. Whenever the application of strict formal contract rules led to morally unacceptable results, *bona fides* was invoked to counteract the formalism of contract law doctrine with a substantive social morality. Contracts were performed in good faith when the participants behaved in accordance with accepted standards of moral behaviour" (*op. cit.*, at 23). His observation is particular true with respect to German contract law, in that the good faith provision in the German Civil Code (1900) played a very particular role in the development of German contract law during the 20th century. What should be of interest to the English contract student is how a single concept permitted the judges to decide factual situations through intermediary notions that themselves were justified, in terms of positive law, by the good faith provision. Here in essence is the methodology of the Continental legal systems.

4. Good faith is not just a general principle as stated in PECL, art.1.201. It is also to be found in the following other PECL articles dealing with: interpretation (arts 1.106, 5.102); reasonableness (art.1.108); imputed knowledge (art.1.305); pre-contractual negotiations (art.2.301); mistake (art.4.103); fraud (art.4.107); unfair advantage (art.4.109); unfair terms and exclusion clauses (arts 4.110, 4.118, 8.109); implied obligations (art.6.102); change of circumstances (art.6.111); assignment (art.11.204, 11.308); and conditions (art.16.102). It clearly underlies the duty to co-operate as well (art.1.202).

3.4 Good faith: English law

Despite an observation by Lord Watson that "Bona fides [is] an implied term in every mercantile contract" (in *Glynn, Mills Currie & Co v East & West India Dock Co* (1882), at 615), it is generally asserted that English contract law knows of no such general principle. The position has been summarised by Bingham L.J. (as he then was).

Interfoto Picture Library Ltd v Stiletto Visual Programmes Ltd **[1989] Q.B. 433, CA**

(For facts and other extracts, see p.402.)

124

Bingham L.J.: "In many civil law systems, and perhaps in most legal systems outside the common law world, the law of obligations recognises and enforces an overriding principle that in making and carrying out contracts parties should act in good faith. This does not simply mean that they should not deceive each other, a principle which any legal system must recognise; its effect is perhaps most aptly conveyed by such metaphorical colloquialisms as 'playing fair', 'coming clean' or 'putting one's cards face upwards on the table'. It is in essence a principle of fair and open dealing. In such a forum it might, I think, be held on the facts of this case that the plaintiffs were under a duty in all fairness to draw the defendants' attention specifically to the high price payable if the transparencies were not returned in time and, when the 14 days had expired, to point out to the defendants the high cost of continued failure to return them.

English law has, characteristically, committed itself to no such overriding principle but has developed piecemeal solutions in response to demonstrated problems of unfairness. Many examples could be given. Thus equity has intervened to strike down unconscionable bargains. Parliament has stepped in to regulate the imposition of exemption clauses and the form of certain hire-purchase agreements. The common law also has made its contribution, by holding that certain classes of contract require the utmost good faith, by treating as irrecoverable what purport to be agreed estimates of damage but are in truth a disguised penalty for breach, and in many other ways.

The well known cases on sufficiency of notice are in my view properly to be read in this context. At one level they are concerned with a question of pure contractual analysis, whether one party has done enough to give the other notice of the incorporation of a term in the contract. At another level they are concerned with a somewhat different question, whether it would in all the circumstances be fair (or reasonable) to hold a party bound by any conditions or by a particular condition of an unusual and stringent nature . . .

The tendency of the English authorities has, I think, been to look at the nature of the transaction in question and the character of the parties to it; to consider what notice the party alleged to be bound was given of the particular condition said to bind him; and to resolve whether in all the circumstances it is fair to hold him bound by the condition in question. This may yield a result not very different from the civil law principle of good faith, at any rate so far as the formation of the contract is concerned . . ."

NOTE

Bingham L.J.'s last sentence may well be true in some situations, but it must be treated with care in that there are cases to be found in the English law reports that might well have been decided differently in civil law jurisdictions. Two particular cases are *Smith v Hughes* (1871) (p.262) and *Bell v Lever Brothers* (1932) (p.250), but the next two cases are of interest as well.

University of Nottingham v Eyett **[1999] 2 All E.R. 437, Ch D**

Hart J.: "This is an appeal by the University of Nottingham (the university) against a determination dated 8 July 1998 of the Pensions Ombudsman, whereby the Pensions Ombudsman upheld a complaint by Mr Eyett (the complainant) that the university, in its capacity as employer of Mr Eyett, had been guilty of maladministration of the university's pension scheme (the scheme).

Under the rules of the scheme as applied with effect from 1 January 1992 the complainant was entitled, with the university's consent, to take early retirement on or after reaching the age of 60 with immediate payment of pension unreduced for early payment. His 60th birthday, being in July 1994, he inquired in early 1994 of the university as to what his pension entitlement would be if he were to retire on 31 July 1994. In response to that inquiry, he was supplied with a quotation showing what the position would then be, depending on whether or not he took part of the then projected pension as a lump sum . . .

Armed with that information, which was entirely accurate, the complainant, in April 1994, notified the university of his intention to retire on 31 July 1994. The university consented to that course and the complainant duly retired as contemplated on 31 July 1994 and received a pension correctly reflecting his entitlement under the scheme.

What the complainant had not realised was that he would have been better off had he sought to defer the date of his retirement to the earliest date after 31 July 1994 to which the university would have been agreeable, which would in fact have been 31 August. Had he done that, his final pensionable salary would have been calculated by reference to his salary levels at 1 August 1992, 1 August 1993 and 1 August 1994 which, because of a salary increase which was subsequently announced and backdated to 1 April 1994, would have raised his final pensionable salary to £15,354 and his consequent pension to £5,118.

The complaint, therefore, was that the university had been at fault in not having alerted him at any stage to the fact that he would be better off in pension terms if he were to make this different choice . . .

In the final analysis, the question for determination comes down to this: does the implied term include a positive obligation on the employer to warn an employee who is proposing to exercise important rights in connection with his contract of employment that the way in which he is proposing to exercise them may not be financially the most advantageous way in the particular circumstances? Expressed in those terms, it can be seen that the recognition of such a duty has potentially far reaching consequences for the employment relationship. A degree of caution is therefore required.

In my judgment, a proper caution requires the court to examine how such a positive obligation would cohere with other default obligations implied by law in the employment context. The answer is 'not well' . . .

It is . . . rightly conceded that *Scally's* case provides no support for the complainant. He undoubtedly knew of the existence of his early retirement rights. He was also able, pace the ombudsman, to have worked out for himself how best to avail himself of those rights by carefully studying the information set out in the explanatory booklet. There is no suggestion that he ever asked for advice as to whether the choice he was making was a suitable one, nor, as I have already indicated, was there any finding that the university knew that he was making a decision under the influence of any mistake.

The fact that *Scally's* case provides no support for the complainant's contention in my judgment tends to subvert, rather than assist, the proposition that the implied term of mutual trust and confidence includes within it a positive obligation to give advice of the kind which is now asserted. In addition, the authorities on the duties of pension fund trustees, who may be subject to a similar implied term, to give advice to beneficiaries do not encourage the idea that the term imposes any such obligation on them. See, for example, the judgment of Carnwath J in *Miller v Stapleton* [1996] 2 All ER 449 at 463.

In my judgment, the authorities neither compel nor indeed justify me in holding that the university was in breach of contract in failing to alert the complainant to the possibility that he was making a financial mistake in seeking the university's permission for him to cease service on the first available date following his 60th birthday. I reach that conclusion with some, but not much, regret. The mistake made by the complainant could easily have been avoided had the university had a standardised procedure for warning employees contemplating retirement of the particular significance of choosing a retirement date one side or the other of 1 August in any particular year. On the other hand, had the complainant continued in employment for the additional month, he would have enjoyed at least two financial advantages which must have been manifest to him, but which he was plainly deciding were not worth the candle of a month's additional service. The most obvious of these was his enjoyment during that month of his salary (about £1,263 before tax at the old 1993 rate) as opposed to his pension, about £411 before tax, an immediate sacrifice by the complainant of some £850 or so. In addition, he would have earned another month's pensionable service. He could not for a moment claim that he was unaware of these advantages or of the fact that he was foregoing them. Had it applied its mind to the question (which it did not), the university might in those circumstances be forgiven for having assumed that the complainant had carefully reckoned the financial consequences of his selected retirement date. The additional pension foregone by the mistake amounted to some £15 per month before tax.

For the reasons I have given, the university's appeal will be allowed."

QUESTIONS

1. Does this case confirm that *Smith v Hughes* (1871) (p.262) is still good law?

2. If the PECL were applied to the facts of *Eyett*, would the result be different?

3. Is *Eyett* really a good faith case, or is it a causation problem?

NOTE

Eyett is not an isolated case.

Reid v Rush & Tompkins Plc [1990] 1 W.L.R. 212, CA

This was an action for damages by an employee against his employer (the more detailed facts are given by Ralph Gibson L.J.). The Court of Appeal (Ralph Gibson, May and Neill L.JJ.) held the employer not liable.

> **Ralph Gibson L.J.:** ". . . The plaintiff on 26 January 1984 suffered severe injuries while driving the defendant's Landrover vehicle on a road in Ethiopia in the course of his employment by the defendant as a quarry foreman on the Armati Diversion Project. His injuries were caused by a collision between the Landrover and a lorry which was being driven along the road in the opposite direction by some person whose identity is not known. The defendant was in no way responsible for the happening of the accident of which the sole cause was the negligence of the lorry driver. The plaintiff has alleged that the defendant was in breach of its duty of care as employer in failing either to insure the plaintiff so as to provide suitable benefits to him in the event of his being injured, as a result of the negligence of a third party, in such a traffic accident or to advise the plaintiff to obtain such insurance cover for himself. His case is that if he had been so advised he would have obtained personal accident cover . . .
>
> In my judgment it is impossible to hold on the facts pleaded that an implied term arose on the particular relationship of this plaintiff to this defendant as his employer. The only facts are the offer and acceptance of the employment and the defendant's knowledge both of the circumstances in which the plaintiff would in Ethiopia be exposed to the special risk and of the plaintiff's ignorance of that risk. If the parties had been asked what the position was with reference to the risk of the plaintiff suffering injury in the course of his employment by the negligence of another driver, for whom the defendant was not responsible, and from whom the plaintiff could recover no damages, it is impossible to be confident, on the facts pleaded, that either side would have answered that the defendant had undertaken a duty to deal specifically with the matter, whether by advice or otherwise. Both parties must have expected and intended that the plaintiff and the defendant would respectively perform the express terms set out in the contract and would comply with any other obligations arising out of their mutual relationship as master and servant. As in *Lister v Romford Ice and Cold Storage Co Ltd* [1957] AC 555, according to the view of the majority, Viscount Simonds, Lord Morton of Henryton and Lord Tucker, the term on which the plaintiff in

this case claims to rely cannot, in my judgment, be implied as a term agreed between the two individuals, and, if it is to be implied at all, must be implied by law . . . It is, however, impossible, in my judgment, to imply in this case a term as a matter of law in the form contended for, namely, a specific duty to advise the plaintiff to obtain specific insurance cover. Such a duty seems to me inappropriate for incorporation by law into all contracts of employment in the circumstances alleged. The length of time during which the servant will work abroad and the nature of his work may vary greatly between one job and another and hence the extent to which the servant would be exposed to the special risk. Further, having regard to the many different ways in which a servant working abroad may run the risk of uncompensated injury caused by the wrongdoing of a third party, apart from a traffic accident, it seems to me impossible to formulate the detailed terms in which the law could incorporate into the general relationship of master and servant a contractual obligation to the effect necessary to cover the plaintiff's claim. I have considered whether the implied term could be limited to the risk from injuries in a traffic accident, but then the question is raised whether the obligation should arise upon any difference between the total protection provided in this country by compulsory third party insurance and the MIB scheme, on the one hand, and such protection as exists in the foreign country, on the other hand, or only upon the total absence of the protection provided in this country . . . For my part I am unable to accept that the court could properly incorporate such a term by law into contracts of employment. It seems to me that it would require of employers, many of whom may have no such resources of advice or experience as may be available to this defendant, and who may employ only one or two servants, to discover much information about foreign legal and social systems in order to decide whether such a term requires action on their part. The usefulness of the principle contended for seems to me, in social terms, to be plain enough; but to incorporate the duty by law into contracts of employment would, in my view, require, if it were to work fairly, exemptions and limitations which can only properly be achieved by legislation . . .

I have had much difficulty in concluding that the general duty at common law upon a master to take care for the protection of his servant's physical well being cannot be extended by decision of the courts to include protection for the financial well being of his servant in special circumstances where the foreseeable financial loss arises from foreseeable physical injury suffered in the course of the employment and the duty claimed would extend only to a warning of a special risk. If this view be right the only way in which an employer's general duty of care—and I emphasise that I am referring only to the general duty of care which arises out of the relationship—will be capable of extension to cover financial loss will be by legislation, or by a contractual term, express or implied on the particular facts, or by a term which the court is able to say must be implied by law . . ."

NOTE

It is most unlikely that this case would have been decided the same way in France. The duty of good faith would surely have placed an obligation upon the employer to look after the health interest of his employee, even if strictly speaking the actual claim could be classified as financial (less important in France). Indeed, even if it was accepted that the claim was based strictly on the employee's financial interest, it is still difficult to imagine a civil law jurisdiction absolving the employer. In fact it is difficult to imagine an English court arriving at the decision it did, given that this is a relational contract in which the employer normally, as a fact, advised its employees going abroad on the insurance position. If one ever needed a case to illustrate that English law knows nothing of good faith, *Rush & Tompkins* is it. A further extract from this grim decision can be found in C&MT, p.50.

QUESTIONS

1. Is an employee under a duty to protect, as far as he can, the financial interests of his employer? For example, if he saw that one of the employer's Land Rovers had been damaged by a car thief, would he be under a duty to inform his employer of this damage?

2. Would this case have been decided differently (in England) if the PECL applied to it?

3. Is good faith actually a substantive principle of contract law, or is it a notion that operates only at the level of contractual remedies?

R. (European Roma Rights) v Prague Immigration Officer [2005] 2 A.C. 1, HL

Lord Hope: ". . . **59** The limited way in which the principle [of good faith] operates can be seen in the field of private law, where its origins lie. The modern theory of contract is derived from the consensual contracts of Roman law which are said to have been governed by the principle of bona fides: *Zimmermann, The Law of Obligations* (1992), p 674. There are differences between the legal systems as to how extensive and how powerful the penetration of the principle has been. They range from systems in the civilian tradition where as a guideline for contractual behaviour the principle is expressly recognised and acted upon, to those of the common law where a general obligation to conform to good faith is not recognised. In an appeal in a Scottish case, *Smith v Bank of Scotland* 1997 SC (HL) 111, 121B Lord Clyde referred to 'the broad principle in the field of contract law of fair dealing in good faith'. The preferred approach in England is to avoid any commitment to over-arching principle, in favour of piecemeal solutions in response to demonstrated problems of unfairness: *Interfoto Picture Library Ltd v Stiletto Visual Programmes Ltd* [1989] QB 433, 439, per Bingham LJ. The same result is reached by other means: *Lando and Beale, Principles of European Contract Law, Parts I and II* (2000), p 116, note 1; *Ewan McKendrick, Contract Law* (2003), pp 533–535.

60 But, as Hector MacQueen, 'Delict, Contract, and the Bill of Rights: A Perspective from the United Kingdom' (2004) 121 South African LJ 359, 382, points out, good faith in Scottish contract law, as in South African law, is generally an underlying principle of an explanatory and legitimating rather than an active or creative nature: see also his chapter on good faith in the Scots law of contract in *Good Faith in Contract and Property Law*, ed ADM Forte (1999). That was so in Roman law, which distinguished between obligations bonae fidei and stricti iuris, and enabled the iudex in the former case to provide remedies on grounds of good faith in bonae fidei judicia: *Buckland, A Text-Book of Roman Law*, 2nd ed (1932), pp 678, 704. It was a distinction which applied properly to the remedy, rather than to the obligation. It was not a source of obligation in itself. That remains generally true today in the civilian systems, which recognise the principle . . ."

NOTE

Unfair clauses is one area of English law into which good faith has been specifically imported thanks to the Directive on unfair contract terms (see p.364).

Director General of Fair Trading v First National Bank plc [2002] 1 A.C. 481, HL

Lord Bingham: "1. My Lords, First National Bank plc ('the bank') is licensed to carry on consumer credit business. It is a major lender in the market and has lent large sums to borrowers under credit agreements regulated under the Consumer Credit Act 1974. Such agreements are made on its printed form which contains a number of standard terms. The Director General of Fair Trading ('the Director'), in exercising powers conferred on him by regulation 8 of the Unfair Terms in Consumer Contracts Regulations 1994 (SI 1994/3159) ('the regulations'), sought an injunction to restrain use of or reliance on one such standard term on the ground that it was unfair. The bank resisted the Director's application on two grounds. The first, rejected by Evans-Lombe J at first instance ([2000] 1 WLR 98) and the Court of Appeal (Peter Gibson, Waller and Buxton L JJ) ([2000] QB 672), was that the fairness provisions of the regulations did not apply to the term in question. The second, accepted by the judge but partially rejected by the Court of Appeal, was that the term in question was not unfair. In this appeal to the House the bank again relies on both these arguments. The Director seeks to uphold the decision of the Court of Appeal but contends that the term was more fundamentally unfair than the Court of Appeal held it to be. Thus there are two broad questions before the House. (1) Do the fairness provisions of the regulations apply to the term in question? (2) If so, is the term unfair and, if it is, on what ground? . . .

4. To ensure that they were able to recover not only the full sum of principal outstanding but also any interest accruing on that sum after judgment as well as

before, it became the practice for lenders to include in their credit agreements a term to the effect of the term here in issue. If such a provision had not been included, a lender seeking to enforce a loan agreement against a borrower in the High Court would suffer prejudice only to the extent that the statutory rate of interest on judgment debts at the material time is lower than the contractual interest rate, because the High Court has, since 1838, had power to award statutory interest on a judgment debt until payment . . .

12. In agreement with the judge and the Court of Appeal, I do not accept the bank's submission on this issue. The regulations, as Professor Sir Guenter Treitel QC has aptly observed (*Treitel The Law of Contract*, 10th ed, 1999, p 248) 'are not intended to operate as a mechanism of quality or price control' and regulation 3(2) is of 'crucial importance in recognising the parties' freedom of contract with respect to the essential features of their bargain' (ibid, at p 249). But there is an important 'distinction between the term or terms which express the substance of the bargain and 'incidental' (if important) terms which surround them' (*Chitty on Contracts*, 28th ed, 1999, 'Unfair Terms in Consumer Contracts', p 747, para 15–025). The object of the regulations and the directive is to protect consumers against the inclusion of unfair and prejudicial terms in standard-form contracts into which they enter, and that object would plainly be frustrated if regulation 3(2)(b) were so broadly interpreted as to cover any terms other than those falling squarely within it. In my opinion the term, as part of a provision prescribing the consequences of default, plainly does not fall within it. It does not concern the adequacy of the interest earned by the bank as its remuneration but is designed to ensure that the bank's entitlement to interest does not come to an end on the entry of judgment. I do not think the bank's argument on merger advances its case. It appears that some judges in the past have been readier than I would be to infer that a borrower's covenant to pay interest was not intended to extend beyond the entry of judgment. But even if a borrower's obligation were ordinarily understood to extend beyond judgment even in the absence of an independent covenant, it would not alter my view of the term as an ancillary provision and not one concerned with the adequacy of the bank's remuneration as against the services supplied. It is therefore necessary to address the second question . . .

17. The test laid down by regulation 4(1), deriving as it does from article 3(1) of the directive, has understandably attracted much discussion in academic and professional circles and helpful submissions were made to the House on it. It is plain from the recitals to the directive that one of its objectives was partially to harmonise the law in this important field among all member states of the European Union. The member states have no common concept of fairness or good faith, and the directive does not purport to state the law of any single member state. It lays down a test to be applied, whatever their pre-existing law, by all member states. If the meaning of the test were doubtful, or vulnerable to the possibility of differing interpretations in differing member states, it might be desirable or necessary to seek a ruling from the European Court of Justice on its

interpretation. But the language used in expressing the test, so far as applicable in this case, is in my opinion clear and not reasonably capable of differing interpretations. A term falling within the scope of the regulations is unfair if it causes a significant imbalance in the parties' rights and obligations under the contract to the detriment of the consumer in a manner or to an extent which is contrary to the requirement of good faith. The requirement of significant imbalance is met if a term is so weighted in favour of the supplier as to tilt the parties' rights and obligations under the contract significantly in his favour. This may be by the granting to the supplier of a beneficial option or discretion or power, or by the imposing on the consumer of a disadvantageous burden or risk or duty. The illustrative terms set out in Schedule 3 to the regulations provide very good examples of terms which may be regarded as unfair; whether a given term is or is not to be so regarded depends on whether it causes a significant imbalance in the parties' rights and obligations under the contract. This involves looking at the contract as a whole. But the imbalance must be to the detriment of the consumer; a significant imbalance to the detriment of the supplier, assumed to be the stronger party, is not a mischief which the regulations seek to address. The requirement of good faith in this context is one of fair and open dealing. Openness requires that the terms should be expressed fully, clearly and legibly, containing no concealed pitfalls or traps. Appropriate prominence should be given to terms which might operate disadvantageously to the customer. Fair dealing requires that a supplier should not, whether deliberately or unconsciously, take advantage of the consumer's necessity, indigence, lack of experience, unfamiliarity with the subject matter of the contract, weak bargaining position or any other factor listed in or analogous to those listed in Schedule 2 of the regulations. Good faith in this context is not an artificial or technical concept; nor, since Lord Mansfield was its champion, is it a concept wholly unfamiliar to British lawyers. It looks to good standards of commercial morality and practice. Regulation 4(1) lays down a composite test, covering both the making and the substance of the contract, and must be applied bearing clearly in mind the objective which the regulations are designed to promote . . .

20. In judging the fairness of the term it is necessary to consider the position of typical parties when the contract is made. The borrower wants to borrow a sum of money, often quite a modest sum, often for purposes of improving his home. He discloses an income sufficient to finance repayment by instalments over the contract term. If he cannot do that, the bank will be unwilling to lend. The essential bargain is that the bank will make funds available to the borrower which the borrower will repay, over a period, with interest. Neither party could suppose that the bank would willingly forgo any part of its principal or interest. If the bank thought that outcome at all likely, it would not lend. If there were any room for doubt about the borrower's obligation to repay the principal in full with interest, that obligation is very clearly and unambiguously expressed in the conditions of contract. There is nothing unbalanced or detrimental to the consumer in that

obligation; the absence of such a term would unbalance the contract to the detriment of the lender . . .

24. . . . Regulation 4 is directed to the unfairness of a contract term, not the use which a supplier may make of a term which is in itself fair. It is readily understandable that a borrower may be disagreeably surprised if he finds that his contractual interest obligation continues to mount despite his duly paying the instalments ordered by the court, but it appears that the bank seeks to prevent that surprise by sending what is described in the evidence as a standard form of letter . . . On balance, I do not consider that the term can properly be said to cause a significant imbalance in the parties' rights and obligations under the contract to the detriment of the consumer in a manner or to an extent which is contrary to the requirement of good faith . . ."

Lord Steyn: ". . . 36. . . . The twin requirements of good faith and significant imbalance will in practice be determinative. Schedule 2 to the Regulations, which explains the concept of good faith, provides that regard must be had, amongst other things, to the extent to which the seller or supplier has dealt fairly and equitably with the consumer. It is an objective criterion. Good faith imports, as Lord Bingham has observed in his opinion, the notion of open and fair dealing: see also *Interfoto Picture Library Ltd v Stiletto Visual Programmes Ltd* [1989] QB 433. And helpfully the commentary to *Lando & Beale, Principles of European Contract Law, Parts I and II* (combined and revised 2000), p 113 prepared by the Commission of European Contract Law, explains that the purpose of the provision of good faith and fair dealing is 'to enforce community standards of fairness and reasonableness in commercial transactions'; a fortiori that is true of consumer transactions. Schedule 3 to the Regulations (which corresponds to the Annex to the directive) is best regarded as a check list of terms which must be regarded as potentially vulnerable. The examples given in Schedule 3 convincingly demonstrate that the argument of the bank that good faith is predominantly concerned with procedural defects in negotiating procedures cannot be sustained. Any purely procedural or even predominantly procedural interpretation of the requirement of good faith must be rejected.

37. That brings me to the element of significant imbalance. It has been pointed out by Hugh Collins that the test 'of a significant imbalance of the obligations obviously directs attention to the substantive unfairness of the contract': 'Good Faith in European Contract Law,' (1994), 14 Oxford Journal of Legal Studies 229, 249. It is however, also right to say that there is a large area of overlap between the concepts of good faith and significant imbalance . . ."

QUESTIONS

1. Does the result of this case support Lord Hope's view in the *Roma Rights* case that the doctrine of good faith operates in a limited way?

2. Does the result of this case drain good faith of much of its intended meaning with respect to unfair terms? Ought not the bank to be under a positive duty

to bring the interest situation very clearly to the attention of any potential borrower before the contract is signed?

3. Could "good faith" be replaced by "reasonableness"?

Law Commission Report, *Unfair Terms in Contracts* **Law Com. No. 292, Cm. 6464, 2004 (footnotes omitted)**

"3.84 When a term is subject to the UCTA controls and is not of no effect [void], under English law it must satisfy the requirements of reasonableness in section 11 if it is to be effective. Under Scots law the test as defined in section 24 is whether it was 'fair and reasonable' to incorporate the term into the contract. The test in the UTCCR is whether the term is unfair. Regulation 5 (1) provides:--

'A contractual term which has not been individually negotiated shall be regarded as unfair if, contrary to the requirement of good faith, it causes a significant imbalance in the parties' rights and obligations arising under the contract, to the detriment of the consumer.'

3.85 In the Consultation Paper, we took the view that there is very little difference between the 'requirement of reasonableness' ['fair and reasonable' test] under UCTA and the test of 'fairness' used in the UTCCR. Our provisional proposal was that the new legislation would give the greatest possible guidance by combining and expanding the two tests.

3.86 We thought that it was neither necessary nor desirable to include an explicit reference to good faith. First, the question of 'forms and methods' of implementation of EU Directives is a matter for each Member State as long as the intended result is ultimately achieved. Secondly, good faith is a concept which is unfamiliar to English and Scots lawyers in this area of law.

3.87 Slightly more than half of our respondents agreed with the provisional proposal. Those who did so tended to favour the absence of a specific reference to good faith on the grounds that it was confusing and likely to mislead.

3.88 Those who did not agree with our proposals felt that it would be a retrograde step to remove the reference to good faith. They questioned whether the Directive would be implemented effectively in its absence. They also considered that in the ongoing process of unification and codification of European contract law, our proposals should refer to good faith which is a standard generally recognised in Civilian systems.

3.89 As we explained in the Consultation Paper, we consider that our proposed test does meet the requirements of the Directive. It will be easier for UK lawyers to apply than a more 'European' test which makes express reference to good faith. Therefore we still recommend that the test should be one of 'fairness and reasonableness'."

NOTE

One area where good faith has played an important role in some civil law systems is pre-contractual negotiations (cf. *Walford v Miles* (1992), p.174). This will be examined in the next chapter (at **4.5**).

3.5 Reasonableness

In addition to the article on good faith (see above, p.122), the PECL also have the following article in their first chapter.

Principles of European Contract Law

"Article 1:302 Reasonableness

Under these Principles reasonableness is to be judged by what persons acting in good faith and in the same situation as the parties would consider to be reasonable. In particular, in assessing what is reasonable the nature and purpose of the contract, the circumstances of the case, and the usages and practices of the trades or professions involved should be taken into account."

NOTES AND QUESTIONS

1. English law may not recognise any general principle of good faith, but the idea that a person should behave reasonably does find considerable expression in the English law of obligations, especially the law of tort. Leaving aside for the moment any problems of definition, the difficulty with respect to contract is in locating the level at which reasonableness might operate. There are several possibilities:

    (a) Is a party under a duty to behave reasonably in negotiating or performing his contractual promises?
    (b) Should any goods or services supplied under a contract be of reasonable quality?
    (c) Should any enforcement procedures or remedies be reasonable?
    (d) Should the contract itself be reasonable?

    In other words, reasonableness can attach to the various institutions of contract law: that is, to the person (*persona*), to any thing supplied (*res*), to any action (*actio*) pursued, or indeed to the contract itself (*obligation*).

2. Now it may at first sight seem reasonable that reasonableness should operate at all of these institutional levels; but because the notion is objective as well as subjective, it can come into conflict with the principle of party autonomy and

freedom of contract. Should not parties have the right to make an *unreasonable* contract if they so wish? Lord Bramwell's response to such a question (see above, p.118) was to say that it was for the parties, particularly if they were business people, to determine their own contracts, and whatever contracts they decided to make would by definition be reasonable. However, once it was recognised, during the second half of the last century, that consumers were often in a weak bargaining position (see Lord Denning, above, at p.119), the idea of reasonableness took on an objective meaning with respect to such consumer contracts. Clauses must be reasonable (see **8.4**). Yet the problem of reasonableness is not confined to contracts where there is inequality of the bargaining power; there are a considerable number of cases that will be found in the chapters that follow where it might be said that the court is being asked to pass judgement on "reasonableness".

3. At this preliminary stage, then, the contract student might reflect upon the following questions:

(a) Is a party entitled to behave unreasonably at the negotiating stage of a contract? (Cf. *Walford v Miles* (1992), p.174.)

(b) Ought a party to be free to insert a term in a contract that he be entitled to put an end to the contract for even the most minor breaches of certain other terms, even if the minor breaches might not be judged unreasonable by an objective bystander? Ought the court always to uphold such repudiation clauses even if it thinks the breach, in the circumstances, was not that unreasonable?

(c) Ought a party to be allowed to insert into a contract terms giving him unreasonable discretionary powers over the other party? Ought the court to be able to sanction any unreasonable exercise of such powers?

(d) Is a party entitled to enforce a contractual right "for a good reason, a bad reason or no reason at all"? (Cf. Pearson L.J. in *Chapman v Honig* (1963), at 520; and see *White & Carter (Councils) v McGregor* (1962), p.386.)

(e) Ought a purchaser of a product or a service to be forced to accept such a product or service which does not conform exactly to the contract and which the purchaser subjectively deems unreasonable, on the ground that it would be objectively unreasonable not to accept it? (Cf. *Ruxley Electronics v Forsyth* (1996), p.442.)

(f) Ought a party to be denied a contractual remedy on the ground that it would be economically unreasonable to grant it? (Cf. *Co-operative Ins Soc v Argyll* (1998), p.566.)

(g) Ought a buyer to be able to resist a claim in debt for goods or services supplied under a contract on the ground that the price is economically unreasonable in the circumstances?

(h) Ought a person to be liable in contract because it is reasonable in the circumstances to hold him liable? (Cf. *Blackpool & Fylde Aero Club v Blackpool BC* (1990), p.177.)

(i) Ought a contract that was once reasonable to be set aside on the ground that, owing to changed economic circumstances, the contract has become unreasonable? (Cf. *Staff AHA v S Staffs Waterworks* (1978), p.428.)

This list of questions about reasonableness is by no means exhaustive, but it should give a flavour of how problems of "reasonableness" can manifest themselves in contract.

4. As revealed by some of the questions above, one way in which reasonableness of behaviour can manifest itself in contract is with respect to the enforcement of rights. In civil law systems, one who insists on enforcing a right in circumstances where there is no legitimate interest in doing so might be liable to pay damages in tort if such an abusive enforcement causes damage (see, e.g., the Spanish Civil Code, art. 7(2)). English law is generally said to recognise no such principle of abuse of rights (*Bradford Corporation v Pickles* (1895)), and this would appear to apply just as much to contractual rights as to those arising in the law of property. Thus in 1963, a Court of Appeal judge declared that he "should be sorry to find a new concept of law introduced that a man may unreasonably exercise his right of termination, which was clearly given to him by the contract" (Upjohn L.J. in *Financings Ltd v Baldock* (1963), at 115). In the same year another Court of Appeal judge expressed the view that a "person who has a right under a contract . . . is entitled to exercise it . . . for a good reason or a bad reason or no reason at all" (Pearson L.J. in *Chapman v Honig* (1963), at 520). However, according to Lord Reid, it *may* be that equity might intervene to prevent the enforcement of a contractual stipulation or remedy when the right-holder has no interest in doing so (see *White & Carter (Councils) v McGregor* (1962), p.491). Other cases which could be seen as 'abuse of right' problems are perhaps *Hong Kong Fir Shipping* (1962) (p.336), *D & C Builders v Rees* (1966) (p.195), and maybe even *Williams v Roffey* (1991) (p.190). In civil law thinking, abuse of contractual rights appears now to be merging with good faith.

Formation of contracts

In order for a contract to form, a number of conditions have to be fulfilled. However, these conditions, or essential elements, are not the same in all systems because the normative focal point can vary according to the theory upon which contract is based. In Roman law, for example, the formation model was built upon *causa*; contracts were based either upon a number of transactions, or upon set words (*stipulatio*). In the later civil law this model changed in that the focal point shifted off *causa* and on to *conventio* (agreement). Contracts were formed by consensual agreement. This is not to say that *causa* became irrelevant, for, as we have seen, the specific transactions remained of importance, and even today exert an important influence on contractual thinking (see **3.1.2**).

In the common law, the position is more complex because of a history centred on different forms of action. The two pillars upon which the English model was constructed were trespass and debt, the former mutating into a particular form of action called *assumpsit*. The idea behind this action was damage caused by a failure to do what one promised and, arguably, this idea of promise remains the starting point for the English formation model (see extract from Zweigert and Kötz, at p.11). As a result there are three possible formation models in European thinking: (i) the model based upon transactions (*causae*); (ii) the model based upon agreement (*conventio*); and (iii) the model based upon promise (see UC&TO, pp.37–41).

4.1 Promise versus agreement

Now there is no doubt that English law, particularly during the 19th century, used civilian ideas to develop a general theory of contract, as we have seen from earlier extracts (see **Chapter 1**). But, as just mentioned, English contract law focuses more on promise than agreement, and this point is worth developing since the dichotomy between promise and agreement will keep recurring throughout this book. The difference can have practical consequences, as the next extract shows.

Gibson v Manchester City Council **[1978] 1 W.L.R. 520, CA; [1979] 1 W.L.R. 294, HL**

(See also p.149.)

> **Lord Denning M.R.** (Court of Appeal): ". . . We have had much discussion as to whether Mr Gibson's letter of 18th March 1971 was a new offer or whether it was

an acceptance of the previous offer which had been made. I do not like detailed analysis on such a point. To my mind it is a mistake to think that all contracts can be analysed into the form of offer and acceptance. I know in some of the textbooks it has been the custom to do so; but, as I understand the law, there is no need to look for a strict offer and acceptance. You should look at the correspondence as a whole and at the conduct of the parties and see therefrom whether the parties have come to an agreement on everything that was material. If by their correspondence and their conduct you can see an agreement on all material terms, which was intended thencefoward to be binding, then there is a binding contract in law even though all the formalities have not been gone through . . ."

Lord Diplock (House of Lords): ". . . My Lords, there may be certain types of contract, although I think they are exceptional, which do not fit easily into the normal analysis of a contract as being constituted by offer and acceptance; but a contract alleged to have been made by an exchange of correspondence between the parties in which the successive communications other than the first are in reply to one another is not one of these. I can see no reason in the instant case for departing from the conventional approach of looking at the handful of documents relied on as constituting the contract sued on and seeing whether on their true construction there is to be found in them a contractual offer by the council to sell the house to Mr Gibson and an acceptance of that offer by Mr Gibson. I venture to think that it was by departing from this conventional approach that the majority of the Court of Appeal was led into error . . ."

QUESTIONS

1. Was Lord Denning attempting to replace the promise thesis with the theory that contract was a matter of agreement? Was this attempt rejected in the House of Lords?

2. Is contractual liability to be found within the actual facts of a dispute, or is it to be found within the intention of the parties? In a case like *Gibson*, does a court have to look only at the documents or must it look beyond the documents?

NOTE

The distinction between a formation model based on agreement and one based on promise is a distinction that will constantly recur in this book (and see UC&TO, pp.39–41). It explains, for example, why English contract law never developed a theory of mistake; instead it focused on promise—that is to say, on the statement(s) made by the parties at the time of negotiation—and used words rather than the mind as the starting point for providing remedies (see **5.2**). Not all statements made before contract about the subject-matter of the contract amount to contractual promises, and so a distinction developed between statements (representations) that did not amount to contractual promises and those that did (often called "warranties").

Hopkins v Tanqueray (1854) 139 E.R. 369, CP

This was an action for damages by the purchaser, at an auction at Tattersall's, of a horse subsequently found to be unsound and resold at a loss by the purchaser. He claimed that the horse was warranted as sound because of statements by the seller to the purchaser on the day previous to the auction; but it was established that horses sold at Tattersall's were not warranted unless so stated in the catalogue, and that the horse in question was not warranted. The jury found in favour of the purchaser, but the Court of Common Pleas (Jervis C.J. and Maule, Creswell and Crowder J.J.) held that there was no evidence to support their finding.

Jervis C.J.: "... I think it is quite clear that what passed amounted to a representation only, and not to a warranty. The facts were simply these: The defendant seeing the plaintiff in the stable on the Sunday prior to the sale, examining the horse's legs, said to him, 'You need not examine his legs: you have nothing to look for: I assure you he is perfectly sound in every respect' to which the plaintiff replied, 'If you say so, I am satisfied.' The plaintiff made no further examination; and he did not employ a veterinary surgeon, relying upon a representation made by an honourable man. The defendant, doubtless, believed the horse to be as he represented it: no fraud is imputed to him: on the contrary, indeed, the plaintiff expressly disclaims it. There is, consequently, no basis on which to rest this action. On the day following, Mr Tattersall announces that he is about to sell California without a warranty: and the defendant becomes the purchaser. It seems to me to be perfectly clear, that, in what took place between them on the Sunday, the defendant did not mean to warrant the horse, but was merely making a representation of that which he bona fide believed to be the fact; and that the plaintiff so understood it. What passed afterwards cannot in any degree affect the case: it only amounts to this, that the parties thought at one time that there had been a warranty. I think the rule must be made absolute."

Crowder J.: I am of the same opinion. The conversation which took place between the parties on the Sunday was a mere representation, and was evidently not made with an intention to warrant the horse. A representation, to constitute a warranty, must be shown to have been intended to form part of the contract. I think it abundantly clear upon the evidence that the matter here relied on was not understood or intended as forming part of the contract which might be made at the auction on the following day, which it was well known to both parties would be without a warranty. It was a mere representation, quite distinct from any intention to warrant the animal. It is unnecessary to consider whether a party may lawfully warrant as between himself and a particular individual under circumstances like these. It is a very grave question whether such a contract could be upheld in a court of justice, in the case of a sale by auction, where all have a right to suppose they are bidding upon equal terms ..."

QUESTIONS

1. "If a man covenant, for a valid consideration, that it shall rain to-morrow, he cannot afterwards say, 'I could not make it rain; I did all I could to make it

rain; but it would not.' He chooses to covenant that such a thing shall happen, and if it does not, he has broken his covenant. If a man enter into a covenant that a thing shall be of a particular quality, it would be no answer to say, 'it is impossible the thing can be of that quality'" (Maule J. in *Canham v Barry* (1855), at 106). Would a promise that it shall rain tomorrow be capable of forming the basis of a contract in Roman and French law?

2. "When a person has been induced to enter into a contract by a representation which, whether wilfully or not, was a mistake, equity will give relief . . ." (Byles J. in *Stears v South Essex Gaslight & Coke Co* (1861), at 55). Could the plaintiff in *Hopkins v Tanqueray* have claimed relief in equity? (Cf **5.2.**)

3. "If there is one principle more clear than another, it is, that if a man has made a deliberate statement, and another has acted upon it, he cannot be at liberty to deny the truth of the statement he has made." (Bramwell B. in *McCance v L & NW Ry* (1861), at 71). Is this a principle that is reflected both in common law (contract and deceit) and in equity (estoppel)?

4. What is the value in distinguishing between a "mere representation" and a "warranty"? Was the court in *Hopkins* in effect treating the representation as a mere "puff" which would not attract legal liability?

NOTE

In civilian systems, as we have seen in **Chapter 1**, it is agreement which acts as the formation model, and this is the model adopted by the PECL (see p.9).

> **Unidroit Principles for International Commercial Contracts**
>
> *"Article 2.1 Manner of Formation*
>
> A contract may be concluded either by the acceptance of an offer or by conduct of the parties that is sufficient to show agreement."

NOTE

It may well be that PECL, art.2:101(1) does not represent English law, but PECL, art.2:101(2) probably does (see above, p.9). A contract can be formed by words and does not normally have to be evidenced in writing. There are exceptions, of course, of which a contract for the sale of an interest in land is possibly the most important (see p.213).

QUESTIONS

1. If either the PECL or UNIDROIT governed the factual situation in *Gibson v Manchester CC*, would there have been an enforceable contract?

2. "A promise which is intended to be legally binding without acceptance is binding" (PECL, art.2:107). Does this reflect English law?

Law of Property (Miscellaneous Provisions) Act 1989 (c 34)

"**1. Deeds and their execution**

(1) Any rule of law which—

    (a) restricts the substances on which a deed may be written;

    (b) requires a seal for the valid execution of an instrument as a deed by an individual; or

    (c) requires authority by one person to another to deliver an instrument as a deed on his behalf to be given by deed,

is abolished.

(2) An instrument shall not be a deed unless—

    (a) it makes it clear on its face that it is intended to be a deed by the person making it or, as the case may be, by the parties to it (whether by describing itself as a deed or expressing itself to be executed or signed as a deed or otherwise); and

    (b) it is validly executed as a deed by that person or, as the case may be, one or more of those parties.

(3) An instrument is validly executed as a deed by an individual if, and only if—

    (a) it is signed—

        (i) by him in the presence of a witness who attests the signature; or

        (ii) at his direction and in his presence and the presence of two witnesses who each attest the signature; and

    (b) it is delivered as a deed by him or a person authorised to do so on his behalf.

NOTES

1. The possibility of creating an enforceable promise by deed is a hangover from the old writ of covenant, which was simply an action to enforce an agreement, although it was overtaken by actions for debt and detinue (Milsom, *Historical Foundations of the Common Law* (2nd edn, (Butterworths, 1981), pp.246–50). Some say that it was England's earliest contract action. The procedure is still alive and has been simplified by the above Act. But just as covenant got eclipsed by trespass and debt, so this statutory form of contracting seems completely overshadowed by the common law's general theory of contracting (which of course developed out of trespass and debt).

2. For s.2 of the 1989 Act, see p.213.

QUESTION

Does this section create a statutory form of contracting?

4.2 Formation: objective approach

There are three essential elements for the formation of an ordinary contract in English law. These are:

(a) offer and acceptance;

(b) consideration; and

(c) intention to create legal relations.

These three elements will each be examined in more detail, but before looking at these formation requirements the following provision must be borne in mind, since even in civilian jurisdictions it is not possible to see into the actual minds of the parties.

> ***Principles of European Contract Law***
>
> *"Article 2:102 Intention*
>
> The intention of a party to be legally bound by contract is to be determined from the party's statements or conduct as they were reasonably understood by the other party."

NOTE

Compare PECL, art.2:102 with the position in English law, as reflected in the next extract.

> ***Paal Wilson & Co v Partenreederei Hannah Blumenthal* [1983] A.C. 854, HL**
>
> **Lord Diplock:** ". . . To the formation of the contract of abandonment, the ordinary principles of the English law of contract apply. To create a contract by exchange of promises between two parties where the promise of each party constitutes the consideration for the promise of the other, what is necessary is that the intention of each *as it has been communicated to and understood by the other* (even though that which has been communicated does not represent the actual state of mind of the communicator) should coincide. That is what English lawyers mean when they resort to the Latin phrase consensus ad idem and the words that I have italicised are essential to the concept of consensus ad idem, the lack of which prevents the formation of a binding contract in English law.
>
> Thus if A (the offeror) makes a communication to B (the offeree) whether in writing, orally or by conduct, which, in the circumstances at the time the communication was received, (1) B, if he were a reasonable man, would understand as stating A's intention to act or refrain from acting in some specified manner if B will promise on his part to act or refrain from acting in some manner

144

also specified in the offer, and (2) B does in fact understand A's communication to mean this, and in his turn makes to A a communication conveying his willingness so to act or to refrain from acting which mutatis mutandis satisfies the same two conditions as respects A, the consensus ad idem essential to the formation of a contract in English law is complete.

The rule that neither party can rely upon his own failure to communicate accurately to the other party his own real intention by what he wrote or said or did, as negativing the consensus ad idem, is an example of a general principle of English law that injurious reliance on what another person did may be a source of legal rights against him. I use the broader expression 'injurious reliance' in preference to 'estoppel' so as to embrace all circumstances in which A can say to B: 'You led me reasonably to believe that you were assuming particular legally enforceable obligations to me,' of which promissory or *High Trees* estoppel [*Central London Property Trust Ltd v High Trees House Ltd* [1947] KB 130] affords another example; whereas 'estoppel,' in the strict sense of the term, is an exclusionary rule of evidence, though it may operate so as to affect substantive legal rights *inter partes*."

NOTE

A more recent case highlights this objective approach.

Centrovincial Estates plc v Merchant Investors Assurance Co Ltd **[1983] Com. L.R. 158, CA**

This was an action for a declaration that there was no legally binding contract arising out of a letter sent by the claimants to the defendants. The defendants were tenants of offices let to them by the claimants and the tenancy contract contained a rent review clause. When the time came for a rent review, the claimants' solicitors sent a letter inviting the defendants to agree a new rent of £65,000, a figure below the rent they were already paying, and the defendants accepted the offer. The claimants then contacted the defendants pointing out that their letter contained an error and that the figure should have been £126,000, a new letter with the correct figure subsequently being sent to the defendants. The defendants refused to agree to this new sum and claimed that there was a binding contract for £65,000. The Court of Appeal (Slade and Robert Goff L.JJ.) refused to grant the declaration and held that the claimants were not entitled to summary judgment.

Slade LJ: ". . . It is a well-established principle of the English law of contract that an offer falls to be interpreted not subjectively by reference to what has actually passed through the mind of the offeror, but objectively, by reference to the interpretation which a reasonable man in the shoes of the offeree would place on the offer. It is an equally well-established principle that ordinarily an offer, when unequivocally accepted according to its precise terms, will give rise to a legally binding agreement as soon as acceptance is communicated to the offeror in the manner contemplated by the offer, and cannot thereafter be revoked without the consent of the other party. Accepting, as they do, that they have not yet proved that the defendants knew, or ought reasonably to have known, of their error at the relevant time, how can the plaintiffs assert that the defendants have no realistic hope of establishing an agreement of the relevant nature by virtue of the two letters of the 22nd and 23rd June 1982? . . .''

NOTES

1. This decision is not holding that the claimants were contractually bound by the letter stating a figure of £65,000. What was decided was that the claimants were not entitled to summary judgment and that the defendants would be allowed at the actual trial to raise the defence that there was a binding contract. Much, no doubt, would depend on the state of the defendants' knowledge with respect to the £65,000 figure. If it was obvious to any reasonable defendant that the figure was wrong, it is unlikely that there would be a binding contract for £65,000 (*Hartog v Colin & Shields* (1939)).

2. See further Steyn L.J. in *Trentham Ltd v Archital Luxfer* (1993).

QUESTIONS

1. Is this case another example of English law's refusal to recognise a doctrine of good faith? Were the defendants behaving reasonably?

2. What if the letter had contained the figure of £6,500? (Cf. *Hartog v Colin & Shields* (1939).)

3. If the mistake in the letter was made by the claimants' solicitors and the contract was subsequently held to be valid, would the claimants have a good claim against their solicitors for their losses?

4. If the mistake was due to an employee of the claimants, and the contract for £65,000 was subsequently upheld, could the claimants have sued the employee for their losses for breach of his or her contract of employment? (Cf. *Lister v Romford Ice & Cold Storage Co* (1957).)

4.3 Offer and acceptance

In both civil and common law jurisdictions, the principal way of determining if a contract has been formed is through offer and acceptance.

Shogun Finance Ltd v Hudson **[2004] 1 A.C. 919, HL**

(For facts, see p.265.)

Lord Phillips: ". . . **123** A contract is normally concluded when an offer made by one party ('the offeror') is accepted by the party to whom the offer has been made ('the offeree'). Normally the contract is only concluded when the acceptance is communicated by the offeree to the offeror. A contract will not be concluded unless the parties are agreed as to its material terms. There must be 'consensus ad idem'. Whether the parties have reached agreement on the terms is not determined by evidence of the subjective intention of each party. It is, in large measure, determined by making an objective appraisal of the exchanges between the parties. If an offeree understands an offer in accordance with its natural meaning and accepts it, the offeror cannot be heard to say that he intended the words of his offer to have a different meaning. The contract stands according to the natural meaning of the words used. There is one important exception to this principle. If the offeree knows that the offeror does not intend the terms of the offer to be those that the natural meaning of the words would suggest, he cannot, by purporting to accept the offer, bind the offeror to a contract: *Hartog v Colin & Shields* [1939] 3 All ER 566; *Smith v Hughes* (1871) LR 6 QB 597. Thus the task of ascertaining whether the parties have reached agreement as to the terms of a contract can involve quite a complex amalgam of the objective and the subjective and involve the application of a principle that bears close comparison with the doctrine of estoppel. Normally, however, the task involves no more than an objective analysis of the words used by the parties. The object of the exercise is to determine what each party *intended*, or must be deemed to have *intended*.

124 The task of ascertaining whether the parties have reached agreement as to the terms of a contract largely overlaps with the task of ascertaining what it is that the parties have agreed. The approach is the same. It requires the construction of the words used by the parties in order to deduce the *intention* of the parties—see *Chitty on Contracts*, 28th ed (1999), vol 1, p 604, paras 12–042, 12–043 and the cases there cited. This is true, whether the contract is oral or in writing. The words used fall to be construed having regard to the relevant background facts and extrinsic evidence may be admitted to explain or interpret the words used. Equally, extrinsic evidence may be necessary to identify the subject matter of the contract to which the words refer.

125 Just as the parties must be shown to have agreed on the terms of the contract, so they must also be shown to have agreed the one with the other. If A makes an offer to B, but C purports to accept it, there will be no contract. Equally, if A makes an offer to B and B addresses his acceptance to C there will be no contract. Where there is an issue as to whether two persons have reached an agreement, the one with the other, the courts have tended to adopt the same approach to resolving that issue as they adopt when considering whether there has been agreement as to the terms of the contract. The court asks the questionwhether each *intended*, or must be deemed to have *intended*, to contract with the other. That approach gives rise to a problem where one person is mistaken as to the identity of the person with whom he is dealing, as the cases demonstrate . . ."

NOTE

The starting point for the formation of a contract is the two notions of "offer" and "acceptance". Each of these elements needs examination, as does a third aspect, that of *consensus ad idem*.

4.3.1 Offer: general considerations

What amounts to an offer for the purposes of the law of contract?

Principles of European Contract Law

"*Article 2:201 Offer*

(1) A proposal amounts to an offer if:

(a) it is intended to result in a contract if the other party accepts it, and
(b) it contains sufficiently definite terms to form a contract.

(2) An offer may be made to one or more specific persons or to the public.
(3) A proposal to supply goods or services at stated prices made by a professional supplier in a public advertisement or a catalogue, or by a display of goods, is presumed to be an offer to sell or supply at that price until the stock of goods, or the supplier's capacity to supply the service, is exhausted."

NOTES

1. See also UNIDROIT, art.2.1.2.

2. Article 2:201 of the PECL only partially represents English law. It says nothing directly about an 'invitation to treat', which must be distinguished from an offer, particularly in respect of para.(3) of art.2:201. An invitation to treat is an invitation to another to make an offer. Thus the 'display of goods', as far as English contract law is concerned, probably does not amount to an offer; it is an invitation to treat, and it is the potential customer who must make the offer. However, one should note that both the PECL and UNI-DROIT state that the offer must be 'sufficiently definite'. This might cause friction between PECL, art.2:103 (above, p.10) and art.2:201(1)(b).

Gibson v Manchester City Council **[1979] 1 W.L.R. 294, HL**

(See also p.139.)

This was an action for specific performance by a potential purchaser of a council house against a local authority which, after a number of preliminary letters indicating a willingness to sell, and setting out the steps to be followed, suddenly, and as a result of a change of political control, refused to carry on with the sale. The Court of Appeal granted the specific performance, but an appeal to the House of Lords (Lords Diplock, Edmund-Davies, Fraser, Russell and Keith) was allowed.

> **Lord Diplock:** ". . . My Lords, the words . . . make it quite impossible to construe this letter as a contractual offer capable of being converted into a legally enforceable open contract for the sale of land by Mr Gibson's written acceptance of it. The words 'may be prepared to sell' are fatal to this . . .
>
> My Lords, the application form and letter of March 18, 1971 were relied on by Mr Gibson as an unconditional acceptance of the council's offer to sell the house; but this cannot be so unless there was a contractual offer by the council available for acceptance, and, for the reason already given I am of opinion that there was none . . ."

QUESTIONS

1. Could there have been "sufficient agreement" for the purposes of PECL, art.2:103?

2. Ought the words "may be prepared to sell" to be construed within the context of the actual behaviour of the council: if they were going ahead with all sales to those who were responding to their "may be prepared to sell" letter, might not this evidence of subjective agreement?

NOTE

English law does recognise that an offer may be made to the public at large, as the next (famous) case illustrates.

Carlill v Carbolic Smoke Ball Co **[1893] 1 Q.B. 256, CA**

This was an action in debt against manufacturers who had inserted in newspapers an advertisement offering "£100 reward" to anyone who caught influenza after using their smoke ball inhalant as per directions for two weeks. The advert also stated that £1,000 had been deposited with the Alliance Bank, "showing our sincerity in the matter". On the faith of the advertisement the plaintiff bought one of the inhalants and used it as directed for two weeks; the product proved ineffective and the defendants insincere. The plaintiff sued for the £100 and the Court of Appeal (Bowen, Lindley and A.L. Smith L.JJ.) allowed her to recover.

Bowen L.J.: ". . . It is . . . contended that the advertisement is rather in the nature of a puff or a proclamation than a promise or offer intended to mature into a contract when accepted. But the main point seems to be that the vagueness of the document shows that no contract whatever was intended. It seems to me that in order to arrive at a right conclusion we must read this advertisement in its plain meaning, as the public would understand it. It was intended to be issued to the public and to be read by the public. How would an ordinary person reading this document construe it? It was intended unquestionably to have some effect, and I think the effect which it was intended to have, was to make people use the smoke ball, because the suggestions and allegations which it contains are directed immediately to the use of the smoke ball as distinct from the purchase of it. It did not follow that the smoke ball was to be purchased from the defendants directly, or even from agents of theirs directly. The intention was that the circulation of the smoke ball should be promoted, and that the use of it should be increased . . . And it seems to me that the way in which the public would read it would be this, that if anybody, after the advertisement was published, used three times daily for two weeks the carbolic smoke ball, and then caught cold, he would be entitled to the reward . . .

Was it intended that the £100 should, if the conditions were filled, be paid? The advertisement says that £1,000 is lodged at the bank for the purpose. Therefore, it cannot be said that the statement that £100 would be paid was intended to be a mere puff. I think it was intended to be understood by the public as an offer which was to be acted upon.

But it was said there was no check on the part of the persons who issued the advertisement, and that it would be an insensate thing to promise £100 to a person who used the smoke ball unless you could check or superintend his manner of using it. The answer to that argument seems to me to be that if a person chooses to make extravagant promises of this kind he probably does so because it pays him to make them, and, if he has made them, the extravagance of the promises is no reason in law why he should not be bound by them . . ."

A.L. Smith L.J.: ". . . In my judgment, the advertisement was an offer intended to be acted upon, and when accepted and the conditions performed constituted a binding promise on which an action would lie, assuming there was consideration for that promise. The defendants have contended that it was a promise in honour or an agreement or a contract in honour—whatever that may mean. I understand that if there is no consideration for a promise, it may be a promise in honour, or, as we should call it, a promise without consideration and *nudum pactum*; but if anything else is meant, I do not understand it. I do not understand what a bargain or a promise or an agreement in honour is unless it is one on which an action cannot be brought because it is *nudum pactum*, and about *nudum pactums* I will say a word in a moment . . ."

150

NOTES

1. This most famous of contract cases remains of central importance to English contract law for several reasons. First, it indicates, once again, how objective promise rather than subjective agreement acts as the foundation of liability. The defendants were liable because they launched on to the consumer market (so to speak) a promise, and this promise was taken up by a consumer who, as an individual, was never known to the promisors.

2. Secondly, the decision shows that an offer made to the world at large, or at least to a class, does not have to be specifically accepted by verbal communication by the person taking up the offer. All that the promisee has to do, if he or she wants what is promised, is to perform the required act which will constitute the consideration moving from the promisee (see **4.6**).

3. Thirdly, *Carlill* established an important role for the collateral contract in the world of commerce and consumer affairs. Mrs Carlill did not buy the product from the manufacturers; she probably purchased it from her local chemist, and thus if it had been defective, causing her injury, she would probably have sued the shop under the contract of sale for breach of an implied term (cf. *Frost v Aylesbury Dairy* (1905), at p.61). Collateral contracts continue to have an important role in the area of formation of contracts.

4. Fourthly, the case illustrates the importance of conditions in contracts (see **Chapter 7**). If Mrs Carlill had not caught influenza, she could not have sued for the money.

5. The case is also of importance in terms of the remedy. Mrs Carlill was not seeking compensation for breach of contract (the company never promised that she would not get influenza); she was in effect seeking the specific enforcement of a contractual primary obligation. She was demanding that the defendants do what they actually promised to do (see **11.2**).

QUESTIONS

1. In what circumstances might a manufacturer of a product be liable, on the basis of an advertising campaign, to compensate a consumer in damages? Can you draft such an advertisement so that it amounts to an offer to the public?

2. Would these facts have given rise to a contractual obligation in a system where contract is founded on agreement rather than promise?

3. A sign outside a pub restaurant states that "If you do not like our delicious food you don't have to pay for it". Mitch orders a meal in the pub and, having eaten it, declares that he did not like it and refuses to pay. Can the pub sue Mitch for the price of the meal?

4.3.2 Offers and the consumer

In theory, the way to determine if a proposition amounts to an offer is to consider the proposition itself and to ask two basic questions: Is it sufficiently definite to form an offer? And, even if relatively definite, is it actually an offer and not an invitation to treat? This second question can raise difficulties, since there appears to be an element of policy attached to the distinction between offers and invitations to treat. For example, a passing taxi with its 'for hire' light on, would seem at first sight to be an offer waiting to be accepted by the first person who hails it. However, it would appear that the light indicates only that it is an invitation to treat, and so the taxi that refuses to stop would seemingly not to be in danger of falling foul of the law of contract. The policy of the law seems to be to give the taxi driver the choice of making or refusing a contract, a situation not shared by all European legal systems.

Given this policy dimension, it might be useful to approach offers from the position of several established factual situations. The first is the supplier of goods. Here, as we have seen, goods displayed in a shop-window do not amount to offers but only to invitations to treat: *Fisher v Bell* (1961) (at p.35). One might compare this situation to the language of PECL, art.2:201(3) (at p.10). What is the situation in supermarkets?

Pharmaceutical Society of Great Britain v Boots [1953] 1 Q.B. 401, CA

This was a prosecution brought against Boots for the way they sold certain drugs in their self-service stores. The Court of Appeal (Somervell, Birkett and Romer L.JJ.) upheld a judgment that no offence had been committed.

Somervell L.J.: ". . . The point taken by the plaintiffs is this: it is said that the purchase is complete if and when a customer going round the shelves takes an article and puts it in the receptacle which he or she is carrying, and that therefore, if that is right, when the customer comes to the pay desk, having completed the tour of the premises, the registered pharmacist, if so minded, has no power to say: 'This drug ought not to be sold to this customer.' Whether and in what circumstances he would have that power we need not inquire, but one can, of course, see that there is a difference if supervision can only be exercised at a time when the contract is completed.

Whether the view contended for by the plaintiffs is a right view depends on what are the legal implications of this layout—the invitation to the customer. Is a contract to be regarded as being completed when the article is put into the receptacle, or is this to be regarded as a more organised way of doing what is done already in many types of shops—and a bookseller is perhaps the best example—namely, enabling customers to have free access to what is in the shop, to look at the different articles, and then, ultimately, having got the ones which they wish to buy, to come up to the assistant saying: 'I want this'? The assistant in 999 times out of 1,000 says: 'That is all right,' and the money passes and the transaction is completed. I agree with what the Lord Chief Justice has said, and with the reasons which he has given for his conclusion, that in the case of an ordinary shop, although goods are displayed and it is intended that customers should go and choose what they want, the contract is not completed until, the customer having indicated the articles which he needs, the shopkeeper, or someone on his behalf, accepts that offer. Then the contract is completed. I can see no reason at all, that being clearly the normal position, for drawing any different implication as a result of this layout.

The Lord Chief Justice, I think, expressed one of the most formidable difficulties in the way of the plaintiffs' contention when he pointed out that, if the plaintiffs are right, once an article has been placed in the receptacle the customer himself is bound and would have no right, without paying for the first article to substitute an article which he saw later of a similar kind and which he perhaps preferred. I can see no reason for implying from this self-service arrangement any implication other than that which the Lord Chief Justice found in it, namely, that it is a convenient method of enabling customers to see what there is and choose, and possibly put back and substitute, articles which they wish to have, and then to go up to the cashier and offer to buy what they have so far chosen. On that conclusion the case fails . . ."

QUESTIONS

1. We have already seen that in a French case involving a bottle of lemonade, which exploded just as the customer was handling it to the cashier, the French courts decided that a contract for the sale of goods in a supermarket is complete as soon as the customer takes the goods from the shelf and puts it in the trolley or basket provided. The customer was thus able to recover damages in contract for her injury (Cass.civ.20.10.1964; DS.1965.62, above p.90). Why do you think the French courts took this approach? What problems might arise from the French rule? How would English law have dealt with the facts of the French case? Do you think this French case is still good law in France? What if a customer is injured in an English supermarket, say by slipping on some spilt yoghurt? (Cf. *Ward v Tesco Stores* (1976), p.183.)

2. A customer in a supermarket is covered in orange juice when a bottle explodes for some unexplained reason, just as he is lifting out of the trolley to present to the cashier. Can the customer sue the supermarket for damages?

3. Are goods displayed in a shop window contractual offers if they have a ticket attached saying "special offer"? What is the position under the PECL?

4. What legal problems might Virtual Reality shopping present to future contract lawyers?

5. A shopkeeper rings up on his till the price of a packet of cigarettes, before realising that the customer buying the cigarettes is under age: must the shopkeeper hand over the cigarettes to the customer?

6. Goods advertised for sale in newspapers or on the web: are they offers?

4.3.3 **Offers made to the public at large**

In the consumer world, it would appear that in many situations it is the consumer who must make the offer. But, as we have seen, some advertisements can amount to contractual offers.

Carlill v Carbolic Smoke Ball Co [1893] 1 Q.B. 256, CA
(For facts and other extracts, see p.149.)

> **Lindley L.J.:** "... Then it is contended that it is not binding. In the first place, it is said that it is not made with anybody in particular. Now that point is common to the words of this advertisement and to the words of all other advertisements offering rewards. They are offers to anybody who performs the conditions named in the advertisement, and anybody who does perform the condition accepts the offer. In point of law this advertisement is an offer to pay £100 to anybody who will perform these conditions, and the performance of the conditions is the acceptance of the offer. That rests upon a string of authorities, the earliest of which is *Williams v Carwardine*, which has been followed by many other decisions upon advertisements offering rewards . . ."

> **Bowen L.J.:** "... It was also said that the contract is made with all the world— that is, with everybody; and that you cannot contract with everybody. It is not a contract made with all the world. There is the fallacy of the argument. It is an offer made to all the world; and why should not an offer be made to all the world which is to ripen into a contract with anybody who comes forward and performs the condition? It is an offer to become liable to any one who, before it is retracted, performs the condition, and, although the offer is made to the world, the contract is made with that limited portion of the public who come forward and perform the condition on the faith of the advertisement. It is not like cases in which you offer to negotiate, or you issue advertisements that you have got a stock of books to sell, or houses to let, in which case there is no offer to be bound by any contract. Such advertisements are offers to negotiate—offers to receive offers—offers to chaffer, as, I think, some learned judge in one of the cases has said. If this is an offer to be bound, then it is a contract the moment the person fulfils the condition . . ."

QUESTION

Given this reasoning, is there any technical reason why a taxi with its "for hire" sign on is not making an offer to the public at large?

NOTE

Auctions can involve offers being made to the public at large: see *Barry v Davies* (2000).

PROBLEM

Basil makes a bid for a musical Christmas tree up for auction on an Internet auction site, but is beaten at the last moment by one other higher bidder. This successful bidder never contacts the seller of the Christmas tree and never responds to any communication from the seller. Can the seller subsequently claim that Basil is contractually bound to buy the Christmas tree?

4.3.4 Revocation and lapse of offers

Once a valid offer has been made, how long does it stay in force? Can it be revoked by the offeror?

Principles of European Contract Law

"*Article 2:202 Revocation of an Offer*

(1) An offer may be revoked if the revocation reaches the offeree before it has dispatched its acceptance or, in cases of acceptance by conduct, before the contract has been concluded under Article 2:205(2) or (3).
(2) An offer made to the public can be revoked by the same means as were used to make the offer.
(3) However, a revocation of an offer is ineffective if:

  (a) the offer indicates that it is irrevocable; or
  (b) it states a fixed time for its acceptance; or
  (c) it was reasonable for the offeree to rely on the offer as being irrevocable and the offeree has acted in reliance on the offer."

NOTES

1. See also UNIDROIT, arts 2.1.3–2.1.5. These code articles go some way in expressing English law, but care must be taken. First, it is a rule of common law that an offer can be revoked at any time before acceptance, even if the offeror has stated a fixed time for its duration or that it is "irrevocable". The reason is that there is no consideration to support this promise. However, equity may well intervene with its doctrine of estoppel (see p.193) in order to prevent an offeror revoking an offer in certain situations where the offeree is relying upon the offer remaining in existence. The classic situation is the unilateral contract, in which acceptance occurs only when the promisee has performed. If D offers C £100 if he completes the London Marathon, D cannot place himself close to the finish and shout a withdrawal as C enters the final stage of the run. D will be estopped in equity from withdrawing the offer until C has had a reasonable chance to complete. So it may be that PECL art 2:202(3) and UNIDROIT, art.2.1.4(2) go far in expressing the position in England.

2. Secondly, a counter-offer will destroy the original offer, and thus an original offer cannot be accepted if the counter-offer is rejected by the original offeror.

3. Thirdly, an offer probably lapses after a reasonable time.

QUESTIONS

1. Does an offer lapse if the offeror dies?

2. Must the revocation of the offer reach the actual offeree, or will its reaching a third party sometimes be sufficient?

Financings Ltd v Stimson [1962] 1 W.L.R. 1184, CA

This was an action for damages for breach of contract, brought by a finance company against a defendant who had signed a hire-purchase form at the premises of a motor dealer, paid a deposit and then took possession of a car. The hire-purchase form stated that the hire-purchase contract would become binding only upon acceptance by the finance company. The defendant later returned the car to the dealer saying that he was dissatisfied with it and that he did not want to go on with the agreement; he also offered to forgo his deposit. Before the finance company had signed the agreement, but after the car had been returned to the dealer, the vehicle was stolen from the dealer's premises and severely damaged. The finance company then signed the agreement and claimed there was a contract. A majority of the Court of Appeal (Lord Denning M.R. and Donovan L.J.; Pearson L.J. dissenting in part) dismissed the finance company's claim for damages.

> **Donovan L.J.:** "The dealer in this case was clearly the plaintiff finance company's agent to do a variety of things: to receive an offer of hire-purchase; to tell the proposed hire purchaser, the defendant, that the plaintiffs would accept the business; to ensure that comprehensive insurance was effected by the defendant; and thereafter to deliver the car to him. In the written hire-purchase form of agreement there was no clause negativing agency between the plaintiffs and the dealer. In these circumstances, authority to receive a notice of revocation of the hire-purchase offer was, in my opinion, within the dealer's authority as ostensible agent for the plaintiffs . . .
>
> Then was a notice of revocation given before the offer was accepted? That acceptance must be taken to have taken place not earlier than 25th March 1961. Before then, namely, on 20th March, the defendant had taken the car back to the dealer, told him he did not want to go on with the transaction and offered to forfeit his deposit. The dealer said words to the effect that he would get in touch with the plaintiffs to see what could be arranged, and told the defendant that he himself should also communicate with the plaintiffs, which the defendant did not do. Clearly both parties were under the impression that what was in view was the rescission of an existing concluded contract, whereas at this moment there was no contract at all. But it is conceded, and I think rightly so, that, if an offeror makes it clear that he does not want to go on with the transaction, it is properly treated as a revocation of his offer, notwithstanding that the words used would be more appropriate to a case of rescission. Thus one reaches the stage that an offer here

has been revoked before acceptance and the revocation communicated to the ostensible agent of the offeree. There is thus an end of the matter in favour of the defendant.

But if this view be wrong, I would agree that the offer here was on the basis that the car remained substantially in the same condition until acceptance, and that this did not happen . . .

QUESTIONS

1. Should this case be classified under offer and acceptance, or mistake?

2. What if the car had been defective and the defendant had been injured while driving it back to the dealer? Could the defendant have sued the plaintiffs in contract for his injuries?

4.3.5 Acceptance

The next element that needs examination is "acceptance".

Principles of European Contract Law

"*Article 2:204 Acceptance*

(1) Any form of statement or conduct by the offeree is an acceptance if it indicates assent to the offer.
(2) Silence or inactivity does not in itself amount to acceptance."

NOTES

1. See also UNIDROIT, art.2.1.6.

2. Both paragraphs of PECL, art.2:204 give expression to English law. Thus conduct can amount to acceptance (*Brogden v Metropolitan Railway Co* (1877)) and silence or inactivity is no acceptance. The main point to be emphasised, however, is that there must be an unequivocal act of acceptance: see *Firstpost Homes Ltd v Johnson* (1995) (read in law report).

4.3.6 Acceptance and conclusion of the contract

Even if there is an unequivocal act of acceptance, a question can still arise about the exact moment when the contract forms.

Principles of European Contract Law

"Article 2:205 Time of Conclusion of the Contract

(1) If an acceptance has been dispatched by the offeree the contract is concluded when the acceptance reaches the offeror.
(2) In case of acceptance by conduct, the contract is concluded when notice of the conduct reaches the offeror.
(3) If by virtue of the offer, of practices which the parties have established between themselves, or of a usage, the offeree may accept the offer by performing an act without notice to the offeror, the contract is concluded when the performance of the act begins."

NOTE

Article 2:205(1) of the PECL (and UNIDROIT, art.2.1.6(2)) only partially represents English law, since a distinction must be made between acceptance by post and acceptance using other means of communication. The general position is set out in the next case extract (the facts of the case are not really important).

Entores Ltd v Miles Far East Corporation **[1955] 2 Q.B. 327, CA**

Denning L.J.: ". . . When a contract is made by post it is clear law throughout the common law countries that the acceptance is complete as soon as the letter is put into the post box, and that is the place where the contract is made. But there is no clear rule about contracts made by telephone or by Telex. Communications by these means are virtually instantaneous and stand on a different footing.

The problem can only be solved by going in stages. Let me first consider a case where two people make a contract by word of mouth in the presence of one another. Suppose, for instance, that I shout an offer to a man across a river or a courtyard but I do not hear his reply because it is drowned by an aircraft flying overhead. There is no contract at that moment. If he wishes to make a contract, he must wait till the aircraft is gone and then shout back his acceptance so that I can hear what he says. Not until I have his answer am I bound . . .

Now take a case where two people make a contract by telephone. Suppose, for instance, that I make an offer to a man by telephone and, in the middle of his reply, the line goes 'dead' so that I do not hear his words of acceptance. There is no contract at that moment. The other man may not know the precise moment when the line failed. But he will know that the telephone conversation was abruptly broken off: because people usually say something to signify the end of the conversation. If he wishes to make a contract, he must therefore get through again so as to make sure that I heard. Suppose next, that the line does not go dead, but it is nevertheless so indistinct that I do not catch what he says and I ask him to repeat it. He then repeats it and I hear his acceptance. The contract is made, not on the first time when I do not hear, but only the second time when I do hear. If he does not repeat it, there is no contract. The contract is only complete when I have his answer accepting the offer.

Lastly, take the Telex. Suppose a clerk in a London office taps out on the teleprinter an offer which is immediately recorded on a teleprinter in a Manchester office, and a clerk at that end taps out an acceptance. If the line goes dead in the middle of the sentence of acceptance, the teleprinter motor will stop. There is then obviously no contract. The clerk at Manchester must get through again and send his complete sentence. But it may happen that the line does not go dead, yet the message does not get through to London. Thus the clerk at Manchester may tap out his message of acceptance and it will not be recorded in London because the ink at the London end fails, or something of that kind. In that case, the Manchester clerk wild not know of the failure but the London clerk will know of it and will immediately send back a message 'not receiving'. Then, when the fault is rectified, the Manchester clerk will repeat his message. Only then is there a contract. If he does not repeat it, there is no contract. It is not until his message is received that the contract is complete.

In all the instances I have taken so far, the man who sends the message of acceptance knows that it has not been received or he has reason to know it. So he must repeat it. But, suppose that he does not know that his message did not get home. He thinks it has. This may happen if the listener on the telephone does not catch the words of acceptance, but nevertheless does not trouble to ask for them to be repeated: or the ink on the teleprinter fails at the receiving end, but the clerk does not ask for the message to be repeated: so that the man who sends an acceptance reasonably believes that his message has been received. The offeror in such circumstances is clearly bound, because he will be estopped from saying that he did not receive the message of acceptance. It is his own fault that he did not get it. But if there should be a case where the offeror without any fault on his part does not receive the message of acceptance—yet the sender of it reasonably believes it has got home when it has not—then I think there is no contract.

My conclusion is, that the rule about instantaneous communications between the parties is different from the rule about the post. The contract is only complete when the acceptance is received by the offeror: and the contract is made at the place where the acceptance is received.

In a matter of this kind, however, it is very important that the countries of the world should have the same rule. I find that most of the European countries have substantially the same rule as that I have stated. Indeed, they apply it to contracts by post as well as instantaneous communications. But in the United States of America it appears as if instantaneous communications are treated in the same way as postal communications. In view of this divergence, I think that we must

159

consider the matter on principle: and so considered, I have come to the view I have stated, and I am glad to see that Professor Winfield in this country (55 *Law Quarterly Review*, 514), and Professor Williston in the United States of America (Contracts, § 82, p 239), take the same view . . ."

NOTES AND QUESTIONS

1. There can be no formal contract between two parties until there has been offer and acceptance. Yet what is the position if one of the parties thinks that there is a contract and incurs expenditure, or acts in some other way, in carrying out what he thinks is his contractual duty? Obviously, the person incurring the expenditure or doing the act cannot found any claim upon the non-existent contract; but he might be able to found a claim in some other area of the law of obligations. Much will depend upon the behaviour of the other party, as Denning L.J. indicates in his famous *obiter dictum* in *Entores*. Thus, if the other party is somehow at fault and this fault can be seen as a cause of the claimant's expenditure loss, a claim might lie in the tort of negligence, although the economic loss rule will present a serious obstacle (no duty of care) (UC&TO, pp.111–114). Alternatively, as we shall see, the claimant may be able to claim any benefit conferred on the other party via a quasi-contractual debt claim (see **1.3.5**). Another possibility, of course, is estoppel. Yet how can one be estopped from denying the existence of a contract? Does the existence of such an equitable principle confirm, yet again, that English law is based on promise rather than agreement?

2. Can a person be liable in damages for breach of a non-existent contract simply on the basis that such a person is estopped from denying the existence of a contract? If this kind of situation is possible, is it better to talk of equity awarding damages, or would such talk undermine the essence of the doctrine of estoppel?

3. Is *Entores* relevant for contractual negotiations carried out by fax? What about e-mail?

4. Why was the nephew in *Beswick* (see p.23) not estopped from denying the existence of an obligation to pay Mrs Beswick?

5. Does the posting rule apply to telex or e-mail communications? (See *Brinkibon Ltd v Stahag Stahl GmbH* (1983).)

6. One obvious difference between the PECL (and UNIDROIT) code provisions and Denning L.J.'s analysis in *Entores*, is that it would seem that there is an exception when the post is used: a contract is concluded when the acceptance is posted rather than received. However, this rule probably applies only when it is reasonable to use the post as a means of acceptance and when the offer itself does not contain a stipulation (express or implied) to the contrary (see *Holwell Security v Hughes* (1974)). One leading authority for the posting rule is *Household Fire Insurance v Grant* (1879), which is worth reading in the law

report not just for the majority judgments but equally for Bramwell L.J.'s dissent. One imagines that trying to prove that one has posted a letter of acceptance might be problematic on occasions.

FURTHER QUESTION

What is the position if the offeror stipulates a time limit for acceptance?

Principles of European Contract Law

"*Article 2:206 Time Limit for Acceptance*

(1) In order to be effective, acceptance of an offer must reach the offeror within the time fixed by it.
(2) If no time has been fixed by the offeror acceptance must reach it within a reasonable time.
(3) In the case of an acceptance by an act of performance under article 2:205(3), that act must be performed within the time for acceptance fixed by the offeror or, if no such time is fixed, within a reasonable time.

Article 2:207 Late Acceptance

(1) A late acceptance is nonetheless effective as an acceptance if without delay the offeror informs the offeree that he treats it as such.
(2) If a letter or other writing containing a late acceptance shows that it has been sent in such circumstances that if its transmission had been normal it would have reached the offeror in due time, the late acceptance is effective as an acceptance unless, without delay, the offeror informs the offeree that it considers its offer as having lapsed."

NOTE

See also UNIDROIT, arts 2.1.7–2.1.9.

QUESTIONS

1. Do you think these code provisions represent English law?

2. How would English law normally deal with the problem envisaged by PECL, art.2:207(2) (and UNIDROIT, art.2.1.9(2))?

4.3.7 Modified acceptance and battle of forms

The normal rule is that an acceptance, to be effective, must be in exact conformity with an offer.

Principles of European Contract Law

"Article 2:208 Modified Acceptance

(1) A reply by the offeree which states or implies additional or different terms which would materially alter the terms of the offer is a rejection and a new offer.
(2) A reply which gives a definite assent to an offer operates as an acceptance even if it states or implies additional or different terms, provided these do not materially alter the terms of the offer. The additional or different terms then become part of the contract.
(3) However, such a reply will be treated as a rejection of the offer if:

(a) the offer expressly limits acceptance to the terms of the offer; or
(b) the offeror objects to the additional or different terms without delay; or
(c) the offeree makes its acceptance conditional upon the offeror's assent to the additional or different terms, and the assent does not reach the offeree within a reasonable time.

Article 2:209 Conflicting General Conditions

(1) If the parties have reached agreement except that the offer and acceptance refer to conflicting general conditions of contract, a contract is nonetheless formed. The general conditions form part of the contract to the extent that they are common in substance.
(2) However, no contract is formed if one party:

(a) has indicated in advance, explicitly, and not by way of general conditions, that it does not intend to be bound by a contract on the basis of paragraph (1); or
(b) without delay, informs the other party that it does not intend to be bound by such contract.

(3) General conditions of contract are terms which have been formulated in advance for an indefinite number of contracts of a certain nature, and which have not been individually negotiated between the parties.

Article 2:210 Professional's Written Confirmation

If professionals have concluded a contract but have not embodied it in a final document, and one without delay sends the other a writing which purports to be a confirmation of the contract but which contains additional or different terms, such terms will become part of the contract unless:

(a) the terms materially alter the terms of the contract; or
(b) the addressee objects to them without delay."

NOTES

1. See also UNIDROIT, art.2.1.11.

162

2. Two types of problem can arise with respect to acceptances that do not conform to their offers. The first is a straightforward difference in the price: S offers to sell his car to B for £500, and B replies by "accepting" the offer for £450. According to English law and UNIDROIT, this is not a valid acceptance; it is a counter-offer, which S can either reject or accept. Moreover, in English law such a counter-offer destroys the original offer, and so if S rejects the £450 counter-offer, B cannot there and then accept the first offer for £500. But what if B replies to the £500 offer by stating that he accepts for £499 (because that is all the cash he has in his pocket)? In English law this probably is just as much a counter-offer which destroys the original offer; but in civil law thinking, as the two codes suggest, things may not be so simple. Because there is a general civilian principle in favour of contracts (rather than their non-existence), it may be that the £499 reply is enough to establish a contractual nexus, but with the option that S can deny the contract if he acts quickly.

3. The second problem is often called a "battle of forms" and largely concerns contracts between commercial organisations where each firm has its own standard-form contractual documents.

Butler Machine Tool Co Ltd v Ex-Cell-O Corporation [1979] 1 W.L.R. 401, CA

This was an action in debt by sellers of a machine in respect of an amount over and above the original sale price of the machine. The sellers claimed they were entitled to this extra sum as a result of a price variation clause contained in their original written offer of sale; but the buyers claimed that the contract was governed by their written acceptance form, which did not contain a price variation clause and which contained a tear-off acknowledgment slip which the claimants had returned. The Court of Appeal (Lord Denning M.R., Lawton and Bridge L.JJ.), allowing an appeal, held that the claimants were not entitled to recover.

Lord Denning M.R.: ". . . If those documents are analysed in our traditional method, the result would seem to me to be this: the quotation of May 23, 1969, was an offer by the sellers to the buyers containing the terms and conditions on the back. The order of May 27, 1969, purported to be an acceptance of that offer in that it was for the same machine at the same price, but it contained such additions as to cost of installation, date of delivery and so forth that it was in law a rejection of the offer and constituted a counter-offer. That is clear from _Hyde v Wrench_ (1840) 3 Beav 334. As Megaw J said in _Trollope & Colls Ltd v Atomic Power Constructions Ltd_ [1963] 1 WLR 333, 337: '. . . the counter-offer kills the original offer.' The letter of the sellers of June 5, 1969, was an acceptance of that counter-offer, as is shown by the acknowledgment which the sellers signed and returned to the buyers. The reference to the quotation of May 23 referred only to the price and identity of the machine . . .

I have much sympathy with the judge's approach to this case. In many of these cases our traditional analysis of offer, counter-offer, rejection, acceptance and so forth is out of date. This was observed by Lord Wilberforce in *New Zealand Shipping Co Ltd v AM Satterthwaite & Co Ltd* [1975] AC 154, 167. The better way is to look at all the documents passing between the parties—and glean from them, or from the conduct of the parties, whether they have reached agreement on all material points—even though there may be differences between the forms and conditions printed on the back of them . . .

Applying this guide, it will be found that in most cases when there is a 'battle of forms' there is a contract as soon as the last of the forms is sent and received without objection being taken to it . . . The difficulty is to decide which form, or which part of which form, is a term or condition of the contract. In some cases the battle is won by the man who fires the last shot. He is the man who puts forward the latest term and conditions: and, if they are not objected to by the other party, he may be taken to have agreed to them . . . In some cases, however, the battle is won by the man who gets the blow in first . . . There are yet other cases where the battle depends on the shots fired on both sides . . .

In the present case the judge thought that the sellers in their original quotation got their blow in first; especially by the provision that 'These terms and conditions shall prevail over any terms and conditions in the Buyer's order.' It was so emphatic that the price variation clause continued through all the subsequent dealings and that the buyer must be taken to have agreed to it. I can understand that point of view. But I think that the documents have to be considered as a whole. And, as a matter of construction, I think the acknowledgment of June 5, 1969 is the decisive document. It makes clear that the contract was on the buyers' terms and not on the sellers' terms: and the buyers' terms did not include a price variation clause . . ."

Lawton L.J.: ". . . In my judgment, the battle has to be conducted in accordance with set rules. It is a battle more on classical 18th century lines when convention decided who had the right to open fire first rather than in accordance with the modern concept of attrition . . .

. . . It cannot be said that the buyers accepted the counter-offer by reason of the fact that ultimately they took physical delivery of the machine. By the time they took physical delivery of the machine, they made it clear by correspondence that they were not accepting that there was any price escalation clause in any contract which they had made with the plaintiffs."

NOTE

This could well be a common event in the commercial world. One firm buys, say, raw materials from another firm, both companies using conflicting contractual documents, which in theory means that no contract can be concluded on the basis of the documents. The seller of the raw material delivers it to the buyer, who then uses it in its manufacturing process. The delivery and use will amount to a contract of sale, but on what terms? If no dispute ever arises then it probably does not matter; but the moment one party wishes to rely on a written term, the court will have to construct an offer, counter-offer and acceptance scenario, since it cannot simply say the whole contract is non-existent and void.

QUESTION

What if the sellers in *Butler* had inserted into their standard contract document the following clause: 'Acceptance on delivery of any machine supplied by us constitutes not just an unquestioning acceptance of all terms and conditions in our contractual sale document but the overriding of any term or condition whatsoever in any contractual document of the buyer which conflicts with our terms and conditions, even with respect to any buyer document apparently accepted by us after the issuing of our contractual document'?

4.3.8 Withdrawal of acceptance

It is possible for an acceptance to be revoked.

> *Unidroit Principles for International Commercial Contracts*
>
> *"Article 2.1.10 Withdrawal of Acceptance*
>
> An acceptance may be withdrawn if the withdrawal reaches the offeror before or at the same time as the acceptance would have become effective."

QUESTION

If this provision represented English law, would it not conflict with the posting rule? (Cf. *Countess of Dunmore v Alexander* (1830).)

4.3.9 Consensus ad idem

Offer and acceptance are not actually enough to constitute the formation of a binding contract. There must also be a mental element of consent flowing between the two parties. Thus if S one day writes to B offering to sell his car for £1,000, and B by chance happens to write to S offering to buy his car for £1,000, the two letters crossing in the post (cross-offers), there will not be a contract.

4.3.10 Absence of offer and acceptance

In *Gibson v Manchester CC* (1979) (see pp.139, 149), Lord Diplock suggests that there might be the odd exceptional situation where a contract can form without there being any offer and acceptance. In civilian systems, where the basis of contract is sufficient agreement rather than identifiable promises, such "exceptional" situations must be a real possibility, as the next extract seemingly confirms.

Principles of European Contract Law

"*Article 2:211 Contracts not Concluded through Offer and Acceptance*

The rules in this section apply with appropriate adaptations even though the process of conclusion of a contract cannot be analysed into offer and acceptance."

NOTE

There are one or two English cases where the conclusion of a contract cannot easily be analysed into offer and acceptance.

Clarke v Dunraven (The Satanita) **[1897] A.C. 59, HL**

This was an action by one yacht owner against another yacht owner for "all damages" arising out of the sinking of the claimant's yacht by the defendant's boat during a regatta. The defendant had argued that the damages payable were limited by a statute governing collisions at sea, but the Court of Appeal allowed the claimant to succeed. An appeal to the House of Lords (Lords Halsbury L.C., Herschell, Macnaghten, Shand and Davey) was dismissed.

Lord Herschell (House of Lords): ". . . I cannot entertain any doubt that there was a contractual relation between the parties to this litigation. The effect of their entering for the race, and undertaking to be bound by these rules to the knowledge of each other, is sufficient, I think, where those rules indicate a liability on the part of the one to the other, to create a contractual obligation to discharge that liability. That being so, the parties must be taken to have contracted that a breach of any of these rules would render the party guilty of that breach liable, in the language of rule 24, to 'pay all damages,' in the language of rule 32, to be 'liable for all damages arising therefrom.' The language is somewhat different in the two rules; but I do not think they were intended to have, with regard to payment or liability to damages, any different effect. It is admitted that the appellant broke one of those rules, and, having broken or disobeyed that rule, it is quite clear, on the assumption of a contract such as I have described, that there arose the liability to 'pay all damages,' or 'to be liable for all damages arising therefrom.' . . .

My Lords, it has been said that a contract such as the Court below have held to exist is a very unlikely contract for the parties to have entered into. I confess I am not satisfied of that either. The parties here are yacht-owners who are entering their yachts for a race in which other yachts will be engaged. I do not think there is anything extraordinary in their entering for that race upon the terms that they shall be liable for all damage, because the contract gives of course the correlative right of being entitled to all damage. The question to whom that contract would be an advantage would depend on the size of the injured vessel and the injuring vessel in the particular case, which could not be foreseen; therefore it does not seem to me extraordinary that a contract of this sort should be entered into. And again, whilst it is a most uncommon thing for merchant vessels engaged in an adventure to be actually navigated by the owner, that is not at all an uncommon thing in the case of yachts. Of course, if the yacht were navigated by the owner and there were negligent navigation, he would be liable for all damages; and that may have been a consideration which led to a contract of this description being made a condition of yachts entering for the race. It puts upon a level, upon an equality as regards liability to one another, a yacht which is being navigated by the owner and a yacht which is being navigated by some other person on his behalf or employed by him. Therefore, there seems to me to be nothing monstrous, nothing absurd, in the contract which has been held to exist by the Court below, which would justify this House, or any tribunal, in saying that the parties never could have intended to enter into a contract of this description, and that it must have some other interpretation. My Lords, I go no further than that—I do not know whether that was the reason—I do not care whether that was the reason why the provision in question was inserted; but when you seek to cut down what is the prima facie meaning of a contract, and to impose a limitation upon the general words which are used in it, if you seek to do so by considerations such as those which have been urged upon your Lordships with great force by the learned counsel for the appellant, then you must make it manifest that it is a contract which there could be no reasonable ground for the parties to have entered into."

QUESTIONS

1. Was the action really one for damages, or was it in effect one in debt on a contract?

2. Did the owner of *The Satanita* make a promise to the owner of the *Valkyrie*, or to the yacht club? Was the owner of the *Valkyrie* aware of any promise made to him by the owner of *The Satanita* when he entered into the regatta?

3. In *Beswick v Beswick* (1968) (see p.23), why did the buyer's promise to pay an annuity to the seller's wife not constitute a contract between the buyer and the wife? The buyer (the nephew) did in fact make one payment to the wife after Mr Beswick's death and the wife accepted this payment: could this not be seen as two acts confirming a contract between the nephew and the wife? Is this analysis any more artificial than the analysis in *Clarke v Dunraven*?

4. *Clarke v Dunraven* has been considered as a case raising problems about the existence of offer and acceptance as between the various entrants to the regatta. But is the analysis really any more complex or difficult than the one in *Carlill* (pp.149, 154)? Did not each entrant make an offer via the regatta form

167

to all other entrants that he would pay "all damages" if certain conditions were fulfilled, those conditions occurring in the case of the owners of the two yachts involved in the case?

5. What if the owner of a passing yacht, on seeing the race, simply decided to join in the fun but fouled one of the official entrants and sank her? Could the owner of the lost yacht sue the owner of the interloper for the whole of his damage, or would he be limited by the statutory provision?

6. What about the insurance position? Can you formulate a policy with respect to insurance, yachts and the regatta rules?

4.4 Certainty of terms

Even if an offer and an acceptance can be identified, it is possible that a contract might fail if there is not sufficient certainty as to the essential promises.

Unidroit Principles for International Commercial Contracts

"*Article 2.1.13 Conclusion of Contract Dependent on Agreement on Specific Matters or in a Specific Form*

Where in the course of negotiations one of the parties insists that the contract is not concluded until there is agreement on specific matters or in a specific form, no contract is concluded before agreement is reached on those matters or in that form.

Article 2.1.14 Contract with Terms Deliberately Left Open

(1) If the parties intend to conclude a contract, the fact that they intentionally leave a term to be agreed upon in further negotiations or to be determined by a third person does not prevent a contract from coming into existence.
(2) The existence of the contract is not affected by the fact that subsequently:

(a) the parties reach no agreement on the terms; or
(b) the third person does not determine the term, provided that there is an alternative means of rendering the term definite that is reasonable in the circumstances, having regard to the intention of the parties."

NOTE

In Roman law there could be no contract of sale unless the price had been fixed (*sine pretio nulla venditio est*: D.18.1.2.1). English law is more ambiguous.

168

Sale of Goods Act 1979 (c.54)

"8. Ascertainment of price

(1) The price in a contract of sale may be fixed by the contract, or may be left to be fixed in a manner agreed by the contract, or may be determined by the course of dealing between the parties.
(2) Where the price is not determined as mentioned in subsection (1) above the buyer must pay a reasonable price.
(3) What is a reasonable price is a question of fact dependent on the circumstances of each particular case.

9. Agreement to sell at valuation

(1) Where there is an agreement to sell goods on the terms that the price is to be fixed by the valuation of a third party, and he cannot or does not make the valuation, the agreement is avoided; but if the goods or any part of them have been delivered to and appropriated by the buyer he must pay a reasonable price for them.
(2) Where the third party is prevented from making the valuation by the fault of the seller or buyer, the party not at fault may maintain an action for damages against the party at fault."

Supply of Goods and Services Act 1982 (c.29)

"14. Implied term about time of performance

(1) Where, under a contract for the supply of a service by a supplier acting in the course of a business, the time for the service to be carried out is not fixed by the contract, left to be fixed in a manner agreed by the contract or determined by the course of dealing between the parties, there is an implied term that the supplier will carry out the service within a reasonable time.
(2) What is a reasonable time is a question of fact.

15. Implied term about consideration

(1) Where, under a contract for the supply of a service, the consideration for the service is not determined by the contract, left to be determined in a manner agreed by the contract or determined by the course of dealing between the parties, there is an implied term that the party contracting with the supplier will pay a reasonable charge.
(2) What is a reasonable charge is a question of fact."

QUESTIONS

1. Basil enters Tony's bookshop and orders a copy of Geoffrey's book, *My Hundred Favourite Tax Cases*. When the book arrives, Basil refuses to buy it

on the ground that its price of £250 is grossly unreasonable. Can Tony sue Basil for damages for breach of contract?

2. Pierre says to Geoffrey, "take whatever you please from my bookcase and pay me what you think it is worth". Geoffrey takes a copy of Domat's *Les Loix civiles dans leur ordre naturel*, but later tries to return it to Pierre on the ground that it is boring. Is there a binding contract to buy the book? (Cf. D.18.1.35.1.)

NOTE

The lack of any agreement over a price can be fatal.

Courtney Ltd v Tolaini Bros Ltd [1975] 1 W.L.R. 297, CA

This was an action for damages for breach of an alleged contract to employ the claimant, or at least to enter into negotiations with him. The judge held that there was such a contract, but an appeal to the Court of Appeal (Lord Denning M.R., Lord Diplock and Lawton L.J.) was allowed.

Lord Denning M.R.: "The question in this case is whether two letters give rise to a concluded contract.

Mr Tolaini, managing director of the defendants, wanted to develop a site in Hertfordshire. It was the Thatched Barn Hotel together with five acres of land. He got in touch with a property developer, a Mr Courtney, the managing director of the plaintiffs. It appears that Mr Courtney was well placed to obtain finance for building development. He was also a building contractor himself. The two met and discussed ways and means at the office of Mr Sacks, an architect. The proposal was that Mr Courtney should introduce some one to provide the money and lend it to Mr Tolaini. Mr Tolaini was to develop the site by building a motel and other things. But he was to employ Mr Courtney or his company to do the construction work . . .

. . . In the end Mr Tolaini did not employ Mr Courtney or his company to do the construction work. Mr Tolaini instructed other contractors and they completed the motel and other works. But then Mr Tolaini took advantage of the finance which Mr Courtney had made possible, but he did not employ Mr Courtney's company to do the work. Naturally enough, Mr Courtney was very upset. He has brought this action in which he says that there was a contract by which his company were to be employed as builders for the work, and it was a breach of contract by Mr Tolaini or his company to go elsewhere and employ somebody else . . .

I am afraid that I have come to a different view from the judge. The reason is because I can find no agreement on the price or on any method by which the price was to be calculated. The agreement was only an agreement to 'negotiate' fair and reasonable contract sums . . . All was left to be agreed in the future. It was to be agreed between the parties themselves. If they had left the price to be agreed by a third person such as an arbitrator, it would have been different. But here it was to be agreed between the parties themselves.

Now the price in a building contract is of fundamental importance. It is so essential a term that there is no contract unless the price is agreed or there is an agreed method of ascertaining it, not dependent on the negotiations of the two parties themselves. In a building contract both parties must know at the outset, before the work is started, what the price is to be, or, at all events, what agreed estimates are. No builder and no employer would ever dream of entering into a building contract for over £200,000 without there being an estimate of the cost and an agreed means of ascertaining the price . . ."

NOTE

In *May and Butcher v R* (1921), Viscount Dunedin said (at 21):

"To be a good contract there must be a concluded bargain, and a concluded contract is one which settles everything that is necessary to be settled and leaves nothing to be settled by agreement between the parties. Of course it may leave something which still has to be determined, but then that determination must be a determination which does not depend upon the agreement between the parties. In the system of law in which I was brought up, that was expressed by one of those brocards of which perhaps we have been too fond, but which often express very neatly what is wanted: 'Certum est quod certum reddi potest [What can be rendered certain is certain].' Therefore, you may very well agree that a certain part of the contract of sale, such as price, may be settled by some one else. As a matter of the general law of contract all the essentials have to be settled. What are the essentials may vary according to the particular contract under consideration."

QUESTIONS

1. Can a contract to contract never be a contract? (Cf. *Blackpool & Fylde Aero Club v Blackpool BC* (1990), at p.177.)

2. Paula, having seen John's house for sale for £400,000, says to John: "If you refrain from selling your house to anyone else but me, I will pay you the full asking price." John replies "OK." When John subsequently sells the house to Elsbeth for £415,000, can Paula sue John for damages?

4.5 Pre-contractual negotiations

A contract is normally concluded when a valid offer is validly accepted. Once formed the legal position is clear: the contract is binding (see UNIDROIT, art.1.3, p.385). The logic is also perfectly clear. Yet logic would further seemingly dictate that any negotiating behaviour which impacts upon the other party *before* the contract is formed *cannot* by definition result in *contractual* liability. The position is not so simple.

4.5.1 Negotiations in good faith

The principle of good faith (see **3.3** and **3.4**) has been extended in some civilian systems to the pre-contractual stage of contract. This development has been reflected in the following extract.

Principles of European Contract Law

"Article 2:301 Negotiations Contrary to Good Faith

(1) A party is free to negotiate and is not liable for failure to reach an agreement.
(2) However, a party who has negotiated or broken off negotiations contrary to good faith and fair dealing is liable for the losses caused to the other party.
(3) It is contrary to good faith and fair dealing, in particular, for a party to enter into or continue negotiations with no real intention of reaching an agreement with the other party.

Article 2:302 Breach of Confidentiality

If confidential information is given by one party in the course of negotiations, the other party is under a duty not to disclose that information or use it for its own purposes whether or not a contract is subsequently concluded. The remedy for breach of this duty may include compensation for loss suffered and restitution of the benefit received by the other party."

NOTES

1. See also UNIDROIT, arts 2.1.15–2.1.16.

2. It would appear that PECL, art.2.301(2) and UNIDROIT, art.2.1.15(2) do not represent English law.

Pitt v PHH Asset Management Ltd [1994] 1 W.L.R. 327, CA

Sir Thomas Bingham M.R.: ". . . For very many people their first and closest contact with the law is when they come to buy or sell a house. They frequently find it a profoundly depressing and frustrating experience. The vendor puts his house on the market. He receives an offer which is probably less than his asking price. He agonises over whether to accept or hold out for more. He decides to accept, perhaps after negotiating some increase. A deal is struck. Hands are shaken. The vendor celebrates, relaxes, makes plans for his own move and takes his house off the market. Then he hears that the purchaser who was formerly pleading with him to accept his offer has decided not to proceed. No explanation is given, no apology made. The vendor has to embark on the whole dreary process of putting his house on the market all over again.

For the purchaser the process is, if anything, worse. After a series of futile visits to unsuitable houses he eventually finds the house of his dreams. He makes an offer, perhaps at the asking price, perhaps at what the agent tells him the vendor is likely to accept. The offer is accepted. A deal is done. The purchaser instructs solicitors to act. He perhaps commissions an architect to plan alterations. He makes arrangements to borrow money. He puts his own house on the market. He makes arrangements to move. He then learns that the vendor has decided to sell to someone else, perhaps for the price already offered and accepted, perhaps for an increased price achieved by a covert, unofficial auction. Again, no explanation, no apology. The vendor is able to indulge his self-interest, even his whims, without exposing himself to any legal penalty.

The reasons why purchaser and vendor can act in this apparently unprincipled manner are to be found in two legal rules of long standing: first, the rule that contracts for the sale and purchase of land must be evidenced (or now made) in writing; secondly, the rule that terms agreed subject to contract do not give rise to a binding contract. These rules are deeply imbedded in statute and authority. They make possible the behaviour I have described, but the validity and merits of those rules are not, and could not be, the subject of challenge in this appeal.

For the purchaser there is, however, one means of protection: to make an independent agreement by which the vendor agrees for a clear specified period not to deal with anyone other than that purchaser. The effect is to give that purchaser a clear run for the period in question. The vendor does not agree to sell to that purchaser, such an agreement would be covered by section 2 of the [Law of Property (Miscellaneous Provisions) Act 1989], but he does give a negative undertaking that he will not for the given period deal with anyone else. That, I am quite satisfied, is what happened here, as the judge rightly held. The vendor and the prospective purchaser made what has come to be called a 'lock out agreement'. That was a contract binding on them both. The vendor broke it. He is liable to the prospective purchaser for damages which remain to be assessed. I would dismiss the appeal."

NOTES

1. Sir Thomas Bingham mentions two reasons why there is no contract. With respect to the first reason (the requirement for writing), see *Firstpost Homes v Johnson* (1995). The second reason is the "subject to contract" rule. This rule can be seen within a variety of contexts:

   (a) First, it can be seen as an application of the intention to create legal relations requirement (see **4.7**); the parties (or one party at least) do not intend a binding contract until formal exchange of contracts.

173

   (b) Secondly, it can be seen as a variation of the *consensus ad idem* rule (see **4.3.9**); the parties are not to be considered "at one" until exchange.

   (c) Thirdly, it could, perhaps, be seen in terms of the rule of certainty; there is no contract until all the major terms are agreed upon, and this does not happen formally until exchange of contracts (see **4.4**). Thus even if a party has "agreed" a price with a buyer, this price is not regarded as a certainty until exchange.

2. The point of raising these different contexts is that they are very important factual perspectives to contract. There are many relationships which are ambiguous: the 'contract' in which a price is yet to be fixed; the 'contract' where some further details are yet to be negotiated (see e.g. *May & Butcher Ltd v R.* (1934)); the 'contract' where parties have worked out all the terms in great detail but still do not as yet wish to be contractually bound. How should the law of obligations deal with these kinds of situations? If one party to a sale 'contract' has actually delivered the goods to the other party despite the fact that the two parties have not agreed a price, is there a contract? In many situations the question may not be that important; even if there were to be no contract the buyer will normally be liable in restitution to pay a reasonable sum (but see Sale of Goods Act 1979, s.8 and see *BSC v Cleveland Bridge* (1984) (at p.185)). But if there is no contract—as in the *Tolaini* case (see p.170) or in the pre-exchange period with respect to the sale of land—ought the parties to be under some kind of duty to each other? Clearly the PECL think that there should be a duty to negotiate in good faith.

3. However, the idea of a pre-contractual duty to negotiate in good faith seems to have been completely rejected by the House of Lords.

Walford v Miles [1992] 2 A.C. 128, HL

This was an action for damages for misrepresentation and breach of contract, brought by disappointed prospective purchasers of a business against the owners of the business who had eventually sold it, not to the plaintiffs, but to a third party. The plaintiffs claimed that the defendants had orally agreed to negotiate only with the plaintiffs and were thus in breach of this "lock-out" agreement when they sold the business to the third party. The trial judge awarded damages for breach of contract and misrepresentation, but a majority of the Court of Appeal allowed an appeal on the breach of contract decision. An appeal to the House of Lords (Lords Keith, Ackner, Goff, Jauncey and Browne-Wilkinson) was dismissed.

Lord Ackner: ". . . The [plaintiffs] relied upon an oral agreement, collateral to the negotiations which were proceeding to purchase the company and land it occupied 'subject to contract'. The consideration for this oral agreement was twofold—firstly the [plaintiffs] agreeing to continue the negotiations and not withdraw and secondly, their providing the comfort letter from their bankers in the terms requested . . .

As thus pleaded, the agreement purported to be what is known as a 'lock-out' agreement, providing the plaintiffs with an exclusive opportunity to try and come to terms with the defendants, but without expressly providing any duration for such an opportunity . . .

[Counsel for the plaintiffs] accepted that as the law now stands and has stood for approaching 20 years, an agreement to negotiate is not recognised as an enforceable contract. This was first decided in terms in *Courtney and Fairbairn Ltd v Tolaini Brothers (Hotels) Ltd* [1975] 1 WLR 297 . . .

Before your Lordships it was sought to argue that the decision in *Courtney's* case . . . was wrong. Although the cases in the United States did not speak with one voice your Lordships' attention was drawn to the decision of the United States' Court of Appeal, Third Circuit, in *Channel Home Centers, Division of Grace Retail Corporation v Grossman* (1986) 795 F 2d 291 as being 'the clearest example' of the American cases in the appellants' favour. That case raised the issue whether an agreement to negotiate in good faith, if supported by consideration, is an enforceable contract. I do not find the decision of any assistance. While accepting that an agreement to agree is not an enforceable contract, the Court of Appeal appears to have proceeded on the basis that an agreement to negotiate in good faith is synonymous with an agreement to use best endeavours and as the latter is enforceable, so is the former. This appears to me, with respect, to be an unsustainable proposition. The reason why an agreement to negotiate, like an agreement to agree, is unenforceable, is simply because it lacks the necessary certainty. The same does not apply to an agreement to use best endeavours. This uncertainty is demonstrated in the instant case by the provision which it is said has to be implied in the agreement for the determination of the negotiations. How can a court be expected to decide whether, subjectively, a proper reason existed for the termination of negotiations? The answer suggested depends upon whether the negotiations have been determined 'in good faith'. However the concept of a duty to carry on negotiations in good faith is inherently repugnant to the adverserial position of the parties when involved in negotiations. Each party to the negotiations is entitled to pursue his (or her) own interest, so long as he avoids making misrepresentations. To advance that interest he must be entitled, if he thinks it appropriate, to threaten to withdraw from further negotiations or to withdraw in fact, in the hope that the opposite party may seek to reopen the negotiations by offering him improved terms. [Counsel for the plaintiffs], of course, accepts that the agreement upon which he relies does not contain a duty to complete the negotiations. But that still leaves the vital question—how is a vendor ever to know that he is entitled to withdraw from further negotiations? How is the court to police such an 'agreement?' A duty to negotiate in good faith is as unworkable in practice as it is inherently inconsistent with the position of a negotiating party. It is here that the uncertainty lies. In my judgment, while negotiations are in existence either party is entitled to withdraw from those negotiations, at any time and for any reason. There can be thus no obligation to continue to negotiate until there is a 'proper reason' to withdraw. Accordingly, a bare agreement to negotiate has no legal content . . .

. . . I believe it helpful to make . . . observations about a so-called 'lock-out' agreement. There is clearly no reason in the English contract law why A, for good consideration, should not achieve an enforceable agreement whereby B, agrees for a specified period of time, not to negotiate with anyone except A in relation to the sale of his property. There are often good commercial reasons why A should desire to obtain such an agreement from B . . . But I stress that this is a negative agreement—B by agreeing not to negotiate for this fixed period with a third party, locks himself out of such negotiations. He has in no legal sense locked himself into negotiations with A. What A has achieved is an exclusive opportunity, for a fixed period, to try and come to terms with B, an opportunity for which he has, unless he makes his agreement under seal, to give good consideration . . ."

QUESTIONS

1. *Walford* is a very good case to compare with cases from civilian jurisdictions where, as the PECL indicate, the doctrine of good faith has been used to impose duties upon parties at a pre-contractual stage (see **3.3**). Why is it that English law insists upon a different approach: is it really because the doctrine is "unworkable"? What if A has expended much money on the basis that some kind of contract will be negotiated with B: ought B to be allowed to have the right to disregard completely the interests of A? Ought B to be free to pull out of negotiations without giving reasons? What if B is a public body?

2. Does *Walford* stipulate that there is no principle of pre-contractual liability in English law? Could *Walford* be an obstacle to the harmonisation of the law of obligations in the EU? (Cf. Lord Steyn (1997) 113 L.Q.R. 433.)

3. Is Lord Ackner's analysis of a lock-out agreement convincing? Is B's duty, in Lord Ackner's example, simply one not to negotiate with anyone else?

4. Can the courts imply a "lock-out" agreement? If so, might such an implication be based on reasonableness and fairness?

NOTES

1. Despite Lord Ackner's rejection of a duty to negotiate in good faith (and see also the *Tolaini* case, above at p.170), it would be a mistake to think that English law does not recognise the possible liability attaching to a person negotiating a contract. See **8.7** and in particular *Blackpool & Fylde v Blackpool BC* (1990) (p.177).

2. A contractor can also be liable for any misstatements (misrepresentations) made before contract which cause damage to the other party: see **5.2**.

3. The position with regard to confidential information, as set out in PECL, art.2.302 (and see also UNIDROIT, art.2.1.16), is different from any supposed duty to negotiate in good faith. Here, art.2.302 probably does go some way in representing the position in English law in as much as equity will certainly provide a remedy (see **8.8**). Thus in *Att.-Gen. v Guardian Newspapers Ltd (No.2)* (1990), Lord Goff said (at 281):

> "I realise that, in the vast majority of cases, in particular those concerned with trade secrets, the duty of confidence will arise from a transaction or relationship between the parties—often a contract, in which event the duty may arise by reason of either an express or an implied term of that contract. It is in such cases as these that the expressions 'confider' and 'confidant' are perhaps most aptly employed. But it is well settled that a duty of confidence may arise in equity independently of such cases; and I have expressed the circumstances in which the duty arises in broad terms, not merely to embrace those cases where a third party receives information from a person who is under a duty of confidence in respect of it, knowing that it has been disclosed by that person to him in breach of his duty of confidence, but also to include certain situations, beloved of law teachers—where an obviously confidential document is wafted by an electric fan out of a window into a crowded street, or where an obviously confidential document, such as a private diary, is dropped in a public place, and is then picked up by a passer-by. I also have in mind the situations where secrets of importance to national security come into the possession of members of the public."

4.5.2 Collateral contract

It is possible, as Sir Thomas Bingham indicates in *Pitt* (see **4.5.1**), that the negotiations between the parties at the pre-contractual stage are precise enough to give rise, in themselves, to a pre-contract contract—in other words, to a collateral contract (cf. *Carlill*, at p.149).

Blackpool & Fylde Aero Club Ltd v Blackpool **BC [1990] 1 W.L.R. 1195, CA**

Bingham L.J.: "In this action the plaintiffs ('the club') sued the defendants ('the council') for damages for breach of contract and common law negligence. It was in issue between the parties whether there was any contract between them and whether the council owed the club any duty of care in tort. These issues of liability came before Judge Jolly sitting as a judge of the Queen's Bench Division and he decided them both in favour of the club, all questions of quantum being deferred. The council appeal, contending that the judge was wrong on each point.

177

The council own and manage Blackpool Airport. For purposes of raising revenue they have made it a practice to grant a concession to an air operator to operate pleasure flights from the airport, no doubt largely for the entertainment of holiday-makers. The club, one of whose directors was and is a Mr Bateson, tendered for and were granted this concession in 1975 and again in 1978 and again in 1980. In 1983 the most recently granted concession was due to expire. The council accordingly prepared an invitation to tender. This was sent to the club and to six other parties, all of them in one way or another connected with the airport. This document was headed and began as follows:

'. . . The council do not bind themselves to accept all or any part of any tender. No tender which is received after the last date and time specified shall be admitted for consideration . . . '

Only three of the selected tenderers responded to the council's invitation. One put in a low bid for the lighter size of aircraft only. The second, Red Rose Helicopters Ltd, submitted a larger bid, also for the lighter size of aircraft. Mr Bateson for the club filled in the form of tender, submitting a bid substantially larger, on its face, than the others' for the lighter size of aircraft, and also submitting a bid for the heavier size. He put it in the envelope provided by the council, took it to the town hall and posted it in the town hall letter box at about 11 am on Thursday 17 March. This was about an hour before the advertised deadline expired. The town clerk's staff were supposed to empty the letter box each day at 12 o'clock. They failed to do so. The club's tender accordingly remained in the letter box until the next morning, 18 March, when the letter box was next opened. The envelope was then taken out and date-stamped 18 March 1983 by the town clerk's department. At some time thereafter the word 'late' was written on the envelope, because that is what the club's tender was mistakenly thought to be.

On 29 March 1983 the chairman of the council's relevant committee considered which tender to accept. The club's tender had been recorded as being late, and was in accordance with the council's standing orders excluded from consideration when the chairman made his decision. He accordingly made his choice between the two tenders believed to be in time, recommending acceptance of Red Rose Helicopters' tender, no doubt because it was bigger. An indication that its tender was accepted was given to Red Rose Helicopters. The town clerk wrote to the club to say that their tender was not received until 18 March and was therefore received too late for consideration. Mr Bateson replied that the club's tender had been delivered to the town hall before the deadline. 'You will appreciate,' he wrote, 'that this matter is of some considerable importance to our company.' The council evidently made inquiries and established that the club's tender had been received in time . . .

The judge resolved the contractual issue in favour of the club, holding that an express request for a tender might in appropriate circumstances give rise to an implied obligation to perform the service of considering that tender. Here, the council's stipulation that tenders received after the deadline would not be admitted for consideration gave rise to a contractual obligation, on acceptance by submission of a timely tender, that such tenders would be admitted for consideration . . .

Mr Toulson [counsel for the council] submitted that the warranty contended for by the club was simply a proposition 'tailor-made to produce the desired result' (per Lord Templeman in *CBS Songs Ltd v Amstrad Consumer Electronics Plc* [1988] AC 1013, 1059F) on the facts of this particular case. There was a vital distinction between expectations, however reasonable, and contractual obligations: see *per* Diplock LJ in *Lavarack v Woods of Colchester Ltd* [1967] 1 QB 278, 294. The club here expected its tender to be considered. The council fully intended that it should be. It was in both parties' interests that the club's tender should be considered. There was thus no need for them to contract. The court should not subvert well-understood contractual principles by adopting a woolly pragmatic solution designed to remedy a perceived injustice on the unique facts of this particular case . . .

I found great force in the submissions made by Mr Toulson and agree with much of what he said. Indeed, for much of the hearing I was of opinion that the judge's decision, although fully in accord with the merits as I see them, could not be sustained in principle. But I am in the end persuaded that Mr Toulson's argument proves too much. During the hearing the questions were raised: what if, in a situation such as the present, the council had opened and thereupon accepted the first tender received, even though the deadline had not expired and other invitees had not yet responded? Or if the council had considered and accepted a tender admittedly received well after the deadline? Mr Toulson answered that although by so acting the council might breach its own standing orders, and might fairly be accused of discreditable conduct, it would not be in breach of any legal obligation because at that stage there would be none to breach. This is a conclusion I cannot accept. And if it were accepted there would in my view be an unacceptable discrepancy between the law of contract and the confident assumptions of commercial parties, both tenderers (as reflected in the evidence of Mr Bateson) and invitors (as reflected in the immediate reaction of the council when the mishap came to light).

A tendering procedure of this kind is, in many respects, heavily weighted in favour of the invitor. He can invite tenders from as many or as few parties as he chooses. He need not tell any of them who else, or how many others, he has invited. The invitee may often, although not here, be put to considerable labour and expense in preparing a tender, ordinarily without recompense if he is unsuccessful. The invitation to tender may itself, in a complex case, although again not here, involve time and expense to prepare, but the invitor does not commit himself to proceed with the project, whatever it is; he need not accept the highest tender; he need not accept any tender; he need not give reasons to justify his acceptance or rejection of any tender received. The risk to which the tenderer is exposed does not end with the risk that his tender may not be the highest or, as the case may be, lowest. But where, as here, tenders are solicited from selected parties all of them known to the invitor, and where a local authority's invitation prescribes a clear, orderly and familiar procedure—draft contract conditions available for inspection and plainly not open to negotiation, a prescribed common form of tender, the supply of envelopes designed to preserve the absolute anonymity of tenderers and clearly to identify the tender in question, and an absolute deadline—the invitee is in my judgment protected at least to this extent: if he submits a conforming tender before the deadline he is entitled, not as a matter of mere expectation but of contractual right, to be sure that his tender will after the deadline be opened and considered in conjunction with all other conforming tenders or at least that his tender will be considered if others are. Had the club, before tendering, inquired of the council whether it could rely on any timely and conforming tender being considered along with others, I feel quite sure that the answer would have been 'of course'. The law would, I think, be defective if it did not give effect to that.

It is of course true that the invitation to tender does not explicitly state that the council will consider timely and conforming tenders. That is why one is concerned with implication. But the council do not either say that they do not bind themselves to do so, and in the context a reasonable invitee would understand the invitation to be saying, quite clearly, that if he submitted a timely and conforming tender it would be considered, at least if any other such tender were considered.

I readily accept that contracts are not to be lightly implied ... In all the circumstances of this case, and I say nothing about any other, I have no doubt that the parties did intend to create contractual relations to the limited extent contended for. Since it has never been the law that a person is only entitled to enforce his contractual rights in a reasonable way (*White and Carter (Councils) Ltd v McGregor* [1962] AC 413, 430A, per Lord Reid), Mr Shorrock was in my view right to contend for no more than a contractual duty to consider. I think it plain that the council's invitation to tender was, to this limited extent, an offer, and the club's submission of a timely and conforming tender an acceptance ...

I accordingly agree with the judge's conclusion on the contractual issue, essentially for the reasons which he more briefly gave.

This conclusion makes it unnecessary to consider at length the club's alternative argument, which the judge also accepted, that if there was no contract at all between the parties the council nonetheless owed the club a duty to take reasonable care to see to it that if the club submitted a tender by the deadline it would be considered along with other tenders duly returned when the decision to grant the concession was made . . .

I am reluctant to venture into this somewhat unvirginal territory when it is unnecessary to do so for the purpose of deciding this case. Having heard the argument, I am tentatively of opinion that Mr Toulson's objections are correct and that the club cannot succeed on this point if they fail on the other. But I do not think it necessary or desirable to express a final conclusion.

I would accordingly dismiss the appeal. The practical consequences of deciding the contractual issue on liability in the club's favour must, if necessary, be decided hereafter."

Stocker L.J.: . . . I . . . agree that in all the circumstances of this case there was an intention to create binding legal obligations if and when a tender was submitted in accordance with the terms of the invitation to tender, and that a binding contractual obligation arose that the club's tender would be before the officer or committee by whom the decision was to be taken for consideration before a decision was made or any tender accepted. This would not preclude or inhibit the council from deciding not to accept any tender or to award the concession, provided the decision was bona fide and honest, to any tenderer. The obligation was that the club's tender would be before the deciding body for consideration before any award was made. Accordingly, in my view, the conclusion of the judge and his reasons were correct . . ."

Farquharson L.J.: "I agree."

NOTES AND QUESTIONS

1. This rather extraordinary case is important for a whole range of reasons. First and foremost because it shows that knowledge of law is not simply a matter of knowing rules. Indeed this case seems to defy most of the settled contract rules (cf. *Tolaini* (1975), p.170), yet its process of reasoning is typical of the common law jurist. Bingham L.J. starts from within the facts and works outward towards the notion of an "expectation", which in turn, rather by sleight of hand, becomes a "right". This methodology does not consist of knowing rules and applying them to a set of facts; it starts out with a set of facts and finds the law within them (*ex facto jus oritur*, said a Post-Glossator of this kind of methodology: see the extracts from Roman law below at pp.448, 449). And if *Blackpool & Fylde* does nothing else, it certainly will prove a challenge to those who think that law is amenable to some existing Artificial Intelligence system. Can a *ratio decidendi* be drawn out of this decision?

2. Secondly, the case is important because it indicates the central role of the collateral contract in pre-contractual liability problems. There is the possibility that the court can turn the pre-contractual behaviour into an independent contract in itself. Is the case in effect an example of a contract to negotiate? What damage did the plaintiff suffer? Was it caused by the defendants?

3. Thirdly, the case is interesting because of the status of the defendant. No doubt the decision deserves its place in law of obligations books, but one may ask whether its real place is in works on administrative law. The duty attached to the procedures rather than to the transaction, and while Bingham L.J. recognised that a contracting party is under no duty to exercise his rights in a reasonable way, he nevertheless seems to be intervening to prevent an abuse of position. Note, also, how Stocker L.J. refers to *bona fides*. Public law, both in the case law and in statute, has recognised for some time now that a public body does not have the same contractual rights and liberties as a private person, particularly at the pre-contract stage (see e.g. *R. v Lewisham LBC Ex p. Shell UK* (1988)). If the defendant had been a private commercial body seeking tenders for a private commercial venture, would the result have been the same?

4. "The court should not subvert well-understood . . . principles by adopting a woolly pragmatic solution designed to remedy a perceived injustice on the unique facts of this particular case" (Toulson Q.C., Counsel for Blackpool BC). Did not the House of Lords do just this in *White v Jones* (1995) (C&MT, p.260)?

FURTHER NOTE

Collateral contracts have an important history and, as *Blackpool & Fylde* indicates, remain a means of providing a remedy. Such contracts were important when consumer protection law was not as robust at the statutory level as it is today: see, e.g., *Webster v Higgin* (1948) and *Andrews v Hopkinson* (1957). See also *Wells (Merstham) Ltd v Buckland Sand and Silica Ltd* (1964) and *The Eurymedon* (1975).

4.5.3 **Liability in tort**

The claimant in *Blackpool & Fylde* based its claim not just in contract but also in tort. If the Court had been unable to establish a contract, could the action have succeeded in the tort of negligence? One difficulty would have been to establish a duty of care given that the damage was pure economic loss (UC&TO, pp.112–113). Nevertheless, according to the precedent *Hedley Byrne & Co v Heller & Partners* (1964) (see p.234), a claim might be possible in situations where a defendant has made a negligent misstatement which causes damage to the claimant, provided there existed a special relationship between the two parties (see **1.3.2**). In order for such a relationship to exist there must be an *undertaking* (with respect to the statement made) of responsibility by the defendant vis-à-vis the claimant and *reliance* on this undertaking and statement by the claimant. Were these conditions fulfilled in *Blackpool & Fylde*? Given that both undertaking and reliance have in exceptional cases been interpreted in a liberal manner (*White v Jones* (1995), C&MT, p.260), tortious liability is not inconceivable, provided that the court was satisfied that it was fair and reasonable to impose such a duty of care.

Liability in tort is also possible where one party induces another to contract with him by way of misstatement. In such a situation negligence is now presumed (Misrepresentation Act 1967, s.2(1), below at p.237). But what if a person enters a shop or supermarket and is injured, for example, by slipping on a cabbage leaf or some spilt yoghurt? German judges developed the notion of *culpa in contrahendo* (fault in contracting) to cover this pre-contract of sale period; while French law, as we have seen (at p.90), extended the contract of sale backwards, so to speak, to cover an injury caused by an exploding bottle. What would English law do in this situation?

Ward v Tesco Stores Ltd [1976] 1 W.L.R. 810, CA

Lawton L.J.: "This is an appeal by the defendants from a judgment of His Honour Judge Nance given in the Liverpool County Court . . . whereby he adjudged that the plaintiff should recover against the defendants £178.50 damages and her costs . . . for personal injuries said to have been caused by the negligence of the defendants in the maintenance of the floor in their supermarket at Smithdown Road, Liverpool . . .

The plaintiff went round the store, carrying a wire basket, as shoppers are expected to do in supermarkets. She was doing her shopping at the back of the store when she felt herself slipping. She appreciated that she was slipping on something which was sticky. She fell to the ground, and sustained minor injuries. She had not seen what had caused her to slip. It was not suggested . . . that she had in any way been negligent in failing to notice what was on the floor as she walked along doing her shopping. When she was picking herself up she appreciated that she had slipped on some pink substance which looked to her like yoghourt. It was yoghourt. Later, somebody on the defendants' staff found a carton of yoghourt in the vicinity which was two-thirds empty . . .

That is all the plaintiff was able to prove, save for one additional fact. About three weeks later when she was shopping in the same store she noticed that some orange squash had been spilt on the floor. She kept an eye on the spillage for about a quarter of an hour. During that time nobody came to clear it up.

The trial judge was of the opinion that the facts which I have related constituted a prima facie case against the defendants. I infer that this case, which involves only a small amount of damages, has been brought to this court because the defendants are disturbed that any judge should find that a prima facie case is established merely by a shopper proving that she had slipped on a supermarket floor.

At the trial the defendants called some evidence . . . The defendants did not call any evidence as to when the store floor had last been brushed before the plaintiff's accident. It follows that there was no evidence before the court as to whether the floor had been brushed a few moments before the accident, or an hour, or possibly an hour and a half. The court was left without any information on what may have been an important matter . . .

In this case the floor of this supermarket was under the management of the defendants and their servants. The accident was such as in the ordinary course of things does not happen if floors are kept clean and spillages are dealt with as soon as they occur. If an accident does happen because the floors are covered with spillage, then in my judgment some explanation should be forthcoming from the defendants to show that the accident did not arise from any want of care on their part; and in the absence of any explanation the judge may give judgment for the plaintiff. Such burden of proof as there is on the defendants in such circumstances is evidential, not probative. The trial judge thought that prima facie this accident would not have happened had the defendants taken reasonable care. In my judgment he was justified in taking that view because the probabilities were that the spillage had been on the floor long enough for it to have been cleaned up by a member of the staff . . ."

Megaw L.J.: ". . . It is for the plaintiff to show that there has occurred an event which is unusual and which, in the absence of explanation is more consistent with fault on the part of the defendants than the absence of fault; and to my mind the learned judge was wholly right in taking that view of the presence of this slippery liquid on the floor of the supermarket in the circumstances of this case: . . . that if it should happen . . . it created a serious risk that customers would fall and injure themselves. When the plaintiff has established that, the defendants can still escape from liability . . . if they could show that the accident must have happened, irrespective of the existence of a proper and adequate system . . . to provide for the safety of customers . . . That, in this case, they wholly failed to do . . ."

Ormrod L.J. (dissenting): ". . . I do not think that it was established that this accident was caused by any want of care on the part of the defendants. The accident described by the plaintiff—and she did no more than describe the accident, namely that she slipped in some yoghourt which was on the floor of the supermarket—could clearly have happened no matter what degree of care these defendants had taken. The crucial question is how long before the accident the yoghourt had been on the floor . . ."

QUESTIONS

1. Does *Ward* actually lay down a rule? If so, what is the rule?

2. Why do the judges differ in *Ward*: is it because the majority focus on the operational *system* and the dissenting judge on the actual *yoghourt*?

3. Does *Ward v Tesco* indicate that facts are often much more important than law in the law of obligations?

NOTE

One reason why this case cannot be considered as contractual is the Occupiers' Liability Act 1957, which establishes a common duty of care in tort owed by an occupier of premises towards visitors (but was Mrs Ward injured by the state of the premises?). So statute provides the basis for any pre-contractual liability with respect to the state of shops, supermarkets, pubs, etc. Even without this statute the common duty of care would be provided either by *Donoghue v Stevenson* (1932) (C&MT, p.112) or by the Supply of Goods and Services Act 1982, s 13 (assuming one could construct a collateral contract between emporium and potential customer entering the premises). The 1957 Act equally applies even where there is a main contract: thus a person injured by a premises defect in a cinema or football ground will still have to base the claim on the 1957 Act.

4.5.4 Liability in restitution

A party which has been negotiating a contract may find itself liable in quasi-contract (unjust enrichment) even if no actual contract results from the negotiations.

> *British Steel Corporation v Cleveland Bridge & Engineering Co Ltd* **[1984] 1 All E.R. 504, QBD**
>
> This was a successful action in debt (*quantum meruit*) for work done, at the request of the defendants, in anticipation of a formal contract that never materialised. The defendants entered into negotiations with the claimants in respect of the manufacture of steel nodes, the former sending a letter of intent to the latter requesting the claimants to commence manufacture of the nodes immediately. The claimants began manufacturing and delivering the nodes, but no formal contract was ever agreed because the claimants were not prepared to accept the defendants' standard-form contract which contained an unlimited liability clause in respect of late delivery. The defendants counterclaimed for damages for breach of contract in respect of the late delivery of a batch of nodes, but the judge held that there existed no binding contract between the parties because the parties had not reached agreement on some material terms.
>
> > **Robert Goff J.:** ". . . Now the question whether in a case such as the present any contract has come into existence must depend on a true construction of the relevant communications which have passed between the parties and the effect (if any) of their actions pursuant to those communications. There can be no hard and fast answer to the question whether a letter of intent will give rise to a binding agreement: everything must depend on the circumstances of the particular case. In most cases, where work is done pursuant to a request contained in a letter of intent, it will not matter whether a contract did or did not come into existence, because, if the party who has acted on the request is simply claiming payment, his claim will usually be based on a *quantum meruit*, and it will make no difference whether that claim is contractual or quasi-contractual. Of course, a *quantum meruit* claim (like the old actions for money had and received and for money paid) straddles the boundaries of what we now call contract and restitution, so the mere framing of a claim as a *quantum meruit* claim, or a claim

for a reasonable sum, does not assist in classifying the claim as contractual or quasi contractual. But where, as here, one party is seeking to claim damages for breach of contract, the question whether any contract came into existence is of crucial importance.

As a matter of analysis the contract (if any) which may come into existence following a letter of intent may take one of two forms: either there may be an ordinary executory contract, under which each party assumes reciprocal obligations to the other; or there may be what is sometimes called an 'if' contract, i.e. a contract under which A requests B to carry out a certain performance and promises B that, if he does so, he will receive a certain performance in return, usually remuneration for her performance. The latter transaction is really no more than a standing offer which, if acted on before it lapses or is lawfully withdrawn, will result in a binding contract . . .

In my judgment, the true analysis of the situation is simply this. Both parties confidently expected a formal contract to eventuate. In these circumstances, to expedite performance under that anticipated contract, one requested the other to commence the contract work, and the other complied with that request. If thereafter, as anticipated, a contract was entered into, the work done as requested will be treated as having been performed under that contract; if, contrary to their expectation, no contract was entered into, then the performance of the work is not referable to any contract the terms of which can be ascertained, and the law simply imposes an obligation on the party who made the request to pay a reasonable sum for such work as has been done pursuant to that request, such an obligation sounding in quasi contract or, as we now say, in restitution. Consistently with that solution, the party making the request may find himself liable to pay for work which he would not have had to pay for as such if the anticipated contract had come into existence, e.g. preparatory work which will, if the contract is made, be allowed for in the price of the finished work . . . I only wish to add to this part of my judgment the footnote that, even if I had concluded that in the circumstances of the present case there was a contract between the parties and that that contract was of the kind I have described as an 'if' contract, then I would still have concluded that there was no obligation under that contract on the part of BSC to continue with or complete the contract work, and therefore no obligation on their part to complete the work within a reasonable time. However, my conclusion in the present case is that the parties never entered into any contract at all."

Regalian Properties Plc v London Dockland Development Corporation **[1995] 1 W.L.R. 212, Ch D**

This was an unsuccessful action for reimbursement of expenses incurred by a property company in carrying out preparatory works in respect of a contract that never materialised.

Rattee J.: ". . . I can well understand why Goff J [in *British Steel Corp v Cleveland Bridge and Engineering Co Ltd* [1984] 1 All E.R. 504] concluded that where one party to an expected contract expressly requests the other to perform services or supply goods that would have been performable or suppliable under the expected contract when concluded in advance of the contract, that party should have to pay a *quantum meruit* if the contract does not materialise. The present case is not analogous. The costs for which Regalian seeks reimbursement were incurred by it not by way of accelerated performance of the anticipated contract at the request of LDDC, but for the purpose of putting itself in a position to obtain and then perform the contract . . .

. . . I appreciate that the English law of restitution should be flexible and capable of continuous development. However, I see no good reason to extend it to apply some . . . principle . . . to facts such as those of the present case, where, however much the parties expect a contract between them to materialise, both enter negotiations expressly (whether by use of the words 'subject to contract' or otherwise) on terms that each party is free to withdraw from the negotiations at any time. Each party to such negotiations must be taken to know (as in my judgment Regalian did in the present case) that pending the conclusion of a binding contract any cost incurred by him in preparation for the intended contract will be incurred at his own risk in the sense that he will have no recompense for those costs if no contract results. In other words . . . each accepted that in the event of no contract being entered into, any resultant loss should lie where it fell . . ."

QUESTIONS

1. Is the *Cleveland* case an example of pre-contractual liability?

2. Compare and contrast *Cleveland* with *Blackpool & Fylde* (at p.177). Could the plaintiff in *Blackpool & Fylde* have sued on a quantum meruit for all the expenses incurred in preparing and submitting the tender?

4.6 Consideration

The second formal requirement, after offer and acceptance, for a valid contract in English law is consideration. The standard definition is: "A valuable consideration, in the sense of the law, may consist either in some right, interest, profit, or benefit accruing to one party, or some forbearance, detriment, loss, or responsibility, given, suffered, or undertaken by the other" (Lush J. in *Currie v Misa* (1875), at 162).

4.6.1 Benefit and detriment

As the next extract illustrates, the way consideration functions is to look at each of the parties and ask if each has (i) received a benefit, and (ii) suffered a detriment.

Carlill v Carbolic Smoke Ball Co **[1893] 1 Q.B. 256, CA**

(For facts, see p.149.)

A.L. Smith L.J.: ". . . [I]t was said that there was no consideration, and that it was *nudum pactum*. There are two considerations here. One is the consideration of the inconvenience of having to use this carbolic smoke ball for two weeks three times a day; and the other more important consideration is the money gain likely to accrue to the defendants by the enhanced sale of the smoke balls, by reason of the plaintiff's user of them. There is ample consideration to support this promise. I have only to add that as regards the policy and the wagering points, in my judgment, there is nothing in either of them . . ."

NOTES

1. Several distinctions need to be borne in mind with respect to the requirement of consideration. The first is the distinction between *consideration* and *performance* of the contract. When B enters a newsagent to buy a newspaper, it is tempting to think that the consideration consists of B handing over the money and S handing over the newspaper. Yet this is probably the wrong analysis given that such a contract is bilateral. The consideration is B's *promise* to pay the price in exchange for S's *promise* to pass title in the newspaper to S. The actual handing over of the money and the newspaper is the *performance* of the contract. Of course, in the world of factual reality, performance and promise often become one and the same, but in the world of contract the two must be kept separate. One can test this with reference to the gratuitous loan. B asks L to lend him £5 for the weekend, which L does: why is B contractually bound to repay the loan given the absence of any apparent benefit to L (except, of course, if L is charging interest)? The answer is because it is a question of promises: in the world of contract, L is promising B to lend him £5 if B promises to pay it back.

2. Accordingly, the second distinction to be borne in mind is the one between bilateral and unilateral contracts (cf. **3.1**). The above analysis applies only to bilateral contracts, because in a unilateral contract the consideration moving from the promisee is her *performance*. Thus, as we have seen, Mrs Carlill made no promise whatsoever; her consideration was the performance of using the medical product. Thus if D promises £5 reward to anyone who returns his lost cat "Tibbins", and C finds *and returns* Tibbins, then D must pay the £5 because a contract has come into existence with C's performance. Imagine, however, that C is a private cat detective and is contacted by D who hires him to search for Tibbins. This might well be a bilateral contract, and thus the consideration would be different: it would consist of C's promise to search for the cat in return for D's promise to pay his fee.

4.6.2 Validity of consideration

Yet another distinction is between *adequacy* and *sufficiency* of consideration. The rule here is that consideration need not be adequate but it must be sufficient. The general rule is that consideration must be of some economic value to be sufficient, but this value can be minimal. Thus if a chocolate company offers a "free" musical record in return for three wrappers from one of their chocolate bars, the three wrappers will be sufficient consideration to make this transaction a contract.

***Chappell & Co Ltd v Nestlé Co Ltd* [1960] A.C. 87, HL**

Lord Somervell: ". . . The question . . . is whether the three wrappers were part of the consideration or, as Jenkins LJ held, a condition of making the purchase, like a ticket entitling a member to buy at a co-operative store.

I think they are part of the consideration. They are so described in the offer. 'They,' the wrappers, 'will help you to get smash hit recordings.' They are so described in the record itself—'all you have to do to get such new record is to send three wrappers from Nestlé's 6d milk chocolate bars, together with postal order for 1s 6d' This is not conclusive but, however described, they are, in my view, in law part of the consideration. It is said that when received the wrappers are of no value to Nestlé's. This I would have thought irrelevant. A contracting party can stipulate for what consideration he chooses. A peppercorn does not cease to be good consideration if it is established that the promisee does not like pepper and will throw away the corn. As the whole object of selling the record, if it was a sale, was to increase the sales of chocolate, it seems to me wrong not to treat the stipulated evidence of such sales as part of the consideration. For these reasons I would allow the appeal."

Lord Reid: ". . . It seems to me clear that the main intention of the offer was to induce people interested in this kind of music to buy (or perhaps get others to buy) chocolate which otherwise would not have been bought. It is, of course, true that some wrappers might come from the chocolate which had already been bought or from chocolate which would have been bought without the offer, but that does not seem to me to alter the case. Where there is a large number of transactions—the notice mentions 30,000 records—I do not think we should simply consider an isolated case where it would be impossible to say whether there had been a direct benefit from the acquisition of the wrappers or not. The requirement that wrappers should be sent was of great importance to the Nestlé Co; there would have been no point in their simply offering records for 1s 6d each. It seems to me quite unrealistic to divorce the buying of the chocolate from the supplying of the records. It is a perfectly good contract if a person accepts an offer to supply goods if he (*a*) does something of value to the supplier and (*b*) pays money: the consideration is both (*a*) and (*b*). There may have been cases

---

where the acquisition of the wrappers conferred no direct benefit on the Nestlé Co., but there must have been many cases where it did. I do not see why the possibility that in some cases the acquisition of the wrappers did not directly benefit the Nestlé Co should require us to exclude from consideration the cases where it did. And even where there was no direct benefit from the acquisition of the wrappers there may have been an indirect benefit by way of advertisement . . ."

(Viscount Simonds and Lord Keith dissented.)

QUESTIONS

1. A manufacturer of chocolate bars states in an advert that it will "give away free copies of Camilla's hit song 'Rock Around the Law Reports' to any law student who dyes his or her hair green and sends in, with a photograph of their hair and proof that they are a law student, three wrappers from one of the company's chocolate bars". Esin sends in the photograph, proof and three chocolate wrappers: is there a contract between Esin and the manufacturer; and, if so, is it a conditional contract and what is the consideration? (Consider also *Esso v Customs & Excise* (1976), p.203.)

2. What if a person promises to do something that he is already legally obligated to do?

Williams v Roffey Brothers & Nicholls (Contractors) Ltd [1991] 1 Q.B. 1, CA

This was an action in debt brought by a carpenter for building work done pursuant to a promise to pay an extra sum of money, made by the defendant building contractor. The extra sum had been promised in return for the claimant completing within a specified time limit the refurbishment of 27 flats, a job the carpenter had already contracted to do and was already performing, for an agreed price of £20,000. The defendant claimed that the promise to pay the extra money was unsupported by consideration, but the Court of Appeal (Glidewell, Russell and Purchas L.JJ.) disagreed; the defendants had received a real benefit in return for their promise to pay more.

Glidewell L.J.: ". . . Mr Evans [counsel for the defendants] submits that, though his clients may have derived, or hoped to derive, practical benefits from their agreement to pay the 'bonus', they derived no benefit in law, since the plaintiff was promising to do no more than he was already bound to do by his subcontract, ie, continue with the carpentry work and complete it on time. Thus there was no consideration for the agreement. Mr Evans relies on the principle of law which, traditionally, is based on the decision in *Stilk v Myrick* (1809) 2 Camp 317. That was a decision at first instance of Lord Ellenborough CJ. On a voyage to the Baltic, two seamen deserted. The captain agreed with the rest of the crew that if they worked the ship back to London without the two seamen being replaced, he would divide between them the pay which would have been due to the two deserters. On arrival at London this extra pay was refused, and the plaintiff's action to recover his extra pay was dismissed. Counsel for the defendant argued that such an agreement was contrary to public policy, but Lord Ellenborough CJ's judgment was based on lack of consideration . . .

In *North Ocean Shipping Co Ltd v Hyundai Construction Co Ltd* [1979] QB 705, Mocatta J regarded the general principle of the decision in *Stilk v Myrick*, 2 Camp 317 as still being good law. He referred to two earlier decisions of this court, dealing with wholly different subjects, in which Denning LJ sought to escape from the confines of the rule, but was not accompanied in his attempt by the other members of the court . . .

Accordingly, following the view of the majority in *Ward v Byham* [1956] 1 WLR 496 and of the whole court in *Williams v Williams* [1957] 1 WLR 148 and that of the Privy Council in *Pao On* [1980] AC 614 the present state of the law on this subject can be expressed in the following proposition: (i) if A has entered into a contract with B to do work for, or to supply goods or services to, B in return for payment by B; and (ii) at some stage before A has completely performed his obligations under the contract B has reason to doubt whether A will, or will be able to, complete his side of the bargain; and (iii) B thereupon promises A an additional payment in return for A's promise to perform his contractual obligations on time; and (iv) as a result of giving his promise, B obtains in practice a benefit, or obviates a disbenefit; and (v) B's promise is not given as a result of economic duress or fraud on the part of A; then (vi) the benefit to B is capable of being consideration for B's promise, so that the promise will be legally binding . . ."

Russell L.J.: ". . . [W]hilst consideration remains a fundamental requirement before a contract not under seal can be enforced, the policy of the law in its search to do justice between the parties has developed considerably since the early 19th century when *Stilk v Myrick*, 2 Camp 317 was decided by Lord Ellenborough CJ. In the late 20th century I do not believe that the rigid approach to the concept of consideration to be found in *Stilk v Myrick* is either necessary or desirable. Consideration there must still be but, in my judgment, the courts nowadays should be more ready to find its existence so as to reflect the intention of the parties to the contract where the bargaining powers are not unequal and where the finding of consideration reflect the true intention of the parties . . ."

Purchase L.J.: ". . . In my judgment . . . the rule in *Stilk v Myrick*, 2 Camp 317 remains valid as a matter of principle, namely that a contract not under seal must be supported by consideration. Thus, where the agreement upon which reliance is placed provides that an extra payment is to be made for work to be done by the payee which he is already obliged to perform then unless some other consideration is detected to support the agreement to pay the extra sum that agreement will not be enforceable. The two cases, *Harris v Watson*, Peake 102 and *Stilk v Myrick*, 2 Camp 317 involved circumstances of a very special nature, namely the extraordinary conditions existing at the turn of the 18th century under which seamen had to serve their contracts of employment on the high seas. There were strong public policy grounds at that time to protect the master and owners of a ship from being held to ransom by disaffected crews. Thus, the decision that the promise to pay extra wages even in the circumstances established in those cases, was not supported by consideration is readily understandable. Of course, conditions today on the high seas have changed dramatically and it is at least questionable, as Mr Makey submitted, whether these cases might not well have been decided differently if they were tried today. The modern cases tend to depend more upon the defence of duress in a commercial context rather than lack of consideration for the second agreement. In the present case the question of duress does not arise . . . Nevertheless, the court is more ready in the presence of this defence being available in the commercial context to look for mutual advantages which would amount to sufficient consideration to support the second agreement under which the extra money is paid . . .

The question must be posed: what consideration has moved from the plaintiff to support the promise to pay the extra £10,300 added to the lump sum provision? In the particular circumstances which I have outlined above, there was clearly a commercial advantage to both sides from a pragmatic point of view in reaching the agreement of 9 April. The defendants were on risk that as a result of the bargain they had struck the plaintiff would not or indeed possibly could not comply with his existing obligations without further finance. As a result of the agreement the defendants secured their position commercially. There was, however, no obligation added to the contractual duties imposed upon the plaintiff under the original contract. Prima facie this would appear to be a classic *Stilk v Myrick* case. It was, however, open to the plaintiff to be in deliberate breach of the contract in order to 'cut his losses' commercially. In normal circumstances the suggestion that a contracting party can rely upon his own breach to establish consideration is distinctly unattractive. In many cases it obviously would be and if there was any element of duress brought upon the other contracting party under the modern development of this branch of the law the proposed breaker of the contract would not benefit. With some hesitation . . . I consider that the modern approach to the question of consideration would be that where there were benefits derived by each party to a contract of variation even though one party did not suffer a detriment this would not be fatal to the establishing of sufficient consideration to support the agreement. If both parties benefit from an agreement it is not necessary that each also suffers a detriment. In my judgment, on the facts as found by the judge, he was entitled to reach the conclusion that consideration existed and in those circumstances I would not disturb that finding. This is sufficient to determine the appeal . . ."

PROBLEM

Duncan invites tenders from a number of builders to build a heart-shaped luxury swimming pool in his garden in time for his planned huge party to celebrate a peerage (which he feels sure he will receive having made a large donation to the political party in power). Horatia puts in a tender for the lowest price, which Duncan promptly accepts, but as the summer approaches it is clear that the swimming pool will not be completed in time for the planned party. Horatia admits that she was careless in preparing the tender and that she has seriously miscalculated the costs. She goes on to suggest that she will have to abandon the contract in order to save herself from bankruptcy. Duncan, pointing out the extra income he will make once he is a peer, offers Horatia an additional sum of money if she continues and completes in time. Horatia agrees to continue, and manages to complete by the date stipulated in the original contract, but Duncan informs her that he has had to cancel the party, because no peerage was forthcoming, and that he will not now pay her the extra money because he will not now receive the vastly increased income he could have commanded if he was a peer. When Horatia threatens to sue, Duncan says that he will counter-claim for damages in negligence and for breach of contract. Would you advise Horatia to sue for the extra sum?

4.6.3 **Role of estoppel**

One way of perceiving *Roffey* (see **4.6.2**) is as a modification of contract problem: one party was agreeing to modify the price promised. As we shall see (**10.2**), English law does not recognise a specific doctrine of modification of an existing obligation, with the result that any further promise is regarded as a "new" promise requiring consideration in order to be enforceable at law. Where a contract remains unperformed (unexecuted) by both parties a new promise is unproblematic, because any changes will be regarded as a set of new promises—a new contract—replacing the old contract. Thus if S agrees to sell his car to B for £1,000 (ownership and possession to pass only on payment) and later, because B cannot raise that amount, S agrees to accept £800, then the first contract for £1,000 is discharged (by a discharge contract) and replaced by a second contract for £800 (new contract of sale), each party making a new promise and this exchange generating the required consideration.

However, a problem arises when one party has performed (executed) his promise but the other party has not. If the party who has performed agrees to a modification of the contract there is the possibility that he will gain no benefit, and thus his promise will not be based on a valid consideration. Accordingly, to go back to the car example, if S has delivered, and B has accepted delivery, of the car, he now of course owes S £1,000. If S subsequently agrees to accept £800 in full settlement, this will be a 'promise' unsupported by consideration, for while B benefits, S suffers only a detriment. The result is, at common law, that S, having accepted the £800, could in theory subsequently demand the extra £200. In other words, his promise to accept less, being unsupported by consideration, is unenforceable at common law. However, equity has intervened in this type of situation.

193

Central London Property Trust Ltd v High Trees House Ltd **[1957] 1 K.B. 130, KBD**

This was an action in debt by a landlord company against a tenant company claiming arrears of rent, for the year of 1945 only, in respect of a block of flats let during the war years. The arrears were based on the amount of rent payable as stipulated in the formal lease, but the tenant claimed that the landlord had agreed to take a reduced rent from 1941 because of the difficulty of letting the flats during the war.

> **Denning J.:** ". . . If I were to consider this matter without regard to recent developments in the law, there is no doubt that, had the plaintiffs claimed it, they would have been entitled to recover ground rent at the rate of £2,500 a year from the beginning of the term, since the lease under which it was payable was a lease under seal which, according to the old common law, could not be varied by an agreement by parol (whether in writing or not), but only by deed. Equity, however, stepped in, and said that if there had been a variation of a deed by a simple contract (which in the case of a lease required to be in writing would have to be evidenced by writing), the courts may give effect to it as is shown in *Berry v Berry*. That equitable doctrine, however, could hardly apply in the present case because the variation here might be said to have been made without consideration. With regard to estoppel, the representation made in relation to reducing the rent was not a representation of an existing fact. It was a representation, in effect, as to the future, namely, that payment of the rent would not be enforced at the full rate but only at the reduced rate. Such a representation would not give rise to an estoppel because, as was said in *Jorden v Money*, a representation as to the future must be embodied as a contract or be nothing.
>
> But what is the position in view of developments in the law in recent years? The law has not been standing still since *Jorden v Money*. There has been a series of decisions over the past 50 years which, although they are said to be cases of estoppel are not really such. They are cases in which a promise was made which was intended to create legal relations and which, to the knowledge of the person making the promise, was going to be acted on by the person to whom it was made, and which was in fact so acted on. In such cases the courts have said that the promise must be honoured . . . The logical consequence, no doubt, is that a promise to accept a smaller sum in discharge of a larger sum, if acted upon, is binding notwithstanding the absence of consideration: and if the fusion of law and equity leads to this result, so much the better . . .
>
> I am satisfied that a promise such as that to which I have referred is binding and the only question remaining for my consideration is the scope of the promise in the present case. I am satisfied on all the evidence that the promise here was that the ground rent should be reduced to £1,250 a year as a temporary expedient while the block of flats was not fully, or substantially fully let, owing to the conditions prevailing. That means that the reduction in the rent applied throughout the years down to the end of 1944, but early in 1945 it is plain that the

flats were fully let, and, indeed the rents received from them (many of them not being affected by the Rent Restrictions Acts), were increased beyond the figure at which it was originally contemplated that they would be let. At all events the rent from them must have been very considerable. I find that the conditions prevailing at the time when the reduction in rent was made, had completely passed away by the early months of 1945. I am satisfied that the promise was understood by all parties only to apply under the conditions prevailing at the time when it was made, namely, when the flats were only partially let, and that it did not extend any further than that. When the flats became fully let, early in 1945, the reduction ceased to apply.

In those circumstances, under the law as I hold it, it seems to me that rent is payable at the full rate for the quarters ending September 29 and December 25, 1945.

If the case had been one of estoppel it might be said that in any event the estoppel would cease when the conditions to which the representation applied came to an end, or it also might be said that it would only come to an end on notice. In either case it is only a way of ascertaining what is the scope of the representation. I prefer to apply the principle that a promise intended to be binding, intended to be acted on and in fact acted on, is binding so far as its terms properly apply. Here it was binding as covering the period down to the early part of 1945, and as from that time full rent is payable.

I therefore give judgment for the plaintiff company for the amount claimed."

QUESTIONS

1. Is this an example of equity modifying a contract? Did not the landlord have the contractual right to the full rent? Was the landlord in effect estopped in equity from abusing his common law right?

2. If the facts of *High Trees* arose again today, would recourse to equity still be necessary?

3. What if a party tries to "blackmail" the other party into accepting less than the contract price?

D & C Builders Ltd v Rees [1966] 2 Q.B. 617, CA

This was an action in debt by a firm of builders in respect of money owed for work done. The debtor argued that the plaintiffs had accepted a lesser figure in full and final settlement of the debt. The creditor argued that this lesser sum had been accepted only after the debtor had threatened to pay them nothing at a time when the firm was on the verge of bankruptcy. The Court of Appeal (Lord Denning M.R., Danckwerts and Winn L.JJ.) gave judgment in favour of the builders.

Lord Denning M.R.: ". . . This case is of some consequence: for it is a daily occurrence that a merchant or tradesman, who is owed a sum of money, is asked to take less. The debtor says he is in difficulties. He offers a lesser sum in settlement, cash down. He says he cannot pay more. The creditor is considerate. He accepts the proffered sum and forgives him the rest of the debt. The question arises: Is the settlement binding on the creditor? The answer is that, in point of law, the creditor is not bound by the settlement. He can the next day sue the debtor for the balance: and get judgment. The law was so stated in 1602 by Lord Coke in *Pinnel's* Case (1602) 5 Co Rep 117a—and accepted in 1889 by the House of Lords in *Foakes v Beer* (1884) 9 App Cas 605.

Now, suppose that the debtor, instead of paying the lesser sum in cash, pays it by cheque. He makes out a cheque for the amount. The creditor accepts the cheque and cashes it. Is the position any different? I think not. No sensible distinction can be taken between payment of a lesser sum by cash and payment of it by cheque. The cheque, when given, is conditional payment. When honoured, it is actual payment. It is then just the same as cash. If a creditor is not bound when he receives payment by cash, he should not be bound when he receives payment by cheque . . .

In point of law payment of a lesser sum, whether by cash or by cheque, is not discharge of a greater sum.

This doctrine of the common law has come under heavy fire. It was ridiculed by Sir George Jessel in *Couldery v Bartram* (1881) 19 Ch D 394 at p 399. It was said to be mistaken by Lord Blackburn in *Foakes v Beer*. It was condemned by the Law Revision Committee (Cmd 5449, 1945) paras 20 and 21. But a remedy has been found. The harshness of the common law has been relieved. Equity has stretched out a merciful hand to help the debtor. The courts have invoked the broad principle stated by Lord Cairns in *Hughes v Metropolitan Railway Co*.

> 'It is the first principle upon which all courts of equity proceed that if parties, who have entered into definite and distinct terms involving certain legal results, afterwards by their own act or with their own consent enter upon a course of negotiation which has the effect of leading one of the parties to suppose that the strict rights arising under the contract will not be enforced or will be kept in suspense, or held in abeyance, the person who otherwise might have enforced those rights will not be allowed to enforce them when it would be inequitable having regard to the dealings which have taken place between the parties.'

It is worth noticing that the principle may be applied, not only so as to suspend strict legal rights, but also so as to preclude the enforcement of them.

This principle has been applied to cases where a creditor agrees to accept a lesser sum in discharge of a greater. So much so that we can now say that, when a creditor and a debtor enter upon a course of negotiation, which leads the debtor to suppose that, on payment of the lesser sum, the creditor will not enforce payment of the balance, and on the faith thereof the debtor pays the lesser sum and the creditor accepts it as satisfaction: then the creditor will not be allowed to enforce payment of the balance when it would be inequitable to do so. This was well illustrated during the last war. Tenants went away to escape the bombs and left their houses unoccupied. The landlords accepted a reduced rent for the time they were empty. It was held that the landlords could not afterwards turn round and sue for the balance, see *Central London Property Trust Ltd v High Trees House Ltd*. This caused at the time some eyebrows to be raised in high places. But they have been lowered since. The solution was so obviously just that no one could well gainsay it.

In applying this principle, however, we must note the qualification: The creditor is only barred from his legal rights when it would be inequitable for him to insist upon them. Where there has been a true accord, under which the creditor voluntarily agrees to accept a lesser sum in satisfaction, and the debtor acts upon that accord by paying the lesser sum and the creditor accepts it, then it is inequitable for the creditor afterwards to insist on the balance. But he is not bound unless there has been truly an accord between them.

In the present case, on the facts as found by the judge, it seems to me that there was no true accord. The debtor's wife held the creditor to ransom. The creditor was in need of money to meet his own commitments, and she knew it. When the creditor asked for payment of the £480 due to him, she said to him in effect 'We cannot pay you the £480. But we will pay you £300 if you will accept it in settlement. If you do not accept it on those terms you will get nothing. £300 is better than nothing.' She had no right to say any such thing. She could properly have said: 'We cannot pay you more than £300. Please accept it on account.' But she had no right to insist on his taking it in settlement. When she said: 'We will pay you nothing unless you accept £300 in settlement', she was putting undue pressure on the creditor. She was making a threat to break the contract (by paying nothing) and she was doing it so as to compel the creditor to do what he was unwilling to do (to accept £300 in settlement): and she succeeded. He complied with her demand. That was on recent authority a case of intimidation: see *Rookes v Barnard* and *Stratford (JT) & Son Ltd v Lindley*. In these circumstances there was no true accord so as to found a defence of accord and satisfaction: see *Day v McLea*. There is also no equity in the defendant to warrant any departure from the due course of law. No person can insist on a settlement procured by intimidation.

In my opinion there is no reason in law or equity why the creditor should not enforce the full amount of the debt due to him. I would, therefore, dismiss this appeal."

NOTES AND QUESTIONS

1. *D & C Builders* is obviously a useful case to compare with *Williams v Roffey*. Why was the Court of Appeal prepared to find consideration in one but not in the other? Did the parties in *D & C Builders* not receive a benefit?

2. If the creditor's debt claim had failed in *D & C Builders*, would the defendant have been unjustly enriched? In which chapter in a book on the law of restitution (unjust enrichment) would you expect to find this case?

3. If the plaintiff in *D & C Builders* had suffered considerable financial loss as a result of the defendant's refusal to pay the full bill, could the plaintiff have sued for damages for breach of contract or for a tort? (Cf. *Wadsworth v Lydall* (1981), below at p.518.)

4. The workers at P's factory threaten to go on strike unless P agrees to pay them higher wages. P agrees to the demands because he wishes to fulfil an urgent order. After the order is fulfilled, P wishes to know if he is bound by the promise to pay higher wages. Advise.

5. Would the result of *Roffey* have been different if the defendant had simply threatened not to continue with the building work unless the plaintiff promised to pay more?

Williams v Roffey Brothers & Nicholls (Contractors) Ltd **[1991] 1 Q.B. 1, CA**

(For facts and further extracts, see p.190.)

Glidewell L.J.: ". . . It was suggested to us in argument that, since the development of the doctrine of promissory estoppel, it may well be possible for a person to whom a promise has been made, on which he has relied, to make an additional payment for services which he is in any event bound to render under an existing contract or by operation of law, to show that the promisor is estopped from claiming that there was no consideration for his promise. However, the application of the doctrine of promissory estoppel to facts such as those of the present case has not yet been fully developed . . .

There is, however, another legal concept of relatively recent development which is relevant, namely, that of economic duress. Clearly if a subcontractor has agreed to undertake work at a fixed price, and before he has completed the work declines to continue with it unless the contractor agrees to pay an increased price, the subcontractor may be held guilty of securing the contractor's promise by taking unfair advantage of the difficulties he will cause if he does not complete the work. In such a case an agreement to pay an increased price may well be voidable because it was entered into under duress. Thus this concept may provide another answer in law to the question of policy which has troubled the courts since before *Stilk v Myrick*, 2 Camp 317, and no doubt led at the date of that decision to a rigid adherence to the doctrine of consideration.

This possible application of the concept of economic duress was referred to by Lord Scarman, delivering the judgment of the Judicial Committee of the Privy Council in *Pao On v Lau Yiu Long* [1980] AC 614 . . ."

QUESTIONS

1. Why should the builder who promised the extra payment not be estopped from claiming that there was no consideration? Is not this kind of development to be found in *D & C Builders* (p.195) and *Entores* (p.158)?

2. Is *D & C Builders* (p.195) an economic duress case? (Cf. **6.2.**)

4.6.4 Estoppel and property rights: "contract" without consideration

Estoppel is said to be a shield and not a sword—that is to say, it is only a defence and not a cause of action. However, the doctrine can be used to create indirectly not just obligation (contract) rights but also property rights.

Crabb v Arun DC **[1976] Ch. 179, CA**

This was an action for a declaration that the plaintiff had a right of access over the defendants' land in order to reach one of his plots which no longer had an access owing to the sale of part of his land. The plaintiff claimed that he would not have gone ahead with the sale of part of his property if the council representative had not given the clear impression in discussions that the plaintiff would be granted access at point B. The council at first left a gap at point B, but later fenced it off, denying the plaintiff access unless he paid £3,000 for such a right. The Court of Appeal (Lord Denning M.R., Lawton and Scarman L.JJ.) granted the declaration.

Lord Denning M.R.: ". . . When counsel for Mr Crabb said that he put his case on an estoppel, it shook me a little, because it is commonly supposed that estoppel is not itself a cause of action. But that is because there are estoppels and estoppels. Some do give rise to a cause of action. Some do not. In the species of estoppel called proprietary estoppel, it does give rise to a cause of action. We had occasion to consider it a month ago in *Moorgate Mercantile Co Ltd v Twitchings* where I said that the effect of estoppel on the true owner may be that:

'his own title to the property, be it land or goods, has been held to be limited or extinguished, and new rights and interests have been created therein. And this operates by reason of his conduct—what he has led the other to believe—even though he never intended it.'

The new rights and interests, so created by estoppel in or over land, will be protected by the courts and in this way give rise to a cause of action . . .

The basis of this proprietary estoppel—as indeed of promissory estoppel—is the interposition of equity. Equity comes in, true to form, to mitigate the rigours of strict law. The early cases did not speak of it as 'estoppel'. They spoke of it as 'raising an equity' . . .

What then are the dealings which will preclude him from insisting on his strict legal rights? If he makes a binding contract that he will not insist on the strict legal position, a court of equity will hold him to his contract. Short of a binding contract, if he makes a promise that he will not insist upon his strict legal rights—even though that promise may be unenforceable in point of law for want of consideration or want of writing—and if he makes the promise knowing or intending that the other will act upon it, and he does act upon it, then again a court of equity will not allow him to go back on that promise: see *Central London Property Trust Ltd v High Trees House Ltd* and *Charles Rickards Ltd v Oppenheim*. Short of an actual promise, if he, by his words or conduct, so behaves as to lead another to believe that he will not insist on his strict legal rights—knowing or intending that the other will act on that belief—and he does so act, that again will raise an equity in favour of the other, and it is for a court of equity to say in what way the equity may be satisfied. The cases show that this equity does not depend on agreement but on words or conduct. In *Ramsden v Dyson* Lord Kingsdown spoke of a verbal agreement 'or what amounts to the same thing, an expectation, created or encouraged'. In *Birmingham and District Land Co v London and North Western Railway Co*, Cotton LJ said that '. . . what passed did not make a new agreement, but what took place . . . raised an equity against him' . . .

The question then is: were the circumstances here such as to raise an equity in favour of Mr Crabb? True the council on the deeds had the title to their land, free of any access at point B. But they led Mr Crabb to believe that he had or would be granted a right of access at point B . . .

The council actually put up the gates at point B at considerable expense. That certainly led Mr Crabb to believe that they agreed that he should have the right of access through point B without more ado . . .

The council knew that Mr Crabb intended to sell the two portions separately and that he would need an access at point B as well as point A. Seeing that they knew of his intention—and they did nothing to disabuse him, but rather confirmed it by erecting gates at point B—it was their conduct which led him to act as he did; and this raises an equity in favour against them . . ."

QUESTIONS

1. Did the claimant gain a *ius in rem* (property right) as a result of the injunction? Would a Continental lawyer classify this case in the law of obligations?

2. Was there not promise and consideration in this case?

3. To what extent can estoppel be used as a "cause of action"?

Amalgamated Investment & Property Co Ltd v Texas Commerce International Bank Ltd
[1982] Q.B. 84, CA

This was an action for a declaration brought by the liquidator of the plaintiff company that a guarantee given by the plaintiff did not cover a particular loan that had been made by the defendants, not actually to the plaintiff company directly, but to a subsidiary company of the plaintiff. The guarantee itself referred only to the plaintiff company and not the subsidiary, but it was assumed by both the plaintiff and the defendants that the guarantee would cover the actual loan. The Court of Appeal (Lord Denning M.R., Eveleigh and Brandon L.JJ.) held that the plaintiff was estopped from denying the guarantee.

> **Lord Denning M.R.:** ". . . The doctrine of estoppel is one of the most flexible and useful in the armoury of the law. But it has become overloaded with cases. That is why I have not gone through them all in this judgment. It has evolved during the last 150 years in a sequence of separate developments: proprietary estoppel, estoppel by representation of fact, estoppel by acquiescence, and promissory estoppel. At the same time it has been sought to be limited by a series of maxims: estoppel is only a rule of evidence, estoppel cannot give rise to a cause of action, estoppel cannot do away with the need for consideration, and so forth. All these can now be seen to merge into one general principle shorn of limitations. When the parties to a transaction proceed on the basis of an underlying assumption— either of fact or of law—whether due to misrepresentation or mistake makes no difference—on which they have conducted the dealings between them—neither of them will be allowed to go back on that assumption when it would be unfair or unjust to allow him to do so. If one of them does seek to go back on it, the courts will give the other such remedy as the equity of the case demands.
>
> That general principle applies to this case. Both the plaintiffs and the bank proceeded for years on the basis of the underlying assumption that the guarantee of the plaintiffs applied to the $3,250,000 advanced by the bank for the Nassau Building. Their dealings in rearranging the portfolio, in releasing properties and moneys, were all conducted on that basis. On that basis the bank applied the surplus of $750,000 (on the English properties) in discharge of the obligations of the plaintiffs under the guarantee. It would be most unfair and unjust to allow the liquidator to depart from that basis and to claim back now the $750,000 . . ."

QUESTION

Is it feasible—or could it ever be feasible—to talk of a person being liable to pay a debt or damages for breach of a contract that never actually existed at common law? Would such a contract be seen to "exist" in equity?

4.6.5 Present and past consideration

Yet another distinction that needs to me made is that between present and past consideration. In *Pao On v Lau Yiu Long* (1980), Lord Scarman, delivering the judgment of the Privy Council, said (at 629): "An act done before the giving of a promise to make a payment or to confer some other benefit can sometimes be consideration for the promise. The act must have been done at the promisors' request: the parties must have understood that the act was to be remunerated either by a payment or the conferment of some other benefit: and payment, or the conferment of a benefit, must have been legally enforceable had it been promised in advance." And he later said (at 630): "Their Lordships agree that the mere existence or recital of a prior request is not sufficient in itself to convert what is prima facie past consideration into sufficient consideration in law to support a promise: as they have indicated, it is only the first of three necessary preconditions." In other words, there must be a sufficient causal connection between a promise given and the act or past promise made which is to serve as the consideration for the promise given.

Thus if Horatia sees Geoffrey's cat "Tibbins" far from its home and returns it to Geoffrey, the latter being so grateful that he promises to buy Horatia a tee shirt, this promise is prima facie not supported by consideration. The act of returning the cat is said to be past consideration. The difficulty here, of course, is that such a rule seemingly threatens the enforceability of many professional transactions: often one person will do an act for another without specifically asking the other person if he agrees to that actual job. For example, a regular window cleaner might clean a person's windows, without getting specific permission for the job, but expecting to be paid all the same. If the owner of the house returns just after the job is completed and, being pleased, promises to send a cheque to the window cleaner, this will not be a matter of past consideration. For the window cleaner did the job *expecting* to be paid (whereas the act of returning Tibbins is probably one where the actor was not expecting to be paid).

4.7 Intention to create legal relations

The third formal requirement for a contract to come into existence is an intention to create legal relations. Here several situations must be distinguished:

(a) First, there are those situations where the "contractual" document (or other associated document) contains a statement or clause that the agreement will not be enforceable as a contract.

(b) Secondly, there are those situations where the context will determine whether or not there is an intention to create legal relations.

(c) Thirdly, there are a number of situations where the law, for reasons of policy or expediency, holds that there is no intention.

(d) Fourthly, statute may declare certain agreements to be unenforceable.

4.7.1 Specific denial of an intention

A document may contain a clause denying an intention to create legal relations. Thus in *Jones v Vernon's Pools Ltd* (1938), a football coupon contained an "honour clause" which stated: ". . . the sending in of the coupon or any transaction entered into in respect of the pool should not be attended by or give rise to any legal relationship, rights, duties or consequences whatsoever, or be legally enforceable or the subject of litigation, but that all such arrangements, agreements and transactions should be binding in honour only". It was held by the judge that there was no enforceable contract between pools company and a person claiming to be a winner. See also *Pitt v PHH Asset Management Ltd* (1994) (at p.172).

4.7.2 **Intention and context**

With respect to transactions occurring in a commercial and (or) consumer context, there is normally a presumption that there is an intention to create legal relations.

Esso Petroleum v Commissioners of Customs & Excise **[1976] 1 WLR 1, HL**

Viscount Dilhorne: "My Lords, the only question for decision in this appeal is whether the coins distributed by the respondents to garage proprietors, for them to give to customers who bought four gallons or more of petrol, were coins 'produced in quantity for general sale.' If they were, then they came within Group 25 in Schedule 1 to the Purchase Tax Act 1963, and the respondents are liable to pay purchase tax on them to the amount of some £200,000.

That the coins were produced in quantity and for general distribution is clear and not disputed. Were they produced for sale? They were sold by the respondents to some 4,900 retailers of petrol for £3 per thousand, but that does not determine the tax liability. The question to be decided is, were they sold or intended to be sold by the garage proprietors to purchasers of petrol? . . .

If the coins were a free gift to every customer who purchased four gallons of petrol or multiples of that quantity, then the appeal must be dismissed. If, on the other hand, a legal contract was entered into between the customer and the dealer which, in addition to the supply of petrol, involved the dealer in a legally binding obligation to transfer a coin or coins to the customer, and if that legal contract amounted to a sale, then the appeal must be allowed. . . .

If what was described as being a gift, which would be given if something was purchased, was something of value to the purchaser, then it could readily be inferred that there was a common intention to enter into legal relations. But here, whatever the cost of production, it is clear that the coins were of little intrinsic value.

I do not consider that the offer of a gift of a free coin is properly to be regarded as a business matter in the sense in which that word was used by Scrutton LJ . . .

Nor do I see any reason to impute to every motorist who went to a garage where the posters were displayed to buy four gallons of petrol any intention to enter into

---

a legally binding contract for the supply to him of a coin. On the acceptance of his offer to purchase four gallons there was no doubt a legally binding contract for the supply to him of that quantity of petrol, but I see again no reason to conclude that because such an offer was made by him, it must be held that, as the posters were displayed, his offer included an offer to take a coin. The gift of a coin might lead to a motorist returning to the garage to obtain another one, but I think the facts in this case negative any contractual intention on his part and on the part of the dealer as to the coin and suffice to rebut any presumption there may be to the contrary."

Lord Simon: ". . . I am, however, my Lords, not prepared to accept that the promotion material put out by Esso was not envisaged by them as creating legal relations between the garage proprietors who adopted it and the motorists who yielded to its blandishments. In the first place, Esso and the garage proprietors put the material out for their commercial advantage, and designed it to attract the custom of motorists. The whole transaction took place in a setting of business relations. In the second place, it seems to me in general undesirable to allow a commercial promoter to claim that what he has done is a mere puff, not intended to create legal relations (cf *Carlill v Carbolic Smoke Ball Co* [1893] 1 QB 256). The coins may have been themselves of little intrinsic value; but all the evidence suggests that Esso contemplated that they would be attractive to motorists and that there would be a large commercial advantage to themselves from the scheme, an advantage to which the garage proprietors also would share. Thirdly, I think that authority supports the view that legal relations were envisaged. . . .

. . . The law happily matches the reality. The garage proprietor is saying, 'If you will buy four gallons of my petrol, I will give you one of these coins.' None of the reasons which have caused the law to consider advertising or display material as an invitation to treat rather than an offer applies here. What the garage proprietor says by his placards is in fact and in law an offer of consideration to the motorist to enter into a contract of sale of petrol. Of course, not every motorist will notice the placard, but nor will every potential offeree of many offers be necessarily conscious that they have been made. However, the motorist who does notice the placard, and in reliance thereon drives in and orders the petrol, is in law doing two things at the same time. First, he is accepting the offer of a coin if he buys four gallons of petrol. Secondly, he is himself offering to buy four gallons of petrol: this offer is accepted by the filling of his tank . . ."

Lord Fraser (dissenting): ". . . I recognise that the reason why an advertisement or display of goods for sale at a stated price is only an invitation to treat and not an offer for sale (as explained by my noble and learned friend, Lord Russell of Killowen, in his speech) has no application to the advertisement of the coins, because the petrol retailer could always remove the advertisement if the supply of coins threatened to run out. But while that is so, I do not regard it as a sufficient reason for declining to recognise what seems to me a simple operation of acquiring four gallons of petrol and a coin as a sale of both articles in one transaction, nor as a reason for breaking it up into two separate operations, a sale of the petrol and a collateral contract for acquiring the coin. . . ."

Lord Russell: ". . . The subject matter was trivial: the proprietor was directly interested in the success of the scheme and would be in the highest degree unlikely to renege on the free gift offer, and indeed there is no suggestion that a motorist who qualified and wanted a medal ever failed to get one: from the motorist's viewpoint, if this had ever happened, I cannot think that he would have considered that he had a legal grievance, though he might have said that he would not patronise that outlet again: similarly in my opinion if a garage advertised 'Free Air' and after buying petrol or oil the motorist was told that the machine was out of order that day. In my opinion, the incentive for the garage proprietor to carry out the scheme was such as to make it quite unnecessary to invest, or for Esso to intend to invest, the transaction with the additional compulsion of a contractual obligation, and in all the circumstances of the case I am unable to regard that which under the scheme was intended by Esso to take place in relation to the medals, and did take place, as something which would be intended to or regarded as creating a legal contractual relationship. In forming that opinion I regard the minimal intrinsic value of a medal as important. I would not wish it to be thought that my opinion, if correct, would, in other cases in which a sales promotion scheme involves substantial benefits, give carte blanche to participants to renege on 'free' offers. I am simply of opinion, in agreement with the Court of Appeal, though not I fear with the majority of your Lordships, that in the instant case, because of the absence of any contractual element, it should not be said that any medal was produced for general sale."

QUESTIONS

1. If the top judges are unable to agree on the legal status of a fairly common consumer transaction, can there ever be any real certainty within the law of obligations with respect to the categorisation of facts and the application of the law?

2. Is the legal reasoning in this case effectively based on analogy and image: was the supply of the football coins analogous to the 'free air' sometimes offered by garages? Or was it a solid thing, capable of forming the object of a contract of sale? When a garage provides free air, is there a change of ownership in the air when a customer puts it in his tyre?

3. To what extent should triviality be a determinant of whether or not a transaction has legal status? Always, sometimes or never?

4. What if one of the coins subsequently proved to be dangerous when sucked by a child? If the child suffered serious injury, would he be able sue the garage and (or) Esso?

NOTE

The commercial context presumption can be rebutted.

Kleinwort Benson Ltd v Malaysia Mining Corporation Berhad **[1989] 1 W.L.R. 379, CA**

This was an appeal against an award of damages for breach of a contract said to arise out of a "comfort letter". The Court of Appeal (Fox, Ralph Gibson and Nicholls L.JJ.) allowed the appeal.

> **Ralph Gibson L.J.:** "This is an appeal by the defendants, Malaysia Mining Corporation Berhad, from the decision of Hirst J of 21 December 1987, by which the plaintiffs, Kleinwort Benson Ltd, obtained judgment for damages for breach of contract against the defendants for £12.26 million, including interest. The defendants ask that the judgment be set aside and that the plaintiffs' claim be dismissed on the ground that the defendants did not enter into any relevant contractual obligations to the plaintiffs. . . .
>
> The plaintiffs are merchant bankers of high reputation and long experience. The defendants are a public limited company incorporated under the laws of Malaysia in which the Republic of Malaysia has at all material times held a controlling interest. In 1983 the defendants caused to be incorporated under the laws of England a company, called MMC Metals Ltd ('Metals'), as a wholly owned but indirect subsidiary to operate as a ring dealing member of the London Metal Exchange. The paid up capital of Metals was £1.5 million. To carry out trading upon the London Metal Exchange much larger funds would be required. There were negotiations for the provision of funds by the plaintiffs to Metals. The plaintiffs sought from the defendants assurances as to the responsibility of the defendants for the repayment by Metals of any sums lent by the plaintiffs. A 'comfort letter' dated 21 August 1984 was provided by the defendants as part of an acceptance credit/multi-currency cash loan facility granted by the plaintiffs to Metals to a maximum of £5 million. That letter contained, among other statements, the assertion by the defendants that 'It is our policy to ensure that the business of [Metals] is at all times in a position to meet its liabilities to you under the above arrangements.' This case turns upon the proper construction, in its context, of that assertion by the defendants. In 1985 the facility was increased by the plaintiffs to a maximum of £10 million in reliance upon a second comfort letter, dated 7 May 1985, which was in substantially identical terms.
>
> . . . In my judgment the defendants made a statement as to what their policy was, and did not in paragraph 3 of the comfort letters expressly promise that such policy would be continued in future. It is impossible to make up for the lack of express promise by implying such a promise, and indeed, no such implied promise was pleaded. My conclusion rests upon what, in my judgment, are the proper effect and meaning which, on the evidence, are to be given to paragraph 3 of the comfort letters . . .

The concept of a comfort letter was, as Mr Stamler acknowledged, not shown to have acquired any particular meaning at the time of the negotiations in this case with reference to the limits of any legal liability to be assumed under its terms by a parent company . . . The comfort letter was drafted in terms which in paragraph 3 do not express any contractual promise and which are consistent with being no more than a representation of fact. If they are treated as no more than a representation of fact, they are in that meaning consistent with the comfort letter containing no more than the assumption of moral responsibility by the defendants in respect of the debts of Metals. There is nothing in the evidence to show that, as a matter of commercial probability or common sense, the parties must have intended paragraph 3 to be a contractual promise, which is not expressly stated, rather than a mere representation of fact, which is so stated.

As I have said, the absence of express words of promise does not by itself prevent a statement from being treated as a contractual promise. The example given in argument by Mr Waller, namely, of the shop stating by a notice that it is its policy to accept, within 14 days of purchase, the return in good condition of any goods bought, and to refund the price without question, seems to me to be a case in which a court would be likely to hold that the notice imported a promise that the policy would continue over the 14-day period. It would be difficult on those facts to find any sensible commercial explanation for the notice other than a contractual promise not to change the policy over the 14–day period. It would not be satisfactory or convincing to regard the notice as no more than the assumption of a moral responsibility by the shop giving such a notice to its customers. In such a case, and in the absence of any relevant factual context indicating otherwise, it seems to me that the court would probably hold that the statement was shown to have been intended to be a contractual promise.

In the present case, however, the opposite seems to me to be clear . . .”

NOTE

Questions of intention to create legal relations can become intertwined with questions of certainty and the like when what is at issue is an implied contract: see *Blackpool & Fylde Aero Club* (1990) (at p.177) and the next case.

Baird Textiles Holdings Ltd v Marks & Spencer plc **[2001] 1 All E.R. (Comm) 737, CA**

This was an action for damages brought by a supplier of clothes against a famous high-street chain store. The Court of Appeal (Sir Andrew Morrit V.C., Mance and Judge L.JJ.) held that the suppliers had no claim either in contract or based on estoppel.

Sir Andrew Morritt V.C.: “[1] Baird Textile Holdings Ltd (Baird) had been one of the principal suppliers of garments to Marks and Spencer plc (M&S) for 30 years when, on 19 October 1999, M&S, without warning, determined all supply arrangements between them with effect from the end of the then current production season. On 10 January 2000 Baird commenced these proceedings against M&S, contending that M&S was precluded by both contract and estoppel from determining such arrangements without reasonable notice. M&S applied under CPR 24.2 for summary judgment against Baird on the ground that it had no reasonable prospect of succeeding on either claim. On 29 June 2000 Morison J dismissed the claim in so far as it was based on contract but directed that it proceed to trial in so far as it was based on estoppel. Each party appeals, with the permission of Morison J, from that part of his order which is against it. Accordingly the issues which arise are whether Baird has a real prospect of succeeding on its claim based on (1) contract, and (2) estoppel, or, if not, whether there is some other compelling reason why that claim or issue should be disposed of at a trial. . . .

[30] I agree with the conclusion of the judge. The alleged obligation on M&S to acquire garments from Baird is insufficiently certain to found any contractual obligation because there are no objective criteria by which the court could assess what would be reasonable either as to quantity or price. This is not a case in which, the parties having evidently sought to make a contract, the court seeks to uphold its validity by construing the terms to produce certainty. Rather it is a case in which the lack of certainty confirms the absence of any clear evidence of an intention to create legal relations. The allegation in para 9.28 also confirms the lack of intention to create legal relations, for if there had been the requisite certainty because of the objective criteria, then to that extent there would have been a detailed contract and a loss of flexibility. It cannot be said, let alone with confidence, that the conduct of the parties is more consistent with the existence of the contract sought to be implied than with its absence. The implication of the alleged contract is not necessary to give business reality to the commercial relationship between M&S and Baird. In agreement with the judge, I do not think that Baird has a real prospect of success on its claim in contract. . . .

[38] In my view English law, as presently understood, does not enable the creation or recognition by estoppel of an enforceable right of the type and in the circumstances relied on in this case. First, it would be necessary for such an obligation to be sufficiently certain to enable the court to give effect to it. That such certainty is required in the field of estoppels such as is claimed in this case as well as in contract was indicated by the House of Lords in *Woodhouse AC Israel Cocoa Ltd SA v Nigerian Produce Marketing Co Ltd*, [1972] AC 741 and by Ralph Gibson LJ in *Troop v Gibson* [1986] 1 EGLR 1 at 6. For the reasons I have already given I do not think that the alleged obligation is sufficiently certain. Second, in my view, the decisions in the three Court of Appeal decisions on which M&S rely do establish that such an enforceable obligation cannot be established by estoppel in the circumstances relied on in this case. This conclusion does not involve the categorisation of estoppels but is a simple application of the principles established by those cases to the obligation relied on in this. I do not consider

that any of the dicta in the line of cases relied on by Baird could entitle this court to decline to apply those principles.

[39] Counsel for M&S was, at one stage, inclined to concede that if we considered that the House of Lords, after the facts had been found at a trial, might adopt the propositions formulated by Mason CJ, Wilson and Brennan JJ in the *Waltons Stores* case, then it might be said that there was a real prospect of succeeding on the estoppel issue so that judgment under CPR 24.2 should not be given at this stage. In reply he submitted that the possibility that the House of Lords might adopt those propositions was an inadequate reason for allowing a trial. I agree. If I am right in believing that English law, as it now stands, does not permit the enforcement of an estoppel in the form alleged in this case then it is the duty of this court to apply it, notwithstanding that it may be developed by the House of Lords, who are not bound by any of the cases relied on, in the future. . . ."

Mance L.J.: ". . . **[61]** An intention to create legal relations is normally presumed in the case of an express or apparent agreement satisfying the first requirement: see *Chitty on Contracts* (28th edn, 1999) vol 1, para 2–146. It is otherwise when the case is that an implied contract falls to be inferred from parties' conduct: *Chitty*, para 2–147. It is then for the party asserting such a contract to show the necessity for implying it. As Morison J. said in his para.12(1), if the parties would or might have acted as they did without any such contract, there is no necessity to imply any contract. It is merely putting the same point another way to say that no intention to make any such contract will then be inferred. . . .

[68] When the suggested long-term contract is put in these terms, it becomes clear that it would, in case of any dispute, involve the court writing a 'reasonable' contract for the parties, after making a complete review of their situations, needs, abilities and expectations. It could only become relevant to seek to identify the impact of such long-term obligations in a situation where actual co-operation had broken down or one or the other party wanted to reduce its commitment to the minimum. So the court would be expected to undertake the exercise in the very situation where the parties' actual behaviour could no longer serve as a guide to the answer. I agree with the Vice-Chancellor that this is not an exercise that the court can or should undertake, or, indeed, which the parties can objectively be taken to have intended. The presence in the suggested contractual formulation of implied duties of good faith is an additional barrier in the way of the conclusion for which Baird contends, in view of English law's general refusal to recognise any duty of this nature as an implied contractual term.

[69] Objectively, the only sensible analysis of the present situation is in my judgment that the parties had an extremely good long-term commercial relationship, but not one which they ever sought to express, or which the court would ever seek to express, in terms of long-term contractual obligations. The upshot is that I agree with the judge's conclusion that there was never here any agreement on essentials . . . .

[77] For all these reasons, therefore, I consider that the judge was correct to rule that Baird had no real prospect of success in establishing the contract pleaded in para 9. . . ."

QUESTIONS

1. How might this case have been decided if the PECL applied to it?

2. Does this case suggest indirectly that *Blackpool & Fylde* might have been wrongly decided, or are there some important differences between the two cases?

3. Do you think that the long-term relationship between Baird and M&S ought to have been given greater recognition by the law of obligations?

NOTE

With respect to promises and agreements made within the family, there is a presumption that there is no intention to create legal relations: see *Jones v Padavatton* (1969) (p.75). The presumption can, of course, be rebutted.

Simpkins v Pays [1955] 1 W.L.R. 975, Chester Assizes

This was an action by a claimant who had participated in a newspaper competition, to recover one-third of the prize money won by the defendant in whose name the competition coupon had actually been entered.

Sellers J.: "Happily this is an unusual type of case to come before a court of law, and it arises out of what seems to be a popular occupation of the public—taking part in a competition run by a Sunday newspaper. In this particular case there was a contest, No 397, in the Sunday Empire News, of June 27, 1954, whereby readers were invited to place in order of merit, attraction or beauty, eight fashions, or articles of attire. Both the plaintiff and the defendant, along with the defendant's granddaughter, Miss Esme Pays, sent in a coupon with three forecasts on it. The middle line of the second forecast was successful and won the prize of £750. This action is brought to recover one-third of that amount, £250. . . .

It may well be there are many family associations where some sort of rough and ready thing is said which would not, on a proper estimate of the circumstances, establish a contract which was contemplated to have legal consequences, but I do not so find here. I think there was here a mutuality in the arrangement between the parties. It was not very formal, but certainly in effect it was agreed that every week the forecast should go in in the name of the defendant, and that if there was success, no matter who won, all should share equally. That seems to be the implication from or the interpretation of what was said, that this was in the nature of a very informal syndicate so that they should all get the benefit of success. It would be equally wrong, I think, to say from what was arranged that because the granddaughter's forecast was the one which was successful of those submitted by the defendant that the plaintiff and the defendant were to get nothing. Although she was not a party before the court and I have not had the benefit of her evidence, as far as I can see, on this arrangement she would be as entitled to the third share as the others, certainly, so far as the plaintiff is concerned. Esme was not, apparently, present when this bargain was made, but both the others knew, at any rate soon after the outset, that she was coming in. It is possible, of course, although the plaintiff is not concerned in it, that the granddaughter's effort was only to assist the defendant, her grandmother. She may accept that, but it makes no difference, so far as I can see, to the fact that the plaintiff and the defendant entered into an agreement to share. The plaintiff does not seek to say: 'Esme was only aiding Mrs Pays,' in asking for half the shares, but she was entitled to one-third, and I so find and give judgment to the amount of £250."

QUESTIONS

1. Do you think this case is still an important precedent half a century later? (Clue: think lottery.)

2. What if the person in whose name a competition coupon was to be entered carelessly forgot to post the coupon: could those others who had contributed to competition coupon sue him or her for damages for loss of a chance of winning? What if it became evident that the coupon would have won had it been posted?

4.7.3 Policy and statute

The courts may refuse to recognise an intention to create legal relations for reasons of policy and (or) because the relationship is covered by statute.

Norweb plc v Dixon **[1995] 1 W.L.R. 636, QBD Div. C**

Dyson J.: ". . . I deal first with the general question whether an agreement for the supply of electricity between a tariff customer and a public electricity supplier (i.e. not a special agreement within the meaning of section 22) is a contract. . . .

. . . [T]here are . . . cases in which a relationship created by legal compulsion is clearly not contractual. Thus a person whose property is compulsorily acquired against his will does not make a contract with the acquiring authority, even though he receives compensation: see *Sovmots Investments Ltd v Secretary of State for the Environment* [1977] QB 411, 443. In Pfizer Corporation v Ministry of Health [1965] AC 512 the House of Lords held that a patient to whom medicines are supplied under the National Health Service does not make a contract to buy them either from the chemist or the Minister of Health even if he pays a subscription charge. The transaction is sui generis, the creation of statute and not a sale pursuant to a contract.

The issue in this case is: which side of the line does the relationship between a tariff customer and a public electricity supplier fall? In my judgment, the legal compulsion as to both the creation of the relationship and the fixing of its terms is inconsistent with the existence of a contract . . .

The justices were of the opinion that, if there was no contract between the parties, there would be no basis in law for the supplier to recover debts owed to it. In my view, they were mistaken. Paragraph 1(1) of Schedule 6 gives the supplier the power to recover any charges due to it. There is, therefore, no need to have recourse to contract.

I have already mentioned *Willmore v South Eastern Electricity Board* [1957] 2 Lloyd's Rep 375. In that case, electricity was supplied by the defendant electricity board to the plaintiffs. It was alleged by the plaintiffs that the defendant was in breach of its contract to supply adequate current. The claim was put on the basis of breach of a term of the supply agreement, and in the alternative breach of a collateral warranty. Dealing with the first point, Glyn-Jones J said, at p 380:

> 'I am unable to accept Mr Lawson's arguments based upon the language of the application form. It seems to me significant that the supply for which the consumer applies is expressed to be "subject to the conditions imposed by statute, order or regulation with respect to supplies of electricity by the board." I have come to the conclusion that Mr Jukes is right and that I ought to treat the supply of electricity by the board not as the acceptance of an offer by the plaintiffs to take and pay for a supply, so as to create a contract, but as given in pursuance of the board's statutory duty to give a supply to any consumer who, being entitled, demands it.'

Mrs Cover submits that that authority is distinguishable since the statutory obligation to supply electricity was different from that under consideration in the present case. That is, of course, true, but our attention was not drawn to any provisions of the Electricity Act 1947 which are materially different from the provisions of the Act of 1989. In my view, that case was correctly decided. . . .

It must follow that there was no contract between the appellants and the respondent, nor was the debt claimed under a contract. That is because, in the absence of any findings to support a special agreement, the relationship between the appellants and the respondent (both actual and claimed) could only be that of public electricity supplier/tariff customer. For the reasons already given, in my view such a relationship is not founded in contract. . . ."

(McCowen L.J. agreed.)

QUESTIONS

1. What is the policy in play in this case? Ought not this judicial policy to have changed with privatisation?

2. Do you think a "National Health Service contract" is a contract at common law? (Cf. National Health Service and Community Care Act 1990, s.4.)

NOTE

Some statutory provisions can specifically negative any intention to create legal relations.

Trade Union and Labour Relations (Consolidation) Act 1992 (c.52)

"*179. Whether agreement intended to be legally enforceable contract*

(1) A collective agreement shall be conclusively presumed not to have been intended by the parties to be a legally enforceable contract unless the agreement—

(a) is in writing, and
(b) contains a provision which (however expressed) states that the parties intend that the agreement shall be a legally enforceable contract.

(2) A collective agreement which does satisfy those conditions shall be conclusively presumed to have been intended by the parties to be a legally enforceable contract."

4.8 Formal requirements

At common law a contract, in order to be enforceable, requires only offer and acceptance, consideration and an intention to create legal relations. However, with respect to certain contracts, statute requires that they also be in writing and perhaps conform to certain other formal requirements: see e.g. *Wilson v First County Trust* (2004) (at p.44). One of the most important classes of contracts which need to be in writing are contracts for the sale of land or an interest in land.

Law of Property (Miscellaneous Provisions) Act 1989 (c.34)

"*2. Contracts for sale etc of land to be made by signed writing*

(1) A contract for the sale or other disposition of an interest in land can only be made in writing and only by incorporating all the terms which the parties have expressly agreed in one document or, where contracts are exchanged, in each.

> (2) The terms may be incorporated in a document either by being set out in it or by reference to some other document.
>
> (3) The document incorporating the terms or, where contracts are exchanged, one of the documents incorporating them (but not necessarily the same one) must be signed by or on behalf of each party to the contract. . . ."

NOTE

See *Firstpost Homes v Johnson* (1995).

4.9 Note on capacity

In French contract law capacity is one of the essential elements for the formation of contract (CC art.1108). In English law capacity is, on the whole, not an essential requirement but a vitiating factor, in as much as it will normally render a contract only voidable and not void (cf. **5.1**). However, in the case of corporate incapacity (*ultra vires*) the contract will be void, and thus it could be said that it is something of a foundational condition.

5 Obstacles to formation and vitiating factors (1): misrepresentation and mistake

In systems where contract is based on agreement rather than promise (see **4.1**), any obstacle that prevents a meeting of the minds must logically prevent the formation of a contract. Such obstacles are principally mistake, fraud and duress. Accordingly, these three vitiating factors are seen as problems attaching to the formation of contracts. In systems where contract is based on *causa* or on promise the same logic does not necessarily apply, for it does not follow that a promise given under a mistake or induced by fraud, or even made under duress, is necessarily void. The cause or promise itself might remain valid even if the mistake, fraud or duress acts as a focal point for certain legal remedies. Thus in the common law, as Robert Goff L.J. once observed (see p.31), vitiating factors like fraud are not treated as part of the formation of the contract as such. Nevertheless, they do often attach as a matter of fact to the giving of the contractual promise, and so it will be useful, for comparative law purposes, to treat them as an aspect of formation. One should add that mistake, fraud (including misrepresentation) and duress are not the only vitiating factors: incapacity and illegality can equally be seen as factors that affect the validity of a contract. These topics will, then, also be dealt with under the heading "Obstacles to formation" (**Chapter 6**).

5.1 Void, voidable and unenforceable contracts

Before examining in substance the different vitiating factors, it is important to distinguish at the outset between the *effects* that a factor might have on a contract.

5.1.1 Void contracts

Sometimes a vitiating factor like mistake can make a contract *void*.

Islington LBC v Uckac **[2006] 1 W.L.R. 1303, CA**

Dyson L.J.: ". . . **25** In my judgment, Mr Arden's submissions must be rejected largely for the reasons given by Mr Seitler. It is important to keep in mind the fundamental difference between a contract which is void and one which is voidable. A void contract is strictly a contradiction in terms, because if an agreement is truly void, it is not a contract; but the term is a useful one and well understood by lawyers: see *Chitty on Contracts*, 29th ed (2004), para 1–070. A contract which is void is no contract at all. Since it never exists, it is not something which, to use the language of section 82(1) of the 1985 Act, can be 'brought to an end' . . ."

NOTE

The various vitiating factors do not impact on contract in the same way. Some, like mistake, *might* on occasions result in no contract forming, with the result that such a "contract" is said to be *void*. As Dyson L.J. points out, such an expression is a contradiction in terms because the "contract" is one that never existed. To draw an analogy with marriage, a void marriage is one where the partners were never married even if they thought that they were. Most void contracts do result from a serious defect at the formation stage.

Shogun Finance Ltd v Hudson **[2004] 1 A.C. 919, HL**

Lord Millett (dissenting): ". . . **63** It is trite law, as Devlin LJ explained . . . that before a contract can come into existence there must be offer and acceptance, and these must correspond. The offer must be addressed to the offeree, either as an individual or as a member of a class or of the public. The acceptance must come from one who is so addressed and must itself be addressed to the offeror. It is not possible in law for a person to accept an offer made to someone else; or to intercept an acceptance of someone else's offer and treat it as an acceptance of his own . . ."

(See also extract from Lord Phillips on p.147; for facts, see p.265.)

NOTES

1. Imagine the following situation. Louis, who is extremely short-sighted, wishes to marry Horatia, and accordingly makes a proposal to a woman whom he believes to be Horatia. In fact the woman to whom he has made the proposal is not Horatia but Camilla, who is pretending to be Horatia. Camilla, imitating Horatia's voice, accepts the proposal. It is not difficult to conclude that no binding contract to marry would come into existence between Louis and Camilla. No contractual bond could form because there is no *consensus ad idem*. It is like two cross-offers passing each other in the post. This marriage example is an extreme situation of course, but it is a useful analogy

for testing whether a purported contract should be treated as having come into existence.

2. The point can be of the utmost importance on occasions, because contract, as we have seen (**1.3.3**), acts as a means of conveying ownership in moveable property. If a purported contract of sale turns out to be void, this has as a logical consequence that any conveyance is equally void, with the result that a "buyer" never becomes owner of the goods "bought" even if he obtains possession of them. Now, like all logic, everything depends upon the premise from which one starts; accordingly there is nothing to stop a legal system asserting that even if a contract is void, ownership can still pass thanks to law of property rules. Roman law said just this (see e.g. D.41.1.36; C.2.3.20) and this model has been adopted by German law (and see also Brazilian CC, art.620). In France the position at first sight looks identical to that of English law: the contract itself passes ownership (CC arts 1138, 1583). However, the French Civil Code has an article which states that "in the case of movables, possession is equivalent to title" (CC art.2279); consequently, a third party who buys in good faith from a possessor who is not the actual owner will nevertheless prima facie get good title.

5.1.2 Voidable contracts

Most vitiating factors, like misrepresentation, duress and undue influence, make a contract *voidable*.

Islington LBC v Uckac [2006] 1 W.L.R. 1303, CA

Dyson L.J.: ". . . 26 A contract may be voidable *inter alia* for misrepresentation. A contract which is voidable exists until and unless it is set aside by an order of rescission made by the court at the instance of a party seeking to terminate it or bring it to an end. A representee who has been induced by misrepresentation, whether fraudulent, negligent or innocent, to enter into a contract with the representor has, on discovery of the true facts, a right of election: he may affirm or disaffirm the contract: *Halsbury's Laws of England*, 4th ed, vol 31 (2003 reissue), para 784. If the representee affirms the contract, then he loses his right to rescind and the contract continues to have full force and effect. If he disaffirms and seeks to bring the contract to an end, the court may make an order of rescission, but in some circumstances will refuse to do so. If the contract is rescinded, then the contract is avoided *ab initio*: it is treated as if it never had effect. But that is not to say that, until it is rescinded, it does not have effect. None of this is controversial law. But it needs to be emphasised, because it is important to have in mind the fundamental difference between contracts which are void and those which are voidable . . ."

NOTES

1. The right to rescind is actually the result, historically and conceptually, of the existence of a remedy in equity called rescission in equity (see **12.3**), whereby the Chancellor would set aside a contract if he felt that it would be inequitable to allow enforcement of it. A good example of this remedy is to be found in the case of *Credit Lyonnais Bank Nederland v Burch* (1997) (above, at p.34); the contract was perfectly valid at common law (and thus not *void*), but it was inequitable in equity and thus *voidable* via rescission in equity. The important property point to be made with respect to a voidable contract is that, because a contract comes into existence and remains valid until rescinded, title to goods can pass. Thus if S sells to B a car under a voidable contract, and B soon after resells the car to C, C will get good title.

2. A useful guide, therefore, is to say that void contracts are a matter for the common law (did the contract exist?), while voidable contracts are a matter for equity (rescission). This division may not be perfect, as some judgments suggest that rescission is now a remedy available at common law as well as in equity (see e.g. *Halpern v Halpern (No.2)* (2006)) and certainly contracts can be voidable under statute: see, e.g., the Companies Act 1985, s.322A. But it might be helpful to the student to think in terms of rescission arising from a vitiating factor (misrepresentation, duress and undue influence) as being a matter for equity. One should note, however, that the right to "rescission" arising from the serious breach of a contract (see **10.4**) is a common law remedy to be clearly differentiated from any right to rescind arising from a vitiating factor.

5.1.3 Unenforceable contracts

Certain vitiating factors, in particular illegality, may result in contracts that are neither void nor voidable. Instead they are *unenforceable*. The idea of a contract being unenforceable is based on the distinction, which goes back to Roman law, between a right (*jus*) and a remedy (*actio*): a contract might exist at the level of rights but the courts will refuse to enforce such a right at the level of remedies (cf. **11.1**). In appearance such contracts may seem at first sight similar to void ones, and indeed statute on occasion uses the expression "void" when it may probably mean "unenforceable" (but see the Surrogacy Arrangements Act 1985, s.1A; Financial Services and Markets Act 2000, s.26).

Shell UK Ltd v Lostock Garage Ltd **[1976] 1 W.L.R. 1187, CA**

(For facts, see p.367.)

Lord Denning M.R.: ". . . It is said that 'a covenant in restraint of trade is invalid *ab initio*, or valid *ab initio*. There cannot come a moment at which it passes from the class of invalid into that of valid covenants': see *Gledhow Autoparts Ltd v Delaney* [1965] 1 WLR 1366, 1377 by Diplock LJ. But there is a fallacy in this argument. It is a mistake to say that a covenant in unreasonable restraint of trade is 'invalid' or 'void' *ab initio*. It is nothing of the sort. It is only unenforceable. Lord Reid made this clear in *Esso Petroleum Co Ltd v Harper's Garage (Stourport) Ltd* [1968] AC 269, 297, when he said:

> 'One must always bear in mind that an agreement in restraint of trade is not generally unlawful if the parties choose to abide by it: it is only unenforceable if a party chooses not to abide by it.'

And all the members of the House were careful to use the word 'unenforceable' rather than 'void' or 'invalid': see Lord Morris at p 304: Lord Hodson at p 321: Lord Pearce at p 324: and Lord Wilberforce at p 333.

Once it is recognised that the covenant itself is not invalid or void, but only unenforceable, the position becomes clear. It operates in two situations. First, when *at the time of* making the contract, it is seen that it may *in the future* operate unfairly or unreasonably, the courts will not enforce it. Secondly, when it is found *afterwards* to operate unreasonably or unfairly—in circumstances which were not envisaged beforehand—the courts will not enforce it. At the time of making the contract, the court has to speculate whether or not the restraint will operate unfairly or unreasonably: but if it afterwards turns out to have operated in fact unfairly or unreasonably, there is no need to speculate. The facts are known. The court never speculates as to what may happen when it knows for certain what has happened: see *Williamson v John L Thornycroft & Co Ltd* [1940] 2 KB 658. The court should, therefore, not enforce a covenant in restraint of trade if circumstances afterwards arise in which it would be unreasonable or unfair to enforce it. This reasoning finds its exact parallel in the modern law as to exemption clauses, already in contracts for the sale of goods, and it may be extended to other fields as well. In the sale of goods, a party is not entitled to rely on an exemption clause which is seen at the time of the contract to be unfair or unreasonable. In addition, he is not entitled to rely on an exemption clause which, although superficially reasonable at the time of the contract, nevertheless is prayed in aid in circumstances when it is unfair or unreasonable for him to rely on it: see the Supply of Goods (Implied Terms) Act 1973, bringing a new section 55A into section 55 of the Sale of Goods Act 1893: and the *Second Report of the Law Commission and the Scottish Law Commission on Exemption Clauses* (1975) (Cmnd. 605), in paragraphs 178 to 183, pp 69–71, which are well worth reading in this context: and my own few words in *Gillespie Bros & Co Ltd v Roy Bowles Transport Ltd* [1973] QB 400, 415–416.

Applying this test, what do we find here? Shell stipulated in 1966 that the garage owner should be tied to Shell and buy petrol only from Shell for five years at the schedule price (less a rebate) and should keep open the garage all day and every day during that time. That stipulation appeared superficially to be fair and reasonable at the time of the contract in 1966. But at the end of 1975, Shell started to subsidise two neighbouring Shell garages to such an extent that they were able to, and did, undercut Lostock. This meant that customers would flock to the other two Shell garages and not buy from Lostock at all: unless Lostock reduced their prices to a competitive level, and this would cause Lostock serious loss. To insist on the tie in these circumstances—and forcing Lostock to keep open paying wages to men—was most unfair and unreasonable. So much so that I think the courts should decline to enforce it. At any rate, they should not enforce it so long as Shell operated their support scheme to the prejudice of Lostock. This was the view of the judge and I agree with it . . ."

NOTES

1. Lord Denning's "novel" view did not attract support from the other members of the Court of Appeal in this case. But it is extracted here because it brings out the difference between a "void" and an "unenforceable" contract. One reason for distinguishing between void and unenforceable contracts is that unenforceability allows the law to be more flexible, especially with regard to those contracts regulated by statute: see, e.g., the Consumer Credit Act 1974, s.127.

2. Statute seems to recognise a distinction between void and unenforceable contracts: see, e.g., the Property Misdescriptions Act 1991, s.1(4).

3. Another important reason for distinguishing between a void and an unenforceable contract is with respect to property rights. In a void sale contract, as we have stated, no title can pass, but this may not be true with respect to an unenforceable contract. Because the contract exists at the level of rights, this may be enough to allow title to pass.

Singh v Ali [1960] A.C. 167, PC

Lord Denning: "The plaintiff, Sardara Ali, is a lorry-driver living at No 132, Lorong Panjang, Malacca. The defendant, Sajan Singh, is a haulier living at Bukit Asahan Estate, Malacca. The two of them entered into an illegal transaction about a lorry. They broke the regulations which governed the transfer and use of motor-vehicles. The question is what are their rights consequent on this illegality . . .

It is not, perhaps, strictly accurate to say that the action was laid in trespass. It was an action for a declaration coupled with a claim in detinue. In order to get a declaration, it was essential for the plaintiff to show that he was the owner of the lorry, and that it was an authorised vehicle. In order to succeed in detinue, it was essential for the plaintiff to show that he had the right to immediate possession of the lorry at the time of commencing the action, arising out of an absolute or special property in it; see Bullen & Leake, 3rd ed (1868), p 312. And in detinue their Lordships think he succeeded. Although the transaction between the plaintiff and the defendant was illegal, nevertheless it was fully executed and carried out: and on that account it was effective to pass the property in the lorry to the plaintiff. There are many cases which show that when two persons agree together in a conspiracy to effect a fraudulent or illegal purpose—and one of them transfers property to the other in pursuance of the conspiracy—then, so soon as the contract is executed and the fraudulent or illegal purpose is achieved, the property (be it absolute or special) which has been transferred by the one to the other remains vested in the transferee, notwithstanding its illegal origin: see *Scarfe v Morgan* ((1838) 4 M & W 270, 281), per Parke B. The reason is because the transferor, having fully achieved his unworthy end, cannot be allowed to turn round and repudiate the means by which he did it—he cannot throw over the transfer. And the transferee, having obtained the property, can assert his title to it against all the world, not because he has any merit of his own, but because there is no one who can assert a better title to it. The court does not confiscate the property because of the illegality—it has no power to do so—so it says, in the words of Lord Eldon: 'Let the estate lie where it falls'; see *Muckleston v Brown* ((1801) 6 Ves 52, 69). This principle was applied by the Court of Appeal recently in *Bowmakers Ltd v Barnet Instruments Ltd* ([1945] KB 65, 70). The parties to the fraud are, of course, liable to be punished for the part they played in the illegal transaction, but nevertheless the property passes to the transferee.

The plaintiff would have been entitled to an order for the return of the vehicle or its value. As it had not been returned, he was clearly entitled to its value. That is the order made by the Court of Appeal and their Lordships agree with it.

Their Lordships would only add this: if the law were not to allow the plaintiff to recover in this case, it would leave the defendant in possession of both the lorry and the money he received for it. Their Lordships are glad to have been able to reach the conclusion that, on the facts of the present case, this is not the law."

(Lord Denning was delivering the opinion of the Privy Council which consisted of Lords Denning, Cohen and Jenkins.)

QUESTION

Why did the defendant in *Shogun Finance v Hudson* (2004) (see p.265) not get good title to the car that was transferred to him under a defective contract?

5.2 Misrepresentation

We have seen that a statement made before the formation of a contract—for example a horse seller who says, "I assure you he is perfectly sound in every respect" (*Hopkins v*

Tanqueray (1854), at p.141)—can be treated as not forming part of the contract itself. In such a situation the statement is either a "mere puff" (cf. *Carlill v Carbolic Smoke Ball Co* (1893), at p.149), which has no legal effect, or a representation. If the statement amounts to a representation and turns out to be untrue, it will be a "misrepresentation". Sometimes, however, the courts are prepared to treat a pre-contractual statement either as part of the main contract, or as a separate collateral contract. For example, a statement describing goods on sale by description will be treated as a contract term as well as a representation (Sale of Goods Act 1979, s.13).

5.2.1 Definition and general effects of a misrepresentation

Misrepresentation is a major vitiating factor in English contract law, and the general effect is set out in the next extracts.

Brown v Raphael **[1958] Ch. 636, CA**

Lord Evershed M.R.: "... In order that he may succeed on such a ground [of misrepresentation] it is, of course, necessary that three things should be established. He must, first, show that the language relied upon does import or contain a representation of some material fact. Second, he must show that the representation is untrue, and, third, he must show that the plaintiff in entering into the contract was induced so to do in reliance upon it. ...."

Witter Ltd v TBP Industries **[1996] 2 All E.R. 573, Ch D**

Jacob J.: "... The law concerning non-fraudulent misrepresentation which induces a party to enter into a contract is that embodied under the common law (including equity) as modified by the 1967 Act as amended by the 1977 Act. Before the 1967 Act the remedy where a non-fraudulent misrepresentation of fact had been made and relied upon lay in equity. Equity could not provide damages: it provided rescission where this was possible. It was not in some cases for certain; in others there was doubt as to the law. It remains the law that a misrepresentation as to law, opinion, or a mere puff will not give rise to a remedy. The misrepresentation must be one of fact, not a mere unfulfilled promise. Nor is there a remedy unless the representee relies upon the representation. By 1967 there may also have been a remedy in negligence, where the misrepresentation of fact was negligently made and there was some kind of special relationship between the parties. *Hedley Byrne & Co Ltd v Heller & Partners Ltd* [1964] AC 465 had recently been decided. Liability for negligent misrepresentation had become part of the law but its scope was not fully resolved. ...."

222

Howard Marine v Ogden & Sons **[1978] Q.B. 574, CA**

Lord Denning M.R. (dissenting): ". . . This enactment [Misrepresentation Act 1967] imposes a new and serious liability on anyone who makes a representation of fact in the course of negotiations for a contract. If that representation turns out to be mistaken—then however innocent he may be—he is just as liable as if he made it fraudulently. But how different from times past! For years he was not liable in damages at all for innocent misrepresentation: see *Heilbut, Symons & Co v Buckleton* [1913] AC 30. Quite recently he was made liable if he was proved to have made it negligently: see *Esso Petroleum Co Ltd v Mardon* [1976] QB 801. But now with this Act he is made liable—unless he proves—and the burden is on him to prove—that he had reasonable ground to believe and did in fact believe that it was true. . . ."

NOTES

1. *Types of misrepresentation*. Misrepresentation as a contractual topic is, as the above extract hints, complex, and the reason for this is that it has been shaped by a rather fragmented history (although whether it is strictly part of contract law is open to question). First, one has to distinguish between *types* of misrepresentation: there are fraudulent, negligent and innocent misrepresentations. The reason for these distinctions is rooted in differing causes of action (deceit, negligence, contract and statute), sources of legal rules (common law, equity and statute) and remedies available (see below).

2. *Remedies for misrepresentation*. Secondly, two quite distinct *remedies* are available to a victim of a misrepresentation. Equity might grant rescission (cf. **12.3**), while the common law might grant *damages* (cf. **11.3**). Before 1964, equity would in principle grant rescission for *any* misrepresentation (fraudulent, negligent or innocent), but the common law would grant damages only if the misrepresentation was fraudulent (tort of deceit) or if the statement was regarded as contractual (breach of contract). After 1964, as Jacob J. indicates in *Witter* (above), damages might be available for a negligent misrepresentation thanks to the decision in *Hedley Byrne v Heller* (see p.234). Since 1967, thanks to statute, not only are damages available for fraudulent and negligent misrepresentations, but all misrepresentations are presumed to be negligent; to escape liability the defendant must effectively prove that the statement was not made carelessly (Misrepresentation Act 1967, s.2(1), below at p.237).

3. *Damages in lieu of rescission*. What if the defendant can prove that the statement was not made negligently? In such a situation *damages at common law* will not be available. In other words, it remains true to say that in principle damages are not awarded for innocent misrepresentation, unless the statement can be treated as a contractual term (enforceable promise) thus giving rise to a claim for damages for breach of a contractual promise (see e.g. *Dick Bentley* (1965), below at p.230). However, statute has given a court

power, in the case of *non-fraudulent* misrepresentations, to award damages *in lieu of rescission in equity* (Misrepresentation Act 1967, s.2(2), below at p.237). Now, given that rescission is in theory available for all misrepresentations, it is possible that a victim could be awarded damages in lieu of rescission; that is to say, the victim might be awarded *damages in equity*. As Jacob J. observes, damages cannot normally be awarded in equity, but this has become possible thanks to statutes which allow a court to refuse an equitable remedy but give damages instead (see **11.6.2**).

4. *Fact and law*. Jacob J. states that the misrepresentation must be one of *fact*. This was true when he gave his judgment, but it may no longer be true thanks to a major House of Lords decision in the law of restitution which has probably abolished the old distinction between mistakes of fact and mistakes of law (*Kleinwort Benson Ltd v Lincoln CC* (1999)).

5.2.2 Silence

Given the availability of these remedies, the first major issue is actually to define the limits of misrepresentation. The first limit is that silence does not normally amount to a misrepresentation.

***English v Dedham Vale Properties Ltd* [1978] 1 W.L.R. 93, Ch D**

This was an action for damages and (or) an account of profits in equity brought by the vendor of a bungalow and land against the purchaser, a property company. Before conveyance of the property the purchaser had, without the knowledge of the vendor, successfully applied for planning permission using the name of the vendor, and the plaintiff became aware of what had happened only after conveyance. The judge held that the property company was not guilty of fraud and not liable in damages for misrepresentation. However, he went on to hold that it was liable in equity to account to the plaintiff vendor for the profit it had made as a result of the increase in the value of the land on the granting of planning permission.

Slade J.: ". . . Secondly, and alternatively, it was submitted that the defendant is liable to Mrs English in damages for fraudulent misrepresentation on the grounds that, even if the representations made to her by Mr Harrington in relation to the prospects of planning permission at or before the meeting of May 21, 1971, were not false to his knowledge at the date when they were made, he acquired knowledge that they were false either when he made the planning application in July 1971, or, alternatively, when planning permission was obtained in October 1971; he thus, it was submitted, became under a duty to disclose the change of circumstances. In this context, Mr Scrivener referred me to the decision of the Court of Appeal in *With v O'Flanagan* [1936] Ch 575. This case illustrates that if, during the course of negotiations for a contract, one of the parties has made a

---

statement which is at the time false in fact, but which he believes to be true and which is material to the contract, and during the course of the negotiations he discovers the falsity of the statement, he becomes under an obligation to correct his erroneous representation. It further shows that if during such negotiations a party makes a material statement which was true at the time it was made, but which before the conclusion of any contract becomes untrue, then if the person who made it discovers before conclusion of any contract that it has become untrue, he becomes under an obligation to disclose to the other the change in circumstances. In either situation, his wrongful failure to disclose may be treated as a deemed misrepresentation.

. . . [T]he principle of *With v O'Flanagan* did not in my judgment itself impose any obligation on him to disclose to her the making of the planning application, though, as I have already indicated, I think he was under an obligation to obtain her consent to the making of the application before contract, for other reasons. A fortiori, in my judgment, the principle of *With v O'Flanagan* did not itself impose on Mr Harrington or the defendant any obligation to disclose in October 1971, the fact that planning permission had been obtained; for by that time Mrs English was already committed to the contract. . . ."

NOTES

There are exceptions to this silence rule. These are: (i) insurance contracts, where there is a duty to disclose; (ii) partial statements, which will trigger a duty to disclose all (in other words, one must keep totally silent or make full disclosure); (iii) changes of circumstance with regard to a statement true when made, again triggering a duty to inform about the change; and (iv) concealment, which will be treated as a positive "statement". Note also that although the plaintiff in *Dedham* may not have been able to succeed in the action for damages, this did not mean that she was left without a remedy: see p.246.

5.2.3 **Opinion**

Statements of opinion are not normally regarded as statements of fact and thus are not prima facie misrepresentations. However, much will depend on the actual statement itself together with the status of the parties.

Esso Petroleum Co Ltd v Mardon **[1976] Q.B. 801, CA**

This was an action in debt and for repossession of premises by an oil company against a tenant of a petrol station. The tenant counterclaimed for damages for misrepresentation. The defendant tenant, before entering into the tenancy with the plaintiff oil company, was given an estimate by an employee of the plaintiff as to the amount of petrol throughput the garage would be likely to generate, and the defendant relied on this information when making the decision to enter into the agreement. The estimate proved very inaccurate and the defendant suffered heavy losses, resulting in non-payment for petrol supplied. The Court of Appeal (Lord Denning M.R., Ormrod and Shaw L.JJ.) held the plaintiff liable in damages for breach of a collateral warranty.

Lord Denning M.R.: "... Ever since *Heilbut, Symons & Co v Buckleton* [1913] AC 30, we have had to contend with the law as laid down by the House of Lords that an innocent misrepresentation gives no right to damages. In order to escape from that rule, the pleader used to allege—I often did it myself—that the misrepresentation was fraudulent, or alternatively a collateral warranty. At the trial we nearly always succeeded on collateral warranty. We had to reckon, of course, with the dictum of Lord Moulton, at p 47, that 'such collateral contracts must from their very nature be rare.' But more often than not the court elevated the innocent misrepresentation into a collateral warranty: and thereby did justice—in advance of the Misrepresentation Act 1967. I remember scores of cases of that kind, especially on the sale of a business. A representation as to the profits that had been made in the past was invariably held to be a warranty. Besides that experience, there have been many cases since I have sat in this court where we have readily held a representation—which induces a person to enter into a contract—to be a warranty sounding in damages ...

[Counsel for the oil company cited] *Bisset v Wilkinson* [1927] AC 177, where the Privy Council said that a statement by a New Zealand farmer that an area of land 'would carry 2,000 sheep' was only an expression of opinion. He submitted that the forecast here of 200,000 gallons was an expression of opinion and not a statement of fact: and that it could not be interpreted as a warranty or promise.

Now I would quite agree with Mr Ross-Munro that it was not a warranty—in this sense—that it did not *guarantee* that the throughput *would* be 200,000 gallons. But, nevertheless, it was a forecast made by a party—Esso—who had special knowledge and skill. It was the yardstick (the eac) by which they measured the worth of a filling station. They knew the facts. They knew the traffic in the town. They knew the throughput of comparable stations. They had much experience and expertise at their disposal. They were in a much better position than Mr Mardon to make a forecast. It seems to me that if such a person makes a forecast, intending that the other should act upon it—and he does act upon it, it can well be interpreted as a warranty that the forecast is sound and reliable in the sense that they made it with reasonable care and skill. It is just as if Esso said to Mr Mardon: 'Our forecast of throughput is 200,000 gallons. You can rely upon it as being a sound forecast of what the service station should do. The rent is calculated on that footing.' If the forecast turned out to be an unsound forecast such as no person of skill or experience should have made, there is a breach of warranty. .... It is very different from the New Zealand case where the land had never been used as a sheep farm and both parties were equally able to form an opinion as to its carrying capacity: see particularly *Bisset v Wilkinson* [1927] AC 177, 183–184.

In the present case it seems to me that there was a warranty that the forecast was sound, that is, Esso made it with reasonable care and skill. That warranty was broken. Most negligently Esso made a 'fatal error' in the forecast they stated to Mr Mardon, and on which he took the tenancy. For this they are liable in damages. . . ."

Shaw L.J.: ". . . Mr Ross-Munro submitted, the *Hedley Byrne* principle had no application. It would follow that, notwithstanding the fact that one party to the negotiations induced the other by a negligent misrepresentation to enter into the contract, the other would have no remedy unless one were available under the Misrepresentation Act 1967. As the matters of which Mr Mardon complained occurred in 1963 his only available means of redress would be such as his contract with Esso afforded: so that if there was no warranty he would have no remedy at all.

It is difficult to see why, in principle, a right to claim damages for negligent misrepresentation which has arisen in favour of a party to a negotiation should not survive the event of the making of a contract as the outcome of that negotiation. . . .

. . . Thus Mr Mardon is entitled in my view to damages for breach of warranty or for negligent misrepresentation. . . ."

NOTE

This case illustrates that a statement made before contract that causes loss may fall into one or more of several categories. It may be (i) a statement of opinion giving rise to no liability; (ii) a collateral contract (warranty) giving rise to a liability in contract; (iii) a negligent misstatement giving rise to liability in the tort of negligence (*Hedley Byrne v Heller* (1964); see p.234); (iv) a misrepresentation giving rise to liability under s.2(1) of the Misrepresentation Act 1967. Note also that a statement may also give rise to estoppel in equity.

QUESTIONS

1. There are to be found on the second-hand market many old binoculars carrying the logo of Carl Zeiss, Jena, indicating normally an instrument of very high quality. Most are genuine Zeiss glasses but some are not, a false top-plate carrying the Zeiss logo having at some point in the past been put onto an inferior quality instrument. Camilla buys from a shop dealing mainly in second-hand cameras, a binocular carrying the Zeiss logo. If Camilla later discovers that the instrument is not a Zeiss, can she demand rescission of the contract? Can she demand damages? Would the price paid for the binocular be of any relevance?

2. What if Geoffrey were to discover in a charity shop a very rare Zeiss binocular, worth several thousand pounds, on sale for £5? Would Geoffrey be under a legal obligation to inform the charity shop of the true value the instrument? What if the assistant in the shop were to say that she did not think it to be very valuable since it was so old, and Geoffrey (an expert on Zeiss) stated that he agreed? (Cf. **8.7.**)

5.2.4 **Statement of future intention**

A statement about one's future intention does not, it seems, amount to a representation of fact.

R. v Sunair Holidays Ltd **[1973] 1 W.L.R. 1105, CA**

This was an appeal by a tour operator against a conviction under the Trade Descriptions Act 1968. The complainant had booked a holiday for himself and his family, relying upon statements made in the defendants' brochure. This brochure had promised a comfortable hotel with good food and a swimming pool; push chairs and special meals for children were also said to be available. On arrival the complainant found a swimming pool devoid of water and no children's meals; push chairs could only be hired from a local shop. The appeal against conviction was allowed by the Court of Appeal (Stephenson L.J., Thesiger and MacKenna JJ.).

Mackenna J.: ". . . A statement that a fact exists now, or that it existed in the past, is either true or false at the time when it is made. But it is not the case with a promise or a prediction about the future. A prediction may come true or it may not. A promise to do something in the future may be kept or it may be broken. But neither the prediction nor the promise can be said to have been true or false at the time when it was made. We conclude that section 14 of the Trade Descriptions Act 1968 does not deal with forecasts or promises as such. . . .

What we have said about section 14 of the Act of 1968 agrees with the law of deceit, whether civil or criminal. In a civil action of deceit the plaintiff must prove that there was a false representation of fact as distinct from the failure to fulfil a promise: see *Salmond, Law of Torts*, 15th ed. (1969), pp. 514–517 . . .

. . . A statement about the quality of a service already provided is a statement of past fact and is covered by the section. A statement of existing fact may also be covered, as, for example, if a hotel advertises that its services currently provided include the provision of afternoon tea; if that service is not being provided at the time when the statement is made in that case an offence may be committed. A statement about existing facts would not cease to be within the section because the person making it warranted that it was true and that the facts would continue to exist in the future. In that limited sense the section can apply to warranties.

But it does not apply to promises about the future unless, as we said earlier, the promise can be construed as an implied statement of a present intention or the like. . .

. . . [W]e hold that section 14 is limited to statements of fact, past or present, and does not include assurances about the future . . ."

QUESTIONS

1. If the claimant had brought a claim in damages based on s.2(1) of the Misrepresentation Act 1967, would the claim have failed?

2. Does not a statement in a hotel advertising brochure claiming that the hotel has a swimming pool, imply that that pool will contain water? Is a "swimming pool" without water a "swimming pool"?

3. "A prediction may come true or it may not. A promise to do something in the future may be kept or it may be broken. But neither the prediction nor the promise can be said to have been true or false at the time when it was made." Do you think a philosopher would heartily approve of this statement (and the logical conclusion that seems to follow from it in the case), or might she reply: "There's glory for you" (or as the Papacy used to say: *sic transit gloria mundi*)?

4. Will this case protect an airline company, which operates a system of overbooking, against liability in (a) contract, (b) tort (including misrepresentation), and (c) criminal law if it turns away a passenger, having assured him earlier on the Internet that a seat had been booked? (Cf. *British Airways Board v Taylor* (1976).)

5.2.5 Liability in contract

Once a statement is held to be a misrepresentation, the next issue is one of liability. If the statement is deemed either to be part of the contract itself or collateral to the main contract (i.e. a collateral contract: see Lord Denning in *Esso v Mardon* (1976), above at p.225), then, if the statement is untrue, this will amount to a breach of contract giving rise to the remedy of damages. However, in what circumstances will the courts treat a misrepresentation as a contractual promise?

Principles of European Contract Law

"Article 6:101 Statements giving rise to contractual obligation

(1) A statement made by one party before or when the contract is concluded is to be treated as giving rise to a contractual obligation if that is how the other party reasonably understood it in the circumstances, taking into account:

(a) the apparent importance of the statement to the other party;

(b) whether the party was making the statement in the course of business; and

(c) the relative expertise of the parties.

(2) If one of the parties is a professional supplier who gives information about the quality or use of services or goods or other property when marketing or advertising them or otherwise before the contract for them is concluded, the statement is to be treated as giving rise to a contractual obligation unless it is shown that the other party knew or could not have been unaware that the statement was incorrect.

(3) Such information and other undertakings given by a person advertising or marketing services, goods or other property for the professional supplier, or by a person in earlier links of the business chain, are to be treated as giving rise to a contractual obligation on the part of the professional supplier unless it did not know and had no reason to know of the information or undertaking."

QUESTION

Does art.6:101 of the PECL accurately represent English law?

Dick Bentley Productions Ltd v Harold Smith (Motors) Ltd [1965] 1 W.L.R. 623, CA

Lord Denning M.R.: "The plaintiff, Charles Walter Bentley, sometimes known as Dick Bentley, brings an action against Harold Smith (Motors) Ltd for damages for breach of warranty on the sale of a car . . . The county court judge found that there was a warranty, that it was broken, and that the damages were more than £400; but as the claim was limited to £400, he gave judgment for the plaintiff for that amount.

The first point is whether this representation, namely, that it had done 20,000 miles only since it had been fitted with a replacement engine and gearbox, was an innocent misrepresentation (which does not give rise to damages), or whether it was a warranty. It was said by Holt CJ, and repeated in *Heilbut, Symons & Co v Buckleton*, that: 'An affirmation at the time of the sale is a warranty, provided it appear on evidence to be so intended'. But that word 'intended' has given rise to difficulties. I endeavoured to explain in *Oscar Chess Ltd v Williams* that the question whether a warranty was intended depends on the conduct of the parties, on their words and behaviour, rather than on their thoughts. If an intelligent bystander would reasonably infer that a warranty was intended, that will suffice. What conduct, then? What words and behaviour lead to the inference of a warranty?

Looking at the cases once more as we have done so often, it seems to me that if a representation is made in the course of dealings for a contract for the very purpose of inducing the other party to act upon it, and actually inducing him to act upon it, by entering into the contract, that is prima facie ground for inferring that it was intended as a warranty. It is not necessary to speak of it as being collateral. Suffice it that it was intended to be acted upon and was in fact acted on. But the maker of the representation can rebut this inference if he can show that it really was an innocent misrepresentation, in that he was in fact innocent of fault in making it, and that it would not be reasonable in the circumstances for him to be bound by it. In the *Oscar Chess* case the inference was rebutted. There a man had bought a second-hand car and received with it a log-book which stated the year of the car, 1948. He afterwards resold the car. When he resold it he simply repeated what was in the log-book and passed it on to the buyer. He honestly believed on reasonable grounds that it was true. He was completely innocent of any fault. There was no warranty by him, but only an innocent misrepresentation. Whereas in the present case it is very different. The inference is not rebutted. Here we have a dealer, Smith, who was in a position to know, or at least to find out, the history of the car. He could get it by writing to the makers. He did not do so. Indeed, it was done later. When the history of this car was examined, his statement turned out to be quite wrong. He ought to have known better. There was no reasonable foundation for it . . .

The judge found that the representations were not dishonest. Smith was not guilty of fraud. But he made the statement as to 20,000 miles without any foundation. And the judge was well justified in finding that there was a warranty . . .

It seems to me that on this point there is nothing wrong in the way the judge has dealt with the case, and therefore . . . I would hold the appeal fails and should be dismissed."

Danckwerts L.J.: "I agree with the judgment of Lord Denning MR."

Salmon L.J.: "I agree. I have no doubt at all that the judge reached a correct conclusion when he decided that Smith gave a warranty to the plaintiff and that that warranty was broken. Was what Smith said intended and understood as a legally binding promise? If so, it was a warranty and as such may be part of the contract of sale or collateral to it. In effect, Smith said: 'If you will enter into a contract to buy this motor car from me for £1,850, I undertake that you will be getting a motor car which has done no more than 20,000 miles since it was fitted with a new engine and a new gearbox'. I have no doubt at all that what was said by Smith was so understood and was intended to be so understood by Bentley. I accordingly agree that the appeal should be dismissed."

QUESTIONS

1. "Where there is a contract for the sale of goods by description, there is an implied condition [now 'term'] that the goods will correspond with the description" (Sale of Goods Act 1979, s 13(1)). Why did the claimant in *Dick Bentley* not seek damages under this section?

2. Is *Dick Bentley* a collateral contract case?

3. If these facts of *Dick Bentley* occurred again today, would the claimant have to rely upon the law of contract in order to get damages?

4. Did the plaintiff get what he contracted for in (i) *Hopkins v Tanqueray* (1854) (see p.141); and (ii) *Dick Bentley*?

5. To what extent was the status of the defendant of importance in *Dick Bentley*?

6. If *Hopkins v Tanqueray* (1854) (see p.141) had arisen after the Sales of Goods Act 1893, would the result have been different?

NOTE

Even if the statement does not amount to a contractual promise, damages may still be available in contract (so it would seem) according to the PECL.

> *Principles of European Contract Law*
>
> "*Article 4:106 Incorrect information*
>
> A party who has concluded a contract relying on incorrect information given it by the other party may recover damages in accordance with Article 4:117(2) and (3) even if the information does not give rise to a right to avoid the contract on the ground of mistake under Article 4:103, unless the party who gave the information had reason to believe that the information was correct.
>
> *Article 4:117 Damages*
>
> (1) A party who avoids a contract under this Chapter may recover from the other party damages so as to put the avoiding party as nearly as possible into the same position as if it had not concluded the contract, provided that the other party knew or ought to have known of the mistake, fraud, threat or taking of excessive benefit or unfair advantage.
>
> (2) If a party has the right to avoid a contract under this Chapter, but does not exercise its right or has lost its right under the provisions of Articles 4:113 or 4:114, it may recover, subject to paragraph (1), damages limited to the loss caused to it by the mistake, fraud, threat or taking of excessive benefit or unfair advantage. The same measure of damages shall apply when the party was misled by incorrect information in the sense of Article 4:106.
>
> (3) In other respects, the damages shall be in accordance with the relevant provisions of Chapter 9, Section 5, with appropriate adaptations."

QUESTION

If a court were to award damages under PECL, art.4:117, would these damages be for a breach of a contractual or non-contractual obligation?

5.2.6 Liability in the tort of deceit

If the misrepresentation was a deliberate lie, that is to say if it was a fraudulent misrepresentation, anyone suffering loss as a result of the lie can sue in the tort of deceit. The requirements of this tort are set out in the next extract.

Downs v Chappell **[1997] 1 W.L.R. 426, CA**

"**Hobhouse L.J.**: ". . . I will take the tort of deceit first. For a plaintiff to succeed in the tort of deceit it is necessary for him to prove that (1) the representation was fraudulent, (2) it was material and (3) it induced the plaintiff to act (to his detriment). A representation is material when its tendency, or its natural and probable result, is to induce the representee to act on the faith of it in the kind of way in which he is proved to have in fact acted. The test is objective. . . ."

NOTE

See also *Bradford Building Society v Borders* (1941) (C&MT, p.287).

QUESTIONS

1. Should a fraudulent misrepresentation attract a larger award of damages than would be the case if the misrepresentation were non-fraudulent? (See the extracts of judgments from Lords Browne-Wilkinson and Steyn in *Smith New Court Securities Ltd v Scrimgeour Vickers Ltd* (1997), extracted in C&MT, p.288.)

2. Is a claim for damages founded upon s.2(1) of the Misrepresentation Act 1967 technically a claim in the tort of deceit? If so, will damages be awarded on the basis of fraud?

Smith New Court Securities Ltd v Scrimgeour Vickers Ltd **[1997] A.C. 254, HL**

"**Lord Steyn**: ". . . At the risk of being side-tracked I must now refer to two Court of Appeal decisions which were discussed in argument. In *Royscot Trust Ltd v Rogerson* [1991] 2 QB 297 the Court of Appeal held that under section 2(1) of the Misrepresentation Act 1967 damages in respect of an honest but careless representation are to be calculated as if the representation had been made fraudulently. The question is whether the rather loose wording of the statute compels the court to treat a person who was morally innocent as if he was guilty of fraud when it comes to the measure of damages. There has been trenchant academic criticism of the *Royscot* case: see Richard Hooley, 'Damages and the Misrepresentation Act 1967' (1991) 107 LQR 547. Since this point does not directly arise in the present case, I express no concluded view on the correctness of the decision in the *Royscot* case. The second case is the decision of the Court of Appeal in *Downs v Chappell* [1997] 1 WLR 426. The context is the rule that in an action for deceit the plaintiff is entitled to recover all his loss directly flowing from the fraudulently induced transaction. In the case of a negligent misrepresentation the rule is narrower: the recoverable loss does not extend beyond the consequences flowing from the negligent misrepresentation: see *Banque Bruxelles Lambert SA v Eagle Star Insurance Co Ltd* [1997] AC 191. In *Downs v Chappell*

233

[1997] 1 WLR 426, Hobhouse LJ applied this narrower rule to an action for deceit. He enunciated the following 'qualification' of the conventional rule, at p 443:

'In my judgment, having determined what the plaintiffs have lost as a result of entering into the transaction—their contract with Mr Chappell—it is still appropriate to ask the question whether that loss can properly be treated as having been caused by the defendants' torts, notwithstanding that the torts caused the plaintiffs to enter into the transaction.'

That led Hobhouse LJ, at p 444, 'to compare the loss consequent upon entering into the transaction with what would have been the position had the represented, or supposed, state of affairs actually existed.' The correctness of this proposition in a case of deceit was debated at the bar. Counsel for Citibank in whose interest it was to adopt this proposition felt some difficulty in doing so. In my view the orthodox and settled rule that the plaintiff is entitled to all losses directly flowing from the transaction caused by the deceit does not require a revision. In other words, it is not necessary in an action for deceit for the judge, after he had ascertained the loss directly flowing from the victim having entered into the transaction, to embark on a hypothetical reconstruction of what the parties would have agreed had the deceit not occurred. The rule in deceit is justified by the grounds already discussed. I would hold that on this point *Downs v Chappell* was wrongly decided. . . .

NOTE

The facts of this important case, and further extracts, can be found in C&MT, p.288.

5.2.7 Liability in the tort of negligence

In order to obtain damages in the tort of deceit, fraud had to be proved (*Derry v Peek* (1887)). If the defendant had only been negligent, before 1964, no damages could be obtained in the law of tort. This was the reason why victims of misrepresentation tried to establish that the statement was a collateral warranty (see *Dick Bentley Productions Ltd v Harold Smith (Motors) Ltd* (1965), at p.230). The position changed with the next case.

Hedley Byrne & Co v Heller & Partners Ltd **[1964] A.C. 465, HL**

This was an action for damages brought by a firm of advertising agents against a bank in respect of financial loss incurred by the agents when one of their clients, to whom they had extended credit, went into liquidation. The advertising agents had extended the credit on the basis of a credit reference supplied by the defendant bank. The bank denied liability on the ground either that they owed no duty of care to the agency, or that they were protected by an exclusion clause. The House of Lords (Lords Reid,

Morris, Hodson, Devlin and Pearce), while giving judgment for the bank on the basis of the clause, nevertheless decided that such facts could give rise to a duty of care.

Lord Reid: "My Lords, this case raises the important question whether and in what circumstances a person can recover damages for loss suffered by reason of his having relied on an innocent but negligent misrepresentation. . . .

It must now be taken that *Derry v Peek* ((1889) 14 App Cas. 337) did not establish any universal rule that in the absence of contract an innocent but negligent misrepresentation cannot give rise to an action. It is true Lord Bramwell said (14 App Cas. 337, 347): 'To found an action for damages there must be a contract and breach, or fraud.' And for the next 20 years it was generally assumed that *Derry v Peek* decided that. But it was shown in this House in *Nocton v Lord Ashburton* ([1914] AC 932) that that is much too widely stated. We cannot, therefore, now accept as accurate the numerous statements to that effect in cases between 1889 and 1914, and we must now determine the extent of the exceptions to that rule.

In *Nocton v Lord Ashburton* a solicitor was sued for fraud. Fraud was not proved but he was held liable for negligence. . . . It hardly needed *Donoghue v Stevenson* ([1932] AC 562) to show that that process can still operate . . .

A reasonable man, knowing that he was being trusted or that his skill and judgment were being relied on, would, I think, have three courses open to him. He could keep silent or decline to give the information or advice sought: or he could give an answer with a clear qualification that he accepted no responsibility for it or that it was given without that reflection or inquiry which a careful answer would require: or he could simply answer without any such qualification. If he chooses to adopt the last course he must, I think, be held to have accepted some responsibility for his answer being given carefully, or to have accepted a relationship with the inquirer which requires him to exercise such care as the circumstances require . . ."

Lord Devlin: ". . . The respondents in this case cannot deny that they were performing a service. Their sheet anchor is that they were performing it gratuitously and therefore no liability for its performance can arise. My Lords, in my opinion this is not the law. A promise given without consideration to perform a service cannot be enforced as a contract by the promisee; but if the service is in fact performed and done negligently, the promisee can recover in an action in tort . . .

. . . I think that today the result can and should be achieved by the application of the law of negligence and that it is unnecessary and undesirable to construct an artificial consideration. I agree with Sir Frederick Pollock's note on the case of *De La Bere v Pearson Ltd* where he said in Contracts, 13th ed, p. 140, that 'the cause of action is better regarded as arising from default in the performance of a voluntary undertaking independent of contract.'

My Lords, it is true that this principle of law has not yet been clearly applied to a case where the service which the defendant undertakes to perform is or includes the obtaining and imparting of information. But I cannot see why it should not be: and if it had not been thought erroneously that *Derry v Peek* negatived any liability for negligent statements, I think that by now it probably would have been. It cannot matter whether the information consists of fact or of opinion or is a mixture of both, nor whether it was obtained as a result of special inquiries or comes direct from facts already in the defendant's possession or from his general store of professional knowledge. One cannot, as I have already endeavoured to show, distinguish in this respect between a duty to inquire and a duty to state.

I think therefore that there is ample authority to justify your Lordships in saying now that the categories of special relationships which may give rise to a duty to take care in word as well as in deed are not limited to contractual relationships or to relationships of fiduciary duty, but include also relationships which in the words of Lord Shaw in *Nocton v Lord Ashburton* are 'equivalent to contract', that is, where there is an assumption of responsibility in circumstances in which, but for the absence of consideration, there would be a contract. Where there is an express undertaking, an express warranty as distinct from mere representation, there can be little difficulty. The difficulty arises in discerning those cases in which the undertaking is to be implied. In this respect the absence of consideration is not irrelevant. Payment for information or advice is very good evidence that it is being relied upon and that the informer or adviser knows that it is. Where there is no consideration, it will be necessary to exercise greater care in distinguishing between social and professional relationships and between those which are of a contractual character and those which are not. It may often be material to consider whether the adviser is acting purely out of good nature or whether he is getting his reward in some indirect form. The service that a bank performs in giving a reference is not done simply out of a desire to assist commerce. It would discourage the customers of the bank if their deals fell through because the bank had refused to testify to their credit when it was good . . ."

NOTE

It is possible to see *Hedley Byrne* as (i) an extension of the tort of deceit; (ii) an extension of the law of contract; (iii) an extension of the equitable notion of fiduciary relationship; or (iv) an extension of the *Donoghue v Stevenson* (1932) principle (C&MT, p.112). If one examines the wording of the Misrepresentation Act 1967, s.2(1), it is tempting to think that the starting point for extending pre-contractual liability for misrepresentation is (i). And there seems little doubt that the case has established a liability at common law for loss suffered by the victim of a misrepresentation: see *Esso v Mardon* (1976) (above, at p.225).

236

5.2.8 Liability under statute

The whole problem of whether or not damages are available for negligent misrepresentation has now been settled by statute.

Misrepresentation Act 1967 (c.7)

"1. Removal of certain bars to rescission for innocent misrepresentation
Where a person has entered into a contract after a misrepresentation has been made to him, and—

(a) the misrepresentation has become a term of the contract; or
(b) the contract has been performed;

or both, then, if otherwise he would be entitled to rescind the contract without alleging fraud, he shall be so entitled, subject to the provisions of this Act, notwithstanding the matters mentioned in paragraphs (a) and (b) of this section.

2. Damages for misrepresentation
(1) Where a person has entered into a contract after a misrepresentation has been made to him by another party thereto and as a result thereof he has suffered loss, then, if the person making the misrepresentation would be liable to damages in respect thereof had the misrepresentation been made fraudulently, that person shall be so liable notwithstanding that the misrepresentation was not made fraudulently, unless he proves that he had reasonable ground to believe and did believe up to the time the contract was made that the facts represented were true.

(2) Where a person has entered into a contract after a misrepresentation has been made to him otherwise than fraudulently and he would be entitled, by reason of the misrepresentation, to rescind the contract, then, if it is claimed, in any proceedings arising out of the contract, that the contract ought to be or has been rescinded, the court or arbitrator may declare the contract subsisting and award damages in lieu of rescission, if of opinion that it would be equitable to do so, having regard to the nature of the misrepresentation and the loss that would be caused by it if the contract were upheld, as well as to the loss that rescission would cause to the other party.

(3) Damages may be awarded against a person under subsection (2) of this section whether or not he is liable to damages under subsection (1) thereof, but where he is so liable any award under the said subsection (2) shall be taken into account in assessing his liability under the said subsection (1)."

QUESTIONS

1. Is misrepresentation part of the law of contract, or of tort?

2. Are all breaches of contract torts?

3. Is a claim for damages under s.2(1) of the 1967 Act a claim in the tort of deceit as modified by the statute?

4. Can one now get damages for innocent misrepresentation?

Witter Ltd v TBP Industries [1996] 2 All E.R. 573, ChD

Jacob J.: ". . . The 1967 Act essentially widened the remedies available. By s 1 it was made clear that the remedies are available even if the misrepresentation has become a term of the contract (a point doubtful before) or if the contract has been performed. By s 2 a remedy in damages was created, both for negligent and non-negligent misrepresentation. As a result it now seldom matters whether a misrepresentation is made fraudulently or not: the 1967 Act confers substantial remedies in respect of non-fraudulent misrepresentation. The principal difference may now lie in relation to clauses attempting to exclude liability for misrepresentation. . . .

Both ss 2(1) and 2(2) provide for damages for misrepresentation. Section 2(1) provides a defence for the misrepresentor—a defence which I shall for brevity call 'innocence' but which involves proof of belief and reasonable grounds for belief that the representation was true. Thus, it is sometimes said that s 2(1) relates to 'negligent' misrepresentation in the sense that it has the 'innocence' defence. Section 2(2) provides no such defence. However, damages are only available 'in lieu of rescission'.

The defendants . . . argued that the discretion under s 2(2) to award damages crucially depends upon the rescission remedy remaining extant at the time the court comes to consider the question. Whether that argument is right has been a moot point since the Act was passed. The leading article of the time, Atiyah and Treitel 'Misrepresentation Act 1967' [1967] MLR 369, noticed the point at once. I found the argument unattractive: rescission might or might not be available at the time of trial depending on a host of factors which have nothing to do with behaviour of either party. I was not surprised to find that the authors of *Chitty on Contracts* (27th edn, 1994) para 6–058, p 372 found the suggested construction 'strange' even though Mustill J had apparently accepted it obiter in *Atlantic Lines and Navigation Co Inc v Hallam Ltd, The Lucy* [1983] 1 Lloyd's Rep 188 and one of the plaintiffs conceded it in *Alman v Associated Newspapers Ltd* (20 June 1980, unreported).

The argument assumes that the Act is referring to the remedy of 'rescission', though this is not clear. If it were only the remedy referred to then it is difficult to understand the reference to 'has been rescinded' in the section. It seemed to me that the reference might well be to a claim by the representee that he was entitled to rescission, in which case it would be enough for the court to find that the agreement was 'rescissionable' at least by the date when the representee first claimed rescission or at any time. There was enough ambiguity here to look to see what was said in Parliament at the time of the passing of the Act, pursuant to the limited new-found freedom given by *Pepper (Inspector of Taxes) v Hart* [1993] 1 All ER 42, [1993] AC 593. . . .

So the Solicitor General told the House of Commons that it was his view that damages could be awarded under s 2(2) when there was an impossibility of restitution. Accordingly, I hold that the power to award damages under s 2(2) does not depend upon an extant right to rescission—it only depends upon a right having existed in the past. . . .

Given that construction of s 2(2), it may be asked: what is the difference between s 2(2) and s 2(1)? In particular, since s 2(1) has a defence of 'innocence' is that in practical terms useless because damages can be had under s 2(2)? There is, of course, overlap between the two subsections on any construction, and s 2(3) explicitly recognises this. But if my construction covered all the cases covered by s 2(1) then the latter would be pointless and my construction would probably be wrong. However, I do not think there is complete overlap. First, under s 2(1) damages can be awarded in addition to rescission. So if there is 'innocence' the representor cannot have both remedies and never could, whatever the date of the decision. Secondly, the question of an award of damages under s 2(2) is discretionary and the court must take into account the matters referred to in the concluding words of the subsection. Thirdly, the measure of damages under the two subsections may be different—s 2(3) certainly contemplates that this may be so and moreover contemplates that s 2(1) damages may be more than s 2(2) damages and not the other way round. It is fair to say, as *Chitty* para 6–059, p 373 observes, that 'the Act gives little clue as to how damages are to be assessed under this subsection if they are not to be assessed in the same way as under subsection (1)'. However both *Chitty* and Treitel *Law of Contract* (8th edn, 1991) p 326 (see also Atiyah and Treitel [1967] MLR 369 at 376) suggest that damages under s 2(2) may be limited to the loss in value of what is bought under the contract whereas s 2(1) damages may also include consequential loss.

I reach my conclusion under s 2(2) without misgivings: as between the person making the innocent misrepresentation and his misrepresentee, the 'merits' favour the latter. The constant and justified academic criticism of the Act indicates a subject well worth the attention of the Law Commission. Fortunately, so far as I am concerned, in the circumstances of this case there can be no difference between the two subsections, for no consequential loss is claimed. . . ."

QUESTION

Is s.2(2) of the Misrepresentation Act 1967 designed to take account of the interests of the misrepresentor as much as the interests of the victim of the misrepresentation?

William Sindall Plc v Cambridgeshire County Council **[1994] 1 W.L.R. 1016, CA**

(For facts, see p.253.)

> **Evans L.J.:** ". . . In my judgment, it is not correct that the measure of damages under section 2(2) for the loss that would be caused by the misrepresentation if the contract were upheld is the same measure as under section 2(1). The latter is established by the common law and it is the amount required to compensate the party to whom the misrepresentation was made for all the losses which he has sustained by reason of his acting upon it at the time when he did. But the damages contemplated by section 2(2) are damages in lieu of rescission. The starting point for the application of the sub-section is the situation where a plaintiff has established a right to rescind the contract on grounds of innocent misrepresentation: its object is to ameliorate for the innocent misrepresentor the harsh consequences of rescission for a wholly innocent (meaning, non-negligent as well as non-fraudulent) misrepresentor, in a case where it is fairer to uphold the contract and award damages against him. Such an award of damages was not permitted in law or equity before 1967. The court, therefore, exercises a statutory jurisdiction and it does so having regard to the circumstances at the date of the hearing, when otherwise rescission would be ordered. . . ."

QUESTION

Does s.2(2) of the Misrepresentation Act 1967 represent a victory of the common law over equity?

NOTE

See also **11.6**.

5.2.9 Rescission in equity

Any misrepresentation (fraudulent, negligent or innocent) will in principle give rise to the remedy of equitable rescission.

Redgrave v Hurd **(1881) 20 Ch.D. 1, CA**

This was an action, brought by the seller, for specific performance of a contract to buy a house and solicitor's practice. The defendant counterclaimed for rescission of the contract on the basis that the plaintiff had seriously misrepresented the amount of income from the business. It appeared that the defendant had not examined the books of the business to see if the plaintiff's representations were accurate; and the trial judge gave judgment for the plaintiff on the basis that the defendant ought to have examined the books and papers. An appeal to the Court of Appeal (Sir George Jessel M.R., Baggallay and Lush L.JJ.) was allowed.

Jessel M.R.: ". . . As regards the rescission of a contract, there was no doubt a difference between the rules of courts of equity and the rules of courts of common law—a difference which, of course, has now disappeared by the operation of the Judicature Act, which makes the rules of equity prevail. According to the decisions of court of equity it was not necessary, in order to set aside a contract obtained by material false representation, to prove that the party who obtained it knew at the time when the representation was made that it was false. It was put in two ways, either of which was sufficient. One way of putting the case was, 'A man is not to be allowed to get a benefit from a statement which he now admits to be false. He is not to be allowed to say, for the purpose of civil jurisdiction, that when he made it he did not know it to be false; he ought to have found that out before he made it.' The other way of putting it was this: 'Even assuming that moral fraud must be shown in order to set aside a contract, you have it where a man, having obtained a beneficial contract by a statement which he now knows to be false, insists upon keeping that contract. To do so is a moral delinquency: no man ought to seek to take advantage of his own false statements.' The rule in equity was settled, and it does not matter on which of the two grounds it was rested . . .

There is another proposition of law of very great importance which I think it is necessary for me to state, because, with great deference to the very learned judge from whom this appeal comes, I think it is not quite accurately stated in his judgment. If a man is induced to enter into a contract by a false representation it is not a sufficient answer to him to say, 'If you had used due diligence you would have found out that the statement was untrue. You had the means afforded you of discovering its falsity, and did not choose to avail yourself of them.' I take it to be a settled doctrine of equity, not only as regards specific performance but also as regards rescission, that this is not an answer . . .

[W]hen a person makes a material representation to another to induce him to enter into a contract, and the other enters into that contract, it is not sufficient to say that the party to whom the representation is made does not prove that he entered into the contract relying upon the representation. If it is a material representation calculated to induce him to enter into the contract, it is an inference of law that he was induced by the representation to enter into it, and in order to take away his title to be relieved from the contract on the ground that the representation was untrue, it must be shown either that he had knowledge of the facts contrary to the representation, or that he stated in terms, or showed clearly by his conduct, that he did not rely on the representation. If you tell a man, 'You may enter into partnership with me, my business is bringing in between £300 and £400 a year', the man who makes that representation must know that it is a material inducement to the other to enter into the partnership, and you cannot investigate as to whether it was more or less probable that the inducement would operate on the mind of the party to whom the representation was made. Where you have neither evidence that he knew facts to show that the

241

statement was untrue, or that he said or did anything to show that he did not actually rely upon the statement, the inference remains that he did so rely, and the statement being a material statement, its being untrue is a sufficient ground for rescinding the contract . . ."

QUESTIONS

1. Who caused the defendant's damage?

2. Has the difference between the rules of the court of equity and the rules of the courts of common law actually disappeared?

3. There are certain bars to rescission. What do you think they are? For example, if Louis buys a car from Horatia and immediately resells it to Duncan, can the contract between Louis and Horatia be rescinded if Louis discovers that a statement made by Horatia about the car was a serious misrepresentation? Can Duncan (who is aware of Horatia's misrepresentation) rescind the contract with Louis, even if Louis made no statement whatsoever about the car? Does it make any difference if Duncan was aware of Horatia's statement (a) before he bought the car from Louis, or (b) only after he had bought the car?

4. Can time be a bar to rescission?

Leaf v International Galleries [1950] 2 K.B. 86, CA

This was a rescission action brought by the purchaser of a painting. In 1944 the plaintiff purchased a picture called "Salisbury Cathedral" from the defendant for £85. At the time of the purchase the defendant said that the picture was by Constable; but when the plaintiff came to sell the painting five years later, he was informed that it had not been painted by Constable. The Court of Appeal (Lord Evershed M.R., Denning and Jenkins L.JJ.) dismissed the plaintiff's claim.

Denning L.J.: "The question is whether the plaintiff is entitled to rescind the contract on the ground that the picture in question was not painted by Constable. I emphasise that it is a claim to rescind only: there is no claim in this action for damages for breach of condition or breach of warranty. The claim is simply one for rescission . . . No claim for damages is before us at all. The only question is whether the plaintiff is entitled to rescind. . . .

In my opinion, this case is to be decided according to the well known principles applicable to the sale of goods. This was a contract for the sale of goods. There was a mistake about the quality of the subject-matter, because both parties believed the picture to be a Constable; and that mistake was in one sense essential or fundamental. But such a mistake does not avoid the contract: there was no mistake at all about the subject-matter of the sale. It was a specific picture,

'Salisbury Cathedral'. The parties were agreed in the same terms on the same subject-matter, and that is sufficient to make a contract: see *Solle v Butcher*.

There was a term in the contract as to the quality of the subject-matter: namely, as to the person by whom the picture was painted—that it was by Constable. That term of the contract was, according to our terminology, either a condition or a warranty. If it was a condition, the buyer could reject the picture for breach of the condition at any time before he accepted it, or is deemed to have accepted it; whereas, if it was only a warranty, he could not reject it at all but was confined to a claim for damages.

I think it right to assume in the buyer's favour that this term was a condition, and that, if he had come in proper time he could have rejected the picture, but the right to reject for breach of condition has always been limited by the rule that, once the buyer has accepted, or is deemed to have accepted, the goods in performance of the contract, then he cannot thereafter reject, but is relegated to his claim for damages: see s 11, sub-s 1 (c) of the Sale of Goods Act 1893, and *Wallis, Son & Wells v Pratt & Haynes*.

The circumstances in which a buyer is deemed to have accepted goods in performance of the contract are set out in s 35 of the Act, which says that the buyer is deemed to have accepted the goods, amongst other things, 'when, after the lapse of a reasonable time, he retains the goods without intimating to the seller that he has rejected them'. In this case the buyer took the picture into his house and, apparently, hung it there, and five years passed before he intimated any rejection at all. That, I need hardly say, is much more than a reasonable time. It is far too late for him at the end of five years to reject this picture for breach of any condition. His remedy after that length of time is for damages only, a claim which he has not brought before the court.

Is it to be said that the buyer is in any better position by relying on the representation, not as a condition, but as an innocent misrepresentation? . . .

Although rescission may in some cases be a proper remedy, it is to be remembered that an innocent misrepresentation is much less potent than a breach of condition; and a claim to rescission for innocent misrepresentation must at any rate be barred when a right to reject for breach of condition is barred. A condition is a term of the contract of a most material character, and if a claim to reject on that account is barred, it seems to me *a fortiori* that a claim to rescission on the ground of innocent misrepresentation is also barred.

So, assuming that a contract for the sale of goods may be rescinded in a proper case for innocent misrepresentation, the claim is barred in this case for the self-same reason as a right to reject is barred. The buyer has accepted the picture. He had ample opportunity for examination in the first few days after he had bought it. Then was the time to see if the condition or representation was fulfilled. Yet he has kept it all this time. Five years have elapsed without any notice of

> rejection. In my judgment he cannot now claim to rescind. His only claim, if any, as the county court judge said, was one for damages, which he has not made in this action. In my judgment, therefore, the appeal should be dismissed."

QUESTIONS

1. Could the plaintiff in *Leaf* have sued the defendant for damages?

2. If the facts of *Leaf* occurred again today, could the claimant get damages under s.2(2) of the Misrepresentation Act 1967?

3. Section 35 of the Sale of Goods Act 1979 has now been amended by s.2 of the Sale and Supply of Goods Act 1994. How might the new s.35 affect the facts of *Leaf*?

4. What if the misrepresentation is made by a third party?

TSB Bank Plc v Camfield [1995] 1 W.L.R. 430, CA

This was an action by a bank for possession of a matrimonial home, which had been mortgaged by a husband and his wife to the bank for security of a business loan made to the husband. The wife had agreed to the security as a result of an innocent misrepresentation made by the husband to his wife that liability would be limited to £15,000. The bank had failed to ensure that the wife was given independent legal advice or that she understood that liability was in fact unlimited. The wife sought rescission of the mortgage transaction on the basis of misrepresentation, but the judge held that she was liable up to £15,000 and awarded possession of the house to the bank. An appeal against this judgment was allowed by the Court of Appeal (Nourse, Roch and Henry L.JJ.).

> **Roch L.J.:** ". . . If this analysis, which, as I understand it, is the analysis adopted by Ferris J in *Allied Irish Banks Plc v Byrne*, 1 February 1994 is correct, then the provisions of the Misrepresentation Act 1967 become, in my view, of the utmost significance. Section 1 of that Act is in terms consistent with the right to rescind for misrepresentation being that of the person to whom the misrepresentation has been made. Section 2(2) gives the court power, where such a person has rescinded or is entitled to rescind a contract, to declare the contract subsisting and to award damages in lieu of rescission in certain circumstances. That implies that but for that subsection the court does not have the power to declare the contract to be subsisting when, as in this case, the representee has exercised her right to set aside the transaction.
>
> In this case Judge Meier did not consider it appropriate to declare the contract to be subsisting and to award damages, although he gave no reason for that conclusion. The absence of reasons, in my view, is explained by the fact that in this case an award of damages against Mr Camfield would have been an empty

remedy, and no court could have formed the opinion that in this case it would be equitable to exercise its power under section 2(2). The loss to the wife by upholding the legal charge in exchange for an award of damages against her husband would have far outweighed the loss that rescission would cause to Mr Camfield. The judge decided to limit the extent to which the transaction—that is to say, the legal charge—was enforceable by the bank against the wife, namely, to the extent of £15,000. The judge was, in effect, declaring the legal charge to be subsisting and depriving the wife of her right to rescind it on terms that the enforceability of the charge against her would be limited to £15,000. In my judgment the judge has no power to do that. Once it was proved that the wife had the right to rescind the transaction, she could not be deprived of that right by the court unless hers was a case which fell within section 2(2) of the Act of 1967.

The judge found that had the true nature of the legal charge been known to the wife she would not have entered into the charge and the enjoyment of her home would never have been at risk. But for the bank's failure to take reasonable steps, the wife would have known the true nature of the proposed legal charge and the potential risk to her interest in the family home, and she would have refused to enter into that transaction. The wife is entitled to be placed in the position she would have been in had the misrepresentation not been made and had she been made aware of the true nature of the legal charge.

This conclusion is not one which need strike terror into the hearts of banks and other lenders, for they can avoid a situation where their legal charge is liable to be rescinded by taking the simple steps indicated in *O'Brien's* case; in other words, by following good banking practice.

For those reasons, I agree that this appeal should be allowed."

QUESTIONS

1. Is rescission in equity a self-help remedy? (*Cf.* **12.6.**)

2. Can a court order partial rescission of a contract? (See PECL below; but *cf. De Molestina v Ponton* (2002).)

NOTES

1. The steps that a bank should take are set out by Lord Nicholls in *Royal Bank of Scotland v Etridge (No.2)* (2002) (see p.299).

2. Certain rules regarding rescission have been set out in the PECL.

Principles of European Contract Law

"*Article 4:112 Notice of avoidance*

Avoidance must be by notice to the other party.

Article 4:113 Time limits

(1) Notice of avoidance must be given within a reasonable time, with due regard to the circumstances, after the avoiding party knew or ought to have known of the relevant facts or became capable of acting freely.

(2) However, a party may avoid an individual term under Article 4:110 if it gives notice of avoidance within a reasonable time after the other party has invoked the term.

Article 4:114 Confirmation

If the party who is entitled to avoid a contract confirms it, expressly or impliedly, after it knows of the ground for avoidance, or becomes capable of acting freely, avoidance of the contract is excluded.

Article 4:115 Effect of avoidance

On avoidance either party may claim restitution of whatever it has supplied under the contract, provided it makes concurrent restitution of whatever it has received. If restitution cannot be made in kind for any reason, a reasonable sum must be paid for what has been received.

Article 4:116 Partial avoidance

If a ground of avoidance affects only particular terms of a contract, the effect of an avoidance is limited to those terms unless, giving due consideration to all the circumstances of the case, it is unreasonable to uphold the remaining contract."

QUESTION

How many of these principles represent English law?

5.2.10 Liability in account

Even if damages and rescission are not available, it may be that equity will allow an action for an account of profits (*cf.* **11.6.1**).

English v Dedham Vale Properties Ltd **[1978] 1 W.L.R. 93, Ch D**

(For facts, see p.224.)

Slade J.: ". . . In my judgment, in the end the question of the liability, if any, of the defendants to account must depend on the view which the court takes as to the nature of the relationship subsisting between them and the plaintiffs at the date when the planning application was made. The liability to account would, in my judgment, arise if, though only if, the relationship was in the eyes of equity a fiduciary one in the sense that it imposed relevant fiduciary duties on the defendants towards the plaintiffs . . .

Counsel for the defendants in effect submitted that the mere making of a planning application could not by itself have given rise to any such relationship when none would have otherwise existed. I see the force of this submission but am not in the end convinced by it. My reasons may be put in the form of two general propositions. (1) Where during the course of negotiations for a contract for the sale and purchase of property, the proposed purchaser, in the name of and purportedly as agent on behalf of the vendor, but without the consent or authority of the vendor, takes some action in regard to the property . . . which, if disclosed to the vendor, might reasonably be supposed to be likely to influence him in deciding whether or not to conclude the contract, a fiduciary relationship in my judgment arises between the two parties. (2) Such fiduciary relationship gives rise to the consequences that there is a duty on the proposed purchaser to disclose to the vendor before the conclusion of the contract what he has done as the vendor's purported agent, and correspondingly, in the event of non-disclosure, there is a duty on him to account to him for any profit made in the course of the purported agency, unless the vendor consents to his retaining it . . .

On my analysis of the facts of the present case, the plaintiffs never consented to the defendants . . . purporting to make the planning application as their agent before contract; the fact that this had been done was never disclosed to them before the exchange of contracts; and they never consented to the defendants retaining the profit ultimately received by them as a result of the making of the planning application. In these circumstances, they are in my judgment account-able for such profit . . ."

NOTES

1. In *Reading v R* (1949), Asquith L.J. said (at 236): "When a servant, or agent, by a breach of duty damnifies his master or principal, the latter can, of course, recover in an ordinary action for breach of contract for any loss he has actually suffered. But there is a well established class of cases in which he can so recover, whether or not he has suffered any detriment in fact. These are cases in which the servant or agent has realised a secret profit, commission or bribe in the course of his employment; and the amount recoverable is a sum equal to such profit . . . This amount the plaintiff can recover, either as money had and received to his use, or as an equitable debt . . ."

2. For further extracts and discussion concerning the remedy of account, see **11.6.1**.

QUESTION

Is equity confined to the remedy of account when it rescinds a contract and seeks to restore each party to its pre-contractual position? Or does it have a power to award damages? (*Cf. Mahoney v Purnell* (1996).)

5.3 Mistake

Many misrepresentation cases can equally be classed under mistake. Yet what if there is a mistake made by one or both parties to the contract but no actual misrepresentation? Does English law have, in addition to the law governing misrepresentations, a theory of mistake? This is by no means an easy question to answer; and the complexity is increased by the fact that there are different classes or categories of mistake.

5.3.1 General introduction

Mistake in contract is one area where the distinction between agreement and promise is fundamental (*cf.* **4.1**). In civil law systems, where contract is based on agreement, a serious mistake must logically act as an obstacle to formation, as the extract below indicates.

> **Robert Pothier, *Traité des obligations* (1761) (translation Bernard Rudden)**
>
> "17. Mistake is the great vice of agreements (*conventions*); for agreements are formed by the consent of the parties and there can be no consent when the parties have erred on the object of their agreement, *non videntur qui errant consentire.*
>
> That is why if someone intends to sell me something and I intend to take it as a loan or a present there is in such a case no sale, nor loan nor gift. If someone intends to sell or to give me a certain thing and I intend to buy some other thing from him or to accept something else as a gift, there is neither sale nor gift. If someone intends to sell me a thing for a certain price and I intend to buy it at a lower price there is no sale; for in all these cases there is no consent. . . .
>
> 18. Mistake annuls the agreement not only when it goes to the thing itself but when it goes to the quality of the thing which the contracting parties had principally in mind, and which forms the substance of this thing.
>
> 19. . . . Mistake as to the person annuls the agreement on every occasion that the consideration of the person enters into the agreement. In contrast, when . . . the contract [is a contract] that I would have wanted to make . . . with any person whoever they were, as with the person that I believed to contract with, the contract must be valuable."

NOTES

1. In this extract Pothier identifies three types of contractual error: (i) an error as to the thing itself (*error in corpore*); (ii) an error as to the quality of the thing (*error in substantia*); and (iii) an error as to the person with whom one is contracting (*error in persona*). Note, with respect to (iii), the distinction made by Pothier: one might ask if this distinction has found its way into English law

(see *Shogun*, at p.265). Other kinds of error, not mentioned in this extract, are mistakes about what was orally agreed (*error in verbis*), mistakes concerning the nature of a document signed by a contracting party (*error in negotio*) and mistakes as to the cause upon which one contracts (*error in causa*).

2. Because mistake (error) goes to the formation process itself, one can talk, in the civil law, of a general theory of mistake, as the next extracts indicate.

Code civil (1804)

"**Art 1109.** There is no valid consent if the consent has been given only by error, or if it has been extorted by duress (*violence*) or obtained by deceit (*dol*).

Art 1110. Error is a cause of nullity of the agreement only when it falls on the substance itself of the thing which is the object of the agreement.

It is not a cause of nullity when it falls only the person with whom one intended to contract, unless the consideration of this person was the principal reason for the agreement.

Art 1117. The agreement contracted by error, duress or deceit is not void as a matter of law; it gives rise only to an action in nullity or rescission . . ."

Principles of European Contract Law

"*Article 4:103 Mistake as to facts or law*

(1) A party may avoid a contract for mistake of fact or law existing when the contract was concluded if:

(a) (i) the mistake was caused by information given by the other party; or
    (ii) the other party knew or ought to have known of the mistake and it was contrary to good faith and fair dealing to leave the mistaken party in error; or
    (iii) the other party made the same mistake, and

(b) the other party knew or should have known that the mistaken party, had it known the truth, would not have entered the contract or would have done so only on fundamentally different terms.

(2) However a party may not avoid the contract if:

(a) in the circumstances his mistake was inexcusable, or
(b) the risk of the mistake was assumed, or in the circumstances should be borne, by it."

NOTE

The major question facing the English contract lawyer is whether this PECL provision equally represents English law. The cases that follow in the next sub-sections should be tested against this PECL article.

5.3.2 *Error in causa*

It might be useful to start with a problem which can be classified under *error in causa*, because what is undoubtedly the leading case on mistake in the common law actually concerns this kind of problem. In addition the case raises an interesting issue about the effects, if any, of silence (a problem already encountered in *English v Dedham Vale Properties* (1978), above at p.224).

> ### *Bell v Lever Brothers Ltd* [1932] A.C. 161, HL
>
> This was an action for rescission of two contracts, together with a claim for the repayment of monies paid thereunder, made between a company and two of its directors, whereby the directors terminated their employment contracts in return for large compensation payments. After the compensation payments had been made, the company discovered that they could legally, and without compensation, have dismissed the two directors for breaches of their employment contracts. The jury found that the two directors had not fraudulently concealed their breaches. The trial judge, Court of Appeal and two Law Lords (Viscount Hailsham and Lord Warrington) thought that the compensation contracts were void for mistake; a majority of the House of Lords (Lords Blanesburgh, Atkin and Thankerton) thought that they were not.
>
> > **Lord Atkin:** ". . . Two points present themselves for decision. Was the agreement of March 19, 1929, void by reason of a mutual mistake . . . ?
> >
> > Could the agreement of March 19, 1929, be avoided by reason of the failure of Mr Bell to disclose his misconduct . . . ?
> >
> > My Lords, the rules of law dealing with the effect of mistake on contract appear to be established with reasonable clearness. If mistake operates at all it operates so as to negative or in some cases to nullify consent. The parties may be mistaken in the identity of the contracting parties, or in the existence of the subject-matter of the contract at the date of the contract, or in the quality of the subject-matter of the contract. These mistakes may be by one party, or by both, and the legal effect may depend upon the class of mistake above mentioned. Thus a mistaken belief by A that he is contracting with B whereas in fact he is contracting with C, will negative consent where it is clear that the intention of A was to contract only with B . . .
> >
> > Mistake as to quality of the thing contracted for raises more difficult questions. In such a case a mistake will not affect assent unless it is the mistake of both parties, and is as to the existence of some quality which makes the thing without the quality essentially different from the thing as it was believed to be . . .
> >
> > It is essential on this part of the discussion to keep in mind the finding of the jury acquitting the defendants of fraudulent misrepresentation or concealment in

procuring the agreements in question. Grave injustice may be done to the defendants and confusion introduced into the legal conclusion, unless it is quite clear that in considering mistake in this case no suggestion of fraud is admissible and cannot strictly be regarded by the judge who has to determine the legal issues raised. The agreement which is said to be void is the agreement contained in the letter of March 19, 1929, that Bell would retire from the Board of the Niger Company . . . and that in consideration of his doing so Levers would pay him as compensation the sum of £30,000 in full satisfaction . . . I have come to the conclusion that it would be wrong to decide that an agreement to terminate a definite specified contract is void if it turns out that the agreement had already been broken and could have been terminated otherwise. The contract released is the identical contract in both cases, and the party paying for release gets exactly what he bargains for. It seems immaterial that he could have got the same result in another way, or that if he had known the true facts he would not have entered into the bargain. A buys B's horse; he thinks the horse is sound and he pays the price of a sound horse; he would certainly not have bought the horse if he had known, as the fact is, that the horse is unsound. If B has made no representation as to soundness and has not contracted that the horse is sound, A is bound and cannot recover back the price. A buys a picture from B; both A and B believe it to be the work of an old master, and a high price is paid. It turns out to be a modern copy. A has no remedy in the absence of representation or warranty . . . A buys a roadside garage business from B abutting on a public thoroughfare: unknown to A, but known to B it has already been decided to construct a by-pass road which will divert substantially the whole of the traffic from passing A's garage. Again A has no remedy. All these cases involve hardship on A and benefit B, as most people would say, unjustly. They can be supported on the ground that it is of paramount importance that contracts should be observed, and that if parties honestly comply with the essentials of the formation of contracts ie, agree in the same terms on the same subject-matter they are bound, and must rely on the stipulations of the contract for protection from the effect of facts unknown to them.

[His Lordship then went on to hold that the defendants owed no duty to the Lever Company to disclose the impugned transactions.]"

Lord Thankerton: ". . . [I]n the present case, there being no obligation to disclose [misconduct], Bell and Snelling, if they had had their misconduct in mind, would have been entitled to say nothing and Lever would have been bound by the contract. I have difficulty in seeing how the fact that Bell and Snelling did not remember at the time is to put Lever in a better position . . ."

QUESTIONS

1. Is the decision in this case inevitable given that English law does not in general treat silence as a misrepresentation?

2. Did the plaintiff company consent to the payments to the two directors, or did it consent only on the basis of certain conditions?

3. Did the directors unjustly enrich themselves at the expense of the plaintiff?

4. Did the contract agreed by the company actually lack the "cause" upon which the company negotiated and contracted (i.e. that the directors had water-tight contracts)?

NOTES

1. It is by no means clear that if *Bell v Lever Brothers Ltd* had been governed by PECL, art.4:103 the result would have been the same. According to art.4:103(1), the two directors would, it seems, have been under a duty to disclose their misconduct.

2. One reason for the difference of approach between the civil and the common law is to be found in the distinction between agreement and promise (*cf.* **4.1**). In French law, where contract is based on consent and agreement, it logically follows that mistake ought in principle to be a vitiating factor: for if the parties have agreed on the basis of an error then there cannot be true agreement. In a system where promise is the basis of a contract it does not logically have to follow that mistake will nullify the contract, since a promise is a promise even if based on a mistake (see the hypothetical examples given by Lord Atkin). In other words, one does not need to look into the minds of one or both of the parties; one need only look at the objective promise. Here is the reason why the common law has no doctrine of mistake.

3. However, as Evans L.J. points out in *William Sindall* (1994) (see below, p.253), there are some situations where the court will seemingly set aside a contract based on mistake; these cases are not, it must be stressed, in theory based on some substantive doctrine of error. They are either offer and acceptance problems, where the court holds that the mistake vitiates the formation of a contract, or implied condition precedent problems, where the court holds that there is an implied condition that, for example, the object of the contract is in existence or is of a certain quality (see *Financings Ltd v Stimson* (1962), at p.156). In these situations the common law is saying either that there never was a contract, or, if there was, that it has imploded as a result of the condition precedent (but *cf. The Great Peace* (2003), below at p.255). The common law, in other words, is declaring the contract *void*.

4. Another difference between the civil and the common law is to be found in the general methodological approach. The civilian starts off from a general principle (e.g. PECL, art.4:103) and applies this principle to the facts of the case; one goes, in other words, from the general to the particular. This is not really Lord Atkin's approach. He justifies his decision not by reference to some axiomatic principle, but by analogy to a series of hypothetical factual situations where he asserts that the contract would remain valid. This is casuistic reasoning (see p.94).

PROBLEMS

1. Basil sees an old painting in a junk shop and asks Esin, the owner, how much she wants for it. Esin says she thinks the painting is by a minor artist and is worth around £500, and she offers it to Basil for £480, which Basil readily accepts. Having purchased the picture, Basil takes it to an antiques expert for a valuation, and the expert says that the picture is a missing masterpiece by a major artist and is worth at least £1 million. The find is widely reported in the press and Esin is much put out. Can Esin ask for the contract to be set aside? Would your answer be different if Basil had orally agreed with Esin that the painting was by a minor artist, knowing full well that it was not?

2. Pierre is on his way to a dinner party, intending to purchase a bottle of good wine to present to the host. He passes Roderick's Wine Emporium and sees in the window a particular bottle of chateau-bottled wine that he knows is supposed to be excellent. The bottle carries a price tag of £50. Pierre mentions to Roderick that the price seems expensive, but nevertheless buys the wine. After leaving the Emporium, Pierre comes across another wine shop in whose window he sees the identical bottle of wine (same year and everything) selling for £20. Pierre returns to Roderick's shop demanding that the contract to buy the bottle for £50 be rescinded on the grounds of mistake. Assuming the contract is governed by the PECL, does Pierre have a good legal claim?

5.3.3 *Error in substantia*

Another category of mistake is error as to the quality of the thing sold. The principle of *Bell v Lever Brothers Ltd* (1932) would appear equally to apply to this class of case.

William Sindall Plc v Cambridgeshire County Council **[1994] 1 W.L.R. 1016, CA**

Evans L.J.: "This could be a textbook case on the law of mistake in contract. Cambridgeshire sold 6.71 acres of land, which had been used for nearly 20 years as a school playing field, to a firm of builders, Sindall, who intended to develop an estate of about 70 houses and 30 flats. The sale was duly completed in March 1989 but then Sindall's troubles began. Obtaining detailed planning permission took longer than had been expected and by October 1990 that process was far from complete. Meanwhile, the value of the land, even with planning permission, had fallen dramatically due to the general decline in market prices. The contract price in 1988 was £5,082,500. The value in 1990 was less than half that figure. Sindall had borrowed the whole of the amount which they had paid, and interest rates were high.

Then came the chance discovery in October 1990 of a sewage pipe crossing the land diagonally about two metres below the surface. Because the land had been

253

used as a playing field, the manhole which would have revealed its existence had been covered and grassed over. The pipe carried foul sewage, as opposed to surface water drainage, from a neighbouring block of flats owned by the Cambridge City Council. It discharged into a public sewer outside the boundary on the far corner of the site. It also served a building, the youth centre, which had been constructed on that part of the site but which would inevitably be demolished in order to make room for the housing development planned.

Neither Sindall nor the officers of Cambridgeshire at the time of the sale knew of the existence of the sewer. Sindall seek to set aside the contract and thus to recover the sum of £5,082,500 which they paid in 1989, on grounds of misrepresentation and mistake. The judge held that they are entitled to do so, and Cambridgeshire now appeals, contending that Sindall are not entitled to any remedy, or alternatively, that Sindall should be restricted to a claim for damages under section 2(1) of the Misrepresentation Act 1967.

First, mistake. There are certain circumstances in which the courts will hold that an agreement made between two parties, each labouring under fundamental mistake, is invalid as a contract, that is to say, it has no legal effect. The judge applied the test established by the majority judgments of the House of Lords in *Bell v Lever Brothers* [1932] AC 161 as defined by Steyn J in *Associated Japanese Bank (International) Ltd v Crédit du Nord SA* [1989] I WLR 255, and he reached the following conclusion: 'there are undoubtedly important differences between what was contracted for and what was purchased. They do not, as it seems to me, meet the essential test of being essentially and radically different.' There is no appeal against that finding or against the judge's conclusion that the builders failed to establish any common law remedy on the basis of mistake. I would add merely this, that the concept of a factual situation 'essentially and radically different' from that by reference to which the parties made their agreement is the same concept, in my view, as that which may lead to frustration of the contract where there has been a change in circumstances due to a supervening event. . . .

[Hoffmann and Russell L.JJ. also held that the contract was valid.]"

QUESTION

If this case had been governed by PECL, art.4:103, would not a court have had to set aside the contract? What provision in art.4:103 might be of help to a court wishing to arrive at the same conclusion as the Court of Appeal in *Sindall*?

NOTE

The whole doctrine of mistake has been quite recently reviewed and modified by the Court of Appeal.

Great Peace Shipping Ltd v Tsavliris Salvage (International) Ltd (The Great Peace)
[2003] Q.B. 679, CA

This was an action for debt brought by the owner of a ship against a salvage company for money owing under a contract for the hire of the ship. An alternative claim for damages for wrongful repudiation of the hire contract was also entered. The salvage company claimed that the contract was either void at common law or voidable in equity for mistake, the ship being much further away from where the parties believed it to be when the contract was made. The Court of Appeal (Lord Phillips M.R., May and Laws L.JJ.) dismissed an appeal from Toulson J. holding the defendants liable in debt; the contract was not void at common law and the doctrine of equitable rescission for mistake was irreconcilable with the common law authority of *Bell v Lever Brothers* [1932] A.C. 161.

Lord Phillips M.R. (delivering the judgment of the court): ". . . 28. A mistake can be simply defined as an erroneous belief. Mistakes have relevance in the law of contract in a number of different circumstances. They may prevent the mutuality of agreement that is necessary for the formation of a contract. In order for two parties to conclude a contract binding in law each must agree with the other the terms of the contract. Whether two parties have entered into a contract in this way must be judged objectively, having regard to all the material facts. It may be that each party mistakenly believes that he has entered into such a contract in circumstances where an objective appraisal of the facts reveals that no agreement has been reached as to the terms of the contract. Such a case was *Raffles v Wichelhaus* (1864) 2 H & C 906. The parties believed that they had entered into a contract for the purchase and sale of a cargo of cotton to arrive 'ex Peerless from Bombay'. That term was capable of applying equally to a cargo of cotton on two different ships, each called Peerless and each having sailed from Bombay, one in September and one in December. The court accepted that parol evidence could be adduced to prove which shipment the parties had intended to be the subject of the contract. Had one party intended the October shipment and the other the December shipment, the agreement necessary for a binding contract would have been absent.

29. *Raffles v Wichelhaus* was a case of latent ambiguity. More commonly an objective appraisal of the negotiations between the parties may disclose that they were at cross-purposes, so that no agreement was ever reached. In such a case there will be a mutual mistake in that each party will erroneously believe that the other had agreed to his terms. This case is not concerned with the kind of mistake that prevents the formation of agreement.

30. Another type of mistake is that where the parties erroneously spell out their contract in terms which do not give effect to an antecedent agreement that they have reached. Such a mistake can result in rectification of the contract. Again, this case is not concerned with that type of mistake.

31. In the present case the parties were agreed as to the express terms of the contract. The defendants agreed that the *Great Peace* would deviate towards the *Cape Providence* and, on reaching her, escort her so as to be on hand to save the lives of her crew, should she founder. The contractual services would terminate when the salvage tug came up with the casualty. The mistake relied upon by the defendants is as to an assumption that they claim underlay the terms expressly agreed. This was that the *Great Peace* was within a few hours sailing of the *Cape Providence*. They contend that this mistake was fundamental in that it would take the *Great Peace* about 39 hours to reach a position where she could render the services which were the object of the contractual adventure.

32. Thus what we are here concerned with is an allegation of a common mistaken assumption of fact which renders the service that will be provided if the contract is performed in accordance with its terms something different from the performance that the parties contemplated. This is the type of mistake which fell to be considered in *Bell v Lever Bros Ltd* [1932] AC 161. We shall describe it as 'common mistake', although it is often alternatively described as 'mutual mistake'. . . . [Lord Phillips discussed *Bell v Lever Bros* and the authorities on which it was based.]

61. We conclude that the two authorities to which Lord Atkin referred provided an insubstantial basis for his formulation of the test of common mistake in relation to the quality of the subject matter of a contract. Lord Atkin advanced an alternative basis for his test: the implication of a term of the same nature as that which was applied under the doctrine of frustration, as it was then understood. In so doing he adopted the analysis of Scrutton LJ in the Court of Appeal. It seems to us that this was a more solid jurisprudential basis for the test of common mistake that Lord Atkin was proposing. At the time of *Bell v Lever Bros Ltd* [1932] AC 161 the law of frustration and common mistake had advanced hand in hand on the foundation of a common principle. Thereafter frustration proved a more fertile ground for the development of this principle than common mistake, and consideration of the development of the law of frustration assists with the analysis of the law of common mistake . . .

73. What do [the] developments in the law of frustration have to tell us about the law of common mistake? First that the theory of the implied term is as unrealistic when considering common mistake as when considering frustration. Where a fundamental assumption upon which an agreement is founded proves to be mistaken, it is not realistic to ask whether the parties impliedly agreed that in those circumstances the contract would not be binding. The avoidance of a contract on the ground of common mistake results from a rule of law under which, if it transpires that one or both of the parties have agreed to do something which it is impossible to perform, no obligation arises out of that agreement.

74. In considering whether performance of the contract is impossible, it is necessary to identify what it is that the parties agreed would be performed. This

involves looking not only at the express terms, but at any implications that may arise out of the surrounding circumstances. In some cases it will be possible to identify details of the 'contractual adventure' which go beyond the terms that are expressly spelt out, in others it will not.

75. Just as the doctrine of frustration only applies if the contract contains no provision that covers the situation, the same should be true of common mistake. If, on true construction of the contract, a party warrants that the subject matter of the contract exists, or that it will be possible to perform the contract, there will be no scope to hold the contract void on the ground of common mistake.

76. If one applies the passage from the judgment of Lord Alverstone CJ in *Blakeley v Muller & Co* 19 TLR 186 . . . it suggests that the following elements must be present if common mistake is to avoid a contract: (i) there must be a common assumption as to the existence of a state of affairs; (ii) there must be no warranty by either party that that state of affairs exists; (iii) the non-existence of the state of affairs must not be attributable to the fault of either party; (iv) the non-existence of the state of affairs must render performance of the contract impossible; (v) the state of affairs may be the existence, or a vital attribute, of the consideration to be provided or circumstances which must subsist if performance of the contractual adventure is to be possible. . . .

81. In *William Sindall plc v Cambridgeshire County Council* [1994] 1 WLR 1016, 1035 Hoffmann LJ commented that such allocation of risk can come about by rules of general law applicable to contract, such as 'caveat emptor' in the law of sale of goods or the rule that a lessor or vendor of land does not impliedly warrant that the premises are fit for any particular purpose, so that this risk is allocated by the contract to the lessee or purchaser.

82. Thus, while we do not consider that the doctrine of common mistake can be satisfactorily explained by an implied term, an allegation that a contract is void for common mistake will often raise important issues of construction. Where it is possible to perform the letter of the contract, but it is alleged that there was a common mistake in relation to a fundamental assumption which renders performance of the essence of the obligation impossible, it will be necessary, by construing the contract in the light of all the material circumstances, to decide whether this is indeed the case. . . .

85. Circumstances where a contract is void as a result of common mistake are likely to be less common than instances of frustration. Supervening events which defeat the contractual adventure will frequently not be the responsibility of either party. Where, however, the parties agree that something shall be done which is impossible at the time of making the agreement, it is much more likely that, on true construction of the agreement, one or other will have undertaken responsibility for the mistaken state of affairs. This may well explain why cases where contracts have been found to be void in consequence of common mistake are few and far between. . . ."

The result in this case

"162. . . . It was unquestionably a common assumption of both parties when the contract was concluded that the two vessels were in sufficiently close proximity to enable the *Great Peace* to carry out the service that she was engaged to perform. Was the distance between the two vessels so great as to confound that assumption and to render the contractual adventure impossible of performance? If so, the defendants would have an arguable case that the contract was void under the principle in *Bell v Lever Bros Ltd* [1932] AC 161.

165. Next Mr Reeder submitted that it was not legitimate for the judge to have regard to the fact that the defendants did not want to cancel the agreement with the *Great Peace* until they knew whether they could get a nearer vessel to assist. We do not agree. This reaction was a telling indication that the fact that the vessels were considerably further apart than the defendants had believed did not mean that the services that the *Great Peace* was in a position to provide were essentially different from those which the parties had envisaged when the contract was concluded. The *Great Peace* would arrive in time to provide several days of escort service. The defendants would have wished the contract to be performed but for the adventitious arrival on the scene of a vessel prepared to perform the same services. The fact that the vessels were further apart than both parties had appreciated did not mean that it was impossible to perform the contractual adventure.

166. The parties entered into a binding contract for the hire of the *Great Peace*. That contract gave the defendants an express right to cancel the contract subject to the obligation to pay the 'cancellation fee' of five days' hire. When they engaged the *Nordfarer* they cancelled the *Great Peace*. They became liable in consequence to pay the cancellation fee. There is no injustice in this result.

167. For the reasons that we have given, we would dismiss this appeal."

NOTES

1. *Preliminary.* Before proceeding further with this case, it might be useful to pause and to reflect on aspects of this important judgment of the Court of Appeal. The judgment might seem complex, but that is because mistake in English law was itself traditionally complex. And there are several reasons for this complexity.

2. *Rights and remedies.* When viewed from the position of the English substantive law of contract (rights), mistake may seem to lack any fundamental principles. If one shifts to the law of remedies the position changes quite dramatically, in that there are a number of remedies which become (or became) available depending on the kind of error in issue. If the source of the error is a statement by one of the contracting parties ("this painting is by Constable", or "this car has done only 20,000 miles") then there may be remedies for

misrepresentation or, sometimes, for breach of contract (see *Dick Bentley* (1965), above at p.230). If the source of the error cannot be attributed to a pre-contractual statement, one of the parties will usually be seeking either to have the contract declared *void* (an action for a declaration) or to enforce a contract that the other party is refusing to perform (specific performance or damages). If the error concerns a document, a special defence of *non est factum* (this is not my deed) comes into play (see **5.3.7**); and if the mistake concerns the identity of a person the tort of conversion is usually the remedy in play since mistake of identity often involves property problems (see **5.3.6**). In fact many cases involving *non est factum* and mistake of identity deserve to be classed more in the law of property than the law of obligations.

3. *Rescission in equity*. One fundamental distinction that must always be borne in mind when dealing with *misrepresentation* problems is, as we have seen, the difference between the remedy of damages at common law and the remedy of rescission in equity. A party who has entered a contract under a misrepresentation made by the other party can in principle ask the court to rescind the contract in equity; and such rescission will be available irrespective of fault. Now, the equitable remedy of rescission was also available for *mistake* as well as misrepresentation thanks to the decision of *Solle v Butcher* (1950). Thus there were once two doctrines of mistake in contract: there was the position at common law (offer and acceptance and implied condition precedent) and the position in equity (remedy of rescission). However, it appears that equitable rescission is no longer available for pure mistake cases (i.e. where there is no misrepresentation).

***Great Peace Shipping Ltd v Tsavliris Salvage (International) Ltd (The Great Peace)* [2003] Q.B. 679, CA**

(For facts, see p.255.)

Lord Phillips M.R. (delivering the judgment of the court): ". . . 95. In *Solle v Butcher* [1950] 1 KB 671 Denning LJ held that a court has an equitable power to set aside a contract that is binding in law on the ground of common mistake. . . .

153. A number of cases, albeit a small number, in the course of the last 50 years have purported to follow *Solle v Butcher* [1950] 1 KB 671, yet none of them defines the test of mistake that gives rise to the equitable jurisdiction to rescind in a manner that distinguishes this from the test of a mistake that renders a contract void in law, as identified in *Bell v Lever Bros Ltd* [1932] AC 161. . . .

154. In *Solle v Butcher* Denning LJ identified the requirement of a common misapprehension that was 'fundamental', and that adjective has been used to describe the mistake in those cases which have followed *Solle v Butcher*. We do not find it possible to distinguish, by a process of definition, a mistake which is

259

'fundamental' from Lord Atkin's mistake as to quality which 'makes the thing [contracted for] essentially different from the thing [that] it was believed to be': [1932] AC 161, 218.

155. A common factor in *Solle v Butcher* and the cases which have followed it can be identified. The effect of the mistake has been to make the contract a particularly bad bargain for one of the parties. Is there a principle of equity which justifies the court in rescinding a contract where a common mistake has produced this result?

156. ... [T]he premise of equity's intrusion into the effects of the common law is that the common law rule in question is seen in the particular case to work injustice, and for some reason the common law cannot cure itself. But it is difficult to see how that can apply here. Cases of fraud and misrepresentation, and undue influence, are all catered for under other existing and uncontentious equitable rules. We are only concerned with the question whether relief might be given for common mistake in circumstances wider than those stipulated in *Bell v Lever Bros Ltd* [1932] AC 161. But that, surely, is a question as to where the common law should draw the line; not whether, given the common law rule, it needs to be mitigated by application of some other doctrine. The common law has drawn the line in *Bell v Lever Bros Ltd*. The effect of *Solle v Butcher* [1950] 1 KB 671 is not to supplement or mitigate the common law: it is to say that *Bell v Lever Bros Ltd* was wrongly decided.

157. Our conclusion is that it is impossible to reconcile *Solle v Butcher* with *Bell v Lever Bros Ltd*. ... If coherence is to be restored to this area of our law, it can only be by declaring that there is no jurisdiction to grant rescission of a contract on the ground of common mistake where that contract is valid and enforceable on ordinary principles of contract law. ..."

QUESTIONS

1. Is this case an example of the Court of Appeal overruling one of its own decisions? Is it entitled to do this?

2. Read *Solle v Butcher* (1950) in the law report. Was one of the parties attempting justly or unjustly to enrich himself at the other's expense? If the attempt was unjustified, was it not right that equity should intervene with one of its remedies?

3. Read paras 96–117 of Lord Phillips' judgment in the law report. Were the members of House of Lords in *Bell v Lever Brothers Ltd* really directing their minds towards the question of whether rescission in equity might or might not be available in mistake cases?

4. If PECL, art.4:103 was adopted as part of English law, would it effectively "restore" equitable mistake as part of English contract law?

5.3.4 *Error in verbis*

Equitable rescission may no longer be available to a contracting party who is the victim of a mistake, but the equitable remedy of rectification of a document might still come to a victim's aid if the mistake is one that attaches to a contractual document. The Court of Chancery has traditionally been prepared to rectify a contractual document if satisfied that the document does not reflect what was actually agreed (or promised) between the parties.

***Thomas Bates & Son Ltd v Wyndham's (Lingerie) Ltd* [1981] 1 W.L.R. 505, CA**

This was an action by a landlord for rectification of a lease which, to the knowledge of the tenant, did not actually reflect what had been agreed between them during negotiations. The Court of Appeal (Buckley, Eveleigh and Brightman L.JJ.) held that the lease should be rectified.

> **Buckley L.J.:** ". . . The landlords claim rectification in the present case on the basis of a principle enunciated by Pennycuick J in *A Roberts & Co Ltd v Leicestershire Council* [1961] Ch 555, 570 where he said:
>
>> 'The second ground rests upon the principle that a party is entitled to rectification of a contract upon proof that he believed a particular term to be included in the contract, and that the other party concluded the contract with the omission or a variation of that term in the knowledge that the first party believed the term to be included . . .
>>
>> The principle is stated in Snell on *Equity*, 25th ed (1960), p 569 as follows: "By what appears to be a species of equitable estoppel, if one party to a transaction knows that the instrument contains a mistake in his favour but does nothing to correct it, he (and those claiming under him) will be precluded from resisting rectification on the ground that the mistake is unilateral and not common."'
>
> For this doctrine—that is to say the doctrine of *A Roberts & Co Ltd v Leicestershire County Council*—to apply I think it must be shown: first, that one party A erroneously believed that the document sought to be rectified contained a particular term or provision, or possibly did not contain a particular term or provision which, mistakenly, it did contain; secondly, that the other party B was aware of the omission or the inclusion and that it was due to a mistake on the part of A; thirdly, that B has omitted to draw the mistake to the notice of A. And I think there must be a fourth element involved, namely, that the mistake must be one calculated to benefit B. If these requirements are satisfied, the court may regard it as inequitable to allow B to resist rectification to give effect to A's intention on the ground that the mistake was not, at the time of execution of the document, a mutual mistake . . .

> For these reasons I think that the judge . . . reached the right conclusion on the matter relating to rectification. I would accordingly uphold that part of his order which directed rectification . . ."

QUESTIONS

1. Is rectification a form of estoppel?

2. Is *Thomas Bates* an unjust enrichment case?

3. Is the remedy of rectification governed by rules?

4. "The equitable remedy of rectification . . . is only one aspect of a much wider equitable jurisdiction to relieve from the consequences of mistake" (Millett J. in *Gibbon v Mitchell* (1990), at p.1307). Is this statement still good law?

5. Is *Thomas Bates* relevant to the problem in *Centrovincial Estates plc v Merchant Investors Assurance Co Ltd* (1983) (p.145)?

5.3.5 *Error in corpore*

Some mistakes go not to the quality of an object forming the subject-matter of the contract but to the *nature* of the thing supplied. Of course some quality mistakes can be analysed in this way: thus in Roman law a sale of wine contract would not be void if the wine proved to be sour; but if it was all along vinegar then the contract would be void because one commodity was being sold for another (D.18.1.9.2). One central question, then, is this: did the buyer get the object he bargained for?

Smith v Hughes (1871) L.R. 6 Q.B. 597, QB

This was an action in debt brought by a farmer for the price of new oats sold to the defendant, a trainer of racehorses. The defendant did not want "new" oats—as the farmer knew—and thus he argued that he was not bound by the contract; but the plaintiff claimed that the defendant had offered to buy "good oats", making no mention of the word "old". The jury returned a verdict for the defendant and the plaintiff appealed. The Court of Queen's Bench (Cockburn C.J., Blackburn and Hannen JJ.) ordered a new trial.

Cockburn C.J.: ". . . [W]e must assume that nothing was said on the subject of the defendant's manager desiring to buy old oats, nor of the oats having been said to be old; while, on the other hand, we must assume that the defendant's manager believed the oats to be old oats, and that the plaintiff was conscious of the existence of such belief, but did nothing, directly or indirectly, to bring it about, simply offering his oats and exhibiting his sample, remaining perfectly passive as to what was passing in the mind of the other party. The question is whether, under such circumstances, the passive acquiescence of the seller in the self-deception of the buyer will entitle the latter to avoid the contract. I am of opinion that it will not.

The oats offered to the defendant's manager were a specific parcel, of which the sample submitted to him formed a part. He kept the sample for twenty-four hours, and had, therefore, full opportunity of inspecting it and forming his judgment upon it. Acting on his own judgment, he wrote to the plaintiff, offering him a price. Having this opportunity of inspecting and judging of the sample, he is practically in the same position as if he had inspected the oats in bulk. It cannot be said that, if he had gone and personally inspected the oats in bulk, and then, believing—but without anything being said or done by the seller to bring about such a belief—that the oats were old, had offered a price for them, he would have been justified in repudiating the contract, because the seller, from the known habits of the buyer, or other circumstances, had reason to infer that the buyer was ascribing to the oats a quality they did not possess, and did not undeceive him.

I take the true rule to be, that where a specific article is offered for sale, without express warranty, or without circumstances from which the law will imply a warranty—as where, for instance, an article is ordered for a specific purpose—and the buyer has full opportunity of inspecting and forming his own judgment, if he chooses to act on his own judgment, the rule caveat emptor applies . . . The question is not what a man of scrupulous morality or nice honour would do under such circumstances . . ."

Blackburn J.: ". . . The jury were directed that, if they believed the word 'old' was used, they should find for the defendant—and this was right; for if that was the case, it is obvious that neither did the defendant intend to enter into a contract on the plaintiff's terms, that is, to buy this parcel of oats without any stipulation as to their quality; nor could the plaintiff have been led to believe he was intending to do so.

But the second direction raises the difficulty. I think that, if from that direction the jury would understand that they were first to consider whether they were satisfied that the defendant intended to buy this parcel of oats on the terms that it was part of his contract with the plaintiff that they were old oats, so as to have the warranty of the plaintiff to that effect, they were properly told that, if that was so, the defendant could not be bound to a contract without any such warranty unless the plaintiff was misled. But I doubt whether the direction would bring to the minds of the jury the distinction between agreeing to take the oats under the belief that they were old, and agreeing to take the oats under the belief that the plaintiff contracted that they were old.

The difference is the same as that between buying a horse believed to be sound, and buying one believed to be warranted sound; but I doubt if it was made obvious to the jury, and I doubt this the more because I do not see much evidence to justify a finding for the defendant on this latter ground if the word 'old' was not used . . . I agree, therefore, in the result that there should be a new trial."

QUESTIONS

1. Is this case authority for the proposition that English contract law has no doctrine of good faith?

2. Who caused the buyer's loss?

3. Is this case authority for the proposition that silence is no misrepresentation?

4. Would this case be decided the same way today? What if the PECL, art.4:103 (see p.249) governed the facts of *Smith v Hughes*: would the result of the case have to be different?

5. Is this case further evidence in support of the idea that English contract law is based on promise rather than agreement?

6. Had s.14 of the Sale of Goods Act 1979 (or indeed 1893) been in force, would this have led to a different result in *Smith v Hughes*?

PROBLEM

Pierre, who has a habit of talking aloud to himself, goes to a local hardware shop to buy a can of paint to paint his garden fence. Standing before the rows of paint, Pierre chooses one and declares aloud to himself: 'this is just what I need for my fence!'. The shop assistant overhears him saying this but at no point warns him that the paint he has taken down from the shelf and is intending to buy is quite unsuitable for outdoor fences. A couple of weeks later Pierre returns to the shop with the empty paint tin, demanding his money back because the paint was unsuitable. Is the shop legally obliged to give him his money back?

FURTHER QUESTION

What if the thing forming the subject-matter of the contract does not actually exist?

Sale of Goods Act 1979 (c.54)

"6. Goods which have perished

Where there is a contract for the sale of specific goods, and the goods without the knowledge of the seller have perished at the time when a contract is made, the contract is void."

NOTES

1. In *Associated Japanese Bank (International) Ltd v Crédit du Nord* (1989), Steyn J. said (at p.269): "The non-existence of the subject matter of the principal contract is . . . of fundamental importance."

2. Strictly speaking, there is no doctrine of mistake in English law (especially now that mistake in equity has been suppressed). Those cases where contracts have been set aside for "mistake" can usually be classified within other areas of contract law, namely: (i) offer and acceptance (*Financings Ltd v Stimson* (1962), at p.156); (ii) misrepresentation (see e.g. *Leaf v International Galleries* (1950), at p.242); or (iii) implied condition precedent (*Associated Japanese Bank (International) Ltd v Crédit du Nord* (1989) and *Financings Ltd v Stimson* (1962)). This idea of an implied condition precedent is probably the conceptual idea that underpins s.6 of the Sale of Goods Act 1979.

PROBLEM

Tony agrees to sell a wrecked ship to Bernard and supplies Bernard with details of its position on some reef in the ocean. Bernard spends much time and money looking for the wreck but is never able to locate it. Can Bernard sue Tony for breach of contract? Would your answer be different if one was applying to this problem a civilian contract system based on agreement rather than promise? (See *Associated Japanese Bank (International) Ltd v Crédit du Nord* (1989); but *cf. McRae v Commonwealth Disposals Commission* (1951).)

5.3.6 *Error in persona*

One can be mistaken not just about the object (*res*) of some contract but also about the identity of the other contracting party (*persona*). Such mistakes usually arise, of course, because someone misrepresents himself as another, thus giving rise to the remedy of rescission. However, rescission makes the contract only *voidable*, with the result that if the contract was one of sale, title in the goods would pass to the representor, allowing him, in turn, to pass good title to a third party. Now if the mistake was such as to make the contract *void*, title in any goods could not pass; the original "seller" would remain owner and could sue any third party in the tort of conversion.

Shogun Finance Ltd v Hudson [2004] 1 A.C. 919, HL

This was an action for damages in the tort of conversion brought by the owner of a motor vehicle, a finance company, against a private purchaser who had bought it in good faith from a fraudster. The fraudster had obtained possession of the vehicle from a dealer by pretending to be the person named on a stolen driving licence and thereby entering into an apparent hire-purchase transaction with the claimants.

Having got possession of the vehicle from the dealer, the fraudster sold it to the defendant before the fraud was discovered. The defendant resisted the claim by relying on s.27 of the Hire Purchase Act 1964, but a majority of the House of Lords (Lords Hobhouse, Phillips and Walker; Lords Nicholls and Millett dissenting) held that this section was applicable only where there had been a valid hire-purchase contract between the person selling the vehicle (the fraudster) and the finance company owner. As there was no such valid contract, the defendant was liable in damages for the value of the vehicle.

Lord Nicholls (dissenting): "**1** My Lords, this appeal raises a difficult problem about the effect of fraudulent misrepresentation on the formation of a contract. If a crook (C) fraudulently represents to the owner of goods (O) that he is another identifiable person (X) and on that basis O parts with goods to C by way of sale, is there in law a contract between O and C? Does the answer to this question differ according to whether O and C communicated face-to-face, or by correspondence, or over the telephone, or by e-mail? The law on cases involving this type of fraudulent conduct, euphemistically described as cases of 'mistaken identity', is notoriously unsatisfactory. The reported decisions are few in number and they are not reconcilable. In the present case Sedley LJ said the law has tied itself into a Gordian knot. Brooke LJ said the law is in a 'sorry condition' which only Parliament or your Lordships' House can remedy: see [2002] QB 834, 847, 855, paras 23, 51.

2 Two features are usually present when cases of this type come before the court. The first feature is that a seller of goods is concerned with the creditworthiness of the proposed buyer. The seller wants to be sure he will be paid for the goods he is handing over. Here the common law seems to have drawn a distinction between two kinds of fraudulent misrepresentation. The common law distinguished between a case (1) where a crook fraudulently asserts he is creditworthy and a case (2) where a crook fraudulently asserts he is someone else known to be creditworthy. One might suppose there is no difference of substance between these two cases. These are merely two ways a crook may assert a spurious creditworthiness. But, historically, the law seems to have been otherwise. In case (1), when the seller parts with his goods he does so pursuant to a *voidable* contract. This is said to be a case of mistake as to a person's attributes. In case (2), in some circumstances but not all, the seller has been held to part with his goods pursuant to a *void* contract, that is, no contract at all. This is said to be a case of mistake as to a person's identity.

3 The second feature usually present in cases of this type is that the crook then sells the goods to an innocent third party. This feature explains why the distinction between a voidable and a void contract matters. Having fraudulently acquired the goods from their owner, the crook then sells them to an unsuspecting third party. The rights of this innocent third party may depend upon the nice distinction between a voidable contract and a void contract. In case (1), where the crook fraudulently misrepresents his own financial standing, the loss falls on the unfortunate owner of the goods who was tricked into parting with them to the crook. . . .

4 This outcome is to be contrasted with case (2), where the crook asserts he is someone else. In such a case the loss sometimes, but not always, falls upon the unfortunate third party who also was a victim of the crook's trickery. The third party paid for the goods in all honesty, but he must return them to their original owner or pay their value. . . .

5 The distinction in outcome thus drawn between these two kinds of fraudulent misrepresentation, one as to 'attributes' and the other as to 'identity', is unconvincing. It has been described as a reproach to the law. To a considerable extent the distinction has now been eroded. *Cundy v Lindsay* 3 App Cas 459 was decided over a century ago, and since then there have been significant developments in this area of case law. Unfortunately these developments have left the law in a state of disarray. The question before the House on this appeal is whether this distinction, so far as it remains, should still be regarded as good law. . . .

34 Accordingly, if the law of contract is to be coherent and rescued from its present unsatisfactory and unprincipled state, the House has to make a choice: either to uphold the approach adopted in *Cundy v Lindsay* and overrule the decisions in *Phillips v Brooks Ltd* and *Lewis v Averay*, or to prefer these later decisions to *Cundy v Lindsay*.

35 I consider the latter course is the right one, for a combination of reasons. It is in line with the direction in which, under the more recent decisions, the law has now been moving for some time. It accords better with basic principle regarding the effect of fraud on the formation of a contract. It seems preferable as a matter of legal policy. As between two innocent persons the loss is more appropriately borne by the person who takes the risks inherent in parting with his goods without receiving payment. This approach fits comfortably with the intention of Parliament in enacting the limited statutory exceptions to the proprietary principle of nemo dat quod non habet . . . And this course makes practical sense. In a case such as the present the owner of goods has no interest in the identity of the buyer. He is interested only in creditworthiness. It is little short of absurd that a subsequent purchaser's rights depend on the precise manner in which the crook seeks to persuade the owner of his creditworthiness and permit him to take the goods away with him. This ought not to be so. The purchaser's rights should not depend upon the precise form the crook's misrepresentation takes . . ."

Lord Hobhouse: ". . . **53** The final point was the fact that the purported customer's signature was not in truth that of Mr Durlabh Patel. The supposed hire-purchase agreement therefore from the outset lacked an essential ingredient and within the terms of the document was never an offer eligible for acceptance. A forged signature is neither the signature of the purported signatory nor of the forger. There may be an exception where the 'forger' had the authority of the actual party to sign on his behalf and in his name, in which case it probably would not be a forgery unless there was some dishonest intent to deceive. The same applies to using a 'mere pseudonym' or a trading name. But that is not this case.

54 It follows that the appeal must be dismissed and the majority judgment of the Court of Appeal affirmed.

55 But, before I leave this case, I should shortly summarise why the argument of the appellant's counsel was so mistaken. The first reason was that they approached the question as if it was simply a matter of sorting out the common law authorities relating to the sale of goods. They did not treat it as a matter of applying a statutory exception to the basic common law rule, nemo dat quod non habet. Further, they did not analyse the structure of the overall transaction and the consumer credit agreement within it. Accordingly, they misrepresented the role of the dealer, wrongly treating him as the contracting agent of the finance company which he was not. They never analysed the terms of the written document and had no regard at all to the offer and acceptance clause it contained which, if there was any contract between a 'debtor' and the finance company, governed their relationship and which expressly set out the *only* way in which such a contract could come into existence. They made submissions which contradicted the express written contract and were therefore contrary to principle and long established English mercantile law. They submitted that *Cundy v Lindsay* 3 App Cas 459 was wrongly decided and should be overruled, substituting for it a general rule which, in disregard of the document or documents which constitute the agreement (if any), makes everything depend upon a factual inquiry into extraneous facts not known to both of the parties thus depriving documentary contracts of their certainty. They sought to convert a direct documentary contract with the finance company into a face-to-face oral contract made through the dealer as the contracting agent of the finance company, notwithstanding that the dealer was never such an agent of the finance company. Finally they sought, having bypassed the written contract, to rely upon authorities on oral contracts for the sale of goods, made face-to-face and where the title to the goods had passed to the 'buyer', notwithstanding that this was a documentary consumer credit transaction not a sale and, on any view, no title had ever passed to R. In the result they have invited a review of those authorities by reference to the particular facts of each of them. They have sought to draw your Lordships into a discussion of the evidential tools, eg, rebuttable presumptions of fact and the so-called face-to-face 'principle', used by judges in those cases to assist them in making factual decisions (see also the dictum of Gresson P in *Fawcett v Star Car Sales Ltd* [1960] NZLR 406, 413), notwithstanding that the present case concerns the construction of a written contract. They forget that the, presently relevant, fundamental principles of law to be applied—consensus ad idem, the correspondence of the contractual offer and the contractual acceptance, the legal significance of the use of a written contract—are clear and are not in dispute. Inevitably over the course of time there have been decisions on the facts of individual 'mistaken identity' cases which seem now to be inconsistent; the further learned, but ultimately unproductive, discussion of them will warm academic hearts. But what matters is the principles of law. They are clear and sound and need no revision. To cast doubt upon them can only be a disservice to English law. Similarly, to attempt to use this appeal to advocate, on the basis of continental legal systems which are open to cogent criticism, the abandonment of the soundly based nemo dat quod non habet rule (statutorily adopted) would be not only improper but even more damaging."

Lord Millett (dissenting): "**57** Generations of law students have struggled with this problem. They may be forgiven for thinking that it is contrived by their tutors to test their mettle . . .

61 My Lords, I think that the time has come to follow the lead given by Lord Denning MR more than 30 years ago in *Lewis v Averay* [1972] 1 QB 198. He roundly rejected the theory that if a party is *mistaken* as to the identity of the person with whom he is contracting there is no contract, or that if there is a contract it is null and void so that no property can pass under it: see pp 206–207. He thought that the doctrine, derived from the writings of Pothier, should not be admitted as part of English law but should be 'dead and buried'. As he observed, it gives rise to fine distinctions which do no good to the law, and it is unjust that an innocent third party, who knows nothing of what passed between the rogue and his vendor, should have his title depend on such refinements. . . .

81 In my opinion, once one accepts that there are two questions involved: (i) did a contract come into existence at all? and (ii) if so was the contract vitiated by fraud or mistake? there is only one principled conclusion. Whatever the medium of communication, a contract comes into existence if, on an objective appraisal of the facts, there is sufficient correlation between offer and acceptance to make it possible to say that the impostor's offer has been accepted by the person to whom it was addressed. While a person cannot intercept and accept an offer made to some one else, he should normally be treated as intending to contract with the person with whom he is dealing. Provided that the offer is made to him, then whether his acceptance of the offer is obtained by deception or mistake, and whether his mistake is as to the identity of the offeror or some material attribute of his, the transaction should result in a contract, albeit one which is voidable.

82 This rule is easy to apply and accords with principle by distinguishing between the formation of a contract as a question of fact to be determined objectively and the consequences of mistake or fraud which depend on its effect on the mind of the person affected. It avoids undesirable refinements and gives a measure of protection to innocent third parties. Of course, someone has to bear the loss where there is fraud, but it is surely fairer that the party who was actually swindled and who had an opportunity to uncover the fraud should bear the loss rather than a party who entered the picture only after the swindle had been carried out and who had none. In the present case, the claimant could easily have exposed the fraud by writing to Mr Patel, whose address it had been given, and asking him to confirm his intention to proceed with the proposed transaction. If it had been one for which statute required a cooling-off period, it no doubt it would have done . . ."

Lord Phillips: ". . . **119** The critical issue in this case is whether a hire-purchase agreement was ever concluded between Shogun and the rogue. If an agreement was concluded, then the rogue was the 'debtor' under section 27 of the 1964 Act and passed good title in the vehicle to Mr Hudson. If no agreement was concluded, then the rogue stole the vehicle by deception and passed no title to Mr Hudson . . .

178 . . . [T]he correct approach in the present case is to treat the agreement as one concluded in writing and to approach the identification of the parties to that agreement as turning upon its construction. The particulars given in the agreement are only capable of applying to Mr Patel. It was the intention of the rogue that they should identify Mr Patel as the hirer. The hirer was so identified by Shogun. Before deciding to enter into the agreement they checked that Mr Patel existed and that he was worthy of credit. On that basis they decided to contract with him and with no one else. Mr Patel was the hirer under the agreement. As the agreement was concluded without his authority, it was a nullity. The rogue took no title under it and was in no position to convey any title to Mr Hudson . . ."

Lord Walker: ". . . **191** However, the present appeal is, as my noble and learned friend, Lord Hobhouse, has demonstrated, easier to resolve. Shogun Finance had no doubt never heard of the real Mr Patel before the day on which the written contract was signed by the rogue, forging Mr Patel's signature. But by the time it accepted the written offer it had, by efficient information technology, confirmed that Mr Patel existed and had learned a good deal of relevant information about him, including his creditworthiness. The form of contract made quite clear that Shogun Finance's intention was to accept an offer made by the real Mr Patel, and no one else . . ."

(For further extracts, see p.48, p.147 and p.216.)

QUESTIONS

1. Do car manufacturers, car dealers and hire-purchase finance companies want to sell as many cars as possible? If so, do they really care about the identity of buyers?

2. Who was in the best position to stop this kind of fraud and the loss that it causes?

3. What if the fraudster had been badly injured while driving the car away from the dealers as a result of the vehicle being defective: could he sue anyone for his injuries?

4. Is this case a mistake or an offer and acceptance problem?

5.3.7 *Error in negotio*

Similar property problems can arise in cases where a person who signs a document is mistaken about the nature of the document.

Avon Finance Co Ltd v Bridger **[1985] 2 All E.R. 281, CA**

The plaintiffs brought an action for possession of the defendants' house which had been charged to the plaintiffs as security for a loan. The charge had been signed by the defendants, but only because they had been misled as to the nature of the document by their son. The judge dismissed the plaintiffs' action on the basis of non est factum and an appeal to the Court of Appeal (Lord Denning M.R., Brandon and Brightman L.JJ.) was unsuccessful.

Lord Denning M.R.: "A few years ago we had a case about old Herbert Bundy, a father who was let down by his son. Now we have the case of George Bridger, a postman, who has also been let down by his son . . .

It is plain that the son was a very bad lot. He went missing. He owed debts all round. Newspapers reported him as saying that his life had crumbled; that he had been sleeping in his car; and so forth. It seems to me that the legal position was not fully canvassed before the county court judge. One could not expect Mr Bridger to understand the law. He set out the facts. In his pleadings he was only bound to set out the material facts. The case was argued as though it depended on the legal doctrine of *non est factum* . . . The judge thought that the issue depended on whether or not Mr and Mrs Bridger were careless in not checking the documents and unreasonable in trusting their son . . .

The judge . . . held that it was a case of *non est factum* and that the parents were not liable.

Now I am afraid I cannot agree with the judge about *non est factum*. The doctrine is of very limited application as was explained in the Court of Appeal in *Saunders v Anglia Building Society, sub nom Gallie v Lee* . . . as modified by Lord Pearson in the House of Lords . . . In that case Mrs Gallie's signature was obtained by fraud just as Mr and Mrs Bridger's was here. Yet the plea of *non est factum* did not prevail.

But I think the case should be considered on a different footing altogether, namely on the principle of 'inequality of bargaining' as set out in *Lloyds Bank Ltd v Bundy* . . .

271

Here this son brought undue pressures on his parents for the benefit of the plaintiffs, and for himself of course, because he wanted the loan. They left it all to him. They said that he was to procure the execution of the deed. He brought undue pressure to bear on his parents by giving them an entirely misleading account of the documents. It seems to me that the parents' bargaining power was impaired by their own ignorance, and that this court should not uphold the transaction. On this ground I would uphold the judge's decision.

I would just like to comment on a point which was not canvassed in the court below. We were referred to the Consumer Credit Act 1974, which now replaces many of the provisions of the old Moneylenders Acts 1900 to 1927 which were in force. Without going into the details of the sections . . . it seems to me that under the statute now, in regard to an agreement such as the one in this case, if it grossly contravenes the ordinary principles of fair dealing, and if regard is had to factors such as the age, experience and business capacity of Mr and Mrs Bridger, this is a case which may well come within the provisions of the 1974 Act. The agreement should be regarded as extortionate and the court can set aside the whole of the obligation. It is unnecessary to consider those matters in detail because they were not gone into. But, as far as I can see, if that statute were considered in detail, it is very likely that the same result would be reached as I would reach in this case, which is that the plaintiffs in these circumstances cannot enforce this legal charge against the parents."

Brandon L.J.: "The deputy county court judge found in favour of the defendants on the basis of the defence *non est factum*. I would not agree with the decision of the deputy county court judge on that aspect of the case. A defendant can only rely on that plea when he has exercised reasonable care in the circumstances in connection with the transaction. The deputy county court judge found as a fact that the defendants had exercised reasonable care; but his decision on that matter, although one of fact, was a decision based on an inference from primary facts which are not in dispute, and this court is as well placed to draw the appropriate inference as was the deputy county court judge. In my judgment, it is impossible on the facts of this case to find that the defendants exercised such reasonable care as was appropriate in the circumstances in entering into the transaction. I would therefore find it impossible to support the judgment on the ground on which it was given.

In this court, however, a different defence has been discussed, which I think it is right the court should consider because the defendants were in person and were not in a position to put all the relevant legal arguments before the court below. That defence is that the transaction relating to the second mortgage is voidable in equity . . .

The matters which seem to me to give rise to an equity in favour of the defendants are three. The first matter is that the plaintiffs chose to appoint the son, who was the debtor, to procure from his parents the security which he and they needed to further the transaction on which they were engaged. It was for the plaintiffs' benefit to have this security because they are in business for money lending, and they wanted a good secure money-lending contract. They chose to appoint the son, a young accountant in the prime of life, to procure this contract from his parents, both of whom were old-age pensioners, much less well educated than he was. The person whom they chose to appoint, being a son, could be expected to have some influence over his elderly parents, and that is something of which the plaintiffs could or should have been aware. In fact, the son was fraudulent. He deceived his parents, and by his deception induced them to enter into this transaction. We have those two matters, the procurement of the security by the son and the relationship between the son and his elderly parents of different educational attainment. Finally we have the third factor of the absence of any independent advice.

The fact is that there was no independent advice, and, in so far as the plaintiffs thought there was independent advice, they were in error . . .''

QUESTIONS

1. Where is the line to be drawn between error and undue influence (see **6.3**)? Does it matter?

2. Was the son acting as agent of the plaintiffs?

3. Could the plaintiffs sue the son for their legal expenses incurred in the action against the parents?

4. Is this a mistake case? If so, which party was labouring under a mistake?

5. How much of Lord Denning's judgment is good law?

NOTES AND FURTHER QUESTIONS

1. The defence of *non est factum* (this is not my document) was originally a matter of proof in the writ of debt rather than part of the law of mistake (see D. Ibbetson, *A Historical Introduction to the Law of Obligations* (OUP, 1999), p.20). However, the 'centuries-old defence of *non est factum*, denying the efficacy of a purported deed under seal, was generalised to apply to all written documents and interpreted as another example of mistake, shifting the case where a document was made under some misapprehension as to its contents from the margin of the defence to its central core' (Ibbetson, p.228). The reason for this shift, says Ibbetson, was the unified theory seemingly fashioned by Pothier (see extract on p.248).

2. As Lord Denning indicated, the leading authority on the defence of *non est factum* is *Saunders v Anglia Building Society* (1971). This was an action for possession of a house brought by a building society against an elderly widow. The widow had signed a document, without reading it carefully because her spectacles were broken, assigning the house to a man called Lee; the widow

signed because she thought, on the basis of a fraudulent misrepresentation made by Lee to her, that she was assigning the house to her nephew. Lee mortgaged the house to the plaintiff building society and then defaulted on the payments. The widow counter-claimed for a declaration that the assignment was void on the basis of the plea of *non est factum*. The House of Lords rejected the counter-claim on the ground that the document she thought she was signing and the document she actually signed were not radically different. Should property title be dependent upon pure chance: that is to say, upon radical difference between what the signor thought she was signing and the document she actually signed?

3. "That delivery did not create any bailment of the car by the finance company to the rogue. The rogue was a thief. Albeit by an elaborate but effective course of action, he stole the car from the possession of the dealer just as surely as if he was a thief stealing it from the forecourt" (Lord Hobhouse in *Shogun*, at § 52). Did not Lee "steal" the house in just the same way? And if so, why should the third party get title in *Saunders* but not in *Shogun*?

5.3.8 Mistake: concluding observations

Even with the suppression of rescission in equity as a remedy for mistake, the area remains complex and difficult mainly because there is no overarching general principle or theory applicable. The Court of Appeal in *The Great Peace* (2003) (p.255) has tried to address this question by drawing an analogy with the doctrine of frustration (see **10.5**), for this was an area of the common law, like mistake, which was once based on the idea of an implied condition precedent. In § 76 of his judgment (above, p.257), Lord Phillips attempts to lay down a general set of rules with respect to mistake at common law. These rules might be compared to those set out in the following extract.

> *Unidroit Principles for International Commercial Contracts*
>
> *"Article 3.3 Initial Impossibility*
>
> (1) The mere fact that at the time of the conclusion of the contract the performance of the obligation assumed was impossible does not affect the validity of the contract.
>
> (2) The mere fact that at the time of the conclusion of the contract a party was not entitled to dispose of the assets to which the contract relates does not affect the validity of the contract.
>
> *Article 3.4 Definition of Mistake*
>
> Mistake is an erroneous assumption relating to facts or to law existing when the contract was concluded.

274

Article 3.5 Relevant Mistake

(1) A party may only avoid the contract for mistake if, when the contract was concluded, the mistake was of such importance that a reasonable person in the same situation as the party would not have concluded it at all if the true state of affairs had been known, and

  (a) the other party made the same mistake, or caused the mistake, or knew or ought to have known of the mistake and it was contrary to reasonable commercial standards of fair dealing to leave the mistaken party in error; or

  (b) the other party had not at the time of avoidance acted in reliance on the contract.

(2) However, a party may not avoid the contract if

  (a) it was grossly negligent in committing the mistake; or

  (b) the mistake relates to a matter in regard to which the risk of mistake was assumed or, having regard to the circumstances, should be borne by the mistaken party.

Article 3.6 Error in Expression or Transmission

An error occurring in the expression or transmission of a declaration is considered to be a mistake of the person from whom the declaration emanated.

Article 3.7 Remedies for Non-Performance

A party is not entitled to avoid the contract on the ground of mistake if the circumstances on which that party relies afford, or could have afforded, a remedy for non-performance."

QUESTION

How might *Bell v Lever Brothers* (1932) (p.250) and *Smith v Hughes* (1871) (p.262) be decided under these UNIDROIT principles?

6 Obstacles to formation and vitiating factors (2): unacceptable behaviour

This second chapter devoted to obstacles to formation and vitiating factors will focus, for the most part, on various kinds of behaviour which can generate remedies on behalf of the victim of the behaviour and (or) affect the enforceability of the agreement. In general this chapter will primarily be concerned with voidable and unenforceable contracts, since the forms of behaviour covered will rarely (if at all) make a contract void (in the sense of never existing). Perhaps, then, one should not talk of 'obstacles to formation'. However, a vitiating factor like fraud or duress can be seen as affecting consent (and this is the reason why rescission at common law seems to have developed: see *Halpern v Halpern (No.2)* (2006)), and thus the civil lawyer would regard these factors as going to the formation of the contract. From a European perspective, therefore, it is not misleading to talk of obstacles to the formation of the contract.

6.1 Fraud

As Goff L.J. pointed out in *Whittaker v Campbell* (1984) (above, at p.31), there is no general principle in English law that fraud vitiates consent. It does not. What it does is to give rise to the equitable remedy of rescission. Moreover, if the fraud results from a misrepresentation (as most do), a victim may also be able to obtain damages through the tort of deceit: see *Smith New Court Securities Ltd v Scrimgeour Vickers Ltd* (1997) (C&MT, p.288). Most fraud cases are, accordingly, to be found in **Chapter 5** on misrepresentation under the heading of 'fraudulent misrepresentation', as the next extract suggests.

> **Unidroit Principles for International Commercial Contracts**
>
> *"Article 3.8 Fraud*
>
> A party may avoid the contract when it has been led to conclude the contract by the other party's fraudulent representation, including language or practices, or

fraudulent non-disclosure of circumstances which, according to reasonable commercial standards of fair dealing, the latter party should have disclosed.

Article 3.18 Damages

Irrespective of whether or not the contract has been avoided, the party who knew or ought to have known of the ground for avoidance is liable for damages so as to put the other party in the same position in which it would have been if it had not concluded the contract."

QUESTIONS

1. Is fraudulent non-disclosure (silence) a ground for rescission in English law?

2. Can fraud ever give rise to a claim for damages for breach of contract?

Mahmud v BCCI [1998] A.C. 20, HL

This was an action for damages by two ex-employees against their employer, a bank, which had been guilty of fraudulent and corrupt practices. The House of Lords (Lords Goff, Mackay, Nicholls, Steyn and Mustill) held that they had a good claim.

Lord Nicholls: "My Lords, this is another case arising from the disastrous collapse of Bank of Credit and Commerce International SA in the summer of 1991. Thousands of people around the world suffered loss. Depositors lost their money, employees lost their jobs. Two employees who lost their jobs were Mr Raihan Nasir Mahmud and Mr Qaiser Mansoor Malik. They were employed by BCCI in London. They claim they lost more than their jobs. They claim that their association with BCCI placed them at a serious disadvantage in finding new jobs. So in March 1992 they sought to prove for damages in the winding up of BCCI. The liquidators rejected this 'stigma' head of loss in their proofs. Liability for notice money and statutory redundancy pay was not in dispute . . .

A dishonest and corrupt business

These questions are best approached by focusing first on the particular conduct of which complaint is made. The bank operated its business dishonestly and corruptly. On the assumed facts, this was not a case where one or two individuals, however senior, were behaving dishonestly. Matters had gone beyond this. They had reached the point where the bank itself could properly be identified with the dishonesty. This was a dishonest business, a corrupt business.

It is against this background that the position of an innocent employee has to be considered. In my view, when an innocent employee of the bank learned the true nature of the bank's business, from whatever source, he was entitled to say: 'I wish to have nothing more to do with this organisation. I am not prepared to help this business, by working for it. I am leaving at once.' This is my intuitive response in the case of all innocent employees of the business, from the most senior to the most junior, from the most long serving to the most recently joined. No one could be expected to have to continue to work with and for such a company against his wish.

This intuitive response is no more than a reflection of what goes without saying in any ordinary contract of employment, namely, that in agreeing to work for an employer the employee, whatever his status, cannot be taken to have agreed to work in furtherance of a dishonest business. This is as much true of a doorkeeper or cleaner as a senior executive or branch manager.

An implied obligation

Two points can be noted here. First, as a matter of legal analysis, the innocent employee's entitlement to leave at once must derive from the bank being in breach of a term of the contract of employment which the employee is entitled to treat as a repudiation by the bank of its contractual obligations. That is the source of his right to step away from the contract forthwith.

In other words, and this is the necessary corollary of the employee's right to leave at once, the bank was under an implied obligation to its employees not to conduct a dishonest or corrupt business. This implied obligation is no more than one particular aspect of the portmanteau, general obligation not to engage in conduct likely to undermine the trust and confidence required if the employment relationship is to continue in the manner the employment contract implicitly envisages. Second, I do not accept the liquidators' submission that the conduct of which complaint is made must be targeted in some way at the employee or a group of employees. No doubt that will often be the position, perhaps usually so. But there is no reason in principle why this must always be so. The trust and confidence required in the employment relationship can be undermined by an employer, or indeed an employee, in many different ways. I can see no justification for the law giving the employee a remedy if the unjustified trust-destroying conduct occurs in some ways but refusing a remedy if it occurs in others. The conduct must, of course, impinge on the relationship in the sense that, looked at objectively, it is likely to destroy or seriously damage the degree of trust and confidence the employee is reasonably entitled to have in his employer. That requires one to look at all the circumstances.

Breach

The objective standard just mentioned provides the answer to the liquidators' submission that unless the employee's confidence is actually undermined there is no breach. A breach occurs when the proscribed conduct takes place: here, operating a dishonest and corrupt business. Proof of a subjective loss of confidence in the employer is not an essential element of the breach, although the time when the employee learns of the misconduct and his response to it may affect his remedy.

Remedies: (1) acceptance of breach as repudiation

The next step is to consider the consequences which flow from the bank being in breach of its obligation to its innocent employees by operating a corrupt banking business. The first remedy of an employee has already been noted. The employee may treat the bank's conduct as a repudiatory breach, entitling him to leave. He is not compelled to leave. He may choose to stay. The extent to which staying would be more than an election to remain, and would be a waiver of the breach for all purposes, depends on the circumstances.

I need say no more about waiver in the present case. The assumed facts do not state whether the appellants first learned of the corrupt nature of BCCI after their dismissal on 3 October 1991, or whether they acquired this knowledge earlier, in the interval of three months between the appointment of the provisional liquidators on 5 July 1991 and 3 October 1991. If anything should turn on this, the matter can be investigated further in due course.

In the nature of things, the remedy of treating the conduct as a repudiatory breach, entitling the employee to leave, can only avail an employee who learns of the facts while still employed. If he does not discover the facts while his employment is still continuing, perforce this remedy is not open to him. But this does not mean he has no remedy. In the ordinary course breach of a contractual term entitles the innocent party to damages . . ."

(For further extracts, see p.375 and p.546.)

NOTE

For implied terms generally, see **7.5**.

6.2 Duress

Duress covers situations where a contractor has been induced to enter into a contract by a threat: "Sign this contract or 'Tibbins' [the cat] gets it." If the person threatened signs the contract, two immediate questions arise: Is there a contract given that there was no free consent? And if there is a contract, does the threatened party have any remedies?

6.2.1 Introduction to duress

English law takes the view that such a contract is not void but is voidable (thanks to the equitable remedy of rescission). However, the nature of the duress is important, and thus three broad types of threat need to be examined. There is duress to the person, duress to goods and economic duress. Can the whole area be encapsulated by a single rule?

Principles of European Contract Law

"Article 4:108 Threats

A party may avoid a contract when it has been led to conclude it by the other party's imminent and serious threat of an act:

(a) which is wrongful in itself, or
(b) which it is wrongful to use as a means to obtain the conclusion of the contract, unless in the circumstances the first party had a reasonable alternative."

NOTE

See also UNIDROIT, art.3.9.

QUESTIONS

1. Do both these articles treat duress as an obstacle to formation, or simply as a ground for rescission? Does it matter?

2. Are there any significant differences between the PECL and UNIDROIT articles?

6.2.2 Duress to the person

The most serious form of duress is to the person. Here the law takes the same approach towards the right to rescind as is does for fraudulent misrepresentation (*cf. Redgrave v Hurd* (1881), p.240).

Barton v Armstrong **[1976] A.C. 104, PC**

This was an action for a declaration that a deed executed on behalf of a company to buy shares for cash from its former chairman was void (*sic*) for duress to the person. The deed had been executed by the managing director of the company after he had been threatened with death by the ex-chairman if the deed was not executed. However, there was evidence that the managing director might have executed the deed even if no threat had been made. A majority of the Privy Council (Lords Cross, Kilbrandon and Sir Garfield Barwick; Lords Wilberforce and Simon dissenting) held that the declaration should issue.

Lord Cross: ". . . The scope of common law duress was very limited and at a comparatively early date equity began to grant relief in cases where the disposition in question had been procured by the exercise of pressure which the Chancellor considered to be illegitimate—although it did not amount to common law duress. There was a parallel development in the field of dispositions induced by fraud. At common law the only remedy available to the man defrauded was an action for deceit but equity in the same period in which it was building up the doctrine of 'undue influence' came to entertain proceedings to set aside dispositions which had been obtained by fraud: see *Holdsworth, A History of English Law*, vol V (1924), pp 328–329. There is an obvious analogy between setting aside a disposition for duress or undue influence and setting it aside for fraud. In each case—to quote the words of Holmes J in *Fairbanks v Snow* (1887) 13 NE Reporter 596, 598—'the party has been subjected to an improper motive for action.' Again the similarity of the effect in law of metus and dolus in connection with dispositions of property is noted by Stair in his *Institutions of the Law of Scotland*, New ed (1832), Book IV, title 40.25. Had Armstrong made a fraudulent misrepresentation to Barton for the purpose of inducing him to execute the deed of January 17, 1967, the answer to the problem which has arisen would have been clear. If it were established that Barton did not allow the representation to affect his judgment then he could not make it a ground for relief even though the representation was designed and known by Barton to be designed to affect his judgment. If on the other hand Barton relied on the misrepresentation Armstrong could not have defeated his claim to relief by showing that there were other more weighty causes which contributed to his decision to execute the deed, for in this field the court does not allow an examination into the relative importance of contributory causes.

"Once make out that there has been anything like deception, and no contract resting in any degree on that foundation can stand': *per* Lord Cranworth LJ in *Reynell v Sprye* (1852) 1 De GM & G 660, 708—see also the other cases referred to in *Cheshire and Fifoot's Law of Contract*, 8th ed (1972), pp 250–251. Their Lordships think that the same rule should apply in cases of duress and that if Armstrong's threats were 'a' reason for Barton's executing the deed he is entitled to relief even though he might well have entered into the contract if Armstrong had uttered no threats to induce him to do so.

It remains to apply the law to the facts. What was the state of Barton's mind when he executed the deed is, of course, a question of fact and a question the answer to which depended largely on Barton's own evidence . . . If Barton had to establish that he would not have made the agreement but for Armstrong's threats then their Lordships would not dissent from the view that he had not made out his case. But no such onus lay on him. On the contrary it was for Armstrong to establish, if he could, that the threats which he was making and the unlawful pressure which he was exerting for the purpose of inducing Barton to sign the agreement and which Barton knew were being made and exerted for this purpose in fact contributed nothing to Barton's decision to sign. . . . The proper inference to be drawn from the facts found is, their Lordships think, that though it may be that Barton would have executed the documents even if Armstrong had made no threats and exerted no unlawful pressure to induce him to do so the threats and unlawful pressure in fact contributed to his decision to sign the documents and to recommend their execution by Landmark and the other parties to them. . . .

In the result therefore the appeal should be allowed and a declaration made that the deeds in question were executed by Barton under duress and are void so far as concerns him . . ."

Lord Wilberforce and Lord Simon (dissenting): "The reason why we do not agree with the majority decision is, briefly, that we regard the issues in this case as essentially issues of fact . . .

The point is not whether the agreement was financially advantageous to one side or the other (we would not venture any pronouncement as to this) but whether it was thought to be advantageous by Barton and his associates. That it was so thought is both found by the judge as a matter of fact, and shown by overwhelming evidence. Before the agreement was signed. Barton and his friends thought that the arrangement would be the salvation of the company, and that it was vital to get Armstrong to sign as soon as possible . . ."

QUESTIONS

1. Did the duress exercised in this case actually make the contract 'void'?

2. Does the victim of duress have to be put into some fear by the threat?

3. Could the managing director have sued the chairman for damages in tort?

6.2.3 Duress to goods

The remedy of rescission is equally available where the threat is directed not to the victim's person but to his or her goods or other property. This area has been largely absorbed into economic duress.

6.2.4 Economic duress

It is clear from the PECL, art.4:108 and UNIDROIT, art.3.9 not only that the threat to do a wrong will amount to duress, but also that any threat that is wrongful to use may equally be duress.

Dimskal Shipping Co v International Transport Workers Federation (The Evia Luck)
[1992] 2 A.C. 152, HL

This was, primarily, an action brought against a trade union for a declaration that certain contracts were voidable and for restitution of money paid by shipowners to the union. The House of Lords (Lords Keith, Ackner, Goff and Lowry; Lord Templeman dissenting) gave judgment for the shipowners. The detailed facts are set out in Lord Templeman's dissenting judgment.

> **Lord Templeman** (dissenting): "My Lords, the appellant federation is a trade union which seeks to prevent the employment of cheap labour on vessels flying flags of convenience. The respondents own the *Evia Luck* which was registered in Panama and employed a crew recruited in Greece and in the Philippines on terms which were inferior to those approved by the federation. The *Evia Luck* put into a port in Sweden and the federation blacked the ship by persuading local workers not to load the ship or to assist her to depart the port until the owners entered into contracts with the federation and the crew whereby the owners paid compensation to the federation for the crew in respect of past wages, entered into fresh contracts of employment with the crew on terms approved by the federation and made a contribution to the welfare fund of the federation.
>
> The contracts entered into by the owners as a result of the blacking organised by the federation were expressed to be governed by English law. In this appeal the owners seek to uphold the decision of the Court of Appeal (McCowan LJ and Sir Roger Ormrod, Neill LJ dissenting) whereby the Court of Appeal ordered the federation to pay the owners $111,743 with interest and declared that the agreements to which the federation and the owners were parties were void. The Court of Appeal [1990] ICR 694 by a majority thus reversed the judgment of Phillips J [1989] 1 Lloyd's Rep 166 who had dismissed the action by the owners . . .
>
> Under the English common law an employer has never been guilty of economic duress if at a time when unemployment is high and workers are weak wages are low. Under the English common law a trade union is guilty of economic duress if the union forces an employer to increase wages by procuring a boycott of the employer's business. Parliament has intervened to restrict the common law rights of employers and to confer immunities on trade unions and other persons engaged in industrial action . . .
>
> In my opinion the owners are not entitled to succeed in this country. In the first place the courts of this country should not concern themselves with industrial action lawfully carried out in the place where that action occurred. In the second place as Lord Diplock pointed out there is no difference between tort and restitution. Moneys paid as a result of conduct lawful where committed and irrecoverable in this country under the law of tort should not be recoverable in this country under the law of restitution. The contents of a bottle cannot be changed by altering the label . . ."

Lord Goff: ". . . We are here concerned with a case of economic duress. It was at one time thought that, at common law, the only form of duress which would entitle a party to avoid a contract on that ground was duress of the person. The origin for this view lay in the decision of the Court of Exchequer in *Skeate v Beale* (1841) 11 Ad & El 983. However, since the decisions of Kerr J in *Occidental Worldwide Investment Corporation v Skibs A/S Avanti (The Siboen and The Sibotre)* [1976] 1 Lloyd's Rep 293, of Mocatta J in *North Ocean Shipping Co Ltd v Hyundai Construction Co Ltd.* [1979] QB 705, and of the Judicial Committee of the Privy Council in *Pao On v Lau Yiu Long* [1980] AC 614, that limitation has been discarded; and it is now accepted that economic pressure may be sufficient to amount to duress for this purpose, provided at least that the economic pressure may be characterised as illegitimate and has constituted a significant cause inducing the plaintiff to enter into the relevant contract (see *Barton v Armstrong* [1976] AC 104, 121, *per* Lord Wilberforce and Lord Simon of Glaisdale (referred to with approval in *Pao On v Lau Yiu Long* [1980] AC 614, 635, *per* Lord Scarman) and *Crescendo Management Pty Ltd v Westpac Banking Corporation* (1988) 19 NSWLR 40, 46, *per* McHugh JA). It is sometimes suggested that the plaintiff's will must have been coerced so as to vitiate his consent. This approach has been the subject of criticism: see Beatson, The *Use and Abuse of Unjust Enrichment* (1991), pp 113–117; and the notes by Professor Atiyah in (1982) 98 LQR 197–202, and by Professor Birks in [1990] 3 LMCLQ 342–351. I myself, like McHugh JA, doubt whether it is helpful in this context to speak of the plaintiff's will having been coerced. It is not however necessary to explore the matter in the present case. Nor is it necessary to consider the broader question of what constitutes illegitimate economic pressure, for it is accepted that blacking or a threat of blacking, such as occurred in the present case, does constitute illegitimate economic pressure in English law, unless legitimised by statute. The question which has fallen for decision by your Lordships is whether, in considering the question whether the pressure should be treated as legitimised, the English courts should have regard to the law of Sweden (where the relevant pressure was exerted on the owners by the agents of the ITF) under which such pressure was lawful . . .

. . . We know, of course, that by English law a contract induced by duress is voidable by the innocent party; and that one form of duress is illegitimate economic pressure, including the blacking or the threat of blacking of a ship. I can see no reason in principle why, prima facie at least, blacking or the threat of blacking a ship should not consitute duress for this purpose, wherever it is committed—whether within the English jurisdiction or overseas; for in point of fact its impact upon the contract does not depend upon the place where the relevant conduct occurs.

It follows therefore that, prima facie at least, whether or not economic pressure amounts to duress sufficient to justify avoidance of the relevant contract by the innocent party is a matter for the proper law of the contract, wherever that pressure has been exerted. Here, of course, the proper law is English law. Moreover in the present case there was at the relevant time no applicable statutory provision of English law which required that blacking or the threat of blacking should not be regarded as duress. So, unencumbered by any such provision, we are left simply with an English contract which is voidable by the innocent party if the formation of the contract has been induced by duress in the form of blacking or the threat of blacking a vessel. The question then arises whether there is any basis in law for rejecting this simple approach, on the ground that the conduct in question was lawful by the law of the place where it occurred, viz Swedish law . . .

Before your Lordships, as in the courts below, the ITF relied upon the analogy of tort. Under English law, since the decision of your Lordships' House in *Boys v Chaplin* [1971] AC 356, conduct in a foreign country is only actionable as a tort in this country if it is both so actionable in English law (ie would be so actionable if the relevant conduct had occurred in this country), and so actionable by the law of the foreign country where the relevant conduct occurred: see rule 205 of *Dicey & Morris*, vol 2, pp 1365 et seq and cases there cited. So, it was suggested, by parity of reasoning regard should be paid to the law of Sweden in the present case, in order to decide whether the conduct of the ITF constituted duress rendering an English contract voidable on that ground. I am bound to say however that I do not find the analogy compelling. In the first place it is not to be forgotten that conduct does not have to be tortious to constitute duress for the purpose of English law; this is so even at common law, and still more so if one has regard to the equitable doctrine of undue influence as an extended form of duress. It is by no means difficult to envisage categories of duress or undue influence which might render a contract voidable by English law as the proper law of the contract, but would not do so by the law of some other country where the relevant conduct in fact occurred. It is difficult to see what relevance the analogy of the English rule of the conflict of laws applicable in the case of tort can have to such a case. . . .

What other reason can be adduced? The judge was impressed by another argument advanced on behalf of the ITF, which was that a man ought to be able safely to regulate his conduct by complying with the laws of the country in which he finds himself. This may be true so far as the criminal law is concerned; but I cannot see that it applies in the case of matters which may affect the validity of a contract governed by some other system of law. If a person enters into such a contract, he has for most purposes to accept the regime of the proper law of the contract; and if under that regime a particular form of conduct constitutes duress, or for that matter undue influence, rendering the contract voidable wherever the relevant conduct occurs, he has in my opinion to accept the consequences of his conduct under that system of law. He should not assume that, simply because his conduct is lawful in the place overseas where it is performed, it cannot for that reason render an English contract voidable for duress."

QUESTIONS

1. An employer, desperate to complete a contract with one of his customers, agrees to pay higher wages to his employees who have taken industrial action in respect of better pay and conditions. The employees return to work and the contract is fulfilled. Can the employer now rescind the agreement to pay higher wages and sue for the return of the extra money paid?

2. Why could the trade union not claim justification? Were they not pursuing a legitimate interest? Could they have raised such a claim if sued in tort by the shipowners for damages?

3. Are there situations where one has a right to make threats? For example, can an employer, club or trade union threaten to dismiss or expel a member unless he pays a fine after having committed a breach of the rules? (*Cf. Thorne v MTA* (1937).)

4. Read *Mogul SS v McGregor, Gow & Co* (1889), either in the law report or in C&MT, p.84. Is there one law for employers and another for trade unions when it comes to commercial pressure? (*Cf. Allen v Flood* (1898).)

5. Take the facts of *Interfoto Picture Library Ltd v Stiletto Visual Programmes Ltd* (1989) (see p.402) and imagine that the firm that had hired the photographic transparencies had said this to the claimants: 'If you do not reduce the invoice sum from £3,783.50 to a reasonable amount, we will see to it that no advertising agency anywhere in the UK will ever hire your pictures again.' Assuming that the threat is a real one given (let us imagine) close personal contacts between those in the advertising industry, is this an example of economic duress?

6. Does this case now mean that judges will never be able to go on strike or take industrial action, however low their salaries fall?

NOTE

A threat to break a contract will amount to duress because it is a threat to commit a wrong: see e.g. *D & C Builders v Rees* (1966) (at p.195). Equally, a threat to commit a crime or a tort will amount to duress: see e.g. *Rookes v Barnard* (1964) (C&MT, p.88). However, the difficulty with economic duress is in trying to distinguish commercial pressure from economic duress, as the next case indicates.

CTN Cash and Carry Ltd v Gallaher Ltd [1994] 4 All E.R. 714, CA

Steyn L.J.: "A buyer paid a sum of money to his supplier. The sum of money was in truth not owed by the buyer to the supplier. The buyer paid the sum as a result of the supplier's threat to stop the buyer's credit facilities in their future dealings if the sum was not paid. The supplier acted in the bona fide belief that the sum was owing. Does the doctrine of economic duress enable the buyer to recover the payment? In a judgment given on 8 August 1991 Judge Michael Kershaw QC gave a negative answer to this question. This appeal challenges the correctness of the deputy judge's conclusion . . .

Miss Heilbron QC, who appeared for the plaintiffs, submitted that the deputy judge erred in rejecting the plea of duress. She submitted that the payment was made under illegitimate pressure. She emphasised that there was objectively no legal basis for demanding the price of the goods, and the threat of withdrawing the credit facilities was made solely in order to obtain the payment. The threat was powerful because the removal of credit would have seriously jeopardised the plaintiffs' business. The clear purpose, she said, was to extort money to which the plaintiffs were in truth not entitled. In the circumstances, the threat was illegitimate and the case of duress was made out.

Miss Heilbron cited a number of authorities which illustrate developments in this branch of the law. While I found the exercise of interest, I was reminded of the famous aphorism of Oliver Wendell Holmes that general propositions do not solve concrete cases. It may only be a half-truth, but in my view the true part applies to this case. It is necessary to focus on the distinctive features of this case, and then to ask whether it amounts to a case of duress.

The present dispute does not concern a protected relationship. It also does not arise in the context of dealings between a supplier and a consumer. The dispute arises out of arm's length commercial dealings between two trading companies. It is true that the defendants were the sole distributors of the popular brands of cigarettes. In a sense the defendants were in a monopoly position. The control of monopolies is, however, a matter for Parliament. Moreover, the common law does not recognise the doctrine of inequality of bargaining power in commercial dealings (see *National Westminster Bank plc v Morgan* [1985] AC 686). The fact that the defendants were in a monopoly position cannot therefore by itself convert what is not otherwise duress into duress.

A second characteristic of the case is that the defendants were in law entitled to refuse to enter into any future contracts with the plaintiffs for any reason whatsoever or for no reason at all. Such a decision not to deal with the plaintiffs would have been financially damaging to the defendants, but it would have been lawful. *A fortiori*, it was lawful for the defendants, for any reason or for no reason, to insist that they would no longer grant credit to the plaintiffs. The defendants' demand for payment of the invoice, coupled with the threat to withdraw credit, was neither a breach of contract nor a tort.

A third, and critically important, characteristic of the case is the fact that the defendants *bona fide* thought that the goods were at the risk of the plaintiffs and that the plaintiffs owed the defendants the sum in question. The defendants exerted commercial pressure on the plaintiffs in order to obtain payment of a sum which they bona fide considered due to them. The defendants' motive in threatening withdrawal of credit facilities was commercial self-interest in obtaining a sum that they considered due to them.

Given the combination of these three features, I take the view that none of the cases cited to us assist the plaintiffs' case. Miss Heilbron accepted that there is no decision which is in material respects on all fours with the present case. It is therefore unnecessary to disinter all those cases and to identify the material distinctions between each of those decisions and the present case. But Miss Heilbron rightly emphasised to us that the law must have a capacity for growth in this field. I entirely agree.

I also readily accept that the fact that the defendants have used lawful means does not by itself remove the case from the scope of the doctrine of economic duress . . .

We are being asked to extend the categories of duress of which the law will take cognisance. That is not necessarily objectionable, but it seems to me that an extension capable of covering the present case, involving 'lawful act duress' in a commercial context in pursuit of a *bona fide* claim, would be a radical one with far-reaching implications. It would introduce a substantial and undesirable element of uncertainty in the commercial bargaining process. Moreover, it will often enable *bona fide* settled accounts to be reopened when parties to commercial dealings fall out. The aim of our commercial law ought to be to encourage fair dealing between parties. But it is a mistake for the law to set its sights too highly when the critical inquiry is not whether the conduct is lawful but whether it is morally or socially unacceptable. That is the inquiry in which we are engaged. In my view there are policy considerations which militate against ruling that the defendants obtained payment of the disputed invoice by duress.

Outside the field of protected relationships, and in a purely commercial context, it might be a relatively rare case in which 'lawful act duress' can be established. And it might be particularly difficult to establish duress if the defendant *bona fide* considered that his demand was valid. In this complex and changing branch of the law I deliberately refrain from saying 'never'. But as the law stands, I am satisfied that the defendants' conduct in this case did not amount to duress.

It is an unattractive result, inasmuch as the defendants are allowed to retain a sum which at the trial they became aware was not in truth due to them. But in my view the law compels the result.

For these reasons, I would dismiss the appeal."

Farquharson L.J.: "I agree."

Sir Donald Nicholls V-C: "I also agree. It is important to have in mind that the sole issue raised by this appeal and argued before us was duress. The plaintiff claims payment was made by it under duress and is recoverable accordingly. I agree, for the reasons given by Steyn LJ, that the claim must fail. When the defendant company insisted on payment, it did so in good faith. It believed the risk in the goods had passed to the plaintiff company, so it considered it was entitled to be paid for them. The defendant company took a tough line. It used its commercial muscle. But the feature underlying and dictating this attitude was a genuine belief on its part that it was owed the sum in question. It was entitled to be paid the price for the goods. So it took the line: the plaintiff company must pay in law what it owed, otherwise its credit would be suspended.

Further, there is no evidence that the defendant's belief was unreasonable. Indeed, we were told by the defendant's counsel that he had advised his client that on the risk point the defendant stood a good chance of success. I do not see how a payment demanded and made in those circumstances can be said to be vitiated by duress.

So that must be an end to this appeal . . ."

QUESTIONS

1. How does *CTN* differ from *D & C Builders v Rees* (1966) (p.195)?

2. If the defendants in *CTN* had decided to withdraw the credit facilities out of malice, would this have been a tort? What would be the position if the defendants did not genuinely believe they were owed the money by the plaintiffs?

3. The disputed invoice in *CTN* arose because the suppliers had delivered cigarettes to the plaintiffs—but to the wrong warehouse—and these cigarettes were stolen from the plaintiffs' warehouse. What ought to be the insurance position with respect to the theft of the cigarettes, and how, if at all, might the insurance position be of importance to the case? Could the plaintiffs sue the defendants for breach of contract or negligence because of the misdelivery?

4. If English contract law had a doctrine of good faith, would *CTN* have been decided differently? What if the PECL had been applicable?

5. Read *Atlas Express Ltd v Kafko Ltd* (1989) in the law report. If this case had been heard after *CTN*, would the result be different? How do the two cases differ? If the facts of *Kafko* had fallen to be decided under the PECL, would the result have been the same?

6. Does the threat of legal action amount to duress when the person making the threat knows full well that he has no legal basis for his threat?

7. Can a threat to withdraw from pre-contractual negotiations ever amount to duress?

8. Is it duress for a trade union to threaten industrial action? If so, can any person who suffers loss as a result of the duress obtain, at common law,

damages? What about equity: will it always allow rescission of any contract entered into as a result of a threat of industrial action?

6.3 Undue influence

Equity was prepared to go further than the common law in respect of what amounts to "duress". Equity was prepared to treat some types of relationship as giving rise to a form of "equitable duress" called undue influence. Thus the relationship of employer and employee was enough in itself to allow the contract of mortgage to be rescinded in *Credit Lyonnais v Burch* (1997) (see p.34). Even some commercial relationships can give rise to a relationship of trust and confidence, entailing equitable rescission if the equitable duty is breached: see *Lloyds Bank v Bundy* (1975) (at p.72).

6.3.1 Undue influence and excessive advantage

In addition to focusing on the relationship between the parties, one can also look at the benefits and advantages obtained by the party exercising the influence. This is the approach taken by European texts.

Principles of European Contract Law

"Article 4:109 Excessive benefit or unfair advantage

(1) A party may avoid a contract if, at the time of the conclusion of the contract:

    (a) it was dependent on or had a relationship of trust with the other party, was in economic distress or had urgent needs, was improvident, ignorant, inexperienced or lacking in bargaining skill, and

    (b) the other party knew or ought to have known of this and, given the circumstances and purpose of the contract, took advantage of the first party's situation in a way which was grossly unfair or took an excessive benefit.

(2) Upon the request of the party entitled to avoidance, a court may if it is appropriate adapt the contract in order to bring it into accordance with what might have been agreed had the requirements of good faith and fair dealing been followed.

(3) A court may similarly adapt the contract upon the request of a party receiving notice of avoidance for excessive benefit or unfair advantage, provided that this party informs the party who gave the notice promptly after receiving it and before that party has acted in reliance on it."

NOTES

1. This provision can be compared with UNIDROIT, art.3.10.

2. One difficulty with these code provisions is that they extend to "economic distress", which is a category different from undue influence. For a party can find itself in economically distressful circumstances even if there is no relationship of trust and confidence between the parties. One question that will need to be considered, then, is whether English law will permit a contract to be rescinded in this extended circumstance.

6.3.2 Nature and effect of undue influence in English law

There is no actual principle of excessive advantage or gross disparity as such in English law. Indeed, adequacy of consideration is generally said to be irrelevant (see **4.6.2**). There is only the equitable doctrine of undue influence. A general summary of this doctrine and its effects is given the next extract.

> ***Royal Bank of Scotland plc v Etridge (No.2)* [2002] 2 A.C. 773, HL**
>
> (See also pp.294, 295, 299.)
>
> **Lord Nicholls:** ". . . 6 The issues raised by these appeals make it necessary to go back to first principles. Undue influence is one of the grounds of relief developed by the courts of equity as a court of conscience. The objective is to ensure that the influence of one person over another is not abused. In everyday life people constantly seek to influence the decisions of others. They seek to persuade those with whom they are dealing to enter into transactions, whether great or small. The law has set limits to the means properly employable for this purpose. To this end the common law developed a principle of duress. Originally this was narrow in its scope, restricted to the more blatant forms of physical coercion, such as personal violence.
>
> 7 Here, as elsewhere in the law, equity supplemented the common law. Equity extended the reach of the law to other unacceptable forms of persuasion. The law will investigate the manner in which the intention to enter into the transaction was secured: 'how the intention was produced', in the oft repeated words of Lord Eldon LC, from as long ago as 1807 (*Huguenin v Baseley* 14 Ves 273, 300). If the intention was produced by an unacceptable means, the law will not permit the transaction to stand. The means used is regarded as an exercise of improper or 'undue' influence, and hence unacceptable, whenever the consent thus procured ought not fairly to be treated as the expression of a person's free will. It is impossible to be more precise or definitive. The circumstances in which one person acquires influence over another, and the manner in which influence may be exercised, vary too widely to permit of any more specific criterion.

8 Equity identified broadly two forms of unacceptable conduct. The first comprises overt acts of improper pressure or coercion such as unlawful threats. Today there is much overlap with the principle of duress as this principle has subsequently developed. The second form arises out of a relationship between two persons where one has acquired over another a measure of influence, or ascendancy, of which the ascendant person then takes unfair advantage. An example from the 19th century, when much of this law developed, is a case where an impoverished father prevailed upon his inexperienced children to charge their reversionary interests under their parents' marriage settlement with payment of his mortgage debts: see *Bainbrigge v Browne* (1881) 18 Ch D 188.

9 In cases of this latter nature the influence one person has over another provides scope for misuse without any specific overt acts of persuasion. The relationship between two individuals may be such that, without more, one of them is disposed to agree a course of action proposed by the other. Typically this occurs when one person places trust in another to look after his affairs and interests, and the latter betrays this trust by preferring his own interests. He abuses the influence he has acquired. In *Allcard v Skinner* (1887) 36 Ch D 145, a case well known to every law student, Lindley LJ, at p 181, described this class of cases as those in which it was the duty of one party to advise the other or to manage his property for him. In *Zamet v Hyman* [1961] 1 WLR 1442, 1444–1445 Lord Evershed MR referred to relationships where one party owed the other an obligation of candour and protection.

10 The law has long recognised the need to prevent abuse of influence in these 'relationship' cases despite the absence of evidence of overt acts of persuasive conduct. The types of relationship, such as parent and child, in which this principle falls to be applied cannot be listed exhaustively. Relationships are infinitely various. Sir Guenter Treitel QC has rightly noted that the question is whether one party has reposed sufficient trust and confidence in the other, rather than whether the relationship between the parties belongs to a particular type: see *Treitel, The Law of Contract*, 10th ed (1999), pp 380–381. For example, the relation of banker and customer will not normally meet this criterion, but exceptionally it may: see *National Westminster Bank plc v Morgan* [1985] AC 686, 707–709.

11 Even this test is not comprehensive. The principle is not confined to cases of abuse of trust and confidence. It also includes, for instance, cases where a vulnerable person has been exploited. Indeed, there is no single touchstone for determining whether the principle is applicable. Several expressions have been used in an endeavour to encapsulate the essence: trust and confidence, reliance, dependence or vulnerability on the one hand and ascendancy, domination or control on the other. None of these descriptions is perfect. None is all embracing. Each has its proper place.

12 In *CIBC Mortgages plc v Pitt* [1994] 1 AC 200 your Lordships' House decided that in cases of undue influence disadvantage is not a necessary ingredient of the cause of action. It is not essential that the transaction should be disadvantageous to the pressurised or influenced person, either in financial terms or in any other way. However, in the nature of things, questions of undue influence will not usually arise, and the exercise of undue influence is unlikely to occur, where the transaction is innocuous. The issue is likely to arise only when, in some respect, the transaction was disadvantageous either from the outset or as matters turned out."

NOTE

As this extract makes clear, undue influence is an offshoot of duress and thus does not as such depend upon disparity and disadvantage. But clearly these elements do have a role to play.

Royal Bank of Scotland plc v Etridge (No.2) [2002] 2 A.C. 773, HL

(See also pp.292, 295, 299.)

Lord Nicholls: ". . . 21 As already noted, there are two prerequisites to the evidential shift in the burden of proof from the complainant to the other party. First, that the complainant reposed trust and confidence in the other party, or the other party acquired ascendancy over the complainant. Second, that the transaction is not readily explicable by the relationship of the parties . . .

24 . . . The second prerequisite . . . is good sense. It is a necessary limitation upon the width of the first prerequisite. It would be absurd for the law to presume that every gift by a child to a parent, or every transaction between a client and his solicitor or between a patient and his doctor, was brought about by undue influence unless the contrary is affirmatively proved. Such a presumption would be too far-reaching. The law would be out of touch with everyday life if the presumption were to apply to every Christmas or birthday gift by a child to a parent, or to an agreement whereby a client or patient agrees to be responsible for the reasonable fees of his legal or medical adviser. The law would be rightly open to ridicule, for transactions such as these are unexceptionable. They do not suggest that something may be amiss. So something more is needed before the law reverses the burden of proof, something which calls for an explanation. When that something more is present, the greater the disadvantage to the vulnerable person, the more cogent must be the explanation before the presumption will be regarded as rebutted . . ."

6.3.3 Proving undue influence

One of the difficulties, then, is proving undue influence. Normally such a burden is on the person who alleges it.

Royal Bank of Scotland plc v Etridge (No.2) [2002] 2 A.C. 773, HL

(See also p.294.)

Lord Nicholls: ". . . 13 Whether a transaction was brought about by the exercise of undue influence is a question of fact. Here, as elsewhere, the general principle is that he who asserts a wrong has been committed must prove it. The burden of proving an allegation of undue influence rests upon the person who claims to have been wronged. This is the general rule. The evidence required to discharge the burden of proof depends on the nature of the alleged undue influence, the personality of the parties, their relationship, the extent to which the transaction cannot readily be accounted for by the ordinary motives of ordinary persons in that relationship, and all the circumstances of the case.

14 Proof that the complainant placed trust and confidence in the other party in relation to the management of the complainant's financial affairs, coupled with a transaction which calls for explanation, will normally be sufficient, failing satisfactory evidence to the contrary, to discharge the burden of proof. On proof of these two matters the stage is set for the court to infer that, in the absence of a satisfactory explanation, the transaction can only have been procured by undue influence. In other words, proof of these two facts is prima facie evidence that the defendant abused the influence he acquired in the parties' relationship. He preferred his own interests. He did not behave fairly to the other. So the evidential burden then shifts to him. It is for him to produce evidence to counter the inference which otherwise should be drawn . . .

16 Generations of equity lawyers have conventionally described this situation as one in which a presumption of undue influence arises. This use of the term 'presumption' is descriptive of a shift in the evidential onus on a question of fact. When a plaintiff succeeds by this route he does so because he has succeeded in establishing a case of undue influence. The court has drawn appropriate inferences of fact upon a balanced consideration of the whole of the evidence at the end of a trial in which the burden of proof rested upon the plaintiff. The use, in the course of the trial, of the forensic tool of a shift in the evidential burden of proof should not be permitted to obscure the overall position. These cases are the equitable counterpart of common law cases where the principle of res ipsa loquitur is invoked. There is a rebuttable evidential presumption of undue influence. . . .

18 The evidential presumption discussed above is to be distinguished sharply from a different form of presumption which arises in some cases. The law has adopted a sternly protective attitude towards certain types of relationship in which one party acquires influence over another who is vulnerable and dependent and where, moreover, substantial gifts by the influenced or vulnerable person are not normally to be expected. Examples of relationships within this special class are parent and child, guardian and ward, trustee and beneficiary, solicitor and

client, and medical adviser and patient. In these cases the law presumes, irrebuttably, that one party had influence over the other. The complainant need not prove he actually reposed trust and confidence in the other party. It is sufficient for him to prove the existence of the type of relationship.

19 It is now well established that husband and wife is not one of the relationships to which this latter principle applies . . ."

NOTE

In an earlier case an attempt was made to categorise the various types of undue influence situations: see Lord Browne-Wilkinson in *Barclays Bank plc v O'Brien* (1994) (read in law report) and consider the comments of Lord Scott in *Royal Bank of Scotland plc v Etridge (No.2)* (2002), §§ 157–162 (read in law report).

6.3.4 Undue influence and third parties

There is a considerable body of English case law dealing with the problem of undue influence coming from a person other than the actual contracting party. The PECL identify two situations.

Principles of European Contract Law

"Article 4:111 Third persons
(1) Where a third person for whose acts a party is responsible, or who with a party's assent is involved in the making of a contract:

    (a) causes a mistake by giving information, or knows of or ought to have known of a mistake,
    (b) gives incorrect information,
    (c) commits fraud,
    (d) makes a threat, or
    (e) takes excessive benefit or unfair advantage,

remedies under this Chapter will be available under the same conditions as if the behaviour or knowledge had been that of the party itself.

(2) Where any other third person:

    (a) gives incorrect information,
    (b) commits fraud,
    (c) makes a threat, or
    (d) takes excessive benefit or unfair advantage,

remedies under this Chapter will be available if the party knew or ought to have known of the relevant facts, or at the time of avoidance it has not acted in reliance on the contract.

NOTES

1. See also UNIDROIT, art.3.11.

2. The question is, of course, the extent to which these code provisions give expression to English law. Certainly a contracting party can find itself faced with a rescission claim even if this party was not itself guilty of misrepresentation and undue influence, as the next leading authority indicates.

Barclays Bank Plc v O'Brien **[1994] 1 A.C. 180, HL**

This was an action by a bank for possession of a matrimonial home, which had been used as security for an overdraft extended to a company in which the husband, but not the wife, had an interest. The wife resisted the possession action on the ground that she signed the charge documents in reliance on her husband's false representation that it was limited to £60,000. The Court of Appeal held that the wife was entitled to special protection in equity and that the charge was enforceable against her only to the extent of £60,000. The House of Lords (Lords Templeman, Lowry, Browne-Wilkinson, Slynn and Woolf), although not agreeing with the special protection in equity, dismissed an appeal.

> **Lord Browne-Wilkinson:** ". . . Up to this point I have been considering the right of a claimant wife to set aside a transaction as against the wrongdoing husband when the transaction has been procured by his undue influence. But in surety cases the decisive question is whether the claimant wife can set aside the transaction, not against the wrongdoing husband, but against the creditor bank. Of course, if the wrongdoing husband is acting as agent for the creditor bank in obtaining the surety from the wife, the creditor will be fixed with the wrongdoing of its own agent and the surety contract can be set aside as against the creditor. Apart from this, if the creditor bank has notice, actual or constructive, of the undue influence exercised by the husband (and consequentially of the wife's equity to set aside the transaction) the creditor will take subject to that equity and the wife can set aside the transaction against the creditor (albeit a purchaser for value) as well as against the husband: see *Bainbrigge v Browne* (1881) 18 ChD 188 and *Bank of Credit and Commerce International SA v Aboody* [1990] 1 QB 923, 973. Similarly, in cases such as the present where the wife has been induced to enter into the transaction by the husband's misrepresentation, her equity to set aside the transaction will be enforceable against the creditor if either the husband was acting as the creditor's agent or the creditor had actual or constructive notice. . . .
>
> *Summary*
>
> I can therefore summarise my views as follows. Where one cohabitee has entered into an obligation to stand as surety for the debts of the other cohabitee and the creditor is aware that they are cohabitees: (1) the surety obligation will be valid

and enforceable by the creditor unless the suretyship was procured by the undue influence, misrepresentation or other legal wrong of the principal debtor; (2) if there has been undue influence, misrepresentation or other legal wrong by the principal debtor, unless the creditor has taken reasonable steps to satisfy himself that the surety entered into the obligation freely and in knowledge of the true facts, the creditor will be unable to enforce the surety obligation because he will be fixed with constructive notice of the surety's right to set aside the transaction; (3) unless there are special exceptional circumstances, a creditor will have taken such reasonable steps to avoid being fixed with constructive notice if the creditor warns the surety (at a meeting not attended by the principal debtor) of the amount of her potential liability and of the risks involved and advises the surety to take independent legal advice.

I should make it clear that in referring to the husband's debts I include the debts of a company in which the husband (but not the wife) has a direct financial interest. . . ."

QUESTIONS

1. Can one commercial corporation be guilty of undue influence over another commercial corporation?

2. "Equity in this jurisdiction acts upon the conscience of the creditor. In coming to the conclusion whether it would be unconscionable for the creditor to enforce the charge against the surety, all the circumstances involving the relationships between the creditor, the debtor and the surety will be taken into account" (Purchas L.J. in the Court of Appeal (1992)). Does this mean that the equitable remedy of rescission is not governed by specific rules as such?

3. Is *Barclays Bank v O'Brien* a policy decision (*cf.* p.14)? If so, what is the policy?

NOTE

The facts of *Barclays Bank v O'Brien* are typical of the type of third party problem that makes up the bulk of the recent English case law. As Lord Bingham has observed: "The problem has arisen in the context of wives guaranteeing payment of their husband's business debts. In recent years judge after judge has grappled with the baffling question whether a wife's guarantee of her husband's bank overdraft, together with a charge on her share of the matrimonial home, was a transaction manifestly to her disadvantage" (*Royal Bank of Scotland plc v Etridge (No.2)* (2002), at § 27). The case in which Lord Bingham made his observation was a consolidated appeal dealing with a number of these husband–wife–bank mortgage transactions.

Royal Bank of Scotland plc v Etridge (No.2) **[2002] 2 A.C. 773, HL**

In this case the House of Lords (Lords Bingham, Nicholls, Clyde, Hobhouse and Scott) reviewed the law concerning undue influence and the husband and wife mortgage transactions.

Lord Nicholls: ". . . 53 My Lords, it is plainly neither desirable nor practicable that banks should be required to attempt to discover for themselves whether a wife's consent is being procured by the exercise of undue influence of her husband. This is not a step the banks should be expected to take. Nor, further, is it desirable or practicable that banks should be expected to insist on confirmation from a solicitor that the solicitor has satisfied himself that the wife's consent has not been procured by undue influence. As already noted, the circumstances in which banks are put on inquiry are extremely wide. They embrace every case where a wife is entering into a suretyship transaction in respect of her husband's debts. Many, if not most, wives would be understandably outraged by having to respond to the sort of questioning which would be appropriate before a responsible solicitor could give such a confirmation. In any event, solicitors are not equipped to carry out such an exercise in any really worthwhile way, and they will usually lack the necessary materials. Moreover, the legal costs involved, which would inevitably fall on the husband who is seeking financial assistance from the bank, would be substantial. To require such an intrusive, inconclusive and expensive exercise in every case would be an altogether disproportionate response to the need to protect those cases, presumably a small minority, where a wife is being wronged.

54 The furthest a bank can be expected to go is to take reasonable steps to satisfy itself that the wife has had brought home to her, in a meaningful way, the practical implications of the proposed transaction. This does not wholly eliminate the risk of undue influence or misrepresentation. But it does mean that a wife enters into a transaction with her eyes open so far as the basic elements of the transaction are concerned . . .

84 The crucially important question raised by this wider application of the *O'Brien* principle concerns the circumstances which will put a bank on inquiry. A bank is put on inquiry whenever a wife stands as surety for her husband's debts. It is sufficient that the bank knows of the husband-wife relationship. That bare fact is enough. The bank must then take reasonable steps to bring home to the wife the risks involved. What, then, of other relationships where there is an increased risk of undue influence, such as parent and child? Is it enough that the bank knows of the relationship? For reasons already discussed in relation to husbands and wives, a bank cannot be expected to probe the emotional relationship between two individuals, whoever they may be. Nor is it desirable that a bank should attempt this. Take the case where a father puts forward his daughter as a surety for his business overdraft. A bank should not be called upon to evaluate

highly personal matters such as the degree of trust and confidence existing between the father and his daughter, with the bank put on inquiry in one case and not in another. As with wives, so with daughters, whether a bank is put on inquiry should not depend on the degree of trust and confidence the particular daughter places in her father in relation to financial matters. Moreover, as with wives, so with other relationships, the test of what puts a bank on inquiry should be simple, clear and easy to apply in widely varying circumstances. This suggests that, in the case of a father and daughter, knowledge by the bank of the relationship of father and daughter should suffice to put the bank on inquiry. When the bank knows of the relationship, it must then take reasonable steps to ensure the daughter knows what she is letting herself into . . .

88 Different considerations apply where the relationship between the debtor and guarantor is commercial, as where a guarantor is being paid a fee, or a company is guaranteeing the debts of another company in the same group. Those engaged in business can be regarded as capable of looking after themselves and understanding the risks involved in the giving of guarantees.

89 By the decisions of this House in *O'Brien* and the Court of Appeal in *Credit Lyonnais Bank Nederland NV v Burch* [1997] 1 All ER 144, English law has taken its first strides in the development of some such general principle. It is a workable principle. It is also simple, coherent and eminently desirable. I venture to think this is the way the law is moving, and should continue to move. Equity, it is said, is not past the age of child-bearing. In the present context the equitable concept of being 'put on inquiry' is the parent of a principle of general application, a principle which imposes no more than a modest obligation on banks and other creditors. The existence of this obligation in all non-commercial cases does not go beyond the reasonable requirements of the present times. In future, banks and other creditors should regulate their affairs accordingly."

Lord Hobhouse: ". . . 111 . . . It must be remembered that the equitable doctrine of undue influence has been created for the protection of those who are sui juris and competent to undertake legal obligations but are nevertheless vulnerable and liable to have their will unduly influenced. It is their weakness which is being protected not their inability to comprehend . . ."

Lord Scott: ". . . 144 . . . If contractual consent has been procured by undue influence or misrepresentation for which a party to the contract is responsible, the other party, the victim, is entitled, subject to the usual defences of change of position, affirmation, delay etc, to avoid the contract. But the case is much more difficult if the undue influence has been exerted or the misrepresentation has been made not by the party with whom the victim has contracted, but by a third party. It is, in general, the objective manifestation of contractual consent that is critical. Deficiencies in the quality of consent to a contract by a contracting party, brought about by undue influence or misrepresentation by a third party, do not, in general, allow the victim to avoid the contract. But if the other contracting party had had actual knowledge of the undue influence or misrepresentation the victim would not, in my opinion, be held to the contract (see *Commission for the New Towns v Cooper (Great Britain) Ltd* [1995] Ch 259, 277–280 and *Banco Exterior Internacional SA v Thomas* [1997] 1 WLR 221, 229). But what if there had been no actual knowledge of the third party's undue influence or misrepresentation but merely knowledge of facts or circumstances that, if investigated, might have led to actual knowledge? In what circumstances does the law expect a contracting party to inquire into the reasons why the other party is entering into the contract or to go behind the other party's apparent agreement, objectively ascertained, to enter into the contract? These are the questions that Lord Browne-Wilkinson had to answer in *O'Brien*. They are contractual questions, not questions relating to competing property interests . . .

164 . . . But in the ordinary case the facts of which the bank is aware, or must be taken to be aware, point to no more than the existence of the inevitable risk that there may have been undue influence or some other impropriety and are not facts sufficient by themselves to give rise to a presumption of undue influence. In such a case the bank does not have to take steps to satisfy itself that there is no undue influence. It must take steps to satisfy itself that the wife understands the nature and effect of the transaction . . .

165 Lord Browne-Wilkinson [1994] 1 AC 180, 197 made clear that it would only be in exceptional cases 'where a creditor has knowledge of further facts which render the presence of undue influence not only possible but probable' that a bank would, to be safe, have to insist that the wife be separately advised. In other cases it would suffice if the bank took steps 'to bring home to the wife the risk she is running by standing as surety and to advise her to take independent advice' (p 196). He added that, as to past transactions—and each of the cases now before the House involves a past transaction—it would depend on the facts of each case whether the bank had satisfied the reasonable steps test. I would emphasise and repeat that the purpose of the steps, in the ordinary surety wife case, would be to satisfy the bank that the wife understood the nature and effect of the transaction she was entering into. . . ."

QUESTION

If a bank can establish that it was aware only of there being a *risk* of undue influence, is the bank under a duty only to advise the wife of the risk she is running in signing the mortgage contract?

NOTE

In *Yorkshire Bank plc v Tinsley* (2004), Longmore L.J. said (at 2389) about *Etridge* that "that case holds that it is not sufficient in a case of this kind for a bank to know that a solicitor has been retained. Banks must take further steps to satisfy themselves that the solicitor has been instructed to give independent advice on the transaction to the wife".

6.4 Illegality

Illegality is a vitiating factor to the extent that it can render a contract unenforceable, and as a result, the case law to be found in this area tends to be concerned more with the consequences of illegality than with the notion of illegality itself. It is arguable, therefore, that this case law belongs to the law of restitution and not to the law of contract, although of course making a rigid distinction between these two areas of the law of obligations is probably unrealistic (as PECL, art.15:104 confirms). This restitution point is not, however, to be dismissed, because the principle of unjust enrichment has a key role to play in the problems created by illegal contracts.

6.4.1 Introduction to contractual illegality

Illegal contracts form an area of law that can be approached from a variety of perspectives; but whatever the perspective chosen, various distinctions must be made. The first perspective is that of the transaction itself, where illegality needs to be divided up into various categories depending upon the nature and type of illegal contract in issue. The main classes or categories of illegal transactions are:

(a) Contracts that are illegal *per se* (*mala in se*). These are contracts where the transaction is one involving the committing of a serious criminal offence—for example a contract to have someone killed or to sell an illegal drug. These contracts may possibly even be void, although it might not always be helpful to treat them as such; much will depend, anyway, on the nature of the crime in question.

(b) Contracts that are not illegal *per se*, but which become illegal as a result of the motive of one or both parties—for example a contract for the hire of a vehicle where both parties know it is to be used for prostitution (*Pearce v Brooks* (1866)) or a contract to buy rat poison where the buyer (but not the seller) knows that it is to be used to commit murder. The contracts in both of these situations are perfectly legal *per se*, but they become tainted with illegality as a result of the motive or knowledge of one or both of the parties.

(c) Contracts that are illegal in their performance. In this situation the contract itself is perfectly legal, but it is performed in a way that is illegal—for example a contract to transport goods in an overloaded ship or lorry (see *Ashmore, Benson, Pease & Co v Dawson* (1973), below p.308).

(d) Contracts that are illegal because they infringe a regulatory statute (*mala prohibita*). These contracts are technically the same as contracts that are illegal *per se*, but the breach of the criminal law may be much less potent in moral terms and, indeed, one or both of the parties might be unaware that the contract is technically illegal. However, the courts might still take a strong line with respect to unenforceability, since to allow a claim would undermine the policy behind the statute (see e.g. *Awwad v Geraghty (A Firm)* (2000)).

(e) Contracts that are "void" for public policy reasons. This class of contract probably should not be classed as "illegal" but simply as "unenforceable"—for example, a contract in restraint of trade is "void" (unenforceable?) for being against the public interest (see *Shell UK Ltd v Lostock Garage Ltd* (1976), above at p.367).

A second perspective is that of remedies (*cf.* **Chapters 11 and 12**). As has been mentioned, most of the cases to be found in this area of illegality are concerned with the consequences of illegality, and these consequences find themselves being expressed through the remedy in issue. Several different remedies can find themselves in play:

(a) *Debt*. In debt cases a party to the illegal contract is normally trying to claim the price for goods sold, or the hire fee for something hired. However, another form of debt claim is one in quasi-contract; in this situation the claimant might be attempting to recover payment for services rendered or goods supplied (see e.g. *Mohamed v Alaga & Co (A Firm)* (2000); *cf. Awwad v Geraghty (A Firm)* (2000)).

(b) *Damages*. In damages cases a party might be trying to claim compensation for harm suffered as a result of a breach of an illegal contract, or for the wrongful interference with the claimant's title in goods. In this latter situation, the action is one where the claimant is in effect attempting to recover goods transferred to the other party to the illegal contract (see e.g. *Bowmakers v Barnet Instruments* (1945)).

(c) *Possessory action*. A party to an illegal contract might try to reclaim possession of real property transferred under a contract tainted by illegality (see e.g. *Tinsley v Milligan* (1994), below at p.310). Here, of course, the claim is one sounding in the law of property rather than the law of obligations.

(d) *Specific performance in equity*. A party to an illegal contract might ask the court to grant the remedy of specific performance despite the contract being tainted by illegality. Such a claim is likely to fail unless there are unjust enrichment circumstances that override the rules regarding unenforceability.

(e) *Declaration*. A party to an illegal contract might ask the court to declare that the contract in question is illegal, thus relieving the claimant from having to perform any of its contractual obligations (see e.g. *Tinsley v Milligan* (1994), below at p.310).

(f) *Account of profits*. It is possible that equity might allow one party to an illegal contract to recover a sum of money from the other party if such a remedy would prevent an unjustified enrichment (*Attorney-General v Blake* (2001), p.552).

A third perspective is that of the cause of action in issue. A party to an illegal contract might be able to avoid unenforceability if it can base its claim on a cause of action independent of the contract. Accordingly the main causes of action that need to be identified are:

(a) *Contract*. If the party's claim for debt, damages or specific performance is based on a cause of action arising out of the illegal contract itself then of course in all likelihood the claim will fail, since illegal contracts are generally unenforceable (see the extract from *Hall v Woolston Hall Leisure Ltd* (2001), below at p.305). However, if it can be shown that the illegality arises from a breach of a statute and that it was not the purpose of this statute to render such contracts unenforceable, the contractual claim might succeed (see e.g. *Archbolds (Freightage) Ltd v Spanglett Ltd* (1961)). Moreover, if the claimant is able to establish a contract collateral to the illegal one, the court might allow a claim based on the breach of this collateral contract (see e.g. *Strongman (1945) Ltd v Sincock* (1955); *St John Shipping Corp v Joseph Rank Ltd* (1957)).

(b) *Tort*. A party to an illegal contract might be able to obtain damages in tort if it can show, for example, that the other party has committed fraud (deceit) or has converted the claimant's goods (see e.g. *Bowmakers v Barnet Instruments* (1945)).

(c) *Property*. If the claimant can establish a cause of action in the law of property (that is to say a property right in the property transferred under an illegal contract) then the court may give effect to this claim (see *Tinsley v Milligan* (1994), below at p.310). Much will depend upon the particular circumstances of the case.

(d) *Equity*. It is possible that equity might grant one of its remedies (e.g., account of profits or specific performance) if this would prevent a clear case of unjustified enrichment by one party to an illegal contract.

Having reflected upon all of these distinctions, one question that might be considered is whether they can be reduced to a single code provision, like the one to be found in the following extract.

Principles of European Contract Law

"Article 15:102 Contracts Infringing Mandatory Rules
(1) Where a contract infringes a mandatory rule of law applicable under Article 1:103 of these Principles, the effects of that infringement upon the contract are the effects, if any, expressly prescribed by that mandatory rule.

(2) Where the mandatory rule does not expressly prescribe the effects of an infringement upon a contract, the contract may be declared to have full effect, to have some effect, to have no effect, or to be subject to modification.

(3) A decision reached under paragraph (2) must be an appropriate and proportional response to the infringement, having regard to all relevant circumstances, including:

> (a) the purpose of the rule which has been infringed;
> (b) the category of persons for whose protection the rule exists;
> (c) any sanction that may be imposed under the rule infringed;
> (d) the seriousness of the infringement;
> (e) whether the infringement was intentional; and
> (f) the closeness of the relationship between the infringement and the contract.

NOTE

Whether or not this provision actually represents English law, it certainly sets out in para.(3) a range of circumstances that are of relevance in deciding many illegal contract cases in the common law courts.

6.4.2 Illegality and unenforceability

The general approach of English law is set out in the next extract.

Hall v Woolston Hall Leisure Ltd [2001] 1 W.L.R. 225, CA

> **Peter Gibson L.J.:** ". . . 28 There can be no doubt but that under English law a claim, whether in contract or in tort, may be defeated on the ground of illegality or, in the Latin phrase, ex turpi causa non oritur actio. The classic statement of the principle was by Lord Mansfield CJ in *Holman v Johnson* (1775) 1 Cowp 341, 343:
>
> > 'No court will lend its aid to a man who founds his cause of action upon an immoral or an illegal act. If, from the plaintiff's own stating or otherwise, the cause of action appears to arise ex turpi causa, or the transgression of a positive law of this country, there the court says he has no right to be assisted.'
>
> 29 Although we are not directly concerned with a claim in contract, it is helpful to consider the applicability of the defence of illegality to a contractual claim before considering the more directly relevant position of a claim in tort. In contract the decision of the House of Lords in *Tinsley v Milligan* [1994] 1 AC 340 has reaffirmed that the claimant cannot found his claim on an unlawful act. But when the claimant is not seeking to enforce an unlawful contract but founds his case on collateral rights acquired under the contract the court is neither bound nor entitled to reject the claim unless the illegality of necessity forms part of the claimant's case: p 377 per Lord Browne-Wilkinson.
>
> 30 In two types of case it is well established that illegality renders a contract unenforceable from the outset. One is where the contract is entered into with the intention of committing an illegal act; the other is where the contract is expressly or implicitly prohibited by statute: *St John Shipping Corpn v Joseph Rank Ltd* [1957] 1 QB 267, 283 per Devlin J.

31 In a third category of cases a party may be prevented from enforcing it. That is where a contract, lawful when made, is illegally performed and the party knowingly participated in that illegal performance. In *Ashmore, Benson, Pease & Co Ltd v A V Dawson Ltd* [1973] 1 WLR 828, 833 Lord Denning MR said:

'Not only did [the plaintiff's transport manager] know of the illegality. He participated in it by sanctioning the loading of the vehicle with a load in excess of the regulations. That participation in the illegal performance of the contract debars [the plaintiff] from suing [the defendant] on it or suing [the defendant] for negligence.'

So too Scarman LJ, at p 836: 'But knowledge by itself is not . . . enough. There must be knowledge plus participation . . . For these reasons I think the performance was illegal . . . ""

Mance L.J.: ". . . **73** Lord Browne-Wilkinson observed in *Tinsley v Milligan*, at p 374: 'The effect of illegality is not substantive but procedural.' But this was a statement made when explaining how an equitable interest might pass under an illegal transaction, though remaining unenforceable in some circumstances. I would not myself view the concept of 'procedure' as an appropriate characterisation of the relevant rule of public policy when, for example, considering the scope allowed under the EC Treaty to domestic courts in procedural matters. The description of the doctrine of illegality as involving 'personal disability' appears more appropriate: *cf Hardy v Motor Insurers' Bureau* [1964] 2 QB 745.

74 Although the underlying principle is as applicable to tort as to contract, its impact differs. So much so that in its recent Consultation Paper No 154, Illegal Transactions: The Effect of Illegality on Contracts and Trusts (1999), the Law Commission said that it was not aware that the law on illegality in relation to tort claims gave rise to any concern, and focused its attention on contracts and trusts. In contract the scope for the existence or commission of relevant illegality—whether in the aim, nature or performance of the contract—is necessarily greater than is the case in tort . . ."

NOTE

Two principles govern the enforceability and restitutionary problems that arise out of illegality. Each of these principles needs separate examination, although they undoubtedly overlap in scope.

6.4.3 *Ex turpi causa non oritur actio*

The *ex turpi causa* rule states quite simply that no action can arise out of an illegal cause.

Geismar v Sun Alliance and London Insurance Ltd [1978] Q.B. 383, QBD

Talbot J.: "By three policies of insurance dated August 30, 1968, September 27, 1971, and March 15, 1973, the plaintiff insured with the defendants the contents of his house at 116, Station Road, London, SW 13, and the defendants agreed to indemnify him against losses by theft. Copies of the relevant policies are contained in the agreed bundle of documents.

On December 7, 1974, whilst the policies were in force, the articles set out in paragraph 5 of the statement of claim were stolen from the plaintiff's house and have not been recovered. Seven articles are the subject of the dispute between the parties and in a schedule to the claim form there are set out the countries where each of these articles was purchased, the date of purchase and the price paid. Each of these articles was imported into this country by the plaintiff and though each article was dutiable and should have been declared on entry by the plaintiff to the customs and excise officers the plaintiff did not declare them and has not paid duty upon them. Furthermore, from what was said by the plaintiff to Mr Mackrill, a loss adjuster acting for the defendants, he had no intention of paying the required customs duty if he could avoid it and it is conceded that duty ought to have been paid on each item.

These are the short, undisputed facts of this case and the point, though short, is a difficult one. It is whether the defendants should, in these circumstances, be called upon to indemnify the plaintiff. . . .

The main point that emerges from [the] submissions is that the plaintiff insured will be in a better position and therefore derive an advantage by reason of the defendants' indemnity. No authority need be cited to support the proposition that in general courts refuse to enforce a claim for a benefit which results from the commission of a crime or a tort or a claim to be indemnified against the consequences of such act, this being an application of the maxim *ex turpi causa non oritur action*. It would be wrong, it was submitted, to allow the plaintiff to obtain a benefit or a profit and would be contrary to public policy because he would, in effect, be profiting from his crime of illegal importation of these articles. . . .

So far as the defendants were concerned, they being unaware of the illegal importation, the policies were not tainted with illegality, but the question is: ought the court to enforce these policies against them in favour of the plaintiff? . . .

I am not concerned with cases of unintentional importation or of innocent possession of uncustomed goods. I would think that different considerations would apply in those cases. But where there is a deliberate breach of the law I do not think the court ought to assist the plaintiff to derive a profit from it, even though it is sought indirectly through an indemnity under an insurance policy.

The claim therefore fails so far as the disputed items are concerned."

QUESTIONS

1. Is one result of this case that the insurance company was enriched at the expense of the public purse?

2. Is this an example of the civil law being used to punish a person for a criminal offence?

3. What if the insurance company discovered that the stolen items had been smuggled only after it had paid out under the policy: could the insurance company have brought an action to reclaim the money?

4. Is this case an example of only part of the contract being illegal?

Principles of European Contract Law

"Article 15:103 Partial Ineffectiveness
(1) If only part of a contract is rendered ineffective under Articles 15:101 or 15:102, the remaining part continues in effect unless, giving due consideration to all the circumstances of the case, it is unreasonable to uphold it.

(2) Articles 15:104 and 15:105 apply, with appropriate adaptations, to a case of partial ineffectiveness."

6.4.4 *In pari delicto potior est conditio defendentis* (or *possidentis*)

The in *pari delicto* rule states that when both parties are equally in the wrong (*in pari delicto*), the defendant (or possessor) is in the better position.

Ashmore, Benson, Pease & Co Ltd v AV Dawson Ltd **[1973] 1 W.L.R. 828, CA**

This was an action for damages by the owner of a heavy piece of machinery against a firm of road hauliers, for damage done to the machine arising from a road accident. The Court of Appeal (Lord Denning M.R., Phillimore and Scarman L.JJ.) gave judgment for the defendant.

Lord Denning M.R.: "In February 1967 a big piece of engineering equipment called a tube bank was being carried from Stockton-on-Tees to Hull where it was to be shipped to Poland. It was very heavy. It weighed 25 tons. It was loaded on an articulated lorry. Halfway to Hull that lorry with its load tipped over. Damage was done to the load. It cost £2,225 to repair. The manufacturers claim damages from the hauliers. In answer the hauliers plead that the load was too heavy for the vehicle: and that the contract of carriage, or the performance of it, was illegal.

The relevant regulations are the Motor Vehicles (Construction and Use) Regulations 1966 (SI 1966 No 1288). They were made by virtue of the Road

Traffic Act 1960, section 64. Subsection (2) of section 64 says: '. . . it shall not be lawful to use on a road a motor vehicle or trailer which does not comply with any such regulations as aforesaid . . . '

In the present case the vehicle was an articulated vehicle with a tractor and trailer. Under regulation 73(2) the maximum weight laden was specified as 30 tons. Now the unladen weight of the vehicle was 10 tons. This load (consisting of the tube bank) was 25 tons. So the total weight laden was 35 tons. So it was five tons over the regulation weight. Furthermore, the tube bank was top heavy. It had fittings on the top which made its centre of gravity high. Not only was it in breach of the regulations, but it was a dangerous and unsafe load to be carried on this vehicle along the roads of England. The evidence showed clearly that the only vehicle suitable for this load was a 'low loader', which is underslung so that it can take heavier weights and bigger loads. So the expedition was certainly illegal . . .

On that evidence I think that Mr Bulmer [the transport manager for the claimants] must have known that these articulated lorries of Dawsons were only permitted to carry 20 tons. Nevertheless, realising that 25 tons was too heavy—much too heavy—for them, he was content to let them carry the loads because it had happened before without trouble. He was getting the transport done cheaper too by £30 saved on each trip by each load. Not only did Mr Bulmer know of the illegality. He participated in it by sanctioning the loading of the vehicle with a load in excess of the regulations. That participation in the illegal performance of the contract debars Ashmores from suing Dawsons on it or suing Dawsons for negligence. I know that Dawsons were parties to the illegality. They knew, as well as Mr Bulmer, that the load was overweight in breach of the regulations. But in such a situation as this, the defendants are in a better position. In pari delicto, potior est conditio defendentis. I would therefore allow the appeal and enter judgment for the defendants."

NOTE

This case might seemingly be used equally to illustrate the *ex turpi causa* rule, but it fits better within the *in pari delicto* rule because, as Lord Denning indicates, the key fact that prevented the claimant from succeeding was its own involvement (via Mr Bulmer, its employee) in the wrongdoing. Moreover the contract was not itself illegal, and thus there was no illegal "cause" so to speak; it was the way it was performed that was wrongful.

QUESTIONS

1. What if the accident had resulted in (a) injury to a passing motorist; (b) damage to neighbouring land; and (c) financial loss to local traders as a result of the road being closed for several hours? Could the motorist, landowner and traders bring claims for damages against the owners of the machine?

2. What if it could be shown that over the previous few years the owners of the machine had managed to save themselves a large sum of money because they

had participated in transport contracts in which overloaded lorries were used: should the owners be allowed to retain this money? If not, who should be able to claim it? At whose expense was this profit made?

3. What if the transport firm had not had an accident but had appropriated the machine for themselves, subsequently selling it and keeping the money: would the owners be able to sue the transport company for damages?

4. Does *Ashmore* reflect the spirit of PECL, art.15:105?

Principles of European Contract Law

"Article 15:105 Damages
(1) A party to a contract which is rendered ineffective under Articles 15:101 or 15:102 may recover from the other party damages putting the first party as nearly as possible into the same position as if the contract had not been concluded, provided that the other party knew or ought to have known of the reason for the ineffectiveness.

(2) When considering whether to award damages under paragraph (1), regard must be had to the factors referred to in Article 15:102(3).

(3) An award of damages may be refused where the first party knew or ought to have known of the reason for the ineffectiveness."

QUESTION

Is the spirit of this article (or at least part of it) reflected in the next case?

Tinsley v Milligan **[1994] 1 A.C. 340, HL**

Lord Jauncey: "My Lords, the parties to this appeal lived together for some years in a house in mid-Glamorgan which they ran as a lodging-house. The purchase price of the house was provided by a mortgage loan from the bank and a sum of money which was provided jointly by the parties. It was, however, agreed between them that the title should be taken in the sole name of the appellant in order to facilitate the making by the respondent of false claims upon the DSS. In 1988 the parties fell out and the appellant moved out of the house. She subsequently raised the present action claiming possession of the property and the respondent counterclaimed for a declaration to the effect that the appellant held the property on trust for the respondent and the appellant in equal shares. The judge in the county court dismissed the claim and found for the defendant on the counterclaim and the Court of Appeal by a majority (Ralph Gibson LJ dissenting) dismissed the appellant's appeal. The issues in the courts below and before this House revolved round the illegal purpose of taking the title of the house in the name of the appellant alone. . . .

The ultimate question in this appeal is, in my view, whether the respondent in claiming the existence of a resulting trust in her favour is seeking to enforce unperformed provisions of an unlawful transaction or whether she is simply relying on an equitable proprietary interest that she has already acquired under such a transaction. . . . So long as that agreement remained unperformed neither party could have enforced it against the other. However, as soon as the agreement was implemented by the sale to the appellant alone she became trustee for the respondent who can now rely on the equitable proprietary interest which has thereby been presumed to have been created in her favour and has no need to rely on the illegal transaction which led to its creation.

My Lords, I have had the advantage of reading in draft the speech of my noble and learned friend, Lord Browne-Wilkinson. I agree with it and for the reasons contained therein as well as for the reasons in this speech I would dismiss the appeal."

Lord Goff (dissenting): ". . . I have already expressed my respectful disagreement with the view expressed by my noble and learned friend, Lord Browne-Wilkinson, that the law has already developed at least in the direction of the conclusion which he favours. I have nevertheless considered whether your Lordships' House should in the present case develop the law, with a view to qualifying the principle by the application to it of the *Bowmakers* rule. I can see the temptation of doing so, if one focuses only on the facts of the present case in which it seems particularly harsh not to assist the respondent to establish her equitable interest in the house where not only was the appellant implicated in precisely the same fraud on the Department of Social Security, but the fraud in question can be regarded as relatively minor and indeed all too prevalent, and the respondent has readily confessed her wrongdoing to the Department and has made amends to them. Furthermore it is probable that, if the appeal should be allowed, the effect will be that she will lose all her capital. But it is not to be forgotten that other cases in this category will not evoke the same sympathy on the part of the court. There may be cases in which the fraud is far more serious than that in the present case, and is uncovered not as a result of a confession but only after a lengthy police investigation and a prolonged criminal trial. Again there may be cases in which a group of terrorists, or armed robbers, secure a base for their criminal activities by buying a house in the name of a third party not directly implicated in those activities. In cases such as these there will almost certainly be no presumption of advancement. Is it really to be said that criminals such as these, or their personal representatives, are entitled to invoke the assistance of a court of equity in order to establish an equitable interest in property? It may be said that these are extreme cases; but I find it difficult to see how, in this context at least, it is possible to distinguish between degrees of iniquity. At all events, I cannot think that the harsh consequences which will arise from the application of the established principle in a case such as the present provide a satisfactory basis for developing the law in a manner which will open the door to far more unmeritorious cases, especially as the proposed development in the law appears to me to be contrary to the established principle underlying the authorities. . . ."

Lord Browne-Wilkinson: "My Lords, I agree with the speech of my noble and learned friend, Lord Goff of Chieveley, that the consequences of being a party to an illegal transaction cannot depend, as the majority in the Court of Appeal held, on such an imponderable factor as the extent to which the public conscience would be affronted by recognising rights created by illegal transactions. However, I have the misfortune to disagree with him as to the correct principle to be applied in a case where equitable property rights are acquired as a result of an illegal transaction.

Neither at law nor in equity will the court enforce an illegal contract which has been partially, but not fully, performed. However, it does not follow that all acts done under a partially performed contract are of no effect. In particular it is now clearly established that at law (as opposed to in equity), property in goods or land can pass under, or pursuant to, such a contract. If so, the rights of the owner of the legal title thereby acquired will be enforced, provided that the plaintiff can establish such title without pleading or leading evidence of the illegality. It is said that the property lies where it falls, even though legal title to the property was acquired as a result of the property passing under the illegal contract itself . . .

From [the] authorities the following propositions emerge: (1) property in chattels and land can pass under a contract which is illegal and therefore would have been unenforceable as a contract; (2) a plaintiff can at law enforce property rights so acquired provided that he does not need to rely on the illegal contract for any purpose other than providing the basis of his claim to a property right; (3) it is irrelevant that the illegality of the underlying agreement was either pleaded or emerged in evidence: if the plaintiff has acquired legal title under the illegal contract that is enough. . . .

I have stressed the common law rules as to the impact of illegality on the acquisition and enforcement of property rights because it is the appellant's contention that different principles apply in equity. In particular it is said that equity will not aid Miss Milligan to assert, establish or enforce an equitable, as opposed to a legal, proprietary interest since she was a party to the fraud on the DSS. The house was put in the name of Miss Tinsley alone (instead of joint names) to facilitate the fraud. Therefore, it is said, Miss Milligan does not come to equity with clean hands: consequently, equity will not aid her. . . .

. . . More than 100 years has elapsed since law and equity became fused. The reality of the matter is that, in 1993, English law has one single law of property made up of legal and equitable interests. Although for historical reasons legal estates and equitable estates have differing incidents, the person owning either type of estate has a right of property, a right in rem not merely a right in personam. If the law is that a party is entitled to enforce a property right acquired under an illegal transaction, in my judgment the same rule ought to apply to any property right so acquired, whether such right is legal or equitable. . . .

. . . The carrying out of the illegal purpose cannot, by itself, destroy the pre-existing equitable interest. The doctrine of locus poenitentiae therefore demonstrates that the effect of illegality is not to prevent a proprietary interest in equity from arising or to produce a forfeiture of such right: the effect is to render the equitable interest unenforceable in certain circumstances. The effect of illegality is not substantive but procedural. The question therefore is, 'In what circumstances will equity refuse to enforce equitable rights which undoubtedly exist.' . . .

. . . In my judgment the time has come to decide clearly that the rule is the same whether a plaintiff founds himself on a legal or equitable title: he is entitled to recover if he is not forced to plead or rely on the illegality, even if it emerges that the title on which he relied was acquired in the course of carrying through an illegal transaction.

As applied in the present case, that principle would operate as follows. Miss Milligan established a resulting trust by showing that she had contributed to the purchase price of the house and that there was common understanding between her and Miss Tinsley that they owned the house equally. She had no need to allege or prove why the house was conveyed into the name of Miss Tinsley alone, since that fact was irrelevant to her claim: it was enough to show that the house was in fact vested in Miss Tinsley alone. The illegality only emerged at all because Miss Tinsley sought to raise it. Having proved these facts, Miss Milligan had raised a presumption of resulting trust. There was no evidence to rebut that presumption. Therefore Miss Milligan should succeed. . . .

I would therefore dismiss the appeal.

[Lord Keith also dissented; Lord Lowry concurred.]"

NOTE

See also *Tribe v Tribe* (1995).

QUESTIONS

1. If these facts occurred again today, could the house be seized under the Proceeds of Crime Act 2002?

2. Is this case an example of a person being able to benefit from her own wrong?

3. Is Lord Goff's methodological approach in this case consistent with his methodological approach in *White v Jones* (1995) (C&MT, p.260)?

4. If all the other Law Lords had agreed with Lord Goff, would this have led to a decision whose effect would be that crime could indeed pay (for some)? In not adopting his approach, does this equally mean that crime can indeed pay (for others)?

5. Does this case conflict with *D & C Builders v Rees* (1966) (see p.195)?

6. Does *Tinsley* reflect (at least to some extent) the spirit of PECL, art.15:104?

Principles of European Contract Law

"Article 15:104 Restitution
(1) When a contract is rendered ineffective under Articles 15:101 or 15:102, either party may claim restitution of whatever that party has supplied under the contract, provided that, where appropriate, concurrent restitution is made of whatever has been received.

(2) When considering whether to grant restitution under paragraph (1), and what concurrent restitution, if any, would be appropriate, regard must be had to the factors referred to in Article 15:102(3).

(3) An award of restitution may be refused to a party who knew or ought to have known of the reason for the ineffectiveness.

(4) If restitution cannot be made in kind for any reason, a reasonable sum must be paid for what has been received.

6.4.5 Contract void for reasons of public policy

A contract can be defective not just because it is illegal or tainted with illegality, but also because it contravenes the public interest. Such contracts are said to be "void", but this is probably a misdescription; such contracts are probably unenforceable rather than non-existent. The background is explained in the next extract.

David Ibbetson, *A Historical Introduction to the Law of Obligations* (OUP, 1999), pp.212–213 (footnotes omitted)

"Behind the prohibition of illegal contracts there was a far wider jurisdiction to refuse to enforce contracts contrary to public policy. There was no predetermined limit to the concept of public policy, and the general principle of not enforcing such contracts is often stated without qualification. Within this broad compass certain categories can be discerned: contracts interfering with freedom of marriage (including marriage brocage contracts and agreements in restraint of marriage), contracts interfering with freedom of trade (agreements in restraint of trade, manipulation of public auctions, and other forms of market), contracts interfering with legal process (such as agreements to suppress criminal prosecutions), and contracts contrary to good government (buying and selling of public offices). Sometimes public policy was reflected in statutes, such as the Gaming Acts or the Statutes of Usury, though the courts exercised a discretion outside the boundaries fixed by these legislative regimes.

By the use of this form of reasoning the judges were able to mould the law of contract around their ideas of social needs and interests. Perceptions of social interests were not constant, however, and the judicial application of the notion of public policy changed substantially through time (and, indeed, from judge to judge). The idea of what constituted an unacceptable restraint of trade at the beginning of the seventeenth century was emphatically not the same as that found at the beginning of the eighteenth or at the beginning of the nineteenth. It was, though, this very flexibility of application that enabled the rules to develop as apparently changeless entities, and to become sufficiently firmly established that they could be incorporated into the fabric of the new law of contract articulated in the nineteenth century. . . ."

QUESTION

Gambling contracts have traditionally been unenforceable. Are they still unenforceable or void? (*Cf.* Gambling Act 2005, s.335.)

NOTE

With regard to contracts in restraint of trade (on which see *Shell UK Ltd v Lostock Garage Ltd* (1976), above at p.218), the general position has been summarised by a Law Lord in a judgment delivered at the end of the 19th century.

Nordenfelt v Maxim Nordenfelt Guns & Ammunition Co Ltd [1894] A.C. 535, HL

Lord MacNaghten: ". . . In the age of Queen Elizabeth all restraints of trade, whatever they were, general or partial, were thought to be contrary to public policy, and therefore void (*Colgate v Bacheler*). In time, however, it was found that a rule so rigid and far-reaching must seriously interfere with transactions of every-day occurrence. Traders could hardly venture to let their shops out of their own hands; the purchaser of a business was at the mercy of the seller; every apprentice was a possible rival. So the rule was relaxed. It was relaxed as far as the exigencies of trade for the time being required, gradually and not without difficulty, until it came to be recognised that all partial restraints might be good, though it was thought that general restraints, that is, restraints of general application extending throughout the kingdom, must be bad. Why was the relaxation supposed to be thus limited? Simply because nobody imagined in those days that a general restraint could be reasonable, not because there was any inherent or essential distinction between the two cases . . .

The true view at the present time I think, is this: The public have an interest in every person's carrying on his trade freely: so has the individual. All interference with individual liberty of action in trading, and all restraints of trade of themselves, if there is nothing more, are contrary to public policy, and therefore void. That is the general rule. But there are exceptions: restraints of trade and interference with individual liberty of action may be justified by the special circumstances of a particular case. It is a sufficient justification, and indeed it is the only justification, if the restriction is reasonable—reasonable, that is, in reference to the interests of the parties concerned and reasonable in reference to the interests of the public, so framed and so guarded as to afford adequate protection to the party in whose favour it is imposed, while at the same time it is in no way injurious to the public. That, I think, is the fair result of all the authorities . . ."

QUESTION

To what extent can this doctrine of contracts in restraint of trade be used to set aside an unconscionable contract?

A Schroeder Music Publishing Co Ltd v Macaulay [1974] 1 W.L.R. 1308, HL

Lord Reid: "My Lords, the appellants are publishers of music. The respondent is a writer of songs. On July 12, 1966, they entered into a somewhat elaborate agreement under which the appellants engaged the exclusive services of the respondent for a term of five years which in a certain event was to be extended to 10 years. In 1970 the respondent raised the present action claiming a declaration that the agreement is contrary to public policy and void. He also made various alternative claims which your Lordships have found it unnecessary to consider. Plowman J made the declaration claimed and his decision was affirmed by the Court of Appeal . . .

The law with regard to the validity of agreements in restraint of trade was fully considered by this House in *Esso Petroleum Co Ltd v Harper's Garage (Stourport) Ltd* [1968] AC 269, and I do not intend to restate the principles there set out or to add to or modify what I said myself. I think that in a case like the present case two questions must be considered. Are the terms of the agreement so restrictive that either they cannot be justified at all or they must be justified by the party seeking to enforce the agreement? Then, if there is room for justification, has that party proved justification—normally by showing that the restrictions were no more than what was reasonably required to protect his legitimate interests . . .

The public interest requires in the interests both of the public and of the individual that everyone should be free so far as practicable to earn a livelihood and to give to the public the fruits of his particular abilities. The main question to be considered is whether and how far the operation of the terms of this agreement is likely to conflict with this objective. The respondent is bound to assign to the appellants during a long period the fruits of his musical talent. But what are the appellants bound to do with those fruits? Under the contract nothing. If they do use the songs which the respondent composes they must pay in terms of the contract. But they need not do so. As has been said they may put them in a drawer and leave them there.

No doubt the expectation was that if the songs were of value they would be published to the advantage of both parties. But if for any reason the appellants chose not to publish them the respondent would get no remuneration and he could not do anything. Inevitably the respondent must take the risk of misjudgment of the merits of his work by the appellants. But that is not the only reason which might cause the appellants not to publish. There is no evidence about this so we must do the best we can with common knowledge. It does not seem fanciful and it was not argued that it is fanciful to suppose that purely commercial consideration might cause a publisher to refrain from publishing and promoting promising material. He might think it likely to be more profitable to promote work by other composers with whom he had agreements and unwise or too expensive to try to publish and popularise the respondent's work in addition. And there is always the possibility that less legitimate reasons might influence a decision not to publish the respondent's work. . . .

Any contract by which a person engages to give his exclusive services to another for a period necessarily involves extensive restriction during that period of the common law right to exercise any lawful activity he chooses in such manner as he thinks best. Normally the doctrine of restraint of trade has no application to such restrictions: they require no justification. But if contractual restrictions appear to be unnecessary or to be reasonably capable of enforcement in an oppressive manner, then they must be justified before they can be enforced.

In the present case the respondent assigned to the appellants 'the full copyright for the whole world' in every musical composition 'composed created or conceived' by him alone or in collaboration with any other person during a period of five or it might be 10 years. He received no payment (apart from an initial £50) unless his work was published and the appellants need not publish unless they chose to do so. And if they did not publish he had no right to terminate the agreement or to have copyrights re-assigned to him. I need not consider whether in any circumstances it would be possible to justify such a one-sided agreement. It is sufficient to say that such evidence as there is falls far short of justification. It must therefore follow that the agreement so far as unperformed is unenforceable."

Lord Diplock: ". . . It is, in my view, salutary to acknowledge that in refusing to enforce provisions of a contract whereby one party agrees for the benefit of the other party to exploit or to refrain from exploiting his own earning power, the public policy which the court is implementing is not some 19th-century economic theory about the benefit to the general public of freedom of trade, but the protection of those whose bargaining power is weak against being forced by those whose bargaining power is stronger to enter into bargains that are unconscionable. Under the influence of Bentham and of laissez-faire the courts in the 19th century abandoned the practice of applying the public policy against unconscionable bargains to contracts generally, as they had formerly done to any contract considered to be usurious; but the policy survived in its application to penalty clauses and to relief against forfeiture and also to the special category of contracts in restraint of trade. If one looks at the reasoning of 19th-century judges in cases about contracts in restraint of trade one finds lip service paid to current economic theories, but if one looks at what they said in the light of what they did, one finds that they struck down a bargain if they thought it was unconscionable as between the parties to it and upheld it if they thought that it was not.

So I would hold that the question to be answered as respects a contract in restraint of trade of the kind with which this appeal is concerned is: 'Was the bargain fair?' The test of fairness is, no doubt, whether the restrictions are both reasonably necessary for the protection of the legitimate interests of the promisee and commensurate with the benefits secured to the promisor under the contract. For the purpose of this test all the provisions of the contract must be taken into consideration. . . .

Standard forms of contracts are of two kinds. The first, of very ancient origin, are those which set out the terms upon which mercantile transactions of common occurrence are to be carried out. Examples are bills of lading, charterparties, policies of insurance, contracts of sale in the commodity markets. The standard clauses in these contracts have been settled over the years by negotiation by representatives of the commercial interests involved and have been widely adopted because experience has shown that they facilitate the conduct of trade. Contracts of these kinds affect not only the actual parties to them but also others who may have a commercial interest in the transactions to which they relate, as buyers or sellers, charterers or shipowners, insurers or bankers. If fairness or reasonableness were relevant to their enforceability the fact that they are widely used by parties whose bargaining power is fairly matched would raise a strong presumption that their terms are fair and reasonable.

The same presumption, however, does not apply to the other kind of standard form of contract. This is of comparatively modern origin. It is the result of the concentration of particular kinds of business in relatively few hands. The ticket cases in the 19th century provide what are probably the first examples. The terms of this kind of standard form of contract have not been the subject of negotiation between the parties to it, or approved by any organisation representing the interests of the weaker party. They have been dictated by that party whose bargaining power, either exercised alone or in conjunction with others providing similar goods or services, enables him to say: 'If you want these goods or services at all, these are the only terms on which they are obtainable. Take it or leave it.'

To be in a position to adopt this attitude towards a party desirous of entering into a contract to obtain goods or services provides a classic instance of superior bargaining power. It is not without significance that on the evidence in the present case music publishers in negotiating with song writers whose success has been already established do not insist upon adhering to a contract in the standard form they offered to the respondent. The fact that the appellants' bargaining power vis-à-vis the respondent was strong enough to enable them to adopt this take-it-or-leave-it attitude raises no presumption that they used it to drive an unconscionable bargain with him, but in the field of restraint of trade it calls for vigilance on the part of the court to see that they did not.

[Viscount Dilhorne, Lords Simon and Kilbrandon agreed with Lords Reid and Diplock.]"

QUESTIONS

1. Was the House of Lords laying down a general common law principle that unfair clauses in standard form contracts might be void?

2. Was the House of Lords recognising a common law principle with respect to inequality of the bargaining power?

3. Would this contract now be covered by the Unfair Terms in Consumer Contracts Regulations 1999 (see pp.364, 353)?

6.5 Incapacity

In French law capacity is an essential element in the formation of a contract (CC art.1108). This is not the position in English law, save perhaps in one situation, namely corporations acting *ultra vires* (but see now the Companies Act 1985, s.35(1)). In English law incapacity is normally a vitiating factor which makes the contract voidable rather than void. Incapacity applies to four main types of contracting party: minors, persons under the influence of drink, persons lacking mental capacity (Mental Capacity Act 2005) and corporations acting *ultra vires*. However, as with illegal contracts, it is the consequences of incapacity that tend to present the greatest challenges for the law.

Kleinwort Benson Ltd v Glasgow CC [1996] Q.B. 678, CA

Millett L.J.: ". . . Every legal system has to make provision for contracts which are defective for one reason or another. They may lack the necessary legal formalities; they may be contrary to public policy or illegal; they may be made by a party without capacity or by an agent without authority; they may contain some unresolved uncertainty or ambiguity, or be incomplete in some material particular; or the consent of one of the parties may be vitiated by mistake or misrepresentation or duress or some other factor. The consequences of these defects may differ. Some may make the contract void; others may make it voidable; still others may make it merely unenforceable. But these are merely useful shorthand methods of describing the different legal consequences which follow from the defect in question. A defect which renders a contract void in one jurisdiction may merely make it voidable in another. A voidable contract which is avoided may be treated as void ab initio in one jurisdiction and not in another.

In English law want of capacity, like mistake, sometimes makes a contract void and sometimes makes it voidable. A contract entered into by a party acting ultra vires is void; a contract entered into by a minor, or a person under the influence of drink, or a person of unsound mind, is voidable. A contract which is properly described as void is not necessarily a complete nullity. A contract which is entered into by an agent without authority, for example, does not impose any legal obligations upon the principal, but it may afterwards be ratified by him. . . ."

NOTE

Contracts made with minors (that is persons under 18 years of age) present special restitutionary problems in as much as some contracts are valid.

Sale of Goods Act 1979 (c.54)

"3. Capacity to buy and sell
(2) Where necessaries are sold and delivered to a minor or to a person who by reason of mental incapacity or drunkenness is incompetent to contract, he must pay a reasonable price for them.

(3) In subsection (2) above 'necessaries' means goods suitable to the condition in life of the minor or other person concerned and to his actual requirements at the time of the sale and delivery."

QUESTIONS

1. Is the sale of drink to an alcoholic suffering from mental incapacity at the time of the sale an enforceable contract?

2. Can the seller of a non-necessary item to a minor recover back from the minor money received for the item when the minor resold it to another minor? Can the seller recover the item from the second minor?

Minors' Contracts Act 1987 (c.13)

"3. Restitution
(1) Where—

(a) a person ('the plaintiff') has after the commencement of this Act entered into a contract with another ('the defendant'), and

(b) the contract is unenforceable against the defendant (or he repudiates it) because he was a minor when the contract was made,

the court may, if it is just and equitable to do so, require the defendant to transfer to the plaintiff any property acquired by the defendant under the contract, or any property representing it.

(2) Nothing in this section shall be taken to prejudice any other remedy available to the plaintiff.

PROBLEMS

1. Muriel, an enterprising 16-year-old, sets up her own stall at a boot fair to sell what she thinks is mainly junk that she has herself purchased at jumble sales and charity shops. She sells an old picture, which she had purchased from a charity shop, to Nicholas, who quickly realises that it is a work by a famous 19th-century Canadian artist. Nicholas seeks your advice as to whether he is entitled to sell the picture for a large sum of money and, if so, whether anyone might have a claim on any sale money that he receives. Advise Nicholas.

2. Steve sells on credit to Roland, a 15-year-old, very keen photographer, an old Leica camera for a price of £200. After 18 months Roland has still not paid a penny for the camera, but old Leica cameras have during this period shot up in value. Advise Steve as to whether he can claim back (a) the camera; (b) the value of the camera (now estimated to be £500); or (c) the price of £200.

6.6 Effects of rescission and voidness

We have seen that one of the main institutional focal points in this chapter on vitiating factors is the remedy. Many of the rules have been formulated around the equitable remedy of rescission, and the question that then arises is what happens next. Can the parties get back what they may have transferred under the voidable contract? Similar restitution problems arise, as we have seen, with respect to illegal contracts and contracts affected by incapacity. Remedies will be considered in more depth in **Chapters 11 and 12**, but it might, by way of summary, be useful to look at the main remedies that come into play when contracts are avoided as a result of a vitiating factor.

6.6.1 Rescission and restitution

When a contract is rescinded in equity for fraud, duress or undue influence, it seems evident that the parties should be restored to their original positions.

Principles of European Contract Law

> **"Article 4:115 Effect of avoidance**
> On avoidance either party may claim restitution of whatever he has supplied
> under the contract or the part of it avoided, provided he makes concurrent
> restitution of whatever he has received under the contract or the part of it
> avoided. If restitution cannot be made in kind for any reason, a reasonable sum
> must be paid for what has been received."

NOTE

This article probably represents the general position in English law, although it may be
important to determine which remedy is the most suitable vehicle to achieve
restitution: an action for money had and received (a quasi-contractual debt claim: see
e.g. *Rowland v Divall* (1923), at p.340); an action in account (see **11.4.1**); or perhaps
even a tracing action (see **12.8**). The restitutionary position arising out of contracts
being declared void for *ultra vires* incapacity has, however, received much attention
from the UK courts: see e.g. *Westdeutsche Landesbank Girozentrale v Islington LBC*
(1996); *Kleinwort Benson Ltd v Birmingham CC* (1997); *Kleinwort Benson Ltd v Lincoln
CC* (1999). It would appear, though, that this restitutionary aspect to defective
contracts is no longer part of the law of contract but belongs, controversially, to the
separate regime of restitution and unjust enrichment.

Kleinwort Benson Ltd v Glasgow CC [1999] 1 A.C. 153, HL

> **Lord Clyde:** ". . . The claim which is being made by Kleinwort in the present case
> is simply and solely a claim for restitution. That is not a claim based on contract
> but a claim based on the principle of unjust enrichment. The remedy of
> restitution is in a category distinct from that of contractual remedies. That
> appears to be the position not only in England and Scotland but also in at least a
> number of other states in Europe. That the parties purported to enter into a
> contract which turned out to be void ab initio is a matter of background history,
> too remote from the claim now made to be related to a contract in the sense
> intended by article 5(1), even if what is now agreed to be a void contract can
> properly be called a contract at all. In the present case the plaintiffs do not seek
> to found on any contract; indeed their claim is one which is pursued in the
> absence of any contract. There is no contractual obligation forming the basis of
> their claim. . . ."

> **Lord Nicholls** (dissenting): ". . . It would be surprising and unfortunate if, having
> decided that the contract is null and void, the same court cannot proceed to
> decide on the restitutionary consequences following directly from this. What
> matters is not whether the consequential relief is classified by English or Scottish
> law or the law of some other contracting state as part of its national law of

contract or part of its national law of restitution. What matters is that, however labelled, the relief is no more than part of the effective determination of a dispute relating to a contract. It is one facet of a single dispute. . . ."

QUESTION

Is this separation between "contract" and "unjust enrichment" in the context of defective contracts really realistic?

Stephen Waddams, *Dimensions of Private Law: Categories and Concepts in Anglo-American Legal Reasoning* (CUP, 2003), p.165 (footnotes omitted)

"To assign unjust enrichment and contracts to separate 'areas' of a conceptual map is to introduce the possibility—indeed the certainty—of conflict between them, and to make it necessary to determine if and when one of them is supplemental, subordinate, secondary or subsidiary to the other, or when they may be combined. This would require a complex new set of terminology that would be by no means self-applying, and not obviously necessary or desirable in an uncodified system.

Nor is it quite satisfactory to say that unjust enrichment is excluded until the contract has 'first' been set aside. Tests commonly used for setting aside a contract for unconscionability are whether the party with superior bargaining power has taken an 'undue advantage', or derived an 'immoderate gain'. These are not tests to be distinguished or applied separately from unjust enrichment; they *are* tests of unjust enrichment. Unfairness and mistake are reasons for reversing enrichment, but these are not principles that can be applied independently of contract law, for almost every disadvantageous contract may be said to be unfair, or to involve a mistake of some kind by the party disadvantaged. The contractual view of the matter and the unjust enrichment view are different aspects of the same question. . . .

It is, indeed, the very impurity, or mixture, of concepts that has enabled the courts in many cases to reach the results they have considered just. . . ."

NOTE

Professor Waddams must surely be right. If contract is about "justified enrichment" then any rule about voidness, voidability or unenforceability must often (if not always) be about preventing contract from becoming a form of "unjustified enrichment". The idea that one can create a completely closed coherent and conceptual model in which "tort" (wrongs), "contract" and "unjust enrichment" are considered alternative (rather than cumulative) categories, is nothing short of epistemological fantasy. Such fantasy is usually indulged in by those unable to distinguish between legal taxonomy and zoological taxonomy (*cf.* Samuel (2000) 49 I.C.L.Q. 297).

6.6.2 Damages

Another possible remedy that can come into play in situations where a contract is undermined by a vitiating factor is damages.

Principles of European Contract Law

"**Article 4:106 Incorrect information**
A party who has concluded a contract relying on incorrect information given it by the other party may recover damages in accordance with Article 4:117(2) and (3) even if the information does not give rise to a right to avoid the contract on the ground of mistake under Article 4:103, unless the party who gave the information had reason to believe that the information was correct.

Article 4:117 Damages
(1) A party who avoids a contract under this Chapter may recover from the other party damages so as to put the avoiding party as nearly as possible into the same position as if it had not concluded the contract, provided that the other party knew or ought to have known of the mistake, fraud, threat or taking of excessive benefit or unfair advantage.

(2) If a party has the right to avoid a contract under this Chapter, but does not exercise its right or has lost its right under the provisions of Articles 4:113 or 4:114, it may recover, subject to paragraph (1), damages limited to the loss caused to it by the mistake, fraud, threat or taking of excessive benefit or unfair advantage. The same measure of damages shall apply when the party was misled by incorrect information in the sense of Article 4:106.

(3) In other respects, the damages shall be in accordance with the relevant provisions of Chapter 9, Section 5, with appropriate adaptations."

NOTE

The problem facing those wishing to obtain damages in English law is that they must establish a cause of action. In the case of fraud, there are the torts of deceit and negligence; indeed, as we have seen, a victim might even be able to sue for breach of contract (*Mahmud v BCCI* (1998), above at p.278). But what about duress and undue influence? Some forms of duress might well amount to an economic tort (see *Rookes v Barnard* (1964) (C&MT, p.88), but as equity could not traditionally award damages it is much more difficult to obtain compensation in undue influence situations (and, anyway, the victim would have to prove loss or damage). However, an account of profits might be available in some situations (see **11.4.1**).

7 Structure and interpretation of contracts

One purpose of this chapter is to look at the internal structure of a contract. As we have seen, the foundation upon which English contract law is based is promise (see **4.1**). However, a contract rarely consists of just one promise in exchange for another; there are usually a number of sub- or collateral promises in addition to the main promise, some of which may be express while others are implied. For example, a sale transaction in a shop does not consist only of a promise to transfer ownership in the thing sold in return for a promise to pay the price. The seller is making other promises (whether it likes it or not) in respect of, for example the quality of the goods (Sale of Goods Act 1979, s.14). In some civil law systems the seller might also be giving undertakings about the state of the shop itself. Even the domestic window cleaner is promising to do more than just clean the windows; he or she is promising in addition not to be careless (Supply of Goods and Services Act 1982, s.13).

In fact commercial contracts and leases tend to consist of book-like documents full of express written promises. To this extent, even in England, a contract can look like a form of private legislation between the contracting parties (*cf.* CC art.1134) and, as such, will need to be interpreted, since language often turns out to be ambiguous in the face of factual reality. Another purpose of this chapter is, accordingly, to look at the rules of interpretation in contract. However, "interpretation" stretches beyond language and reaches into the nature of the undertakings themselves, and so structure and interpretation of contracts can merge. Consequently a topic such as implied terms can be seen as an aspect both of structure and of interpretation.

One particularly difficult area of interpretation is with respect to exclusion and limitation clauses. However, because these clauses limit the effects of the contract, the topic will be dealt with in the next chapter rather than in this present one (see **7.3**). Nevertheless some of the rules falling within this chapter will be more than relevant when it comes to looking at the problem of exclusion clauses.

7.1 Terms

An English contract consists, then, of promises. However, the general expression used by contract lawyers to describe these contractual promises is not "promise" as such but "terms". Thus the structure and contents of a contract consists of a bundle of terms (promises).

7.1.1 Nature and status of terms

These terms do not have the same status, since some are more important than others and one or two might be "fundamental" to the whole contract itself (see *Rowland v Divall* (1923), at p.340). Moreover, it has to be recalled that not all statements made by a contractual party amount to contractual promises (i.e. terms); some are merely "representations" which, if untrue, give rise not to a contractual action but to a claim for rescission in equity or (and) damages (see **5.2**). As for terms themselves, the way they have come to structure contract can really be understood only from an historical perspective.

> **David Ibbetson, *A Historical Introduction to the Law of Obligations* (OUP, 1999), pp.83–84, 86 (footnotes omitted)**
>
> "The parties' contractual obligations were in principle determined by their agreement. If the contract was based on a written document, then all that was required was to construe the words, applying routine canons of construction, such as that any ambiguities should be resolved against the maker of the document. The Common-law courts would not allow written terms to be varied by a purely oral agreement of the parties, but there is good reason to think that the Chancery might have been willing to go behind the document. So far as unwritten agreements were concerned, there was not a great deal of room for legal rules to determine the content of the contract: difficult questions could invariably be concealed behind the general issue and the defendant's wager of law or a general verdict of the jury.
>
> In some types of contracts, most importantly contracts of sale, there might be terms collateral to the primary obligations arising under the contract, such as undertakings as to the quality of goods sold. Such terms were commonly known as 'warranties'. . . .
>
> Cutting across the treatment of terms as actionable warranties, it might be agreed between the parties that some term should operate as a condition of the whole validity of the contract. . . . The sale of a horse might be expressed to be subject to a condition that the bargain be void if the horse was not sound or the sale of a cow might be subject to a condition that it be in milk. Such a claim was functionally different from a claim that there was a warranty. It did not ground an action for damages, but either underpinned a defence that there should be no liability on the contract since it was subject to an unfulfilled condition or entitled those who had performed their side of a putative bargain to reclaim any money paid or property passed. . . ."

NOTE

Accordingly, a contractual promise (term) might fall into one of two categories: it might be a "warranty", or it might be a "condition". If the latter, it was a promise upon which the whole validity of the contract depended. Consequently, if a condition was breached, the whole contract would, logically speaking, collapse.

7.1.2 Condition

Conditions thus came to describe the fundamental or foundational terms (promises) of a contract. However, as the next extract indicates, the word "condition" is ambiguous, because it can mean several different things in different contexts.

L Schuler AG v Wickman Machine Tool Sales Ltd [1974] A.C. 235, HL

This was an action for damages for breach of contract by an English company (Wickman) against a German company (Schuler), after the latter terminated a contract claiming that Wickman was in breach of a condition. The question before the court was whether Schuler was entitled to repudiate a contract for breach of a term of the written contract, described as a "condition", whereby a certain number of visits would be made by employees of Wickman to clients in respect of promoting Schuler's products. Most of the visits were made by Wickman, but on a few occasions they failed to make the required number of visits stipulated for in the contract. The arbitrator held that Schuler was not entitled to repudiate or terminate the contract, and a majority of the House of Lords (Lords Reid, Morris, Simon and Kilbrandon; Lord Wilberforce dissenting) confirmed this decision.

"**Lord Reid**: ". . . Schuler maintains that the word 'condition' has now acquired a precise legal meaning; that, particularly since the enactment of the Sale of Goods Act 1893, its recognised meaning in English law is a term of a contract any breach of which by one party gives to the other party an immediate right to rescind the whole contract. Undoubtedly the word is frequently used in that sense. There may, indeed, be some presumption that in a formal legal document it has that meaning. But it is frequently used with a less stringent meaning. One is familiar with printed 'conditions of sale' incorporated into a contract and with the words 'For conditions see back' printed on a ticket. There it simply means that the 'conditions' are terms of the contract.

In the ordinary use of the English language 'condition' has many meanings, some of which have nothing to do with agreements. In connection with an agreement it may mean a pre-condition: something which must happen or be done before the agreement can take effect. Or it may mean some state of affairs which must continue to exist if the agreement is to remain in force. The legal meaning on which Schuler relies is, I think, one which would not occur to a layman; a condition in that sense is not something which has an automatic effect. It is a term the breach of which by one party gives to the other an option either to terminate the contract or to let the contract proceed and, if he so desires, sue for damages for the breach.

Schuler maintains that the use of the word 'condition' is in itself enough to establish this intention. No doubt some words used by lawyers do have a rigid inflexible meaning. But we must remember that we are seeking to discover intention as disclosed by the contract as a whole. Use of the word 'condition' is an indication—even a strong indication—of such an intention but it is by no means conclusive.

The fact that a particular construction leads to a very unreasonable result must be a relevant consideration. The more unreasonable the result the more unlikely it is that the parties can have intended it, and if they do intend it the more necessary it is that they shall make that intention abundantly clear.

Clause 7(*b*) requires that over a long period each of the six firms shall be visited every week by one or other of two named representatives. It makes no provision for Wickman being entitled to substitute others even on the death or retirement of one of the named representatives. Even if one could imply some right to do this, it makes no provision for both representatives being ill during a particular week. And it makes no provision for the possibility that one or other of the firms may tell Wickman that they cannot receive Wickman's representative during a particular week. So if the parties gave any thought to the matter at all they must have realised the probability that in a few cases out of the 1,400 required visits a visit as stipulated would be impossible. But if Schuler's contention is right, failure to make even one visit entitle them to terminate the contract however blameless Wickman might be.

This is so unreasonable that it must make me search for some other possible meaning of the contract. If none can be found then Wickman must suffer the consequences. But only if that is the only possible interpretation.

If I have to construe clause 7 standing by itself then I do find difficulty in reaching any other interpretation. But if clause 7 must be read with clause 11 the difficulty disappears. The word 'condition' would make any breach of clause 7(*b*), however excusable, a material breach. That would then entitle Schuler to give notice under clause 11(*a*)(i) requiring the breach to be remedied. There would be no point in giving such a notice if Wickman were clearly not in fault but if it were given Wickman would have no difficulty in showing that the breach had been remedied. If Wickman were at fault then on receiving such a notice they would have to amend their system so that they could show that the breach had been remedied. If they did not do that within the period of the notice then Schuler would be entitled to rescind.

In my view, that is a possible and reasonable construction of the contract and I would therefore adopt it. The contract is so obscure that I can have no confidence that this is its true meaning but for the reasons which I have given I think that it is the preferable construction. It follows that Schuler was not entitled to rescind the contract as it purported to do. So I would dismiss this appeal . . ."

"**Lord Morris:** ". . . Subject to any legal requirements businessmen are free to make what contracts they choose but unless the terms of their agreement are clear a court will not be disposed to accept that they have agreed something utterly fantastic. If it is clear what they have agreed a court will not be influenced by any suggestion that they would have been wiser to have made a different agreement. If a word employed by the parties in a contract can have only one possible meaning, unless any question of rectification arises, there will be no problem. If a word either by reason of general acceptance or by reason of judicial construction has come to have a particular meaning then, if used in a business or technical document, it will often be reasonable to suppose that the parties intended to use the word in its accepted sense. But if a word in a contract may have more than one meaning then, in interpreting the contract, a court will have to decide what was the intention of the parties as revealed by or deduced from the terms and subject-matter of their contract. . . ."

Lord Wilberforce (dissenting): ". . . The general rule is that extrinsic evidence is not admissible for the construction of a written contract; the parties' intentions must be ascertained, on legal principles of construction, from the words they have used . . .

There are of course exceptions. I attempt no exhaustive list of them . . . [E]vidence may be admitted of surrounding circumstances or in order to explain technical expressions or to identify the subject-matter of an agreement; or (an overlapping exception) to resolve a latent ambiguity. But ambiguity in this context is not to be equated with difficulty of construction, even difficulty to a point where judicial opinion as to meaning has differed. This is, I venture to think, elementary law . . .

I would only add that, for my part, to call the clause arbitrary, capricious or fantastic, or to introduce as a test of its validity the ubiquitous reasonable man (I do not know whether he is English or German) is to assume, contrary to the evidence, that both parties to this contract adopted a standard of easygoing tolerance rather than one of aggressive, insistent punctuality and efficiency . . ."

QUESTIONS

1. Does this case suggest that a contractor will not be permitted to exercise his right to repudiate a contract if it is unreasonable for him to do so? Was Schuler's action in terminating the agreement out of all proportion to the extent of the breach of promise by Wickman? Was Schuler acting in bad faith when it terminated the contract?

2. Is this case an example of the courts remaking a contract for two commercial parties?

3. Could Schuler have sued Wickman for damages? If so, how much would it have got?

PROBLEM

Pierre contracts to paint Geoffrey's house for a fixed price. The written contract stipulates that it is a "condition" that only a particular named type of paint is used. Pierre paints the building but does not use the paint stipulated for in the contract. Can Geoffrey refuse to pay Pierre? What if the paint, although not the one stipulated for in the contract, is a better quality and more expensive paint?

NOTE

"In civilian legal systems", observed Lord Steyn, "a condition is sharply distinguished from the actual terms of a contract. It is reserved for an external fact upon which the existence of the contract depends. . . . In English law a condition frequently means an actual term of the agreement. It is therefore necessary to distinguish between promissory and contingent conditions" (*Total Gas v Arco British* (1998), at 220). When used as a term, "condition" represents a promise that, if broken by one party, will give the other party a right to terminate the contract for breach. However, the term can be used in another sense, that is to say as a "contingent condition".

Principles of European Contract Law

"**Article 16:101 Types of Condition**
A contractual obligation may be made conditional upon the occurrence of an uncertain future event, so that the obligation takes effect only if the event occurs (suspensive condition) or comes to an end if the event occurs (resolutive condition).

Article 16:102 Interference with Conditions
(1) If fulfilment of a condition is prevented by a party, contrary to duties of good faith and fair dealing or co-operation, and if fulfilment would have operated to that party's disadvantage, the condition is deemed to be fulfilled.

(2) If fulfilment of a condition is brought about by a party, contrary to duties of good faith and fair dealing or co-operation, and if fulfilment operates to that party's advantage, the condition is deemed not to be fulfilled.

Article 16:103 Effect of Conditions
(1) Upon fulfilment of a suspensive condition, the relevant obligation takes effect unless the parties otherwise agree.

(2) Upon fulfilment of a resolutive condition, the relevant obligation comes to an end unless the parties otherwise agree."

NOTES

1. In *Carlill v Carbolic Smoke Ball Co* (1893) (see p.149), the contract arising out of the advertisement was subject to the condition that the consumer caught

influenza. If Mrs Carlill had not caught this illness, the Carbolic Smoke Ball Co would not have been under any obligation whatsoever to pay her £100. Equally, if Mrs Carlill had not used the product during the stipulated period, and according to the supplied directions, there would have been no obligation to pay. In *Carlill*, then, the expression "condition" is being used in the sense set out in PECL, art.16:103(1).

2. Alternatively a condition can operate to undermine a contract: see e.g. *Associated Japanese Bank (International) Ltd v Crédit du Nord* (1989). Here a condition is operating (more) in the sense of PECL, art.16:103(2).

3. Consequently care must be taken when using the word "condition". Does it describe the status of a promise, or does it apply to an event that may or may not occur? To quote Lord Steyn again: "This is a source of recurring confusion. But the prospects of persuading lawyers to adopt a more rational terminology are bleak. After all, as a distinguished commentator has observed, 'there is probably no change in the law harder to achieve than one of terminology': GH Treitel 'Conditions' and 'Conditions Precedent,' 106 LQR 185 at p 192' (*Total Gas v Arco British* (1998), at 220).

7.1.3 Warranty

Conditions are, inter alia, terms that are fundamental to the contract. Terms that are not fundamental have attracted the name "warranty".

Sale of Goods Act 1979 (c.54)

"11. When condition to be treated as warranty
(3) Whether a stipulation in a contract of sale is a condition, the breach of which may give rise to a right to treat the contract as repudiated, or a warranty, the breach of which may give rise to a claim for damages but not a right to reject the goods and treat the contract as repudiated, depends in each case on the construction of the contract; and a stipulation may be a condition, although called a warranty in the contract."

QUESTION

In *Schuler v Wickman Tools* (1974), was the court treating a condition as a warranty?

L Schuler AG v Wickman Machine Tool Sales Ltd **[1974] A.C. 235, HL**

(See above, p.327.)

"Lord Morris: "... Words are but the instruments by which meanings or intentions are expressed. Often the same word has in differing contexts to do

331

service to convey differing meanings. In contracts of insurance an insurer will often wish to stipulate that his acceptance of a risk is strictly contingent upon the complete accuracy of some statement or representation that has been made to him. The word 'warranty' if used by a proposer or an insured person in reference to such a statement or representation may denote much more than a promise for the breach of which (if the statement or representation is inaccurate) damages might be sought. So the word 'warranty' may be used to denote one of the meanings that can be given to the word 'condition.' An insurer may provide that he will only be liable if his insured does this or that: even if 'this or that' is not of special importance a court may decide that it was clearly the intention of the parties that there should only be liability if this or that had been done. If in the contract it is stated that such performance is a condition precedent to a right to recover the intention of the parties may be clearly revealed: see *London Guarantie Co v Fearnley* (1880) 5 App Cas 911 . . .

Just as the word 'warranty' may have differing meanings according to the context so may the word 'condition.' The words 'condition precedent' may have a specific meaning. But the 'conditions' of a contract may be no more than its terms or provisions. A condition of a contract may according to the context be a term of it or it may denote something to be satisfied before the contract comes into operation or it may denote something basic to its continuing operation."

NOTE

One of the problems with the word "condition", as we have seen, is that it can mean different things in different contexts. The same is true of the word "warranty". Sometimes it is used simply to mean a contractual term rather than a mere representation (see *Dick Bentley v Harold Smith (Motors) Ltd* (1965), above at p.230); sometimes it is used to mean "condition" (Marine Insurance Act 1906, s.33(3)). In the Sale of Goods Act 1979 it is used for a particular purpose, namely, to determine whether or not a contractor is entitled to use the self-help remedy of termination of a contract for the other party's breach (see **10.4**).

QUESTION

What if a contractor tries to take abusive advantage of the fact that the other party is (seemingly) in breach of a "condition"?

***Cehave NV v Bremer Handelsgesellschaft mbH (The Hansa Nord)* [1976] Q.B. 44, CA**

This was an action in debt to claim back the price paid for goods which turned out on arrival to be damaged. The buyers had paid £100,000 for a cargo of pellets to be used by them for animal feed, but when the pellets arrived in Rotterdam half of the cargo (stored in one hold of a ship) was damaged and the buyers rejected the whole cargo (including pellets in a second hold that were undamaged). The pellets were then sold to a third party for £30,000, and this third party resold them to the claimants for the same price, the claimants using them for their original purpose, namely, animal feed. The trial judge held that the rejection of the goods was justified for breach of s.14 of the Sale of Goods Act 1893, but an appeal to the Court of Appeal (Lord Denning M.R., Roskill and Ormrod L.JJ.) was allowed.

Lord Denning M.R.: ". . . These citrus pulp pellets were bought for cattle food. That was the purpose for which such pellets are commonly bought. They were as fit for that purpose as it was reasonable to expect. That is shown by the fact that they were actually used for that purpose. Some of them arrived damaged, but not to such an extent that the buyer was entitled to reject the cargo in both holds, or either of them. That damage was such as to entitle the buyer to an allowance off the price for breach of the clause 'shipped in good condition': but not such as to entitle him to reject the lot on the ground that it was not of 'merchantable quality.' That is, I think, what the board of appeal meant when they found that the goods were 'merchantable' on arrival at Rotterdam in a commercial sense, though at a lower price than would be paid for sound goods. In short, the buyers are entitled to an allowance or damages for the damaged goods, but not entitled to reject the lot. This makes commercial good sense. It often happens that the market price falls between the making of the contract and the time for delivery. In such a situation, it is not fair that a buyer should be allowed to reject a whole consignment of goods just because a small quantity are not up to the contract quality or condition. The proper remedy is a price allowance and not complete rejection. I feel sure that is what the board of appeal thought in this case. They only found otherwise because they thought the law constrained them to do so. Their instinct was right. Having found that in a commercial sense the goods were merchantable, there was no breach of section 14(2) . . ."

Ormrod L.J.: ". . . We have all been brought up since our student days to ask the question in the form: 'Is this stipulation a condition or a warranty?' But before the Sale of Goods Act 1893 was passed the question was whether the buyer was bound to accept the goods. The answer depended, to use modern language, on whether the stipulation 'went to the root of the contract,' although it was differently phrased, e.g., 'the buyer was entitled to get what he bargained for' or 'the seller had failed to perform an essential term of the contract.' The words 'condition' and 'warranty' were used in various senses in different cases but the distinction depended largely on the old rules of pleading. Section 11(1)(b) of the Act was clearly intended to remove this confusion of terminology but the essential dichotomy was not affected; it was and is, between the right to reject or the right to damages. The modern form of the question tends to put the cart before the horse and to obscure the issue. . . .

The result may be summarised in this way. When a breach of contract has taken place the question arises: 'Is the party who is not in breach entitled in law to treat the contract as repudiated or, in the case of a buyer, to reject the goods'? . . .

If this approach is permissible in the present case I would unhesitatingly hold that the stipulation in clause 7 that the goods were to be shipped in good condition was not a condition, and that on the facts of this case the breach did not go to the root of the contract, and that, consequently, the buyers were not entitled to reject the goods.

If, on the contrary, I have to make an exclusive choice between condition and warranty I would categorise the relevant part of clause 7 as a warranty, mainly because I find it unrealistic to hold that parties who have expressly stipulated in clause 5 that terms as to quality shall be treated, in effect, as warranties, except in the special circumstances defined by the clause itself, should have intended the general stipulation as to condition of the goods on shipment to have any greater effect. . . .''

QUESTION

Would life be easier if this part of English law were governed by the PECL?

Principles of European Contract Law

"**Article 9:301 Right to Terminate the Contract**
"(1) A party may terminate the contract if the other party's non-performance is fundamental.

Article 9:307 Recovery of Money Paid
On termination of the contract a party may recover money paid for a performance which it did not receive or which it properly rejected.

Article 9:308 Recovery of Property
On termination of the contract a party who has supplied property which can be returned and for which it has not received payment or other counter-performance may recover the property.

Article 9:401 Right to Reduce Price
(1) A party who accepts a tender of performance not conforming to the contract may reduce the price. This reduction shall be proportionate to the decrease in the value of the performance at the time this was tendered compared to the value which a conforming tender would have had at that time.

(2) A party who is entitled to reduce the price under the preceding paragraph and who has already paid a sum exceeding the reduced price may recover the excess from the other party.

(3) A party who reduces the price cannot also recover damages for reduction in the value of the performance but remains entitled to damages for any further loss it has suffered so far as these are recoverable under Section 5 of this Chapter.''

QUESTIONS

1. Imagine that these Principles had governed the facts of *The Hansa Nord*. Discuss.

2. Ought conditions and warranties to be placed in the chapter on "Non-performance of Contracts" rather than in a chapter on 'Structure and Interpretation'?

PROBLEMS

1. Camilla, who runs a one-woman flying company, contracts with Elspeth to advertise Elspeth's processed broad beans by flying over Wigan in her aeroplane pulling an advert that says "Eat Elspeth's Broad Beans". The contract is to run for a year, and it contains a stipulation that before any flight Camilla "warrants" that she will telephone Elspeth to get clearance for the flight. On one occasion, two months into the contract, Camilla fails to telephone. Can Elspeth terminate the contract?

2. Assuming that Elspeth has not terminated the contract (if she ever had the right to), on another occasion (a month later) Camilla sets out for a flight but, again, forgets to telephone Elspeth. Meanwhile, in the centre of Wigan, it is Armistice Day, and as people are standing to attention during the two-minute silence, the quiet is interrupted by the chugging of an aeroplane; those whose eyes turn to the sky observe Camilla's brightly coloured little aeroplane pulling its message, "Eat Elspeth's Broad Beans". Elspeth's office is subsequently inundated with telephone complaints, and the local newspaper exhorts the population of Wigan to boycott Elspeth's beans. Can Elspeth terminate the contract? (*Cf. Aerial Advertising Co v Batchelors Peas Ltd* (1938).)

3. What if, on Armistice Day, Camilla had in fact telephoned Elspeth and Elspeth had given clearance for the flight?

7.1.4 **Innominate term**

The condition/warranty approach appeals to contract lawyers (or at least to those who love "certainty") because it provides a rational model from which a remedial question (*cf.* PECL, art.9:301) can be answered simply through logic. If the breach turns out to be the breach of a promise that has the status of a "condition", the victim of the breach has the right to terminate. In other words, using the language of PECL, art.9:301, the breach would automatically (logically) be classed as "fundamental". However, if the term (promise) broken has the status only of a "warranty", the victim has no right to terminate. None the less, as some of the cases extracted above suggest, logic does not always mirror reality. Sometimes the breach of a condition can result in damage that cannot be classed as fundamental (*The Hansa Nord* (1976)); sometimes the breach of a warranty can have serious consequences (*Aerial Advertising Co v Batchelors Peas Ltd* (1938)). This difficulty was recognised in the next extract.

Hong Kong Fir Shipping Co Ltd v Kawasaki Kishen Kaisha Ltd [1962] 2 Q.B. 26, CA

This was an action for damages by the owners of a ship against the charterers of the vessel for wrongful repudiation of the charterparty. The charterers claimed they were entitled to repudiate the contract because the ship was unseaworthy and the crew inadequate. The trial judge held that the owners were in breach of contract, but that the charterers had not been entitled to repudiate. An appeal to the Court of Appeal (Diplock, Upjohn and Sellers L.JJ.) was dismissed.

Diplock L.J.: ". . . Every synallagmatic contract contains in it the seeds of the problem: in what event will a party be relieved of his undertaking to do that which he has agreed to do but has not yet done? . . .

The test whether an event has this effect or not has been stated in a number of metaphors all of which I think amount to the same thing: does the occurrence of the event deprive the party who has further undertakings still to perform of substantially the whole benefit which it was the intention of the parties as expressed in the contract that he should obtain as the consideration for performing those undertakings? . . .

There are . . . many contractual undertakings of a more complex character which cannot be categorised as being 'conditions' or 'warranties', if the late nineteenth century meaning adopted in the Sale of Goods Act, 1893, and used by Bowen LJ in *Bentsen v Taylor, Sons & Co* be given to those terms. Of such undertakings all that can be predicated is that some breaches will and others will not give rise to an event which will deprive the party not in default of substantially the whole benefit which it was intended that he should obtain from the contract; and the legal consequences of a breach of such an undertaking, unless provided for expressly in the contract, depend upon the nature of the event to which the breach gives rise and do not follow automatically from a prior classification of the undertaking as a 'condition' or a 'warranty.' For instance, to take Bramwell B's example in *Jackson v Union Marine Insurance Co Ltd* itself, breach of an undertaking by a shipowner to sail with all possible dispatch to a named port does not necessarily relieve the charterer of further performance of his obligation under the charterparty, but if the breach is so prolonged that the contemplated voyage is frustrated it does have this effect . . .

As my brethren have already pointed out, the shipowners' undertaking to tender a seaworthy ship has, as a result of numerous decisions as to what can amount to 'unseaworthiness', become one of the most complex of contractual undertakings. It embraces obligations with respect to every part of the hull and machinery, stores and equipment and the crew itself. It can be broken by the presence of trivial defects easily and rapidly remediable as well as by defects which must inevitably result in a total loss of the vessel.

Consequently the problem in this case is, in my view, neither solved nor soluble by debating whether the shipowner's express or implied undertaking to tender a seaworthy ship is a 'condition' or a "warranty'. It is like so many other contractual terms an undertaking one breach of which may give rise to an event which relieves the charterer of further performance of his undertakings if he so elects and another breach of which may not give rise to such an event but entitle him only to monetary compensation in the form of damages . . ."

Upjohn L.J.: ". . . Why is this apparently basic and underlying condition of seaworthiness not, in fact, treated as a condition? It is for the simple reason that the seaworthiness clause is breached by the slightest failure to be fitted 'in every way' for service. Thus, to take examples from the judgments in some of the cases I have mentioned above, if a nail is missing from one of the timbers of a wooden vessel or if proper medical supplies or two anchors are not on board at the time of sailing, the owners are in breach of the seaworthiness stipulation. It is contrary to common sense to suppose that in such circumstances the parties contemplated that the charterer should at once be entitled to treat the contract as at an end for such trifling breaches . . .

It is open to the parties to a contract to make it clear either expressly or by necessary implication that a particular stipulation is to be regarded as a condition which goes to the root of the contract, so that it is clear that the parties contemplate that any breach of it entitles the other party at once to treat the contract as at an end. That matter has to be determined as a question of the proper interpretation of the contract . . . Where, however, upon the true construction of the contract, the parties have not made a particular stipulation a condition, it would in my judgment be unsound and misleading to conclude that, being a warranty, damages is necessarily a sufficient remedy. . . .

If I have correctly stated the principles, then as the stipulation as to the seaworthiness is not a condition in the strict sense the question to be answered is, did the initial unseaworthiness as found by the judge, and from which there has been no appeal, go so much to the root of the contract that the charterers were then and there entitled to treat the charterparty as at an end? The only unseaworthiness alleged, serious though it was, was the insufficiency and incompetence of the crew, but that surely cannot be treated as going to the root of the contract for the parties must have contemplated that in such an event the crew could be changed and augmented. In my judgment, on this part of his case counsel for the charterers necessarily fails . . ."

NOTES AND QUESTIONS

1. Read *Lister v Romford Ice & Cold Storage Co* (1957) in the law report (or in C&MT, p.52). Could the employers have dismissed the employee for his breach of contract in injuring his fellow employee?

2. Could the hirers of the motor launch in *Reed v Dean* (1949) (below, at p.471) have repudiated the contract of hire the moment they discovered there was no fire extinguisher on the vessel?

337

3. Was the hairdresser in *Ingham v Emes* (1955) (below, at p.457) in breach of any contractual term? If so, was it a breach of a condition or a warranty?

4. The difficulty facing lawyers is one of determining when a breach is serious (or "fundamental", to use the PECL expression). Basically there are two approaches to the problem: either the breach can be measured in relation to the status of the particular promise (term) broken, or it can be measured in relation to the actual consequences of the breach itself. The former approach, developed in respect of sale of goods contracts, was, until *Hong Kong Fir*, considered good for all contracts; however, it gave rise to logical problems, in that the breach of a serious term, labelled a 'condition' (on which see *Schuler v Wickman Tools* (1974), above at p.327), might lead to little or no damage. Consequently, the courts started to take account of the consequences flowing from the breach. Did this new approach invent a new type of term that was neither a "condition" nor a "warranty"? Or did it simply require the courts to look at the consequences of the breach?

Bunge Corpn v Tradax SA [1981] 1 W.L.R. 711, HL

This was an action for damages for breach of contract, brought by the sellers of soya bean meal against the buyers. The buyers had been five or so days late in giving notice of readiness of a ship, and the sellers treated this as a repudiation of the contract. One question that arose was whether the lateness in giving notice amounted to a breach of condition, and the House of Lords (Lords Wilberforce, Fraser, Scarman, Lowry and Roskill) held that it did.

Lord Roskill: ". . . My Lords, the central question in this appeal is whether the appellants' obligation under clause 7 completed as I have completed it, are of such a character that a breach of them by the appellants such as, in my view, undoubtedly took place, entitled the respondents forthwith to rescind and claim damages. Put into lawyers' language—is the appellants' obligation to give the required 15 days' notice a condition or not? . . .

My Lords, the judgment of Diplock LJ in the *Hongkong Fir* case is, if I may respectfully say so, a landmark in the development of one part of our law of contract in the latter part of this century. Diplock LJ showed by reference to detailed historical analysis, contrary to what had often been thought previously, that there was no complete dichotomy between conditions and warranties and that there was a third class of term, the innominate term. . . .

My Lords, I venture to doubt whether much help is necessarily to be derived in determining whether a particular term is to be construed as a condition or as an innominate term by attaching a particular label to the contract. Plainly there are terms in a mercantile contract . . . which are not to be considered as conditions.

But the need for certainty in mercantile contracts is often of great importance and sometimes may well be a determining factor in deciding the true construction of a particular term in such a contract . . .

. . . I agree with Mr Staughton that in a mercantile contract when a term has to be performed by one party as a condition precedent to the ability of the other party to perform another term, especially an essential term such as the nomination of a single loading port, the term as to time for the performance of the former obligation will in general fall to be treated as a condition. Until the 15 consecutive days' notice had been given, the respondents could not know for certain which loading port they should nominate so as to ensure that the contract goods would be available for loading on the ship's arrival at that port before the end of the shipment period."

Lord Scarman: ". . . A condition is a term, the failure to perform which entitles the other party to treat the contract as at an end. A warranty is a term, breach of which sounds in damages but does not terminate, or entitle the other party to terminate, the contract. An innominate or intermediate term is one, the effect of non-performance of which the parties expressly or (as is more usual) impliedly agree will depend upon the nature and the consequences of breach. In the *Hongkong Fir* case the term in question provided for the obligation of seaworthiness, breach of which it is well known may be trivial (eg one defective rivet) or very serious (eg a hole in the bottom of the ship). It is inconceivable that parties when including such a term in their contract could have contemplated or intended (unless they expressly say so) that one defective rivet would entitle the charterer to end the contract or that a hole in the bottom of the ship would not. I read the *Hongkong Fir* case as being concerned as much with the construction of the contract as with the consequences and effect of breach. . . .

. . . Unless the contract makes it clear, either by express provision or by necessary implication arising from its nature, purpose, and circumstances ('the factual matrix' as spelt out, for example, by Lord Wilberforce in his speech in the Reardon Smith case [1976] 1 WLR 989, 995–997), that a particular stipulation is a condition or only a warranty, it is an innominate term, the remedy for a breach of which depends upon the nature, consequences, and effect of the breach . . .

The difficulty in the present case is, as Mr Buckley's excellent argument for the appellants revealed, to determine what is the true construction of the completed clause 7 of GAFTA form 119, which the parties incorporated in their contract. After some hesitation, I have concluded that the clause was intended as a term, the buyer's performance of which was the necessary condition to performance by the seller of his obligations. The contract, when made, was, to use the idiom of Diplock LJ [1962] 2 QB 26, 65 and Demosthenes (Oratt. Attici, Reiske 867.11), 'synallagmatic,' ie a contract of mutual engagements to be performed in the future, or, in the more familiar English/Latin idiom, an 'executory' contract. The seller needed sufficient notice to enable him to choose the loading port: the parties were agreed that the notice to be given him was 15 days: this was a mercantile contract in which the parties required to know where they stood not merely later with hindsight but at once as events occurred. Because it makes commercial sense to treat the clause in the context and circumstances of this contract as a condition to be performed before the seller takes his steps to comply with the bargain, I would hold it to be not an innominate term but a condition."

QUESTION

Are the judges really talking about the status of terms (promises), or are they really talking about the nature and the severity of failures to perform promises?

7.1.5 Fundamental term

A condition is often described as a term that is fundamental to the contract. However, just to make matters more complex, the courts developed the expression "fundamental term" to mean something different from a condition. According to Devlin J., a fundamental term "must be something . . . narrower than a condition of the contract . . . It is . . . something which underlies the whole contract so that, if it is not complied with, the performance becomes something totally different from that which the contract contemplates" (*Smeaton Hanscomb v Sassoon I Setty* (1953), at 1473). This term of art meaning was implied by the notion of a "fundamental breach" of a contract, mentioned by Lord Denning in the *George Mitchell v Finney Lock Seeds* (1983) case (above, at p.119). As Lord Denning observes, the fundamental breach doctrine was developed (mainly by him) as a means of combating exclusion clauses; however, it was subsequently disapproved of by the House of Lords in *Photo Production v Securicor* (1980) (below, at p.406). Does this mean that the concept of a "fundamental term" has now disappeared? As a term of art to be used against exclusion clauses, the notion of a fundamental term has probably been drained of much of its significance. But the idea that there are some terms or promises that are so basic that a breach of them will amount to a "total failure of consideration" has probably not disappeared.

Rowland v Divall [1923] 2 K.B. 500, CA

This was an action in debt for money had and received by a purchaser of a car, which subsequently turned out to be stolen and had to be surrendered to its true owner, for the return of the price paid. The Court of Appeal (Atkin, Scrutton and Bankes L.JJ.) allowed the purchaser to recover the full price.

Atkin L.J.: ". . . It seems to me that in this case there has been a total failure of consideration, that is to say that the buyer has not got any part of that for which he paid the purchase money. He paid the money in order that he might get the property, and he has not got it. It is true that the seller delivered to him the de facto possession, but the seller had not got the right to possession and consequently could not give it to the buyer. Therefore the buyer, during the time that he had the car in his actual possession had no right to it, and was at all times liable to the true owner for its conversion. Now there is no doubt that what the buyer had a right to get was the property in the car, for the Sale of Goods Act expressly provides that in every contract of sale there is an implied condition that the seller has a right to sell; and the only difficulty that I have felt in this case arises out of the wording of s 11, sub-s 1(c), which says that: 'Where a contract of sale is not severable, and the buyer has accepted the goods . . . the breach of any condition to be fulfilled by the seller can only be treated as a breach of warranty, and not as a ground for rejecting the goods and treating the contract as repudiated, unless there be a term of the contract, express or implied, to that effect.' It is said that this case falls within that provision, for the contract of sale was not severable and the buyer had accepted the car. But I think that the answer is that there can be no sale at all of goods which the seller has no right to sell. The whole object of a sale is to transfer property from one person to another. And I think that in every contract of sale of goods there is an implied term to the effect that a breach of the condition that the seller has a right to sell the goods may be treated as a ground for rejecting the goods and repudiating the contract notwithstanding the acceptance, within the meaning of the concluding words of sub-s (c); or in other words that the subsection has no application to a breach of that particular condition. It seems to me that in this case there must be a right to reject, and also a right to sue for the price paid as money had and received on failure of the consideration, and further that there is no obligation on the part of the buyer to return the car, for *ex hypothesi* the seller had no right to receive it. Under those circumstances can it make any difference that the buyer has used the car before he found out that there was a breach of the condition? To my mind it makes no difference at all. The buyer accepted the car on the representation of the seller that he had a right to sell it, and inasmuch as the seller had no such right he is not entitled to say that the buyer has enjoyed a benefit under the contract. In fact the buyer has not received any part of that which he contracted to receive—namely, the property and right to possession—and, that being so, there has been a total failure of consideration. The plaintiff is entitled to recover the £334 which he paid."

QUESTIONS

1. What is meant by total failure of consideration? Was the consideration for the promise to pay the price that title actually be transferred? If not, surely there must have been consideration for the sale contract? Or is "consideration" being used in a special (empirical) sense?

2. Was the plaintiff's claim based on contract?

3. Was the seller in breach of a "fundamental" term?

4. Would *Rowland v Divall* be decided the same way today? (See *Barber v NWS Bank* (1996).)

5. The purchaser of the car got six months' free use of the vehicle. Was he not unjustly enriched?

7.2 Express terms: interpretation of contracts

Express terms are those that the parties have expressly put into the contract. However, because language can be ambiguous, disputes easily arise as to the meaning of a word or a phrase, as indeed we have already seen in cases like *Schuler v Wickman Tools* (1974) (above, p.327). In fact much of the work of the courts throughout Europe is about interpreting language, since the intention of those who draft statutes, contracts, wills and other legal documents is, and can be, expressed only through language. In civil law systems the interpretation of contracts is an exercise analogous to the interpretation of statutes; it is all about interpreting texts. Indeed the meaning of language has been a central aspect of legal knowledge since Roman times (see D.50.16).

7.2.1 Interpretation of contracts: general approaches

The same should be true of English law, and not just because the interpretation of statutes has attracted its own mass of rules to be found in textbooks. As the great majority of cases that come before the UK courts are statutory interpretation cases, one would have thought that the courts would have established a body of clear rules applicable to contractual texts. Yet traditionally it was not easy to find chapters in contract textbooks headed "Interpretation of contracts". Why this is (or was) is interesting, and reasons for the lack of a fully developed body of independent interpretation rules will emerge in this chapter. But had there been such chapters in contract textbooks, would the rules have looked something like those to be found in the following extract?

Principles of European Contract Law

"Article 5:101 General Rules of Interpretation
(1) A contract is to be interpreted according to the common intention of the parties even if this differs from the literal meaning of the words.

(2) If it is established that one party intended the contract to have a particular meaning, and at the time of the conclusion of the contract the other party could not have been unaware of the first party's intention, the contract is to be interpreted in the way intended by the first party.

(3) If an intention cannot be established according to (1) or (2), the contract is to be interpreted according to the meaning that reasonable persons of the same kind as the parties would give to it in the same circumstances.

Article 5:102 Relevant Circumstances
In interpreting the contract, regard shall be had, in particular, to:

(a) the circumstances in which it was concluded, including the preliminary negotiations;
(b) the conduct of the parties, even subsequent to the conclusion of the contract;
(c) the nature and purpose of the contract;
(d) the interpretation which has already been given to similar clauses by the parties and the practices they have established between themselves;
(e) the meaning commonly given to terms and expressions in the branch of activity concerned and the interpretation similar clauses may already have received;
(f) usages; and
(g) good faith and fair dealing

Article 5.103 Contra Proferentem Rule
Where there is doubt about the meaning of a contract term not individually negotiated, an interpretation of the term against the party who supplied it is to be preferred.

Article 5:104 Preference to Negotiated Terms
Terms which have been individually negotiated take preference over those which are not.

Article 5:105 Reference to Contract as a Whole
Terms are interpreted in the light of the whole contract in which they appear.

Article 5:106 Terms to Be Given (Full) Effect
An interpretation which renders the terms of the contract lawful, or effective, is to be preferred to one which would not.

Article 5:107 Linguistic Discrepancies
Where a contract is drawn up in two or more language versions none of which is stated to be authoritative, there is, in case of discrepancy between the versions, a preference for the interpretation according to the version in which the contract was originally drawn up."

NOTE

Article 5:101(1) of the PECL reflects the general position in the civil law world (see e.g. CC art.1156). English law is traditionally said to have taken the opposite approach: that is to say, one *does stop* at the literal meaning of words and one does not search for the actual intention of the parties.

Genossenschaftsbank v Burnhope **[1995] 1 W.L.R. 1580, HL**

(See p.98.)

> **Lord Steyn** (dissenting): "... It is true the objective of the construction of a contract is to give effect to the intention of the parties. But our law of construction is based on an objective theory. The methodology is not to probe the real intentions of the parties but to ascertain the contextual meaning of the relevant contractual language. Intention is determined by reference to expressed rather than actual intention. The question therefore resolves itself in a search for the meaning of language in its contractual setting. That does not mean that the purpose of a contractual provision is not important. The commercial or business object of a provision, objectively ascertained, may be highly relevant: see *Prenn v Simmonds* [1971] 1 WLR 1381, 1385B, *per* Lord Wilberforce; *Reardon Smith Line Ltd v Yngvar Hansen-Tangen (trading as HE Hansen-Tangen)* [1976] 1 WLR 989, 996, *per* Lord Wilberforce. But the court must not try to divide the purpose of the contract by speculating about the real intention of the parties. It may only be inferred from the language used by the parties, judged against the objective contextual background. It is therefore wrong to speculate about the actual intention of the parties in this case ..."

NOTE

Two years later, however, Lord Steyn seems to have modified his position.

Mannai Investment Co v Eagle Star Life Assurance **[1997] A.C. 749, HL**

> **Lord Steyn:** "... In determining the meaning of the language of a commercial contract, and unilateral contractual notices, the law ... generally favours a commercially sensible construction. The reason for this approach is that a commercial construction is more likely to give effect to the intention of the parties. Words are therefore interpreted in the way in which a reasonable commercial person would construe them. And the standard of the reasonable commercial person is hostile to technical interpretations and undue emphasis on niceties of language. ..."

QUESTION

Is there really such a person as the "reasonable commercial person"?

7.2.2 Interpretation and the literal approach

It would appear at first sight that Lord Steyn, if not contradicting himself in the two extracts set out at **7.2.1** above, is at least moving more towards a civilian view of contractual interpretation. Yet the problem is really one of method. A person faced with having to interpret a text can adopt one of several methodological approaches. The interpreter can try to extract a meaning simply from the words themselves: they can adopt a *literal method*.

President of India v Jebsens (UK) Ltd (The General Capinpin) [1991] 1 Lloyd's Rep.1, HL

Lord Goff: ". . . [I]t must not be forgotten that a charter-party is not like legislation, forced upon parties against their wills; it is bargained for, and if any particular provision is perceived to favour one or other party, that can be taken into account when negotiating the contractual consideration. Furthermore, in the commercial world contracting parties have to look after their own interests. Shipowning, and (in the case of regular charterers) chartering, are highly professional occupations; and in any event the services of brokers are available to both. It is up to them to assess the probable impact of any particular clause upon their interest, and to act accordingly when negotiating the charter.

. . . [O]nce a clause is embodied in a commercial contract, it has simply to be construed in its context, from the objective point of view of reasonable persons in the shoes of the contracting parties. Of course it has to be construed sensibly, and regard has to be had to its practical effect. But the objective interpretation is of paramount importance in commercial affairs; commercial men have frequently to take important decisions with some speed, and it is of great importance that they all know that they can rely on Courts and arbitrators, if any dispute should later arise, to adopt the same objective approach as they themselves have to adopt in the daily administration of their contracts."

NOTE

The literal approach is, then, not without its merits. It is not for the court to involve itself in the pre-contractual negotiations of the parties in an attempt to fathom what each was thinking; it is to be assumed that the contracting parties knew exactly what they were doing and that their intentions are to be found in the text itself and not beyond it. It would appear that this is true even with respect to long-term contracts: in a "relational contract . . . there are no special rules of interpretation applicable to such contracts . . . That is not to say that in an appropriate case a Court may not take into account that, by reason of the changing conditions affecting such a contract, a flexible approach may best match the reasonable expectations of the parties. But, as in the case of all contracts, loyalty to the contractual text viewed against its relevant contextual background is the first principle of construction" (Lord Steyn in *Total Gas v Arco British* (1998), at 218). The policy reason for such a literal approach is well expressed in the next extract.

> **A/S Awilco v Fulvia SpA di Navigazione (The Chikuma) [1981] 1 W.L.R. 314, HL**
>
> **Lord Bridge:** ". . . It has often been pointed out that shipowners and charterers bargain at arm's length. Neither class has such a preponderance of bargaining power as to be in a position to oppress the other. They should be in a position to look after themselves by contracting only on terms which are acceptable to them. Where, as here, they embody in their contracts common form clauses, it is, to my mind, of overriding importance that their meaning and legal effect should be certain and well understood. The ideal at which the courts should aim, in construing such clauses, is to produce a result, such that in any given situation both parties seeking legal advice as to their rights and obligations can expect the same clear and confident answer from their advisers and neither will be tempted to embark on long and expensive litigation in the belief that victory depends on winning the sympathy of the court. This ideal may never be fully attainable, but we shall certainly never even approximate to it unless we strive to follow clear and consistent principles and steadfastly refuse to be blown off course by the supposed merits of individual cases. . . ."

QUESTION

A literal approach has, then, as one of its objectives certainty. But can it be assumed that a text will always reflect the intentions of the parties and (or) that a literal approach will always result in certainty?

7.2.3 Interpretation and an "actional" approach

In a case in 1963, a will made by a Dr Rowland, leaving all his property to his wife unless her death preceded his or was "coinciding with" his own death, became the object of interpretation. A literal approach would no doubt come up with other phrases, such as "at the same time" or "simultaneous with". Yet what happened in the case of Dr Rowland was that he and his wife seemingly died when a ship in which they were travelling disappeared. Were their deaths "coinciding"? In other words, did they die "at the same time"? The literal approach seemed of little use to Lord Denning.

> **Re Rowland [1963] Ch. 1, CA**
>
> **Lord Denning M.R.** (dissenting): ". . . I decline . . . to ask myself: what do the words mean to a grammarian? I prefer to ask: What did Dr Rowland and his wife mean by the word 'coincide' in their wills? When they came to make their wills it is not difficult to piece together the thoughts that ran through their minds. The doctor might well say: 'We are going off for three years to these far off places and in case anything happens to either of us we ought to make our wills. If I die before you, I would like everything to go to you, but if you die before me, I

346

should like it to go to my brother and his boy'. She might reply: 'Yes, but what if we both die together. After all, one of those little ships might run on the rocks or something and we might both be drowned; or we might both be killed in an aeroplane crash'. 'To meet that,' he would say, 'I will put in that if your death coincides with mine, it is to go to my brother and his boy just the same'. He would use the words 'coinciding with', not in the narrow meaning of 'simultaneous', but in the wider meaning of which they are equally capable, especially in this context, as denoting death on the same occasion by the same cause. It would not cross Dr Rowland's mind that anyone would think of such niceties as counsel for the first defendant has presented to us. . . ."

NOTE

In the above extract Lord Denning abandons the literal approach and adopts, instead, what might be described as an *"actional"* approach. That is to say, it is a method whereby one constructs a hypothetical person and then uses this person as an "actor", through which one arrives at some desired subjective meaning or interpretation. Lawyers often have recourse to such actors: the "reasonable man" test is used as a means of deciding if certain behaviour is careless or not, or if a certain head of damage is "foreseeable". In contract such a constructed actor is the "reasonable commercial party" or "reasonable businessman": see Bingham L.J.'s judgment in *Blackpool & Fylde Aero Club v Blackpool BC* (1990) (above, at p.177) and Lord Steyn (above, at p.344).

Cehave NV v Bremer Handelsgesellschaft mbH (The Hansa Nord) [1976] Q.B. 44, CA

(For facts, see p.332.)

Lord Denning M.R.: ". . . In applying that definition, it is as well to remember that, by the statute, we are dealing with an implied *condition*, strictly so called, and not a warranty. For any breach of it, therefore, the buyer is entitled to *reject* the goods: or, alternatively, if he chooses to accept them or has accepted them, he has a remedy in damages. In these circumstances, I should have thought a fair way of testing merchantability would be to ask a commercial man: was the breach such that the buyer should be able to reject the goods? In answering that question the commercial man would have regard to the various matters mentioned in the new statutory definition. He would, of course, have regard to the purpose for which goods of that kind are commonly bought. If a buyer buys 'waste silk' and it is of no use for the purpose of 'waste silk,' he can reject it: see *Gardiner v Gray* (1815) 4 Camp 144. If he buys dates for food and they are of no use for food, he can reject them: see *Asfar & Co v Blundell* [1896] 1 QB 123, 127. But if he buys groundnuts for cattlefood, and they can reasonably be used for cattlefood, he may not be able to reject them, even though they are not suitable for poultry; see *Hardwick Game Farm v Suffolk Agricultural Poultry Producers Association* [1969] 2

AC 31. The commercial man would also, of course, have regard to the description applied to them. If motor horns are sold, expressly or impliedly, as 'new' and then the buyer finds that they are dented and scratched, he ought to be able to reject them: see *Jackson v Rotax Motor and Cycle Co* [1910] 2 KB 937. If they are sold as 'second hand' or 'shop soiled.' then he must take them as they are: see *Bartlett v Sidney Marcus Ltd* [1965] 1 WLR 1013; unless there is something radically wrong with them. He would also have regard to the price. If they are sold at the market price, the buyer would expect them to be of good quality and condition; and, if they were not, he would be able to reject them: see *Jones v Just* (1868) LR 3 QB 197 (much better reported in 9 B & S 141); and *B.S. Brown & Son Ltd v Craiks Ltd* [1970] 1 WLR 752, 754–755, *per* Lord Reid: but, if they are sold at a 'cut' price or 'bargain' price, or a lower price, he would have to put up with something less. He would not be entitled to reject them simply because they were not perfect. The commercial man would also have regard to any other relevant circumstances. If there was a clause, express or implied, which would give the buyer an allowance off the price for the particular shortcomings, such that a commercial man would say: 'The buyer is entitled to a price allowance but not to reject them'—again the goods would be of merchantable quality. The buyer would be entitled to an allowance or damages in lieu, but not entitled to reject the lot. . . .''

QUESTION

Would not the "commercial man" be more interested in getting goods normally costing £100,000 for £30,000?

NOTE

See further Lord Denning MR in *Staffs Area HA v S Staffs Waterworks* (1978) (below, at p.428).

7.2.4 Methodological individualism versus methodological holism

In contrast to Lord Denning's approach in *Re Rowland* (above p.346), another judge in the same case adopted a very different approach (and accordingly arrived at a different result).

Re Rowland **[1963] Ch. 1, CA**

Russell L.J.: ". . . If the evidence was that the testator and his wife were below decks in their cabin and the vessel plunged abruptly to the bottom of the sea, the view might be taken that their deaths were, metaphysics apart, coincident in point of time. But we simply do not know what happened to them. Counsel for the appellants could not suggest, in the case of either spouse, whether the correct inference was death by drowning, trapped in the ship, or death by drowning, sucked down by the sinking ship after going overboard, or death by shark or similar fish, or by thirst, or by drowning after swimming about or floating for a greater or less period with or without a lifebelt. This makes it plain that there is no evidence at all that the deaths were coincident in point of time (in the natural sense of simultaneous) in the mind of the ordinary man. . . .”

NOTE

The object of interpretation for Russell L.J. is not actually the word(s) in the text but the facts. This judge constructed a factual situation very different from the one envisaged by Lord Denning. Whereas the latter saw the sinking as a single event in terms both of cause and of time, the former envisages the tragedy as a series of individual events occurring at different times. Russell L.J. adopts what is sometimes called a "nominalistic" or individualistic approach (in contrast to Lord Denning's 'holistic' approach) to the facts. Is the sinking of a ship, or the explosion and crash of an aeroplane, a single event in which everyone dies at the same time from the same cause, or is it an event that can be divided up into a series of sub-events where people die at different moments and possibly from different causes? Lord Denning has one view, while Russell L.J. has another.

QUESTION

If one contracts to buy a flock of sheep, is one contracting to buy an existing thing or is one contracting to buy just a mass of individual animals?

7.2.5 Dialectical interpretative method

A third approach to interpretation is *dialectical*. That is to say, the interpreter reduces the problem to an "either/or" situation: either the word or phrase means X, or it means Y. A good example of this approach is to be found in situations where the disputed word can be made to cover the factual situation before the court, but the court does not wish to adopt this wider meaning. The way to avoid having to adopt the wider approach is to say that the word in question can have two different meanings (either this or that) and that one meaning is to be preferred in contrast to the other.

Young v Sun Alliance and London Insurance Ltd **[1977] 1 W.L.R. 104, CA**

This was a claim by a householder for an indemnity under his household insurance in respect of the expense incurred in remedying an ingress of water into his bathroom which left the room covered in three inches of water. The claim was rejected by the Court of Appeal (Shaw, Lawton and Cairns L.JJ.).

Shaw L.J.: ". . . The plaintiff appeals to this court on the ground that the judge erred in his construction of the word 'flood' in the context in which it appeared in the policy. Mr Jacob has put before this court a most able argument, and an almost persuasive one, to the effect that in this context, notwithstanding the juxtaposition of those three words, 'storm, tempest or flood' which appear to denote different forms of violent manifestation of some natural phenomenon, 'flood' here, when one is considering its application in relation to a private dwelling, ought to be construed in a wide rather than a narrow sense. First because the language was adopted by the insurers so that the contra proferentem principle should apply, and secondly because, so far as a householder is concerned, if he finds that in part of his property he cannot walk about except by putting his feet into 3 inches of water, and if that happens in a significant part of his property, then he is entitled to say that it has been flooded; and if any damage results from it, the damage has resulted from or has been caused by flood.

At first sight—or perhaps I should say at second sight having heard Mr Jacob's argument—that appears to be a plausible proposition. But on further consideration it seems apparent that what the policy was intending to cover, whatever may be the colloquial use of the word 'flood' in common parlance, were three forms of natural phenomena which were related not only by the fact that they were natural, but also that they were unusual manifestations, certainly of those phenomena: that is to say, 'storm' meant 'rain accompanied by strong wind'; 'tempest' denoted an even more violent storm; and 'flood' was not something which came about by seepage or by trickling or dripping from some natural source, but involved 'an overflowing or irruption of a great body of water' as one of the definitions in the Shorter Oxford English Dictionary, 3rd ed (1944), puts it. The slow movement of water, which can often be detected so that the loss threatened can be limited, is very different from the sudden onset of water where nothing effective can be done to prevent the loss, for it happens too quickly. . . ."

Lawton L.J.: "This appeal raises a semantic problem which has troubled many philosophers for centuries, and it can, I think, be expressed in the aphorism that an elephant is difficult to define but easy to recognise. I find difficulty in defining the word 'flood' as used in this policy; I have no difficulty in looking at the evidence in this case and coming to the conclusion, as I do, that the water in the lavatory was not a flood within the meaning of paragraph 8 of this policy. . . ."

Cairns L.J.: ". . . I think in such circumstances one's first impression may be the best guide to the real meaning. Giving oneself for the moment the credit of assuming that one is an ordinary Englishman, when I first looked at this case my reaction to it was: 'No; you really could not call this a flood.' But when one began to analyse it, and to listen to the argument of Mr Jacob, I, like Shaw LJ, was almost persuaded that this could be called a flood. That it could be called a flooded floor, that an ordinary man or an ordinary housewife would say, 'The water is flooding my floor,' I have no doubt. But we come back to the question: Is it a flood? Is it a flood in a clause which refers also to 'storm and tempest'?— which I think, contributes to giving a colour to the meaning of it. . . ."

QUESTIONS

1. What prevented the plaintiff from recovering? Was it (i) the small amount of water; (ii) the wording of the policy; or (iii) the visual imagination of the judges?

2. Would the result have been different if (i) the whole of the plaintiff's ground floor, or (ii) the whole of the neighbourhood had been submerged under three inches of water (by seepage and not by a storm)?

3. What if the claimant had taken out his household policy on the basis of a television advertising campaign which stated that the insurance company "did not make a drama out of a crisis": do you think the claimant would have a contractual expectation to be indemnified, given the damage he suffered?

4. Why was the *contra proferentem* rule not applied?

5. An elephant is difficult to define but easy to recognise. Does this suggest that knowledge cannot be completely reduced to linguistic propositions?

6. Did this case also involve an "actional" interpretative approach?

PROBLEM

Geoffrey enters into an insurance contract for a fire insurance policy to cover his new sailing boat called *Hello Sailor*. A clause in the policy states that the insurance company will be liable for damage or destruction "by fire howsoever caused". *Hello Sailor* is destroyed by an explosion when it strikes an old World War I mine, but the insurance company refuses to pay out, saying that it is not liable. In a claim brought by Geoffrey against the insurance company, the judge at first instance states: "This case raises a semantic problem which has troubled many philosophers for centuries, and it can, I think, be expressed in the aphorism that an elephant is difficult to define but easy to recognise. I find difficulty in defining the word 'fire' as used in this policy; I have no difficulty in looking at the evidence in this case and coming to the conclusion, as I do, that an explosion was not a fire within the meaning of this policy." Would you advise Geoffrey to appeal against this decision? (*Cf. Hughes v Lord Advocate* (1963).)

7.2.6 Interpretation and the functional approach

Another approach is to look not so much at the word itself but at the function of the term, or, indeed, at the contract as a whole.

Photo Production Ltd v Securicor Transport Ltd **[1980] A.C. 827, HL**

(For facts and other extracts, see p.406.)

> **Lord Wilberforce:** ". . . Securicor undertook to provide a service of periodical visits for a very modest charge . . . It did not agree to provide equipment. It would have no knowledge of the value of Photo Productions' factory; that and the efficacy of their fire precautions, would be known to Photo Productions. In these circumstances nobody could consider it unreasonable that as between these two equal parties the risk assumed by Securicor should be a modest one, and that Photo Productions should carry the substantial risk of damage or destruction . . ."
>
> **Lord Salmon:** ". . . I think that any businessman entering into this contract could have had no doubt as to the real meaning of this clause and would have made his insurance arrangements accordingly . . ."

NOTE

In *Photo Production* the court looked at the function of the exclusion clause and decided that in the context of the contract as a whole its purpose was commercially reasonable, namely to determine the insurance risk.

QUESTION

If the House of Lords in this case (see p.406) had applied PECL, art.5:103, would the result have had to be different?

PROBLEM

Geoffrey enters into an insurance contract for a fire insurance policy to cover his new sailing boat, bought to replace his old one which was destroyed by an explosion. A clause in the policy states that the insurance company will be liable for damage or destruction "by fire howsoever caused". This new boat, called *Hello Sailor II*, is destroyed by an explosion when it strikes an old World War II mine, but the insurance company refuses to pay out saying that it is not liable. In a claim brought by Geoffrey against the insurance company, the judge at first instance states: "The premium payable for this fire policy was a very modest one indeed compared with what one would normally pay for this type of insurance and thus nobody could consider it unreasonable that as between these two parties the risk assumed by the insurance company in respect of *Hello Sailor II* should be a modest one." Would you advise Geoffrey to appeal against this decision?

7.2.7 *Contra proferentem* **rule**

According to the PECL, where "there is doubt about the meaning of a contract term not individually negotiated, an interpretation of the term against the party who supplied it is to be preferred" (art.5:103). Despite *Photo Production* (1980) (above p.351 and below p.406), *contra proferentem* is an English law, as well as a civil law, rule. It was developed mainly in respect of exclusion clauses rather than as a general interpretation rule: see e.g. *Adams v Richard & Starling Ltd* (1969), where Salmon L.J.

said that the clause in issue should be construed strictly *contra proferentem*. There is now a general obligation to write terms clearly so that they can be understood by the consumer. In case of doubt, the *contra proferentem* rule will come into play.

Unfair Terms in Consumer Contracts Regulations 1999 (SI 1999/2083)

"7. Written contracts
(1) A seller or supplier shall ensure that any written term of a contract is expressed in plain, intelligible language.

(2) If there is doubt about the meaning of a written term, the interpretation which is most favourable to the consumer shall prevail . . ."

Unfair Contract Terms Bill 2004

"8. Ambiguity
(1) If it is reasonable to read a written term of a consumer contract in two (or more) ways, the term is to be read in whichever of those ways it is reasonable to think the more (or the most) favourable to the consumer . . ."

QUESTION

If these rules had been in force at the time of *Adams v Richards & Starling* (1969) (read in law report), might they have affected the outcome?

7.2.8 Abandonment of the literal rule

In isolating various different methodological approaches (literal, actional, functional, etc.), it is not being suggested that one method necessarily excludes another. Often several methods are intermixed, as indeed the case of *Young v Sun Alliance Ins* (1977) (p.349) suggests. However, the overriding question that needs to be asked with regard to interpretation of contracts is whether or not the literal approach has now been modified or, indeed, abandoned.

Mannai Investment Co v Eagle Star Life Assurance **[1997] A.C. 749, HL**

Lord Hoffmann: ". . . In the case of commercial contracts, the restriction on the use of background has been quietly dropped. There are certain special kinds of evidence, such as previous negotiations and express declarations of intent, which for practical reasons which it is unnecessary to analyse, are inadmissable in aid of construction. They can be used only in an action for rectification. But apart from these exceptions, commercial contracts are construed in the light of all the background which could reasonably have been expected to have been available to the parties in order to ascertain what would objectively have been understood to be their intention: *Prenn v Simmonds* [1971] 1 WLR 1381, 1383. The fact that the words are capable of a literal application is no obstacle to evidence which demonstrates what a reasonable person with knowledge of the background would have understood the parties to mean, even if this compels one to say that they used the wrong words. In this area, we no longer confuse the meaning of words with the question of what meaning the use of the words was intended to convey. . . ."

NOTE

Lord Hoffmann developed this approach in a subsequent decision.

Investors Compensation Scheme v West Bromwich Building Society **[1998] 1 W.L.R. 896, HL**

Lord Hoffmann: ". . . I do not think that the fundamental change which has overtaken this branch of the law, particularly as a result of the speeches of Lord Wilberforce in *Prenn v Simmonds* [1971] 1 WLR 1381, 1384–1386 and *Reardon Smith Line Ltd v Yngvar Hansen-Tangen* [1976] 1 WLR 989, is always sufficiently appreciated. The result has been, subject to one important exception, to assimilate the way in which such documents are interpreted by judges to the common sense principles by which any serious utterance would be interpreted in ordinary life. Almost all the old intellectual baggage of 'legal' interpretation has been discarded. The principles may be summarised as follows.

(1) Interpretation is the ascertainment of the meaning which the document would convey to a reasonable person having all the background knowledge which would reasonably have been available to the parties in the situation in which they were at the time of the contract.

(2) The background was famously referred to by Lord Wilberforce as the 'matrix of fact,' but this phrase is, if anything, an understated description of what the background may include. Subject to the requirement that it should have been reasonably available to the parties and to the exception to be mentioned next, it includes absolutely anything which would have affected the way in which the language of the document would have been understood by a reasonable man.

(3) The law excludes from the admissible background the previous negotiations of the parties and their declarations of subjective intent. They are admissible only in an action for rectification. The law makes this distinction for reasons of practical policy and, in this respect only, legal interpretation differs from the way we would interpret utterances in ordinary life. The boundaries of this exception are in some respects unclear. But this is not the occasion on which to explore them.

(4) The meaning which a document (or any other utterance) would convey to a reasonable man is not the same thing as the meaning of its words. The meaning of words is a matter of dictionaries and grammars; the meaning of the document is what the parties using those words against the relevant background would reasonably have been understood to mean. The background may not merely enable the reasonable man to choose between the possible meanings of words which are ambiguous but even (as occasionally happens in ordinary life) to conclude that the parties must, for whatever reason, have used the wrong words or syntax: see *Mannai Investments Co Ltd v Eagle Star Life Assurance Co Ltd* [1997] AC 749.

(5) The 'rule' that words should be given their 'natural and ordinary meaning' reflects the common sense proposition that we do not easily accept that people have made linguistic mistakes, particularly in formal documents. On the other hand, if one would nevertheless conclude from the background that something must have gone wrong with the language, the law does not require judges to attribute to the parties an intention which they plainly could not have had . . .

If one applies these principles, it seems to me that the judge must be right and, as we are dealing with one badly drafted clause which is happily no longer in use, there is little advantage in my repeating his reasons at greater length. The only remark of his which I would respectfully question is when he said that he was 'doing violence' to the natural meaning of the words. This is an over-energetic way to describe the process of interpretation. Many people, including politicians, celebrities and Mrs Malaprop, mangle meanings and syntax but nevertheless communicate tolerably clearly what they are using the words to mean. If anyone is doing violence to natural meanings, it is they rather than their listeners . . ."

NOTE

In principle (3) Lord Hoffmann is referring to the "parole evidence" rule.

QUESTION

Is Lord Hoffmann saying that the literal approach has been abandoned?

7.3 Unfair terms

Many contractual interpretation cases are to be found in the chapter in contract textbooks dealing with exclusion and limitation clauses. For example, it was largely with respect to these types of clauses that the *contra proferentem* rule was developed (see *Adams v Richard & Starling* (1969)). Unfair terms do not, however, include just exclusion clauses; the expression covers any term that restricts a party's rights or places a burden on him which might be considered unfair. These clauses, now regulated by legislation, will be dealt with in detail the next chapter since they go to the effects of a contract (see **8.4**). However, it may be useful to indicate the main categories of unfair terms and some of the important interpretation issues that attach to them.

7.3.1 **Exclusion and limitation clauses**

These have been defined by the legislator as terms excluding or restricting liability, but the following terms are also classed within this category.

Unfair Contract Terms Act 1977 (c.50)

"13. Varieties of exemption clause
(1) To the extent that this Part of this Act prevents the exclusion or restriction of any liability it also prevents—

(a) making the liability or its enforcement subject to restrictive or onerous conditions;
(b) excluding or restricting any right or remedy in respect of the liability, or subjecting a person to any prejudice in consequence of his pursuing any such right or remedy;
(c) excluding or restricting rules of evidence or procedure;

and (to that extent) sections 2 and 5 to 7 also prevent excluding or restricting liability by reference to terms and notices which exclude or restrict the relevant obligation or duty.

(2) But an agreement in writing to submit present or future differences to arbitration is not to be treated under this Part of this Act as excluding or restricting any liability.

QUESTION

Would clause 7 in the *Schuler v Wickman Tools* (1974) case (above, p.327) fall within s.13 of the 1977 Act?

NOTE

See Lord Denning M.R.'s judgment in *George Mitchell (Chesterhall) Ltd v Finney Lock Seeds Ltd* (1983) (above, p.119).

7.3.2 **Penalty clauses**

A contract may contain a term that requires a party in breach of the contract to pay a specific sum of money to the other party as a debt. If the sum payable is a reasonable estimation of the damage suffered as a result of a breach, the term will be classed as a "liquidated damages clause" and thus enforceable as a debt. However, if the sum is excessive, in that it bears no relation to the damage suffered, it may well be classed as a penalty. Such penalties are in theory valid at common law, but equity intervened and refused to enforce them. The position is set out in the next extract.

Workers Trust Bank Ltd v Dojap Ltd **[1993] A.C. 573, PC**

This was an action in equity for relief against forfeiture of a deposit. The Privy Council (Lords Keith, Jauncey, Donaldson and Browne-Wilkinson, and Sir Christopher Slade) granted the relief.

> **Lord Browne-Wilkinson:** "This case raises the question whether a deposit in excess of 10 per cent paid under a contract for the sale of land can be lawfully forfeited by the vendor in the event of a failure by the purchaser to complete on the due date. . . .
>
> In general, a contractual provision which requires one party in the event of his breach of the contract to pay or forfeit a sum of money to the other party is unlawful as being a penalty, unless such provision can be justified as being a payment of liquidated damages being a genuine pre-estimate of the loss which the innocent party will incur by reason of the breach. One exception to this general rule is the provision for the payment of a deposit by the purchaser on a contract for the sale of land. Ancient law has established that the forfeiture of such a deposit (customarily 10 per cent of the contract price) does not fall within the general rule and can be validly forfeited even though the amount of the deposit bears no reference to the anticipated loss to the vendor flowing from the breach of contract.
>
> This exception is anomalous and at least one textbook writer has been surprised that the courts of equity ever countenanced it: see *Farrand, Contract and Conveyance*, 4th ed (1983), p 204. The special treatment afforded to such a deposit derives from the ancient custom of providing an earnest for the performance of a contract in the form of giving either some physical token of earnest (such as a ring) or earnest money. The history of the law of deposits can be traced to the Roman law of arra, and possibly further back still: see *Howe v Smith* (1884) 27 Ch D 89, 101–102, per Fry LJ. Ever since the decision in Howe v Smith, the nature of such a deposit has been settled in English law. Even in the absence of express contractual provision, it is an earnest for the performance of the contract: in the event of completion of the contract the deposit is applicable towards payment of the purchase price; in the event of the purchaser's failure to complete in accordance with the terms of the contract, the deposit is forfeit, equity having no power to relieve against such forfeiture.
>
> However, the special treatment afforded to deposits is plainly capable of being abused if the parties to a contract, by attaching the label 'deposit' to any penalty, could escape the general rule which renders penalties unenforceable. . . .

. . . It is not possible for the parties to attach the incidents of a deposit to the payment of a sum of money unless such sum is reasonable as earnest money. The question therefore is whether or not the deposit of 25 per cent in this case was reasonable as being in line with the traditional concept of earnest money or was in truth a penalty intended to act in terrorem. . . .

Their Lordships agree with the Court of Appeal that this evidence falls far short of showing that it was reasonable to stipulate for a forfeitable deposit of 25 per cent of the purchase price or indeed any deposit in excess of 10 per cent. . . .''

QUESTION

Is a penalty clause simply deemed not to exist, or is it a valid term but enforceable only up to the limit of the damage suffered by the victim of the breach?

Principles of European Contract Law

"**Article 9:509 Agreed Payment for Non-performance**
(1) Where the contract provides that a party who fails to perform is to pay a specified sum to the aggrieved party for such non-performance, the aggrieved party shall be awarded that sum irrespective of its actual loss.

(2) However, despite any agreement to the contrary the specified sum may be reduced to a reasonable amount where it is grossly excessive in relation to the loss resulting from the non-performance and the other circumstances."

QUESTION

Does this PECL provision represent in substance English law?

Jobson v Johnson [1989] 1 W.L.R. 1026, CA

This was an action for specific performance of a retransfer clause in a contract for the sale of shares. The clause stipulated that the shares were to be retransferred to the vendor for £40,000 if the buyer defaulted in the payment of any instalment of the purchase price. The Court of Appeal (Nicholls and Dillon L.JJ.; Kerr L.J. dissenting in part) held that the retransfer clause was a penalty and unenforceable in equity.

Nicholls L.J.: ". . . The particular procedure by which the Court of Chancery prevented a party seeking payment under a penalty clause in a contract, including a bond, from recovering more than his actual loss seems to have differed a little according to whether the penalty was intended to secure only a payment of money on a specified date or was intended to secure the performance of an obligation other than a payment of money. The details are not material for the purpose of this appeal. It suffices to say that an example of the latter type of case is to be found in *Sloman v Walter* (1784) 1 Bro CC 418. The party seeking payment of the penalty was prevented by injunction from recovering, by execution or otherwise, more from his judgment obtained at law on a bond than the amount of his loss as established by an issue of quantum damnificatus directed by the Court of Chancery. In the former case, of a bond securing only a money payment, the Court of Chancery proceeded on the principle that failure to pay the principal on a certain day could be compensated sufficiently by payment of principal, interest and costs on a subsequent day. Thus it was unnecessary to direct an issue of quantum damnificatus. . . . Subsequently the common law courts became obliged to give effect to these equitable principles, under . . . statutes. . . . After the Supreme Court of Judicature Act 1873 came into force these two statutes ceased to be necessary, and eventually they were repealed.

Thus today, when law and equity are administered concurrently in the same courts, and the rules of equity prevail whenever there is any conflict or variance between the rules of equity and the rules of the common law with reference to the same matter (section 49 of the Supreme Court Act 1981), a penalty clause in a contract is, in practice, a dead letter. An obligation to make a money payment stipulated in terrorem will not be enforced beyond the sum which represents the actual loss of the party seeking payment, namely, principal, interest and, if appropriate, costs, in those cases where (to use modern terminology) the primary obligation is to pay money, or where the primary obligation is to perform some other obligation, beyond the sum recoverable as damages for breach of that obligation. . . .

Although in practice a penalty clause in a contract as described above is effectively a dead letter, it is important in the present case to note that, contrary to the submissions of Mr Joseph, the strict legal position is not that such a clause is simply struck out of the contract, as though with a blue pencil, so that the contract takes effect as if it had never been included therein. Strictly, the legal position is that the clause remains in the contract and can be sued upon, but it will not be enforced by the court beyond the sum which represents, in the events which have happened, the actual loss of the party seeking payment. . . .

This is not the occasion to attempt to rationalise the distinction [between penalty and forfeiture clauses]. One possible explanation is that the distinction is rooted in the different forms which the relief takes. In the case of a penalty clause in a contract equity relieves by cutting down the extent to which the contractual obligation is enforceable: the 'scaling down' exercise, as I have described it. In the case of forfeiture clauses equitable relief takes the form of relieving wholly against the contractual forfeiture provision, subject to compliance with conditions imposed by the court. Be that as it may, I see no reason why the court's ability to grant discretionary relief automatically granted in respect of a penalty clause if, exceptionally, a contractual provision has characteristics which enable a defendant to pray in aid both heads of relief. . . ."

Kerr L.J. (dissenting in part): ". . . In my view, the combined effect of law and equity upon penalty clauses is simply that they will not be enforced in favour of a plaintiff without first giving to the defendant a proper opportunity to obtain relief against their penal consequences. . . .

In these circumstances it seems to me that, in equity, the plaintiff is entitled to a further alternative. This would be an order giving effect to paragraph 6(b), but on terms that the plaintiff repays to the defendant, perhaps with interest, the £160,000 which he has received under the agreement. In my view a further option to this effect would do justice to the plaintiff without contravening any principle of equity. It would give effect to the unenforceability of paragraph 6(b) because of its penal nature, but without simply 'blue-pencilling' it, which would be wrong. Secondly, it would provide some compensation to the plaintiff for having lost the opportunity of obtaining an order in terms of paragraph 6(b) because the normal process of an application for relief from forfeiture was frustrated by the defendant's decision to allow his counterclaim to be struck out. Above all, it would result in equitable restitution to both parties, without either enforcing or 'blue-pencilling' paragraph 6(b). . . . Paragraph 6(b) is penal, because its operation takes no account of the sums already received, and to that extent it is unenforceable. But it is enforceable to the extent that it is not a penalty, by requiring full restitution by the plaintiff as a condition of its enforcement. That would not be a case of 'mending men's bargains,' but the enforcement of a penal forfeiture clause by the removal of its penal element, and in a situation where relief from forfeiture can no longer be claimed by the defendant. . . ."

QUESTIONS

1. Which judgment is closer to PECL, art.9:509?

2. If equity was prepared to intervene with respect to penalty clauses, why was it not prepared to do the same thing with exclusion and limitation clauses?

3. What if the contracting party who is claiming relief in equity from a penalty clause is coming to equity without clean hands? (*Cf. D & C Builders v Rees* (1966), at p.195.)

4. Can a clause that turns a relatively minor breach into a breach of "condition" (thus allowing the other party to end the contract and claim damages for the whole loss of the bargain) ever be deemed a penalty? (*Lombard plc v Butterworth* (1987).)

NOTES

1. The equitable doctrine against penalties is one area of substantive contract law where equity makes a direct contribution. In many ways, of course, the doctrine is more a remedy than a right, in as much as it attaches to the creditor's claim in debt and involves enforcement rather than substantive

obligation. Nevertheless, it would probably be incorrect to describe the doctrine as a remedy to be placed alongside injunction and rescission. The doctrine is more like an estoppel: a contractual party is simply prevented from enforcing a debt right that he has at common law.

2. See further *Bridge v Campbell Discount Co* (1962).

7.3.3 Indemnity clauses

An indemnity clause is in some ways like a penalty, in that it places a contracting party under a contractual obligation to pay a sum of money as an indemnifying debt to the other party on the happening of a stipulated event. It is therefore a conditional promise or obligation.

Unfair Contract Terms Act 1977 (c.50)

"2. Negligence liability
(1) A person cannot by reference to any contract term or to a notice given to persons generally or to particular persons exclude or restrict his liability for death or personal injury resulting from negligence.

(2) In the case of other loss or damage, a person cannot so exclude or restrict his liability for negligence except in so far as the term or notice satisfies the requirement of reasonableness.

4. Unreasonable indemnity clauses
(1) A person dealing as consumer cannot by reference to any contract term be made to indemnify another person (whether a party to the contract or not) in respect of liability that may be incurred by the other for negligence or breach of contract, except in so far as the contract term satisfies the requirement of reasonableness.

(2) This section applies whether the liability in question—

(a) is directly that of the person to be indemnified or is incurred by him vicariously;
(b) is to the person dealing as consumer or to someone else."

PROBLEM

Tony hires an excavator and driver from Bernard. The contract states that Tony will indemnify Bernard against any liability that Bernard may incur as a result of the use of the excavator on Tony's premises. John, the driver of the excavator and an employee of Bernard, carelessly runs over Nicholas, a postman delivering letters to Tony, and kills him. Nicholas's wife, Elspeth, successfully sues Bernard for damages under the Fatal Accidents Act 1976. Can Bernard, who was well aware that John was an inexperienced excavator driver, recoup from Tony the damages he has paid to Elspeth?

Thompson v T Lohan (Plant) Ltd [1987] 1 W.L.R. 649

This was an action for damages by a wife against two defendants in respect of the death of her husband who had been killed by the negligence of a Mr Hill. Both the plaintiff's husband and Hill had been employed by the first defendants, working as drivers in a quarry owned by the second defendants. The trial judge held that the first defendants were vicariously liable to the plaintiff's wife, but the first defendants argued that they should be indemnified for this liability by the second defendants, thanks to a contract term. The Court of Appeal (Fox, Dillon and Woolf L.JJ.) upheld the validity of this indemnity clause.

> **Fox L.J.:** ". . . The next question is this. The third party say that, as a general matter of law, a party is only entitled to indemnity against the consequences of his own negligence, or that of his servant, where the indemnity clause relied upon contains an express provision to that effect, or where the words of the clause in their ordinary meaning are wide enough to cover negligence on his part. It is said that a clause does not contain an express provision indemnifying such a party against his or his servant's negligence, unless it contains the word 'negligence' or some synonym for 'negligence.' The authority for that proposition is the decision of the House of Lords in *Smith v South Wales Switchgear Co Ltd* [1978] 1 WLR 165. It is submitted that neither clause 8 nor clause 13, when taken either alone or together, satisfy the requirements of that principle so far as liability in negligence is concerned . . .
>
> We were referred to the decision of this court in *Phillips Products Ltd v Hyland (Note)* [1987] 1 WLR 659. . . .
>
> If one then turns to the present case, the sharp distinction between it and the *Phillips* case is this, that whereas in the *Phillips* case there was a liability in negligence of Hamstead to Phillips (and that was sought to be excluded), in the present case there is no exclusion or restriction of the liability sought to be achieved by reliance upon the provisions of clause 8. The plaintiff has her judgment against Lohan and can enforce it. The plaintiff is not prejudiced in any way by the operation sought to be established of clause 8. All that has happened is that Lohan and the third party have agreed between themselves who is to bear the consequences of Mr Hill's negligent acts. I can see nothing in section 2(1) of the Act of 1977 to prevent that. In my opinion, section 2(1) is concerned with protecting the victim of negligence and, of course, those who claim under him. It is not concerned with arrangements made by the wrongdoer with other persons as to the sharing or bearing of the burden of compensating the victim. In such a case it seems to me there is no exclusion or restriction of the liability at all. The liability has been established by Hodgson J. It is not in dispute and is now unalterable. The circumstance that the defendants have between themselves chosen to bear the liability in a particular way does not affect that liability; it does not exclude it, and it does not restrict it. The liability to the plaintiff is the only

relevant liability in the case, as it seems to me, and that liability is still in existence and will continue until discharge by payment to the plaintiff. Nothing is excluded in relation to the liability, and the liability is not restricted in any way whatever. The liability of Lohan to the plaintiff remains intact. The liability of Hamstead to Phillips was sought to be excluded . . .”

Dillon L.J.: “. . . Lohan and the third party, in their dealings with each other, were not dealing as consumers. So, that seems to me a strong indication that a clause of indemnity, or providing for a person who is liable to transfer his liability to someone else as between the two of them (or recoup that liability from someone else), is outside the scope of section 2 of the Act . . .”

NOTE

In *Smith v South Wales Switchgear Ltd* (1978), Viscount Dilhorne said (at 168): “While an indemnity clause may be regarded as the obverse of an exempting clause, when considering the meaning of such a clause one must, I think, regard it as even more inherently improbable that one party should agree to discharge the liability of the other party for acts for which he is responsible. In my opinion it is the case that the imposition by the proferens on the other party of liability to indemnify him against the consequences of his own negligence must be imposed by very clear words. It cannot be said, in my opinion, that it has been in the present case.”

7.3.4 Surprising terms

The notion of a "surprising term" has been formally introduced into contractual language by the UNIDROIT code.

Unidroit Principles for International Commercial Contracts

“Article 2.20 Surprising Terms
(1) No term contained in standard terms which is of such a character that the other party could not reasonably have expected it, is effective unless it has been expressly accepted by that party.

(2) In determining whether a term is of such a character regard is to be had to its content, language and presentation.”

NOTE

This article regulates the incorporation of such a term at the time of the formation of the contract. Although UNIDROIT does not represent English law, the Court of Appeal has come close to reflecting its spirit: see *Interfoto Picture Library Ltd v Stiletto Visual Programmes Ltd* (1989) (at p.402).

7.3.5 Unfair terms in general

The common law traditionally had no notion of an "unfair" term, despite the name appearing in the title of the 1977 legislation regulating exclusion clauses. The expression was introduced into English law via an EU Directive (5 April 1993: 93/13EEC:L 95/29), which became law as a result of secondary legislation.

Unfair Terms in Consumer Contracts Regulations 1999 (SI 1999/2083)

"4. Terms to which these Regulations apply
(1) These Regulations apply in relation to unfair terms in contracts concluded between a seller or a supplier and a consumer.

(2) These Regulations do not apply to contractual terms which reflect—

(a) mandatory statutory or regulatory provisions (including such provisions under the law of any Member State or in Community legislation having effect in the United Kingdom without further enactment);
(b) the provisions or principles of international conventions to which the Member States or the Community are party.

5. Unfair Terms
(1) A contractual term which has not been individually negotiated shall be regarded as unfair if, contrary to the requirement of good faith, it causes a significant imbalance in the parties' rights and obligations arising under the contract, to the detriment of the consumer.

(2) A term shall always be regarded as not having been individually negotiated where it has been drafted in advance and the consumer has therefore not been able to influence the substance of the term.

(3) Notwithstanding that a specific term or certain aspects of it in a contract has been individually negotiated, these Regulations shall apply to the rest of a contract if an overall assessment of it indicates that it is a pre-formulated standard contract.

(4) It shall be for any seller or supplier who claims that a term was individually negotiated to show that it was.

(5) Schedule 2 to these Regulations contains an indicative and non-exhaustive list of the terms which may be regarded as unfair.

6. Assessment of unfair terms
(1) Without prejudice to regulation 12, the unfairness of a contractual term shall be assessed, taking into account the nature of the goods or services for which the contract was concluded and by referring, at the time of conclusion of the contract,

---

to all the circumstances attending the conclusion of the contract and to all the other terms of the contract or of another contract on which it is dependent.

(2) In so far as it is in plain intelligible language, the assessment of fairness of a term shall not relate—

(a) to the definition of the main subject matter of the contract, or
(b) to the adequacy of the price or remuneration, as against the goods or services supplied in exchange.

SCHEDULE 2

Regulation 5(5)

INDICATIVE AND NON-EXHAUSTIVE LIST OF TERMS WHICH MAY BE REGARDED AS UNFAIR

1. Terms which have the object or effect of—

(a) excluding or limiting the legal liability of a seller or supplier in the event of the death of a consumer or personal injury to the latter resulting from an act or omission of that seller or supplier;

(b) inappropriately excluding or limiting the legal rights of the consumer vis-à-vis the seller or supplier or another party in the event of total or partial non-performance or inadequate performance by the seller or supplier of any of the contractual obligations, including the option of offsetting a debt owed to the seller or supplier against any claim which the consumer may have against him;

(c) making an agreement binding on the consumer whereas provision of services by the seller or supplier is subject to a condition whose realisation depends on his own will alone;

(d) permitting the seller or supplier to retain sums paid by the consumer where the latter decides not to conclude or perform the contract, without providing for the consumer to receive compensation of an equivalent amount from the seller or supplier where the latter is the party cancelling the contract;

(e) requiring any consumer who fails to fulfil his obligation to pay a disproportionately high sum in compensation;

(f) authorising the seller or supplier to dissolve the contract on a discretionary basis where the same facility is not granted to the consumer, or permitting the seller or supplier to retain the sums paid for services not yet supplied by him where it is the seller or supplier himself who dissolves the contract;

(g) enabling the seller or supplier to terminate a contract of indeterminate duration without reasonable notice except where there are serious grounds for doing so;

(h) automatically extending a contract of fixed duration where the consumer does not indicate otherwise, when the deadline fixed for the consumer to express his desire not to extend the contract is unreasonably early;

(i) irrevocably binding the consumer to terms with which he had no real opportunity of becoming acquainted before the conclusion of the contract;

(j) enabling the seller or supplier to alter the terms of the contract unilaterally without a valid reason which is specified in the contract;

(k) enabling the seller or supplier to alter unilaterally without a valid reason any characteristics of the product or service to be provided;

(l) providing for the price of goods to be determined at the time of delivery or allowing a seller of goods or supplier of services to increase their price without in both cases giving the consumer the corresponding right to cancel the contract if the final price is too high in relation to the price agreed when the contract was concluded;

(m) giving the seller or supplier the right to determine whether the goods or services supplied are in conformity with the contract, or giving him the exclusive right to interpret any term of the contract;

(n) limiting the seller's or supplier's obligation to respect commitments undertaken by his agents or making his commitments subject to compliance with a particular formality;

(o) obliging the consumer to fulfil all his obligations where the seller or supplier does not perform his;

(p) giving the seller or supplier the possibility of transferring his rights and obligations under the contract, where this may serve to reduce the guarantees for the consumer, without the latter's agreement;

(q) excluding or hindering the consumer's right to take legal action or exercise any other legal remedy, particularly by requiring the consumer to take disputes exclusively to arbitration not covered by legal provisions, unduly restricting the evidence available to him or imposing on him a burden of proof which, according to the applicable law, should lie with another party to the contract."

QUESTIONS

1. What is meant by "good faith" in reg.5(1)? Is it the same as "reasonableness"?

2. In *Director General of Fair Trading v First National Bank plc* (2002) (above, at p.131), was the disputed term "unfair" in any way?

7.4 Implied terms

In addition to the express promises to be found in a contract, there may also be promises that are unexpressed. These are called implied terms.

7.4.1 **Implied terms in general**

The general nature of an implied term is set out in the following code extracts.

Principles of European Contract Law

"Article 6:102 Implied obligations
In addition to the express terms, a contract may contain implied terms which stem from

(a) the intention of the parties,
(b) the nature and purpose of the contract, and
(c) good faith and fair dealing."

Unidroit Principles for International Commercial Contracts

"Article 5.1 Express and Implied Obligations
The contractual obligations of the parties may be express or implied.

Article 5.2 Implied Obligations
Implied obligations stem from

(a) the nature and purpose of the contract;
(b) practices established between the parties and usages;
(c) good faith and fair dealing;
(d) reasonableness."

NOTE

As we shall see, these articles only partly reflect English law.

Shell UK Ltd v Lostock Garage Ltd **[1976] 1 W.L.R. 1187, CA**

This was an action for an injunction and damages brought by an oil company against a garage for breach of a contract for the supply of petrol. The garage had entered into a 20–year solus agreement, under which the garage agreed to supply only the plaintiff oil company's petrol. However, during a "price war" the defendant garage discovered that the oil company was running a subsidy scheme, which benefited other tied garages in the area but from which the defendant was excluded, forcing it to trade at a loss. The defendant accordingly obtained supplies of petrol from another supplier. In its defence the garage argued that the oil company was in breach of an implied term not to discriminate against it in favour of other garages in the area. A majority of the Court of Appeal (Lord Denning M.R. and Ormrod L.J.; Bridge L.J. dissenting) held that such a term could not be implied. However, a majority (Lord Denning M.R. and Bridge L.J.) also held that an injunction would not issue.

Lord Denning M.R.: ". . . I ventured with some trepidation to suggest that terms implied by law could be brought within one comprehensive category—in which the courts could imply a term such as was just and reasonable in the circumstances: see *Greaves & Co (Contractors) Ltd v Baynham Meikle & Partners* [1975] 1 WLR 1095, 1099–1100; *Liverpool City Council v Irwin* [1976] QB 319, 331–332. But, as I feared, the House of Lords in *Liverpool City Council v Irwin* [1976] 2 WLR 562, have rejected it as quite unacceptable. As I read the speeches, there are two broad categories of implied terms.

(i) The first category

The first category comprehends all those relationships which are of common occurrence. Such as the relationship of seller and buyer, owner and hirer, master and servant, landlord and tenant, carrier by land or by sea, contractor for building works, and so forth. In all those relationships the courts have imposed obligations on one party or the other, saying they are 'implied terms.' These obligations are not founded on the intention of the parties, actual or presumed, but on more general considerations: see *Luxor (Eastbourne) Ltd v Cooper* [1941] AC 108, 137 by Lord Wright; *Lister v Romford Ice and Cold Storage Co Ltd* [1957] AC 555, 576 by Viscount Simonds, and at p 594 by Lord Tucker (both of whom give interesting illustrations); and *Liverpool City Council v Irwin* [1976] 2 WLR 562, 571 by Lord Cross of Chelsea, and at p 579 by Lord Edmund-Davies. In such relationships the problem is not to be solved by asking what did the parties intend? Or would they have unhesitatingly agreed to it, if asked? It is to be solved by asking: has the law already defined the obligation or the extent of it? If so, let it be followed. If not, look to see what would be reasonable in the general run of such cases: see by Lord Cross of Chelsea at p 570H: and then say what the obligation shall be. The House in *Liverpool City Council v Irwin* [1976] 2 WLR 562 went through that very process. They examined the existing law of landlord and tenant, in particular that relating to easements, to see if it contained the solution to the problem: and, having found that it did not, they imposed an obligation on the landlord to use reasonable care. In these relationships the parties can exclude or modify the obligation by express words; but unless they do so, the obligation is a legal incident of the relationship which is attached by the law itself and not by reason of any implied term.

Likewise, in the general law of contract, the legal effect of frustration does not depend on an implied term. It does not depend on the presumed intention of the parties, nor on what they would have answered, if asked: but simply on what the court itself declares to amount to a frustration: see *Davis Contractors Ltd v Fareham Urban District Council* [1956] AC 696, 728 by Lord Radcliffe and *The Eugenia* [1964] 2 QB 226, 238, 239.

(ii) The second category

The second category comprehends those cases which are not within the first category. These are cases—not of common occurrence—in which from the particular circumstances a term is to be implied. In these cases the implication is based on an intention imputed to the parties from their actual circumstances: see *Luxor (Eastbourne) Ltd v Cooper* [1941] AC 108, 137 by Lord Wright. Such an imputation is only to be made when it is necessary to imply a term to give efficacy to the contract and make it a workable agreement in such manner as the parties would clearly have done if they had applied their mind to the contingency which has arisen. These are the 'officious bystander' types of case: see *Lister v Romford Ice and Cold Storage Co Ltd* [1957] AC 555, 594, by Lord Tucker. In such cases a term is not to be implied on the ground that it would be reasonable: but only when it is necessary and can be formulated with a sufficient degree of precision. This was the test applied by the majority of this court in *Liverpool City Council v Irwin* [1976] QB 319. and they were emphatically upheld by the House on this point: see [1976] 2 WLR 562, 571D--H by Lord Cross of Chelsea; p 578G--579A by Lord Edmund-Davies.

There is this point to be noted about *Liverpool City Council v Irwin*. In this court the argument was only about an implication in the second category. In the House of Lords that argument was not pursued. It was only the first category.

Into which of the two categories does the present case come? I am tempted to say that a solus agreement between supplier and buyer is of such common occurrence nowadays that it could be put into the first category: so that the law could imply a term based on general considerations. But I do not think this would be found acceptable. Nor do I think the case can be brought within the second category. If the Shell company had been asked at the beginning: 'Will you agree not to discriminate abnormally against the buyer?' I think they would have declined. It might be a reasonable term, but it is not a necessary term. Nor can it be formulated with sufficient precision. On this point I agree with Kerr J. It should be noticed that in the *Esso* case Mocatta J also refused to make such an implication: see [1966] 2 QB 514, 536–541; and there was no appeal from his decision. In the circumstances, I do not think any term can be implied . . ."

Bridge L.J.: ". . . But it does not follow that in the absence of any such express term the plaintiffs must be at liberty to discriminate against the defendants to any degree. An extreme example will serve to illustrate that such a freedom on the part of the plaintiffs would lead to absurdity. Suppose that an oil company concludes a five-year solus agreement with A at a normal rate of rebate. If on the very next day the company were to conclude two other five-year solus agreements with B and C, A's nearest competitors, giving them in each case a rebate at a rate 10p per gallon higher than the rate of rebate given to A this would make it manifestly impossible for A to trade on the terms expressly agreed. To say that in those circumstances A must still be bound by his contract would be an absurdity. Obviously the parties as reasonable men cannot have intended such in absurdity.

Accordingly, it seems to me to follow that the necessary foundation for the application of the classic doctrine on which terms are implied in contracts is here present. That doctrine, as I understand it, requires that terms should be implied to prevent contractual absurdities which reasonable parties cannot have intended . . .

It is said that lack of precision in the criterion to be embodied in the implied term is fatal to any implication. But it is no novelty in the common law to find that a criterion on which some important question of liability is to depend can only be defined in imprecise terms which leave a difficult question for decision as to how the criterion applies to the facts of a particular case. A clear and distinct line of demarcation may be impossible to draw in abstract terms; yet the court does not shrink from the task of deciding on the facts of any case before it on which side of the line the case falls. This kind of pragmatism is so deeply entrenched in the common law's approach to a multitude of legal problems that I decline to accept that the difficulty of defining with precision what term is to be implied in this case is an insuperable obstacle to the implication of any term limiting the plaintiffs' freedom to discriminate. I am content, in my approach to the further questions arising, to take as the test of the degree of discrimination prohibited by the implied term whether it is such as to render the defendants' commercial operation of their petrol sales business impracticable . . ."

QUESTION

In what circumstances (if ever) can a court imply a term into a contract simply on the ground of the reasonable man test?

Liverpool City Council v Irwin [1977] A.C. 239, HL

This was an action for repossession by a local authority landlord against the tenants of a tower block who were refusing to pay rent because of the bad conditions of the tower block premises. The tenants counterclaimed for damages for breach of an implied term in the tenancy contract. The House of Lords (Lords Wilberforce, Cross, Salmon, Edmund-Davies and Fraser) held that there was an implied term that the landlord keep in reasonable repair the common parts of the tower block, although on the actual facts there was no breach of this term.

Lord Cross: ". . . When it implies a term in a contract the court is sometimes laying down a general rule that in all contracts of a certain type—sale of goods, master and servant, landlord and tenant and so on—some provision is to be implied unless the parties have expressly excluded it. In deciding whether or not to lay down such a prima facie rule the court will naturally ask itself whether in the general run of such cases the term in question would be one which it would be reasonable to insert. Sometimes, however, there is no question of laying down any prima facie rule applicable to all cases of a defined type but what the court is being in effect asked to do is to rectify a particular—often a very detailed—contract by inserting in it a term which the parties have not expressed. Here it is not enough for the court to say that the suggested term is a reasonable one the presence of which would make the contract a better or fairer one; it must be able to say that the insertion of the term is necessary to give—as it is put—'business efficacy' to the contract and that if its absence had been pointed out at the time both parties—assuming them to have been reasonable men—would have agreed without hesitation to its insertion. The distinction between the two types of case was pointed out by Viscount Simonds and Lord Tucker in their speeches in *Lister v Romford Ice and Cold Storage Co Ltd* [1957] AC 555, 579, 594, but I think that Lord Denning MR in proceeding—albeit with some trepidation—to 'kill off' MacKinnon LJ's 'officious bystander' (*Shirlaw v Southern Foundries (1926) Ltd* [1939] 2 KB 206, 227) must have overlooked it. Counsel for the appellant did not in fact rely on this passage in the speech of Lord Denning. His main argument was that when a landlord lets a number of flats or offices to a number of different tenants giving all of them rights to use the staircases, corridors and lifts there is to be implied, in the absence of any provision to the contrary, an obligation on the landlord to keep the 'common parts' in repair and the lifts in working order. But, for good measure, he also submitted that he could succeed on the 'officious bystander' test.

I have no hesitation in rejecting this alternative submission. We are not here dealing with an ordinary commercial contract by which a property company is letting one of its flats for profit. The respondent council is a public body charged by law with the duty of providing housing for members of the public selected because of their need for it at rents which are subsidised by the general body of ratepayers. Moreover the officials in the council's housing department would know very well that some of the tenants in any given block might subject the chutes and lifts to rough treatment and that there was an ever present danger of deliberate damage by young 'vandals'—some of whom might in fact be children of the tenants in that or neighbouring blocks. In these circumstances, if at the time when the respondents were granted their tenancy one of them had said to the council's representative: 'I suppose that the council will be under a legal liability to us to keep the chutes and the lifts in working order and the staircases properly lighted,' the answer might well have been—indeed I think, as Roskill LJ thought [1976] QB 319, 338, in all probability would have been—'Certainly not.' The official might have added in explanation—'Of course we do not expect our tenants to keep them in repair themselves—though we do expect them to use them with care and to co-operate in combating vandalism. The council is a responsible body conscious of its duty both to its tenants and to the general body of ratepayers and we will always do our best in what may be difficult circumstances to keep the staircases lighted and the lifts and chutes working, but we cannot be expected to subject ourselves to a liability to be sued by any tenant for defects which may be directly or indirectly due to the negligence of some of the other tenants in the very block in question.' Some people might think that it would have been, on balance, wrong for the council to adopt such an attitude, but no one could possibly describe such an attitude as irrational or perverse . . .

. . . Can a pregnant woman accompanied by a young child be expected to walk up 15, or for that matter nine, storeys in the pitch dark to reach her home? Unless the law, in circumstances such as these, imposes an obligation upon the council at least to use reasonable care to keep the lifts working properly and the staircase lit, the whole transaction becomes inefficacious, futile and absurd. I cannot go so far as Lord Denning MR and hold that the courts have any power to imply a term into a contract merely because it seems reasonable to do so. Indeed, I think that such a proposition is contrary to all authority. To say, as Lord Reid said in *Young & Marten Ltd v McManus Childs Ltd* [1969] 1 AC 454, 465, that '. . . no warranty ought to be implied in a contract unless it is in all the circumstances reasonable' is, in my view, quite different from saying that any warranty or term which is, in all the circumstances, reasonable ought to be implied in a contract. I am confident that Lord Reid meant no more than that unless a warranty or term is in all the circumstances reasonable there can be no question of implying it into a contract, but before it is implied much else besides is necessary, for example that without it the contract would be inefficacious, futile and absurd . . ."

QUESTIONS

1. Was the status of the landlord (a local authority) of importance in this case? If the local authority decided to sell the block of flats to a private landlord, would this new landlord be subject to exactly the same implied term with respect to the common parts, or might the implied duty be one "to keep the chutes and the lifts in working order and the staircases properly lighted"?

2. In *Birmingham CC v Oakley* (2001), Lord Hoffmann said this (at 628): "My Lords, on the surface, this does not look like a very momentous case. The question is whether Mr and Mrs Oakley's landlord should have provided them with a basin in the WC. The statute which they say made it necessary to install one is ambiguous. The language is capable of bearing such a construction. On the other hand, it is very unlikely that this was what Parliament intended. So the courts have a choice. If they say that Mr and Mrs Oakley should have had a basin, landlords of old houses and flats all over the country will have to install them. Local authorities and housing trusts will have to incur very considerable expense. Under the surface, therefore, the case raises a question of great constitutional importance. When it comes to the expenditure of large sums of public and private money, who should make the decision? If the statute is clear, then of course Parliament has already made the decision and the courts merely enforce it. But when the statute is doubtful, should judges

decide? Or should they leave the decision to democratically elected coun-
cillors or members of Parliament?" Do you think the Law Lords in *Irwin* had
similar considerations at the back of their minds?

7.4.2 Terms implied in particular factual situations

Terms can be implied into a particular contract before the court on the basis of the
particular facts of the case. The leading authority is set out in the next extract.

The Moorcock **(1889) 14 P.D. 64, CA**

This was an action for damages by the owner of a ship against the owners of a wharf
in respect of damage sustained by the ship when she rested on hard ground at low
tide. The Court of Appeal (Lord Esher M.R., Bowen and Fry L.JJ.) held the wharf
owners liable.

> **Bowen L.J.:** ". . . The question which arises here is whether, when a contract is
> made to let the use of this jetty to a ship which can only use it, as is known to
> both parties, by taking the ground, there is any implied warranty on the part of
> the owners of the jetty, and if so, what is the extent of that warranty. Now, an
> implied warranty, or as it is called, a covenant in law, as distinguished from an
> express contract or express warranty, really is in all cases founded on the
> presumed intention of the parties, and upon reason. The implication which the
> law draws from what must obviously have been the intention of the parties, the
> law draws with the object of giving efficacy to the transaction and preventing such
> a failure of consideration as cannot have been within the contemplation of either
> side; and I believe if one were to take all the cases, and they are many, of implied
> warranties and covenants in law, it will be found that in all them the law is raising
> an implication from the presumed intention of the parties with the object of
> giving to the transaction such efficacy as both parties must have intended that in
> all events it should have. In business transactions such as this, what the law
> desires to effect by the implication is to give such business efficacy to the
> transaction as must have been intended at all events by both parties who are
> business men; not to impose on one side all the perils of the transaction, or to
> emancipate one side from all the chances of failure, but to make each party
> promise in law as much, at all events, as it must have been in the contemplation
> of both parties that he should be responsible for in respect of those perils or
> chances.
>
> Now what did each party in a case like this know? For if we are examining into
> their presumed intention, we must examine into their minds as to what the
> transaction was. Both parties knew that this jetty was let for hire, and knew that it
> could only be used under the contract by the ship taking the ground. They must
> have known that it was by grounding that she used the jetty; in fact . . . they must

have known, both of them, that unless the ground was safe the ship would be simply buying an opportunity of danger, and that all consideration would fail unless some care had been taken to see that the ground was safe. In fact the business of the jetty could not be carried on except upon such a basis. The parties also knew that with regard to the safety of the ground outside the jetty the shipowner could know nothing at all, and the jetty owner might with reasonable care know everything. The owners of the jetty, or their servants, were there at high and low tide, and with little trouble they could satisfy themselves, in case of doubt, as to whether the berth was reasonably safe. The ship's owner, on the other hand, had not the means of verifying the state of the jetty, because the berth itself opposite the jetty might be occupied by another ship at any moment.

[I]t may well be said that the law will not imply that the persons who have not control of the place have taken reasonable care to make it good, but it does not follow that they are relieved from all responsibility. They are on the spot. They must know the jetty cannot be used unless reasonable care is taken, if not to make it safe, at all events to see whether it is safe. No one can tell whether reasonable safety has been secured except themselves, and I think if they let out their jetty for use they at all events imply that they have taken reasonable care to see that the berth, which is the essential part of the use of the jetty, is safe, and if it is not safe, and if they have not taken such reasonable care, it is their duty to warn persons with whom they have dealings that they have not done so . . ."

NOTE

The notion of an implied term is central to English contract law since it is the means by which a court can interpret contractual facts in order to insert into the facts a normative element that can then be used to establish liability. Thus the wharf owner was liable not because he was at fault (one possible normative concept), but because he had "promised" (another normative concept) that the berth was safe. The berth was not safe, so the wharf owner was liable to compensate in damages because he was in breach of his promise. Fault and the implied term do, however, often come together: if in *Bolton v Mahadeva* (1972) (see p.454) a fire had accidentally started, the question of the level of duty (fault or strict liability) would have centred on the implied term. Did the heating engineers promise to use care and skill, or did they warrant that the materials they used were safe?

QUESTIONS

1. Is the implied term a means by which courts can remake contracts?
2. What if the owner of the ship had been compensated for the damage by his insurance company: would the court still have implied the term so as to allow the insurance company to recover from the wharf owner via the doctrine of subrogation?

7.4.3 Terms implied into categories of contract

Terms can also be implied into a whole class or category of contract, such as landlord and tenant or sale of goods contracts. One of the most important of such implied terms is to be found in the Sale of Goods Act 1979, s.14 (see p.60). But terms can be implied into a class of contract not only by statute, but also by case law.

Mahmud v BCCI [1998] A.C. 20, HL

(For facts and further extract, see p.278.)

> **Lord Steyn:** ". . . The applicants do not rely on a term implied in fact. They do not therefore rely on an individualised term to be implied from the particular provisions of their employment contracts considered against their specific contextual setting. Instead they rely on a standardised term implied by law, that is, on a term which is said to be an incident of all contracts of employment: *Scally v Southern Health and Social Services Board* [1992] 1 AC 294, 307B. Such implied terms operate as default rules. The parties are free to exclude or modify them. But it is common ground that in the present case the particular terms of the contracts of employment of the two applicants could not affect an implied obligation of mutual trust and confidence. . . .
>
> The evolution of the implied term of trust and confidence is a fact. It has not yet been endorsed by your Lordships' House. It has proved a workable principle in practice. It has not been the subject of adverse criticism in any decided cases and it has been welcomed in academic writings. I regard the emergence of the implied obligation of mutual trust and confidence as a sound development. . . .''

NOTE

Terms can be implied in fact and in law. Or, put another way, there are some contracts where implied promises will automatically apply either because of precedent, or because of legislation. The notion of an implied term can thus become a means of importing objective rules into contractual situations.

QUESTIONS

1. Do employees impliedly promise their employers in their contracts of employment that they will never be negligent? Does an employer impliedly promise to warn employees about any lack of insurance cover when the employer asks the employee to work abroad? Is a university under an implied obligation to take out insurance on behalf of its post-graduate students who go abroad to do research? (*Cf. Reid v Rush & Tompkins Plc* (1990), and see above, p.128)

2. 'Bona fides [is] an implied term in every mercantile contract' (Lord Watson in *Glynn, Mills Currie & Co v East & West India Dock Co* (1882), at 615). Is this actually true?

7.4.4 Implied terms and level of duty

One of the interesting aspects of s.14 of the Sale of Goods Act 1979 is that liability is strict: if the goods sold are not reasonably fit, the seller will be liable even in the absence of fault on his part (see *Frost v Aylesbury Dairy Co Ltd* (1905), above at p.61). In other words, the seller is promising a specific result. It is possible that case law might imply such a specific result promise as well, as the next extract indicates (but see also *Thake v Maurice* (1986), above at p.63).

Hyman v Nye (1881) 6 Q.B.D. 685, QBD

Lindley J.: "The defendant in this case was a job-master at Brighton, letting out carriages and horses for hire. The plaintiff hired of him a landau, and a pair of horses, and a driver, for a drive from Brighton to Shoreham and back. After having driven some way, and whilst the carriage was going down hill and slowly over a newly mended part of the road, a bolt in the underpart of the carriage broke. The splinter-bar became displaced; the horses started off; the carriage was upset; the plaintiff was thrown out and injured, and he brought this action for compensation.

It was proved at the trial that no fault could be imputed to the horses nor to the driver; and although the plaintiff was charged with having caused the accident by pulling the reins, the jury found in the plaintiff's favour on this point, and nothing now turns upon it.

It further appeared that the carriage had been built by a good builder some eight or nine years before the accident; had been repaired by a competent person about 15 months before it; that the defendant had no reason to suppose that there was any defect in the carriage or in any of its bolts; and that the defect, if any, in the bolt which broke could not have been discovered by any ordinary inspection. The bolt itself was not produced at the trial, and the nature of the defect, if any, in it when the carriage started was not proved.

The learned judge at the trial told the jury in substance that the plaintiff was bound to prove that the injury which he had sustained was caused by the negligence of the defendant; and if in their opinion the defendant took all reasonable care to provide a fit and proper carriage their verdict ought to be for him. Being thus directed, the jury found a verdict for the defendant; and in particular they found that the carriage was reasonably fit for the purpose for which it was hired, and that the defect in the bolt could not have been discovered by the defendant by ordinary care and attention. The plaintiff complains of this direction, and of the verdict founded upon it, and we have to consider whether the direction was correct . . .

A careful study of these authorities leads me to the conclusion that the learned judge at the trial put the duty of the defendant too low. A person who lets out carriages is not, in my opinion, responsible for all defects discoverable or not; he is not an insurer against all defects; nor is he bound to take more care than coach proprietors or railway companies who provide carriages for the public to travel in;

376

but in my opinion, he is bound to take as much care as they; and although not an insurer against all defects, he is an insurer against all defects which care and skill can guard against. His duty appears to me to be to supply a carriage as fit for the purpose for which it is hired as care and skill can render it; and if whilst the carriage is being properly used for such purpose it breaks down, it becomes incumbent on the person who has let it out to show that the breakdown was in the proper sense of the word an accident not preventable by any care or skill. If he can prove this, as the defendant did in *Christie v Griggs*, and as the railway company did in *Readhead v Midland Ry Co*, he will not be liable; but no proof short of this will exonerate him. Nor does it appear to me to be at all unreasonable to exact such vigilance from a person who makes it his business to let out carriages for hire. As between him and the hirer the risk of defects in the carriage, so far as care and skill can avoid them, ought to be thrown on the owner of the carriage. The hirer trusts him to supply a fit and proper carriage; the lender has it in his power not only to see that it is in a proper state, and to keep it so, and thus protect himself from risk, but also to charge his customers enough to cover his expenses. . . .

For the above reasons I am of opinion that there should be a new trial.

Mathew J [concurred]."

QUESTION

Is this a negligence case, with the burden of disproving negligence on the owner of the carriage? Is a railway company in truth under the same duty with respect to its carriages?

Readhead v Midland Railway Co **(1869) L.R. 4 Q.B. 379, Ex Chamber**

Montague Smith J. (delivering the judgment of the court): "In this case the plaintiff, a passenger for hire on the defendants' railway, suffered an injury in consequence of the carriage in which he travelled getting off the line and upsetting; the accident was caused by the breaking of the tyre of one of the wheels of the carriage owing to 'a latent defect in the tyre which was not attributable to any fault on the part of the manufacturer, and could not be detected previously to the breaking'.

Does an action lie against the company under these circumstances?

This question involves the consideration of the true nature of the contract made between a passenger and a general carrier of passengers for hire. It is obvious, that for the plaintiff on this state of facts to succeed in this action, he must establish either that there is a warranty, by way of insurance on the part of the carrier to convey the passenger safely to his journey's end, or, as the learned

377

counsel mainly insisted, a warranty that the carriage in which he travels shall be in all respects perfect for its purpose, that is to say, free from all defects likely to cause peril, although those defects were such that no skill, care, or foresight could have detected their existence.

We are of opinion, after consideration of the authorities, that there is no such contract either of general or limited warranty and insurance entered into by the carrier of passengers, and that the contract of such a carrier and the obligation undertaken by him are to take due care (including in that term the use of skill and foresight) to carry a passenger safely. It of course follows that the absence of such care, in other words negligence, would alone be a breach of this contract, and as the facts of this case do not disclose such a breach, and on the contrary negative any want of skill, care or foresight, we think the plaintiff has failed to sustain his action and that the judgment of the Court below in favour of the defendant ought to be affirmed. . . .

An obligation to use all due and proper care is founded on reasons obvious to all, but to impose on the carrier the burden of a warranty that everything he necessarily uses is absolutely free from defects likely to cause peril, when from the nature of things defects must exist which no skill can detect, and the effects of which no care or foresight can avert, would be to compel a man, by implication of law and not by his own will, to promise the performance of an impossible thing, and would be directly opposed to the maxims of law, *lex non cogit ad impossibilia—Nemo tenetur ad impossibilia*. . . .

[The other judges were Kelly C.B., Byles and Keating JJ. and Channell and Bramwell BB.]"

QUESTIONS

1. Why is there one rule for goods (bailment) and another for passengers? (Read the whole of Montague Smith J.'s judgment in the law report.)

2. Why should it be the passengers—and not the railway company (and its shareholders)—who have to carry the risks of faulty trains?

3. In order for a contractor to be in breach of contract, he, she or it must be in breach of one of the actual promises (terms) which go to make up the contract. However, as the above case makes clear, this exercise is one of interpretation not of the parties' minds, but of the law. Yet the parties' minds become one reason for not implying an absolute promise since that would, according to the court, lead to a situation where the parties have promised the impossible. Why, however, does Lindley J. in *Hyman v Nye* (1881) seem to take a different approach?

4. Was Lindley J. in *Hyman v Nye* applying to the facts before him exactly the same rule as the court in *Readhead v Midland Railway Co* applied to the facts before it? If so, why the different result?

5. Did the defendant in *Hyman v Nye* promise the impossible? If so, does Lindley J. offer any justification?

NOTES

French lawyers would readily recognise the distinction to be found between *Readhead v Midland Railway Co* and *Hyman v Nye* (and between s.14 of the Sale of Good Act 1979 and s.13 of the Supply of Goods and Services Act 1982). However, they would talk of a distinction between two different obligations: an *obligation de résultat* and an *obligation de moyens*. This distinction has been specifically adopted by the UNIDROIT code.

Unidroit Principles for International Commercial Contracts

"Article 5.4 Duty to Achieve a Specific Result. Duty of Best Efforts
(1) To the extent that an obligation of a party involves a duty to achieve a specific result, that party is bound to achieve that result.

(2) To the extent that an obligation of a party involves a duty of best efforts in the performance of an activity, that party is bound to make such efforts as would be made by a reasonable person of the same kind in the same circumstances.

Article 5.5 Determination of Kind of Duty Involved
In determining the extent to which an obligation of a party involves a duty of best efforts in the performance of an activity or duty to achieve a specific result, regard shall be had, among other factors, to

(a) the way in which the obligation is expressed in the contract;
(b) the contractual price and other terms of the contract;
(c) the degree of risk normally involved in achieving the expected result;
(d) the ability of the other party to influence the performance of the obligation."

QUESTIONS

1. Does art.5.5 suggest that contractual liability is governed by rules that are actually rather different in nature from those dealing with the formation and contents of a contract?

2. If the facts of *Readhead v Midland Railway Co* occurred in France, do you think the French courts would treat the obligation owed by SNCF to its passengers as an obligation to achieve a specific result (i.e. get passengers to their destination unharmed), or as an obligation of best efforts (i.e. run a service with reasonable care and skill)?

3. In what circumstances might art.5.5 be relevant (or of some relevance at least) for English lawyers?

379

Greaves & Co (Contractors) Ltd v Baynham Meikle & Partners **[1975] 1 W.L.R. 1095, CA**

Lord Denning M.R.: ". . . [I]t has often been stated that the law will only imply a term when it is reasonable and necessary to do so in order to give business efficacy to the transaction; and, indeed, so obvious that both parties must have intended it. But those statements must be taken with considerable qualification. In the great majority of cases it is no use looking for the intention of both parties. If you asked the parties what they intended, they would say that they never gave it a thought; or, if they did, the one would say that he intended something different from the other. So that courts imply—or, as I would say, impose—a term such as is just and reasonable in the circumstances. Take some of the most familiar of implied terms in the authorities cited to us. Such as the implied condition of fitness on a sale of goods at first implied by the common law and afterwards embodied in the Sale of Goods Act 1893. Or the implied warranty of fitness on a contract for work and materials: *Young & Marten Ltd v McManus Childs Ltd*. Or the implied warranty that a house should be reasonably fit for human habitation: see *Hancock v BW Brazier*. And dozens of other implied terms. If you should read the discussions in the cases, you will find that the judges are not looking for the intention of both parties; nor are they considering what the parties would answer to an officious bystander. They are only seeking to do what is 'in all the circumstances reasonable'. That is how Lord Reid put it in *Young & Marten Ltd v McManus Childs Ltd*; and Lord Upjohn said quite clearly that the implied warranty is 'imposed by law'.

Apply this to the employment of a professional man. The law does not usually imply a warranty that he will achieve the desired result, but only a term that he will use reasonable care and skill. The surgeon does not warrant that he will cure the patient. Nor does the solicitor warrant that he will win the case. But, when a dentist agrees to make a set of false teeth for a patient, there is an implied warranty that they will fit his gums: see *Samuels v Davis*.

What then is the position when an architect or an engineer is employed to design a house or a bridge? Is he under an implied warranty that, if the work is carried out to his design, it will be reasonably fit for the purpose? Or is he only under a duty to use reasonable care and skill? This question may require to be answered some day as matter of law . . ."

NOTE

It might be useful to recall how the distinction between result and best efforts is to be found expressed in an English statute.

Supply of Goods and Services Act 1982 (c.29)

"9. Implied terms about quality or fitness
(2) Where . . . the bailor bails goods in the course of a business, there is (. . .) an implied condition that the goods supplied under the contract are of satisfactory quality.

13. Implied term about care and skill
In a contract for the supply of a service where the supplier is acting in the course of a business, there is an implied term that the supplier will carry out the service with reasonable care and skill."

NOTES AND QUESTIONS

1. One reason for the difference between goods and services is to be found in the wording and institutional structure of the statutory provisions. Section 9 of the Supply of Goods and Services Act 1982, like s.14 of the Sale of Goods Act 1979, is framed around the *res* (goods) rather than the *persona* (seller). Thus liability becomes dependent upon the state and condition of the goods. In s.13 of the 1982 Act, however, the rule is framed around the *persona* (supplier), and this automatically brings into play the behaviour of the supplier. The obligation, in other words, attaches to the person rather than to the thing. Imagine that Parliament had wanted to introduce strict liability for services: can you redraft s.13 so as to reflect Parliament's wishes?

2. English contract law is often said to be an obligation of strict liability rather than one that is fault-based; the civilian systems, in contrast, are said to be fault-based. There is truth in this at the level of contractual theory, but in practice it often comes down to interpretation. What did the parties actually promise (common law) or agree (civil law)? And policy has its role as well. Who ought to bear the risk of this damage or loss: the claimant or the defendant? Does, or should, insurance have a role here?

Barclays Bank Plc v Fairclough Building Ltd [1995] Q.B. 214, CA

This was an action in damages for breach of contract, brought by the owner of premises against a firm of contractors who had undertaken to carry out specialist maintenance work with respect to asbestos roofs on the premises. The contract specified that the work should be done by specialist roofing contractors. The defendant contractors, and their sub-contractors, failed to do the work properly, with the result that the plaintiffs incurred very expensive remedial work. The defendants claimed that the damage was caused wholly or in part by the plaintiffs' own negligence. The trial judge held that the defendants were liable but that the damages should be reduced under the Law Reform (Contributory Negligence) Act 1945. On appeal it was argued that the 1945 Act would not apply if the facts disclosed only a liability in contract. The question thus arose as to the nature of the obligation and the level of duty. Was it a duty to achieve a specific result (purely contractual), or was it a duty of care and skill (contractual and tortious)? The Court of Appeal held (Beldam, Simon Brown and Nourse L.JJ.) that the duty was purely contractual and thus that the 1945 Act was not applicable.

Beldam L.J.: ". . . The requirement that the workmanship should be the best of its kind required a standard to be achieved. It would not be satisfied by workmanship of average competence or skill or by the exercise of reasonable care to try to attain the standard. Taken in conjunction with the requirement that roofing work should only be executed by a specialist firm of roofing contractors or by craftsmen of the defendant's properly experienced in such work, it is clear that the specification required the standard to be achieved, not merely that reasonable care should be taken in carrying out the work. It was argued by Mr Butcher for the defendant that it was inapposite to apply the term 'workmanship' to an operation of the kind undertaken to clean the asbestos roofs. In my view 'workmanship' in the context of the specification was intended to cover the whole of the works which the defendant had undertaken to perform. I consider therefore there was a clear breach of the defendant's obligation to carry out the work in accordance with the specification and to achieve the standard specified. The defendant's failure was not simply a failure to exercise reasonable care and skill, although out of caution an implied term to that effect had been pleaded on the plaintiff's behalf. The defendant's failure to comply with the requirements of the Asbestos Regulations of 1987 in breach of condition 5.1 was likewise a breach of a strict contractual term. . . .

. . . In the present case . . . the judge did not consider the character of the obligations broken by the defendant and dealt with the case as if the only breach of duty was breach of a duty to take reasonable care coextensive with the breach of such a duty in tort. For the reasons I have given, I think he was wrong to do so. . . ."

Simon Brown L.J.: ". . . But when . . . the contractual liability . . . is a strict liability arising independently of any negligence on the defendant's part, then there seem to me compelling reasons why the contract, even assuming it is silent as to apportionment, should be construed as excluding the operation of the Act of 1945. The very imposition of a strict liability on the defendant is to my mind inconsistent with an apportionment of the loss. And not least because of the absurdities that the contrary approach carries in its wake. Assume a defendant, clearly liable under a strict contractual duty. Is his position to be improved by demonstrating that besides breaching that duty he was in addition negligent? Take this very case. Is this contract really to be construed so that the defendant is advantaged by an assertion of its own liability in nuisance or trespass as well as in contract? Are we to have trials at which the defendant calls an expert to implicate him in tortious liability, whilst the plaintiff's expert seeks paradoxically to exonerate him? The answer to all these questions is surely 'No.' Whatever arguments exist for apportionment in other categories of case—and these are persuasively deployed in the 1993 Law Commission Report (Law Com No 219)—to my mind there are none in the present type of case and I for my part would construe the contract accordingly."

Nourse L.J.: ". . . It ought to be a cause of general concern that the law should have got into such a state that a contractor who was in breach of two of the main obligations expressly undertaken by him in a standard form building contract was able to persuade the judge in the court below that the building owner's damages should be reduced by 40 per cent because of its own negligence in not preventing the contractor from committing the breaches. In circumstances such as these release, waiver, forbearance or the like are the only defences available to a party to a contract who wishes to assert that the other party's right to recover damages for its breach has been lost or diminished. It ought to have been perfectly obvious that the Law Reform (Contributory Negligence) Act 1945 was never intended to obtrude the defence of contributory negligence into an area of the law where it has no business to be. . . ."

QUESTION

Given that the stipulated standard was not achieved, could the plaintiff, in addition to any other remedy, have refused to pay for the work done by the specialist roofing contractors?

8 Effects of a contract

Once a contract has been validly formed, and assuming that it is free of any vitiating factor, the next general question that arises is this: What are the actual effects of this contract? This question can be broken down into a number of sub-questions. For example, what does a contractual obligation mean to each of the parties in respect of what they can and cannot do? What if the contract purports to confer rights or duties upon a third party who may not be a party to the contract? What is the status and effect of clauses that limit or exclude the obligational effects of a contract? What if circumstances beyond the control of the parties change and this causes hardship for one of the parties? Can the effects of a contract reach beyond the actual contractual obligation itself? Some of the issues that these questions raise have, of course, been dealt with in previous chapters, while others belong more properly in chapters that follow. But examining a contract from the position of its effects on parties and (sometimes) non-parties can be useful when it comes to looking at how contracts function within a world of individuals and their interests, these interests themselves being dependent not just on the behaviour and acts of co-contractors, but equally on the vagaries of external reality.

8.1 Binding nature of a contract

Perhaps the most obvious effect of a contract is its binding nature.

Unidroit Principles for International Commercial Contracts

"Article 1.3 Binding Character of Contract
A contract validly entered into is binding upon the parties. It can only be modified or terminated in accordance with its terms or by agreement or as otherwise provided in these Principles."

NOTE

This may seem an evident provision, but it can have logical consequences that are capable on occasions of causing disquiet.

White & Carter (Councils) Ltd v McGregor **[1962] A.C. 413, HL (Sc)**

This was an action in debt brought against a contractor who had attempted to cancel a validly made contract. The defender did not deny he was in breach but argued that the pursuers should not be allowed to succeed in debt, only in damages. A bare majority of the House of Lords (Lords Reid, Tucker and Hodson; Lords Morton and Keith dissenting) allowed the pursuers to succeed.

Lord Reid: "My Lords, the pursuers supply to local authorities litter bins which are placed in the streets. They are allowed to attach to these receptacles plates carrying advertisements, and they make their profit from payments made to them by the advertisers. The defender carried on a garage in Clydebank and in 1954 he made an agreement with the pursuers under which they displayed advertisements of his business on a number of these bins. In June 1957 his sales manager made a further contract with the pursuers for the display of these advertisements for a further period of three years. The sales manager had been given no specific authority to make this contract and when the defender heard of it later on the same day he at once wrote to the pursuers to cancel the contract. The pursuers refused to accept this cancellation. They prepared the necessary plates for attachment to the bins and exhibited them on the bins from 2nd November 1957 onwards.

The defender refused to pay any sums due under the contract and the pursuers raised the present action in the Sheriff Court craving payment of £196 4s. the full sum due under the contract for the period of three years. After sundry procedure the Sheriff-Substitute on 15th March 1960 dismissed the action . . .

The case for the defender (now the respondent) is that, as he repudiated the contract before anything had been done under it, the appellants were not entitled to go on and carry out the contract and sue for the contract price: he maintains that in the circumstances the appellants' only remedy was damages, and that, as they do not sue for damages, this action was rightly dismissed . . .

The general rule cannot be in doubt. It was settled in Scotland at least as early as 1848 and it has been authoritatively stated time and again in both Scotland and England. If one party to a contract repudiates it in the sense of making it clear to the other party that he refuses or will refuse to carry out his part of the contract; the other party, the innocent party, has an option. He may accept that repudiation and sue for damages for breach of contract, whether or not the time for performance has come; or he may if he chooses disregard or refuse to accept it and then the contract remains in full effect . . .

I need not refer to the numerous authorities. They are not disputed by the respondent but he points out that in all of them the party who refused to accept the repudiation had no active duties under the contract. The innocent party's option is generally said to be to wait until the date of performance and then to claim damages estimated as at that date. There is no case in which it is said that he may, in face of the repudiation, go on and incur useless expense in performing the contract and then claim the contract price. The option, it is argued, is merely as to the date as at which damages are to be assessed . . .

Of course, if it had been necessary for the defender to do or accept anything before the contract could be completed by the pursuers, the pursuers could not and the court would not have compelled the defender to act, the contract would not have been completed and the pursuers' only remedy would have been damages . . .

It might be said that, because in most cases the circumstances are such that an innocent party is unable to complete the contract and earn the contract price without the assent or co-operation of the other party, therefore in cases where he can do so he should not be allowed to do so. I can see no justification for that. . . ."

Lord Keith of Avonholm (dissenting): ". . . If I understand aright, counsel for the appellants would read time of performance as time of performance by the defender after the appellants had discharged their part of performance under the contract. Their claim then becomes a claim, not for damages for breach of contract, but for a debt due by the defender under the contract. In other words, there would be an anticipatory repudiation by the defender which the appellants were not bound to accept as a breach of contract and which did not cease to be anticipatory until the moment when the defender was due to make payment under the contract. This, I think, goes beyond anything that has been decided in the cases where anticipatory repudiation has been considered. It makes an arbitrary distinction and one differing in its consequences according as performance is first called for under the contract from the repudiating party, or from the other party. In the former case there is a plain breach of contract making the repudiating party liable in damages, unless where a claim for specific implement is available. In the latter case, according to the submission made, he is liable contractually for a debt at least where the consideration for performance by the other party is expressed in money. The law of Scotland has always stressed the mutuality of contracts and it should follow, in my opinion, that the consequences of breach of contract by either party should correspond. I would state the position in the case of an anticipatory repudiation not accepted by the other party as a breach of contract thus: If the contract is to take operative effect in the first place by performance of the repudiating party and he maintains his repudiation by refusing, or failing to give performance, the other party has a cause of action for either damages or specific implement. If performance is first to be given by the other party and the time for his performance has arrived he must tender performance, in the sense of showing that he is now ready and able to give performance, and if this tender is still rejected by the repudiating party his only cause of action again arises to him as at that date. . . .

I would refer first to contracts for the sale of goods which were touched on in the course of the debate, for the reason that one of the remedies provided to the seller by the Sale of Goods Act 1893, is an action for the price. This, however, applies only in two cases. One is where the property in the goods has passed to the buyer. But property cannot pass without the intention of the buyer as well as that of the seller and, except in some such cases as fraud or lack of consensus in idem or breach of contract by the seller, no question of repudiation can arise. The contract is completed and finished apart from delivery and nothing remains but payment of the price. The only other case is where parties have contracted for payment on a day certain, irrespective of delivery or the passing of property. This is a clear case of a contractual debt unconditioned by any question of performance by the other party. A much closer parallel with the present case is a contract to sell future, or unascertained goods. In this case there can be no appropriation of, and therefore passing of, property in the goods without the assent of both buyer and seller. If therefore the buyer repudiates the contract before appropriation, or refuses his assent to appropriation, there can be no passing of property. The seller is then confined to an action of damages for breach of contract. This, of course, is a rule of statute. But the Act is largely declaratory of English law, though not of Scots law. So the rule can only be treated as an analogy, but it is an analogy which seems to me to make a hole in the principle contended for by the appellants . . .

I find the argument advanced for the appellants a somewhat startling one. If it is right it would seem that a man who has contracted to go to Hong Kong at his own expense and make a report, in return for remuneration of £10,000, and who, before the date fixed for the start of the journey and perhaps before he has incurred any expense, is informed by the other contracting party that he has cancelled or repudiates the contract, is entitled to set off for Hong Kong and produce his report in order to claim in debt the stipulated sum. Such a result is not, in my opinion, in accordance with principle or authority, and cuts across the rule that where one party is in breach of contract the other must take steps to minimise the loss sustained by the breach . . ."

QUESTIONS

1. Why might it be more advantageous to sue in debt rather than damages? (*Cf.* **11.2.**)

2. Is this an example of specific performance of a contract?

NOTE

Anticipatory breach is discussed in **10.4.4**

8.2 Privity of contract

Sometimes, however, a party who has made a contractual promise is seemingly able to escape from the legally binding nature of the promise: see *Beswick v Beswick* (1968) (above, at p.23). The reason for the contract in *Beswick* lacking effect, at common law, was that the promise had been made to a third party who was not a party to the contract.

8.2.1 Introduction to the privity rule

There is logic to this unenforceability, in as much as a contract creates an obligation *in personam* between the two parties who have made the contract. In another words, it is a personal obligation that is "private" as between the two contractors, resulting in a situation where no third party ought in principle to be affected by such a contract. In civil law thinking this is described as the "relative effect" of a contract; in common law thinking it is described as the rule of privity of contract. The rule can be seen either as a principle attaching to the personal nature of contract itself, or as an aspect of consideration; only those who have provided consideration for the promise should be subject to its legal effects (UC&TO, pp.50–52). The background to the rule is given in the next extract.

Darlington Borough Council v Wiltshier Northern Ltd [1995] 1 W.L.R. 68, CA

(For facts and further extracts, see p.395.)

Steyn L.J.: ". . . The genesis of the privity rule is suspect. It is attributed to *Tweedle v Atkinson* (1861) B & S 393. It is more realistic to say that the rule originated in the misunderstanding of *Tweddle v Atkinson*: see Atiyah, *The Rise and Fall of Freedom of Contract* (1979), p 414 and Simpson, *A History of the Law of Contract: the Rise of the Action of Assumpsit* (1975), p 475. While the privity rule was barely tolerable in Victorian England, it has been recognised for half a century that it has no place in our more complex commercial world. Indeed, as early as 1915, in *Dunlop Pneumatic Tyre Co Ltd v Selfridge & Co Ltd* [1915] AC 847, 855, when the House of Lords restated the privity rule, Lord Dunedin observed in a dissenting speech that the rule made

'it possible for a person to snap his fingers at a bargain deliberately made, a bargain not in itself unfair, and which the person seeking to enforce it has a legitimate interest to enforce.'

Among the majority, Viscount Haldane LC asserted as a self-evident truth, at p 853, that 'only a person who is a party to a contract can sue on it.' Today the doctrinal objection to the recognition of a stipulatio alteri continues to hold sway. While the rigidity of the doctrine of consideration has been greatly reduced in modern times, the doctrine of privity of contract persists in all its artificial technicality.

In 1937 the Law Revision Committee in its Sixth Report (Cmd 5449, para 41–48) proposed the recognition of a right of a third party to enforce the contract

---

which by its express terms purports to confer a benefit directly on him. In 1967, in *Beswick v Beswick* [1968] AC 58, 72, Lord Reid observed that if there was a long period of delay in passing legislation on the point the House of Lords might have to deal with the matter. Twelve years later Lord Scarman, who as a former chairman of the Law Commission usually favoured legislative rather than judicial reform where radical change was involved, reminded the House that it might be necessary to review all the cases which 'stand guard over this unjust rule:' *Woodar Investment Development Ltd v Wimpey Construction UK Ltd* [1980] 1 WLR 277, 300G. See also Lord Keith of Kinkel, at pp 297H--298A. In 1981 Dillon J described the rule as 'a blot on our law and most unjust:' *Forster v. Silvermere Golf and Equestrian Centre* (1981) 125 SJ 397. In 1983 Lord Diplock described the rule as 'an anachronistic shortcoming that has for many years been regarded as a reproach to English private law:' Swain v The Law Society [1983] 1 AC 598, 611D.

But as important as judicial condemnations of the privity rule is the fact that distinguished academic lawyers have found no redeeming virtues in it: see, for example, Markesinis (1987) 103 LQR 354; Reynolds (1989) 105 LQR 1; Beatson (1992) 44 CLP 1 and Adams and Brownsword (1993) 56 MLR 722. And we do well to remember that the civil law legal systems of other members of the European Union recognise such contracts. That our legal system lacks such flexibility is a disadvantage in the single market. Indeed it is a historical curiosity that the legal system of a mercantile country such as England, which in other areas of the law of contract (such as, for example, the objective theory of the interpretation of contracts) takes great account of the interests of third parties, has not been able to rid itself of this unjust rule deriving from a technical conception of a contract as a purely bilateral vinculum juris.

In 1991 the Law Commission revisited this corner of the law. In cautious language appropriate to a consultation paper the Law Commission has expressed the provisional recommendation that 'there should be a (statutory) reform of the law to allow third parties to enforce contractual provisions made in their favour:' Privity of Contract: Conflicts for the Benefit of Third Parties, Consultation Paper No 121, p 132. The principal value of the consultation paper lies in its clear analysis of the practical need for the recognition of a contract for the benefit of third parties, and the explanation of the unedifying spectacle of judges trying to invent exceptions to the rule to prevent demonstrable unfairness. No doubt there will be a report by the Law Commission in the not too distant future recommending the abolition of the privity of contract rule by statute. What will then happen in regard to the proposal for legislation? The answer is really quite simple: probably nothing will happen.

But on this occasion I can understand the inaction of Parliament. There is a respectable argument that it is the type of reform which is best achieved by the courts working out sensible solutions on a case by case basis, e.g., in regard to the exact point of time when the third party is vested with enforceable contractual rights: see Consultation Paper, No 121, para 5.8. But that requires the door to be opened by the House of Lords reviewing the major cases which are thought to have entrenched the rule of privity of contract. Unfortunately, there will be few opportunities for the House of Lords to do so. After all, by and large, courts of law in our system are the hostages of the arguments deployed by counsel. And Mr Furst for the council, the third party, made it clear to us that he will not directly challenge the privity rule if this matter should go to the House of Lords. He said that he is content to try to bring his case within exceptions to the privity rule or what Lord Diplock in *Swain v The Law Society* [1983] 1 AC 598, 611D, described as 'juristic subterfuges . . . to mitigate the effect of the lacuna resulting from the non-recognition of a jus quaesitum tertio . . . ' . . .''

NOTE

Three points might be noted at once in this judgment extract: (i) the *stipulatio alteri* exception in the civil law; (ii) the Law Commission's recommendations; and (iii) the existence of exceptions to the privity rule.

8.2.2 **Stipulation in favour of a third party**

As Steyn L.J. observed in *Darlington BC v Wiltshier* (1995) (**8.2.1** above), the relative effect of contract in the civilian tradition had been largely mitigated by the rule that one could stipulate in favour of a third party. This civilian principle is to be found in the PECL.

Principles of European Contract Law

"Article 6:110 Stipulation in favour of a third party
(1) A third party may require performance of a contractual obligation when its right to do so has been expressly agreed upon between the promisor and the promisee, or when such agreement is to be inferred from the purpose of the contract or the circumstances of the case. The third party need not be identified at the time the agreement is concluded.

(2) If the third party renounces the right to performance the right is treated as never having accrued to it.

(3) The promisee may by notice to the promisor deprive the third party of the right to performance unless:

  (a) the third party has received notice from the promisee that the right has been made irrevocable, or
  (b) the promisor or the promisee has received notice from the third party that the latter accepts the right."

QUESTION

If this rule had been in force in England at the time of *Beswick*, would the wife have been able to sue in debt, and in her own capacity, for the annuity?

8.2.3 Law Commission and *stipulatio alteri*

Soon after Steyn L.J.'s observations in *Darlington BC v Wiltshier* (1995), the Law Commission Report on reform of the privity rule was published (Law Com. No. 242, Cm 3329, 1996). This resulted in legislative intervention.

Contracts (Rights of Third Parties) Act 1999 (c.31)

"1. Right of third party to enforce contractual term
(1) Subject to the provisions of this Act, a person who is not a party to a contract (a 'third party') may in his own right enforce a term of the contract if—

  (a) the contract expressly provides that he may, or
  (b) subject to subsection (2), the term purports to confer a benefit on him.

(2) Subsection (1)(b) does not apply if on a proper construction of the contract it appears that the parties did not intend the term to be enforceable by the third party.

(3) The third party must be expressly identified in the contract by name, as a member of a class or as answering a particular description but need not be in existence when the contract is entered into.

(4) This section does not confer a right on a third party to enforce a term of a contract otherwise than subject to and in accordance with any other relevant terms of the contract.

(5) For the purpose of exercising his right to enforce a term of the contract, there shall be available to the third party any remedy that would have been available to him in an action for breach of contract if he had been a party to the contract (and the rules relating to damages, injunctions, specific performance and other relief shall apply accordingly).

(6) Where a term of a contract excludes or limits liability in relation to any matter references in this Act to the third party enforcing the term shall be construed as references to his availing himself of the exclusion or limitation.

(7) In this Act, in relation to a term of a contract which is enforceable by a third party—

  'the promisor' means the party to the contract against whom the term is enforceable by the third party, and 'the promisee' means the party to the contract by whom the term is enforceable against the promisor.

3. Defences etc available to promisor

(1) Subsections (2) to (5) apply where, in reliance on section 1, proceedings for the enforcement of a term of a contract are brought by a third party.

(2) The promisor shall have available to him by way of defence or set-off any matter that—

(a) arises from or in connection with the contract and is relevant to the term, and
(b) would have been available to him by way of defence or set-off if the proceedings had been brought by the promisee.

(3) The promisor shall also have available to him by way of defence or set-off any matter if—

(a) an express term of the contract provides for it to be available to him in proceedings brought by the third party, and
(b) it would have been available to him by way of defence or set-off if the proceedings had been brought by the promisee.

(4) The promisor shall also have available to him—

(a) by way of defence or set-off any matter, and
(b) by way of counterclaim any matter not arising from the contract,

that would have been available to him by way of defence or set-off or, as the case may be, by way of counterclaim against the third party if the third party had been a party to the contract.

(5) Subsections (2) and (4) are subject to any express term of the contract as to the matters that are not to be available to the promisor by way of defence, set-off or counterclaim.

(6) Where in any proceedings brought against him a third party seeks in reliance on section 1 to enforce a term of a contract (including, in particular, a term purporting to exclude or limit liability), he may not do so if he could not have done so (whether by reason of any particular circumstances relating to him or otherwise) had he been a party to the contract.

4. Enforcement of contract by promisee

Section 1 does not affect any right of the promisee to enforce any term of the contract.

6. Exceptions

(1) Section 1 confers no rights on a third party in the case of a contract on a bill of exchange, promissory note or other negotiable instrument.

(2) Section 1 confers no rights on a third party in the case of any contract binding on a company and its members under section 14 of the Companies Act 1985.

(3) Section 1 confers no right on a third party to enforce—

(a) any term of a contract of employment against an employee,
(b) any term of a worker's contract against a worker (including a home worker), or
(c) any term of a relevant contract against an agency worker.

. . .

(5) Section 1 confers no rights on a third party in the case of—

(a) a contract for the carriage of goods by sea, or
(b) a contract for the carriage of goods by rail or road, or for the carriage of cargo by air, which is subject to the rules of the appropriate international transport convention,

except that a third party may in reliance on that section avail himself of an exclusion or limitation of liability in such a contract.

QUESTIONS

1. Why does this 1999 Act need several pages of text (only extracts are given above) when the PECL need only one article a few lines long?

2. Has the Law Commission "simplified" the law?

3. Consider the facts of the famous tort case *Donoghue v Stevenson* (1932) (C&MT, p.112). If the same facts arose again today, would Mrs Donoghue be able to sue the café for breach of contract in failing to supply goods of satisfactory quality and reasonably fit for their purpose?

4. Does s.1 of the 1999 Act extend s.13 of the Supply of Goods and Services Act 1982 to non-contracting parties?

5. Consider the facts of the tort case *Spartan Steel & Alloys v Martin & Co* (1973) (C&MT, p.137). If the same facts arose today, could the claimants now succeed, using the 1999 Act, in getting all the damages they originally claimed?

6. Why the exception in s.6(5)(b)?

NOTE

David Ibbetson observes that the "formulation of liability in promissory terms provided an opportunity for the law to distance itself from the medieval rules of privity of contract, for it would have been far easier to describe a third-party beneficiary as the recipient of the promise than as party to the contract" (*A Historical Introduction to the Law of Obligations* (OUP, 1999), p.140). The 1999 Act, however miserably drafted in terms of elegant English and control freakishness, is surely trying to make up for lost time and lost opportunities.

8.2.4 Exceptions to the privity rule

Even before the Contracts (Rights of Third Parties) Act 1999, the courts had recognised a number of exceptions to the privity rule.

Darlington Borough Council v Wiltshier Northern Ltd **[1995] 1 W.L.R. 68, CA**

This was an action in damages for breach of contract brought by a local authority (Darlington) against a construction company (Wiltshier) in respect of defects in a building constructed for the authority. The local authority had not contracted directly with the construction company but were assignees of all rights and causes of action from the actual contractor (Morgan Grenfell). The judge held that, as assignees, the local authority was entitled only to nominal damages; the local authority successfully appealed to the Court of Appeal (Dillon, Steyn and Waite L.JJ.) against this judgment.

> **Steyn L.J.:** ". . . The case for recognising a contract for the benefit of a third party is simple and straightforward. The autonomy of the will of the parties should be respected. The law of contract should give effect to the reasonable expectations of contracting parties. Principle certainly requires that a burden should not be imposed on a third party without his consent. But there is no doctrinal, logical or policy reason why the law should deny effectiveness to a contract for the benefit of a third party where that is the expressed intention of the parties. Moreover, often the parties, and particularly third parties, organise their affairs on the faith of the contract. They rely on the contract. It is therefore unjust to deny effectiveness to such a contract. I will not struggle further with the point since nobody seriously asserts the contrary; but see a valuable article by Jack Beatson, a law commissioner, now Rouseball Professor of English Law at Cambridge, 'Reforming the Law of Contracts for the Benefit of Third Parties: a Second Bite at the Cherry' (1992) 45 CLP 1. . . .
>
> There seems no logical or policy reason why recovery of substantial damages for such a breach of contract should be denied. . . .
>
> That brings me to the speech of Lord Browne-Wilkinson in the *Linden Gardens* case [1994] AC 85. In his speech Lord Browne-Wilkinson rested his decision on the exception to the rule that a plaintiff can only recover damages for his own loss which was enunciated in *The Albazero* [1977] AC 774 in the context of carriage of goods by sea, bills of lading and bailment. . . . Relying on the exception recognised in the *Linden Gardens* case, as well as on the need to avoid a demonstrable unfairness which no rational legal system should tolerate, I would rule that the present case is within the rationale of Lord Browne-Wilkinson's

speech. I do not say that the relevant passages in his speech precisely fit the material facts of the present case. But it involves only a very conservative and limited extension to apply it by analogy to the present case. For these reasons I would hold that the present case is covered by an exception to the general rule that a plaintiff can only recover damages for his own loss. . . ."

NOTES

1. Three-party situations have presented problems in the law of contract since Roman times. Both in civil law and in the common law, the idea that one person could use contract to the benefit or the burden of a third party has been only reluctantly overcome and then, usually, by recourse either to fiction or to tort. The reason in the civil law for this reluctance is to be found in the idea of an *in personam* obligation itself: an obligation is a *vinculum juris* (legal chain) which binds only two named parties. If contract could confer rights or duties on third parties then it would become a matter of *iura in rem*. In the common law, which did not inherit the legacy of Roman legal science, the problem of the third party is founded in the notion of consideration which must move from the promisee. *Beswick v Beswick* (1968) (see p.23) indicates that the doctrine remains alive at common law, although legislation has of course intervened. One might note that a number of classic three-party situations—trusts, cheques and life insurance for example—are also well-established exceptions to the privity rule thanks either to precedent or to statute.

2. One way of avoiding the privity rule was to emphasise rules attaching to remedies rather than to contractual rights. Two cases are particularly noteworthy. The first is *Beswick v Beswick* (1968) (see p.23), where the equitable remedy of specific performance came to the aid of the third party (*cf.* **12.1**). The second is set out below.

Jackson v Horizon Holidays Ltd [1975] 1 W.L.R. 1468, CA

This was an action for damages brought by a father against a tour operator in respect of a holiday booked by the father for himself and his family. The father had booked the holiday in reliance upon statements made over the telephone and in the tour operator's brochure. Many of the promised facilities were not available, and the hotel and food were of poor quality. The father sought compensation for mental distress in respect of himself, his wife and his children, and the trial judge, who thought that they had had half a holiday, awarded half the total price of the holiday, plus another £500 for mental distress. An appeal by the defendants as to the amount awarded was dismissed by the Court of Appeal (Lord Denning M.R. and Orr and James L.JJ.).

Lord Denning M.R.: ". . . The judge said that he could only consider the mental distress to Mr Jackson himself, and that he could not consider the distress to his wife and children. He said:

396

'The damages are the plaintiff's . . . I can consider the effect upon his mind of the wife's discomfort, vexation, and the like, although I cannot award a sum which represents her own vexation.'

Mr Davies, for Mr Jackson, disputes that proposition. He submits that damages can be given not only for the leader of the party—in this case, Mr Jackson's own distress, discomfort and vexation—but also for that of the rest of the party.

We have had an interesting discussion as to the legal position when one person makes a contract for the benefit of a party. In this case it was a husband making a contract for the benefit of himself, his wife and children. Other cases readily come to mind. A host makes a contract with a restaurant for a dinner for himself and his friends. The vicar makes a contract for a coach trip for the choir. In all these cases there is only one person who makes the contract. It is the husband, the host or the vicar, as the case may be. Sometimes he pays the whole price himself. Occasionally he may get a contribution from the others. But in any case it is he who makes the contract. It would be a fiction to say that the contract was made by all the family, or all the guests, or all the choir and that he was only an agent for them. Take this very case. it would be absurd to say that the twins of three years old were parties to the contract or that the father was making the contract on their behalf as if they were principals. It would equally be a mistake to say that in any of these instances there was a trust. The transaction bears no resemblance to a trust. There was no trust fund and no trust property. No, the real truth is that in each instance, the father, the host or the vicar, was making a contract himself for the benefit of the whole party. In short, a contract by one for the benefit of third persons.

What is the position when such a contract is broken? At present the law says that the only one who can sue is the one who made the contract. None of the rest of the party can sue, even though the contract was made for their benefit. But when that one does sue, what damages can he recover? Is he limited to his own loss? Or can he recover for the others? Suppose the holiday firm puts the family into a hotel which is only half built and the visitors have to sleep on the floor? Or suppose the restaurant is fully booked and the guests have to go away, hungry and angry, having spent so much on fares to get there? Or suppose the coach leaves the choir stranded halfway and they have to hire cars to get home? None of them individually can sue. Only the father, the host or the vicar can sue. He can, of course, recover his own damages. But can he not recover for the others? I think he can. The case comes within the principle stated by Lush LJ in *Lloyd's v Harper*:

'I consider it to be an established rule of law that where a contract is made with A. for the benefit of B., A. can sue on the contract for the benefit of B., and recover all that B. could have recovered if the contract had been made with B. himself.'

It has been suggested that Lush LJ was thinking of a contract in which A was trustee for B. But I do not think so. He was a common lawyer speaking of

397

common law. His words were quoted with considerable approval by Lord Pearce in *Beswick v Beswick*. I have myself often quoted them. I think they should be accepted as correct, at any rate so long as the law forbids the third persons themselves from suing for damages. It is the only way in which a just result can be achieved. Take the instance I have put. The guests ought to recover from the restaurant their wasted fares. The choir ought to recover the cost of hiring the taxis home. Then is no one to recover from them except the one who made the contract for their benefit? He should be able to recover the expense to which he has been put, and pay it over to them. Once recovered, it will be money had and received to their use. (They might even, if desired, be joined as plaintiffs.) If he can recover for the expense, he should also be able to recover for the discomfort, vexation and upset which the whole party have suffered by reason of the breach of contract, recompensing them accordingly out of what he recovers.

Applying the principles to this case, I think that the figure of £1,100 was about right. It would, I think, have been excessive if it had been awarded only for the damage suffered by Mr Jackson himself. But when extended to his wife and children, I do not think it is excessive. People look forward to a holiday. They expect the promises to be fulfilled. When it fails, they are greatly disappointed and upset. It is difficult to assess in terms of money; but it is the task of the judges to do the best they can. I see no reason to interfere with the total award of £1,100. I would therefore dismiss the appeal."

QUESTIONS

1. If the father had refused to hand over to his wife the damages he had obtained on her behalf, could the wife bring an action in debt against him to recover them?

2. Could the wife and children have sued Horizon Holidays for damages in their own right, in tort or (now) under the 1999 Act?

3. Would it make sense to allow a family to contract, to own property and to sue as a legal subject (*persona*) in itself? Does the family exist as a social reality? Does it have its own interests that the law should recognise?

NOTE

Another means of avoiding the privity rule was through the establishment of a collateral contract.

Lockett v A & M Charles Ltd [1938] 4 All E.R. 170, KB

This was an action for damages by Mr and Mrs Lockett against a restaurant, in respect of food poisoning from the whitebait *hors d'oeuvre*. Mr Lockett had paid the bill. The action was successful.

Tucker J.: ". . . With regard to the female plaintiff's position in respect of breach of warranty, every proprietor of a restaurant is under a duty to take reasonable care to see that the food which he supplies to his guests is fit for human consumption. If he does not take such reasonable steps, and if he is negligent, a person who buys the food which he supplies can recover damages from him based on his negligence. As, however, there is no allegation of such negligence in this case, it must be assumed that the proprietor of the hotel and his servants could not be at fault in any way, and either plaintiff can recover only if he or she establishes that there was a contract between him or her and the proprietor of the hotel . . .

Counsel for the plaintiffs is, in my opinion, right when he submits that, when persons go into a restaurant and order food, they are making a contract of sale in exactly the same way as they are making a contract of sale when they go into a shop and order any other goods. I think that the inference is that the person who orders the food in a hotel or restaurant prima facie makes himself or herself liable to pay for it, and when two people—whether or not they happen to be husband and wife—go into a hotel and each orders and is supplied with food, then, as between those persons and the proprietor of the hotel, each of them is making himself liable for the food which he orders, whatever may be the arrangement between the two persons who are eating at the hotel. On the facts in this case, it is, in my opinion, right to hold that there was a contract implied by the conduct of the parties between the plaintiff, Mrs Lockett, and the defendants when she ordered and was supplied with the whitebait at the Hotel de Paris . . .

If that is so, it follows beyond all doubt that there is an implied warranty that the food supplied is reasonably fit for human consumption. I hold that the whitebait delivered in this case were not reasonably fit for human consumption, and that there was a breach of warranty. Accordingly I give judgment for the male plaintiff for the agreed sum of £98 8s, and for Mrs Lockett for £100."

NOTE

There are a number of other well-established exceptions to the privity rule, of which the most important are trusts, cheques and life assurance. Of particular importance, however, is the tort of negligence, the foundation of which is a precedent that itself can be seen as creating an exception to the privity rule: *Donoghue v Stevenson* (1932) (C&MT, p.112). A contracts with B to perform a service; but A performs the service negligently, causing damage not to B, but to C. A can be said to be in breach of an implied term to perform the contract with skill and care (Supply of Goods and Services Act 1982, s.13), yet this implied term will not extend to C at common law because C is not a party to the contract (but *cf.* the Contracts (Rights of Third Parties) Act 1999). However, the importance of *Donoghue v Stevenson* is that behaviour that amounts to a breach of the implied term of skill and care can now equally amount to the tort of negligence (*Hedley Byrne v Heller* (1964), above at p.234). The only obstacle facing C is that he must show that A owed him a duty of care, which may be difficult in situations where the damage is pure economic loss (*Murphy v Brentwood DC* (1990)) or there is no undertaking and reliance structure (*cf. Lennon* (2004), above p.20). Nevertheless, there are cases where C is owed a duty even where the damage is purely financial (*Smith v Eric Bush* (1990)) and the undertaking/reliance structure weak (*White v Jones* (1995)) (C&MT, p.260).

QUESTIONS

1. Read *Donoghue v Stevenson* (1932) in the law report (or in C&MT, p.112). In what ways does *Lockett* differ from *Donoghue*? Would not Mrs Donoghue have been liable to pay for her bottle of ginger-beer if the friend had not paid?

2. Can the existence of a contract between A and B ever prevent C from suing A for damage caused to C by A's negligence? (*Cf. Marc Rich & Co v Bishop Rock Ltd* (1996); C&MT, p.291.)

3. In a contract of bailment between A and B, A promises B that he will sue neither B nor C for damage or loss caused to the goods bailed by A to B. C carelessly damages the goods. Can A sue C in tort in respect of the damage? What if A had promised B that he (A) would fully insure the goods against any damage howsoever caused, but forgot to do so; if the goods are carelessly damaged by C, could C, if sued by A in tort, counter-claim for breach of the insurance promise?

Morris v CW Martin & Sons Ltd [1966] 1 Q.B. 716, CA

When Beder (see p.113) sent the mink stole to the defendants, he did so under a contract to which the plaintiff (the owner and bailor of the stole) was not a party. This contract contained exclusion clauses, and the question arose as to whether these clauses would protect the defendants against a claim for damages by the owner of the stole. The Court of Appeal (Lord Denning M.R., Diplock and Salmon L.JJ.) held that the clauses would not protect the defendants.

Lord Denning M.R.: ". . . Now comes the question: Can the defendants rely, as against the plaintiff, on the exempting conditions although there was no contract directly between them and her? There is much to be said on each side. On the one hand, it is hard on the plaintiff if her just claim is defeated by exempting conditions of which she knew nothing and to which she was not a party. On the other hand, it is hard on the defendants if they are held liable to a greater responsibility than they agreed to undertake. As long ago as 1601 Lord Coke advised a bailee to stipulate specially that he would not be responsible for theft, see *Southcote's* case (1601) 4 Co Rep 83b a case of theft by a servant. It would be strange if his stipulation was of no avail to him. The answer to the problem lies, I think, in this: the owner is bound by the conditions if he has expressly or impliedly consented to the bailee making a sub-bailment containing those conditions, but not otherwise. Suppose the owner of goods lets them out on hire, and the hirer sends them for repair, and the repairer holds them for a lien. The owner is bound by the lien because he impliedly consented to the repairs being done, since they were reasonably incidental to use of the car: see *Tappenden v Artus*. So also if the owner of a ship accepts goods for carriage on a bill of lading containing exempting conditions (ie, a 'bailment upon terms') the owner of the goods (although not a party to the contract) is bound by those conditions if he impliedly consented to them as being in 'the known and contemplated form,' . . .

In this case the plaintiff agreed that Beder should send the fur to the defendants, and by so doing I think she impliedly consented to his making a contract for cleaning on the terms usually current in the trade. But when I come to study the conditions I do not think they are sufficient to protect the cleaners. We always construe such conditions strictly. Clause 9 applies only to 'goods belonging to customers,' that is, goods belonging to Beder, and not to goods belonging to his customers such as the plaintiff. The conditions themselves draw a distinction between 'customer' and 'his own customer,' see clause 16. Clause 14 only applies to 'the loss of or damage to the goods during processing.' The loss here was not during processing. It was before or after processing.

Seeing that the conditions do not protect the defendants, I am of opinion that they are liable for the loss due to the theft by their servant. I would allow the appeal accordingly, and direct judgment to be entered for the value of the stole as found by the judge £200."

NOTE

This case is important not just in respect of its actual result (the clauses were ineffective), but equally with regard to Lord Denning's comments as to when a bailor *will* be bound by clauses in a contract to which he is not a party: see *The Pioneer Container* (1994).

PROBLEM

In *New Zealand Shipping Co v AM Satterthwaite & Co (The Eurymedon)* (1975) (above, p.96), S (a shipper) contracted with C (a carrier) to transport a machine owned by O from Liverpool to New Zealand. The contract contained a clause exempting C and any of C's servants, agents or independent contractors from any liability unless the action was brought within one year. Stevedores employed by C negligently damaged the machine while unloading it in New Zealand. O brought an action for damages against the stevedores outside the exclusion clause time limit and the question arose as to whether O was bound by the clause. A majority of the Privy Council held that the exclusion clause was a unilateral (collateral) contractual promise made by O, via C, to the stevedores, who accepted the promise (and provided consideration) when they unloaded the machine, such unloading being a benefit to O. Smith and Thomas, *A Casebook on Contract*, 11th edn, (Sweet & Maxwell, 2000), state (at p.304) in respect of this case that the 'third party to the contract containing the exemption clause was the plaintiff, so the 1999 Act would have no application to this situation. It does not enable the contracting parties to impose any burden on the third parties'. Do you agree that the 1999 Act would have no application?

QUESTIONS

1. Read *Scruttons Ltd v Midland Silicones Ltd* (1962) in the law report. Would the 1999 Act now apply to these facts?

2. Would the 1999 Act have helped the defendants in *Morris v Martin*?

3. Could the courts have used collateral contracts, specific performance in equity and (or) estoppel to develop a legal situation in which the 1999 Act would have been unnecessary?

4. Imagine that Lord Denning's statements in *Beswick* (p.23), *Jackson* (p.396) and *Morris* (p.400) were all regarded as very sound law. Would the 1999 Act have been unnecessary?

8.3 Incorporating terms and clauses

In order for a contractual promise (term) to be effective and binding it must actually have been incorporated into the contract. Thus a promise made after the contract is formed, or a promise not brought to the other party's attention, might well be ineffective through lack of incorporation in the contract.

Interfoto Picture Library Ltd v Stiletto Visual Programmes Ltd **[1989] Q.B. 433, CA**

This was an action in debt by the owners of photographic transparencies, against the hirers of them, for a sum of money calculated on the basis of a clause in the contract charging a high daily fee if the transparencies were not returned in time. The Court of Appeal (Dillon and Bingham L.JJ.) held that the claimants were entitled only to a much lower sum of money calculated on a *quantum meruit* basis.

Dillon L.J.: ". . . The plaintiffs run a library of photographic transparencies. The defendants are engaged in advertising. On 5 March 1984 Mr Beeching, a director of the defendants, wanting photographs for a presentation for a client, telephoned the plaintiffs, whom the defendants had never dealt with before. He spoke to a Miss Fraser of the plaintiffs and asked her whether the plaintiffs had any photographs of the 1950s which might be suitable for the defendants' presentation. Miss Fraser said that she would research his request, and a little later on the same day she sent round by hand to the defendants 47 transparencies packed in a jiffy bag. Also packed in the bag, among the transparencies, was a delivery note which she had typed out . . .

Having received the transparencies, Mr Beeching telephoned the plaintiffs at about 3.10 on the afternoon of 5 March, and told Miss Fraser . . . that he was very impressed with the plaintiffs' fast service, that one or two of the transparencies could be of interest, and that he would get back to the plaintiffs.

Unfortunately, he did not get back on to the plaintiffs and the transparencies seem to have been put on one side and overlooked by the defendants. The plaintiffs tried to telephone Mr Beeching on 20 and again on 23 March, but only spoke to his secretary. In the upshot the transparencies, which the defendants did not use for their presentation, were not returned to the plaintiffs until 2 April.

The plaintiffs thereupon sent an invoice to the defendants for £3,783.50 as a holding charge for the transparencies. The invoice was rejected by the defendants, and accordingly in May 1984 the plaintiffs started this action claiming £3,783.50, the amount of the invoice. That is the sum for which the judge awarded the plaintiffs judgment by his order now under appeal. The plaintiffs' claim is based on conditions printed on their delivery note . . .

The sum of £3,783.50 is calculated by the plaintiffs in strict accordance with condition 2 as the fee for the retention of 47 transparencies from 19 March to 2 April 1984. It is of course important to the plaintiffs to get their transparencies back reasonably quickly, if they are not wanted, since if a transparency is out with one customer it cannot be offered to another customer, should occasion arise. It has to be said, however, that the holding fee charged by the plaintiffs by condition 2 is extremely high, and in my view exorbitant. The judge held that on a *quantum meruit* a reasonable charge would have been £3.50 per transparency per week, and not £5 per day . . .

The question is therefore whether condition 2 was sufficiently brought to the defendants' attention to make it a term of the contract which was only concluded after the defendants had received, and must have known that they had received the transparencies and the delivery note. . . .

Condition 2 of these plaintiffs' conditions is in my judgment a very onerous clause. The defendants could not conceivably have known, if their attention was not drawn to the clause, that the plaintiffs were proposing to charge a 'holding fee' for the retention of the transparencies at such a very high and exorbitant rate.

At the time of the ticket cases in the last century it was notorious that people hardly ever troubled to read printed conditions on a ticket or delivery note or similar document. That remains the case now. In the intervening years the printed conditions have tended to become more and more complicated and more and more one-sided in favour of the party who is imposing them, but the other parties, if they notice that there are printed conditions at all, generally still tend to assume that such conditions are only concerned with ancillary matters of form and are not of importance. In the ticket cases the courts held that the common

403

law required that reasonable steps be taken to draw the other parties' attention to the printed conditions or they would not be part of the contract. It is, in my judgment, a logical development of the common law into modern conditions that it should be held, as it was in *Thornton v Shoe Lane Parking Ltd* [1971] 2 QB 163, that, if one condition in a set of printed conditions is particularly onerous or unusual, the party seeking to enforce it must show that that particular condition was fairly brought to the attention of the other party.

In the present case, nothing whatever was done by the plaintiffs to draw the defendants' attention particularly to condition 2; it was merely one of four columns' width of conditions printed across the foot of the delivery note. Consequently condition 2 never, in my judgment, became part of the contract between the parties.

I would therefore allow this appeal and reduce the amount of the judgment which the judge awarded against the defendants to the amount which he would have awarded on a quantum meruit on his alternative findings, ie the reasonable charge of £3.50 per transparency per week for the retention of the transparencies beyond a reasonable period, which he fixed at 14 days from the date of their receipt by the defendants."

Bingham L.J.: ". . . Turning to the present case, I am satisfied for reasons which Dillon LJ has given that no contract was made on the telephone when the defendants made their initial request. I am equally satisfied that no contract was made on delivery of the transparencies to the defendants before the opening of the jiffy bag in which they were contained. Once the jiffy bag was opened and the transparencies taken out with the delivery note, it is in my judgment an inescapable inference that the defendants would have recognised the delivery note as a document of a kind likely to contain contractual terms and would have seen that there were conditions printed in small but visible lettering on the face of the document. To the extent that the conditions so displayed were common form or usual terms regularly encountered in this business, I do not think the defendants could successfully contend that they were not incorporated into the contract.

The crucial question in the case is whether the plaintiffs can be said fairly and reasonably to have brought condition 2 to the notice of the defendants. The judge made no finding on the point, but I think that it is open to this court to draw an inference from the primary findings which he did make. In my opinion the plaintiffs did not do so. They delivered 47 transparencies, which was a number the defendants had not specifically asked for. Condition 2 contained a daily rate per transparency after the initial period of 14 days many times greater than was usual or (so far as the evidence shows) heard of. For these 47 transparencies there was to be a charge for each day of delay of £235 plus value added tax. The result would be that a venial period of delay, as here, would lead to an inordinate liability. The defendants are not to be relieved of that liability because they did not read the condition, although doubtless they did not; but in my judgment they are to be relieved because the plaintiffs did not do what was necessary to draw this unreasonable and extortionate clause fairly to their attention. I would accordingly allow the defendants' appeal and substitute for the judge's award the sum which he assessed upon the alternative basis of *quantum meruit*.

In reaching the conclusion I have expressed I would not wish to be taken as deciding that condition 2 was not challengeable as a disguised penalty clause. This point was not argued before the judge nor raised in the notice of appeal. It was accordingly not argued before us. I have accordingly felt bound to assume, somewhat reluctantly, that condition 2 would be enforceable if fully and fairly brought to the defendants' attention."

(For further extract, see p.124.)

QUESTIONS

1. On what legal ground was the debt clause in *Interfoto* set aside: because it was onerous, or because it was not incorporated into the contract?

2. If parties are under a duty only to plead the facts, why is it that a court cannot raise any question of law (e.g., whether the clause is a penalty) to be found in the facts?

3. Is this an unjust enrichment case?

4. Is this a good faith case?

NOTES AND FURTHER QUESTIONS

1. In *Thornton v Shoe Lane Parking* (1971), the user of a car park was badly injured in the car park owing to the negligence of the car park owners. When sued for damages by the injured person, the owners denied liability on the basis of an exclusion clause printed on the ticket, dispensed from a machine, issued on arrival at the car park and also displayed on a notice inside the premises. The Court of Appeal held that the clause was ineffective because the contract was concluded with the machine before the customer could read the condition printed on it; consequently it was not incorporated in the contract. What if the claimant had used the car park on previous occasions and was thus well aware of the existence of the exclusion clause? (*Cf. British Crane Hire Corpn v Ipswich Plant Hire Ltd* (1975).)

2. If facts similar to *Thornton* arose again today, and the clause was displayed clearly in flashing neon lights on a notice outside the car park, the owners would still not be able to rely on the clause thanks to the Unfair Contract Terms Act 1977, s.2(1). But what if the car park user suffered not personal

405

injury, but damage to his car as a result of the owners' negligence: might such a clause be valid?

3. Does *Interfoto* give expression to PECL, art.2:104?

Principles of European Contract Law

"Article 2:104 Terms not individually negotiated
(1) Contract terms which have not been individually negotiated may be invoked against a party who did not know of them only if the party invoking them took reasonable steps to bring them to the other party's attention before or when the contract was concluded.

(2) Terms are not brought appropriately to a party's attention by a mere reference to them in a contract document, even if that party signs the document."

QUESTION

If this article applied to the facts of *Director General of Fair Trading v First National Bank* (2002) (p.131), would the disputed clause in the case have to be deemed ineffective?

8.4 Limiting and excluding the effects of a contract

We have already seen that in principle a party can incorporate a term in a contract excluding or limiting the effects of the contract. In particular a party can, at common law, draft a clause that limits or excludes liability.

8.4.1 Contractual freedom and exclusion clauses

The freedom to do this is guaranteed by the general principle of freedom of contract, a point reconfirmed by the House of Lords.

Photo Production Ltd v Securicor Transport Ltd [1980] A.C. 827, HL

This was an action for damages brought by the owners of a factory (or more precisely their insurance company) against a security company in respect of a fire deliberately started by one of the security company's patrolmen. The fire completely destroyed the plaintiffs' factory, but the security company resisted liability on the basis of a clause in the contract which stipulated that 'under no circumstances' were the defendants to be 'responsible for any injurious act or default by any employee unless such act or default could have been foreseen and avoided by the exercise of due diligence on the part of the [defendants] as his employer; nor, in any event, [were the defendants to] be held responsible for any loss suffered by the [plaintiffs] through fire or any other cause, except in so far as such loss [was] solely attributable to the negligence of the [defendants'] employees acting within the course of their employment.' The trial judge gave judgment for the security company; the Court of Appeal reversed this decision; an appeal to the House of Lords (Lords Diplock, Wilberforce, Salmon, Keith and Scarman) was allowed.

Lord Diplock: ". . . My Lords, the contract in the instant case was entered into before the passing of the Unfair Contract Terms Act 1977. So what we are concerned with is the common law of contract, of which the subject-matter is the legally enforceable obligations as between the parties to it of which the contract is the source . . .

A basic principle of the common law of contract, to which there are no exceptions that are relevant in the instant case, is that parties to a contract are free to determine for themselves what primary obligations they will accept. They may state these in express words in the contract itself and, where they do, the statement is determinative; but in practice a commercial contract never states all the primary obligations of the parties in full; many are left to be incorporated by implication of law from the legal nature of the contract into which the parties are entering. But if the parties wish to reject or modify primary obligations which would otherwise be so incorporated, they are fully at liberty to do so by express words.

Leaving aside those comparatively rare cases in which the court is able to enforce a primary obligation by decreeing specific performance of it, breaches of primary obligations give rise to substituted secondary obligations on the part of the party in default, and, in some cases, may entitle the other party to be relieved from further performance of his own primary obligations. These secondary obligations of the contract breaker and any concomitant relief of the other party from his own primary obligations also arise by implication of law, generally common law, but sometimes statute, as in the case of codifying statutes passed at the turn of the century, notably the Sale of Goods Act 1893. The contract, however, is just as much the source of secondary obligations as it is of primary obligations; and like primary obligations that are implied by law secondary obligations too can be modified by agreement between the parties, although, for reasons to be mentioned later, they cannot, in my view, be totally excluded. In the instant case, the only secondary obligations and concomitant reliefs that are applicable arise by implication of the common law as modified by the express words of the contract.

Every failure to perform a primary obligation is a breach of contract. The secondary obligation on the part of the contract breaker to which it gives rise by implication of the common law is to pay monetary compensation to the other party for the loss sustained by him in consequence of the breach . . .

My Lords, an exclusion clause is one which excludes or modifies an obligation, whether primary, or secondary, that would otherwise arise under the contract by implication of law. Parties are free to agree to whatever exclusion or modification of obligations they please within the limits that the agreement must retain the legal characteristics of a contract and must not offend against the equitable rule against penalties, that is to say, it must not impose on the breaker of a primary obligation a general secondary obligation to pay to the other party a sum of money that is manifestly intended to be in excess of the amount which would fully compensate the other party for the loss sustained by him in consequence of the breach of the primary obligation. Since the presumption is that the parties by entering into the contract intended to accept the implied obligations, exclusion clauses are to be construed strictly and the degree of strictness appropriate to be applied to their construction may properly depend on the extent to which they involve departure from the implied obligations. Since the obligations implied by law in a commercial contract are those which, by judicial consensus over the years or by Parliament in passing a statute, have been regarded as obligations which a reasonable businessman would realise that he was accepting when he entered into a contract of a particular kind, the court's view of the reasonableness of any departure from the implied obligations which would be involved in construing the express words of an exclusion clause in one sense that they are capable of bearing rather than another is a relevant consideration in deciding what meaning the words were intended by the parties to bear. But this does not entitle the court to reject the exclusion clause, however unreasonable the court itself may think it is, if the words are clear and fairly susceptible of one meaning only.

My Lords, the reports are full of cases in which what would appear to be very strained constructions have been placed on exclusion clauses, mainly in what today would be called consumer contracts and contracts of adhesion. As Lord Wilberforce has pointed out, any need for this kind of judicial distortion of the English language has been banished by Parliament's having made these kinds of contracts subject to the Unfair Contract Terms Act 1977. In commercial contracts negotiated between businessmen capable of looking after their own interests and of deciding how risks inherent in the performance of various kinds of contract can be most economically borne (generally by insurance), it is, in my view, wrong to place a strained construction on words in an exclusion clause which are clear and fairly susceptible of one meaning only even after due allowance has been made for the presumption in favour of the implied primary and secondary obligations.

Applying these principles to the instant case, in the absence of the exclusion clause a primary obligation of Securicor under the contract, which would be implied by law, would be an absolute obligation to procure that the visits by the night patrol to the factory were conducted by natural persons who would exercise reasonable skill and care for the safety of the factory. That primary obligation is modified by the exclusion clause. Securicor's obligation to do this is not to be absolute, but is limited to exercising due diligence in their capacity as employers of the natural persons by whom the visits are conducted, to procure that those persons shall exercise reasonable skill and care for the safety of the factory.

For the reasons given by Lord Wilberforce it seems to me that this apportionment of the risk of the factory being damaged or destroyed by the injurious act of an employee of Securicor while carrying out a visit to the factory is one which reasonable businessmen in the position of Securicor and Photo Productions might well think was the most economical . . . The risk that a servant of Securicor would damage or destroy the factory or steal goods from it, despite the exercise of all reasonable diligence by Securicor to prevent it, is what in the context of maritime law would be called a 'misfortune risk', is something which reasonable diligence of neither party to the contract can prevent. Either party can insure against it. It is generally more economical for the person by whom the loss will be directly sustained to do so rather than that it should be covered by the other party by liability insurance . . ."

(For further extracts, see pp.70, 351.)

QUESTIONS

1. 'Leaving aside those comparatively rare cases in which the court is able to enforce a primary obligation by decreeing specific performance of it, breaches of primary obligations give rise to substituted secondary obligations on the part of the party in default, and, in some cases, may entitle the other party to be relieved from further performance of his own primary obligations.' Why might this be a very inaccurate account of the operation of English contract law?

2. Did the court focus on risk rather than fault? Whose insurance policy ought to bear the risk of the factory burning down?

3. Why was the *contra proferentem* rule not applied?

4. Would the plaintiffs have to pay for the services rendered by Securicor?

5. Did Securicor commit a trespass?

NOTES

1. In *Watford Electronics Ltd v Sanderson CFL Ltd* (2001), Chadwick L.J. said (at § 55): 'Where experienced businessmen representing substantial companies of equal bargaining power negotiate an agreement, they may be taken to have had regard to the matters known to them. They should, in my view, be taken to be the best judge of the commercial fairness of the agreement which they have made, including the fairness of each of the terms in that agreement. They should be taken to be the best judge on the question whether the terms of the agreement are reasonable.' (*Cf.* Lord Bramwell, above at p.118.)

2. Lord Denning M.R.'s judgment in *George Mitchell v Finney Lock* (1983) (above, p.119) gives a brief history of the problem of exclusion clauses in English law.
3. In civilian legal thinking unfair clauses are now quite strictly controlled.

Principles of European Contract Law

"Article 4:110 Unfair Terms Which Have Not Been Individually Negotiated
(1) A party may avoid a term which has not been individually negotiated if, contrary to the requirements of good faith and fair dealing, it causes a significant imbalance in the parties' rights and obligations arising under the contract to the detriment of that party, taking into account the nature of the performance to be rendered under the contract, all the other terms of the contract and the circumstances at the time the contract was concluded.

(2) This Article does not apply to:

(a) a term which defines the main subject matter of the contract, provided the term is in plain and intelligible language; or to
(b) the adequacy in value of one party's obligations compared to the value of the obligations of the other party.

Article 4:118 Exclusion or Restriction of Remedies
(1) Remedies for fraud, threats and excessive benefit or unfair advantage-taking, and the right to avoid an unfair term which has not been individually negotiated, cannot be excluded or restricted.

(2) Remedies for mistake and incorrect information may be excluded or restricted unless the exclusion or restriction is contrary to good faith and fair dealing.

Article 8:109 Clause Limiting or Excluding Remedies
Remedies for non-performance may be excluded or restricted unless it would be contrary to good faith and fair dealing to invoke the exclusion or restriction."

QUESTION

What if a term in a contract which defines the main subject-matter of the contract is a term that has not been individually negotiated and causes a significant imbalance in the parties' rights and obligations under the contract to the detriment of the party subject to it?

8.4.2 Control of exclusion clauses and business liability

Although exclusion clauses are perfectly valid at common law provided they have been incorporated into the contract and are correctly drafted, legislation has subjected them to legal control. The Unfair Contract Terms Act 1977 basically does one of two things with regard to exclusion clauses in certain contracts: it either (i) treats some types of clause in some types of contract as void from the start, or (ii) subjects an exclusion clause to the test of reasonableness. The first question that might reasonably be asked is what clauses are actually covered by the 1977 Act—an issue regulated by s.13 of the Act (above, p.356). The next question is to discover what contracts fall under the Act.

Unfair Contract Terms Act 1977 (c.50)

"1. Scope of Part I
(2) This Part of this Act is subject to Part III; and in relation to contracts, the operation of sections 2 to 4 and 7 is subject to the exceptions made by Schedule 1.

(3) In the case of both contract and tort, sections 2 to 7 apply (except where the contrary is stated in section 6(4)) only to business liability, that is liability for breach of obligations or duties arising—

  (a) from things done or to be done by a person in the course of a business (whether his own business or another's); or
  (b) from the occupation of premises used for business purposes of the occupier;

and references to liability are to be read accordingly [but liability of an occupier of premises for breach of an obligation or duty towards a person obtaining access to the premises for recreational or educational purposes, being liability for loss or damage suffered by reason of the dangerous state of the premises, is not a business liability of the occupier unless granting that person such access for the purposes concerned falls within the business purposes of the occupier].

(4) In relation to any breach of duty or obligation, it is immaterial for any purpose of this Part of this Act whether the breach was inadvertent or intentional, or whether liability for it arises directly or vicariously.

QUESTION

The key point to note in this section is the notion of "business liability". Will this cover a non-profit making community activity organised by a local authority?

Unfair Contract Terms Act 1977 (c.50)

"14. Interpretation of Part I
In this Part of this Act—

'business' includes a profession and the activities of any government department or local or public authority;

'goods' has the same meaning as in [the Sale of Goods Act 1979];

'hire-purchase agreement' has the same meaning as in the Consumer Credit Act 1974;

'negligence' has the meaning given by section 1(1);

'notice' includes an announcement, whether or not in writing, and any other communication or pretended communication; and

'personal injury' includes any disease and any impairment of physical or mental condition.

8.4.3 Negligence liability

Many of the exclusion clause cases to be found in the law reports are concerned with situations where a defendant is claiming the protection of an exclusion clause against an action for injury or damage arising from negligence (see e.g. *Thornton v Shoe Lane Parking* (1971), at p.405). The 1977 Act deals specifically with such negligence liability.

Unfair Contract Terms Act 1977 (c.50)

"1. Scope of Part I
(1) For the purposes of this Part of this Act, 'negligence' means the breach—

    (a) of any obligation, arising from the express or implied terms of a contract, to take reasonable care to exercise reasonable skill in the performance of the contract;
    (b) of any common law duty to take reasonable care or exercise reasonable skill (but not any stricter duty);
    (c) of the common duty of care imposed by the Occupiers' Liability Act 1957 or the Occupiers' Liability Act (Northern Ireland) 1957. . . .

2. Negligence liability
(1) A person cannot by reference to any contract term or to a notice given to persons generally or to particular persons exclude or restrict his liability for death or personal injury resulting from negligence.

(2) In the case of other loss or damage, a person cannot so exclude or restrict his liability for negligence except in so far as the term or notice satisfies the requirement of reasonableness.

(3) Where a contract term or notice purports to exclude or restrict liability for negligence a person's agreement to or awareness of it is not of itself to be taken as indicating his voluntary acceptance of any risk.

QUESTION

Imagine facts similar to those in *Attia v British Gas Plc* (1988) (read in law report). Imagine also that a clause in the contract states: "British Gas will accept full

412

responsibility for any personal injury or property damage arising out of the contract of installation, but it cannot be liable for any psychological or emotional damage arising out of a contracting party experiencing serious harm to his property or to his patrimony as a result of any event linked to this contract." Would the clause be void?

NOTE

Section 2 demonstrates how the 1977 Act declares some clauses void from the start (s.2(1)) while others are subject to the reasonableness test (s.2(2)). What differentiates the two approaches in s.2 is, of course, the nature of the damage. Thus personal injury must be distinguished from other types of damage.

8.4.4 Contractual liability: general

With respect to contracts generally, the 1977 Act makes a number of distinctions. First, there is the distinction between consumer and non-consumer contracts. Secondly, there is a distinction between standard-form contracts and non standard-form contracts.

> **Unfair Contract Terms Act 1977 (c.50)**
>
> **"3. Liability arising in contract**
> (1) This section applies as between contracting parties where one of them deals as consumer or on the other's written standard terms of business.
>
> (2) As against that party, the other cannot by reference to any contract term—
>
> (a) when himself in breach of contract, exclude or restrict any liability of his in respect of the breach; or
> (b) claim to be entitled—
>
> > (i) to render a contractual performance substantially different from that which was reasonably expected of him, or
> > (ii) in respect of the whole or any part of his contractual obligation, to render no performance at all,
>
> except in so far as (in any of the cases mentioned above in this subsection) the contract term satisfies the requirement of reasonableness."

PROBLEMS

1. Tony contracts with Basil for a loan using one of Basil's standard-form contracts. The contract contains a clause allowing Basil to alter the rate of interest at any time. Basil increases the rate well beyond the standard bank rate. Tony claims that the clause is unreasonable under s.3 of the 1977 Act. Basil replies that s.3 applies only to Basil's performance and not to Tony's performance in paying interest. Tony replies to this argument by saying that "performance" includes any Basil demand ("you will pay . . .") in respect of

any sum payable under the contract. Who is right? (*Cf. Paragon Finance plc v Staunton* (2002).)

2. Ian contracts with Harm's Happy Holidays Ltd for a package holiday in France. All of Harm's advertisements stress that what they provide is a good "holiday" at very cheap prices irrespective of the actual destination. The document signed by Ian is one of Harm's standard-form contracts and contains a clause permitting Harm to change the location of the holiday at any time after the contract is concluded. A day before the flight to France, Harm informs Ian that he will be going to the Croatian coast and not to the French coast. When Ian objects, Harm points out that food, wine and "other pleasures" will actually be cheaper than in France, and anyway, what matters is the quality of the holiday in relation to the price (which Ian admits is quite cheap). Is the clause permitting Harm's Happy Holidays to make this change caught by s.3 of the 1977 Act?

QUESTIONS

1. It is clear from this section that the 1977 Act covers not just contracts with consumers, but also some commercial contracts. Does this mean that contracts between commercial organisations have to achieve a certain level of reasonableness?

2. Ought the law to distinguish between small and large businesses? (*Cf.* Unfair Contract Terms Bill 2004.)

3. What is actually meant by 'written standard terms of business'? Could s.3 have been of any relevance to *Butler Machine Tool Co Ltd v Ex-Cell-O Corporation* (1979) (see p.163)?

8.4.5 Supply of goods contracts

Another important distinction is between contracts for the supply of goods and contracts for the supply of a service.

Unfair Contract Terms Act 1977 (c.50)

6. Sale and hire-purchase
(1) Liability for breach of the obligations arising from—

(a) section 12 of the Sale of Goods Act 1979 (seller's implied undertakings as to title, etc);
(b) section 8 of the Supply of Goods (Implied Terms) Act 1973 (the corresponding thing in relation to hire-purchase),

cannot be excluded or restricted by reference to any contract term.

(2) As against a person dealing as consumer, liability for breach of the obligations arising from—

   (a) section 13, 14 or 15 of the 1979 Act (seller's implied undertakings as to conformity of goods with description or sample, or as to their quality or fitness for a particular purpose);

   (b) section 9, 10 or 11 of the 1973 Act (the corresponding things in relation to hire-purchase),

cannot be excluded or restricted by reference to any contract term.

(3) As against a person dealing otherwise than as consumer, the liability specified in subsection (2) above can be excluded or restricted by reference to a contract term, but only in so far as the term satisfies the requirement of reasonableness.

(4) The liabilities referred to in this section are not only the business liabilities defined by section 1(3), but include those arising under any contract of sale of goods or hire-purchase agreement.

7. Miscellaneous contracts under which goods pass

(1) Where the possession or ownership of goods passes under or in pursuance of a contract not governed by the law of sale of goods or hire-purchase, subsections (2) to (4) below apply as regards the effect (if any) to be given to contract terms excluding or restricting liability for breach of obligation arising by implication of law from the nature of the contract.

(2) As against a person dealing as consumer, liability in respect of the goods' correspondence with description or sample, or their quality or fitness for any particular purpose, cannot be excluded or restricted by reference to any such term.

(3) As against a person dealing otherwise than as consumer, that liability can be excluded or restricted by reference to such a term, but only in so far as the term satisfies the requirement of reasonableness.

(3A) Liability for breach of the obligations arising under section 2 of the Supply of Goods and Services Act 1982 (implied terms about title etc in certain contracts for the transfer of the property in goods) cannot be excluded or restricted by references to any such term.

(4) Liability in respect of—

   (a) the right to transfer ownership of the goods, or give possession; or

   (b) the assurance of quiet possession to a person taking goods in pursuance of the contract,

cannot (in a case to which subsection (3A) above does not apply) be excluded or restricted by reference to any such term except in so far as the term satisfies the requirement of reasonableness."

QUESTIONS

1. Does s.6 cover sales at car boot fairs?

2. Do ss.6(1) and 7(3A) give indirect legislative support to *Rowland v Divall* (1923) (p.340)?

8.4.6 **Consumer contracts**

As we have seen, where one the contracting parties deals as a consumer, the protection offered in respect of exclusion clauses is considerable. This protection is increased thanks to a second piece of legislation that gives effect to the EU Directive on Unfair Terms of 5 April 1993. Moreover, the protection offered extends beyond exclusion clauses to cover unfair terms in general.

Unfair Terms in Consumer Contracts Regulations 1999 (SI 1999/2083)

"8. Effect of unfair term
(1) An unfair term in a contract concluded with a consumer by a seller or supplier shall not be binding on the consumer.

(2) The contract shall continue to bind the parties if it is capable of continuing in existence without the unfair term."

NOTE

See also reg.5 (what amounts to an unfair term) (above, at p.364), reg.4 (terms to which the Regulations apply (above, at p.364), reg.6 (assessment of unfair terms) (above, at p.364) and reg.7 (interpretation of written terms) (above, at p.353).

QUESTION

Do the 1999 Regulations define a consumer in way similar to the definition in the 1977 Act?

Unfair Terms in Consumer Contracts Regulations 1999 (SI 1999/2083)

"3. Interpretation
(1) In these Regulations—

'the Community' means the European Community;

'consumer' means any natural person who, in contracts covered by these Regulations, is acting for purposes which are outside his trade, business or profession;

. . .

'seller or supplier' means any natural or legal person who, in contracts covered by these Regulations, is acting for purposes relating to his trade, business or profession, whether publicly owned or privately owned;

'unfair terms' means the contractual terms referred to in regulation 5.

Unfair Contract Terms Act 1977 (c.50)

"12. 'Dealing as consumer'

(1) A party to a contract 'deals as consumer' in relation to another party if—

    (a) he neither makes the contract in the course of a business nor holds himself out as doing so; and

    (b) the other party does make the contract in the course of a business; and

    (c) in the case of a contract governed by the law of sale of goods or hire-purchase, or by section 7 of this Act, the goods passing under or in pursuance of the contract are of a type ordinarily supplied for private use or consumption.

(2) But on a sale by auction or by competitive tender the buyer is not in any circumstances to be regarded as dealing as consumer.

(3) Subject to this, it is for those claiming that a party does not deal as consumer to show that he does not."

Unfair Contract Terms Bill 2004

"26. 'Consumer contract' and 'business contract'

(1) 'Consumer contract' means a contract (other than one of employment) between—

    (a) an individual ('the consumer') who enters into it wholly or mainly for purposes unrelated to a business of his, and

    (b) a person ('the business') who enters into it wholly or mainly for purposes related to his business."

PROBLEMS

1. Geoffrey and Jennifer run a small limited company importing and selling plastic flowers. They purchase a car, in the company's name, from Mitch's Motors, which they intend to use for both private and business purposes; however, the car proves defective and fails to function six months after purchase. When Geoffrey and Jennifer complain, Mitch of Mitch Motors points to a clause in the sale contract excluding any liability with respect to the quality and fitness of the vehicle. Is the clause in the contract excluding liability void, as against Geoffrey and Jennifer (i) under the 1977 Act, and (ii)

under the 1999 Regulations? (*Cf. R & B Customs Brokers Co Ltd v United Dominions Trust Ltd* (1988).)

2. Having finally managed to repair the car, Geoffrey and Jennifer decide to sell it, again under the company's name, and are contacted by Paula, who shows interest in the vehicle. Geoffrey and Jennifer point out that they are not in the business of selling cars and that is the reason why the selling price is low. It is, they say, a "private sale". Paula purchases the car, having been informed in writing that, given the price, the seller can accept no responsibility with regard to its quality and fitness, but soon finds that it will not go anywhere much because of its unreliability. Can Paula sue Geoffrey and Jennifer's company for damages for breach of s.14 of the Sale of Goods Act 1979? (*Cf. Stevenson v Rogers* (1999).)

8.4.7 Reasonableness test

Many of the clauses caught by the 1977 Act will be ineffective only if they are unreasonable.

Unfair Contract Terms Act 1977 (c.50)

"11. The 'reasonableness' test
(1) In relation to a contract term, the requirement of reasonableness for the purposes of this Part of this Act, section 3 of the Misrepresentation Act 1967 and section 3 of the Misrepresentation Act (Northern Ireland) 1967 is that the term shall have been a fair and reasonable one to be included having regard to the circumstances which were, or ought reasonably to have been, known to or in the contemplation of the parties when the contract was made.

(2) In determining for the purposes of section 6 or 7 above whether a contract term satisfies the requirement of reasonableness, regard shall be had in particular to the matters specified in Schedule 2 to this Act; but this subsection does not prevent the court or arbitrator from holding, in accordance with any rule of law, that a term which purports to exclude or restrict any relevant liability is not a term of the contract.

(3) In relation to a notice (not being a notice having contractual effect), the requirement of reasonableness under this Act is that it should be fair and reasonable to allow reliance on it, having regard to all the circumstances obtaining when the liability arose or (but for the notice) would have arisen.

(4) Where by reference to a contract term or notice a person seeks to restrict liability to a specified sum of money, and the question arises (under this or any other Act) whether the term or notice satisfies the requirement of reasonableness, regard shall be had in particular (but without prejudice to subsection (2) above in the case of contract terms) to—

(a) the resources which he could expect to be available to him for the purpose of meeting the liability should it arise; and

(b) how far it was open to him to cover himself by insurance.

(5) It is for those claiming that a contract term or notice satisfies the requirement of reasonableness to show that it does.

SCHEDULE 2

'GUIDELINES' FOR APPLICATION OF REASONABLE TEST

The matters to which regard is to be had in particular for the purposes of sections 6(3), 7(3) and (4), 20 and 21 are any of the following which appear to be relevant—

(a) the strength of the bargaining positions of the parties relative to each other, taking into account (among other things) alternative means by which the customer's requirements could have been met;

(b) whether the customer received an inducement to agree to the term, or in accepting it had an opportunity of entering into a similar contract with other persons, but without having to accept a similar term;

(c) whether the customer knew or ought reasonably to have known of the existence and extent of the term (having regard, among other things, to any custom of the trade and any previous course of dealing between the parties);

(d) where the term excludes or restricts any relevant liability if some condition is not complied with, whether it was reasonable at the time of the contract to expect that compliance with that condition would be practicable;

(e) whether the goods were manufactured, processed or adapted to the special order of the customer."

NOTE

Compare this test with the one being proposed by the Law Commission.

Unfair Contract Terms Bill 2004

"14. The test
(1) Whether a contract term is fair and reasonable is to be determined by taking into account—

(a) the extent to which the term is transparent, and

(b) the substance and effect of the term, and all the circumstances existing at the time it was agreed.

(2) Whether a notice is fair and reasonable is to be determined by taking into account—

(a) the extent to which the notice is transparent, and
(b) the substance and effect of the notice, and all the circumstances existing at the time when the liability arose (or, but for the notice, would have arisen).

(3) 'Transparent' means—

(a) expressed in reasonably plain language,
(b) legible,
(c) presented clearly, and
(d) readily available to any person likely to be affected by the contract term or notice in question.

(4) Matters relating to the substance and effect of a contract term, and to all the circumstances existing at the time it was agreed, include the following—

(a) the other terms of the contract,
(b) the terms of any other contract on which the contract depends,
(c) the balance of the parties' interests,
(d) the risks to the party adversely affected by the term,
(e) the possibility and probability of insurance,
(f) other ways in which the interests of the party adversely affected by the term might have been protected,
(g) the extent to which the term (whether alone or with others) differs from what would have been the case in its absence,
(h) the knowledge and understanding of the party adversely affected by the term,
(i) the strength of the parties' bargaining positions,
(j) the nature of the goods or services to which the contract relates.

(5) Subsection (4) applies, with any necessary modifications, in relation to a notice as it applies in relation to a contract term.

(6) Schedule 2 contains an indicative and non-exhaustive list of consumer contract terms and small business contract terms which may be regarded as not being fair and reasonable."

NOTE

See extract from the Law Commission Report on *Unfair Terms in Contracts*, Law Com. (No.292, Cm 6464, 2004), above at p.135.

QUESTION

Does "reasonableness" in this statutory context have any relation to "reasonableness" as a behavioural test?

George Mitchell (Chesterhall) Ltd v Finney Lock Seeds Ltd **[1983] 2 A.C. 803, HL**

This was an action for damages by a farmer against the seller of Dutch Winter cabbage seed. The seed, which cost £201.60, turned out to be of inferior quality and useless to the farmer, and he claimed compensation for all his losses when the crop of cabbages had to be destroyed. The sellers relied on a clause on the invoice purporting to limit their liability, should the seed prove defective, to replacing the seed or repaying the price. The trial judge awarded the farmer £61,513.78 damages plus £30,756 interest, and appeals to the Court of Appeal and House of Lords (Lords Diplock, Scarman, Roskill, Bridge and Brightman) were dismissed.

Lord Bridge: "... My Lords, it seems to me, with all due deference, that the judgments of the learned trial judge and of Oliver LJ on the common law issue come dangerously near to re-introducing by the back door the doctrine of 'fundamental breach' which this House in *Securicor 1*, had so forcibly evicted by the front. The learned judge discusses what I may call the 'peas and beans' or 'chalk and cheese' cases, sc. those in which it has been held that exemption clauses do not apply where there has been a contract to sell one thing, eg, a motor car, and the seller has supplied quite another things eg, a bicycle. I hasten to add that the judge can in no way be criticised for adopting this approach since counsel appearing for the appellants at the trial had conceded 'that if what had been delivered had been beetroot seed or carrot seed, he would not be able to rely upon the clause'. Different counsel appeared for the appellants in the Court of Appeal, where that concession was withdrawn ...

This is the first time your Lordships' House has had to consider a modern statutory provision giving the court power to override contractual terms excluding or restricting liability, which depends on the court's view of what is 'fair and reasonable' ... It may ... be appropriate to consider how an original decision of what is 'fair and reasonable' made in the application of any of these [statutory] provisions should be approached by an appellate court. It would not be accurate to describe such a decision as an exercise of discretion. But ... the court must entertain a whole range of considerations, put them in the scales on one side or the other and decide at the end of the day on which side the balance comes down ...

The question of relative bargaining strength under paragraph (a) and of the opportunity to buy seeds without a limitation of the seedsman's liability under paragraph (b) were inter-related. The evidence was that a similar limitation of liability was universally embodied in the terms of trade between seedsmen and farmers and had been so for very many years. The limitation had never been negotiated between representative bodies but, on the other hand, had not been the subject of any protest by the National Farmers' Union. These factors, if considered in isolation, might have been equivocal. The decisive factor, however, appears from the evidence of four witnesses called for the appellants, two independent seedsmen, the chairman of the appellant company, and a director of a sister company (both being wholly-owned subsidiaries of the same parent). They said that it had always been their practice, unsuccessfully attempted in the instant case, to negotiate settlements of farmers' claims for damages in excess of the price of the seeds, if they thought that the claims were 'genuine' and 'justified'. This evidence indicated a clear recognition by seedsmen in general, and the appellants in particular, that reliance on the limitation of liability imposed by the relevant condition would not be fair or reasonable.

Two further factors, if more were needed, weight the scales in favour of the respondents. The supply of autumn, instead of winter, cabbage seeds was due to the negligence of the appellants' sister company. Irrespective of its quality, the autumn variety supplied could not, according to the appellants' own evidence, be grown commercially in East Lothian. Finally, as the trial judge found, seedsmen could insure against the risk of crop failure caused by supplying the wrong variety of seeds without materially increasing the price of seeds.

My Lords, even if I felt doubts about the statutory issue, I should not, for the reasons explained earlier, think it right to interfere with the unanimous original decision of that issue by the Court of Appeal. As it is, I feel no such doubts. If I were making the original decision, I should conclude without hesitation that would not be fair or reasonable to allow the [defendants] to rely on the contractual limitation of their liability . . ."

QUESTIONS

1. Did fault play a central role in determining the outcome of this case? If so, how can this be reconciled with risk, which is, surely, the notion that underpins insurance?

2. Did the House of Lords base their decision on an issue of fact?

3. Is it now in the contracting parties' interests to consider the insurance position when negotiating contracts?

4. In *Smith v Eric Bush* (1990), Lord Templeman, when considering the reasonableness test in the 1977 Act, said (at 854): 'The public are exhorted to purchase their homes and cannot find houses to rent. . . . In these circumstances it is not fair and reasonable for building societies and valuers to agree together to impose on purchasers the risk of loss arising as a result of incompetence or carelessness on the part of valuers.' Is 'reasonableness' being used here in the same way as it is being used in the *George Mitchell* case?

8.4.8 Reform of exclusion clause legislation

The Law Commission has proposed replacing the two current statutes regulating unfair terms with a single Act. Some of the provisions have already been encountered; others are set out in the next extract.

Unfair Contract Terms Bill 2004

"4. Terms of no effect unless fair and reasonable
(1) If a term of a consumer contract is detrimental to the consumer, the business cannot rely on the term unless the term is fair and reasonable.

(2) But subsection (1) does not apply to a term which defines the main subject matter of a consumer contract, if the definition is—

(a) transparent, and
(b) substantially the same as the definition the consumer reasonably expected.

(3) Nor does subsection (1) apply to a term in so far as it sets the price payable under a consumer contract, if the price is—

(a) transparent,
(b) payable in circumstances substantially the same as those the consumer reasonably expected, and
(c) calculated in a way substantially the same as the way the consumer reasonably expected.

(4) Nor does subsection (1) apply to a term which—

(a) is transparent, and
(b) leads to substantially the same result as would be produced as a matter of law if the term were not included.

(5) The reference to the price payable under a consumer contract does not include any amount, payment of which would be incidental or ancillary to the main purpose of the contract.

(6) 'Price' includes remuneration.

9. Written standard terms
(1) This section applies where one party to a business contract ('A') deals on the written standard terms of business of the other ('B').

(2) Unless the term is fair and reasonable, B cannot rely on any of those terms to exclude or restrict its liability to A for breach of the contract.

(3) Unless the term is fair and reasonable, B cannot rely on any of those terms to claim that it has the right—

(a) to carry out its obligations under the contract in a way substantially different from the way in which A reasonably expected them to be carried out, or
(b) not to carry out all or part of those obligations.

11. Non-negotiated terms
(1) This section applies where there is a small business contract and—

(a) the terms on which one party ('A') deals include a term which the other party ('B') put forward during the negotiation of the contract as one of its written standard terms of business,

(b) the substance of the term was not, as a result of negotiation, changed in favour of A, and

(c) at the time the contract is made, A is a small business.

(2) If that term is detrimental to A, B cannot rely on the term unless the term is fair and reasonable.

(3) But subsection (2) does not apply to a term which defines the main subject matter of a small business contract, if the definition is—

(a) transparent, and

(b) substantially the same as the definition A reasonably expected.

(4) Nor does subsection (2) apply to a term in so far as it sets the price payable under a small business contract, if the price is—

(a) transparent,

(b) payable in circumstances substantially the same as those A reasonably expected, and

(c) calculated in a way substantially the same as the way A reasonably expected.

(5) Nor does subsection (2) apply to a term which—

(a) is transparent, and

(b) leads to substantially the same result as would be produced as a matter of law if the term were not included.

(6) The reference to the price payable under a small business contract does not include any amount, payment of which would be incidental or ancillary to the main purpose of the contract.

(7) 'Price' includes remuneration.

NOTE

See extract from Law Commission Report on *Unfair Terms in Contracts*, Law Com. (No.292, Cm 6464, 2004), above at p.135

8.5 Unenforceable provisions

We have already seen in the previous chapter that certain terms are unenforceable in English law. The main classes of terms are those in restraint of trade (see **5.1.3**; **6.4.5**) and penalty clauses (**7.3.2**). With respect to the latter, see *Workers Trust Bank Ltd v Dojap Ltd* (1993) (p.357); *Jobson v Johnson* (1989) (p.358). One interesting question is whether a breach of contract is essential before equity can intervene with respect to the clause. On this issue, see *Bridge v Campbell Discount Co Ltd* (1962) (read in law report).

8.6 Change of circumstances and hardship

One problem that has troubled contract lawyers for centuries is change of circumstances. This is a problem that affects long-term contracts (see **2.3.3**) and is often dealt with under the Latin heading of *clausula rebus sic stantibus*.

8.6.1 Civil law: *clausula rebus sic stantibus*

We have already seen, with respect to the contents of a contract (see PECL, arts 16:101–16:103, above at p.330), that a condition, in civilian thinking, is a future event that is uncertain in that it may or may not occur. And thus a "contractual obligation may be made conditional upon the occurrence of an uncertain future event, so that the obligation takes effect only if the event occurs (suspensive condition) or comes to an end if the event occurs (resolutive condition)" (PECL, art.16:101). This notion of a condition can be of particular conceptual importance in situations where an unexpected event occurs which destabilises a contractual obligation for one or both of the parties. Can the court imply into the contract a condition that the obligation is dependent upon events remaining the same (*rebus sic stantibus*)?

The canonists and Post-Glossators were prepared to recognise such an implied condition, and this was to be taken up by the subsequent schools of civil law, with the result that the idea found acceptance in German and Italian law (Pichonnaz, *Impossibilité et exorbitance* (Éditions Universitaires Fribourg Suisse, 1997)). In France the position was different. In private law the theory of imprévision was rejected by the *Cour de cassation* in a case where monetary inflation had undermined the commercial viability of a contract, although the *Conseil d'État* took a different view for an administrative contract where inflation threatened to destroy the company that supplied gas to Bordeaux. In this latter situation it was in the public interest that the company should be kept commercially viable. The contemporary *lex mercatoria* has adopted the more liberal approach, and thus while the PECL reaffirm the importance of the binding nature of contractual obligations "even if performance has become more onerous" because of increased costs or devaluation (art.6:111(1)), there is a duty to renegotiate where performance has become "excessively onerous" (art.6:111(2)). A similar duty to renegotiate is to be found in the UNIDROIT code, where a subsequent event "alters the equilibrium" of the contract (art.6.6.2). These international provisions seem now conceptually to be divorced from the implied condition theory, but the power of the court to grant remedies where a party unreasonably fails to renegotiate is historically rooted in the implied agreement of the parties which found its expression in the condition or *clausula rebus sic stantibus*.

8.6.2 English law: no doctrine of change of circumstances

In English law there is no doctrine of change of circumstances, despite the efforts of Lord Denning M.R. to try to introduce one (see *Staffs AHA* (1978), below at p.428). The problem is treated, in so far as it is treated, either as a non-performance and dissolution issue (frustration of contracts: see **10.5**) or as an interpretation question, as the next two extracts well illustrate.

Davis Contractors Ltd v Fareham Urban District Council **[1956] A.C. 696, HL**

This was an action in quasi contractual debt (*quantum meruit*) by a firm of building contractors for expenditure incurred over and above the agreed contract price of £92,425 to build 78 houses. The extra expenditure had been incurred as a result of an unforeseen serious shortage of skilled labour and building materials; and the plaintiffs claimed that the contract itself had been frustrated by these unforeseen shortages. The House of Lords (Viscount Simonds and Lords Morton, Reid, Radcliffe and Somervell) held that the contract had not been not frustrated.

> **Lord Radcliffe:** ". . . Here is a building contract entered into by a housing authority and a big firm of contractors in all the uncertainties of the post-war world. Work was begun shortly before the formal contract was executed and continued, with impediments and minor stoppages but without actual interruption, until the 78 houses contracted for had all been built. After the work had been in progress for a time the appellants raised the claim, which they repeated more than once, that they ought to be paid a larger sum for their work than the contract allowed; but the respondents refused to admit the claim and, so far as appears, no conclusive action was taken by either side which would make the conduct of one or the other a determining element in the case.
>
> That is not in any obvious sense a frustrated contract . . . The contract, it is said, was an eight month contract, as indeed it was. Through no fault of the parties it turned out that it took 22 months to do the work contracted for. The main reason for this was that, whereas both parties had expected that adequate supplies of labour and material would be available to allow for completion in eight months, the supplies that were in fact available were much less than adequate for the purpose. Hence, it is said, the basis or the footing of the contract was removed before the work was completed; or, slightly altering the metaphor, the footing of the contract was so changed by the circumstance that the expected supplies were not available and the contract built upon that footing became void . . .
>
> Two things seem to me to prevent the application of the principle of frustration to this case. One is that the cause of the delay was not any new state of things which the parties could not reasonably be thought to have foreseen. On the contrary, the possibility of enough labour and materials not being available was

before their eyes and could have been the subject of special contractual stipulation. It was not made so. The other thing is that, though timely completion was no doubt important to both sides, it is not right to treat the possibility of delay as having the same significance for each. The owner draws up his conditions in detail, specifies the time within which he requires completion, protects himself both by a penalty clause for time exceeded and by calling for the deposit of a guarantee bond and offers a certain measure of security to a contractor by his escalator clause with regard to wages and prices. In the light of these conditions the contractor makes his tender, and the tender must necessarily take into account the margin of profit that he hopes to obtain upon his adventure and in that any appropriate allowance for the obvious risks of delay. To my mind, it is useless to pretend that the contractor is not at risk if the delay does occur, even serious delay. And I think it a misuse of legal terms to call in frustration to get him out of his unfortunate predicament . . ."

NOTE

What the building firm was trying to do in this case was to say that the contract had disappeared because of a frustrating event (see **10.5**). The contract having disappeared, the contractors would then be entitled to sue in quasi-contract for a sum of money that represented their actual costs. However, the House of Lords said there was no frustration and the contract thus remained valid; the contractors were therefore entitled only to the agreed contract price and the change of circumstances was a risk that they had to bear (for a similar attitude see *William Sindall Plc v Cambridgeshire County Council* (1994), above at p.253). What this case indicates, then, is that there is no doctrine of change of circumstances known to English law; there is only frustration.

QUESTIONS

1. Why should the contractor in *Davis* and not the local authority be the one to shoulder the risk of the unforeseen shortages? Would it be in the public interest to bankrupt the private contractor? Were the shortages to be foreseen or not? Ought they to have been foreseen? What if the houses had been only partially completed and the builders were facing bankruptcy unless the local authority agreed to pay more?

2. Is it a material fact that the builders were a "big firm of contractors"?

3. Could not the courts have implied into a contract a term that if there was a change of circumstances that caused hardship for one of the parties, the contract price could be re-negotiated?

Staffordshire Area Health Authority v South Staffordshire Waterworks [1978] 1 W.L.R. 1387, CA

This was an action for a declaration that an agreement made in 1929 between a water company and a local area health authority could be determined by the water company on reasonable notice and without the consent of the area health authority. The problem arose because the contract to supply the water was made in 1929 at a fixed price that by the 1970s had become unrealistic. Thus the "water company feel that the time has come when the hospital authorities should pay a more reasonable rate. In order to accomplish this, they assert that the 1929 agreement is determinable by six months' notice. Accordingly, on 30th September 1975 they gave notice to the hospital authorities to terminate the agreement as from 30th April 1976. They said that they were quite prepared to supply 5,000 gallons a day free of charge, but they would have to charge for the excess at their normal rate. The area health authority refused to accept this notice as valid. So an originating summons was taken out to determine the matter. Foster J held that the agreement of 1929 was to last forever: and that the hospital authorities could take all the water they desired from the mains at the rate of seven old pence (that is 2.9p) per 1,000 gallons in perpetuity. The water company appeal to this court" (Lord Denning M.R.). The Court of Appeal (Lord Denning M.R., Goff and Cumming-Bruce L.JJ.) granted the declaration.

Lord Denning M.R.: ". . . In 1857 the House of Lords in *Grey v Pearson* ((1857) 6 HL Cas 61) by a majority laid down the so-called 'golden rule' of construction of written instruments. It was said by Lord Cranworth LC (at p 78) that the courts should 'adhere as rigidly as possible to the express words that are found and to give those words their natural and ordinary meaning'. Lord Wensleydale (at p 106) echoed it by saying that 'the grammatical and ordinary sense of the words is to be adhered to'.

That golden rule was the rule of the strict constructionists. It had great influence for the next 100 years. It is still very influential over some minds. It was decisive to the mind of Foster J in this case. The words 'at all times hereafter' were, he said, a 'plain and unambiguous phrase'. They could only mean 'forever or in perpetuity'. He added that 'the mere fact that the agreement has proved to be extremely costly to one of the parties cannot lead the court to change the meaning of plain words'.

Now I quite agree that, if that rule of construction were in force today, Foster J would be right. There is a great deal to be said for his view that the words 'at all times hereafter' are plain and that they mean 'forever or in perpetuity'. Subtle arguments were adduced before us to limit this meaning. Such as that they meant 'at all times during the day and night', or 'at all times during the subsistence of the agreement'. But I confess that, as a matter of strict construction, I cannot read any such limitation into the words.

The rule has now been changed

But I think that the rule of strict construction is now quite out of date. It has been supplanted by the rule that written instruments are to be construed in relation to the circumstances as they were known to or contemplated by the parties; and that even the plainest words may fall to be modified if events occur which the parties never had in mind and in which they cannot have intended the agreement to operate. . . . As I understand this modern rule, we are no longer to go by the strict construction of the words as judges did in the 19th century. We are to put ourselves in the same situation as the parties were in at the time they drew up the instrument, to sit in their chairs with our minds endowed with the same facts as theirs were, and envisage the future with the same degree of foresight as they did. So placed we have to ask ourselves: what were the circumstances in which the contract was made? Does it apply in the least to the new situation which has developed? If events occur for which they have made no provision, and which were outside the realm of their speculations altogether, or of any reasonable persons sitting in their chairs, then the court itself must take a hand and hold that the contract ceases to bind. Such was the rule which I suggested long ago in *British Movietonenews Ltd v London and District Cinemas Ltd* ([1951] 1 KB 190) without success at that time: but which seems to have come into its own now . . .

Contracts which contain no provision for determination

We were taken through six cases which considered contracts which contained no provision for determination. On going through them, they seem to show that, when a person agrees to supply goods or services continuously over an unlimited period of time in return for a fixed monthly or yearly payment, the courts shrink from holding it to be an agreement in perpetuity. The reason is because it is so unequal. The cost of supply of goods and services goes up with inflation through the rooftops: and the fixed payment goes down to the bottom of the well so that it is worth little or nothing. Rather than tolerate such inequality, the courts will construe the contract so as to hold that it is determinable by reasonable notice. They do this by reference to the modern rule of construction. They say that in the circumstances as they have developed, which the parties never had in mind, the contract ceases to bind the parties forever. It can be determined on reasonable notice. . . .

Inflation

From . . . [the] cases it is possible to detect a new principle emerging as to the effect of inflation and the fall in the value of money. In the ordinary way this does not affect the bargain between the parties. . . . But times have changed. We have since had mountainous inflation and the pound dropping to cavernous depths . . . The time has come when we may have to revise our views about the principle of nominalism, as it is called. Dr FA Mann in his book, *The Legal Aspect of Money* (3rd ed (1971), p 100), said: 'If the trend of inflation which has clouded the last few decades continues some relief in the case of long-term obligations will become unavoidable.' That was written in 1971. Inflation has been more rampant than ever since that time. Here we have in the present case a striking instance of a long term obligation entered into 50 years ago. It provided for yearly payments for water supplied at seven old pence a 1,000 gallons. In these 50 years, and especially in the last 10 years, the cost of supplying the water has increased twentyfold. It is likely to increase with every year that passes. Is it right that the hospital should go on forever only paying the old rate of 50 years ago? . . .

So here the situation has changed so radically since the contract was made so many years ago that the term of the contract 'at all times hereafter' ceases to bind: and it is open to the court to hold that the contract is determined by reasonable notice.

Conclusion

I do not think that the water company could have determined the agreement immediately after it was made. That cannot have been intended by the parties. No rule of construction could sensibly permit such a result. But, in the past 50 years, the whole situation has changed so radically that one can say with confidence: 'The parties never intended that the supply should be continued in these days at that price.' Rather than force such unequal terms on the parties, the court should hold that the agreement could be and was properly determined in 1975 by the reasonable notice of six months. This does not mean, of course, that on the expiry of the notice the water company can cut off the supply to the hospital. It will be bound to continue it. All that will happen is that the parties will have to negotiate fresh terms of payment. These should take into account the history from the 1909 Act onwards. In the light of that history, it seems to me plain that the 1929 agreement should be up-dated so as to have regard to the effect of inflation. The hospital should be entitled to 5,000 gallons a day free of charge and pay for the excess at a rate which is 70 per cent of the current market rate. I would commend this solution to these two public authorities in the hope that it will settle their difficulties without troubling the courts further.

So I would grant a declaration in respect of the contract being determinable by reasonable notice but I will say nothing about the declaration as to payment. I would allow the appeal accordingly."

Goff L.J.: "I agree with the result, but I think in some respects my reasoning is not the same as that of Lord Denning MR. . . .

Having weighed all [the] considerations, which I think cover all the ground, I have finally reached the conclusion that the fact that the hospital authorities were not . . . purchasing a facility for a capital cash consideration, that they were being given an unlimited supply at a concessionary rate including the first 5,000 gallons per day entirely free, and that the price was to be fixed once and for all, though it was not so fixed under the 1909 Act, do require the inference of a power to determine on reasonable notice, and outweigh all indications to the contrary. . . .

I agree, therefore, that the appeal should be allowed and that we should make a declaration that the agreement was determinable by reasonable notice and was determined by the letter of 30th September 1975, but that failing agreement between the parties we should refer the question of the effect of determination back to the judge."

Cumming-Bruce L.J.: ". . . I agree with the analysis . . . proposed by Goff LJ and cannot usefully add anything. With all respect to Lord Denning MR, I do not found my decision on the existence of an implied term that the agreement should not continue to bind the parties on the emergence of circumstances which the parties did not then foresee . . ."

QUESTIONS

1. Is *Staffs AHA* (i) a contractual interpretation case (*cf.* **7.2**); (ii) an implied term case (*cf.* **5.5**); or (iii) a hardship case?

2. Was Lord Denning in *Staffs AHA* in effect applying the old implied term theory of frustration (*cf.* **10.5**)? Does *Staffs AHA* conflict with the *Davis Contractors* case (see p.426)? Was Lord Denning getting close to utilising rescission in equity to deal with this contractual problem? Ought the equitable remedy of rescission to be available to deal with change of circumstances problems?

3. If, in *Staffs AHA*, the two parties had been private commercial bodies, would the result of the case have been the same?

4. What method of interpretation does Lord Denning apply in place of the Golden Rule?

5. Is *Staffs AHA* dealing with the public rather than the private interest? Is this important?

NOTE

The rule in *Staffs AHA* seems to have been incorporated into European contract law.

Principles of European Contract Law

"Article 6:109 Contract for an Indefinite Period
A contract for an indefinite period may be ended by either party by giving notice of reasonable length."

8.6.3 **European contract law**

Civil lawyers tend to distinguish between change of circumstances (*imprévision*) and impediment. However, this does not mean that, say, a French court would not reach a result similar to the one reached by the House of Lords in *Davis v Fareham* (1956) (see Cass.Civ 6.3.1876; D.1876.1.193). It is just that impossibility (*impossibilia*) is seen as not being the same as hardship (*difficultas*). The distinction between change of circumstances (hardship) and impediment is a rational one once one distinguishes (which contract theory cannot easily do) between instantaneous and long-term contracts (*cf.* **2.3.3**). Civil lawyers take the view not only that contractual relationships are to be supported wherever possible, but also that the parties to a contract must act in good faith. When these two principles are put together it is easy to see how long-term contracts can give rise to rather special problems. Of course it does not follow that the civil lawyers will automatically set aside a contractual obligation as soon as the going gets tough for one party, and the sanctity of the obligation is given support by UNIDROIT, art.1.3 (above p.385) and art.6.2.1 (below, p.433). But where, say, inflation or shortages become so severe that they threaten the economic existence of one of the parties, it may be that it is not in the general interest that such a party should be allowed to go bankrupt.

Principles of European Contract Law

"**Article 6:111 Change of Circumstances**

(1) A party is bound to fulfil its obligations even if performance has become more onerous, whether because the cost of performance has increased or because the value of the performance it receives has diminished.

(2) If, however, performance of the contract becomes excessively onerous because of a change of circumstances, the parties are bound to enter into negotiations with a view to adapting the contract or terminating it, provided that:

(a) the change of circumstances occurred after the time of conclusion of the contract,

(b) the possibility of a change of circumstances was not one which could reasonably have been taken into account at the time of conclusion of the contract, and

(c) the risk of the change of circumstances is not one which, according to the contract, the party affected should be required to bear.

(3) If the parties fail to reach agreement within a reasonable period, the court may:

(a) terminate the contract at a date and on terms to be determined by the court; or

(b) adapt the contract in order to distribute between the parties in a just and equitable manner the losses and gains resulting from the change of circumstances.

In either case, the court may award damages for the loss suffered through a party refusing to negotiate or breaking off negotiations contrary to good faith and fair dealing."

Unidroit Principles for International Commercial Contracts

"Article 6.2.1 Contract to be Observed
Where the performance of a contract becomes more onerous for one of the parties, that party is nevertheless bound to perform its obligations subject to the following provisions on hardship.

Article 6.2.2 Definition of Hardship
There is hardship where the occurrence of events fundamentally alters the equilibrium of the contract either because the cost of a party's performance has increased or because the value of the performance a party receives has diminished, and

(a) the events occur or become known to the disadvantaged party after the conclusion of the contract;
(b) the events could not reasonably have been taken into account by the disadvantaged party at the time of the conclusion of the contract;
(c) the events are beyond the control of the disadvantaged party; and
(d) the risk of the events was not assumed by the disadvantaged party.

Article 6.2.3 Effects of Hardship
(1) In case of hardship the disadvantaged party is entitled to request renegotiations. The request shall be made without undue delay and shall indicate the grounds on which it is based.

(2) The request for renegotiation does not itself entitle the disadvantaged party to withhold performance.

(3) Upon failure to reach agreement within a reasonable time either party may resort to the court.

(4) If the court finds hardship it may, if reasonable,

(a) terminate the contract at a date and on terms to be fixed; or
(b) adapt the contract with a view to restoring its equilibrium.

QUESTION

Could it be said that these code provisions reflect Lord Denning's judgment in *Staffs AHA*?

8.7 Pre-contractual effects

Logically a contract should be effective only from the point of its formation. However, we have seen that statements made before formation, even if such statements do not ultimately form part of the subsequent contract, can impact upon the contract (see **5.2**). Such statements, if untrue, amount to misrepresentations, allowing the representee to rescind the contract in equity (see *Redgrave v Hurd* (1881), above at p.240). In addition, the representee may be able to sue in tort for damages (Misrepresentation Act 1967, s.2(1), above at p.237). Rescission may equally be available in situations where, before the formation of the contract, a party had exercised duress or undue influence.

Given the existence of these remedies, it becomes possible to talk in terms of pre-contractual duties or obligations. In the civil law the subsequent contract can of itself impose certain pre-contractual obligations, and these obligations can broadly be said to be of two kinds. First, in the German model, there has been recognised a duty by, for example, the owners of commercial premises to ensure that a potential customer is safe from harm while on the premises. Secondly, in the French model, there is now not just an obligation not to make false or misleading statements before contract, but also a positive duty to disclose certain information to the other party. The obvious question for the European contract lawyer is the extent to which English law gives expression to these pre-contractual effects of a contract. With respect to dangerous premises, the duty does not arise from the contract but from the law of tort (see *Ward v Tesco Stores* (1976), above at p.183); and such a duty is the common duty of care (Occupiers' Liability Act 1957, s.2(1)). Pre-contractual disclosure is more sensitive, as *Bell v Lever Brothers* (1932) (above, p.250) indicates.

Paula Giliker, 'Unifying European Contract Law: Identifying a European Pre-contractual Obligation to Inform' in John Bell and Claire Kilpatrick (eds), *Cambridge Yearbook on European Legal Studies 2004–5* (Hart Publishing, 2006), pp.135, 154, 155–6 (footnotes omitted)

"Reviewing the treatment of the duty of disclosure in English and French law, one notes certain obvious structural differences, but also finds a surprising degree of similarity. The use of contractual warranties may be compared with the concept of *vices cachés*; misrepresentation with *erreur* and *dol*. One sees similar forms of statutory intervention, for example in the field of insurance contracts and comparable treatment of fiduciary contracts. This is taken a step further by the *acquis communautaire*. Certain core European principles of disclosure have been introduced to member States by virtue of EC Directives, notably in the field of consumer law. Amongst the numerous examples, one might note, for example, the impact of the Sale of Consumer Goods Directive of 1999, which protects parties who have relied upon advertising and public statements in purchasing the goods. Equally, Directive 90/314/EEC on Package Travel, Package Holidays, and

Package Tours provides a detailed set of rules that seek to ensure that consumers are fully informed of their rights when entering such contracts. Consumer credit agreements also benefit from the protection given to parties under Directive 87/102/EEC concerning consumer credit. Such provisions affect every Member State and ensure a minimum level of disclosure regardless of pre-existing national law. . . .

My study reveals no structural obstacle to such [a pre-contractual] obligation. It is important not to be distracted by the different legal framework. . . . However, an obstacle does exist that, I submit, provides a real barrier to harmonisation, namely the disparate reasoning of the national courts. . . .

Let me illustrate. For the French courts, with limited exceptions, liability is seen in terms of contractual morality or, if one prefers, a duty of good faith. Ghestin, for example, highlights the inequality of the parties to which good faith requires a response. To take advantage of one's position and allow the other party to enter a contract *knowing* that he or she has a material misunderstanding of the situation is seen as an unfair advantage that the courts should undo. One is thus left with a regime which is openly protective and where the *solidarité* of contract law is seen as a necessary part of any contracting culture.

In contrast, English law manifests a clear reluctance to impose a duty on a party to intervene. A relationship is required—either that of contract or extremely close proximity—before such a step could be contemplated. One notes a continuing regard for the doctrine of freedom of contract, certainty and political liberalism. This may, as has been suggested, derive to a certain extent from the commercial character of much of the litigation that reaches the higher courts, but these values continue to influence the courts' general interpretation of basic contractual concepts. Such analysis has been supported in recent years by economic theory that provides a justification for non-disclosure based on the cost of information acquisition and the social utility of incentives which promote the efficient generation of information. Where one party has invested time and money in gathering information, on what basis, it is asked, should he or she be required to disclose this information gratuitously? . . .

Such economic arguments have, until recently, had limited impact in France. The courts' motivation, as we have seen, is to prevent exploitation. It is *morale*, not economic. Such arguments have also been regarded as 'Anglo-Saxon' and based on the prevalent right wing, market-orientated values of the United States. . . . Fabre-Magnan indeed is one of the few authors to address economic theory. She nevertheless concludes that, whilst helpful, it can only be part of any theory of law and that analysis cannot be taken in isolation from the moral context. Fontaine, reviewing formation of contract in 2002, agrees that 'our legal system prefers other values'. . . ."

QUESTIONS

1. Would you describe Lord Atkin's judgment in *Bell v Lever Brothers* (1932) (p.250) as one influenced by right-wing, market-orientated values of the United States?

2. Is the *acquis communautaire* in respect of pre-contractual obligations a body of law influenced by left-wing anti-market values of certain European countries?

3. Does European contract law treat consumers as lacking in full contractual capacity?

NOTE

See also **4.5**.

8.8 Post-contractual effects

Just as the contractual obligation—especially, in civilian thinking, the obligation of good faith—can reach backward, so to speak, to encompass the pre-contractual stage, so logically the contractual obligation can reach forward to encompass the post-contractual stage. This is particularly true with respect to confidential information obtained by a contractual party during the period when the contract was in operation. When the contract ends (e.g. an employment contract, where an employee leaves one employer for another) certain obligations may well remain alive, such as the obligation with respect to confidential information.

Thomas Marshall Ltd v Guinle [1979] Ch.227, Ch D

This was an action for an injunction brought by an ex-employer against an ex-employee. The employee had been contracted to work for the claimant for 10 years, and there were terms in the contract that he should neither work for any other employer nor disclose confidential information. The defendant resigned from his employment before the end of the 10–year period and the question arose as to whether the terms were still effective despite the ending of the contract. The Vice-Chancellor held that they were.

Sir Robert Megarry V-C: "... I shall take first Mr Hutchison's submission that the defendant's service agreement was terminated by his unilateral repudiation of it on December 5, 1977, even though the company never accepted it as ending the agreement. This is a striking contention. It means that although the defendant and the company contractually bound themselves together for ten years from September 2, 1972, so that the agreement still has over $4\frac{1}{2}$ years to run, the defendant, and also the company, was able at any time, without the consent of the other, to bring the contract to an end simply by saying so; and that is just what the defendant has done. ...

Above all, I think the courts must be astute to prevent a wrongdoer from profiting too greatly from his wrong. If without just cause a servant who has

---

contracted to serve for a term of years refuses to do so, it is easy to see that the court is powerless to make him do what he has contracted to do: neither by decreeing specific performance nor by granting an injunction can the court make the servant perform loyally what he is refusing to do, however wrongfully. If such an order were to be made, the ultimate sanction for disobedience is committal to prison; and this, far from forcing the servant to work for his master, would effectively stop him from doing this. But why should the court's inability to make a servant work for his employer mean that as soon as the servant refuses to do so the court is forthwith disabled from restraining him from committing any breach, however flagrant, of his other obligations during the period of his contract? I would wholly reject the doctrine of automatic determination, whether in its wide form or in its narrowed version.

I accept, of course, that there are difficulties in almost any view that one takes. To say that a contract of service remains in existence despite the servant's resolute refusal to do any work under it produces odd results. Here, however, I am concerned only with the issue whether the servant's wrongful refusal to serve has set him free of the obligations which bound him while his contract of service continued. Furthermore, since what is before me is a mere motion for an interlocutory injunction, strictly speaking all that I have to do before I turn to consider the balance of convenience is to see whether there is a serious question to be tried, and whether the company has any real prospect of succeeding at the trial: see *In re Lord Cable, decd* [1977] 1 WLR 7, 19. To these questions I would answer with an unhesitating Yes. But, as I have mentioned, the interlocutory stage is so important to both parties that I have examined the authorities in some detail, and I think it right, for their assistance, to express my views more fully. I may summarise them as follows. First, in my judgment the service agreement between the parties has not been determined but remains still in force. Second, the defendant is subject to all the obligations that flow from his being bound by the service agreement. Third, as the service agreement is still in force, clause J.2, which provides for the defendant to be free from restrictions when he ceases to be managing director, has not come into operation, and that is so whether or not the two provisos are satisfied. Fourth, there is ample jurisdiction in the court to grant an injunction to restrain the defendant from doing acts contrary to his obligations under the service agreement, subject always to the exercise of the court's discretion whether to grant an injunction at all, and, if so, in what width . . ."

QUESTIONS

1. Is this a good faith case?

2. Is this an unjust enrichment case?

3. Did the terms of the contract continue to live on despite the ending of the employment relationship? Or did the contract actually remain in existence

subject only to the rule that it would not be specifically enforced in equity (*cf.* **12.1**)?

NOTE

On the remedy of injunction, see **12.2**.

9 Performance of a contract

In many ways this chapter is both the key chapter to the whole book yet the most difficult conceptually to construct. The reason for this is that it brings together aspects of all the other chapters—in particular the chapters on structure and content and on remedies—while at the same time raising difficult questions about the nature and effects of a contract, and about the relationship between failures in performance and remedies available. The conceptual difficulty is increased when contract is studied in a European context, because the civil law and the common law often use differing concepts as well as starting out from rather different positions. Yet the comparative approach has its benefits: it can help contract students appreciate the nature and range of problems likely to arise in contractual disputes. Furthermore, performance questions raise issues of method: many cases can depend as much upon the way a problem is analysed and argued in court as upon the actual contractual rules that will come into play. In addition, performance of contracts can encompass questions about the domain of contract; that is to say, performance can raise issues of non-contractual as well as contractual liability. Lastly, performance helps emphasise the important difference between types of contractual terms: there are those that are formulated by the parties themselves; there are those resulting from the nature of the contract and (or) the status of one or both of the parties; and there are those imposed, so to speak, from outside. In short, performance can highlight the contrast between private promises and public regulation.

9.1 Performance and non-performance

Contracts are about performance expectations. The buyer of an onion expects to receive a reasonable onion and the seller expects to be paid. The householder who hires a window cleaner to clean all his 20 windows expects that they will be satisfactorily washed, while the cleaner expects to be paid the agreed price for his work. In the world of commerce, the hirer of a ship expects to receive a seaworthy boat, while the owner of the vessel expects to be paid the hire charge promptly at the end of each month (or whenever). Statistically, most of these expectations are met— most contracts, in other words, are performed satisfactorily—and were this not to be the case, trade, commerce and consumerism would probably grind to a halt. The law could certainly not handle statistically large numbers of unsatisfactorily performed contracts. When small things do go wrong—the consumer goods that are slightly defective, the hired crane that breaks down—the supplier is usually quick to act, either exchanging goods or handing back any money paid. Most of the famous high street stores have not made their names (at least in more recent years) by giving consumers poor value, and when the boss of one such store informed his clientele that his shops sold nothing but "crap", neither he nor his company's chain of stores lasted much longer. But when one talks of "expectations", what exactly is a contracting party entitled to expect?

Principles of European Contract Law

"Article 6:108 Quality of Performance
If the contract does not specify the quality, a party must tender performance of at least average quality."

Unidroit Principles for International Commercial Contracts

"Article 5.6 Determination of Quality of Performance
Where the quality of performance is neither fixed by, nor determinable from, the contract a party is bound to render a performance of a quality that is reasonable and not less than average in the circumstances.

Article 7.1.1 Non-performance Defined
Non-performance is failure by a party to perform any of its obligations under the contract, including defective performance or late performance."

NOTES AND QUESTIONS

1. It is easy enough to state that performance must be reasonable and of average quality, but translating this into factual realities is more difficult. A buyer purchases a new car with a small but annoying scratch on it side. A passenger buys from a station bookstall a magazine or paperback book which turns out to have some torn pages. The window cleaner hired to clean all 20 windows misses out one or two. Can we talk here of reasonable or average quality? How is such a test to be applied? If the car works mechanically, with no problems whatsoever, and the magazine or book is quite readable despite the torn pages, do not these items fulfil their functions? But could it be said that a new car has an aesthetic function as well as a mechanical one? Yet if this is the case, what kind of harm does the buyer of the new car suffer as a result of the scratch? If one says that it is a form of mental rather than mechanical harm then one has to ask the further questions about "expectations". Is the consumer entitled to the fulfilment of mental as well as physical expectations?

2. With respect to services, the position is no easier. What is average quality with regard to window cleaning? Ought not the householder who finds that 19 out of his 20 windows have been cleaned well, be reasonably satisfied?

3. Just as difficult is the relationship between quality and the contract itself. It may be that objectively the consumer has received, physically and econom-

ically, excellent quality, but that this quality does not actually accord with the specifications in the contract. For example, a contractor stipulates very precisely the type and quality of materials to be used in a construction job; if the constructor uses better quality, but different, materials, can it be said that the contractor has received reasonable performance? In other words, are "quality" and "reasonableness" to be judged objectively (what the reasonable bystander might think) or subjectively (what the contractor subjectively desired)? This problem lies at the heart of the next two extracts.

The Liddesdale [1900] A.C. 190, PC

This was an action in debt brought by a firm of ship repairers in respect of repairs carried out on a ship called the *Liddesdale*. The work done was good work, but it was not in accordance with the contract, and the owner of the ship argued that he never agreed to any variation. The Privy Council (Lords Hobhouse, Davey and Robertson, and Sir Richard Couch) dismissed the claim.

> **Lord Hobhouse:** "This suit is in form a proceeding in the Vice-Admiralty Court to make the ship *Liddesdale* answerable for the cost of repairs executed upon her. In substance it does not differ from other litigations between one who has done work on a chattel and the owner of the chattel who denies his liability to pay for it
> . . .
>
> In the case of *Appleby v Myers* Lord Blackburn mentions two conditions under which a contractor for a lump sum who has not performed the stipulated work can recover something under his contract. He can do so if he has been prevented by the defendant from performing his work, or if a new contract has been made that he shall be paid for the work he has actually done. Their Lordships are clearly in agreement with the learned judges below that there is no evidence to support either of these conditions, and it is not necessary to travel into further detail upon this point . . .
>
> . . . There is no doubt that many repairs were executed according to contract; but the cost cannot be recovered, because the contract is an entire one, and in its entirety has never been performed . . .
>
> The result is that their Lordships concur with the learned judge below in his conclusions, and for the most part on the same grounds as are taken by him. It seems hard that the plaintiffs should not be paid for work which they have done; but such is the effect of contracting to work for a lump sum and failing to do the work. It would be hard upon the defendants if they were made to pay for work which they did their best to prevent. And it must be said that the plaintiffs have done a great deal to bring the hardship upon themselves by careless, irregular proceedings in relying on verbal orders, or on the mere presence and knowledge of Watson and Clark, as if they were equivalent to orders coming from the owners, whom the plaintiffs knew to be directing the business. . . ."

QUESTIONS

1. Was the owner of the ship enriched at the expense of the plaintiffs? Was he unjustly enriched?

2. Would this case be decided the same way today?

Ruxley Electronics Ltd v Forsyth **[1996] 1 A.C. 344, HL**

Lord Jauncey: "My Lords, the respondent entered into a contract with the appellants for the construction by them of a swimming pool at his house in Kent. The contract provided for the pool having a maximum depth of 7 feet 6 inches but, as built, its maximum depth was only 6 feet. The respondents sought to recover as damages for breach of contract the cost of demolition of the existing pool and construction of a new one of the required depth. The trial judge made the following findings which are relevant to this appeal: (1) the pool as constructed was perfectly safe to dive into; (2) there was no evidence that the shortfall in depth had decreased the value of the pool; (3) the only practicable method of achieving a pool of the required depth would be to demolish the existing pool and reconstruct a new one at a cost of £21,560; (4) he was not satisfied that the respondent intended to build a new pool at such a cost; (5) in addition such cost would be wholly disproportionate to the disadvantage of having a pool of a depth of only 6 feet as opposed to 7 feet 6 inches and it would therefore be unreasonable to carry out the works; and (6) that the respondent was entitled to damages for loss of amenity in the sum of £2,500.

The Court of Appeal by a majority (Staughton and Mann LJ, Dillon LJ dissenting) allowed the appeal holding that the only way in which the respondent could achieve his contractual objective was by reconstructing the pool at a cost of £21,560 which was accordingly a reasonable venture. . . .

I take the example suggested during argument by my noble and learned friend, Lord Bridge of Harwich. A man contracts for the building of a house and specifies that one of the lower courses of brick should be blue. The builder uses yellow brick instead. In all other respects the house conforms to the contractual specification. To replace the yellow bricks with blue would involve extensive demolition and reconstruction at a very large cost. It would clearly be unreasonable to award to the owner the cost of reconstructing because his loss was not the necessary cost of reconstruction of his house, which was entirely adequate for its design purpose, but merely the lack of aesthetic pleasure which he might have derived from the sight of blue bricks. Thus in the present appeal the respondent has acquired a perfectly serviceable swimming pool, albeit one lacking the specified depth. His loss is thus not the lack of a useable pool with consequent need to construct a new one. Indeed were he to receive the cost of building a new one and retain the existing one he would have recovered not compensation for loss but a very substantial gratuitous benefit, something which damages are not intended to provide.

What constitutes the aggrieved party's loss is in every case a question of fact and degree. Where the contract breaker has entirely failed to achieve the contractual objective it may not be difficult to conclude that the loss is the necessary cost of achieving that objective. Thus if a building is constructed so defectively that it is of no use for its designed purpose the owner may have little difficulty in establishing that his loss is the necessary cost of reconstructing. Furthermore in taking reasonableness into account in determining the extent of loss it is reasonableness in relation to the particular contract and not at large. Accordingly if I contracted for the erection of a folly in my garden which shortly thereafter suffered a total collapse it would be irrelevant to the determination of my loss to argue that the erection of such a folly which contributed nothing to the value of my house was a crazy thing to do. . . .

However where the contractual objective has been achieved to a substantial extent the position may be very different.

It was submitted that where the objective of a building contract involved satisfaction of a personal preference the only measure of damages available for a breach involving failure to achieve such satisfaction was the cost of reinstatement. In my view this is not the case. Personal preference may well be a factor in reasonableness and hence in determining what loss has been suffered but it cannot per se be determinative of what that loss is.

My Lords, the trial judge found that it would be unreasonable to incur the cost of demolishing the existing pool and building a new and deeper one. In so doing he implicitly recognised that the respondent's loss did not extend to the cost of reinstatement. He was, in my view, entirely justified in reaching that conclusion. It therefore follows that the appeal must be allowed. . . .

The second matter relates to the award of £2,500 for loss of amenity made by the trial judge. The respondent argued that he erred in law in making such award. However as the appellant did not challenge it, I find it unnecessary to express any opinion on the matter."

Lord Mustill: ". . . It is a common feature of small building works performed on residential property that the cost of the work is not fully reflected by an increase in the market value of the house, and that comparatively minor deviations from specification or sound workmanship may have no direct financial effect at all. Yet the householder must surely be entitled to say that he chose to obtain from the builder a promise to produce a particular result because he wanted to make his house more comfortable, more convenient and more conformable to his own particular tastes; not because he had in mind that the work might increase the amount which he would receive if, contrary to expectation, he thought it expedient in the future to exchange his home for cash. To say that in order to escape unscathed the builder has only to show that to the mind of the average onlooker, or the average potential buyer, the results which he has produced seem just as good as those which he had promised would make a part of the promise illusory, and unbalance the bargain. In the valuable analysis contained in *Radford v De Froberville* [1977] 1 WLR 1262, Oliver J emphasised, at p 1270, that it was for the plaintiff to judge what performance he required in exchange for the price. The court should honour that choice. Pacta sunt servanda. If the appellant's argument leads to the conclusion that in all cases like the present the employer is entitled to no more than nominal damages, the average householder would say that there must be something wrong with the law.

In my opinion there would indeed be something wrong if, on the hypothesis that cost of reinstatement and the depreciation in value were the only available measures of recovery, the rejection of the former necessarily entailed the adoption of the latter; and the court might be driven to opt for the cost of reinstatement, absurd as the consequence might often be, simply to escape from the conclusion that the promisor can please himself whether or not to comply with the wishes of the promise which, as embodied in the contract, formed part of the consideration for the price. Having taken on the job the contractor is morally as well as legally obliged to give the employer what he stipulated to obtain, and this obligation ought not to be devalued. In my opinion however the hypothesis is not correct. There are not two alternative measures of damage, at opposite poles, but only one; namely, the loss truly suffered by the promisee. In some cases the loss cannot be fairly measured except by reference to the full cost of repairing the deficiency in performance. In others, and in particular those where the contract is designed to fulfil a purely commercial purpose, the loss will very often consist only of the monetary detriment brought about by the breach of contract. But these remedies are not exhaustive, for the law must cater for those occasions where the value of the promise to the promisee exceeds the financial enhancement of his position which full performance will secure. This excess, often referred to in the literature as the 'consumer surplus' (see for example the valuable discussion by Harris, Ogus and Philips (1979) 95 LQR 581) is usually incapable of precise valuation in terms of money, exactly because it represents a personal, subjective and non-monetary gain. Nevertheless where it exists the law should recognise it and compensate the promisee if the misperformance takes it away. The lurid bathroom tiles, or the grotesque folly instanced in argument by my noble and learned friend, Lord Keith of Kinkel, may be so discordant with general taste that in purely economic terms the builder may be said to do the employer a favour by failing to install them. But this is too narrow and materialistic a view of the transaction. Neither the contractor nor the court has the right to substitute for the employer's individual expectation of performance a criterion derived from what ordinary people would regard as sensible. As my Lords have shown, the test of reasonableness plays a central part in determining the basis of recovery, and will indeed be decisive in a case such as the present when the cost of reinstatement would be wholly disproportionate to the non-monetary loss suffered by the employer. But it would be equally unreasonable to deny all recovery for such a loss. The amount may be small, and since it cannot be quantified directly there may be room for difference of opinion about what it should be. But in several fields the judges are well accustomed to putting figures to intangibles, and I see no reason why the imprecision of the exercise should be a barrier, if that is what fairness demands. . . ."

[Lords Lloyd, Bridge and Keith delivered judgments allowing the appeal.]

(For further extracts, see pp.523, 542.)

NOTES AND QUESTIONS

1. Mr Forsyth was not the original claimant in this case. The original action was one in debt for the price of constructing the pool, brought by Ruxley against Mr Forsyth who was refusing to pay because, in his view, Ruxley had not performed their contractual promise. Faced with the action in debt, Mr Forsyth used this action to launch his counterclaim in damages. Why do you think he might have done this? Why did he not just sit tight and say that there had not been contractual performance?

2. Mr Forsyth was a very tall man and wished to be able to dive into his pool without fear of hitting his head on the bottom. Did the claimants (Ruxley) substantially perform the contract according to the legitimate expectation of Mr Forsyth? If they did not, how can one say that "the contractual objective has been achieved"? If the contractual objective had not been achieved, why should Mr Forsyth have to pay for the pool?

3. Should the trial judge ever have been entitled, in a contract case where the contract specified certain measurements, to come to the conclusion that the swimming pool was reasonable? Would a jury (who would have decided this question if the case had arisen in the 19th century) have come to this result?

4. Does *Ruxley* undermine consumer protection rights against builders?

5. Is there now a principle that contracts must be enforced in a reasonable way?

6. Is *Ruxley* (i) a proportionality, and/or (ii) a good faith case?

7. Whose interests and/or expectations were being protected in this breach of contract case?

8. Is *Ruxley* an example of economic theory being used to decide a case?

9. Are the facts of *The Liddesdale* different from those in *Ruxley* in a number of important ways?

FURTHER NOTE

Mr Forsyth's original remedy, as has been mentioned, was the self-help one of refusing to pay (*cf.* **12.6**). A victim of a non-performing contactor has the right to refuse to carry out his obligation, usually an obligation to pay a price: see *Vigers v Cook* (1919) (p.453) and *Bolton v Mahadeva* (1972) (p.554). However, the victim has the right to refuse to pay only if there has been a non-performance of an entire contract, i.e. one that is not divisible into parts where a portion of the total payment is payable on the completion of each part (building contracts are not usually entire contracts). With regard to defective performance of an entire contract, this must be serious enough to amount to a non-performance (*Bolton v Mahadeva* (1972), at p.454). If the performance is "substantial" then the victim does not have the right to refuse to pay.

Hoenig v Isaacs **[1952] 2 All E.R. 176, CA**

This was an action in debt for the balance outstanding in respect of decoration and furnishing work carried out in the defendant's flat. The defendant claimed that the plaintiff had not performed the contract, and it was found at first instance that although the contract had been substantially performed, there were some defects in the workmanship which would cost just under £56 to put right. The Court of Appeal (Somervell, Denning and Romer L.JJ.) held that the plaintiff was entitled to the outstanding balance of £350 less the cost of the defects by way of set-off.

> **Denning L.J.:** ". . . In determining this issue the first question is whether, on the true construction of the contract, entire performance was a condition precedent to payment. It was a lump sum contract, but that does not mean that entire performance was a condition precedent to payment. When a contract provides for a specific sum to be paid on completion of specified work, the courts lean against a construction of the contract which would deprive the contractor of any payment at all simply because there are some defects or omissions. The promise to complete the work is, therefore, construed as a term of the contract, but not as a condition. It is not every breach of that term which absolves the employer from his promise to pay the price, but only a breach which goes to the root of the contract, such as an abandonment of the work when it is only half done. Unless the breach does go to the root of the matter, the employer cannot resist payment of the price. He must pay it and bring a cross-claim for the defects and omissions, or, alternatively, set them up in diminution of the price . . . It is, of course, always open to the parties by express words to make entire performance a condition precedent . . .
>
> Even if entire performance was a condition precedent, nevertheless, the result would be the same, because I think the condition was waived . . . [The defendant] did not refuse to accept the work. On the contrary, he entered into possession of the flat and used the furniture as his own, including the defective items. That was

a clear waiver of the condition precedent. Just as in a sale of goods the buyer who accepts the goods can no longer treat a breach of condition as giving a right to reject but only a right to damages, so also in a contract for work and labour an employer who takes the benefit of the work can no longer treat entire performance as a condition precedent, but only as a term giving rise to damages . . ."

QUESTIONS

1. Is *Ruxley Electronics v Forsyth* (1996) a substantial performance case? If so, why was it not argued along these lines? Are the facts of *Ruxley* and *Hoenig* in reality very different?

2. At what point does non-performance become substantial performance? The window cleaner who cleans only 20 of the 30 windows: has she performed the contract sufficiently enough to entitle her to, say, two-thirds of the agreed contract price?

3. What if, because of a sudden shortage in builders and decorators, the flat owner in *Hoenig* had been given quotes never less than £300 to put the defects right? Would he have been justified in these circumstances in refusing to pay the plaintiff?

9.2 Performance and the role of fault

The performance issue has so far focused on the main contractual promise—the promise to supply goods that meet expectations, the promise to clean all of the windows, or the promise to build something that conforms to the contractual stipulation. However, the notion of performance encompasses much more. What if, for example, the window cleaner manages to break one of the householder's valuable garden gnomes? Or what if the window cleaner falls from his ladder as a result of one of the windows being severely defective? Here performance must be related to implied terms (*cf.* **7.4**). Thus in *The Moorcock* (1889) (above, at p.373), the owner of the damaged ship was, of course, complaining of defective performance of the contract by the wharf owner. Implied terms in turn must be related to the level of duty: what did the contractor promise? Did the contractor promise a result, or just to use skill and care (*cf.* UNIDROIT, art.5.4, above at p.379)? This, in its turn, may well be related to the nature of the contract, contracts of service being differentiated from contracts to supply goods (see **2.3.2**).

9.2.1 Fault in the civil law

There is another way of viewing this problem: one can, as in Roman law, simple start out from the facts and search for fault.

Digest of Roman Law Book 13, Title 6 (*commodati vel contra*)

5. ULPIAN, *Edict,* **book 28** ". . . 2. Now let us see what is to be taken into account in the action on a loan for use, whether it is wilful wrongdoing (*dolus*) or fault (*culpa*) or in fact any risk (*omne periculum*). And indeed in contracts sometimes one is liable for *dolus* alone sometimes for *culpa* as well; *dolus* in deposit, for, because there is no interest (*utilitas*) of the depositee that is engaged, it is right that he is liable for dolus alone; unless perhaps payment is attached (for then, because of an imperial enactment (*constitutio*), fault is taken account of as well) or if it was agreed at the outset that the depositee is to be liable for both *culpa* and *periculum*. But where the interest of each party is advanced such as in sale, hire, dowry, pledge or partnership, one is liable for *dolus* and *culpa*. . . . 4. In fact where something happened through old age or illness, or something is taken by robbers or something similar happens, it is laid down that no liability for this loss is to be imputed to the borrower, unless fault is to be found on his part. Consequently if a fire or collapse of a building happens or some similar fateful damage he is not liable, unless by chance he might have saved the things borrowed, he preferred to save his own. . . . 7. But occasionally loss arising from death falls on the one who asked for the loan: thus if I lend you a horse for you to take to your country house, and you take it to war, you will be held liable on the contract of loan. The same applies with regard to a slave. It is obvious if I lent it so that you were to take it to war the risk (*periculum*) is mine. For if I lend you a slave plasterer and he falls from the scaffolding Namusa holds the risk to be mine. But I think this is right if I have lent him to you in order to work on the scaffolding; but if he was to work on the ground, and you ordered him up the scaffolding, or if the scaffolding is faulty through having been tied together, not by him, with lack of care or with old ropes or poles, I say the accident, which has happened through the fault of the person who asked for the loan, ought to be the responsibility of the borrower himself. For Mela has written, if a borrowed slave stone-cutter died under scaffolding, the artisan is liable to an action on loan for use because he has negligently fastened together the scaffolding. 8. In addition one who puts the thing lent for use to some other use, not only will he be held liable for an action on the loan, but also for an action for theft. . . . 10. It is clear that on occasions the person who asks for a loan will be liable for *dolus* alone, as for instance if this is what he agreed; or if the loan relates only to his interest (*causa*), as by chance to his fiancée or wife so that she might be dressed in a dignified manner when brought to him . . ."

NOTE

The point to note here is that this analysis by the great classical jurist Ulpian is identical to the methodological analysis taken in non-contractual liability cases.

Digest of Roman Law **Book 9, Title 2** (*ad legem aquiliam*)

52. ALFENUS, *Digest, book 2* ". . . 2. On Capitoline hill mules were pulling two loaded wagons; the drivers of the first wagon which had tilted up were supporting it so as to make it easier for the mules to pull it; however while doing this the first cart started to roll backwards and when the drivers, who had been between the two wagons, had got out of the way, the rear cart was hit by the one in front and moved back and crushed someone or other's slave boy. The owner of the slave boy asked me against whom he should claim. I replied that the law was to be found in the facts of the case (*respondi in causa ius esse positum*). For if the drivers who were supporting the wagon got themselves out of the way on their own accord and it was as a result of this fact that the mules were not able to hold the wagon and were themselves dragged back by the load, then no action could be brought against the owner of the mules. However with respect to the men who were holding up the tilted wagon a claim under the *lex Aquilia* could be brought; for it is no less the doing of damage he who voluntarily lets go of something he is holding up so that it hits something; for example if someone who steers an ass does not restrain it, he would do wrongful damage in the same way as if he had discharged a spear or anything else from his hand. But if the mules behaved in the way they did because they were frightened by something, and the drivers left the wagon fearing they would be crushed, while no action could be brought against the men, an action could be brought against the owner of the mules. However if neither mules nor men were the cause, but the mules could not hold up the weight, or while trying slipped and fell and the wagon went backwards and the men had been unable to bear the weight of it when the wagon tilted over, neither the owner of the mules nor the men would be open to an action. What is indeed certain, whatever the situation in this affair, is that no claim could be made against the owner of the mules pulling the wagon behind, for they did not go back on their own accord but because they were hit and pushed backwards."

NOTES

1. The piece of text from D.13.6.5 (Ulpian) might at first sight seem mundane, but it is the foundation for the modern civil law of contractual liability. It establishes that the starting point for such liability is fault, and it shows how, at the level of liability, there is a close relationship between contractual and delictual (tortious) actions (*cf.* D.9.2.52.2). The methodology applicable, in other words, is the same as in the Roman law of tort: Dig.9.2.52.2 (Alfenus) (which could easily have been a contract case as well if, say, the owner of the slave boy was the contractor of the wagons). We shall see that the search for fault lurking beneath contractual facts can be on occasions just as relevant to some English cases: see e.g. *Joseph Constantine v Imperial Smelting Corpn* (1942) (p.467) and *The Moorcock* (1889) (p.373).

2. Modern civil law has moved away from the Roman casuistic approach (reasoning at the level of facts, often by analogy) to an "axiomatic" method

(reasoning by deduction from abstract principles). Accordingly the law expressed in D.13.6.5 and D.9.2.52.2 is set out differently.

Code civil (1804)

"**1147**. A debtor is judged liable, if there are grounds for it, to the payment of damages, either by reason of the non-performance of the obligation or by reason of delay in the performance at all times when he does not prove that the non-performance came from an outside cause (*cause étrangère*) which cannot be imputed to him, and further that there was no bad faith on his part.

1148. No damages arise when, as result of an act of God or of a fortuitous event (*force majeure*), the debtor was prevented from giving or doing that for which he had bound himself, or did what was forbidden to him.

1382. Any human act whatever which causes damage to another obliges him by whose fault it occurred to make reparation."

NOTE

Fault, in short, underpins the theory of *liability* in Continental contract law.

GH Treitel, *Remedies for Breach of Contract: A Comparative Account* (OUP, 1988), p.8 (footnotes omitted)

"9. *Requirement of fault in civil law*. Civil law systems start with the theory that fault is a requirement for the availability of contractual remedies. The theory finds its clearest expression in § 276 of the German Civil Code, which states the general principle that 'the debtor is responsible for deliberate acts and negligence'. The same general principle is accepted in Austria and Switzerland. It can be explained on the ground that contract is regarded by these systems as part of the general law of obligations. Hence the fault principle which (at least until recently) seemed to be an obvious general requirement in delict was carried over to contract. But the general principle is subject to two exceptions, so that there are now many cases in which contractual liability is strict; and the practical importance of these 'exceptional' cases may have become at least as great as that of the cases that fall within the 'general rule' requiring fault. Perhaps for this reason the orthodox approach of a 'general' requirement of fault, subject to these exceptions, has been viewed with scepticism by some civil lawyers. But there is no doubt that the civil law does recognise two categories of cases, ie those in which fault is an essential ingredient of contractual liability, and those in which such liability is strict."

NOTE

See UNIDROIT, art.5.4 (above, p.379).

9.2.2 Fault in the common law

When one turns to the common law, the starting point seems, at first sight, rather different.

> **GH Treitel,** *Remedies for Breach of Contract: A Comparative Account* **(OUP, 1988), pp.8–9 (footnotes omitted)**
>
> "**10.** *Whether fault required in common law systems.* The common law has devoted little attention to the question whether fault is a requirement of contractual liability. The general assumption probably is that there is no such requirement. Thus in England it has been said that: 'In relation to a claim for damages for breach of contract, it is, in general, immaterial why the defendant failed to fulfil his obligations and certainly no defence to plead that he had done his best' [*Raineri v Miles* [1981] AC 1050, 1086]. Moreover, the question whether fault is a requirement is thought to be relevant to definitions of breach (rather than to discussions of remedies); and it is uncommon to find in such definitions any reference to 'fault' . . . The proposition that the failure in performance must occur *'without justification'* leaves open the question whether lack of 'fault' can provide a justification. . . . The common law . . . thus has a structure which is the exact opposite of that of the civil law systems mentioned above: that is, it starts from the general principle of strict liability but this is subject to significant exceptions under which liability is based on fault."

NOTE

Compare s.14 of the Sale of Goods Act 1979 (above, at p.60) with s.13 of the Supply of Goods and Services Act 1982 (above, at p.381). See also *Frost v Aylesbury Dairy* (1905) (p.61); *Thake v Maurice* (1986) (p.63); *Hyman v Nye* (1881) (p.376); *Readhead v Midland Ry* (1869) (p.377); *Greaves & Co (Contractors) Ltd v Baynham Meikle & Partners* (1975) (p.380); and *Barclays Bank Plc v Fairclough Building Ltd* (1995) (p.381).

QUESTION

Is it true to say that the common law has devoted little attention to the question of fault in contract?

> *Joseph Constantine SS Ltd v Imperial Smelting Co Ltd* **[1942] A.C. 154, HL**
>
> (For facts, see p.467.)
>
> **Lord Porter:** ". . . The true principle seems to be, not that all contracts must prima facie be performed whether performance be possible or not but that there are some contracts absolute in their nature where the promisor warrants the

possibility of performance. These he is bound to perform in any event or to pay damages, but there are other cases where the promisor is only obliged to perform if he can. In a contract for personal performance where he dies, or in certain other cases where the subject-matter of the contract is destroyed, he cannot implement his promise. In such cases he is excused unless he be in fault. Of course, if he is in fault because his deliberate act has done away with the subject-matter of the contract, and, perhaps, if he has been negligent, he cannot recover. But prima facie he escapes. To make him liable his fault must be proved by the party which alleges that it destroys his excuse.

It has, I think, long been recognized that a particular contract may or may not impose an absolute undertaking on the promisor. . . .

Where the promisor makes an absolute promise he takes the risk of his ability to fulfil his contract and must do so or pay damages. No question of frustration does or can arise. Whatever occurs the promisor is bound. The very fact, however, that in certain cases impossibility of performance is an excuse shows that in those cases there is no absolute promise. It is conditional on something, ie, the possibility of performance. If, then, in certain contracts the promisor need only fulfil his obligations if performance be possible and this be such a contract, there seems no valid reason for imposing on him the obligation of proving his innocence of fault. In truth, the words 'without default on either side' are not used for the purpose of establishing what has to be proved by either party. Rather they are necessarily inserted to limit the cases to which the doctrine of frustration applies. If a party be in fault the doctrine is not to be invoked by him. If he is not in fault, it may be. But they have no bearing on the onus of proof. They qualify the doctrine; they do not impose on the party seeking to be excused the necessity of proving want of fault either in himself or in his opponent. . . .

I have thought it unnecessary to trouble your Lordships with a discussion of the question whether a contractor should be held liable in a case where the impossibility on which he relies was due to his negligence only or whether some more deliberate act is required if the plea is to be defeated. . . . A contractor who negligently destroys the subject-matter of the contract is not free from blame and in some cases may not be within the exception 'without default' as used in the cases, but I prefer to leave the question for determination until it comes directly in issue."

NOTE

The problem of fault can sometimes emerge out of debt claims where a party who has performed a service, or thinks he has performed a service, is claiming the price for the service performed. The next case is a good example.

Vigers v Cook **[1919] 2 K.B. 475, CA**

This was an action in debt by a funeral undertaker against the defendant in respect of a funeral of the defendant's son. The Court of Appeal (Bankes, Scrutton and Atkin L.JJ.) held that the defendant was justified in refusing to pay the bill.

> **Bankes L.J.:** ". . . The first question is, what was the contract between the parties? . . .
>
> Undertaking an order for a funeral indicates not a single but a complex operation, that is to say, a series of single operations; and naturally there must have been a discussion in reference to these various single operations which went to make up the entire transaction in respect of which the contract was made. For instance, there must have been an intimation as to where the interment was to take place, and as to the kind of coffin desired . . . But, having been concluded, in my opinion it is one entire contract . . . Not a word has been said against the plaintiff in this case. He is an undertaker of repute . . . He took the order, and the order included the supply of the elm shell, the lead coffin, and the oak case . . . On August 1 the lead coffin was soldered down in the mortuary, and the pinhole was left . . . On August 2 the complaint came from the mortuary authorities, and on that day the pinhole was closed. As the natural result of closing the pinhole, the gas accumulated in the lead coffin to such an extent that by the time the coffin arrived at the entrance to the church the lead coffin had burst, and there was a leakage from the coffin, sufficient, to render it extremely undesirable that the body should be taken into the church . . . and as a result the body was not taken in.
>
> In my opinion the contract which was made between the parties included . . . as an essential term the conveying of the body into the church for a part of the service, subject to this condition, that the body was in such a state as to permit of that being done. The body in this coffin was not in that state, but the onus was on the plaintiff to establish that it was not in that state owing to no default on his part. In my opinion he did not discharge that onus . . . I think that, although the plaintiff down to the time of the closing of the aperture did nothing other than what a competent and careful undertaker would do, in the difficult circumstances which arose when he felt it necessary to close the aperture, he has not shown that it was owing to no fault on his part that one essential term of his contract was not fulfilled; and it being one entire contract, in my opinion he fails in proving that he is entitled to any portion of the one entire price which was payable for the entire contract . . ."

NOTES AND QUESTIONS

1. It has been observed many times in this book that the difference between contract in the civil law and in English law is that one is based on agreement and the other is based on promise (see **4.1**). This distinction becomes evident,

once again, in the way failure to perform a contract is envisaged. In French law and in the PECL, all failures to perform are labelled "non-performance" (*inexécution*); but in English law the notion of promise has generated a different expression. A failure to do what one has promised to do is called a "breach" of promise, and this has given rise to the notion of breach of contract (see **10.4**). However, the idea of a non-performance cannot be disregarded in English law, because in a unilateral contract the promisee cannot ever be in breach since such a person has never promised anything. Thus Mrs Carlill (see p.149) could never be in breach of contract; all she could ever be accused of by the Carbolic Smoke Ball Company would be non-performance of the consideration stipulated in the advertisement. Was the Carbolic Smoke Ball Co in breach of the contract with Mrs Carlill, or were they guilty only of a non-performance?

2. From the position of the law of remedies the difference between breach and non-performance can be important. If a contractor wishes to claim damages, it must be established that the other party is in breach of contract and that this breach has caused the claimant's damage. But what if the damage suffered by the claimant as a result of the other party's failure to perform is less than the price that the claimant had agreed to pay for the performance?

Bolton v Mahadeva **[1972] 1 W.L.R. 1009, CA**

This was a debt action for £560 brought by a firm of heating engineers against a householder who had contracted with the engineers to have a central heating system installed in his house for £560. The householder claimed that the work of installation was so defective that it amounted to a non-performance of the contract and that, accordingly, he was not liable to pay anything. The trial judge held that the system was defective and would cost £174.50 to remedy; he gave judgment for £385.50 plus another £46 for extras. The Court of Appeal (Sachs, Buckley and Cairns L.JJ.) allowed an appeal by the householder.

Cairns L.J.: "... The main question in the case is whether the defects in workmanship found by the judge to be such as to cost £174 to repair—that is, between one-third and one-quarter of the contract price—were of such a character and amount that the plaintiff could not be said to have substantially performed his contract. That is, in my view, clearly the legal principle which has to be applied to cases of this kind.

The rule which was laid down many years ago in *Cutter v Powell* in relation to lump sum contracts was that unless the contracting party had performed the whole of his contract, he was not entitled to recover anything. That strong rule must now be read in the light of certain more recent cases . . .

Perhaps the most helpful case is the most recent one of *Hoenig v Isaacs*. That was a case where the plaintiff was an interior decorator and designer of furniture who had entered into a contract to decorate and furnish the defendant's flat for a sum of £750; and, as appears from the statement of facts, the official referee who tried the case at first instance found that the door of a wardrobe required replacing, that a bookshelf which was too short would have to be re-made, which would require alterations being made to a bookcase, and that the cost of remedying the defects was £55 18s. 2p. That is on a £750 contract. The ground on which the Court of Appeal in that case held that the plaintiff was entitled to succeed, notwithstanding that there was not complete performance of the contract, was that there was substantial performance of the contract and that the defects in the work which there existed were not sufficient to amount to a substantial degree of non-performance.

In considering whether there was substantial performance I am of opinion that it is relevant to take into account both the nature of the defects and the proportion between the cost of rectifying them and the contract price. It would be wrong to say that the contractor is only entitled to payment if the defects are so trifling as to be covered by the *de minimis* rule . . .

Now, certainly it appears to me that the nature and amount of the defects in this case were far different from those which the court had to consider in *H Dakin & Co Ltd v Lee* and *Hoenig v Isaacs*. For my part, I find it impossible to say that the judge was right in reaching the conclusion that in those circumstances the contract had been substantially performed. The contract was a contract to install a central heating system. If a central heating system when installed is such that it does not heat the house adequately and is such, further, that fumes are given out, so as to make living rooms uncomfortable, and if the putting right of those defects is not something which can be done by some slight amendment of the system, then I think that the contract is not substantially performed.

The actual amount of expenditure which the judge assessed as being necessary to cure those particular defects were £40 in each case. Taking those matters into account and the other matters making up the total of £174, I have reached the conclusion that the judge was wrong in saying that this contract had been substantially completed; and, on my view of the law, it follows that the plaintiff was not entitled to recover under that contract . . ."

NOTES AND QUESTIONS

1. One of the most effective remedies that a consumer has against a supplier who provides shoddy goods or services is the option not to pay the bill. In effect the consumer is either (a) simply repudiating the contract for serious breach by the other party (see **10.4** and **12.6**), or (b) refusing to perform because the other party has not performed (see **10.4.2**). What is the difference between breach of contract and non-performance of a contract? Were the consumers in *Vigers* and *Mahadeva* refusing to pay because the other party was in breach?

2. If, of course, the consumer is not justified in repudiating because (a) the breach by the supplier does not go to the root of the contract, or (b) the other party has substantially (or reasonably?) performed, the consumer will be in breach of contract. What remedies will the supplier then have against the consumer? If the refusal to pay the bill caused the undertaker or the firm of heating engineers to borrow money at a high rate of interest to stop them going bankrupt, could they claim this interest in a claim for damages against the consumer?

3. In both *Vigers* and *Mahadeva* it could be said that the consumers received something from the suppliers. Ought they to pay for this something? If the house owner in *Mahadeva* had brought in another firm to get the heating working for a price of £100 (1972 prices), would it be just and equitable that the owner could obtain a heating system so cheaply? Had he unjustly enriched himself at the expense of the first heating firm? What if the firm had been a cowboy firm of builders: can one unjustly enrich himself or herself at the expense of a cowboy firm of builders? Is there a policy consideration that might override this unjust enrichment consideration?

4. In *Mahadeva* the refusal to pay was a particularly effective remedy. But what if the heating engineers had not only installed a bad system, but also had caused extensive damage to the owner's house? In this situation the owner would have had to sue for damages for breach of contract, and such a remedy covers only the actual loss suffered by the claimant. Would the court, then, have set off the cost of the pipes, radiators, etc. against the loss suffered by the owner? What if the house owner had suffered nervous shock at seeing his home burn down? (*cf. Attia v British Gas* (1988).)

5. What if it is the claimant who is at fault?

Heil v Hedges [1951] 1 T.L.R. 512, KBD

This was an action for damages brought by the purchaser of a pork chop against the butcher who had sold her the meat. The plaintiff consumed a pork chop for lunch that had been only partly cooked by her maid, and she suffered trichinosis as a result. The plaintiff argued that the chop was neither of merchantable quality nor reasonably fit for its purpose, but the action was unsuccessful.

McNair J.: ". . . The next question is whether the defendant was in breach of the implied condition of reasonable fitness and merchantability under s 14 . . . of the Sale of Goods Act 1893. I have already stated that the evidence satisfies me that if pork infested with trichinella is subjected to a temperature of 131 deg F, or on a more conservative estimate 137 deg F, the trichinella is killed and the pork is innocuous. I am also satisfied on the evidence called by the defendant that it is common knowledge among the general public, as distinct from experts in nutrition and dietectics, that pork should be cooked substantially longer than other meat, given the same temperature, and that the proper way to cook pork is to cook it until it is white. A well-qualified witness called by the defendant told me that she had consulted 40 or 50 cookery books on the subject and that they were all to the same effect. She had also, by way of reinforcing her view, asked a number of housewives of humble station as to their views, and they had unanimously formed the view which she had formed.

In these circumstances it seems to me that, so far as trichinella spiralis is concerned, the implied condition of fitness or merchantability is complied with if the pork, when supplied, is in such condition that if properly cooked according to accepted standards it is innocuous . . .

It being the common contemplation of the parties that the pork will be cooked before consumption, it seems to me that the implied condition must be applied in relation to pork which is not only cooked but properly cooked according to accepted standards. In my opinion, on the facts, it is plain that the pork in question in this case was not properly cooked according to accepted and known standards, but was fit for human consumption and merchantable if so cooked. Accordingly, in my judgment, the plaintiff's allegation that the implied conditions of fitness and merchantability were broken fails.

If liability had been established, I should have assessed the damages recoverable at £209 6s 10d in respect of special damage and £750 as general damages, but as I have taken the view that no liability is established there will be judgment for the defendant."

QUESTIONS

1. If the meat had been lamb rather than pork, would the result have been different? What about chicken?

2. Is this a causation case?

3. Will this decision apply to eggs purchased in the UK? In other words, is a consumer under a duty not to eat raw or undercooked eggs? And if a consumer who eats such eggs suffers salmonella food poisoning, could he or she sue for damages for breach of s 14 of the Sale of Goods Act 1979?

4. Would this case about pork be decided the same way today?

5. What if a customer has a particular allergy with respect to some products?

Ingham v Emes [1955] 2 Q.B. 366, CA

This was an action for damages brought by a customer, Mrs Ingham, against "Maison Emes", a ladies' hairdressers in Godalming. Mrs Ingham had gone to the hairdressers to have her hair dyed by the use of a product called Inecto, a preparation known to be dangerous in some cases, but she had failed to disclose to the hairdressers that she had suffered acute dermatitis when Inecto had been used on her some seven years previously. This second use of the product again caused dermatitis, but the Court of Appeal (Denning, Birkett and Romer L.JJ.) rejected the damages claim.

> **Denning L.J.:** ". . . The difficulty that I have felt is that this looks like a plea of contributory negligence, or a plea that Mrs Ingham was the author of her own misfortune; and that has never been pleaded or found. But I think the same result is reached by saying that the implied term as to fitness is dependent on proper disclosure by the customer of any relevant peculiarities known to her, and in particular of the fact that she knew by experience that Inecto might have a bad effect on her. The way this result is reached in law is this: in a contract for work and materials (such as the present) there is an implied term that the materials are reasonably fit for the purpose for which they are required: see *Myers v Brent Cross Service Co*. This term is analogous to the corresponding term in the sale of goods: see *Stewart v Reavell's Garage*. In order for the implied term to arise, however, the customer must make known to the contractor expressly or by implication the 'particular purpose' for which the materials are required so as to show that he relies on the contractor's skill or judgment. The particular purpose in this case was to dye the hair, not of a normal person, but of a person known to be allergic to Inecto. Mrs Ingham did not make that particular purpose known to the assistant. She cannot therefore recover on the implied term . . ."

QUESTIONS

1. In *Ingham v Emes*, did the plaintiff fail because the hairdresser was not the factual cause of the plaintiff's dermatitis?

2. What if the plaintiff had forgotten that she was allergic to Inecto?

3. What if the plaintiff had suffered the dermatitis for the first time at the defendants' salon, but could not actually prove beyond doubt that Inecto causes dermatitis; she could prove only that there was a 50 per cent chance that her illness was caused by the product?

4. What if a hairdresser accidentally cuts the ear off a customer after having been startled by a car back-firing in the street outside?

5. Could *Ingham v Emes* be seen as a good faith case? (*Cf.* Powell (1956) 9 CLP 16.)

6. Did the plaintiffs in *The Liddesdale* (1900) (above, p.441) have only themselves to blame?

NOTE

Causation in the law of obligations is a complex topic and is normally dealt with at length in tort courses: see C&MT, pp.324–68; UC&TO, pp.145–64. Some of the cases extracted in C&MT will be of relevance to contract, but it would perhaps be an uneconomical use of space to repeat them in this present book. The basic rule is that there must be cause and connection between the defective performance or non-performance and any harm suffered by the other contracting party (see **11.4**). Yet causation as a topic in contract is in some ways even more complex than in tort, in that many cases that actually concern causal issues tend to be hidden behind other contractual concepts such as, for example, self-induced frustration or (as in *Ingham v Emes* (1955)) implied terms.

9.3 Performance by third parties

A glance at the names of the parties in contract cases will soon reveal that in many contract situations, performance of a contractual promise is not actually carried out by the contractor itself but by a third party, often, but not always, an employee of the contractor. This raises the question of when a contractor can escape responsibility for defective performance by claiming that the act or omission that amounts to non- or defective performance is not its act: see e.g. *Photo Production v Securicor* (1980) (pp.70, 406). One might start by looking at the general rule in civil law thinking.

Principles of European Contract Law

"**Article 7:106 Performance by a Third Person**
(1) Except where the contract requires personal performance the obligee cannot refuse performance by a third person if:

(a) the third person acts with the assent of the obligor; or

(b) the third person has a legitimate interest in performance and the obligor has failed to perform or it is clear that it will not perform at the time performance is due.

(2) Performance by the third person in accordance with paragraph (1) discharges the obligor.

Article 8:107 Performance Entrusted to Another
A party who entrusts performance of the contract to another person remains responsible for performance."

QUESTIONS

1. What is meant by "entrusts"?

2. Does art.8:107 represent the position in English law?

Wong Mee Wan v Kwan Kin Travel Services Ltd [1996] 1 W.L.R. 38, PC

This was an action for damages in contract and in negligence brought by a mother in respect of her daughter's death during a package holiday in China offered by the first defendant travel company. The death resulted from a speedboat accident caused by the negligence of the driver, an employee of the third defendant owners of the boat, who had volunteered to take the group across a lake. And the question arose as to whether the first defendant (the travel company), in addition to the other defendants, was to be liable for this death. The Privy Council (Lords Goff, Jauncey, Slynn, Nolan and Hoffmann) held that the first defendant was to be liable.

> **Lord Slynn:** "... There are of course many contracts under which a person agrees to supply services when he may arrange for his obligations to be performed by others, and where it is indeed contemplated that he will do so. ...
>
> The fact that the supplier of services may under the contract arrange for some or all of them to be performed by others does not absolve the supplier from his contractual obligation. He may be liable if the service is performed without the exercise of due care and skill on the part of the sub-contractor just as he would be liable if the sub-contractor failed to provide the service or failed to provide it in accordance with the terms of the contract. The obligation undertaken is thus, if the person undertaking to supply the services performs them himself, that he will do so with reasonable skill and care, and that if, where the contract permits him to do so, he arranges for others to supply the services, that they will be supplied with reasonable skill and care (see *Chitty on Contracts* (27th edn, 1994) pp.987–988, paras 19–046 and 19–047).
>
> The distinction between the two categories of case—where the party agrees merely as agent to arrange for services to be provided and where he undertakes to supply the services—is drawn in *Craven v Strand Holidays (Canada) Ltd* (1982) 40 OR (2d) 186, 142 DLR (3d) 31. ...
>
> It is ... clear that the fact that it is known that another person will or may perform the service or part of them does not mean that the contract is one of agency. In each case it has to be asked as a matter of construction into which category the contract falls. This may not always be easy. ...
>
> [Lord Slynn then discussed *Stewart v Reavell's Garage* [1952] 2 QB 545, *Rogers v Night Riders (a firm)* [1983] RTR 324, *Jarvis v Swans Tours Ltd* [1973] QB 233 and *Wilson v Best Travel Ltd* [1993] 1 All ER 353, 356. *Wall v Silver Wing Surface Arrangements Ltd*, unreported.]
>
> It was clearly always the first defendant's intention that parts of the package tour would be carried out by others and, in particular, in their respective spheres, by the second and third defendants. [The daughter] and her colleagues may have appreciated that someone other than the first defendant would carry out some

parts of the tour. That does not, however, conclude the question. It still has to be considered whether the first defendant was in reality doing no more than 'arranging' the tour so that they undertook no liability for any default by those providing the goods and services or, at most, a liability to take reasonable care in the selection of those who provided the services. In the present case there are in the terms of the brochure, which are treated as part of the contractual arrangements, no clear statements that the first defendant was doing no more than arranging the tour as agent for the travellers. . . .

Taking the contract as a whole their Lordships consider that the first defendant here undertook to provide and not merely to arrange all the services included in the programme, even if some activities were to be carried out by others. . . .

In their Lordships' view it was an implied term of the contract that those services would be carried out with reasonable skill and care. That term does not mean, to use the words of Hodgson J in *Wall v Silver Wing Surface Arrangements Ltd*, that the first defendant undertook an obligation to ensure 'the safety of all the components of the package'. The plaintiff's claim does not amount to an implied term that her daughter would be reasonably safe. It is a term simply that reasonable skill and care would be used in rendering the services to be provided under the contract. The trip across the lake was clearly not carried out with reasonable skill and care in that no steps were taken to see that the driver of the speedboat was of reasonable competence and experience and the first defendant is liable for such breach of contract as found by the trial judge.

Their Lordships of course appreciate the desire of the Court of Appeal to avoid imposing a burden which is 'intolerable' on package tour operators. It must, however, be borne in mind that the tour operator has the opportunity to seek to protect himself against claims made against him in respect of services performed by others by negotiating suitable contractual terms with those who are to perform those services. He may also provide insurance cover. He may include an appropriate exemption clause in his contract with the traveller. It also has to be borne in mind, in considering what is 'tolerable' or reasonable between the parties, that a traveller in the position of [the daughter] could have no influence on the terms negotiated by the tour operator with third parties, and if injured by their lack of care would, if having no right against the package tour operator, be obliged to pursue a claim in a foreign country. The difficulty involved in doing so does not need to be elaborated. In considering what is or is not tolerable as between traveller and tour operator it is of some relevance to not the Package Travel, Package Holidays and Package Tours Regulations 1992, SI 1992/3288, made pursuant to Council Directive (EC) 90/314. [Lord Slynn then quoted section 15 of the Regulations.] . . .

These terms do not of course apply to the present contract but they do throw some light on the contention that an unreasonable burden would be imposed if the contract were held to contain a term that reasonable skill and care would be used. Their Lordships are satisfied that in the present case such a term was to be implied in respect of the services provided, and, to quote Cockburn CJ in *British Waggon Co v Lea & Co* (1880) 5 QBD 149 at 154, whether the work 'is done by the immediate party to the contract, or by someone on his behalf'. Their Lordships accordingly conclude that, if the tour operator agrees that services will be supplied, whether by him or others on his behalf, to imply a term that those services will be carried out with reasonable skill and care is not imposing on the tour operator a burden which is 'intolerable', as the Court of Appeal thought. Nor is it wholly unreasonable, as Hodgson J thought in *Wall v Silver Wing Surface Arrangements Ltd.. . .*"

QUESTIONS

1. What if the driver of the speedboat had assaulted the daughter and thrown her overboard: would the tour operator have been liable?

2. Was the term implied because it was (i) reasonable, or (ii) tolerable to imply it?

3. Could the tour operator sue the owners and/or driver of the speedboat?

4. Could it be said that the tour operator was under a duty to ensure the security of their holidaymakers? Or could the holiday be seen as a "thing" that had to be "reasonably fit for its purpose"?

5. Is this a case of strict liability?

NOTE

Wong Mee involved an action for damages in respect of personal injury inflicted by a third party; the next case involves an action for debt in respect of property damage inflicted by a third party.

Poole v Smith's Car Sales (Balham) Ltd [1962] 1 W.L.R. 744, CA

This was an action in debt by one car dealer against another for the price of a car. The vehicle had been transferred by the plaintiff to the defendants with a view to the latter selling it to one of their customers for £325. Subsequently, the plaintiff, without success, asked for the return of the vehicle, and it was only after a final demand that the car was returned in a very bad condition. It seemed that this damage had been caused by two of the defendants' employees who had used the car without permission. The Court of Appeal (Ormerod, Willmer and Danckwerts L.JJ.) held the defendants liable for the price.

Willmer L.J.: "... Had the defendants returned the car within a reasonable time, and had the plaintiff then refused to accept it because of the damage it had sustained, I think a really interesting question could have arisen. Our attention has been called to *Elphick v Barnes* which shows that where goods delivered under a sale or return contract are lost or damaged without default on the part of the defendant, the plaintiff cannot maintain an action for the price so long as the stipulated time or a reasonable time has not elapsed. For the party to whom the goods are delivered is not an insurer. I accept that. Such party would doubtless be liable in the event of loss or damage occurring through his fault while the goods are in his possession, but not if the damage occurred without any fault on his part. Had the defendants returned this car within a reasonable time in its damaged condition, it would at least have been open to them to contend that the damage was caused by no fault on their part, and that, accordingly, the plaintiff, on the principle of *Elphick v Barnes*, would be bound to accept the return of the car. But that could only be on the basis that the property had never passed under rule 4(b). On the view to which we have come in this case, however, this very interesting question does not, in my judgment, arise. I think that the plaintiff is entitled to recover, quite regardless of the fact of the car having been damaged, on the basis that a reasonable time had elapsed, so that the property had passed to the defendants. Accordingly, the contract price of £325 was, in my judgment, payable.

I would allow the appeal."

QUESTIONS

1. This case illustrates the important difference between a claim in debt and one in damages (see Lord Keith in *White & Carter (Councils) Ltd v McGregor* (1962), above at p.386). In sale cases, the defendant can be liable in contractual debt only if property (ownership) in the goods (the car) has passed to him. If property has not passed the seller can only sue in damages (see e.g. *Lazenby Garages v Wright* (1976), above at p.537). Yet is not the prospective purchaser a bailee of the car on sale or return, and would not the defendant be liable in damages for conversion and/or trespass?

2. Could the defendant garage have claimed that they were not responsible for the acts of the employees who used the car without authority? Could the plaintiff have sued the employees for (a) debt and/or (b) damages? Could the defendant garage have recovered the cost of the car from one or both of the employees?

3. What was the advantage to the plaintiff in suing in debt for the price rather than in damages for the damage to the car?

4. Why could the garage in *Lazenby Garages v Wright* (1976) (above, p.537) not sue in debt for the price of the car? (*Cf.* Lord Keith in *White & Carter (Councils) Ltd v McGregor* (1962), above at p.386.)

9.4 Impediment to performance

What if a contracting party is either hindered or completely prevented from performing his contractual obligations as a result of some outside event over which he had no control? This general question raises both an issue of abstract principle—what effect should such event have on the obligation to perform—and a number of sub-issues about the nature and force of the external event. For example, what amounts to an external event? What if the contracting party promised to achieve a specific result? What if the event only hindered, rather than prevented, performance (*cf.* **8.6**)? Upon whom is the burden of proof in cases where fault of one of the parties is in issue with respect to the event impeding or preventing performance? English contract lawyers may find the raising of this question (or these questions) in a chapter on performance a little strange, for normally intervening events are dealt with in the chapter on dissolution of contract under the sub-heading of frustration (see **10.5**). However, in the civil law things are different, as CC art.1147 indicates (see above, p.450) and the next extract confirms.

Principles of European Contract Law

"Article 8:108 Excuse Due to an Impediment
(1) A party's non-performance is excused if it proves that it is due to an impediment beyond its control and that it could not reasonably have been expected to take the impediment into account at the time of the conclusion of the contract, or to have avoided or overcome the impediment or its consequences.

(2) Where the impediment is only temporary the excuse provided by this article has effect for the period during which the impediment exists. However, if the delay amounts to a fundamental non-performance, the obligee may treat it as such.

(3) The non-performing party must ensure that notice of the impediment and of its effect on its ability to perform is received by the other party within a reasonable time after the non-performing party knew or ought to have known of these circumstances. The other party is entitled to damages for any loss resulting from the non-receipt of such notice.

NOTES

1. See also UNIDROIT, art.7.1.7.

2. It would appear that the civil law influenced the common law.

Taylor v Caldwell (1863) 122 E.R. 309, QB

Blackburn J.: "In this case the plaintiffs and defendants had, on May 27, 1861, entered into a contract by which the defendants agreed to let the plaintiffs have the use of The Surrey Gardens and Music Hall on four days then to come . . . for the purpose of giving a series of four grand concerts . . . and the plaintiffs agreed to take the Gardens and Hall on those days, and pay £100 for each day . . .

After the making of the agreement, and before the first day on which a concert was to be given, the Hall was destroyed by fire. This destruction, we must take it on the evidence, was without the fault of either party, and was so complete that in consequence the concerts could not be given as intended. And the question we have to decide is whether, under these circumstances, the loss which the plaintiffs have sustained is to fall upon the defendants. The parties when framing their agreement evidently had not present to their minds the possibility of such a disaster, and have made no express stipulation with reference to it, so that the answer to the question must depend upon the general rules of law applicable to such a contract.

There seems no doubt that where there is a positive contract to do a thing, not in itself unlawful, the contractor must perform it or pay damages for not doing it, although in consequence of unforeseen accidents, the performance of his contract has become unexpectedly burthensome or even impossible . . . But this rule is only applicable when the contract is positive and absolute, and not subject to any condition either express or implied: and . . . where, from the nature of the contract, it appears that the parties must from the beginning have known that it could not be fulfilled unless when the time for the fulfilment of the contract arrived some particular specified thing continued to exist, so that, when entering into the contract, they must have contemplated such continuing existence as the foundation of what was to be done; there, in the absence of any express or implied warranty that the thing shall exist, the contract is not to be construed as a positive contract, but as subject to an implied condition that the parties shall be excused in case, before breach, performance becomes impossible from the perishing of the thing without default of the contractor.

There seems little doubt that this implication tends to further the great object of making the legal construction such as to fulfil the intention of those who entered into the contract. For in the course of affairs men in making such contracts in general would, if it were brought to their minds, say that there should be such a condition.

Accordingly, in the civil law, such an exception is implied in every obligation of the class which they call *obligatio de certo corpore*. The rule is laid down in the Digest, lib. XLV., tit. 1, *de verborum obligationibus* . . . The general subject is treated of by Pothier, who in his *Traité des Obligations*, Partie 3, Chap. 6, art. 3, 668, states the result to be that the debtor corporis certi is freed from his obligation when the thing has perished, neither by his act, nor his neglect, and before he is in default, unless by some stipulation he has taken on himself the risk of the particular misfortune which has occurred.

Although the civil law is not, of itself, authority in an English court, it affords great assistance in investigating the principles on which the law is grounded. And it seems to us that the common law authorities establish that in such a contract the same condition of the continued existence of the thing is implied by English law.

465

There is a class of contracts in which a person binds himself to do something which requires to be performed by him in person; and such promises, e.g., promises to marry, or promises to serve for a certain time, are never in practice qualified by an express exception of the death of the party . . .

These are instances where the implied condition is of the life of a human being, but there are others in which the same implication is made as to the continued existence of a thing . . .

In none of these cases is the promise in words other than positive, nor is there any express stipulation that the destruction of the person or thing shall excuse the performance; but that excuse is by law implied, because from the nature of the contract it is apparent that the parties contracted on the basis of the continued existence of the particular person or chattel. In the present case, looking at the whole contract, we find that the parties contracted on the basis of the continued existence of the Music Hall at the time when the concerts were to be given; that being essential to their performance.

We think, therefore, that the Music Hall having ceased to exist, without fault of either party, both parties are excused, the plaintiffs from taking the gardens and paying the money, the defendants from performing their promise to give the use of the Hall and Gardens and other things."

NOTES AND QUESTIONS

1. According to the civil law (including the PECL and UNIDROIT), if the defendant can show he is not at fault he may escape liability. Such a principle was imported into English law by Blackburn J. via the notion of an implied term; fault, in other words, got translated into promise. Take the following example. Geoffrey promises his friend Pierre that he will attend Pierre's birthday party "come what may"; on the day of the party Geoffrey does not turn up and Pierre is most put out, until he learns that his friend has been badly injured by a bus while crossing the road on the way to the party. Why is it that Pierre does not "blame" Geoffrey for failing to perform his promise? Is it because there was an implied understanding that Geoffrey's promise to turn up was subject to obvious exceptions? Or is it because Geoffrey was not "at fault"? What if Geoffrey had been careless in crossing the road; would Pierre have good grounds to be put out?

2. Much, of course, depends on the nature of the arrangement or transaction within which the promises are made. If John promises Elsbeth that he will look after Elsbeth's car while she is away, she will no doubt not hold it against John if the car is damaged in a freak thunderstorm. But what if it is damaged by a freak thunderstorm partly because John has failed to put the car in a safe parking place? In these circumstances carelessness on the part of the promisor becomes important because the "institution" (*res*) damaged is Elsbeth's property (and of course John is a bailee: see *Morris v Martin* (1966), at p.113).

466

Ownership and property change the nature of the problem—the nature of the interest—and thus the nature of the promises. Can this be translated into a question of "duty"? What is the duty of John in respect of Elsbeth's car? Does such a notion depend upon fault, or promise? And what if the arrangement was a commercial one: Elsbeth was to pay John for looking after the car. Does Roman law (D.13.6.5, above at p.448) provide any insights?

3. "Although the civil law is not, of itself, authority in an English court, it affords great assistance in investigating the principles on which the law is grounded" (Blackburn J.). Is this statement still true today?

4. Could an English lawyer ever teach English law to a French or German lawyer without the English lawyer having a knowledge of the civil codes?

5. Is Blackburn J.'s implied term theory still good law? (*Cf. Davis Contractors v Fareham UDC* (1956), at p.497.)

PROBLEM

Simon contracts with Horatia to perform in her theatre on a certain night; but when the night arrives Simon fails to turn up, and later claims, and can prove, that he was ill. Will the contract be frustrated if Horatia can prove that he was ill only because he had carelessly neglected to take proper care of himself? What if, before the night he was supposed to perform, Simon had been arrested for possession of illegal drugs and was in custody the night he was supposed to perform? What if part of Simon's immense attraction as a popular singing star is his adherence to a "drug culture"? (*Cf. Shepherd & Co v Jerrom* (1986).)

FURTHER NOTE

As we shall see, frustration is not just an excuse; it automatically brings the contract to an end and thus is a means of discharge of contract. Accordingly, the topic will be dealt with in more detail in the next chapter (**10.5**). However, one further aspect of frustration worth pursuing here, under the title of non-performance, is the difficult question of cause and responsibility that can sometimes arise in these impediment cases. In *Taylor v Caldwell* (1863), Blackburn J. specifically says that the hall burned down through the fault of neither party. But upon whom is the burden of proving fault or its absence? What assumptions should the court make if the evidence is ambiguous?

Joseph Constantine SS Ltd v Imperial Smelting Co Ltd [1942] A.C. 154, HL

This was an action for damages in contract brought by the hirers of a ship (the respondents) against its owners (the appellants). During the period of hire the ship blew up for some unexplained reason. The Court of Appeal held that the owners could rely upon frustration only if they could prove that they were not at fault with regard to the explosion. The House of Lords (Viscounts Simon L.C. and Maugham, and Lords Russell, Wright and Porter) allowed an appeal.

Viscount Simon L.C.: "My Lords, by a charterparty, dated August 5, 1936, the appellants, who were the owners of a steamship called the Kingswood, chartered the ship to agents for the respondents for a voyage with a cargo of ores and concentrates from Port Pirie in South Australia to Europe. The vessel duly sailed for Port Pirie to load her cargo. On January 3, 1937, while she was anchored in the roads at Port Pirie, but before she became an 'arrived ship,' there was an explosion of extreme violence in the neighbourhood of her auxiliary boiler, which caused such damage to the steamer that she could not perform the charterparty, and the appellants gave notice to the respondents to that effect. The respondents claim damages from the appellants, alleging that the latter have broken the charterparty by failing to load a cargo. The appellants set up the defence that the contract was 'frustrated' by the destructive consequences to the Kingswood of the explosion. . . .

After examining three principal theories which were suggested in evidence as possibly accounting for the disaster, the arbitrator declares himself unable to decide whether any one of them provided the true explanation, and he goes on to say that he is not satisfied that the direct cause of the disaster has as yet been suggested at all. His conclusion is that he was not satisfied that any of the servants of the appellants were guilty of negligence. On the other hand, neither was he satisfied that negligence on the part of the servants of the appellants did not cause or contribute to the disaster. It is this nicely balanced conclusion on the facts which provides the question of law which this House has now to decide. That question is whether, when parties have contracted in such circumstances as require a term to be implied in the contract that it shall be determined, and the mutual obligations of the parties discharged, by supervening destruction of essential subject-matter of the contract, the party alleging frustration must prove affirmatively that the destruction has not been brought about by his own neglect or default.

The charterers appealed to the Court of Appeal, which reversed Atkinson J's decision. Scott LJ delivered the first judgment, with which the Master of the Rolls and Goddard LJ agreed. Scott LJ declared that this was a 'very simple case,' and this view is no doubt the explanation of the fact that his judgment does not provide this House with the arguments or authorities which led the Court of Appeal to their conclusion. The only help your Lordships can get is the assertion by the learned Lord Justice that 'a party prima facie guilty of a failure to perform his contract cannot escape under the plea of frustration, unless he proves that the frustration occurred without his default. There is no frustration in the legal sense unless he proves affirmatively that the cause was not brought into operation by his default.' If this assertion is correct, it, of course, disposes of the case. . . .

The question to be answered is not, in my view, a very simple one, and it has not as yet, so far as I can discover, been the subject of direct decision. There is no doubt, of course, that . . . 'self-induced' frustration provides no defence. . . .

All this, however, is really beside the present point, for the question raised by the arbitrator's award is not whether the defence of frustration fails if the frustration is proved to be 'self-induced' (Lord Sumner), or 'due to the act or election of the party' (Lord Wright), or, to use Scott LJ's phrase, 'brought into operation by his default.' The question here is where the onus of proof lies; ie whether, when a supervening event has been proved which would, apart from the defendant's 'default' put an end to the contract, and when at the end of the case no inference of 'default' exists and the evidence is equally consistent with either view, the defence fails because the defendant has not established affirmatively that the supervening event was not due to his default.

I may observe, in the first place, that, if this were correct, there must be many cases in which, although in truth frustration is complete and unavoidable, the defendant will be held liable because of his inability to prove a negative—in some cases, indeed, a whole series of negatives. Suppose that a vessel while on the high seas disappears completely during a storm. Can it be that the defence of frustration of the adventure depends on the owner's ability to prove that all his servants on board were navigating the ship with adequate skill and that there was no 'default' which brought about the catastrophe? Suppose that a vessel in convoy is torpedoed by the enemy and sinks immediately with all hands. Does the application of the doctrine require that the owners should affirmatively prove that those on board were keeping a good look-out, were obscuring lights, were steering as directed, and so forth? There is no reported case which requires us so to hold. The doctrine on which the defence of frustration depends is nowhere so stated as to place this onus of proof on the party relying on it. . . .

In this connection it is well to emphasize that when 'frustration' in the legal sense occurs, it does not merely provide one party with a defence in an action brought by the other. It kills the contract itself and discharges both parties automatically. The plaintiff sues for breach at a past date and the defendant pleads that at that date no contract existed. In this situation the plaintiff could only succeed if it were shown that the determination of the contract were due to the defendant's 'default,' and it would be a strange result if the party alleging this were not the party required to prove it. . . .

The point as to onus of proof is put very clearly in the third paragraph of Article 91 of *Scrutton on Charterparties*, 14th ed, p 297. See also *Carver on Carriage by Sea*, 8th ed, s 78. The decision in *The Northumbria* involves the same conclusion. Another example, from the law of bailment, confirms this view. Assume a bailment of goods to be kept in a named warehouse with an express exception of loss by fire. Proof of destruction by fire would prima facie excuse the bailee. The bailor could counter by alleging either (a) fire caused by the negligence of the bailee or (b) goods when burnt were not stored in the agreed warehouse. But it would be for the bailor not only to allege but to prove either (a) or (b), though he might rely on facts proved or admitted by the bailee as establishing his proposition. . . .

I reach the conclusion that Atkinson J took the right view in this case, and that the Court of Appeal was mistaken in holding that once the frustration in fact was established and any inference of default alleged to arise from the fact that the ship was under the control of the appellants' servants was negatived, it lay on the appellants to go further and satisfy the arbitrator positively that the frustration occurred without their default. . . .

For purposes of clearness and to avoid possible misunderstanding hereafter, I must add (though this is not necessary for the present decision) that I do not think that the ambit of 'default' as an element disabling the plea of frustration to prevail has as yet been precisely and finally determined. 'Self-induced' frustration . . . involves deliberate choice, and those cases amount to saying that a man cannot ask to be excused by reason of frustration if he has purposely so acted as to bring it about. 'Default' is a much wider term and in many commercial cases dealing with frustration is treated as equivalent to negligence. Yet in cases of frustration of another class, arising in connection with a contract for personal performance, it has not, I think, been laid down that, if the personal incapacity is due to want of care, the plea fails. Some day it may have to be finally determined whether a prima donna is excused by complete loss of voice from an executory contract to sing if it is proved that her condition was caused by her carelessness in not changing her wet clothes after being out in the rain. The implied term in such a case may turn out to be that the fact of supervening physical incapacity dissolves the contract without inquiring further into its cause, provided, of course, that it has not been deliberately induced in order to get out of the engagement.

I move that this appeal be allowed and that the order of Atkinson J be restored . . ."

(See also p.457.)

QUESTIONS

1. Does this decision conflict with the rules laid down in the PECL and UNIDROIT?

2. What effect has *Davis Contractors v Fareham UDC* (1956) (p.497) had on *Joseph Constantine*?

3. Is not the hirer of a ship under an absolute duty to supply a seaworthy vessel?

4. Are charterparty contracts different from other kinds of contract?

5. If a ship sinks for some unexplained reason, is a court entitled to assume that it has sunk because it was unseaworthy? (*Cf. The Guardian*, 26 July 2006, p.12, report by Ian Sample; guardian.co.uk/science.)

6. Does the *ratio decidendi* of *Joseph Constantine* apply to the hire of things other than ships?

Reed v Dean [1949] 1 K.B. 188, KBD

This was an action for damages by the hirers of a motor launch who had suffered injury and loss when the boat caught fire.

Lewis J.: ". . . In my view, the present case is governed by cases like *Hyman v Nye* and *Jones v Page*. Where a vessel or other thing is hired there is an implied term that the vessel or thing hired shall be as fit for the purpose as reasonable care and skill can make it. In my view the plaintiffs are right in saying that that term was implied in the present contract.

But it has been argued that the fact that the 'Golden Age' caught fire does not of necessity show that it was not fit for the purpose for which it was hired. I think I am entitled to say that, when a motor launch catches fire, apparently for an entirely unexplained cause, there is a presumption that the launch was not reasonably fit for that purpose. The evidence was that the launch, including the engine, was in perfect condition at the commencement of the hire, except that there was evidence that when the engine was cold the device known as 'tickling the carburettor' was necessary, and that that caused a certain amount of petrol to flow outside the engine into the bilge. It is quite clear that there was a leak of petrol somewhere or somehow. This engine caught fire and, in my view, it is necessary for the defendants to satisfy me that it was not through any fault of theirs. I do not think that the admission by the plaintiff husband to the fireman that he might have spilt some petrol was sufficient to rebut the presumption that there was something wrong with the engine, as is proved by the fact that it caught fire, and the defendant has not discharged the onus of showing that the fire was not caused through any deficiency in the engine.

One other matter has caused me considerable anxiety. There was no form of fire appliance on this vessel, except an extinguisher which was useless. It was argued for the plaintiffs that proper fire-fighting equipment was part of the necessary equipment of a motor launch, that failure to provide such equipment was a breach of the implied warranty of fitness and that the fact that the 'Golden Age' had no proper fire-fighting appliances was therefore a breach of the implied warranty. I was not referred by counsel to any authority directly on the point as to whether the implied warranty of fitness, where there is one, requires that a vessel shall be provided with equipment that is unnecessary to make it go or with equipment such as any reasonable person would supply in order that the vessel should be safe. I do not know; I have tried to find whether there is any such authority and my researches have failed to find any case immediately in point. I venture to suggest that in the case of a ship or motor launch one knows that one of the essentials of the vessel is to have lights. The lights do not assist in making the vessel go, but I should be very much surprised to learn that a vessel which was hired out to be sent to sea without any port or starboard lights was as fit as reasonable care and skill could make it for the purpose for which it was hired. I hold therefore that the defendant was under an implied obligation to make the 'Golden Age' as reasonably safe as care and skill could make it, that that obligation included an obligation to provide fire-fighting equipment and that one of the causes of the loss that the plaintiffs have suffered was the failure by him to provide efficient fire-fighting equipment. There will therefore be judgment for the plaintiffs."

QUESTIONS

1. Is this modest case more important than it looks, in that it goes some way in tackling a problem exposed in the decision of *Joseph Constantine SS Ltd v Imperial Smelting* (1942)? Why could the owners of the motor launch not plead frustration? Could frustration be an effective defence in situations where a consumer product explodes for some unexplained reason?

2. Would the owner of the motor launch be entitled to the hire fee up to the moment the boat sank?

3. Has this decision been modified by the Supply of Goods and Services Act 1982?

4. Could the defendants have raised the defence of contributory negligence?

5. Does reasoning by analogy play an important role in Lewis J.'s decision?

9.5 Effects of non-performance

The effects of a non-performance of a contractual obligation have been well summarised in European contract law.

Principles of European Contract Law

"Article 8:101: Remedies Available
(1) Whenever a party does not perform an obligation under the contract and the non-performance is not excused under Article 8:108, the aggrieved party may resort to any of the remedies set out in Chapter 9.

(2) Where a party's non-performance is excused under Article 8:108, the aggrieved party may resort to any of the remedies set out in Chapter 9 except claiming performance and damages.

(3) A party may not resort to any of the remedies set out in Chapter 9 to the extent that its own act caused the other party's non-performance.

NOTES

1. Chapter 9 in the above extract is of course Chapter 9 of the PECL, which deals with remedies. Remedies in this present book will be dealt with in **Chapters 11** and **12**.

2. Article 8:108 of the PECL can be found extracted above at p.464.

3. Article 8:101 of the PECL represents English law if one understands by non-performance a non-performance that amounts to a breach of contract. Another possibility might be to say that it broadly represents English law if excuse under PECL, art.8:108 is treated as excuse by frustration; but of course in theory frustration is more than an "excuse" in that it "kills the contract" (see *Joseph Constantine* (1942), above at p.467; and **10.5**).

9.6 Non-performance and third parties

The effect of a non-performance of a contractual obligation on a third party has largely been examined in the last chapter under the heading of privity of contract (see **8.2**). Several situations need to be identified:

(a) Non-performances which impact upon third parties who are not parties to the contract and who are not specifically (as an individual or a member of a class) identified by the contract. Here the law of tort may be of relevance in as much as a breach of contract might, vis-à-vis the third party, amount to a breach of a non-contractual duty: see e.g. *Donoghue v Stevenson* (1932); *Smith v Eric Bush* (1990); *White v Jones* (1995); Consumer Protection Act 1987. See generally C&MT.

(b) Non-performances which impact upon third parties who are not parties to the contract but are (or ought to be) contemplated by the contract. Here the Contracts (Rights of Third Parties) Act 1999 (above, p.392) may well be relevant; and see also *Beswick v Beswick* (above, p.23) and *Jackson v Horizon Holidays* (1975) (above, p.396).

(c) Non-performances which impact upon third parties who are not parties to the main contract but may have a separate collateral contractual relationship with the non-performer. See e.g. *Lockett v A & M Charles* (1938) (above, p.398); *New Zealand Shipping Co v Satterthwaite* (1975) (noted above, at p.401).

(d) Non-performances which impact upon third parties who are not parties to the contract but have a bailment relationship with the non-performer. See e.g. *Morris v CW Martin & Sons* (1966) (above, p.113).

10 Discharge of contract

Textbooks on contractual obligations in the civil law systems often do not have a chapter devoted specifically to the discharge or dissolution of contractual obligations. This is because the topic is dealt with at a higher level of abstraction (as well as, of course, to an extent, under performance and non-performance of contracts). Contract is part of the law of obligations, and thus the issue of discharge is one that attaches to the notion of an obligation (the *vinculum iuris*) rather than specifically to contract. Accordingly the topic of discharge is a topic that forms part of the general theory of obligations rather than part of the law of contract. The situation is different in English law thinking because there is not really any general theory of obligations. There are only the categories of contract, tort and restitution, which did not devolve from some generic category. The foundations of the English "law of obligations" are the old forms of action—trespass, debt, actions on the case and so on—which had no connection with the Roman institutional scheme (law of persons, law of property and law of obligations).

Nevertheless, it is worth reflecting on the civilian scheme, in that this scheme and its concepts undoubtedly influenced the common lawyers during the 19th century. The Romans regarded the extinction of the *vinculum iuris* as a matter of form analogous to the formation of the obligation; thus if a contractual obligation has been created by the delivery of a thing then its extinction will occur only on redelivery, and if it has been created by words then its extinction will be either by performance of what was promised or by words (D.46.3.80). Equally, contracts formed by bare agreement can be ended by agreement (D.50.17.35). Two particular means of extinction emerge from this formality: an obligation can be extinguished either by performance, or by agreement. As was mentioned in the previous chapter, most contractual operations are entered into and completed without giving rise to any problem whatsoever. The sale of everyday articles, the use of public transport, the purchase of consumer services are the foundation of commercial life, and even when transactions prove problematic, there is a good chance that they will be settled by agreement. Many sellers simply replace the defective product without the purchaser demanding the cost of a bus fare. Performance and agreement remain, in short, the most important ways of ending an obligation. (One might note here in passing that statistically most non-performances are failures to pay contractual debts.)

However, Roman law also recognised that an obligation could be extinguished indirectly through rules that attach to the *actio*. A creditor who failed to enforce a claim at law would after a certain period of time lose the right to sue through a device known as prescription (in English law see the Limitation Act 1980, especially s.5). The flow of time presumed the extinction of the debt. In situations where the *actio* has not been extinguished by time, the effect of legal proceedings is to put an end to an obligation either through enforced performance or through the payment of damages (see Lord Diplock in *Photo Production v Securicor* (1980), above at p.406). Of course it may be that a defendant will be able to resist a claim for damages on the basis of a *force majeure*, in which case it could be said that an obligation is extinguished as a result of an outside event (*cf.* below **10.5**). However, as has been seen, one traditional explanation of such an extinction is through the notion of a condition, and thus it could be said that the obligation is ended by implied agreement (see e.g. *Taylor v Caldwell* (1863), at p.464). Assignment, once requiring agreement, is yet another means of putting an end to an obligation as far as one of the parties is concerned (although space dictates that this is a topic that cannot be covered in this present book). Perhaps, then, one comes back to Roman law: obligations are ended either by performance (prescription being a negative form of performance), or by agreement. Unfortunately this neat theory can no longer easily be applied to English law (see e.g. *Davis Contractors v Fareham UDC* (1956), below at p.497).

10.1 Discharge by performance

A contract will in principle be discharged when both parties have satisfactorily performed their contractual obligations.

Gareth H Jones and Peter Schlechtriem, 'Breach of Contract' in *International Encyclopedia of Comparative Law*, **Vol.VII, Ch.15 (footnotes omitted)**

"14.—If an obligation is performed properly, ie conforming to its content, it will be discharged and thereby extinguished, so that the other party can no longer be aggrieved by a breach of this obligation. That does not mean, however, that the obligor cannot still feel aggrieved any more at all: If the object of—full and satisfying—performance (eg the purchased and delivered object, the constructed and accepted building) were destroyed later, ie after performance and discharge of the underlying obligation, the recipient of the performance will be 'aggrieved', but not by a breach of an obligation of the promisor. Therefore, discharge or breach are but two sides of the same coin, and it is necessary . . . to know at what point in time and by which acts, behaviour, non-doing etc, a discharge of an obligations is achieved.

This, of course, again depends on the respective obligation and the respective contract . . .

17. *The issue.*—Related to the question of discharge by performance is the problem of determining what constitutes a full performance conforming exactly to the obligation. If the obligor does not perform in time or not completely or performance does not conform to the contract, he will not be discharged and will probably be held to be in breach. . . ."

NOTE

As we have seen in the previous chapter, the difficult problem likely to arise with respect to performance is when one party asserts that the performance is not satisfactory. This, of course, is more a question of remedies than of discharge, but if the non-performance is serious, it may be that the victim will be able to escape from the contract as a result of discharge by breach (see below **10.4**). Another conceptual difficulty is to decide at what point the contract is discharged. In a sale of goods transaction the passing of ownership and possession in the goods from seller to buyer, together with the payment of the price, in one sense completes the transaction. But what if some months later the goods prove defective?

Crowther v Shannon Motor Co **[1975] 1 W.L.R. 30, CA**

This was an action for damages for breach of s.14 of the Sale of Goods Act brought by the purchaser of a second-hand Jaguar car against the dealers who sold it to him. The car had done over 82,000 miles at the time of the sale and the buyer did a further 2,000 miles; however, after this mileage the engine seized up and had to be replaced. The plaintiff called as a witness a previous owner of the Jaguar, who indicated that the engine was in "clapped out" state when the dealers sold it to the plaintiff. The county court judge awarded damages to the plaintiff and an appeal to the Court of Appeal (Lord Denning M.R., Orr and Browne L.JJ.) was dismissed.

Lord Denning M.R.: "... Mr Rudd, who put the case very cogently before us, submitted that a car which had covered 2,354 miles must have been reasonably fit for the purpose of driving along the road. He drew attention to a case some years ago in this court of *Bartlett v Sidney Marcus Ltd* [1965] 1 WLR 1013. We emphasised then that a buyer, when he buys a secondhand car, should realise that defects may appear sooner or later. In that particular case a defect did appear in the clutch. It was more expensive to repair than had been anticipated. It was held by this court that the fact that the defect was more expensive than had been anticipated did not mean that there had been any breach of the implied condition. But that case seems to me to be entirely distinguishable from the present case. In that case it was a minor repair costing £45 after 300 miles. Here we have a very different case. On the dealers' own evidence, a buyer could reasonably expect to get 100,000 miles life out of a Jaguar engine. Here the Jaguar had only done 80,000 miles. Yet it was in such a bad condition that it was 'clapped out' and after some 2,300 miles it failed altogether. That is very different from a minor repair. The dealers themselves said that if they had known that the engine would blow up after 2,000 miles, they would not have sold it. The reason obviously was because it would not have been reasonably fit for the purpose.

Some criticism was made of a phrase used by the judge. He said 'What does "fit for the purpose" mean?' He answered: 'To go as a car for a reasonable time.' I am not quite sure that that is entirely accurate. The relevant time is the time of

477

sale. But there is no doubt what the judge meant. If the car does not go for a reasonable time but the engine breaks up within a short time, that is evidence which goes to show it was not reasonably fit for the purpose at the time it was sold. On the evidence in this case, the engine was liable to go at any time. It was 'nearing the point of failure,' said the expert, Mr Wise. The time interval was merely 'staving off the inevitable.' That shows that at the time of the sale it was not reasonably fit for the purpose of being driven on the road. I think the judge on the evidence was quite entitled to find there was a breach of section 14 (1) of the Sale of Goods Act 1893 and I would therefore dismiss the appeal."

NOTE

This case seems to indicate that the contract of sale had not been discharged as such: there was a continuing performance obligation with respect to the car, lasting for some months after the actual contract of sale had been completed. Yet Lord Denning asserts that the obligation is not actually one that continues for a "reasonable time", for this is an evidence issue with respect to the state of the goods at the time of the contract. Goods which break down before the expiry of a reasonable time are goods that were defective at the time of the sale. Even so, a seller in the course of a business cannot assume that all contractual obligations are discharged once the sale is complete and the price paid, and the same is no doubt true with respect to contracts of service. If a service proves defective several months after the transaction has taken place, this may be evidence of a breach of s.13 of the Supply of Goods and Services Act 1982.

QUESTIONS

1. An employee leaves one employer to go to work for another. Are all contractual obligations on both sides discharged with respect to the first employment contract? (*Cf. Thomas Marshall v Guinle* (1979), at p.436.)

2. Does the Limitation Act 1980, s.5 positively confirm the discharge of all contractual obligations six years after the apparent completed performances of a contract?

10.2 Discharge by agreement

Just as contracts can be formed by agreement (or exchange of promises), so they can be discharged by agreement (or a new exchange of promises). In the civil law the variation or the discharge of a contract presents few problems because the contractual bond depends entirely on consensus and agreement; if the parties freely agree a change or a cancellation of the contract, this will take effect in law in the same way as the formation of a contract by agreement and consent. In the common law it is different because the basis of contract is different. In the common law, just as a contract can be formed only by promise and consideration, so it can be varied or discharged only by promise and consideration. In fact the contract is not in theory varied or cancelled as such; what happens is that a new set of promises—a new contract—replaces the old contract.

Where the old contract remains unperformed (unexecuted) by either side there will be no problem. A new contract varying or cancelling the old contract can be formed because there will be consideration moving from each party (that is to say, benefit and detriment will attach to each party).

Paal Wilson & Co v Partenreederei Hannah Blumenthal **[1983] A.C. 854, HL**

Lord Diplock: ". . . Abandonment of a contract ('the former contract') which is still executory, ie, one in which at least one primary obligation of one or other of the parties remains unperformed, is effected by the parties entering into a new contract ('the contract of abandonment') by which each party promises the other to release that other party from further performance of any primary obligations on his part under the former contract then remaining unperformed, but without such non-performance giving rise to any substituted secondary obligation under the former contract to pay damages . . ."

NOTES

1. However, there will be a problem if one party has performed its obligations under the old contract, in that the new set of promises will lack consideration. Thus in *D & C Builders v Rees* (1966) (see above, p.195) there was an apparent variation of the contract in as much as the builder agreed to accept a sum different from (lower than) the agreed contractual price; this agreement proved unenforceable because it was not supported by consideration. The builder had performed its obligations under the contract and thus there was no benefit to the builder in accepting a sum lower than the agreed price. At common law the old contract remained in force because no new set of enforceable promises had been validly created to replace the old contract.

2. Equity, as we have seen (**4.6.3**), intervened to alleviate any injustice arising out of this strict common law position. Where one party had performed its obligations under the contract, but had freely consented to a subsequent variation, the doctrine of estoppel would prevent this party from going back on his promissory statement (see the *High Trees* (1947) case, above at p.194; and Lord Denning M.R. in *WJ Alan & Co Ltd v El Nasr Export and Import Co* (1972)). Estoppel thus became a means by which partially executed contracts could be varied, or indeed discharged, by agreement. However, if there was evidence of any duress, equity would refuse its aid (*D & C Builders v Rees* (1966), p.195).

3. In addition to this equitable intervention, the common law has recognised a doctrine of waiver of contractual rights.

Charles Rickards Ltd v Oppenhaim [1950] 1 K.B. 616, CA

This was an action in debt for the balance of the price of a car chassis upon which the sellers further contracted to have built a car body. The defendant had stipulated that time was of the essence. There were considerable delays with respect to the carrying out of the work on the car, and in the end the defendant cancelled the contract and refused to pay for the vehicle. The Court of Appeal (Bucknill, Singleton and Denning L.JJ.) held that the defendant was, in the end, entitled to cancel, despite having waived his rights on several successive occasions as to time of delivery.

Denning L.J.: ". . . If this had been originally a contract without any stipulation as to time and, therefore, with only the implication of reasonable time, it may be that the plaintiffs could have said that they had fulfilled the contract; but in my opinion the case is very different when there was an initial contract, making time of the essence of the contract: 'within six or at the most, seven months.' I agree that that initial time was waived by reason of the requests that the defendant made after March, 1948, for delivery; and that, if delivery had been tendered in compliance with those requests, the defendant could not have refused to accept the coach-body. Suppose, for instance, that delivery had been tendered in April, May, or June, 1948: the defendant would have had no answer. It would be true that the plaintiffs could not aver and prove they were ready and willing to deliver in accordance with the original contract. They would have had, in effect, to rely on the waiver almost as a cause of action. At one time there would have been theoretical difficulties about their doing that. It would have been said that there was no consideration; or, if the contract was for the sale of goods, that there was nothing in writing to support the variation. . . but all those difficulties are swept away now. If the defendant, as he did, led the plaintiffs to believe that he would not insist on the stipulation as to time, and that, if they carried out the work, he would accept it, and they did it, he could not afterwards set up the stipulation as to the time against them. Whether it be called waiver or forbearance on his part, or an agreed variation or substituted performance, does not matter. It is a kind of estoppel. By his conduct he evinced an intention to affect their legal relations. He made, in effect, a promise not to insist on his strict legal rights. That promise was intended to be acted on, and was in fact acted on. He cannot afterwards go back on it. I think not only that that follows from *Panoutsos v Raymond Hadley Corporation of New York* a decision of this court, but that it was also anticipated in *Bruner v Moore*. It is a particular application of the principle which I endeavoured to state in *Central London Property Trust Ld. v High Trees House Ld.*

So, if the matter had stopped there, the plaintiffs could have said, notwithstanding that more than seven months had elapsed, that the defendant was bound to accept; but the matter did not stop there, because delivery was not given in compliance with the requests of the defendant. Time and time again the defendant pressed for delivery, time and time again he was assured he would have early delivery; but he never got satisfaction; and eventually at the end of June he gave notice saying that, unless the car were delivered by July 25, 1948, he would not accept it.

The question thus arises whether he was entitled to give such a notice, making time of the essence, and that is the question that Mr Sachs has argued before us . . . It would be most unreasonable if the defendant, having been lenient and waived the initial expressed time, should, by so doing, have prevented himself from ever thereafter insisting on reasonably quick delivery. In my judgment he was entitled to give a reasonable notice making time of the essence of the matter. Adequate protection to the suppliers is given by the requirement that the notice should be reasonable . . .

So here the notice was a perfectly good notice so as to make time of the essence of the contract . . .

On the counterclaim the judge has held that the chassis should be returned or its value paid. I assume that the plaintiffs will exercise their option of paying for the chassis. They will then own the whole car which they can sell for whatever they can realize. I cannot help sharing the regret of the judge that this car was not sold before and the proceeds used to meet the cost of the work. But we have only to determine the strict legal rights of the parties. They are that the plaintiffs made a contract which they have not fulfilled and which the defendant justifiably cancelled. I think the decision of the judge was right and that this appeal should be dismissed."

NOTES AND QUESTIONS

1. Is this a sort of estoppel-at-common-law case?

2. Read *WJ Alan & Co Ltd v El Nasr Export and Import Co* (1972) in the law report. Ought not the common law to develop an independent doctrine of variation of contractual rights? Or are the present concepts of consideration and estoppel perfectly adequate to deal with almost any factual situation?

3. Could it not be argued that once a contract has been formed there comes into existence an independent legal bond (*vinculum iuris*) that transcends the original contractual promises? If so, should not this bond be capable of variation without having to fall back on the notion of promise (and consideration)?

4. Is estoppel effectively capable of creating an equitable doctrine of contract (just as there exists an equitable doctrine of ownership)?

10.3 Discharge by rescission in equity

A contractor who has been induced to enter into a contract as a result of fraud, misrepresentation, duress or undue influence has in principle the right to rescind the contract (see e.g. *Redgrave v Hurd* (1881), at p.240). It may be that time will defeat this right (see e.g. *Leaf v International Galleries* (1950), at p.242), and there are certain other bars to rescission such as restitution impossibility (see e.g. *Long v Lloyd* (1958)). In the case of non-fraudulent misrepresentation the court has power to refuse rescission and to treat the contract as subsisting, awarding damages in lieu (Misrepresentation Act 1967, s.2(2), above, p.237). It is the act of rescission that brings the contract to an end, although the other party can always go to court to challenge the validity of such rescission.

> **TSB Bank Plc v Camfield [1995] 1 W.L.R. 430, CA**
>
> (For facts and further extract, see p.244.)
>
> **Roch L.J.:** ". . . The right to set aside or rescind the transaction is that of the representee, not that of the court. The court's role in a disputed case will be to decide whether the representee has lawfully rescinded the transaction or is entitled to rescind it. Normally, if the representee is entitled to rescind the legal charge, that will have been effected by the representee's pleading that the transaction has been or should be set aside; that is to say, the transaction would have been set aside before the matter reaches the court. The court is not being asked to grant equitable relief; nor is it, in my view, granting equitable relief to which terms may be attached. . . ."

QUESTION

If the right to rescind is now a self-help remedy rather than a remedy granted by a court, is it now irrelevant to talk in terms of "equitable" rescission? Is the right to rescind recognised, equally, by the common law?

10.4 Discharge by breach

We have already seen that a breach of condition will give the innocent party to the contract a right to terminate the contract: see **7.1**. The conceptual basis for this right is actually quite complex.

10.4.1 Civil law analysis

In civil law thinking, right from Roman times, the content of a contract is said to be made up of terms and conditions. The term is a future event which is certain and upon which depends the enforceability or the extinction of the obligation; it may be certain or uncertain in the sense that the date of the future event can be determinable or undeterminable (e.g. the death of a person) (see e.g. Québec CC, art.1508). The condition is a future event that is uncertain in that it may or may not occur. And thus a "contractual obligation may be made conditional upon the occurrence of an uncertain future event, so that the obligation takes effect only if the event occurs (suspensive condition) or comes to an end if the event occurs (resolutive condition)" (PECL, art.16:101). The implied condition is important in respect of two contractual remedies, namely the right either to withhold performance until the other party performs (*exceptio non adimpleti contractus*) or to rescind the obligation for failure of performance by the other party (*si fides servetur*).

10.4.2 **Withholding performance**

The first remedy arose out of the synallagmatic nature of contracts such as sale: one party's undertaking was seen to be conditionally dependent on the other party's undertaking, and so if one party seemed reluctant to perform, this gave the other party the right to withhold his performance. In Roman law itself this particular remedy was very limited—indeed there was no general theory in Roman law about reciprocal obligations—and thus it is to be found only in the contract of sale. As a matter of *bona fides*, a seller was not under an obligation to deliver the goods until the buyer indicated that he was ready to pay (D.19.1.13.8). In the later civil law the idea was developed that each obligation was conditional upon the other and in modern contract law the right to withhold performance is expressed simply as a remedy.

Principles of European Contract Law

"Article 9:201 Right to Withhold Performance
(1) A party who is to perform simultaneously with or after the other party may withhold performance until the other has tendered performance or has performed. The first party may withhold the whole of its performance or a part of it as may be reasonable in the circumstances.

(2) A party may similarly withhold performance for as long as it is clear that there will be a non-performance by the other party when the other party's performance becomes due."

NOTES

1. See also UNIDROIT, arts 7.1.3 and 7.3.4.

2. If one asks whether the above rule represents the common law as well as the civil law, one soon finds that matters become extremely complex: see G.H. Treitel, *Remedies for Breach of Contract: A Comparative Account* (OUP, 1988), pp.245–317. One reason for this complexity is actually empirical (as much as theoretical) in that in many contracts one party has one main obligation, namely to pay the stipulated price for work done or for goods supplied. If the work done or property supplied does not amount to substantial performance then the other party is under no obligation to pay the price.

Sumpter v Hedges [1898] 1 Q.B. 673, CA

A.L. Smith L.J.: In this case the plaintiff, a builder, entered into a contract to build two houses and stables on the defendant's land for a lump sum. When the buildings were still in an unfinished state the plaintiff informed the defendant that he had no money, and was not going on with the work any more. The learned judge has found as a fact that he abandoned the contract. Under such circumstances, what is a building owner to do? He cannot keep the buildings on his land in an unfinished state for ever. The law is that, where there is a contract to do work for a lump sum, until the work is completed the price of it cannot be recovered. Therefore the plaintiff could not recover on the original contract. It is suggested however that the plaintiff was entitled to recover for the work he did on a quantum meruit. But, in order that that may be so, there must be evidence of a fresh contract to pay for the work already done. . . . I think the appeal must be dismissed."

Chitty L.J.: "I am of the same opinion. The plaintiff had contracted to erect certain buildings for a lump sum. When the work was only partly done, the plaintiff said that he could not go on with it, and the judge has found that he abandoned the contract. The position therefore was that the defendant found his land with unfinished buildings upon it, and he thereupon completed the work. That is no evidence from which the inference can be drawn that he entered into a fresh contract to pay for the work done by the plaintiff. If we held that the plaintiff could recover, we should in my opinion be overruling *Cutter v Powell*, and a long series of cases in which it has been decided that there must in such a case be some evidence of a new contract to enable the plaintiff to recover on a quantum meruit. . . ."

Collins L.J.: "I agree. I think the case is really concluded by the finding of the learned judge to the effect that the plaintiff had abandoned the contract. If the plaintiff had merely broken his contract in some way so as not to give the defendant the right to treat him as having abandoned the contract, and the defendant had then proceeded to finish the work himself, the plaintiff might perhaps have been entitled to sue on a quantum meruit on the ground that the defendant had taken the benefit of the work done. But that is not the present case. There are cases in which, though the plaintiff has abandoned the performance of a contract, it is possible for him to raise the inference of a new contract to pay for the work done on a quantum meruit from the defendant's having taken the benefit of that work, but, in order that that may be done, the circumstances must be such as to give an option to the defendant to take or not to take the benefit of the work done. It is only where the circumstances are such as to give that option that there is any evidence on which to ground the inference of a new contract. Where, as in the case of work done on land, the circumstances are such as to give the defendant no option whether he will take the benefit of the work or not, then one must look to other facts than the mere taking the benefit of the

> work in order to ground the inference of a new contract. In this case I see no other facts on which such an inference can be founded. The mere fact that a defendant is in possession of what he cannot help keeping, or even has done work upon it, affords no ground for such an inference. He is not bound to keep unfinished a building which in an incomplete state would be a nuisance on his land. I am therefore of opinion that the plaintiff was not entitled to recover for the work which he had done. . . ."

QUESTIONS

1. If a contractor threatens not to pay until the other party has performed satisfactorily, is this an example of withholding performance until the other party performs?

2. Could Mr Forsyth (above, p.442) have threatened the swimming pool company that he would not pay, say, half the contract price until they provided a swimming pool of the correct depth?

3. Is s.39 of the Sale of Goods Act 1979 an example of the *exceptio non adimpleti contractus* rule in English law? What about s.48B of the 1979 Act?

NOTES

1. *Sumpter v Hedges* is still good law: see *Bolton v Mahadeva* (1972) (above, p.454). It is, however, subject to the substantial performance rule: see *Hoenig v Isaacs* (1952) (above, p.446) and *Ruxley Electronics v Forsyth* (1996) (above, p.442).

2. Treitel writes: "There is . . . the point that while the civil law systems distinguish sharply between the *exceptio non adimpleti contractus* and termination (*résolution, Rücktritt*), the distinction is often blurred in common law systems, in which many of the same rules apply to both remedies. This point is reflected in common law terminology, which often refers to both remedies as "rescission" though the use of that expression has been criticized both in England and in the United States where its use in the present context is declining' (*Remedies for Breach of Contract: A Comparative Account* (OUP, 1988), p.245).

10.4.3 Termination for breach

The self-help remedy to rescind equally did not exist as such in Roman law except where such a clause had been expressly inserted into a contract (see e.g. D.18.1.3; D 41.4.2.5). However, the medieval canonists developed the idea that a synallagmatic contract was dependent upon each party keeping his promise (*frangenti fidem non est fides servanda*), and this was taken up by the late medieval jurisprudence (case law) if not by the Post-Glossators. In the later civil law, Dumoulin and Pothier reconciled the canonist learning with the jurisprudence in basing the remedy on the notion of an implied resolutive condition, and this analysis found its way into the *Code civil*. According to art.1184, a resolutory condition is always implied in a synallagmatic contract where one of the two parties does not satisfy his undertaking. However, the condition does not automatically destroy the contract; the innocent party has the choice either to force the other to perform the undertaking when it is possible, or to claim the rescission with damages. In the modern *lex mercatoria* a party may terminate the contract if the other party's non-performance is fundamental (see PECL, art.9:301, above at p.334). The question, of course, is what amounts to a fundamental non-performance.

Principles of European Contract Law

"Article 8:103 Fundamental Non-Performance
A non-performance of an obligation is fundamental to the contract if:

(a) strict compliance with the obligation is of the essence of the contract; or

(b) the non-performance substantially deprives the aggrieved party of what it was entitled to expect under the contract, unless the other party did not foresee and could not reasonably have foreseen that result; or

(c) the non-performance is intentional and gives the aggrieved party reason to believe that it cannot rely on the other party's future performance."

Unidroit Principles for International Commercial Contracts

"Article 7.3.1 Right to Terminate the Contract
(1) A party may terminate the contract where the failure of the other party to perform an obligation under the contract amounts to a fundamental performance.

(2) In determining whether a failure to perform an obligation amounts to a fundamental non- performance regard shall be had, in particular, to whether

(a) the non-performance substantially deprives the aggrieved party of what it was entitled to expect under the contract unless the other party did not foresee and could not reasonably have foreseen such result;
(b) strict compliance with the obligation which has not been performed is of essence under the contract;
(c) the non-performance is intentional or reckless;
(d) the non-performance gives the aggrieved party reason to believe that it cannot rely on the other party's future performance;
(e) the non-performing party will suffer disproportionate loss as a result of the preparation or performance if the contract is terminated.

(3) In the case of delay the aggrieved party may also terminate the contract if the other party fails to perform before the time allowed under Article 7.1.5 has expired."

NOTES AND QUESTIONS

1. The common law tackles the issue of fundamental and non-fundamental non-performance by referring to the status of the term broken: a breach of condition entitles the other party to terminate (see **7.1.2**), whereas a breach of warranty will not (see **7.1.3**). However, as we have seen in a previous chapter, this strict dichotomy was to cause problems on occasions, with the result that the court would look at the nature of the breach itself, giving rise to the idea of an innominate term (see **7.1.4**). However, to what extent does PECL, art.8:103 or UNIDROIT, art.7.3.1 represent English law?

2. Is there a separate doctrine of termination that attaches uniquely to the breach itself, or are all breaches of contract ultimately to be resolved by reference to the nature of the term broken?

3. Can one say that English law allows the victim of a breach to terminate only if the breach is fundamental?

Decro-Wall International SA v Practitioners in Marketing Ltd **[1971] 1 W.L.R. 361, CA**

This was an action in debt in respect of unpaid bills concerning goods which had been supplied by the plaintiffs, a French company, to the defendants, an English company. There was also a claim for a declaration that the defendants were no longer the sole concessionaires in respect of the plaintiffs' products, the defendants having repudiated the contract by their history of late payment of bills and their refusal to pay the present bills. The defendants counterclaimed for a declaration that they were still concessionaires and an injunction to prevent the plaintiffs from supplying their goods to anyone other than the defendants. The defendants also counterclaimed for damages for breach of contract. The trial judge gave judgment for the plaintiffs in respect of the debt claim, but refused to hold that the contract had been terminated by the defendants' breach. Accordingly he awarded damages on the counterclaim. An appeal to the Court of Appeal (Salmon, Sachs and Buckley L.JJ.) was dismissed.

Salmon L.J.: ". . . The first question to be decided on this appeal is whether the defendants, by failing punctually to pay the bills of exchange prior to April 9, 1970, repudiated the agreement made in March 1967. I have come to the conclusion that the judge was plainly right in holding that there had been no repudiation by the defendants. Clearly the defendants were in breach of the 1967 agreement by failing to pay the bills punctually. A breach of contract may be of such a nature as to amount to repudiation and give the innocent party the right (if he desires to exercise it) to be relieved from any further performance of the contract, or the breach may entitle the innocent party only to damages. How is the legal consequence of a breach to be ascertained? Primarily from the terms of the contract itself. The contract may state expressly or by necessary implication that the breach of one of its terms will go to the root of the contract and

487

accordingly amount to repudiation. Where it does not do so, the courts must look at the practical results of the breach in order to decide whether or not it does go to the root of the contract: see *Mersey Steel & Iron Co Ltd v Naylor, Benzon & Co* (1884) 9 App Cas 434, *per* Lord Blackburn at pp 443, 444; *Hongkong Fir Shipping Co Ltd v Kawasaki Kisen Kaisha Ltd* [1962] 2 QB 26, *per* Diplock LJ at pp 69–71; *The Mihalis Angelos* [1971] 1 QB 164, *per* Lord Denning MR at p 193.

The same test may be and indeed often has been stated in different language, namely: is the term which has been breached of the essence of the contract? Section 10(1) of the Sale of Goods Act 1893 provides that: 'Unless a different intention appears from the terms of the contract, stipulations as to time of payment are not deemed to be of the essence of a contract of sale. . . . ' The present contract is, of course, not a simple contract of sale but, in my view, the same principle is to be applied to it.

I am confident that the terms of the present contract relating to time of payment of the bills cannot properly be regarded as of the essence of the contract, or, to put it the other way, there is nothing expressed in or to be implied from the contract to suggest that a failure punctually to pay the bills goes to the root of the contract and thereby amounts to a repudiation . . .

. . . The case would have been quite different if the defendants' breaches had been such as reasonably to shatter the plaintiffs' confidence in the defendants' ability to pay for the goods with which the plaintiffs supplied them. I think that, in such circumstances, the consequences of the breach could properly have been regarded as most serious, indeed fundamental, and going to the root of the contract so that the plaintiffs would have been entitled to refuse to continue doing business with the defendants . . ."

Buckley L.J.: ". . . Will the consequences of the breach be such that it would be unfair to the injured party to hold him to the contract and leave him to his remedy in damages as and when a breach or breaches may occur? If this would be so, then a repudiation has taken place . . ."

NOTES

1. One can see the danger here of terminating a contract when the breach is not fundamental: the terminator becomes liable for breach of the contract.

2. See also *Schuler v Wickman Tools* (1974) (p.327, 331); *Cehave v Bremer* (1976) (p.332, 347); *Hong Kong Fir Shipping* (1962) (p.336); and *Bunge Corpn v Tradax* (1981) (p.338).

10.4.4 **Anticipatory breach**

The notion of an "anticipatory" breach of contract is set out in the next extract.

Principles of European Contract Law

"**Article 9:304 Anticipatory Non-Performance**
Where prior to the time for performance by a party it is clear that there will be a fundamental non-performance by it the other party may terminate the contract."

NOTE

See also UNIDROIT, art.7.3.3. Anticipatory breach is explained in the next extract.

G.H. Treitel, *Remedies for Breach of Contract: A Comparative Account* **(OUP, 1988), pp.379–80 (footnotes omitted)**

"**279.** *Meaning and availability of termination.* The expression 'anticipatory breach' and 'anticipatory repudiation' are used in common law systems to refer to situations in which a party to a contract, before performance from him has fallen due, either renounces the contract or disables himself from performing it. In such situations, the aggrieved party can either continue to press for performance or he can 'accept' the breach. If he takes the former course, his remedies are governed by the same principles that apply in cases of actual breach, ie where the renunciation or disablement occurs after the defaulting party's performance is due. But if the aggrieved party accepts the breach, the general principle is that his remedies become available at once, ie even though performance from the defaulting has not yet become due. . . . The English position . . . seems to be that an anticipatory breach can justify termination even though the breach is not 'serious' but that it will not do so where the right to terminate arises solely by virtue of an express term of the contract . . ."

QUESTION

It may be that the anticipatory breach does not need to be serious for the option to terminate to operate, but must there be a breach of a 'condition'?

NOTE

What brings the contract to an end is not the breach itself but the election to terminate by the aggrieved party, and this is true not just with anticipatory breaches of contract but with all breaches serious enough to justify termination.

Decro-Wall International SA v Practitioners in Marketing Ltd **[1971] 1 W.L.R. 361, CA**

(For facts, see p.487.)

Sachs L.J.: ". . . The truth of the matter is that there are a great many cases in which it is of no benefit to the innocent party to keep the contract alive for the simple reason that, in the long run, unless the repudiating party can be persuaded or impelled to change his mind and withdraw his repudiation, the only remedy available to the innocent party will lie in damages. So there are vast numbers of cases where the innocent party can in one sense be said to be forced to adopt the only practicable course because any other would be valueless. In such cases it is the range of remedies that is limited, not the right to elect.

That does not alter the position that the innocent party can, if he so chooses, elect not to accept the repudiation and may thus in suitable cases keep open, maybe at certain risks, the chances either that the other party may yet take a different course or that it may be one of those special cases where the court will in its discretion grant some form of declaration or injunction on the basis that the contract has not yet been discharged . . ."

QUESTION

In *White & Carter (Councils) v McGregor* (1962) (p.386), the claimant refused to terminate and performed its contractual promises; it then successfully claimed the price for this performance. What are the limits (if any) to this doctrine? If a defendant householder cancels a contract with a window cleaner before the date of performance, can the window cleaner nevertheless refuse to accept this anticipatory breach and turn up, clean the windows, and claim the price? (*Cf. Hounslow LBC v Twickenham Garden Developments Ltd* (1971).)

Attica Sea Carriers Corp v Ferrostaal Poseidon [1976] 1 Ll. Rep.250, CA

This was an action for debt brought by the owners of a ship against the hirers of the vessel. The hirers were under a contractual duty to redeliver the ship in good repair, but, owing to engine trouble, it transpired that to put the ship in good repair would cost over twice its actual value. The hirers accordingly tried to redeliver the ship without the full repairs being done. The owners refused to accept redelivery and were thus claiming the hire fees for the whole period during which the ship remained unrepaired. The Court of Appeal (Lord Denning M.R., Orr and Browne L.JJ.) held that the owners ought to have accepted redelivery and thus were not entitled to sue in debt. They were entitled only to damages.

Lord Denning M.R.: ". . . [*White & Carter (Councils) Ltd v McGregor*] has no application whatever in a case where the plaintiff ought, in all reason, to accept the repudiation and sue for damages—provided that damages would provide an adequate remedy for any loss suffered by him. The reason is because, by suing for the money, the plaintiff is seeking to enforce specific performance of the contract—and he should not be allowed to do so when damages would be an adequate remedy . . . [The owners] cannot sue for specific performance—either of the promise to pay the charter hire, or of the promise to do the repairs—because damages are an adequate remedy for the breach. What is the alternative which the shipowners present to the charterers? Either the charterers must pay the charter hire for years to come, whilst the vessel lies idle and useless for want of repair. Or the charterers must do the repairs which would cost twice as much as the ship would be worth when repaired—after which the shipowners might sell it as scrap, making the repairs a useless waste of money. In short, on either alternative, the shipowners seek to compel specific performance of one or other of the provisions of the charter—with most unjust and unreasonable consequences—when damages would be an adequate remedy. I do not think the law allows them to do this. . . .”

QUESTIONS

1. Does this case share a common denominator with *Ruxley Electronics v Forsyth* (1996) (p.442) and *Co-operative Insurance Society Ltd v Argyll Stores Ltd* (1998) (p.566)? If so, what is it? (*Cf.* Cunnington (2006) 26 L.S. 369, at 384–9.)

2. Is *Attica* saying that there are some situations where the aggrieved party does not have an option about whether or not to terminate?

3. Is it true to say that English law is reluctant specifically to enforce contracts?

4. Could this case be seen as one where the claimant was not acting in good faith?

5. Was the claimant abusing its right? Did equity prevent the claimant suing in debt?

White & Carter (Councils) Ltd v McGregor **[1962] A.C. 413, HL (Scot.)**

(For facts and further extracts, see p.386.)

Lord Reid: “. . . [Another] ground would be that there is some general equitable principle or element of public policy which requires this limitation of the contractual rights of the innocent party. It may well be that, if it can be shown that a person has no legitimate interest, financial or otherwise, in performing the contract rather than claiming damages, he ought not to be allowed to saddle the other party with an additional burden with no benefit to himself. If a party has no interest to enforce a stipulation, he cannot in general enforce it: so it might be said that, if a party has no interest to insist on a particular remedy, he ought not to be allowed to insist on it. And, just as a party is not allowed to enforce a penalty, so he ought not to be allowed to penalise the other party by taking one course when another is equally advantageous to him. If I may revert to the example which I gave of a company engaging an expert to prepare an elaborate report and then repudiating before anything was done, it might be that the company could show that the expert had no substantial or legitimate interest in carrying out the work rather than accepting damages: I would think that the *de minimis* principle would apply in determining whether his interest was substantial, and that he might have a legitimate interest other than an immediate financial interest. But if the expert had no such interest then that might be regarded as a proper case for the exercise of the general equitable jurisdiction of the court. But that is not this case. Here the respondent did not set out to prove that the appellants had no legitimate interest in completing the contract and claiming the contract price rather than claiming damages; there is nothing in the findings of fact to support such a case, and it seems improbable that any such case could have been proved. It is, in my judgment, impossible to say that the appellants should be deprived of their right to claim the contract price merely because the benefit to them, as against claiming damages and re-letting their advertising space, might be small in comparison with the loss to the respondent: that is the most that could be said in favour of the respondent. Parliament has on many occasions relieved parties from certain kinds of improvident or oppressive contracts, but the common law can only do that in very limited circumstances. Accordingly, I am unable to avoid the conclusion that this appeal must be allowed and the case remitted so that decree can be pronounced as craved in the initial writ."

QUESTIONS

1. Is the notion of a "legitimate interest" really of help in this situation, for will it not always be in a claimant's interest, at least in certain situations where the breach has not caused damage in excess of the price, to sue in debt rather than damages?

2. Did the claimant in *Attica* have an interest in not accepting redelivery of the ship? Was it legitimate? If not, why not?

3. What is the historical or precedent basis of Lord Reid's equitable principle?

10.4.5 Effects of termination

Once a contract has been terminated, questions arise about the rights and obligations of each party.

Principles of European Contract Law

"Article 9:305 Effects of Termination in General
(1) Termination of the contract releases both parties from their obligation to effect and to receive future performance, but, subject to Articles 9:306 to 9:308, does not affect the rights and liabilities that have accrued up to the time of termination.

(2) Termination does not affect any provision of the contract for the settlement of disputes or any other provision which is to operate even after termination.

Article 9:306 Property Reduced in Value
A party who terminates the contract may reject property previously received from the other party if its value to the first party has been fundamentally reduced as a result of the other party's non-performance.

Article 9:307 Recovery of Money Paid
On termination of the contract a party may recover money paid for a performance which it did not receive or which it properly rejected.

Article 9:308 Recovery of Property
On termination of the contract a party who has supplied property which can be returned and for which it has not received payment or other counter-performance may recover the property.

Article 9:309 Recovery for Performance that Cannot be Returned
On termination of the contract a party who has rendered a performance which cannot be returned and for which it has not received payment or other counter-performance may recover a reasonable amount for the value of the performance to the other party."

NOTE

See also UNIDROIT, arts 7.3.5 and 7.3.6.

QUESTIONS

1. Reconsider *Sumpter v Hedges* (1898) (above p.484) and *Bolton v Mahadeva* (1972) (above p.454) in the light of the above articles: could the non-performing party recover for the property left on the other party's premises? Do the above articles reflect English law?

2. Can deposits be recovered? (*Cf. Workers Trust Bank Ltd v Dojap Ltd* (1993) p.357.)

10.5 Discharge by frustration

We have seen that a mere change of circumstances will not discharge a contract in English law, or even give rise to a duty to renegotiate (see **8.6**). However, if the change of circumstances is dramatic and is caused by an outside event unforeseen by the contractors at the time of contracting and arising through the fault of neither party, it may act as a frustrating event that will bring the contract to an end (*cf.* **9.4**).

10.5.1 **Nature of frustration**

The development and definition of the doctrine of frustration has been outlined in a Court of Appeal judgment.

***Great Peace Shipping Ltd v Tsavliris Salvage (International) Ltd* [2003] Q.B. 679, CA**

(For facts, see p.255.)

> **Lord Phillips M.R.** (delivering the judgment of the court): ". . . 62. The foundation of the law of frustration was Blackburn J's famous judgment in *Taylor v Caldwell* (1863) 3 B & S 826. The parties had entered into an agreement for the hire of a music hall for concerts on four specified nights. The hall burnt down before the first of these. Blackburn J, giving the judgment of the Court of Queen's Bench, held that performance of the contract was excused by reason of an implied term . . .
>
> 63. *Taylor v Caldwell* was a case in which the subject matter of the contract was destroyed, so that performance of the letter of the contract was rendered impossible. The principle of frustration thus established, its ambit of operation was then extended. Claims for frustration were advanced, not where a supervening event had made it impossible to perform the letter of the contract, but where performance of the letter of the contract had become something radically different from that which the parties contemplated when it was concluded.
>
> 64. The first such case was *Jackson v Union Marine Insurance Co Ltd* (1874) LR 10 CP 125. There a voyage charterparty from Liverpool to San Francisco was delayed for over six months as a result of the vessel stranding before loading her cargo. The charter was held to have been frustrated upon the jury finding that a voyage undertaken after the ship had been repaired would have been a different adventure from that to which the parties had agreed.
>
> 65. Particularly instructive in the present context are the 'coronation cases'. Many rooms were leased, or seats in stands sold, along the route planned for the coronation procession of King Edward VII. He fell ill and the coronation was cancelled. Spectators who had contracted before he fell ill claimed that their contracts were frustrated. In at least one case, a spectator who had contracted in ignorance of his illness claimed that his contract was void for mistake. These claims succeeded. . . .
>
> 69. Cases where frustration was alleged proved a fruitful source of litigation and, by 1916, Earl Loreburn was able to advance the following proposition in *FA Tamplin Steamship Co Ltd v Anglo-Mexican Petroleum Products Co Ltd* [1916] 2 AC 397, 403–404:
>
> > 'when our courts have held innocent contracting parties absolved from further performance of their promises, it has been upon the ground that there was an

implied term in the contract which entitled them to be absolved. Sometimes it is put that performance has become impossible and that the party concerned did not promise to perform an impossibility. Sometimes it is put that the parties contemplated a certain state of things which fell out otherwise. In most of the cases it is said that there was an implied condition in the contract which operated to release the parties from performing it, and in all of them I think that was at bottom the principle upon which the court proceeded. It is in my opinion the true principle, for no court has an absolving power, but it can infer from the nature of the contract and the surrounding circumstances that a condition which is not expressed was a foundation on which the parties contracted.'

70. Despite Earl Loreburn's words, the doctrine of frustration was patently judge-made law. In *National Carriers Ltd v Panalpina (Northern) Ltd* [1981] AC 675 the House of Lords considered five different explanations for the doctrine of frustration. Lord Hailsham of St Marylebone LC and Lord Roskill favoured the exposition of the doctrine given by Lord Radcliffe in *Davis Contractors Ltd v Fareham Urban District Council* [1956] AC 696, 728 and Lord Simon of Glaisdale advanced the following refinement of that test [1981] AC 675, 700:

'Frustration of a contract takes place when there supervenes an event (without default of either party and for which the contract makes no sufficient provision) which so significantly changes the nature (not merely the expense or onerousness) of the outstanding contractual rights and/or obligations from what the parties could reasonably have contemplated at the time of its execution that it would be unjust to hold them to the literal sense of its stipulations in the new circumstances; in such case the law declares both parties to be discharged from further performance.'

71. Lord Simon's formulation of the doctrine must be read subject to the proviso that the parties may make express provision for what is to happen in the event of what would otherwise be a frustrating event. Such a provision will normally preclude the application of the doctrine of frustration.

72. Initially the effect of frustration was to terminate the parties' respective obligations from the date of the frustrating event, but to leave outstanding any accrued obligations. This harsh result was mitigated to a degree by the decision of the House of Lords in *Fibrosa Spolka Akcyjna v Fairbairn Lawson Combe Barbour Ltd* [1943] AC 32 and to a greater degree by the Law Reform (Frustrated Contracts) Act 1943. . . .

74. In considering whether performance of the contract is impossible, it is necessary to identify what it is that the parties agreed would be performed. This involves looking not only at the express terms, but at any implications that may arise out of the surrounding circumstances. In some cases it will be possible to identify details of the 'contractual adventure' which go beyond the terms that are expressly spelt out, in others it will not. . . .''

NOTES

1. In *Paal Wilson & Co v Partenreederei* (1983), Lord Brandon said (at 909): "The first essential factor is that there must be some outside event or extraneous change of situation, not foreseen or provided for by the parties at the time of contracting, which either makes it impossible for the contract to be performed at all, or at least renders its performance something radically different from what the parties contemplated when they entered into it. The second essential factor is that the outside event or extraneous change of situation concerned, and the consequences of either in relation to the performance of the contract, must have occurred without either the fault or the default of either party to the contract."

2. Lord Phillips in *The Great Peace* compared the doctrine of frustration with the doctrine of mistake at common law (see **5.3**). He said (at § 85): "Circumstances where a contract is void as a result of common mistake are likely to be less common than instances of frustration. Supervening events which defeat the contractual adventure will frequently not be the responsibility of either party. Where, however, the parties agree that something shall be done which is impossible at the time of making the agreement, it is much more likely that, on true construction of the agreement, one or other will have undertaken responsibility for the mistaken state of affairs. This may well explain why cases where contracts have been found to be void in consequence of common mistake are few and far between."

3. Unlike breach, frustration automatically discharges the contract; the parties have no choice in the matter.

National Carriers Ltd v Panalpina (Northern) Ltd **[1981] A.C. 675, HL**

(For facts, see p.500.)

Lord Roskill: ". . . The extension in recent years of government interference in ordinary business affairs, inflation, sudden outbreaks of war in different parts of the world, are all recent examples of circumstances in which the doctrine has been invoked, sometimes with success, sometimes without. Indeed the doctrine has been described as a 'device' for doing justice between the parties when they themselves have failed either wholly or sufficiently to provide for the particular event or events which have happened. The doctrine is principally concerned with the incidence of risk—who must take the risk of the happening of a particular event especially when the parties have not made any or any sufficient provision for the happening of that event? When the doctrine is successfully invoked it is because in the event which has happened the law imposes a solution, casting the incidence of that risk on one party or the other as the circumstances of the particular case may require, having regard to the express provisions of the

496

contract into which the parties have entered. The doctrine is no arbitrary dispensing power to be exercised at the subjective whim of the judge by whom the issue has to be determined. Frustration if it occurs operates automatically. Its operation does not depend on the action or inaction of the parties. It is to be invoked or not to be invoked by reference only to the particular contract before the court and the facts of the particular case said to justify the invocation of the doctrine . . ."

NOTE

The implied term theory of contract was abandoned in the 1950s.

Davis Contractors Ltd v Fareham UDC [1956] A.C. 696, HL

(For facts, see p.426.)

Lord Radcliffe: ". . . The theory of frustration belongs to the law of contract and it is represented by a rule which the courts will apply in certain limited circumstances for the purpose of deciding that contractual obligations, ex facie binding, are no longer enforceable against the parties. The description of the circumstances that justify the application of the rule and, consequently, the decision whether in a particular case those circumstances exist are, I think necessarily questions of law.

It has often been pointed out that the descriptions vary from one case of high authority to another . . .

Lord Loreburn ascribes the dissolution to an implied term of the contract that was actually made. This approach is in line with the tendency of English courts to refer all the consequences of a contract to the will of those who made it. But there is something of a logical difficulty in seeing how the parties could even impliedly have provided for something which *ex hypothesi* they neither expected nor foresaw; and the ascription or frustration to an implied term of the contract has been criticised as obscuring the true action of the court which consists in applying an objective rule of the law of contract to the contractual obligations that the parties have imposed upon themselves . . .

By this time it might seem that the parties themselves have become so far disembodied spirits that their actual persons should be allowed to rest in peace. In their place there rises the figure of the fair and reasonable man. And the spokesman of the fair and reasonable man, who represents after all no more than the anthropomorphic conception of justice, is and must be the court itself. So perhaps it would be simpler to say at the outset that frustration occurs whenever the law recognises that without default of either party a contractual obligation has become incapable of being performed because the circumstances in which performance is called for would render it a thing radically different from that which was undertaken by the contract. *Non haec in foedera veni*. It was not this that I promised to do.

There is, however, no uncertainty as to the materials upon which the court must proceed. 'The data for decision are, on the one hand, the terms and construction of the contract, read in the light of the then existing circumstances, and on the other hand the events which have occurred' . . . But, even so, it is not hardship or inconvenience or material loss itself which calls the principle of frustration into play. There must be as well such a change in the significance of the obligation that the thing undertaken would, if performed, be a different thing from that contracted for. . . ."

QUESTION

"There is nothing so foreseeable as the unforeseeable." If this adage has any validity, does it mean that Lord Radcliffe's analysis, and abandonment of the implied term theory, is not as rational as it might first appear?

10.5.2 **Nature of frustrating event**

Not all intervening events will amount to frustration: see the facts of *Davis*, at p.426. One important distinction is between "commercial basis" and "motive". A frustration of motive will not normally undermine the contract. Thus if a person contracts with a taxi firm to be taken to a friend's house for a party, the cancellation of the party will not result in the frustration of the taxi contract. Yet much may depend on the circumstances.

Krell v Henry **[1903] 2 K.B. 740, CA**

This was an action in debt for rent owing for the use of rooms overlooking Pall Mall. The defendant had contracted to rent the rooms for £75 for two days during the coronation of the King, and had paid the plaintiff £25 in advance. However, when the coronation was cancelled, owing to the illness of the King, the defendant refused to pay the £50 and counterclaimed for the return of his £25. The trial judge gave judgment for the defendant on the claim and counterclaim, and the Court of Appeal (Vaughan Williams, Romer and Stirling L.JJ.) agreed that the contract was frustrated.

Vaughan Williams L.J.: "The real question in this case is the extent of the application in English law of the principle of the Roman law which has been adopted and acted on in many English decisions, and notably in the case of *Taylor v Caldwell* . . . I do not think that the principle of the civil law as introduced into the English law is limited to cases in which the event causing the impossibility of performance is the destruction or non-existence of some thing which is the subject-matter of the contract or of some condition or state of things expressly specified as a condition of it. I think that you first have to ascertain, not necessarily from the terms of the contract, but, if required, from necessary inferences, drawn from surrounding circumstances recognised by both contracting parties, what is the substance of the contract, and then to ask the question whether that substantial contract needs for its foundation the assumption of the existence of a particular state of things. If it does, this will limit the operation of the general words, and in such case, if the contract becomes impossible of performance by reason of the non-existence of the state of things assumed by both contracting parties as the foundation of the contract there will be no breach of the contract thus limited. Now what are the facts of the present case? The contract is contained in two letters of June 20 which passed between the defendant and the plaintiff's agent, Mr Cecil Bisgood. These letters do not mention the coronation, but speak merely of the taking of Mr Krell's chambers, or, rather, of the use of them, in the daytime of June 26 and 27, for the sum of £75, £25 then paid, balance £50 to be paid on the 24th. But the affidavits, which by agreement between the parties are to be taken as stating the facts of the case, show that the plaintiff exhibited on his premises, third floor, 56A, Pall Mall, an announcement to the effect that windows to view the Royal coronation pro-cession were to be let, and that the defendant was induced by that announcement to apply to the housekeeper on the premises, who said that the owner was willing to let the suite of rooms for the purpose of seeing the Royal procession for both days, but not nights, of June 26 and 27. In my judgment the use of the rooms was let and taken for the purpose of seeing the Royal procession. It was not a demise of the rooms, or even an agreement to let and take the rooms. It is a licence to use rooms for a particular purpose and none other. And in my judgment the taking place of those processions on the days proclaimed along the proclaimed route, which passed 56A, Pall Mall, was regarded by both contracting parties as the foundation of the contract; and I think that it cannot reasonably be supposed to have been in the contemplation of the contracting parties, when the contract was made, that the coronation would not be held on the proclaimed days, or the processions not take place on those days along the proclaimed route . . .

I think for the reasons which I have given that the principle of *Taylor v Caldwell* ought to be applied. This disposes of the plaintiff's claim for £50 unpaid balance of the price agreed to be paid for the use of the rooms. The defendant at one time set up a cross-claim for the return of the £25 he paid at the date of the contract. As that claim is now withdrawn it is unnecessary to say anything about it . . ."

QUESTIONS

1. What was the object of the contract in *Krell v Henry*: was it to hire a room, or to hire a viewing place? Is the answer to this question determined by the owner's pre-contractual statement? What if the contract had contained a clause stipulating that it was a contract for the demise of rooms? Might it be said that it is the law of property which determined whether or not the contract was frustrated?

2. Why should the owner of the rooms and not the hirer be the one to shoulder the risk of the coronation being cancelled?

3. Ought the defendant to have been able to reclaim the £25 in debt?

4. Can you reconcile *Krell v Henry* with *Herne Bay SS Co v Hutton* (1903) (read in law report)?

5. Does the doctrine of frustration apply to leases?

National Carriers Ltd v Panalpina (Northern) Ltd [1981] A.C. 675, HL

This was an action in debt by a lessor for rent due from a lessee in respect of the 10–year lease of a warehouse. The lessee had refused to pay the rent on the basis that the lease had been frustrated owing to the closure of the warehouse's access by the local authority; the lessee was unable to use the warehouse for the contemplated purpose. The closure, which seemingly was to last 18 months, had been caused by the unsafe nature of a nearby building requiring demolition. The trial judge gave judgment for the lessor on the basis that according to precedent a lease could not be frustrated. On an appeal direct to the House of Lords (a "leapfrog" appeal), the House (Lords Hailsham, Wilberforce, Simon, Russell and Roskill) dismissed the appeal; the interruption did not amount to a frustrating event. However, a majority of the Law Lords held that a lease could in principle be subject to the doctrine of frustration.

Lord Simon: ". . . The appellants were undoubtedly put to considerable expense and inconvenience. But that is not enough. Whenever the performance of a contract is interrupted by a supervening event, the initial judgment is quantitative—what relation does the likely period of interruption bear to the outstanding period for performance? But this must ultimately be translated into qualitative terms: in the light of the quantitative computation and of all other relevant factors (from which I would not entirely exclude executed performance) would outstanding performance in accordance with the literal terms of the contract differ so significantly from what the parties reasonably contemplated at the time of execution that it would be unjust to insist on compliance with those literal terms? In the instant case, at the most favourable to the appellants' contention, they could, at the time when the road was closed, look forward to pristine enjoyment of the warehouse for about two thirds of the remaining currency of the lease. The interruption would be only one sixth of the total term. Judging by the drastic increase in rent under the rent review clause (more than doubled), it seems likely that the appellants' occupation towards the end of the first quinquennium must have been on terms very favourable to them. The parties can hardly have contemplated that the expressly-provided-for fire risk was the only possible source of interruption of the business of the warehouse—some possible interruption from some cause or other cannot have been beyond the reasonable contemplation of the parties. Weighing all the relevant factors, I do not think that the appellants have demonstrated a triable issue that the closure of the road so significantly changed the nature of the outstanding rights and obligations under the lease from what the parties could reasonably have contemplated at the time of its execution that it would be unjust to hold them to the literal sense of its stipulations . . ."

Lord Russell: ". . . If a principle of achieving justice be anywhere at the root of the principle of frustration, I ask myself why should justice require that a useless site be returned to the lessor rather than remain the property of the lessee? (It is not suggested that a just solution can be achieved by somehow sharing the bad luck between lessor and lessee by, for example, a reduction of rent.) . . ."

Lord Roskill: ". . . The law should not be compartmentalised. In principle a common law doctrine ought not to be held capable of applying only in one field of contract and not in another. To preserve the dichotomy between leases on the one hand and other types of contract on the other can undoubtedly create anomalies. Thus if a ship is demise-chartered for the purpose of storing oil and explodes without fault of either party, the demise charter would clearly be frustrated. If the same demise charterer also leases an adjacent shore installation for the same purpose and the same explosion destroys that installation along with the demise-chartered ship, rent for that storage installation would remain payable in full for the unexpired period of the lease though liability for demise charter hire had ceased upon the frustration of the demise charterparty . . .

My Lords, it follows that on the question of principle I find it impossible to justify compartmentalisation of the law or to agree that the doctrine of frustration applies to every type of contract save a lease. I can see no logical difference between frustration of a demise charterparty and frustration of a lease. In principle the doctrine should be equally capable of universal application in all contractual arrangements . . ."

QUESTIONS

1. If PECL, art.6.111 (see above, p.432) were in force in the UK, would it apply to *Panalpina*?

2. With regard to Lord Russell's question, why should the risk, for that matter, be on the lessee?

3. An increase in expense does not generally amount to frustration (see *Davis Contractors v Fareham UDC* (1956), at p.426). But what about a dramatic increase in expense?

4. Was Lord Roskill being serious when he said that the law should not be "compartmentalized"? (*Cf.* Tony Weir, above at p.59.)

10.5.3 Fault and frustration

One of the key factors in frustration is that the frustrating event should not result from one of the party's acts or omissions. If it does, this will amount to "self-induced frustration".

Maritime National Fish Ltd v Ocean Trawlers Ltd [1935] A.C. 524, PC

This was an action in debt by the owners of a trawler called the *St Cuthbert* against the charterers of the vessel. The charterers, by way of defence, claimed that the contract of hire had been frustrated, for they had been granted only three fishing licences by the Canadian government in respect of a fleet, including the *St Cuthbert*, of five trawlers. The charterers (appellants) had decided to apply the three licences to boats other than the *St Cuthbert*, which meant that this latter vessel became redundant to them, because it could not be used for fishing without a licence. The Privy Council (Lords Atkin, Tomlin, Macmillan and Wright) held that the contract had not been frustrated and that the charterers were accordingly liable for the money owed.

> **Lord Wright:** ". . . It is clear that the appellants were free to select any three of the five trawlers they were operating and could, had they willed, have selected the *St Cuthbert* as one, in which event a licence would have been granted to her. It is immaterial to speculate why they preferred to put forward for licences the three trawlers which they actually selected. Nor is it material, as between the appellants and the respondents, that the appellants were operating other trawlers to three of which they gave the preference. What matters is that they could have got a licence for the *St Cuthbert* if they had so minded. If the case be figured as one in which the *St Cuthbert* was removed from the category of privileged trawlers, it was by the appellants' hand that she was so removed, because it was their hand that guided the hand of the Minister in placing the licences where he did and thereby excluding the *St Cuthbert*. The essence of 'frustration' is that it should not be due to the act or election of the party . . .
>
> . . . [T]heir Lordships are of opinion that the loss of the *St Cuthbert's* licence can correctly be described, quoad the appellants, as 'a self induced frustration.' . . . In truth, it happened in consequence of their election. If it be assumed that the performance of the contract was dependent on a licence being granted, it was that election which prevented performance, and on that assumption it was the appellants' own default which frustrated the adventure: the appellants cannot rely on their own default to excuse them from liability under the contract."

PROBLEMS

1. John runs a van-hire business which consists of 12 ordinary vans of the same type and one extra large van. One Friday, John contracts with 12 customers, including Basil, for the hire of his vans for the following week. He also contracts with Tony to hire out the extra large van for the following week. During the weekend there is a fire at John's premises which destroys six of the 12 ordinary vans and also writes off the extra large van. On the Monday, John decides to let out the six remaining ordinary vans to the first six of the 12 contractors who arrive at his premises. Basil is the seventh to arrive and, on discovering that there is no van, threatens to sue John for breach of contract. Tony also threatens to sue when he discovers that there is no longer a large

van. Can John raise the defence of frustration against Basil and Tony? (See *J Lauritzen AS v Wijsmuller BV (The Super Servant Two)* (1990).)

2. Same facts as above, except for two major differences. First, all of John's vans are destroyed and, secondly, both Basil and Tony suspect that the cause of the fire is John's negligence with regard to the state of his premises. When threatened with legal action, John claims all the contracts are frustrated. Advise Basil and Tony. (*Cf. Joseph Constantine SS Line Ltd v Imperial Smelting* (1942), above at p.467.)

3. John runs a van-hire business and contracts with Geoffrey to hire him a van for the following week. On Monday Geoffrey does not turn up to collect the van, and John subsequently discovers that this was because Geoffrey had been arrested and held on remand for some awful offence committed over the weekend. John is threatening to sue Geoffrey for breach of contract. Advise Geoffrey (in prison) whether or not he can raise the defence of frustration. (*Cf. FC Shepherd & Co Ltd v Jerrom* (1986).)

QUESTIONS

1. Do the rules of causation have an important role to play in frustration cases?

2. What is the difference between termination by breach and termination by self-induced frustration?

NOTES

1. In *Paal Wilson & Co v Partenreederei Hannah Blumenthal* (1983) Kerr L.J. said (at 892): "We were referred to all the classic authorities on self-induced frustration such as *Maritime National Fish Ltd v Ocean Trawlers Ltd* and *Joseph Constantine Steamship Line Ltd v Imperial Smelting Corporation Ltd*, but none of them goes anywhere near suggesting that inaction is to be equated with fault or default when there is no obligation or duty to act. On the contrary, while avoiding any precise definition, they suggest that self-induced frustration requires some deliberate or positive act which renders the performance of the contract impossible, or impossible in the way in which performance had been intended."

2. In *C Czarnikow Ltd v Rolimpex* (1978), Lord Denning said (at 194): "The 'force majeure' clause is contained in a standard form which was designed to regulate contracts between merchants and traders. It is easy to apply the clause in contracts where a government is not a party . . . It is much more difficult to apply the clause when a government itself is one of the parties to the contract, either by itself or by one of its departments. In such a case it can be argued that the 'seller' is the government: that no 'governmental intervention' is beyond the seller's control: because the seller, being the government, can always exercise control over its own intervention. It can intervene or not,

as it pleases. This is a telling argument when the government itself is a party: at any rate when it intervenes so as to escape its own obligations under the contract. It cannot rely on a self-induced 'intervention' any more than it could rely on a self-induced frustration . . ."

10.5.4 **Effects of frustration**

Technically speaking, the rules that come into play after a contract has been discharged for frustration do not belong to the law of contract since there is no longer any contract. They belong to the law of restitution, as the next extract indicates.

> *Fibrosa Spolka Akcyjna v Fairbairn Lawson Combe Barbour Ltd* **[1943] A.C. 32, HL**
>
> **Lord Wright:** "My Lords, the claim in the action was to recover a prepayment of £1,000 made on account of the price under a contract which had been frustrated. The claim was for money paid for a consideration which had failed. It is clear that any civilised system of law is bound to provide remedies for cases of what has been called unjust enrichment or unjust benefit, that is to prevent a man from retaining the money of or some benefit derived from another which it is against conscience that he should keep. Such remedies in English law are generically different from remedies in contract or in tort, and are now recognised to fall within a third category of the common law which has been called quasi-contract or restitution. . . ."

NOTE

Despite these bold words from Lord Wright, the judges were not able to work out a satisfactory set of rules with respect to recovery of money, property and (or) other benefits transferred under a contract later discharged for frustration. Parliament had to intervene.

> **Law Reform (Frustrated Contracts) Act 1943 (6 & 7 Geo VI c.40)**
>
> **"1. Adjustment of rights and liabilities of parties to frustrated contracts**
> (1) Where a contract governed by English law has become impossible of performance or been otherwise frustrated, and the parties thereto have for that reason been discharged from the further performance of the contract, the following provisions of this section shall, subject to the provisions of section two of this Act, have effect in relation thereto.
>
> (2) All sums paid or payable to any party in pursuance of the contract before the time when the parties were so discharged (in this Act referred to as 'the time of discharge') shall, in the case of sums so paid, be recoverable from him as money received by him for the use of the party by whom the sums were paid, and, in the case of sums to payable, cease to be so payable.

Provided that, if the party to whom the sums were so paid or payable incurred expenses before the time of discharge in, or for the purpose of, the performance of the contract, the court may, if it considers it just to do so having regard to all the circumstances of the case, allow him to retain or, as the case may be, recover the whole or any part of the sums paid or payable, not being an amount in excess of the expenses so incurred.

(3) Where any party to the contract has, by reason of anything done by any other party thereto in, or for the purpose of, the performance of the contract, obtained a valuable benefit (other than a payment of money to which the last foregoing subsection applies) before the time of discharge, there shall be recoverable from him by the said other party such sum (if any), not exceeding the value of the said benefit to the party obtaining it, as the court considers just, having regard to all the circumstances of the case and, in particular—

(a) the amount of any expenses incurred before the time of discharge by the benefited party in, or for the purpose of, the performance of the contract, including any sums paid or payable by him to any other party in pursuance of the contract and retained or recoverable by that party under the last foregoing subsection, and

(b) the effect, in relation to the said benefit, of the circumstances giving rise to the frustration of the contract."

QUESTIONS

1. C contracts with D to paint D's house for £1,000. When three-quarters of the house is painted, the building is struck by lightning and totally destroyed. Can C claim any money off D? (*Cf.* Robert Goff J. in *BP Exploration Co (Libya) Ltd v Hunt (No.2)* (1979) (QBD) (affirmed in1983 by the HL).)

2. If the central heating system in *Bolton v Mahadeva* (1972) (see p.454) had not functioned for some unexplained reason and the engineers had been able to prove that they were not at fault, would the 1943 Act have been applicable?

3. If the fire in *Reed v Dean* (1949) (see p.471) had started for some unexplained reason and the owners of the boat had been able to prove that they were not at fault, would this Act have been applicable?

4. Do you think that the principles laid down in the 1943 statute ought sometimes to be available to a court in cases where the non-performance arises out of a breach of contract?

5. Is s.1 of the 1943 Act based upon the remedy of debt (action for money had and received) or account of profits? (See generally **11.4.1.**)

NOTE

Read *Gamerco SA v ICM/Fair Warning (Agency) Ltd* (1995) in the law report.

10.6 Discharge by interpretation

It is, at the level of theory, inaccurate to say that interpretation is a means by which a contract can be discharged. Interpretation is a method and not a means of discharge. But at the level of practicality the judges might well interpret a contract in such a way as to allow one of the parties to terminate it: see *Staffs AHA v S Staffs Waterworks* (1978) (p.428). This interpretative aspect is particularly important in situations where the contract itself contains a *force majeure* clause.

Gareth H Jones and Peter Schlechtriem, 'Breach of Contract' in *International Encyclopedia of Comparative Law*, **Vol.VII, Ch.15 (footnotes omitted)**

"**204** ... However, the parties to a commercial contract may endeavour to anticipate events beyond their control, which may arise after the formation of the contract. A contract may contain a *force majeure* clause which allows an obligor to terminate a contract or suspend performance on the occurrence of such an event. The contents of the *force majeure* clause depends on the terms of the contract. There is much case law construing clauses which excuse a party ... Such clauses do not normally protect a party simply because performance has become more expensive, unless perhaps if it would drive prices up to 'unheard levels'. The burden of proof is on the party who seeks to rely on the *force majeure* clause to bring himself within its terms. Subject to the terms of the particular clause, events which are frequently held to amount to *force majeure* include: strikes; wars; and abnormal weather which impedes shipment of goods by sea."

QUESTIONS

1. Do you think the case law concerning express *force majeure* clauses might ever be relevant to problems concerning the doctrine of frustration?

2. If a contract can contain express *force majeure* clauses, why has it been deemed conceptually impossible in *Davis Contractors v Fareham UDC* (1956) (p.497) for a contract to contain implied *force majeure* clauses?

11 Remedies (1): monetary remedies

When one turns from the substantive rules of contract to the remedies available to a disappointed contractor, faced with a non-performance, two generic categories of remedy immediately emerge. There are monetary remedies and non-monetary remedies. However, before considering the various types of remedy in more depth, a general question needs to be considered: What exactly is meant by the term "remedy"?

11.1 Remedies and rights

This broad question as to the nature of a remedy will need some discussion because the term is used to mean different things in different contexts. In addition, the very existence of the term suggests that a remedy is something that needs to be contrasted with a "right". What is a "remedy", and what is the relationship between remedies and "rights"?

11.1.1 Problems of definition

A number of writers have observed that the expression "remedy" is used in a variety of different senses.

Rafal Zakrzewski, *Remedies Reclassified* (OUP, 2005), pp.1–2 (footnotes omitted)

"The word 'remedy' is constantly on lawyers' lips. Legal remedies are claimed, sought, found, had, requested, elected, chosen, pursued, used, available, refused, allowed, obtained, awarded, dispensed, granted, given, provided, fashioned, and enforced. They are described as common law, equitable, statutory, discretionary, as of right, *in rem*, *in personam*, proprietary, personal, specific, substitutional, monetary, non-monetary, coercive, non-coercive, enforceable, constitutive, declaratory, judicial, non-judicial, self-help, civil, private, public, or administrative. But, rather disturbingly, as Burrows points out '[t]he concept of a remedy has rarely been subjected to rigorous analysis.'

As a consequence, remedy is used synonymously with a wide range of different terms and, what is probably worse, by way of contrast to an equally long and diverse list. It is used synonymously with action, response, redress, and relief. It is used in contradistinction to wrong, injury, cause of action, liability, substance, institution, and doctrine. Most confusingly, it is used both as a synonym of right and in opposition to it. In short, the concept of a remedy is unstable. It comprises a number of different but insufficiently differentiated legal concepts.

Birks drew attention to the promiscuity of this term and identified a number of different senses in which it is used . . ."

NOTES

1. See Birks (2000) 20 O.J.L.S. 1.

2. As we shall see, no precise definition of a remedy will be offered in these chapters. Instead a remedy will be seen as "institutional". In addition, particularly with respect to problem-solving in contract, a remedy might usefully be regarded as "an instrument of attack" (see H.F. Jolowicz, *Roman Foundations of Modern Law* (OUP, 1957), pp.75–81).

3. From the perspective of Roman law learning, it is possible to see a remedy as an "institution". An institution in this sense is something which exists at one and the same time in the world of law and the world of fact, and as such acts as a focal point for legal rules. According to a scheme of thought that has its origins in the *Institutes of Gaius* (a work probably published around A.D. 160 as a student textbook), all law is centred on the 'institution' of either a person (*persona*), or a thing (*res*) or an action (*actio*) (G.I.8; D.1.5.1). Thus, for example, s.14 of the Sale of Goods Act 1979 (see above, p.60) is framed around the institution of the *res* (goods sold), while s.13 of the Supply of Goods and Services Act 1982 (see p.381) uses the *persona* (contractor) as its institutional focal point. The *action* (remedy) is the central institution in s.37(1) of the Supreme Court Act 1981 (p.570).

11.1.2 Forms of action as remedies

None of this is to suggest that English law was directly influenced by Gaius. In fact right and remedy were not easy to distinguish under the old "forms of action" procedure.

R.C. van Caenegem, 'History of European Civil Procedure' in *International Encyclopedia of Comparative Law*, Vol.XVI, Ch.2 (footnotes omitted)

"20. . . . In England relations between adjective and substantive law could not be closer. The forms of process dominated the law and made the great legal textbooks look like treatises on procedure: *Maine's* words are certainly applicable here: 'So great is the ascendancy of the Law of Actions in the infancy of Courts of Justice, that substantive law has at first the look of being gradually secreted in the interstices of procedure'. Substantive law was discussed in terms of procedure and the rights of the parties were expressed in the form of writs and pleading. In the law faculties [of continental Europe] the exact opposite was the case, the rise of an autonomous science of the rules of procedure was one of the striking results of their activity . . .

75. *England.*—The great continental codes had modernized procedure, they had not changed its structure but adapted it to the demands of a new age. What happened in England and the United States of America in the nineteenth century went much further: the ancient Common Law procedure was changed in its very nature and the forms of action, which had been the cradle of the Common Law and the most important characteristic of English medieval law, were abolished. Just as in the late Roman Empire the procedure *extra ordinem* had taken the place of the *legis actiones* and the formulary process, so, in nineteenth century England, the hallowed forms of action were replaced by a uniform, simplified and streamlined procedure, dominated by general rules and concepts. English procedure, which had been among the first to modernize in the twelfth century, was among the slowest to adapt itself and to break away from the past . . .”

NOTE

The forms of action are one reason why the distinction between rights and remedies remains difficult in English law. Indeed, they are also one reason why the definition of a remedy proves difficult—for each form of action defined its own jurisdictional scope, procedure, remedy and right. This has all left its imprint on modern contract and tort law.

David Ibbetson, *A Historical Introduction to the Law of Obligations* (OUP, 1999), p.294 (footnotes omitted)

“Whatever changes have occurred on the surface of the law, and whatever accretions have been incorporated into its fabric, at a deep level the structure of the Common law of obligations has remained remarkably slow-moving. With the exception of the coalescing category of unjust enrichment, the basic divisions of the law found in the twelfth or thirteenth century are reflected in the structure of the law at the end of the twentieth; the uneasy division between contract and tort (or covenant and trespass); the division within the law of contract between actions to vindicate entitlements and actions claiming damages or penalties; the distinction within the law of tort(s) between actions dependent on the causation of economic loss and actions to give effect to rights. Like an ancient building in continual use for centuries but readapted to satisfy the needs of each generation, the medieval ground plan of the Common law of obligations remains visible through all the reordering of its internal features and the change of use of its component rooms. . . ."

NOTES

1. This "medieval ground plan" tends to be particularly visible in the area of contractual remedies. The distinction between an action for debt (writ of debt) and an action for damages (trespass) is one obvious example, but the dichotomy between common law remedies and equitable remedies is another, in as much as the dichotomy exposes the old procedural distinctions between common law and equity.

2. Remedies, then, will be approached as institutions attracting, to an extent, their own rules, principles and interests. Certainly from a contract problem-solving perspective, the remedy is a starting point of analysis. What does the claimant actually want? Is he claiming a debt, or compensation for physical or economic harm; or is he asking the court to rescind the contract or specifically enforce it, or to rectify an error in the written contractual document? Or, again, does he want the defendant to account to him a profit improperly obtained? Perhaps these chapters on remedies should have been placed at the beginning rather than the end of this present book.

11.1.3 Contractual forms of action

Given that the medieval ground plan can still on occasions be visible in modern contract law, it might be valuable to look briefly at the main forms of action upon which a general theory of contract was ultimately constructed, for these forms were also remedies.

Richard Garde, *Analysis of Pleading* (Maxwell, 1841), pp.1, 3–4

"1. An action is the *legal* demand of a person's right . . .

4. Personal actions are those which are brought for the specific recovery of goods and chattels—or for damages, or other redress, for breach of contract, or other injuries of whatever description, except the recovery of lands, &c . . .

14. In personal actions, the most usual of which are assumpsit, debt, covenant, detinue, trespass, trespass on the case, trover, and replevin, the action in the inferior courts must be commenced by a writ of summons or a writ of capias . . .

17. *Action of debt* lies where a person claims the recovery of a *certain* sum of money alleged to be due to him, and is generally founded on some contract alleged to have taken place between the parties, or on some matter of fact from which the law implies a contract between them.

18. *Action of covenant* lies where a party claims damages for breach of *covenant*, ie of a promise under seal.

19. *Action of detinue* lies where a party claims the specific recovery of goods and chattels or deeds and writings detained from him.

20. *Action of assumpsit* lies where a party claims *damages* for a breach of simple contract, ie a promise not under seal. These promises may be expressed or implied, and the law always implies a promise to do that which a party is legally liable to perform.

21. *Action of trespass* lies where a party claims *damages* for a trespass, ie an injury committed with violence against him, and this violence may be either *actual or implied*.

22. *Action of trespass on the case* lies where a party sues for *damages* for any wrong or cause of complaint to which covenant or trespass will not apply.

23. *Action for trover* lies to recover goods and chattels, and in its form it claims damages for these goods and chattels found and converted to the defendant's own use . . .''

NOTES

1. Richard Garde dedicated his little book to Sir Frederick Pollock. On Pollock's contribution to the law of contract, see N. Duxbury, *Frederick Pollock and the English Juristic Tradition* (OUP, 2004), pp.189–224.

2. Claims in contract are thus personal actions. For an example of what was once considered a "real" action, see *Manchester Airport plc v Dutton* (2000) (C&MT, p.370).

EXERCISE

(Re)consider the following cases and statutes in the light of the above list of forms of action: *Carlill v Carbolic Smoke Ball Co* (1893) (p.149); Law of Property (Miscellaneous Provisions) Act 1989, s.1 (p.143); *Morris v CW Martin & Co* (1966) (p.113); *Hedley Byrne v Heller* (1964) (p.234); *Photo Production v Securicor* (1980) (p.406); *Shogun Finance v Hudson* (2004) (p.265). For an interesting tort case in which "forms of action" thinking is still evident, see *Esso Petroleum v Southport Corporation* (1954, CA; 1956, HL) (C&MT, p.4).

11.1.4 Remedies and causes of action

One of the conceptual problems associated with the forms of action was that they did not distinguish between the "cause" and the "action", that is to say between the remedy (action, *actio*) and its causative "right" (cause, *ius*). Thus the writ of debt was both an action (remedy) and a cause of action (and this is still true today: *Overstone v*

Shipway (1962), below p.516). With the abolition of the forms of action in 1852 (and definitively in 1875) and the adoption of a system of causes of action, the separation became more apparent. Nevertheless conceptual problems can still occur (see e.g. Lord Nicholls' judgment in *Mercedes-Benz AG v Leiduck* (1996)).

Normally one cannot obtain a legal remedy without showing a cause of action to support it, but there are some exceptional cases: see e.g. *Jackson v Horizon Holidays* (1975) (at p.396). Remedies can, in other words, sometimes be used to protect a claimant's *interest* even when such a claimant cannot establish a legal *right* (cause of action). Lord Denning also tried to protect such an interest in *Beswick v Beswick* (1966, CA) (at p.15). The notion of an interest has an important role to play in the remedy of damages—for damages protect certain interests (bodily, proprietary, economic, mental, expectation, reliance, restitution and so on)—and thus it is quite easy to slip from talking about "rights" to talking about "interests" (and vice versa) (see further C&MT, pp.381–3). Civil law thinking is governed by the maxim *pas d'intérêt pas d'action* (only those with a legitimate interest in a dispute are entitled to a remedy).

11.1.5 **Classification of remedies**

Various writers have attempted—and are still attempting—to produce highly coherent taxonomies of remedies. No doubt all this is very valuable, although it is unlikely to be of much interest to practitioners, who will continue to use the expression "remedy" to mean different things in different contexts. However, there are a number of broad categories that are of importance to the contract lawyer, especially when it comes to problem-solving. These are:

(a) *Monetary and non-monetary remedies*. The distinction between monetary and non-monetary remedies can be of practical importance in, for example, misrepresentation and mistake: is the claimant seeking just rescission of the contract, or does she also want monetary compensation? The two remedies bring into play different subsections of the Misrepresentation Act 1967 (see p.237). Indeed, with regard to *Leaf v International Galleries* (1950) (p.242), an appreciation of the remedy in issue is vital to an understanding of the decision; had the claimant been seeking a monetary remedy the whole case might have been different.

(b) *Common law and equitable remedies*. History has its role to play with respect to classification. Because the common law courts could, with one exception (repossession of land), offer only monetary remedies, the Court of Chancery felt able to correct this deficiency by developing a range of non-monetary remedies such as injunctions, specific performance, rescission and rectification. However, before concluding that the division between common law and equity is just another way of describing monetary and non-monetary remedies, it has to be remembered that equity can offer damages in lieu of rescission (Misrepresentation Act 1967, s.2(2)) and in lieu of specific performance and injunctions (Supreme Court Act 1981, s.50). In addition, the remedy of account is now considered to be equitable rather than common law, while rescission may now be a common law as well as an equitable remedy. The label "equitable" is important because these remedies are said to be discretionary, although this does not mean that courts can exercise such discretion free of equitable precedents and principle.

(c) *Self-help and judicial remedies*. Some remedies are available to victims of a legal transgression without recourse to the courts, the most famous probably being self-defence. In contractual cases it is, of course, rare that one contractor will have to resort to reasonable violence to protect himself from the other (although see *Barton v Armstrong* (1975), p.281), but the self-help remedy of termination for serious breach is of major importance. As with all self-help remedies, this termination remedy must be exercised with care, because if it transpires that the use of the remedy was unjustified then the person who has resorted to self-help will find himself liable for breach of contract (see e.g. *Hong Kong Fir Shipping* (1962), p.336).

(d) *Compensatory and restitutionary remedies*. A broad distinction can be made between remedies designed to compensate for damage caused to a victim and remedies designed to reverse unjustified enrichments. The first group of remedies—in truth primarily the remedy of damages—looks to the claimant's loss, while the second group of remedies (which may include damages) looks to a defendant's gain. The distinction is discussed by Lord Hobhouse in *Att-Gen v Blake* (2000) (see p.552) and see also *Surrey CC v Bredero Homes* (1993) (p.551); *R. (Kemp) v Denbighshire LHB* (2007), at para.86.

(e) *Proprietary and personal remedies*. The distinction between actions *in rem* (brought against a thing) and *in personam* (brought against another person) is Roman in origin and is to be found only with difficulty in English law. Indeed the common law has never had a *rei vindicatio*, that is to say a remedy exclusively protecting ownership. Nevertheless, there are a number of claims that are, either formally or at least in essence, aimed at a *res* (money or other property) rather than at another person (*persona*). The action for damages in the tort of conversion might, in its substance (although not in its form), be seen as one such claim (see *Shogun Finance v Hudson* (2004), p.265), while tracing and liens are undoubtedly proprietary remedies (liens also being a self-help remedy). Debt claims can also have a proprietary flavour: debts are a form of personal property, and in a debt action the claimant might be said to be "vindicating" his right to a sum of money (see *Lipkin Gorman v Karpnale Ltd* (1991)), even if the action is one that, unlike tracing, does not actually assert a property right in a sum of money in another's patrimony (*cf.* Lord Denning M.R. in *Beswick v Beswick* (1966, CA), p.23).

(f) *Remedies arising from rights and remedies arising from wrongs*. The distinction between a claim based on the invasion of a right and a claim arising out of a wrong overlaps to an extent with the division between proprietary and non-

513

proprietary remedies. However, the two groupings are not synonymous. A claim in damages for trespass, conversion or defamation is a claim based on a right, as is of course an action in debt in contract; yet these claims are proprietary, at best, only in substance. Indeed many trespass claims arise out of invasions to the person (assault and false imprisonment) and thus do not involve property, assuming of course that the body cannot be owned (a Roman law rule: D.9.2.13pr). The distinction between rights and wrongs is explained by Lord Hobhouse in *Three Rivers DC v Bank of England (No.3)* (2003) (C&MT, pp.83–4).

These are not the only classification schemes applicable to remedies, for more elaborate taxonomies are possible. But they are classification dichotomies of some importance to the contract student, and they should be brought to bear on all practical problems in contract. They are one useful starting point for an analysis of facts. However, in this present chapter, and the next, the broad dichotomy adopted is the one between monetary and non-monetary remedies, since this is probably the most useful from a practical point of view. But this distinction must also be considered alongside the one between common law and equity, for the two dichotomies overlap to a large extent.

11.2 Debt

Statistically, by far the most important remedy in contract is an action for debt.

Rafal Zakrzewski, *Remedies Reclassified* (OUP, 2005), p.108 (footnotes omitted)

"An award of a sum due under a contract is the most commonly sought remedy in respect of contracts. This is because the main duty of at least one party to the overwhelming majority of contracts is the duty to pay. It is present in the case of contracts of sale, lease, hire, employment, and for other services. Contracts of loan and insurance place *both* parties under duties to pay. But, as Burrows observes, the remedy is often and 'rather uncomfortably' relegated to discussions of damages in standard contract texts. Sometimes it is omitted altogether. For example, a leading equity text states: 'The only remedy which the common law afforded for breach of contract was an award of damages. In equity, however, the due performance of the contract itself was in many cases enforced upon the ground of inadequacy of the damages recoverable for breach.' This is incorrect. For the vast majority of contracts, due performance of the contract itself was enforced at common law by means of an action in debt culminating in an award of an agreed sum. . . ."

NOTE

It is a common mistake for judges and jurists to state that a claim for damages is the main remedy for breach of contract. Moreover, the forms of action suggest that failure to pay has been a major problem since the birth of the common law, for the writ of debt is one of the oldest actions. The nature of a debt claim, in comparison to an action for damages, is explained in the next extract.

Jervis v Harris [1996] Ch.195, CA

Millett L.J.: ". . . The question . . . is whether the landlord's right to enter the property, effect the repairs himself and then claim to recover the cost of doing so from the tenant is a claim for damages for breach of a covenant by the tenant 'to keep or put in repair during the currency of the lease all or any of the property comprised in the lease.' . . .

The short answer to the question is that the tenant's liability to reimburse the landlord for his expenditure on repairs is not a liability in damages for breach of his repairing covenant all. The landlord's claim sounds in debt not damages; and it is not a claim to compensation for breach of the tenant's covenant to repair, but for reimbursement of sums actually spent by the landlord in carrying out repairs himself. I shall expand on each of these distinctions in turn.

The law of contract draws a clear distinction between a claim for payment of a debt and a claim for damages for breach of contract. The distinction and its consequences are set out in *Chitty on Contracts*, 27th ed (1994), vol 1, p 1046, para 21–031. As there stated, a debt is a definite sum of money fixed by the agreement of the parties as payable by one party to the other in return for the performance of a specified obligation by the other party or on the occurrence of some specified event or condition; whereas damages may be claimed from a party who has broken his primary contractual obligation in some way other than by failure to pay such a debt.

The plaintiff who claims payment of a debt need not prove anything beyond the occurrence of the event or condition on the occurrence of which the debt became due. He need prove no loss; the rules as to remoteness of damage and mitigation of loss are irrelevant; and unless the event on which the payment is due is a breach of some other contractual obligation owed by the one party to the other the law on penalties does not apply to the agreed sum. It is not necessary that the amount of the debt should be ascertained at the date of the contract; it is sufficient if it is ascertainable when payment is due. The landlord's monetary claim under clause 2(10) does not arise unless and until he has carried out the repairs; when it does arise, his claim is for an account and payment, not for damages.

Moreover, the landlord's monetary claim under such a clause is not a claim for compensation for loss suffered by him by reason of the tenant's failure to repair but for reimbursement of expenditure which he incurred in order to avoid such loss. The difference is one of substance. The loss which the landlord suffers by reason of the tenant's failure to repair is the diminution of the value of his interest in the property. Even before the Landlord and Tenant Act 1927 the landlord could not recover more than the diminution in the value of the reversion unless he coupled his claim with a claim for forfeiture of the lease. Even if the landlord left the lease on foot then, having recovered damages for breach of the tenant's repairing covenant, he was not bound to apply them in carrying out repairs. He could choose to leave the property unrepaired; he had been fully compensated for the diminution in the value of his interest, and the tenant would have to live with the diminution in the value of his.

But a clause such as clause 2(10) works very differently. It enables the landlord to take remedial action himself to avoid any loss consequent on the tenant's failure to repair. Once the landlord has carried out the repairs himself, the value of his interest in the property is restored. The work of repair enures to the benefit of the tenant as well as the landlord. The landlord is out of pocket, but that is because he has carried out repairs, not because the property is in disrepair. . . .

The landlord's claim to reimbursement is not triggered by the tenant's breach of covenant but by his own expenditure on carrying out repairs. The fact that the property is in disrepair is not enough. The landlord must have carried out work to remedy the want of repair; and his right to do so does not depend upon the existence of any covenant on the part of the tenant, but simply upon there being a want of repair which the tenant has failed to remedy within the stated period after notice. The fact that the tenant is thereby in breach of covenant is neither here nor there. It merely means that the landlord has an alternative remedy of claiming damages for breach of covenant. But the presence of an alternative remedy which the landlord does not choose to enforce cannot affect the proper characterisation of the remedy which he does. . . ."

NOTES AND QUESTIONS

1. Debt is a difficult notion because it is both a cause of action and a remedy. Thus if a victim of a breach of contract sues in damages, this will not preclude a later, second action, based on the same contractual relationship, from being brought by the same victim. "The two causes of action, namely, that for debt or money due under the contract and that for damages for breach of contract, are", said a Court of Appeal judge, "quite different" (Davies L.J., *Overstone Ltd v Shipway* (1962), at 129). Thus the claimant was able to bring two claims arising out of a breach of the same hire-purchase contract. Does this mean that if the plaintiff in *White & Carter (Councils) v McGregor* (1962) (above, p.386) had lost his debt claim, he could, at a later date, have brought a quite separate damages action?

2. One major advantage in suing in debt rather than damages is that the claimant is under no obligation to mitigate (see below **11.4.4**) his losses. This is because, in terms of classification (above **11.1.5**), a debt claim is one arising out of a "right", whereas a damages action is usually (but not always) seen as

arising out of a "wrong". Could the use of debt to avoid mitigation ever amount to an abuse of a contractual right to a remedy? And if so, could the court intervene? (*Cf.* Lord Reid in *White & Carter (Councils) v McGregor* (1962) (at p.491).)

3. European contract law now seems to have adopted not only the distinction between debt and damages, but also the rule in *White & Carter*.

Unidroit Principles for International Commercial Contracts

"Article 7.2.1 Performance of Monetary Obligation
Where a party who is obliged to pay money does not do so, the other may require payment."

Principles of European Contract Law

"Article 9:101 Monetary Obligations
(1) The creditor is entitled to recover money which is due.

(2) Where the creditor has not yet performed its obligation and it is clear that the debtor will be unwilling to receive performance, the creditor may nonetheless proceed with its performance and may recover any sum due under the contract unless:

(a) it could have made a reasonable substitute transaction without significant effort or expense; or

(b) performance would be unreasonable in the circumstances.

Article 9:307 Recovery of Money Paid
On termination of the contract a party may recover money paid for a performance which it did not receive or which it properly rejected."

QUESTIONS

1. Does the second limb of PECL, art.9:101(2) (the exception to the '*White & Carter*' rule) represent English law?

2. Might a court ever award specific performance in equity of a debt claim? (*Cf. Beswick v Beswick* (1968) (p.564).)

NOTES

1. For some notable debt cases, see: *Carlill v Carbolic Smoke Ball Co* (1893) (p.149); *Rowland v Divall* (1923) (p.340); *Bolton v Mahadeva* (1972) (p.454).

2. Note also that the remedy of debt is not confined to contract; it is an important quasi-contractual (unjust enrichment) action as well. See Lord

Atkin in *United Australia* (1941) (p.30); see also *Rowland v Divall* (1923) (p.340) and *R. (Kemp) v Denbighshire LHB* (2007).

FURTHER QUESTION

What if a debtor's failure to pay the debt causes loss to the creditor: can the creditor recover this loss by way of a claim for damages?

Wadsworth v Lydall [1981] 1 W.L.R. 598, CA

Brightman L.J.: ". . . The second question on the appeal is a little more difficult. It is whether the plaintiff is entitled to recover as special damages the loss which he has suffered as a result of the defendant's failure to pay his debt under the contract on the due date . . . The defendant contends that . . . although interest can be awarded nowadays under [statute], damages cannot be awarded in respect of unpaid indebtness. The plaintiff is confined, the defendant says, to such interest as he is able to claim under the [statute], but is not entitled to damages . . . In my view the court is not so constrained by the decision of the House of Lords. In *London, Chatham and Dover Railway Co v South Eastern Railway Co* [1893] AC 429 the House of Lords was not concerned with a claim for special damages. The action was an action for an account. The House was concerned only with a claim for interest by way of general damages. If a plaintiff pleads and can prove that he has suffered special damages as a result of the defendant's failure to perform his obligation under a contract, and such damage is not too remote on the principle of *Hadley v Baxendale* (1854) 9 Exch 341, I can see no logical reason why such special damage should be irrecoverable merely because the obligation on which the defendant defaulted was an obligation to pay money and not some other type of obligation . . ."

Reeve J.: "I agree."

Ormrod L.J.: ". . . The court has to look not at what this particular defendant knew or contemplated but what a reasonable person in his position would have contemplated . . . This case is not on all fours with—and can be distinguished from—the *London, Chatham and Dover* case and clearly ought to be so distinguished."

NOTE

See now the Late Payment of Commercial Debts (Interest) Act 1998; Late Payment of Commercial Debts Regulations 2002 (SI 2002/1674).

QUESTION

Can a claim for damages be used to recover a debt?

Damon Compania Naviera SA v Hapag-Lloyd **[1985] 1 W.L.R. 435, CA**

This was an action for damages brought by a seller of three ships against prospective buyers who, in breach of a contract concluded via telexes, failed to sign a formal contract of purchase. The telex contract contained a clause that a deposit of 10 per cent would be payable on the signing of the formal contract. The disappointed sellers claimed this 10 per cent by way of damages, and a majority of the Court of Appeal (Fox and Stephenson L.JJ.: Goff L.J. dissenting) upheld their claim.

> **Fox L.J.:** ". . . Damages for breach of contract are a compensation for the loss which the plaintiff has suffered through the breach. Accordingly, the plaintiff is entitled to be placed in the same position as if the contractual obligation had been performed. In the present case, if the obligation had been performed, Hapag-Lloyd could have sued Damon in debt for the amount of the deposit and it seems to me that that should be reflected in the damages recoverable for breach of the obligation."

> **Robert Goff L.J.** (dissenting): ". . . If the repudiation occurred after Damon had paid the deposit, Hapag-Lloyd would be safe: they would have the deposit and could keep it. If the repudiation occurred after the obligation to pay the deposit had accrued due, but before Damon had paid it, Hapag-Lloyd could sue Damon for the deposit as a debt . . . But if the repudiation occurred before Damon's obligation to pay the deposit had fallen due, then Hapag-Lloyd could only recover damages for repudiation, which would fall to be assessed on the usual basis of compensating Hapag-Lloyd for the loss of their bargain . . . The normal measure, in a contract of sale of goods, is of course the difference between the contract and market prices for the goods. I can see no reason for departing from that ordinary measure of damages in the present case. To award Hapag-Lloyd damages assessed on the basis of the amount of the deposit would be to compare their present position with what their position would have been if the contract had only been partially performed (ie, the deposit paid), and not with their position if the contract had been performed in full; if damages were assessed in that way, they would be over-compensated for the loss of their bargain. In truth, the inability of Hapag-Lloyd to obtain the protection of the deposit, in the circumstances of the present case, flows from their contracting on such terms that the deposit was not payable forthwith upon the making of the contract."

> **Stephenson L.J.:** ". . . On the last point I am attracted by the logic of Robert Goff LJ's contrary opinion. But the measure of damages resulting from Damon's repudiatory breach is, in my opinion, the loss directly and naturally resulting from the breach in the ordinary course of events, and I agree with Fox LJ that that loss is the amount of the deposit . . ."

QUESTION

Why was the plaintiff not required to prove its actual loss flowing from the defendants' breach? Is this decision effectively allowing a contractor to enforce a "penalty" through an action for damages?

11.3 Damages (1): general principles

Statistically damages might not be the most important contractual remedy, but it is the one that seems to dominate in the textbooks and casebooks. As a remedy, it also appears to attract more rules than debt.

11.3.1 Definition and role of damages

A claim for damages is a remedy that is not confined to the law of contract: it is the leading remedy in the law of tort. Accordingly, damages as a remedy can cut across the frontier between the two subjects.

> **Cassell & Co v Broome [1972] A.C. 1027, HL**
>
> **Lord Hailsham:** ". . . Of all the various remedies available at common law, damages are the remedy of most general application at the present day, and they remain the prime remedy in actions for breach of contract and tort. They have been defined as 'the pecuniary compensation, obtainable by success in an action, for a wrong which is either a tort or a breach of contract'. They must normally be expressed in a single sum to take account of all the factors applicable to each cause of action . . .
>
> In almost all actions for breach of contract, and in many actions for tort, the principle of *restitutio in integrum* is an adequate and fairly easy guide to the estimation of damage, because the damage suffered can be estimated by relation to some material loss. It is true that where loss includes a pre-estimate of future losses, or an estimate of past losses which cannot in the nature of things be exactly computed, some subjective element must enter in. But the estimate is in things commensurable with one another . . .
>
> The next point to notice is that it has always been a principle in English law that the award of damages when awarded must be a single lump sum in respect of each separate cause of action . . ."
>
> **Lord Diplock:** ". . . The award of damages as the remedy for all civil wrongs was in England the creature of the common law. It is a field of law in which there has been but little intervention by Parliament. It is judge-made law par excellence. Its original purpose in cases of trespass was to discourage private revenge in a primitive society inadequately policed, at least as much as it was to compensate the victim for the material harm occasioned to him . . ."

NOTES AND QUESTIONS

1. Is Lord Hailsham right in saying that "damages are the remedy of most general application" in contract?

2. "The general rule in English law today as to the measure of damages recoverable for the invasion of a legal right, whether by breach of a contract or by commission of a tort, is that damages are compensatory. Their function is to put the person whose right has been invaded in the same position as if it had been respected so far as the award of a sum of money can do so . . ." (Lord Diplock in *The Albazero* (1977), at 841). Is the role of damages only to compensate? See also Lord Blackburn in *Livingstone v Rawyards Coal Co* (1880), at 39, extracted in C&MT, p 380. Was there *restitutio in integrum* in *Damon Compania Naviera SA v Hapag-Lloyd* (1985) (see p.519)?

11.3.2 Contractual right to damages

A contracting party faced with a breach of contract by the other party is entitled to sue for damages. As Lord Diplock has asserted: "Every failure to perform a primary obligation is a breach of contract. The secondary obligation on the part of the contract breaker to which it gives rise by implication of the common law is to pay monetary compensation to the other party for the loss sustained by him in consequence of the breach" (*Photo Production v Securicor* (1980), above at p.406). In European and international contract law, the right has been set out in the following extract.

> *Principles of European Contract Law*
>
> **"Article 9:501 Right to damages**
> (1) The aggrieved party is entitled to damages for loss caused by the other party's non-performance which is not excused under Article 8:108.
>
> (2) The loss for which damages are recoverable includes:
>
> (a) non-pecuniary loss; and
> (b) future loss which is reasonably likely to occur."

NOTES

1. See also UNIDROIT, art.7.4.1.

2. In English law the right to damages arises from a breach of contract rather than a non-performance. Or, put another way, a breach of contract gives rise to a cause of action. On the nature of a "cause of action", see Diplock L.J. in *Letang v Cooper* (1965), extracted in C&MT, pp.3–4.

3. From a "form of action" perspective, the cause of action in damages for breach of contract grew out of the action of *assumpsit*. It was different, of course, for debt; this action grew out of the writ of debt. Both forms of action have been eclipsed by a general theory of contract but, as we have seen, debt is still a different claim from damages.

11.3.3 **Measure of damages**

As for the amount of damages an aggrieved party can obtain, this depends on the nature and amount of the loss suffered.

Principles of European Contract Law

"**Article 9:502 General measure of damages**
The general measure of damages is such sum as will put the aggrieved party as nearly as possible into the position in which it would have been if the contract had been duly performed. Such damages cover the loss which the aggrieved party has suffered and the gain of which he has been deprived."

Unidroit Principles for International Commercial Contracts

"**Article 7.4.2 Full Compensation**
(1) The aggrieved party is entitled to full compensation for harm sustained as a result of the non-performance. Such harm includes both any loss which it suffered and any gain of which it was deprived, taking into account any gain to the aggrieved party resulting from its avoidance of cost or harm.

(2) Such harm may be non-pecuniary and includes, for instance, physical suffering or emotional distress."

NOTE

These code principles certainly reflect English law at the level of general principle. However, common lawyers tend to express these different entitlements in terms of "interests".

Surrey County Council v Bredero Homes Ltd **[1993] 1 W.L.R. 1361, CA**

(For facts, see p.551.)

Steyn L.J.: "... An award of compensation for breach of contract serves to protect three separate interests. The starting principle is that the aggrieved party ought to be compensated for loss of his positive or expectation interests. In other words, the object is to put the aggrieved party in the same financial position as if the contract had been fully performed. But the law also protects the negative interest of the aggrieved party. If the aggrieved party is unable to establish the value of a loss of bargain he may seek compensation in respect of his reliance losses. The object of such an award is to compensate the aggrieved party for expenses incurred and losses suffered in reliance on the contract. These two complementary principles share one feature. Both are pure compensatory principles ...

There is, however, a third principle which protects the aggrieved party's restitutionary interest. The object of such an award is not to compensate the plaintiff for a loss, but to deprive the defendant of the benefit he gained by the breach of contract. The classic illustration is a claim for the return of goods sold and delivered where the buyer has repudiated his obligation to pay the price. It is not traditional to describe a claim for restitution following a breach of contract as damages. What matters is that a coherent law of obligations must inevitably extend its protection to cover certain restitutionary interests . . ."

QUESTION

Why did Mr Forsyth not get damages for his expectation interest in *Ruxley Electronics v Forsyth* (1996) (see p.442)?

Ruxley Electronics Ltd v Forsyth [1996] 1 A.C. 344, HL

(For facts, see p.442.)

Lord Jauncey: ". . . Damages are designed to compensate for an established loss and not to provide a gratuitous benefit to the aggrieved party from which it follows that the reasonableness of an award of damages is to be linked directly to the loss sustained. If it is unreasonable in a particular case to award the cost of reinstatement it must be because the loss sustained does not extend to the need to reinstate. A failure to achieve the precise contractual objective does not necessarily result in the loss which is occasioned by a total failure. . . ."

Lord Lloyd: ". . . Cardozo J's judgment [in *Jacob & Youngs v Kent*, 129 NE 889] is important, because it establishes two principles, which I believe to be correct, and which are directly relevant to the present case; first, the cost of reinstatement is not the appropriate measure of damages if the expenditure would be out of all proportion to the good to be obtained, and, secondly, the appropriate measure of damages in such a case is the difference in value, even though it would result in a nominal award. . . ."

QUESTIONS

1. Would Mr Forsyth have received a gratuitous benefit if the builders had been ordered to rebuild the pool to the required contractual depth?

2. Where a builder constructs a project that does not conform to the contract, is the measure of damages now to be the difference in value between what the contractor stipulated for and what the contractor actually got? If so, does this mean that builders are now, in effect, free to ignore contractual terms, provided they build something that is at least as economically valuable as the project envisaged in the contract?

11.4 Damages (2): limitation of liability

The law imposes a number of limits on the amount of damages that can be claimed for a breach of contract.

11.4.1 Introduction

At a very general level these limits might be summed up in terms of cause and risk.

Banque Bruxelles Lambert SA v Eagle Star Insurance Co Ltd [1997] A.C. 191, HL

Lord Hoffmann: ". . . There is no reason in principle why the law should not penalise wrongful conduct by shifting on to the wrongdoer the whole risk of consequences which would not have happened but for the wrongful act. Hart and Honoré, in *Causation in the Law*, 2nd ed (1985), p 120, say that it would, for example, be perfectly intelligible to have a rule by which an unlicensed driver was responsible for all the consequences of his having driven, even if they were unconnected with his not having a licence. One might adopt such a rule in the interests of deterring unlicensed driving. But that is not the normal rule. One may compare, for example, *The Empire Jamaica* [1955] P 259, in which a collision was caused by a 'blunder in seamanship of . . . a somewhat serious and startling character' (Sir Raymond Evershed MR, at p 264) by an uncertificated second mate. Although the owners knew that the mate was not certificated and it was certainly the case that the collision would not have happened if he had not been employed, it was held in limitation proceedings that the damage took place without the employers' 'actual fault or privity' (section 503 of the Merchant Shipping Act 1894) because the mate was in fact experienced and (subject to this one aberration) competent. The collision was not therefore attributable to his not having a certificate. The owners were not treated as responsible for all the consequences of having employed an uncertificated mate but only for the consequences of his having been uncertificated.

Rules which make the wrongdoer liable for all the consequences of his wrongful conduct are exceptional and need to be justified by some special policy. Normally the law limits liability to those consequences which are attributable to that which made the act wrongful. . . ."

NOTES

1. See also the extract in C&MT, pp.335–56.

2. Three expressions find themselves being employed when it comes to the limitation of damages: cause, risk, and policy. We shall see that a fourth expression, "reasonable", also makes an appearance from time to time (see e.g. *Ruxley Electronics v Forsyth* (1996), at p.523).

11.4.2 Foreseeability

The French Civil Code contains an article that limits the liability of a contractor to pay damages for non-performance of a contract.

Code civil **(1804)**

"1149. Damages due to a creditor are, in general, the loss sustained and the profit foregone, apart from the hereinafter exceptions and modifications.

1150. A debtor is held only to damages which were foreseen or which could have been foreseen at the time of the contract, when it is not by his wilfulness that the obligation is not executed.

1151. Even in the case where the inexecution of the agreement results from the wilfulness of the debtor, damages are to include, with regard to the loss incurred by the creditor and profit foregone, only what is an immediate and direct consequence of the non-performance of the agreement."

NOTE

This foreseeability principle (art.1150) has been adopted by both European and international contract law.

Principles of European Contract Law

"Article 9:503 Foreseeability
The non-performing party is liable only for loss which it foresaw or could reasonably have foreseen at the time of conclusion of the contract as a likely result of its non-performance, unless the non-performance was intentional or grossly negligent."

NOTES

1. See also UNIDROIT, art.7.4.4.

2. The principle set out in CC art.1150 is regarded in France as a kind of limitation of liability clause implied into all contracts. It was imported into the common law in the following leading case.

Hadley v Baxendale **(1854) 156 E.R. 145, Exch**

This was an action for damages by a mill owner against a firm of transporters (Pickfords) in respect of a mill shaft wrongfully delayed five days by the transporter. The shaft had been sent as a pattern for a new shaft and while it was away the mill could not operate; consequently the mill owner put in a claim not just for the value of the shaft but also for his lost profits. The Court of Exchequer held that the plaintiff was not entitled to the lost profits.

Alderson B. (delivering the judgment of the court): ". . . We think the proper rule in such a case as the present is this. Where two parties have made a contract which one of them has broken the damages which the other party ought to receive in respect of such breach of contract should be such as may fairly and reasonably be considered as either arising naturally, ie, according to the usual course of things, from such breach of contract itself, or such as may reasonably be supposed to have been in the contemplation of both parties at the time they made the contract as the probable result of the breach of it. If special circumstances under which the contract was actually made were communicated by the plaintiffs to the defendants, and thus known to both parties, the damages resulting from the breach of such a contract which they would reasonably contemplate would be the amount of injury which would ordinarily follow from a breach of contract under the special circumstances so known and communicated. But, on the other hand, if these special circumstances were wholly unknown to the party breaking the contract, he, at the most, could only be supposed to have had in his contemplation the amount of injury which would arise generally, and in the great multitude of cases not affected by any special circumstances, from such a breach of contract. For, had the special circumstances been known, the parties might have specially provided for the breach of contract by special terms as to the damages in that case; and of this advantage it would be very unjust to deprive them. In the present case, if we are to apply the principles above laid down, we find that the only circumstances here communicated by the plaintiffs to the defendants at the time the contract was made were that the article to be carried awas the broken shaft of a mill and that the plaintiffs were the millers of that mill. But how do these circumstances show reasonably that the profits of the mill must be stopped by an unreasonable delay in the delivery of the broken shaft by the carrier to the third person? Suppose the plaintiffs had another shaft in their possession and that they only wished to send back the broken shaft to the engineer who made it; it is clear that this would be quite consistent with the above circumstances, and yet the unreasonable delay in the delivery would have no effect upon the intermediate profits of the mill.

It follows, therefore, that the loss of profits here cannot reasonably be considered such a consequence of the breach of contract as could have been fairly and reasonably contemplated by both the parties when they made this contract. For such loss would neither have flowed naturally from the breach of this contract in the great multitude of such cases occurring under ordinary circumstances, nor were the special circumstances, which, perhaps, would have made it a reasonable and natural consequence of such breach of contract, communicated to or known by the defendants. The judge ought, therefore, to have told the jury that, upon the facts there before them, they ought not to take the loss of profits into consideration at all in estimating the damages. There must, therefore, be a new trial in this case."

NOTES AND QUESTIONS

1. This famous case remains the starting point for the measure of damages in claims for breach of contract. It has a European flavour, in that it is generally considered to have been influenced by Pothier and by the rule in CC art.1150. However, the use of the word "contemplation" in *Hadley* has attracted much attention, since it appears to mean, in the context of a contractual relationship, something different from the word "forseeability" used, subsequently, in the context of a tort situation (*The Heron II* (1969)). Can one contemplate something that the reasonable man would not foresee? Can one foresee something that the reasonable contractor, at the time of the contract, would not contemplate? How would an English court interpret PECL, art.9:503?

2. What was the claimant's (plaintiff's) expectation interest in *Hadley*? Did the court protect this interest? If not, what interest did the court protect?

3. Tony hired a horse from Basil and used it in battle. The horse proved most unsuitable for war, and as a result Tony was captured and spent five years in captivity. Ought Basil to be liable for the five years in captivity?

4. How many rules are being formulated by Alderson B.?

5. Can one be liable for damage which, although not in the contemplation of the parties at the time of the contract, arises naturally from the breach?

Parsons (Livestock) Ltd v Uttley Ingham & Co [1978] Q.B. 791, CA

A pig farmer brought an action in damages for breach of s.14 of the Sale of Goods Act against the vendor of a hopper used for storing pig food nuts. The vendor of a hopper had failed to remove, when erecting the hopper on the buyer's farm, some sticky tape holding the ventilator closed; the closed ventilator could not be seen from the ground and the nuts stored in the hopper went mouldy. The farmer nevertheless continued to feed the nuts to his pigs, and as a result the herd was destroyed by a very rare disease. The Court of Appeal (Lord Denning M.R., Orr and Scarman L.JJ.) held that the vendor was to be liable in damages not just for the mouldy nuts, but also for the death of the pigs.

Lord Denning M.R.: ". . . . Remoteness of damage is beyond doubt a question of law. In *C Czarnikow Ltd v Koufos* [1969] AC 350 the House of Lords said that, in remoteness of damage, there is a difference between contract and tort. In the case of a breach of contract, the court has to consider whether the consequences were of such a kind that a reasonable man, at the time of making the contract, would contemplate them as being of a very substantial degree of probability. (In the House of Lords various expressions were used to describe this degree of probability, such as, not merely 'on the cards' because that may be too low: but as being 'not unlikely to occur' (see pp 383 and 388); or 'likely to result or at least

527

not unlikely to result' (see p 406); or 'liable to result' (see p 410); or that there was a 'real danger' or 'serious possibility' of them occurring (see p 415).)

In the case of a tort, the court has to consider whether the consequences were of such a kind that a reasonable man, at the time of the tort committed, would foresee them as being of a much lower degree of probability. (In the House of Lords various expressions were used to describe this, such as, it is sufficient if the consequences are 'liable to happen in the most unusual case' (see p 385); or in a 'very improbable' case (see p 389); or that 'they may happen as a result of the breach, however unlikely it may be, unless it can be brushed aside as far-fetched' (see p 422).)

I find it difficult to apply those principles universally to all cases of contract or to all cases of tort: and to draw a distinction between what a man 'contemplates' and what he 'foresees.' I soon begin to get out of my depth. I cannot swim in this sea of semantic exercises—to say nothing of the different degrees of probability— especially when the cause of action can be laid either in contract or in tort. I am swept under by the conflicting currents. I go back with relief to the distinction drawn in legal theory by Professors Hart and Honoré in their book *Causation in the Law* (1959), at pp 281–287. They distinguish between those cases in contract in which a man has suffered no damage to person or property, but only *economic loss*, such as, loss of profit or loss of opportunities for gain in some future transaction: and those in which he claims damages for an *injury actually done* to his person or *damage actually* done to his property (including his livestock) or for ensuing expense (*damnum emergens*) to which he has actually been put. In the law of tort, there is emerging a distinction between economic loss and physical damage: see *Spartan Steel Alloys Ltd v Martin Co (Contractors) Ltd* [1973] QB 27, 36–37. It underlies the words of Lord Wilberforce in *Anns v Merton London Borough Council* [1978] AC 728, recently, where he classified the recoverable damage as 'material, physical damage.' It has been much considered by the Supreme Court of Canada in *Rivtow Marine Ltd v Washington Iron Works and Walkem Machinery Equipment Ltd* [1973] 6 WWR 692 and by the High Court of Australia in *Caltex Oil (Australia) Pty Ltd v Dredge Willemstad* (1976) 51 ALGR 270.

It seems to me that in the law of contract, too, a similar distinction is emerging. It is between loss of profit consequent on a breach of contract and physical damage consequent on it. . . .

Conclusion

The present case falls within the class of case where the breach of contract causes physical damage. The test of remoteness in such cases is similar to that in tort. The contractor is liable for all such loss or expense as could reasonably have been foreseen, at the time of the breach, as a possible consequence of it. Applied to this case, it means that the makers of the hopper are liable for the death of the pigs. They ought reasonably to have foreseen that, if the mouldy pignuts were fed to the pigs, there was a possibility that they might become ill. Not a serious possibility. Nor a real danger. But still a slight possibility. On that basis the makers were liable for the illness suffered by the pigs. They suffered from diarrhoea at the beginning. This triggered off the deadly E coli. That was a far worse illness than could then be foreseen. But that does not lessen this liability. The type or kind of damage was foreseeable even though the extent of it was not: see *Hughes v Lord Advocate* [1963] AC 837. The makers are liable for the loss of the pigs that died and of the expenses of the vet and such like, but not for loss of profit on future sales or future opportunities of gain: see *Simon v Pawson and Leafs Ltd* (1932) 38 Com Cas 151.

So I reach the same result as the judge, but by a different route. I would dismiss the appeal."

Orr L.J.: I agree with Lord Denning MR and also with Scarman LJ, whose judgment I have had the opportunity of reading, that this appeal should be dismissed, but with respect to Lord Denning MR I would dismiss it for the reasons to be given by Scarman LJ and not on the basis that a distinction is to be drawn for the present purposes between loss of profits and physical damage cases. I have not been satisfied that such a distinction is sufficiently supported by the authorities. . . ."

Scarman L.J.: ". . . My conclusion in the present case is the same as that of Lord Denning MR but I reach it by a different route. I would dismiss the appeal. I agree with him in thinking it absurd that the test for remoteness of damage should, in principle, differ according to the legal classification of the cause of action, though one must recognise that parties to a contract have the right to agree on a measure of damages which may be greater, or less, than the law would offer in the absence of agreement. I also agree with him in thinking that, notwithstanding the interpretation put on some dicta in *C Czarnikow Ltd v Koufos* [1969] AC 350, the law is not so absurd as to differentiate between contract and tort save in situations where the agreement, or the factual relationship, of the parties with each other requires it in the interests of justice. I differ from him only to this extent: the cases do not, in my judgment, support a distinction in law between loss of profit and physical damage. Neither do I think it necessary to develop the law judicially by drawing such a distinction. Of course (and this is a reason for refusing to draw the distinction in law) the type of consequence—loss of profit or market or physical injury—will always be an important matter of fact in determining whether in all the circumstances the loss or injury was of a type which the parties could reasonably be supposed to have in contemplation. . . .

This is so, in my judgment, not because there is, or ought to be, a specific rule of law governing cases of physical injury but because it would be absurd to regulate damages in such cases upon the necessity of supposing the parties had a prophetic foresight as to the exact nature of the injury that does in fact arise. . . .

It does not matter, in my judgment, if they thought that the chance of physical injury, loss of profit, loss of market, or other loss as the case may be, was slight, or that the odds were against it, provided they contemplated as a serious possibility the type of consequence, not necessarily the specific consequence, that ensued upon breach. Making the assumption as to breach that the judge did, no more than common sense was needed for them to appreciate that food affected by bad storage conditions might well cause illness in the pigs fed upon it.

As I read the judgment under appeal, this was how the judge, whose handling of the issues at trial was such that none save one survives for our consideration, reached this decision. In my judgment, he was right, upon the facts as found, to apply the first rule in *Hadley v Baxendale*, 9 Exch 341 or, if the case be one of breach of warranty, as I think it is, the rule in section 53(2) of the Sale of Goods Act 1893 without inquiring as to whether, upon a juridical analysis, the rule is based upon a presumed contemplation. At the end of a long and complex dispute the judge allowed common sense to prevail. I would dismiss the appeal."

QUESTIONS

1. What must a contractor contemplate: (i) the actual damage that has occurred; (ii) the class of damage that has occurred (personal injury, physical injury to property); (iii) any damage in general; or (iv) specific economic loss? (*Cf. Victoria Laundry (Windsor) Ltd v Newman Industries Ltd* (1949).)

2. How much should the farmer in *Parsons* get for his dead pigs? Should he get: (i) the cost of replacing the pigs; (ii) the cost of replacing the pigs plus compensation for the trouble and mental distress at seeing, and clearing up, the dead animals; (iii) the sale value of the pigs; (iv) the sale value plus compensation for mental distress, etc.? Does the distinction between *damnum emergens* (consequential loss) and *lucrum cessans* (failure to gain) have any meaning in the *Parsons* case?

4. What if a neighbouring farmer had borrowed (mouldy) nuts from the hopper: should he be able to sue either the vendor or the buyer of the hopper? How much should the neighbouring farmer get if successful?

5. "In cases like *Hadley v Baxendale* or the present case it is not enough that in fact the plaintiff's loss was directly caused by the defendant's breach of contract. It clearly was so caused in both. The crucial question is whether . . . the loss . . . should have been within his contemplation. The modern rule in tort is quite different and it imposes a much wider liability. The defendant will be liable for any type of damage which is reasonably foreseeable as liable to happen even in the most unusual case . . ." (Lord Reid in *The Heron II* (1969), at 385). Did Lord Scarman in *Parsons* actually apply the tort rule rather than the contract rule?

Banque Bruxelles Lambert SA v Eagle Star Insurance Co Ltd [1997] A.C. 191, HL

Lord Hoffmann: ". . . The measure of damages in an action for breach of a duty to take care to provide accurate information must also be distinguished from the measure of damages for breach of a warranty that the information is accurate. In the case of breach of a duty of care, the measure of damages is the loss attributable to the inaccuracy of the information which the plaintiff has suffered by reason of having entered into the transaction on the assumption that the information was correct. One therefore compares the loss he has actually suffered with what his position would have been if he had not entered into the transaction and asks what element of this loss is attributable to the inaccuracy of the information. In the case of a warranty, one compares the plaintiff's position as a result of entering into the transaction with what it would have been if the information had been accurate. Both measures are concerned with the consequences of the inaccuracy of the information but the tort measure is the extent to which the plaintiff is worse off because the information was wrong whereas the warranty measure is the extent to which he would have been better off if the information had been right.

This distinction was the basis of the decision of this House in *Swingcastle Ltd v Alastair Gibson* [1991] 2 AC 223. Simplifying the facts slightly, the plaintiffs were moneylenders who had advanced £10,000 repayable with interest at the rate of 36.51 per cent, rising in the event of default to 45.619 per cent, on the security of a house which had been valued at £18,000. The valuation was admittedly negligent and the property fetched only £12,000. By that time arrears of interest had increased the debt to nearly £20,000 and the lenders claimed £8,000 damages. This House held that the lenders were not entitled to damages which represented the contractual rate of interest. That would be to put them in the position in which they would have been if the valuation had been correct; a measure of damages which could be justified only if they had given a warranty. In an action for breach of a duty of care, they could not recover more than what they would have earned with the money if they had not entered into the transaction. As there was no evidence that they would have been able to obtain the same exorbitant rate of interest elsewhere, the claim in respect of arrears of interest failed. . . ."

NOTE AND QUESTION

One way, then, to consider the difference between contract and tort damages is to go back to the notion of interests (*cf.* below, **11.5**). In a breach of contract case the claimant is normally claiming an expectation interest, while in tort it is a restoration interest. But must the actual expectation interest be in the contemplation of the contract breaker at the time of the contract, or is it assumed?

The Borag [1981] 1 W.L.R. 274, CA

This was an action for damages brought by the owners of a ship against a contractor, who had agreed to manage the ship but who had caused it to be wrongfully arrested. The owners incurred heavy interest charges in getting the ship released and they claimed these charges as damages. The Court of Appeal (Lord Denning M.R., Shaw and Templeman L.JJ.) held that the interest charges were too remote and unreasonable to be recovered.

> **Lord Denning M.R.:** "In this case a vessel was wrongfully arrested. It was afterwards released on the owner providing security. The question is: what is the proper measure of compensation for the owner? . . .
>
> I can understand that in some cases [the] distinction [between damages and mitigation] may be useful and valuable: but for myself, when expenditure is incurred as a result of a wrongful act, the common law has always looked upon it as damages. I need not go through all the cases. In a personal injury case the medical expenditure incurred is regarded as damages. In damage to property, if you have a lorry or motor car which has been damaged and put out of action, the cost of providing a substitute is not regarded as sums expended in mitigation. It is always regarded as sums recoverable by way of damages for the wrongful act.
>
> . . . It seems to me, as a matter of common sense and common law, that expenditure made to obtain the release of a vessel from arrest should be regarded as an item of damages, and not as mitigation. It is the natural way of dealing with it.
>
> . . . Next there was the question of causation or remoteness. I would agree that the overdraft interest was in a sense a consequence of the unlawful arrest. It flowed from it in the sense that, if there had been no unlawful arrest, the overdraft would not have been incurred. But, as we all know, it is not every consequence of a wrongful act which is the subject of compensation. The law has to draw a line somewhere . . . Although the overdraft interest may be a consequence of the initial unlawful arrest, is it such a consequence that ought to be visited in damages?
>
> Upon this point—I do not care whether you call it 'causation' or whether you call it 'remoteness'—causation and remoteness are two different ways of stating the same question. Is the consequence sufficiently closely connected with the cause as to be the subject of compensation or not? To my mind causation and remoteness here are the same . . .
>
> It comes back to what Templeman LJ said in the first hour or two of hearing this appeal: They are entitled to all the reasonable expenditure which they incurred as a result of the wrongful arrest and getting the ship released; but not 'unheard-of' overdraft interest of this kind. . . ."

> **Shaw L.J.:** ". . . [The umpire] looked at the whole matter as should a man of business who was sufficiently informed in regard to the broad legal principles involved in breach of contract and the right and reasonable basis for compensation for the damage occasioned by a particular breach . . ."
>
> **Templeman L.J.:** ". . . The managers, in breach of contract, arrested the owners' vessel to secure payment of the owners' debts. The managers became liable for the reasonably foreseeable damages suffered by the owners as a result of that breach of contract. . . .
>
> Whatever principle is invoked—whether it be the principle of causation or mitigation—the acid test in the present circumstances must have been reasonableness; and, if the interest charges were unreasonable, they were not damages for which the managers are liable . . . [I]f the interest charges were unreasonable—they were too remote; they were not caused by the breach; they were not part of a reasonable form of mitigation—all these matters hang together. . . ."

QUESTIONS

1. Is there now a rule that the head of damage must not only be contemplated but also reasonable?

2. Are causation and remoteness two different ways of stating the same question? In *Parsons*, Lord Denning said: "There is no problem here about causation. The closed ventilator was clearly the cause, or one of the causes, of the deaths of the pigs. There was an unbroken sequence all the way. There was no intervening human action such as gave rise to the discussion on causation in *Weld-Blundell v Stephens* [1920] A.C. 956 or *Dorset Yacht Co Ltd v Home Office* [1970] A.C. 1004, 1030. The only problem here is with remoteness of damage" (at 801). Surely he was treating causation and remoteness as very different questions?

3. Did the Court of Appeal apply the rule in *Hadley v Baxendale* (1854) to the facts of *The Borag*?

11.4.3 Causation and contributory negligence

Where the harm has been caused by the defendant's breach of contract, it is axiomatic that the wrong (breach of contract) must be the cause of the claimant's harm. This is true in both contract and tort (see C&MT, pp.335–51). However, it would appear from the cases extracted above that the causation question often gets merged with the remoteness issue. This is unfortunate, since causation is a question of fact (once decided by the jury) while remoteness is a question of law (decided by the judge). Yet the codes do not seem to separate the two at the level of general principle. Nevertheless the international codes do have a "fault of the victim" provision.

Principles of European Contract Law

"Article 9:504 Loss attributable to aggrieved party
The non-performing party is not liable for loss suffered by the aggrieved party to the extent that the aggrieved party contributed to the non-performance or its effects."

NOTES

1. See also UNIDROIT, art.7.4.7.

2. In English law this topic is dealt with under the heading either of contributory negligence or of mitigation. With respect to contributory negligence, the Law Reform (Contributory Negligence) Act 1945 enables "a court in actions of tort to apportion responsibility for the damage suffered by the plaintiff where there had been fault by both parties". But "in the present state of the law contributory negligence is not a defence to a claim for damages founded on breach of a strict contractual obligation" (see Beldam L.J. in *Barclays Bank Plc v Fairclough Building Ltd* (1995), extracted in C&MT, p.365). Only if the facts disclose a cause of action in tort (as well as contract) will the Act be applicable. However, see the Contributory Negligence Bill (Law Comm. No.219).

3. The facts of *Parsons* (1978) (see p.527) raise a paradox. If the defendants argue that they could not foresee or contemplate the illness and/or death of the pigs then they cannot argue that the farmer should have foreseen or contemplated the illness or deaths. Equally, if the farmer claims that the sellers of the hopper should have contemplated the illness or death then the farmer is leaving himself open to the accusation that he too should have contemplated the possibility. This is why it was better to try to argue that the loss was "directly and naturally resulting . . . from the breach of warranty" (Sale of Goods Act 1979, s.53(2)).

QUESTION

If the vendor in *Parsons* (1978) (p.527) could contemplate the illness of the pigs, why not the farmer? If the farmer should have contemplated the illness of the pigs from mouldy nuts, could it not be said that, by continuing to use the nuts after noticing mould, he caused their death? Why could the seller of the hopper not have pleaded contributory negligence?

11.4.4 Mitigation of damage

Another rule that overlaps with contributory negligence is the rule that a claimant is under a "duty" to mitigate, or reduce, his loss. This rule is equally applicable to damages claims in tort, and thus reference should be made to C&MT, pp.366–8.

Principles of European Contract Law

"Article 9:505 Reduction of loss
(1) The non-performing party is not liable for loss suffered by the aggrieved party to the extent that the aggrieved party could have reduced the loss by taking reasonable steps.

(2) The aggrieved party is entitled to recover any expenses reasonably incurred in attempting to reduce the loss."

NOTES AND QUESTIONS

1. See also UNIDROIT, art.7.4.8.

2. "A plaintiff is under no duty to mitigate his loss, despite the habitual use by the lawyers of the phrase 'duty to mitigate'. He is completely free to act as he judges to be in his best interests. On the other hand, a defendant is not liable for all loss suffered by the plaintiff in consequence of his so acting. A defendant is only liable for such part of the plaintiff's loss as is properly to be regarded as caused by the defendant's breach of duty . . . Whether a loss is avoidable by reasonable action on the part of the plaintiff is a question of fact not law" (Sir John Donaldson M.R. in *The Solholt* (1983), at 608). Is the distinction between "duty" and "interest" helpful in this context? What are the rights of a claimant vis-à-vis a defendant in breach of an obligation? What are the rights of a defendant in these circumstances? If the defendant has certain rights, is not the claimant under certain duties? Can one apply Sir John Donaldson's reasoning in *The Solholt* to the law of obligations in general: for example, could one say that one is under no "duty" in the law of contract to execute one's promises, but that if one does not then one must pay damages?

3. See generally UC&TO, pp.161–62.

PROBLEM

Geoffrey, who runs a souvenir shop, contracts with Basil for the latter to supply him with consignments of musical coffee mugs every month, payment to be made for each consignment within 30 days of delivery. Geoffrey is often late with the payments and Basil terminates the contract for breach. Geoffrey claims that the termination is itself a breach of contract since late payment is not fundamental enough to warrant termination, but Basil replies by offering to continue to supply the mugs on a cash-on-delivery basis. Geoffrey refuses this offer and successfully argues in court that Basil is in breach of contract. Geoffrey claims as damages all of his loss of profit that he would have made from the sale of the mugs had not Basil cut off the supply. Is Geoffrey likely to obtain damages for all of this loss of profit? (*Cf. Payzu Ltd v Saunders* (1919).)

11.5 Damages (3): particular interests

We have seen in Steyn L.J.'s judgment in *Surrey CC v Bredero Homes* (1993) (at p.522) that another way of analysing damages is via the notion of an interest. What interests does an award of damages in contract protect? Steyn L.J. identified three interests—expectation, reliance, and restitution—but the notion of an interest is often used in a more precise empirical sense. It is applied descriptively to different types of harm. "There are", says Tony Weir, "several good things in life, such as liberty, bodily integrity, land, possessions, reputation, wealth, privacy, dignity, perhaps even life itself" and lawyers "call these goods 'interests'". And he noted that these "interests are all good, but they are not all *equally* good" (*A Casebook on Tort*, 10th edn (Sweet & Maxwell, 2004), p.6; and see also C&MT, pp.381–3).

11.5.1 Defining damage

The first point to note is that substantial damages will be available only in situations where the breach of contract has caused damage. A breach that causes no damage—invades no interest—will attract no damages.

> **Unidroit Principles for International Commercial Contracts**
>
> **"Article 7.4.3 Certainty of Harm**
> (1) Compensation is due only for harm, including future harm, that is established with a reasonable degree of certainty.
>
> (2) Compensation may be due for the loss of a chance in proportion to the stability of its occurrence.
>
> (3) Where the amount of damages cannot be established with a sufficient degree of certainty, the assessment is at the discretion of the court."

QUESTION

Does this article represent English law?

NOTES

1. This damage rule has two particular consequences. First, it means that non-compensatory punitive (exemplary) damages cannot be awarded in contract (*cf.* Cunnington (2006) 26 LS 369). Secondly, it means that a damages claim in contract is not well-suited as a vehicle for relieving a contractor of any profits resulting from a breach of contract where such profits do not actually result in damage to the innocent party (*cf. Att-Gen v Blake* (2001), below at p.552).

2. Sometimes it is not easy to decide if the victim of a breach of contract has actually suffered damage, as the next case illustrates.

Lazenby Garages Ltd v Wright **[1976] 1 W.L.R. 459, CA**

Lord Denning M.R.: "Mr Wright works on the land. On 19th February 1974 he went to the showrooms of motor dealers called Lazenby Garages Ltd. He saw some second-hand cars there. He agreed to buy a BMW 2002. He signed a contract to pay £1,670 for it. It was to be delivered to him on 1st March 1974. He went back home to his wife and told her about it. She persuaded him not to buy it. So next day he went back to the garage and said he would not have it after all. They kept it there offering it for resale. Two months later on 23rd April 1974 they resold it for £1,770, that is for £100 more than Mr Wright was going to pay.

Notwithstanding this advantageous resale, the garage sued Mr Wright for damages. They produced evidence that they had themselves bought the car second-hand on 14th February 1974, that is five days before Mr Wright had come in and agreed to buy it. They said that they had bought it for £1,325. He had agreed to buy it from them for £1,670. So they had lost £345 and they claimed that sum as damages.

In answer Mr Wright said: 'You haven't lost anything; you've sold it for a higher price'. The garage people said that they were dealers in second-hand cars; that they had had a number of cars of this sort of age and type, BMW 2002s; and that they had lost the sale of another car. They said that, if Mr Wright had taken this car, they would have been able to sell one of those other cars to the purchaser. So they had sold one car less and were entitled to profit accordingly.

The judge thought that they had not proved that they had sold one car less but that there was a 50:50 chance that they would have sold an extra car. So he gave them damages for half the sum claimed. Instead of £345 he gave them £172.50.

Now there is an appeal to this court. The cases show that if there are a number of new cars, all exactly of the same kind, available for sale, and the dealers can prove that they sold one car less than they otherwise would have done, they would be entitled to damages amounting to their loss of profit on the one car: see the judgment of Upjohn J in *W L Thompson v Robinson (Gunmakers) Ltd*. The same has been held in the United States: *Torkomian v Russell* and *Stewart v Hawsen*; in Canada, *Mason & Risch Ltd v Christner*; and in Australia, *Cameron v Campbell & Worthington*.

But it is entirely different in the case of a second-hand car. Each second-hand car is different from the next, even though it is the same make. The sales manager of the garage admitted in evidence that some second-hand cars, of the same make, even of the same year, may sell better than others of the same year. Some may sell quickly, others sluggishly. You simply cannot tell why. But they are all different.

In the circumstances the cases about new cars do not apply. We have simply to apply to s 50 of the Sale of Goods Act 1893. There is no available market for second-hand cars. So its not sub-s (3) but sub-s (2). The measure of damages is the estimated loss directly and naturally resulting in the ordinary course of events from the buyer's breach of contract. That throws us back to the test of what could reasonably be expected to be in the contemplation of the parties as a natural consequence of the breach. The buyer in this case could not have contemplated that the dealer would sell one car less. At most he would contemplate that, if they resold this very car at a lower price, they would suffer by reason of that lower price and should recover the difference. But if they resold this very car at a higher price, they would suffer no loss. Seeing that these plaintiffs resold this car for £100 more than the sale to Mr Wright, they clearly suffered no damage at all.

In my opinion the appeal should be allowed and judgment entered for the defendant, Mr Wright.

[Lawton and Bridge LJJ agreed.]"

QUESTIONS

1. If the plaintiff in *White & Carter* (1962) (see p.386) was entitled to its "expectation interest" (enforced via an action in debt), why was Lazenby Garages denied its expectation interest?

2. Did the economic "interest" in this case attach itself to the car rather than to the plaintiff? Why is it different with respect to new cars?

3. If Mr Wright had paid a deposit on the car, would Lazenby Garages have been entitled to keep it? What if, according to the sale contract, a deposit of 10 per cent of the price became legally due the moment the contract was agreed: could Lazenby have sued Wright either in debt or in damages for this sum? (*Cf. Damon Compania Naviera SA v Hapag-Lloyd* (1985), above at p.519.)

4. Was not the trial judge right in saying that Lazenby had lost a chance? Is not the loss of a chance an accepted form of damage?

11.5.2 Loss of a chance

Despite the Court of Appeal overturning the trial judge's finding in *Lazenby* that there had been the loss of a chance, this form of damage is recognised by English law (see UC&TO, pp.152–5; and see UNIDROIT, art.7.4.3(2)).

Allied Maples Group Ltd v Simmons & Simmons **[1995] 1 W.L.R. 1602, CA**

Stuart-Smith L.J.: "This is an appeal by the defendants from a judgment of Turner J given on 8 June 1993 on the trial of a preliminary issue as to liability.

The plaintiffs are a subsidiary of Asda Group Plc and are the retailing arm of that group which is concerned with carpets, furniture and soft furnishings. The defendants are a well known firm of solicitors in the City of London with extensive experience in the field of company takeovers and mergers. The proceedings arise from the takeover by the plaintiffs of assets and businesses within the Gillow group of companies.

The plaintiffs brought this action complaining that in the course of the negotiation of the takeover and in the agreement itself they were insufficiently advised in respect of, and protected from, the liabilities that might and did eventuate from leases originally held by one of the companies in the Gillow group and which had been assigned by it prior to the date of the takeover agreement. This species of liability is referred to as 'first tenant liability.' . . .

In these circumstances, where the plaintiffs' loss depends upon the actions of an independent third party, it is necessary to consider as a matter of law what it is necessary to establish as a matter of causation, and where causation ends and quantification of damage begins. . . .

Although there is not a great deal of authority, and none in the Court of Appeal, relating to solicitors failing to give advice which is directly in point, I have no doubt that Mr Jackson's [counsel for the defendants] submission is wrong and the second alternative is correct.

In *Chaplin v Hicks* [1911] 2 KB 786 the defendant's breach of contract prevented the plaintiff from taking part in a beauty contest and deprived her of the chance of winning one of the prizes. The Court of Appeal upheld the judge's award on the basis that, while there was no certainty that she would have won, she lost the chance of doing so.

In *Kitchen v Royal Air Force Association* [1958] 1 WLR 563 the defendant solicitors negligently failed to issue a writ against the tortfeasor with the result that the plaintiff's claim was statute barred. The Court of Appeal upheld the judge's award of £2,000, which was two-thirds of the full liability value of the claim. The court firmly rejected the defendant's contention that she had to establish on a balance of probability that she would have won the action. . . . Mr Jackson made two submissions on those authorities. First, that they should be confined to cases where the plaintiff has lost a valuable right or chose in action; in the present case he said that the plaintiffs had no such right. It is true that in *Chaplin v Hicks* [1911] 2 KB 786 both Vaughan Williams and Fletcher Moulton LJJ referred to the plaintiff losing a valuable right, but I can see no difference in principle between the chance of gaining a benefit and the chance of avoiding a liability.

Secondly, Mr Jackson submitted that the plaintiffs can only succeed if in fact the chance of success can be rated at over 50 per cent. . . .

In *Spring v Guardian Assurance Plc* [1995] 2 AC 296 the House of Lords held that an employer who negligently gave a bad reference for the plaintiff, their ex-employee, might be liable to him in damages. The case was remitted to the Court of Appeal for the assessment of damages, the plaintiff's case being in essence that he failed to obtain employment with a third party because of the adverse reference. The defendant's case was that the third party would not have employed him anyway. Lord Lowry expressed the opinion obiter, at p 327:

'Once the duty of care is held to exist and the defendants' negligence is proved, the plaintiff only has to show that by reason of that negligence he has lost a reasonable chance of employment (which would have to be evaluated) and has thereby sustained loss: *McGregor on Damages*, 14th ed (1980), pp 198–202, paras 276–278 and *Chaplin v Hicks* [1911] 2 KB 786. He does not have to prove that, but for the negligent reference, Scottish Amicable would have employed him.'

I respectfully agree with that statement of the law. . . ."

Hobhouse L.J.: ". . . Negotiations may depend upon the will of the parties and neither party was under any obligation at that stage to agree anything. But it is unrealistic to treat the outcome of further negotiation between commercial parties as arbitrary and wholly unpredictable. Those with experience of commercial negotiation are able, with a reasonable degree of accuracy, to form a view of what can be achieved by such negotiation. The present was such a case. It is possible to make an informed judgment of what the chances were of achieving certain results. The situation is certainly less speculative than that in *Chaplin v Hicks* [1911] 2 KB 786 (the beauty competition case) or *Dunbar v A & B Painters Ltd* [1986] 2 Lloyd's Rep 38 (the underwriters' waiver case). . . ."

Millett L.J. (dissenting in part): ". . . The 'chance' of which the plaintiffs claim to have been deprived is the chance that they might have negotiated better terms from their vendors. In the absence of evidence from Gillow, what would have been the outcome of such negotiations is a matter of pure speculation. No case has gone so far as to allow damages in such a situation, and in my view it would be wrong to do so. The nearest is *Davies v Taylor* [1974] AC 207, where the outcome depended on whether a married couple who had separated would have had a reconciliation; it was held that this was too speculative to sound in damages. I call to mind the words of Vaughan Williams LJ in *Chaplin v Hicks* [1911] 2 KB 786, 792–793:

'There are cases, no doubt, where the loss is so dependent on the mere unrestricted volition of another that it is impossible to say that there is any assessable loss resulting from the breach.'

In my judgment this is just such a case. . . ."

QUESTION

Is loss of a chance simply a causation problem, or does it equally involve how one envisages a *res* (i.e. a "thing" lost)?

11.5.3 **Personal injury and property damage**

A contractor can be liable, as we have seen in *Parsons v Uttley Ingham* (1978) (p.527), not just for the economic loss arising out of defective goods but also for physical damage if it is direct and foreseeable. With respect to personal injury, a breach of contract will give rise to a right to damages, provided that the personal injury flows directly from the breach and is not too remote; see e.g. *Vacwell Engineering Co Ltd v BDH Chemicals Ltd* (1971). As for property damage, the next extract indicates that much will depend upon the circumstances.

> *Lagden v O'Connor* **[2004] 1 A.C. 1067, HL**
>
> **Lord Hope:** ". . . 32 In *Harbutt's 'Plasticine' Ltd v Wayne Tank and Pump Co Ltd* [1970] 1 QB 447 the plaintiffs' factory, which was in an old mill, was destroyed by fire as a result of defects in the design of equipment supplied by the defendants and its having been switched on and the plant left unattended. A new factory had to be built. The plaintiffs had no other option if they were to continue their business of making plasticine. They were not allowed to rebuild the old mill, so they had to put up a new factory. A question was raised as to the measure of damages. The defendants said that it should be limited to the difference in the value of the old mill before and after the fire and that the plaintiffs should not be allowed the cost of replacing it with a new building. This argument was rejected. . . .
>
> 34 Of course, the facts . . . were quite different from those in this case. But I think that the principles on which they were decided are of general application, and it is possible to extract this guidance from them. It is for the defendant who seeks a deduction from expenditure in mitigation on the ground of betterment to make out his case for doing so. It is not enough that an element of betterment can be identified. It has to be shown that the claimant had a choice, and that he would have been able to mitigate his loss at less cost. The wrongdoer is not entitled to demand of the injured party that he incur a loss, bear a burden or make unreasonable sacrifices in the mitigation of his damages. He is entitled to demand that, where there are choices to be made, the least expensive route which will achieve mitigation must be selected. So if the evidence shows that the claimant had a choice, and that the route to mitigation which he chose was more costly than an alternative that was open to him, then a case will have been made out for a deduction. But if it shows that the claimant had no other choice available to him, the betterment must be seen as incidental to the step which he was entitled to take in the mitigation of his loss and there will be no ground for it to be deducted. . . ."

NOTE

The mitigation rule can play an important role in the decision whether or not to protect certain interests, as of course can causal and remoteness rules. In this respect the Court of Appeal judges in *The Borag* (1981) (see p.532) were no doubt correct in saying that it often does not make much difference which limitation rule one employs. The question is whether the claimed particular interest is a reasonable one in the circumstances.

11.5.4 **Mental distress**

A more difficult interest is the non-economic interest of mental distress and disappointment. Here the general rule is that only economic interests are protected by the law of contract: thus damages are not normally available unless physical or economic loss can actually be proved. But the courts have now recognised some important exceptions.

Watts v Morrow **[1991] 1 W.L.R. 1421, CA**

Bingham L.J.: ". . . A contract-breaker is not in general liable for any distress, frustration, anxiety, displeasure, vexation, tension or aggravation which his breach of contract may cause to the innocent party . . . But the rule is not absolute. Where the very object of a contract is to provide pleasure, relaxation, peace of mind or freedom from molestation, damages will be awarded if the fruit of the contract is not provided or if the contrary result is procured instead . . . A contract to survey the condition of a house for a prospective purchaser does not, however, fall within this exceptional category. In cases not falling within this exceptional category, damages are in my view recoverable for physical inconvenience and discomfort caused by the breach and mental suffering directly related to that inconvenience and discomfort . . . But I also agree that awards should be restrained . . ."

NOTE

The breakthrough came with the holiday cases: see *Jarvis v Swans Tours Ltd* (1971) and *Jackson v Horizon Holidays* (1975) (p.396).

Ruxley Electronics Ltd v Forsyth **[1996] 1 A.C. 344, HL**

(For facts, see p.442.)

Lord Lloyd: ". . . *Addis v Gramophone Co Ltd* established the general rule that in claims for breach of contract, the plaintiff cannot recover damages for his injured feelings. But the rule, like most rules, is subject to exceptions. One of the well established exceptions is when the object of the contract is to afford pleasure, as, for example, where the plaintiff has booked a holiday with a tour operator. If the tour operator is in breach of contract by failing to provide what the contract called for, the plaintiff may recover damages for his disappointment: see *Jarvis v Swans Tours Ltd* [1973] QB 233 and *Jackson v Horizon Holidays Ltd* [1975] 1 WLR 1468.

This was, as I understand it, the principle which Judge Diamond applied in the present case. He took the view that the contract was one 'for the provision of a pleasurable amenity.' In the event, Mr Forsyth's pleasure was not so great as it would have been if the swimming pool had been 7 feet 6 inches deep. This was a view which the judge was entitled to take. If it involves a further inroad on the rule in *Addis v Gramophone Co Ltd* [1909] AC 488, then so be it. But I prefer to regard it as a logical application or adaptation of the existing exception to a new situation. I should, however, add this note of warning. Mr Forsyth was, I think, lucky to have obtained so large an award for his disappointed expectations. But as there was no criticism from any quarter as to the quantum of the award as distinct from the underlying principle, it would not be right for your Lordships to interfere with the judge's figure. . . ."

NOTE

The way the House of Lords managed to avoid the expectation interest rule of damages was to effect a shift with respect to the descriptive interest in play. Mr Forsyth was asserting that the damage attached to the swimming pool in that it did not conform to the contract; Lord Lloyd is saying that the damage attached to Mr Forsyth himself. It was his mental interest that was invaded by the breach of contract.

QUESTION

A potential house buyer contracts with a firm of surveyors for the latter to survey the house, the potential buyer specifically requesting that the surveyors report on whether or not the house is under an airport flight path. The surveyors report that the house is not so situated, but when the buyer has purchased the property he discovers that the survey report was wrong. Can the buyer recover damages for his mental distress caused by the aircraft nuisance?

Farley v Skinner [2002] 2 A.C. 732, HL

Lord Steyn: "1. My Lords, the central question is whether a buyer, who employed a surveyor to investigate whether a property in the countryside was seriously affected by aircraft noise, may in principle recover non-pecuniary damages against the surveyor for the latter's negligent failure to discover that the property was so affected. The trial judge answered this question in the affirmative. A two-member Court of Appeal disagreed on it. The point was then re-argued before a three-member Court of Appeal. By a majority the Court of Appeal reversed the decision of the trial judge and ruled that there was no right to recover non-pecuniary damages in such cases. The second Court of Appeal was deluged with authorities. So was the House on the present appeal. The hearings of what was a comparatively simple case took up an exorbitant amount of time. This circumstance underlines the importance, in the quest for coherent and just solutions in such cases, of simple and practical rules. . . .

18. . . . . The plaintiff made it crystal clear to the surveyor that the impact of aircraft noise was a matter of importance to him. Unless he obtained reassuring information from the surveyor he would not have bought the property. That is the tenor of the evidence. It is also what the judge found. The case must be approached on the basis that the surveyor's obligation to investigate aircraft noise was a major or important part of the contract between him and the plaintiff. It is also important to note that, unlike in *Addis v Gramophone Co Ltd* [1909] AC 488, the plaintiff's claim is not for injured feelings caused by the breach of contract. Rather it is a claim for damages flowing from the surveyor's failure to investigate and report, thereby depriving the buyer of the chance of making an informed choice whether or not to buy resulting in mental distress and disappointment. . . .

24. . . . It is obvious, and conceded, that if an architect is employed only to design a staircase, or a surveyor is employed only to investigate aircraft noise, the breach of such a distinct obligation may result in an award of non-pecuniary damages. Logically the same must be the case if the architect or surveyor, apart from entering into a general retainer, concludes a separate contract, separately remunerated, in respect of the design of a staircase or the investigation of aircraft noise. . . . There is no reason in principle or policy why the scope of recovery in the exceptional category should depend on the object of the contract as ascertained from all its constituent parts. It is sufficient if a major or important object of the contract is to give pleasure, relaxation or peace of mind. . . .

25. That brings me to the second issue, namely whether the plaintiff's claim is barred by reason of the fact that the surveyor undertook an obligation to exercise reasonable care and did not guarantee the achievement of a result. . . . I fully accept, of course, that contractual guarantees of performance and promises to exercise reasonable care are fundamentally different. The former may sometimes give greater protection than the latter. Proving breach of an obligation of reasonable care may be more difficult than proving breach of a guarantee. On the other hand, a party may in practice be willing to settle for the relative reassurance offered by the obligation of reasonable care undertaken by a professional man. But why should this difference between an absolute and relative contractual promise require a distinction in respect of the recovery of non-pecuniary damages? Take the example of a travel agent who is consulted by a couple who are looking for a golfing holiday in France. Why should it make a difference in respect of the recoverability of non-pecuniary damages for a spoiled holiday whether the travel agent gives a guarantee that there is a golf course very near the hotel, represents that to be the case, or negligently advises that all hotels of the particular chain of hotels are situated next to golf courses? If the nearest golf

course is in fact 50 miles away a breach may be established. It may spoil the holiday of the couple. It is difficult to see why in principle only those plaintiffs who negotiate guarantees may recover non-pecuniary damages for a breach of contract. It is a singularly unattractive result that a professional man, who undertakes a specific obligation to exercise reasonable care to investigate a matter judged and communicated to be important by his customer can in Lord Mustill's words in *Ruxley Electronics and Construction Ltd v Forsyth* [1996] AC 344, 360 'please himself whether or not to comply with the wishes of the promisee which, as embodied in the contract, formed part of the consideration for the price'. If that were the law it would be seriously deficient. I am satisfied that it is not the law. . . .

26. The final argument was that by failing to move out the plaintiff forfeited a right to claim non-pecuniary damages. This argument was not advanced in the Court of Appeal. It will be recalled that the judge found as a fact that the plaintiff had acted reasonably in making 'the best of a bad job'. The plaintiff's decision also avoided a larger claim against the surveyor. It was never explained on what legal principle the plaintiff's decision not to move out divested him of a claim for non-pecuniary damages. . . . The third argument must also be rejected. . . .

28. In the surveyor's written case it was submitted that the award of £10,000 was excessive. It was certainly high. Given that the plaintiff is stuck indefinitely with a position which he sought to avoid by the terms of his contract with the surveyor I am not prepared to interfere with the judge's evaluation on the special facts of the case. On the other hand, I have to say that the size of the award appears to be at the very top end of what could possibly be regarded as appropriate damages. . . .

29. In agreement with the reasoning of Clarke LJ I would therefore hold that the decision of the majority in the Court of Appeal was wrong. . . ."

Lord Scott: ". . . 86. In summary, the principle expressed in *Ruxley Electronics and Construction Ltd v Forsyth* [1996] AC 344 should be used to provide damages for deprivation of a contractual benefit where it is apparent that the injured party has been deprived of something of value but the ordinary means of measuring the recoverable damages are inapplicable. The principle expressed in *Watts v Morrow* [1991] 1 WLR 1421 should be used to determine whether and when contractual damages for inconvenience or discomfort can be recovered.

87. These principles, in my opinion, provide the answer, not only to the issue raised in the present case, but also to the issues raised in the authorities which were cited to your Lordships. . . .

[Lords Browne-Wilkinson, Clyde and Hutton also agreed that the decision of the Court of Appeal should be reversed.]"

QUESTION

Can an employee sue his employer for the mental distress caused by (i) bullying by a fellow-employee, and/or (ii) over-work?

11.5.5 **Reputation**

An interest analogous in some ways to mental distress (in that it is a non-economic loss) is injury to the reputation interest.

Mahmud v BCCI [1998] A.C. 20, HL

(For facts, see p.278.)

Lord Nicholls: ". . . Can an employee recover damages for breach of the trust and confidence term when he first learns of the breach after he has left the employment? The answer to this question is inextricably bound up with the further question of what damages are recoverable for a breach of this term. In turn, the answer to this further question is inextricably linked with one aspect of the decision in *Addis v Gramophone Co Ltd* [1909] AC 488. . . .

Against this background I turn to the much discussed case of *Addis v Gramophone Co Ltd* [1909] AC 488. Mr Addis, it will be recalled, was wrongfully and contumeliously dismissed from his post as the defendant's manager in Calcutta. At trial he was awarded damages exceeding the amount of his salary for the period of notice to which he was entitled. The case is generally regarded as having decided, echoing the words of Lord Loreburn LC, at p 491, that an employee cannot recover damages for the manner in which the wrongful dismissal took place, for injured feelings or for any loss he may sustain from the fact that his having been dismissed of itself makes it more difficult for him to obtain fresh employment. In particular, *Addis's* case is generally understood to have decided that any loss suffered by the adverse impact on the employee's chances of obtaining alternative employment is to be excluded from an assessment of damages for wrongful dismissal. . . .

In my view [Lord Loreburn's] observations cannot be read as precluding the recovery of damages where the manner of dismissal involved a breach of the trust and confidence term and this caused financial loss. *Addis v Gramophone Co Ltd* was decided in the days before this implied term was adumbrated. Now that this term exists and is normally implied in every contract of employment, damages for its breach should be assessed in accordance with ordinary contractual principles. This is as much true if the breach occurs before or in connection with dismissal as at any other time. . . .

Breach of contract and reputation

I must now turn to two submissions made concerning injury to reputation. The liquidators submitted that injury to reputation is protected by the law of defamation. The boundaries set by the tort of defamation are not to be side-stepped by allowing a claim in contract that would not succeed in defamation: see *Lonrho Plc v Fayed (No 5)* [1993] 1 WLR 1489, 1496, per Dillon LJ. Here, it was submitted, a claim in defamation would not succeed: the bank made no defamatory statements, either referring to the applicants or at all. This submission is misconceived.

I agree that the cause of action known to the law in respect of injury to reputation is the tort of defamation. With certain exceptions this tort provides a remedy, where the necessary ingredients are present, whether or not the injury to a person's reputation causes financial loss. No proof of actual damage is necessary, and damages are at large. If, as a result of the injury to his reputation the plaintiff does in fact suffer financial loss, this may be recoverable in a defamation action as 'special damage.'

All this is commonplace. It by no means follows, however, that financial loss which may be recoverable as special damage in a defamation action is irrecoverable as damages for breach of contract. If a breach of contract gives rise to financial loss which on ordinary principles would be recoverable as damages for breach of contract, those damages do not cease to be recoverable because they might also be recoverable in a defamation action. There can be no justification for artificially excising from the damages recoverable for breach of contract that part of the financial loss which might or might not be the subject of a successful claim in defamation. . . .

Furthermore, the fact that the breach of contract injures the plaintiff's reputation in circumstances where no claim for defamation would lie is not, by itself, a reason for excluding from the damages recoverable for breach of contract compensation for financial loss which on ordinary principles would be recoverable. An award of damages for breach of contract has a different objective: compensation for financial loss suffered by a breach of contract, not compensation for injury to reputation.

Sometimes, in practice, the distinction between damage to reputation and financial loss can become blurred. Damage to the reputation of professional persons, or persons carrying on a business, frequently causes financial loss. None the less, the distinction is fundamentally sound, and when awarding damages for breach of contract courts take care to confine the damages to their proper ambit: making good financial loss. In *Herbert Clayton and Jack Waller Ltd v Oliver* [1930] AC 209, 220, when considering an award of damages to an actor who should have been billed to appear at the London Hippodrome, Lord Buckmaster regarded loss of publicity rather than loss of reputation as the preferable expression. In *Aerial Advertising Co v Batchelors Peas Ltd (Manchester)* [1938] 2 All ER 788, 796–797, where aerial advertising ('Eat Batchelors Peas') took place during Armistice Day services, Atkinson J was careful to confine damages to the financial loss flowing from public boycotting of the defendant's goods and to exclude damages for loss of reputation. Lord Denning MR drew the same distinction in *GKN Centrax Gears Ltd v Matbro Ltd* [1976] 2 Lloyd's Rep 555, 573. . . .

Conclusion

For these reasons I would allow these appeals. The agreed set of assumed facts discloses a good cause of action. Unlike the courts below, this House is not bound by the observations in *Addis v Gramophone Co Ltd* [1909] AC 488 regarding irrecoverability of loss flowing from the manner of dismissal, or by the decision in *Withers v General Theatre Corporation Ltd* [1933] 2 KB 536. . . ."

Lord Steyn: ". . . The speeches of the majority of the House of Lords in *Spring v Guardian Assurance Plc* [1995] 2 AC 296 are also instructive. In that case the majority held that a former employee could recover damages for financial loss which he suffered as a result of his employer's negligent preparation of a reference. The reference affected his reputation. The majority considered that, if the reference had been given while the plaintiff was still employed, his claim could have been brought in contract. On that hypothesis he could have sued in contract for damage to his reputation. The dicta in *Spring v Guardian Assurance Plc* show that there is no rule preventing the recovery of damages for injury to reputation where that injury is caused by a breach of contract. The principled position is as follows. Provided that a relevant breach of contract can be established, and the requirements of causation, remoteness and mitigation can be satisfied, there is no good reason why in the field of employment law recovery of financial loss in respect of damage to reputation caused by breach of contract is necessarily excluded. . . .

. . . [But] even if the employee can establish a breach of this obligation, it does not follow that he will be able to recover damages for injury to his employment prospects. The Law Commission has pointed out that loss of reputation is inherently difficult to prove: Consultation Paper No 132 on Aggravated, Exemplary and Restitutionary Damages, p 22, para 2.15. It is, therefore, improbable that many employees would be able to prove 'stigma compensation.' The limiting principles of causation, remoteness and mitigation present formidable practical obstacles to such claims succeeding. But difficulties of proof cannot alter the legal principles which permit, in appropriate cases, such claims for financial loss caused by breach of contract being put forward for consideration."

QUESTIONS

1. Has *Addis v Gramophone Co* now been overruled?

2. Can damages ever be awarded for injured feelings? (*Cf.* Equality Act 2006 s.68(4).)

11.5.6 Non-compensatory damages

Addis v Gramophone (1909) is also an authority in support of the proposition that exemplary damages—that is non-compensatory damages awarded to punish a defendant—cannot be awarded in contract. They can, however, be awarded in certain circumstances in tort: see C&MT, pp.383–6. Some argue that they should also be available in contract: see e.g. Cunnington (2006) 26 LS 369 (this article will repay its reading). Another form of non-compensatory damages are those awarded not to compensate a victim of a breach of contract but to deprive the party in breach of a profit derived from the breach. The interest in play here is called "restitutionary" (see Lord Steyn, above at p.552) and is now remedied, it would seem, by an action in account (see below).

11.6 Monetary remedies in equity

The common law courts could, on the whole, grant only monetary remedies, and because this could often cause injustice, the Court of Chancery developed a range of non-monetary remedies (which will be discussed in the next chapter). However, there are two monetary remedies employed by equity for use in exceptional situations. The first is an equitable form of debt action, called account of profits, and the second is equitable damages.

11.6.1 **Account**

The action of account is very old and is probably common law in origin. However, it was subsequently appropriated by the Court of Chancery.

F.H. Lawson, *Remedies of English Law*, (2nd edn, Butterworths, 1980), pp.142–3 (footnotes omitted)

"The peculiar organisation of the Chancery, part court and part administrative office, enabled it to develop the special remedy of account, whereby a defendant could be made to furnish the plaintiff with an account of the dealings between them and, if the plaintiff chooses to apply for it, an order to pay the balance that is found to exist. The remedy can now be afforded not only by its descendant, the Chancery Division, but also by any Division of the High Court. The remedy is not universal in scope, but it would probably be granted whenever the plaintiff has some other gorund for seeking equitable relief. . . .

The law relating to account has many dark corners which have not been illuminated in the books or in the course of litigation; and it seems that more use might with advantage be made of the remedy."

NOTE

The late Professor Lawson was writing about account over a quarter of a century ago, and since then there has been a major development: account has been developed as a restitutionary remedy (see *Attorney-General v Blake* (2001), below at p.552). Before this recent development, account was traditionally available in the situations set out in the next extract.

London, Chatham & Dover Railway Co v South Eastern Railway Co [1892] 1 Ch.120, CA

Lindley L.J.: ". . . Before the Judicature Acts a suit for an account could be maintained in equity in the following cases:-- (1) Where the plaintiff had a legal right to have money payable to him ascertained and paid, but which right, owing to defective legal machinery, he could not practically enforce at law. Suits for an account between principal and agent, and between partners, are familiar instances of this class of case. (2) Where the plaintiff would have had a legal right to have money ascertained and paid to him by the defendant, if the defendant had not wrongfully prevented such right from accruing to the plaintiff. In such a case a court of law could only give unliquidated damages for the defendant's wrongful act; and there was often no machinery for satisfactorily ascertaining what would have been due and payable if the defendant had acted properly. In such a case, however, a Court of Equity decreed an account, ascertained what would have been payable if the defendant had acted as he ought to have done and ordered him to pay the amount: *M'Intosh v Great Western Railway Company* ((1865) 4 Giff 683), is the leading authority in this class of case. (3) Where the plaintiff had no legal but only equitable rights against the defendant, and where an account was necessary to give effect to those equitable rights. Ordinary suits by *cestuis que trust* against their trustees and suits for equitable waste fell within this class. (4) Combination of the above cases."

NOTES

1. In *Watson v Holliday* (1882), Kay J. said (at 784): 'He [Lord Westbury] does not treat an account of profits as a remedy in the nature of damages. He treats it as being more like an equitable claim for money had and received, taking the person who has committed the tort as having been in fact in the position of an agent or trustee for the Plaintiff.' Account is, then, closer to a debt claim than to a claim for damages. Indeed, in *Webb v Stenton* (1883) Lindley L.J. asserted (at 526): "Now, I quite agree that the word 'debt' in this order includes not only what was a common law debt before the passing of the Judicature Act, but also what was a mere equitable debt, that is to say a liquidated sum of money owing in equity from one person to another."

2. The role of account has now been further developed: it can be used as an unjust enrichment remedy.

Attorney-General v Guardian Newspapers (No.2) **[1990] A.C. 109, HL**

> **Lord Goff:** ". . . The statement that a man shall not be allowed to profit from his own wrong is in very general terms, and does not of itself provide any sure guidance to the solution of a problem in any particular case. That there are groups of cases in which a man is not allowed to profit from his own wrong, is certainly true . . . The plaintiff's claim to restitution is usually enforced by an account of profits made by the defendant through his wrong at the plaintiff's expense. This remedy of an account is alternative to the remedy of damages . . ."

QUESTION

A contractor secures a large profit through an act which amounts to a breach of contract with the claimant. However, the claimant is unable to prove that he has suffered any damage. Can he nevertheless sue for damages at common law?

Surrey County Council v Bredero Homes Ltd **[1993] 1 W.L.R. 1361, CA**

> **Dillon L.J.:** "This is an appeal by the plaintiffs, the Surrey County Council . . . against a decision of Ferris J given on 21 November 1991 . . . By his decision the judge awarded the plaintiffs nominal damages only against the defendant, Bredero Homes Ltd, for breaches of virtually identical positive covenants contained in transfers by the plaintiffs to the defendant of certain land in Surrey in 1981 . . .
>
> The plaintiffs object to the development of the final 3.64 acres . . . As a legal basis it is said by the plaintiffs, and conceded by the defendant, that in building 77 houses in all under the later planning permission, rather than 72 under the first planning permission, the defendant acted in breach of the covenants in the transfers.
>
> The plaintiffs therefore seek damages. They have never sought an interim injunction to restrain the defendant from developing the land otherwise than in accordance with the first planning permission. They never sought an injunction at the trial requiring the defendant to pull down the completed houses. They recognised that there was never any practical possibility of such an injunction being granted . . . The plaintiffs accept that they have not suffered any damage at all of the nature of damage to adjoining property owned or occupied by them. What they claim as damages is essentially the profit made by the defendant by breaking the covenants and building 77 houses and not just 72 . . .
>
> The starting point, however, in my judgment is that the remedy at common law for a breach of contract is an award of damages, and damages at common law are intended to compensate the victim for his loss, not to transfer to the victim if he has suffered no loss the benefit which the wrongdoer has gained by his breach of contract . . .

Every student is taught that the basis of assessing damages for breach of contract is the rule in *Hadley v Baxendale* (1854) 9 Ex 341, which is wholly concerned with the losses which can be compensated by damages. Such damages may, in an appropriate case, cover profit which the injured plaintiff has lost, but they do not cover an award, to a plaintiff who has himself suffered no loss, of the profit which the defendant has gained for himself by his breach of contract.

In the field of tort there are areas where the law is different and the plaintiff can recover in respect of the defendant's gain. Thus in the field of trespass it is well established that if one person has, without leave of another, been using that other's land for his own purposes he ought to pay for such user. Thus even if he had done no actual harm to the land he was charged for the user of the land . . . The same principle was applied to patent infringement . . . The infringer was ordered to pay by way of damages a royalty for every infringing article because the infringement damaged the plaintiff's property right, that is to say, his patent monopoly. So in a case of detinue the defendant was ordered to pay a hire for chattels he had detained: *Strand Electric and Engineering Co Ltd v Brisford Entertainments Ltd* [1952] 2 QB 246 . . .

As I see it, therefore, there never was in the present case, even before the writ was issued, any possibility of the court granting an injunction . . . The plaintiffs' only possible claim from the outset was for damages only, damages at common law. The plaintiffs have suffered no damage. Therefore on basic principles, as damages are awarded to compensate loss, the damages must be merely nominal. For these reasons, which substantially accord with those of Ferris J I would dismiss this appeal."

Steyn L.J.: ". . . The present case involves no breach of fiduciary obligations. It is a case of breach of contract. The principles governing expectation or reliance losses cannot be invoked. Given the fact of the breach of contract the only question is whether restitution is an appropriate remedy for this wrong. The case does not involve any invasion of the plaintiffs' property interests even in the broadest sense of that word, nor is it closely analogous to the *Wrotham Park* position. I would therefore rule that no restitutionary remedy is available and there is certainly no other remedy available. I would dismiss the appeal."

Rose L.J.: "I agree . . ."

QUESTION

Is this not a case where equity could intervene with its remedy of account?

Attorney-General v Blake [2001] 1 A.C. 268, HL

This was an action for a declaration brought by the Attorney-General against George Blake, a self-confessed traitor who had fled the United Kingdom to live in Russia, that the Crown was beneficially entitled to the copyright in an autobiographical book published by Blake. At the trial the Crown rested its claim on the single cause of action that in writing and having published the book, Blake was in breach of a fiduciary duty owed to the Crown. The trial judge rejected the claim ([1997] Ch 84); the Court of Appeal allowed an appeal, not with respect to the fiduciary duty, but on the basis of an amended statement of claim that stated that the Crown had a claim in public law. In private law Blake was in breach of contract with the Crown, but as the Crown had suffered no loss it had no remedy in damages. The public law claim would, however, give rise to a freezing injunction restraining the defendant from profiting from his breach of the criminal law ([1998] Ch 439). The House of Lords (Lords Nicholls, Goff, Browne-Wilkinson, Steyn and Hobhouse) held that the Court of Appeal had exceeded its jurisdiction in issuing the injunction based on public law since it amounted to a confiscatory order; there is no power at common law to confiscate property without compensation. However, a majority of the House of Lords (Lord Hobhouse dissenting) dismissed the appeal on the basis that the Crown had a remedy in account. This remedy, discretionary in nature, would be available in exceptional circumstances where other normal remedies (damages, specific performance or injunction) were inadequate.

Lord Nicholls: ". . . Prompted by an invitation from your Lordships, the Attorney General advanced an argument that restitutionary principles ought to operate to enable the Crown to recover from Blake his profits arising from his breach of contract. It will be convenient to consider this private law claim first.

. . . The broad proposition that a wrongdoer should not be allowed to profit from his wrong has an obvious attraction. The corollary is that the person wronged may recover the amount of this profit when he has suffered no financially measurable loss. As Glidewell LJ observed in *Halifax Building Society v Thomas* [1996] Ch 217, 229, the corollary is not so obviously persuasive. In these choppy waters the common law and equity steered different courses. The effects of this are still being felt. . . .

Courts of equity went further than the common law courts. In some cases equity required the wrongdoer to yield up all his gains. In respect of certain wrongs which originally or ordinarily were the subject of proceedings in the Court of Chancery, the standard remedies were injunction and, incidental thereto, an account of profits. These wrongs included passing off, infringement of trade marks, copyrights and patents, and breach of confidence. Some of these subjects are now embodied in statutory codes. . . .

Considered as a matter of principle, it is difficult to see why equity required the wrongdoer to account for all his profits in these cases, whereas the common law's response was to require a wrongdoer merely to pay a reasonable fee for use of another's land or goods. In all these cases rights of property were infringed. This difference in remedial response appears to have arisen simply as an accident of history. . . .

I turn to the decision of the Court of Appeal in *Surrey County Council v Bredero Homes Ltd* [1993] 1 WLR 1361. . . .

This is a difficult decision. It has attracted criticism from academic commentators and also in judgments of Sir Thomas Bingham MR and Millett LJ in *Jaggard v Sawyer* [1995] 1 WLR 269. I need not pursue the detailed criticisms. In the *Bredero* case Dillon LJ himself noted, at p 1364, that had the covenant been worded differently, there could have been provision for payment of an increased price if a further planning permission were forthcoming. That would have been enforceable. But, according to the *Bredero* decision, a covenant not to erect any further houses without permission, intended to achieve the same result, may be breached with impunity. That would be a sorry reflection on the law. Suffice to say, in so far as the *Bredero* decision is inconsistent with the approach adopted in the *Wrotham Park* case, the latter approach is to be preferred. . . .

[The] cases illustrate that circumstances do arise when the just response to a breach of contract is that the wrongdoer should not be permitted to retain any profit from the breach. In these cases the courts have reached the desired result by straining existing concepts. Professor Peter Birks has deplored the 'failure of jurisprudence when the law is forced into this kind of abusive instrumentalism': see (1993) 109 LQR 518, 520. Some years ago Professor Dawson suggested there is no inherent reason why the technique of equity courts in land contracts should not be more widely employed, not by granting remedies as the by-product of a phantom 'trust' created by the contract, but as an alternative form of money judgment remedy. That well known ailment of lawyers, a hardening of the categories, ought not to be an obstacle: see 'Restitution or Damages' (1959) 20 Ohio SLJ 175.

My conclusion is that there seems to be no reason, in principle, why the court must in all circumstances rule out an account of profits as a remedy for breach of contract. I prefer to avoid the unhappy expression 'restitutionary damages'. Remedies are the law's response to a wrong (or, more precisely, to a cause of action). When, exceptionally, a just response to a breach of contract so requires, the court should be able to grant the discretionary remedy of requiring a defendant to account to the plaintiff for the benefits he has received from his breach of contract. In the same way as a plaintiff's interest in performance of a contract may render it just and equitable for the court to make an order for specific performance or grant an injunction, so the plaintiff's interest in performance may make it just and equitable that the defendant should retain no benefit from his breach of contract. . . .

The Attorney General's entitlement to an account of Blake's profits does not, in this case, confer on the Crown any proprietary interest in the debt due to Blake from Jonathan Cape. The Crown is entitled, on the taking of the account, to a money judgment which can then be enforced by attachment of the debt in the usual way. . . . The injunction granted by the Court of Appeal will remain in force until Jonathan Cape duly makes payment to the Attorney General. I would dismiss this appeal. . . ."

Lord Steyn: ". . . My Lords, it has been held at first instance and in the Court of Appeal that Blake is not a fiduciary. This is not an issue before the House. But, as my noble and learned friend Lord Nicholls of Birkenhead has observed, the present case is closely analogous to that of fiduciaries: compare *Reading v Attorney-General* [1951] AC 507 . . . I bear in mind that the enduring strength of the common law is that it has been developed on a case-by-case basis by judges for whom the attainment of practical justice was a major objective of their work. It is still one of the major moulding forces of judicial decision-making. These observations are almost banal: the public would be astonished if it was thought that judges did not conceive it as their prime duty to do practical justice whenever possible. A recent example of this process at work is *White v Jones* [1995] 2 AC 207 where by a majority the House of Lords held that a solicitor who caused loss to a third party by negligence in the preparation of a will is liable in damages. Subordinating conceptual difficulties to the needs of practical justice a majority, and notably Lord Goff of Chieveley, at pp. 259G--260H, upheld the claim. For my part practical justice strongly militates in favour of granting an order for disgorgement of profits against Blake. . . ."

Lord Hobhouse (dissenting): ". . . Your Lordships have concluded that this claim should be allowed.

I cannot join your Lordships in that conclusion. I have two primary difficulties. The first is the facts of the present case. . . . Blake has made a financial gain but he has not done so at the expense of the Crown or making use of any property of or commercial interest of the Crown either in law or equity.

My second difficulty is that the reasoning of my noble and learned friend depends upon the conclusion that there is some gap in the existing state of the law which requires to be filled by a new remedy. He accepts that the term 'restitutionary damages' is unsatisfactory but, with respect, does not fully examine why this is so, drawing the necessary conclusions. . . .

. . . [T]he Crown did not apply for an injunction at the time it would have done some good and quite probably stopped the publication of the book. This is the source of the problems for the Crown in achieving its purpose in bringing these proceedings. . . .

My Lords, Mr Clayton was right to say that the exceptional facts of this case have been critical to its decision. The policy which is being enforced is that which requires Blake to be punished by depriving him of any benefit from anything connected with his past deplorable criminal conduct. Your Lordships consider that this policy can be given effect to without a departure from principle. I must venture to disagree. I would allow the appeal and dismiss the cross-appeal."

QUESTIONS

1. What is the present status of "restitutionary damages"? Has such a damages action now been replaced by an action of account (equitable debt claim)?

2. Can account now be used to deprive all criminals of their ill-gotten gains? (*Cf.* Proceeds of Crime Act 2002.)

3. Is *Blake* (i) a breach of contract case; or (ii) an unjust enrichment case; or (iii) a property right case; or (iv) all three?

4. Is *Blake* a sort of exemplary damages case?

5. Is account now a standard contractual remedy?

Attorney-General v Blake **[2001] 1 A.C. 268, HL**

Lord Nicholls: ". . . The main argument against the availability of an account of profits as a remedy for breach of contract is that the circumstances where this remedy may be granted will be uncertain. This will have an unsettling effect on commercial contracts where certainty is important. I do not think these fears are well founded. I see no reason why, in practice, the availability of the remedy of an account of profits need disturb settled expectations in the commercial or consumer world. An account of profits will be appropriate only in exceptional circumstances. Normally the remedies of damages, specific performance and injunction, coupled with the characterisation of some contractual obligations as fiduciary, will provide an adequate response to a breach of contract. It will be only in exceptional cases, where those remedies are inadequate, that any question of accounting for profits will arise. No fixed rules can be prescribed. The court will have regard to all the circumstances, including the subject matter of the contract, the purpose of the contractual provision which has been breached, the circumstances in which the breach occurred, the consequences of the breach and the circumstances in which relief is being sought. A useful general guide, although not exhaustive, is whether the plaintiff had a legitimate interest in preventing the defendant's profit-making activity and, hence, in depriving him of his profit. . . ."

NOTE

See *English v Dedham Vale Properties* (1978) (at p.246).

QUESTION

Could an action in account ever be used as a means of retrieving money obtained by a contractor through a fraudulent misrepresentation?

Ex parte Adamson (1878) 8 Ch.D. 807, CA

> **James and Baggallay L.JJ.:** ". . . The suit was always for an equitable debt or liability in the nature of debt. It was a suit for the restitution of the actual money or thing, or value of the thing, of which the cheated party had been cheated. If a man had been defrauded of any money or property and the cheater afterwards became bankrupt, if the money could be earmarked, or if the thing could be found in specie, or traced, the assignees or trustees were made to give it back, or if it could not be earmarked or traced, then proof was allowed against the estate . . ."

NOTE

On tracing, see **12.8.1**.

11.6.2 Damages in equity

It is generally considered that the Court of Chancery had no inherent power to award damages. Some legal historians dispute this; but whatever the truth, Chancery never wished to see itself in competition with the common law courts and so one does not normally think of damages as an equitable remedy. There is an exception, however, as the next extract illustrates (the facts of the case are not important for the contract lawyer).

Jaggard v Sawyer [1995] 2 All E.R. 189, CA

> **Sir Thomas Bingham M.R.:** ". . . In considering the legal issues in this case, I should acknowledge at the outset my debt to an illuminating article by Professor Jolowicz 'Damages in Equity—A Study of Lord Cairns' Act' [1975] CLJ 224.
>
> Historically, the remedy given by courts of common law was damages. These afforded retrospective compensation for past wrongs. If the wrongs were repeated or continued, a fresh action was needed. Courts of equity, in contrast, were able to give prospective relief by way of injunction or specific performance. A mandatory injunction would require the defendant to observe a legal obligation or undo the effects of a past breach of legal obligation. A negative injunction would restrain a defendant from committing breaches of legal obligation in future. But these courts could not award damages. This anomaly was mitigated by the Common Law Procedure Act 1854, which gave courts of common law a limited power to grant equitable relief as well as damages. It was further mitigated by the Chancery Amendment Act 1858 (Lord Cairns' Act), which gave the Court of Chancery the power to award damages.
>
> Section 2 of Lord Cairns' Act provided:

'In all cases in which the Court of Chancery has jurisdiction to entertain an application for an injunction against a breach of any covenant, contract, or agreement, or against the commission or continuance of any wrongful act, or for the specific performance of any covenant, contract, or agreement, it shall be lawful for the same Court, if it shall think fit, to award damages to the party injured, either in addition to or in substitution for such injunction or specific performance; and such damages may be assessed in such manner as the Court shall direct.'

This enabled the Chancery Court on appropriate facts to award damages for unlawful conduct in the past as well as an injunction to restrain unlawful conduct in the future. It also enabled the Chancery Court to award damages instead of granting an injunction to restrain unlawful conduct in the future. Such damages can only have been intended to compensate the plaintiff for future unlawful conduct, the commission of which, in the absence of any injunction, the court must have contemplated as likely to occur. Despite the repeal of Lord Cairns' Act, it has never been doubted that the jurisdiction thereby conferred on the Court of Chancery is exercisable by the High Court and by county courts. . . .'"

Millett L.J.: "This appeal raises yet again the questions: what approach should the court adopt when invited to exercise its statutory jurisdiction to award damages instead of granting an injunction to restrain a threatened or continuing trespass or breach of a restrictive covenant? And if the court accedes to the invitation, on what basis should damages be assessed?

Before considering these questions, it is desirable to state some general propositions which are established by the authorities and which are, or at least ought to be, uncontroversial.

(1) The jurisdiction was originally conferred by s 2 of the Chancery Amendment Act 1858, commonly known as Lord Cairns' Act. It is now to be found in s 50 of the Supreme Court Act 1981. It is a jurisdiction to award damages 'in addition to, or in substitution for, an injunction or specific performance'.

(2) The principal object of Lord Cairns' Act is well known . . . It was to enable the Court of Chancery, when declining to grant equitable relief and leaving the plaintiff to his remedy at law, to award the plaintiff damages itself instead of sending him to the common law courts to obtain them. From the very first, however, it was recognised that the Act did more than this. The jurisdiction of the Court of Chancery was wider than that of the common law courts, for it could give relief where there was no cause of action at law . . . Damages at common law are recoverable only in respect of causes of action which are complete at the date of the writ; damages for future or repeated wrongs must be made the subject of fresh proceedings. Damages in substitution for an injunction, however, relate to the future, not the past. They inevitably extend beyond the damages to which the plaintiff may be entitled at law . . .

(3) The nature of the cause of action is immaterial; it may be in contract or tort. Lord Cairns' Act referred in terms to 'a breach of any covenant, contract, or agreement, or against the commission or continuance of any wrongful act' . . . Equitable relief, whether by way of injunction or damages under Lord Cairns' Act, is available because the common law remedy is inadequate; but the common law remedy of damages in cases of continuing trespass is inadequate not because the damages are likely to be small or nominal but because they cover the past only and not the future.

(4) The power to award damages under Lord Cairns' Act arises whenever the court 'has jurisdiction to entertain an application' for an injunction or specific performance . . . When the court comes to consider whether to grant an injunction or award damages instead, of course, it must do so by reference to the circumstances as they exist at the date of the hearing.

(5) The former question is effectively one of jurisdiction. The question is whether, at the date of the writ, the court could have granted an injunction, not whether it would have done . . .

(6) It is not necessary for the plaintiff to include a claim for damages in his writ . . . By a parity of reasoning it is not in my opinion necessary for a plaintiff to include a claim for an injunction in order to found a claim for damages under the Act. It would be absurd to require him to include a claim for an injunction if he is sufficiently realistic to recognise that in the circumstances he is unlikely to obtain one and intends from the first to ask the court for damages instead. But he ought to make it clear whether he is claiming damages for past injury at common law or under the Act in substitution for an injunction.

(7) . . . The court can in my judgment properly award damages 'once and for all' in respect of future wrongs because it awards them in substitution for an injunction and to compensate for those future wrongs which an injunction would have prevented. The doctrine of res judicata operates to prevent the plaintiff and his successors in title from bringing proceedings thereafter to recover even nominal damages in respect of further wrongs for which the plaintiff has been fully compensated. . . .

When the plaintiff claims an injunction and the defendant asks the court to award damages instead, the proper approach for the court to adopt cannot be in doubt. Clearly the plaintiff must first establish a case for equitable relief, not only by proving his legal right and an actual or threatened infringement by the defendant, but also by overcoming all equitable defences such as laches, acquiescence or estoppel. If he succeeds in doing this, he is *prima facie* entitled to an injunction. The court may nevertheless in its discretion withhold injunctive relief and award damages instead. How is this discretion to be exercised? [Millett L.J. then referred to A.L. Smith's checklist in the *Shelfer* case] . . .

Reported cases are merely illustrations of circumstances in which particular judges have exercised their discretion . . . Since they are all cases on the exercise of a discretion, none of them is a binding authority on how the discretion should be exercised . . ."

NOTES

1. A court also has power to award damages in lieu of equitable rescission in cases of non-fraudulent misrepresentation: see Misrepresentation Act 1967, s.2(2) (above, at p.237).

2. See *Witter Ltd v TBP Industries* (1996) (p.238) and Evans LJ in *William Sindall v Cambridgeshire CC* (1994) (p.240).

12 Remedies (2): non-monetary remedies

When one turns to the non-monetary remedies available (possibly) to an aggrieved contractor, two types need to be identified at the outset. There are remedies which need to be obtained from a court—judicial remedies—and there are remedies that require no judicial proceedings. These latter are non-judicial or self-help remedies. This is not to say that the use of a self-help remedy will never give rise to legal proceedings; if the other contracting party is of the view that the use of a non-judicial remedy is not supported by the law, this party against whom self-help was exercised may in turn seek the remedy of damages, or a declaration that the self-help action is itself a breach of contract (see e.g. *Hong Kong Fir Shipping* (1962), at p.336).

Most of the judicial non-monetary remedies are equitable in origin, and this means that they have a certain discretionary aspect. If a court is of the view that it would be inequitable to grant the remedy it will be refused, leaving the claimant to pursue his claim at common law in debt or damages (and see PECL, art.9:103). This discretion is not, it must be stressed, open-ended; it is governed by precedent and principle, and thus a judge administering equity must always fully justify his or her decision by reference to other cases and (or) to principle (see e.g. Lord Hoffmann in *Co-operative Insurance Society Ltd v Argyll Stores Ltd* (1998), below at p.566).

12.1 Specific performance in equity

Perhaps the most well-known equitable contractual remedy is an order for specific performance of the contractual promise. This is said to be an exceptional remedy, because it will not be granted when damages at common law would be an adequate remedy.

12.1.1 General rules

The general rules attaching to the remedy of specific performance are set out in the following code extracts.

Principles of European Contract Law

"Article 9:102 Non-monetary Obligations
(1) The aggrieved party is entitled to specific performance of an obligation other than one to pay money, including the remedying of a defective performance.

(2) Specific performance cannot, however, be obtained where:

- (a) performance would be unlawful or impossible; or
- (b) performance would cause the obligor unreasonable effort or expense; or
- (c) the performance consists in the provision of services or work of a personal character or depends upon a personal relationship, or
- (d) the aggrieved party may reasonably obtain performance from another source.

(3) The aggrieved party will lose the right to specific performance if it fails to seek it within a reasonable time after it has or ought to have become aware of the non-performance.

Article 9:103 Damages Not Precluded
The fact that a right to performance is excluded under this Section does not preclude a claim for damages."

NOTES

1. See also UNIDROIT, art.7.2.2.

2. These code articles are valuable in the way in which they summarise the rules regarding the situations where the remedy will not be granted. And note how these code articles recognise the difference between debt and specific performance. In English law, of course, this is a distinction between a common law debt claim and an equitable remedy (but *cf. Beswick v Beswick* (1968), below at p.564). Some of the principles attaching to specific performance are set out in the next extract.

Price v Strange **[1978] Ch.337, CA**

The question before the Court of Appeal in this case was whether a tenant could obtain an order for specific performance of an oral agreement with his landlord to grant a sub-lease. The tenant had performed a substantial part of his side of the agreement (which included certain repairs), but the trial judge dismissed the claim for specific performance for lack of mutuality at the date of the contract. That is to say, as the defendant could not have obtained specific performance in respect of her rights under the agreement, it would be inequitable for the remedy to be available to the other party. The Court of Appeal (Buckley, Scarman and Goff L.JJ.) allowed an appeal and ordered specific performance subject to certain terms.

Buckley L.J.: ". . . I will first deal with the question of mutuality. It is easy to understand that, as the equitable jurisdiction to enforce specific performance of contractual obligations developed, it should have become an accepted rule that equity would not compel one party to perform his obligations specifically in accordance with the terms of the contract unless it could also ensure that any unperformed obligations of the other party would also be performed specifically. For breaches of some kinds of contract, pre-eminently contracts for the sale of land, the common law remedy of damages was inadequate. The courts of equity consequently supplemented the common law by introducing the equitable remedy of specific performance, compelling the defendant to carry out his contract instead of penalising him in damages for failing to do so.

Considering the position *a priori* and apart from authority, it would seem that the questions which should be asked by any court which is invited to enforce specific performance of a contractual obligation should be: (1) is the plaintiff entitled to a remedy of some kind in respect of the alleged breach of contract? (2) if so, would damages be an adequate remedy? (3) if not, would specific performance be a more adequate remedy for the plaintiff? (4) if so, would it be fair to the defendant to order him to perform his part of the contract specifically? The first question goes to the validity and enforceability of the contract. Only if it is answered affirmatively do the subsequent questions arise. If the second question is answered affirmatively there is no occasion for equity to interfere, so that again the subsequent questions do not arise. If the second question is answered in the negative it will not necessarily follow that the third question must be answered affirmatively. For instance, the circumstances may not be such as to admit of specific performance, as where the subject-matter of the contract no longer exists. Only in the event of the third question arising and being answered in the affirmative can the fourth question arise. It is here, as it seems to me, that the alleged principle of mutuality comes in.

If one party were compelled to perform his obligations in accordance with the terms of the contract while the obligations of the other party under the contract, or some of them, remained unperformed, it might be unfair that the former party should be left to his remedy in damages if the latter party failed to perform any of his unperformed obligations. This is a consideration which bears on the appropriateness of specific performance as a remedy in the particular case; it has no bearing on the validity or enforceability of the contract, that is to say, on whether the plaintiff has a cause of action. A contract of which mutual specific performance cannot be enforced may yet afford a good cause of action for a remedy in damages at law . . .

The present case differs from any decided case . . . in this respect, that, although all the agreed repairs have been done, they have not all been done by the plaintiff. In my judgment, however, this is no bar to the plaintiff's right to a grant of the sub-lease in accordance with the contract. That the plaintiff did not do all the work was not due to any default of his; it was due to the defendant's unjustified repudiation of the contract. She was, in my opinion, clearly under an implied obligation not to prevent the plaintiff from performing his part of the contract, but she did so. This was an incident of her wrongful repudiation of her obligation to grant him a sub-lease. The financial consequences of the defendant's having carried out at her own expense work which under the contract should have been done by the plaintiff at his expense could be adjusted by appropriate accounts, enquiries and adjustments under the court's order. . . ."

QUESTIONS

1. Is mutuality a general principle of the law of contract itself?

2. Contracts for the sale of an interest in land had to be in writing (Law of Property Act 1925, s.40, now replaced by the Law of Property (Miscellaneous Provisions) Act 1989, s.2). Why was it, then, that equity was prepared to enforce the oral agreement in *Price v Strange*?

3. Can specific performance be ordered on behalf of a claimant who is not a party to the contract?

12.1.2 Specific performance and debt

We saw in the last chapter that the action for debt is in effect a claim for specific performance at common law where the obligation is to pay a sum of money. But what if for some reason the claim at common law is unenforceable?

Beswick v Beswick **[1968] A.C. 58, HL**

(For facts, see p.23.)

Lord Reid: ". . . [T]he respondent in her personal capacity has no right to sue, but she has a right as administratrix of her husband's estate to require the appellant to perform his obligation under the agreement. He has refused to do so and he maintains that the respondent's only right is to sue him for damages for breach of his contract. If that were so, I shall assume that he is right in maintaining that the administratrix could then recover only nominal damages, because his breach of contract has caused no loss to the estate of her deceased husband. If that were the only remedy available the result would be grossly unjust. It would mean that the appellant keeps the business which he bought and for which he has only paid a small part of the price which he agreed to pay . . .

I am of opinion that specific performance ought to be ordered . . ."

Lord Hodson: ". . . It is no part of the law that in order to sue on a contract one must establish that it is in one's interest to do so . . .

In such a case as this, there having been an unconscionable breach of faith, the equitable remedy sought is apt. The appellant has had the full benefit of the contract and the court will be ready to see that he performs his part . . ."

Lord Pearce: "My Lords, if the annuity had been payable to a third party in the lifetime of Beswick, senior, and there had been default, he could have sued in respect of the breach. His administratrix is now entitled to stand in his shoes and to sue in respect of the breach which has occurred since his death. It is argued that the estate can recover only nominal damages and that no other remedy is open, either to the estate or to the personal plaintiff. Such a result would be wholly repugnant to justice and commonsense. And if the argument were right it would show a very serious defect in the law . . .

The administratrix is entitled, if she so prefers, to enforce the agreement rather than accept its repudiation, and specific performance is more convenient than an action for arrears of payment followed by separate actions as each sum falls due. Moreover, damages for breach would be a less appropriate remedy since the parties to the agreement were intending an annuity for a widow; and a lump sum of damages does not accord with this; and if (contrary to my view) the argument that a derisory sum of damages is all that can be obtained be right, the remedy of damages in this case is manifestly useless. The present case presents all the features which led the equity courts to apply their remedy of specific performance. The contract was for the sale of a business. The appellant could on his part clearly have obtained specific performance of it if Beswick senior or his administratrix had defaulted. Mutuality is a ground in favour of specific performance. Moreover, the appellant on his side has received the whole benefit of the contract and it is a matter of conscience for the court to see that he now performs his part of it . . ."

Lord Upjohn: ". . . In this case the court ought to grant a specific performance order all the more because damages are nominal. [The defendant] has received all the property; justice demands that he pay the price and this can only be done in the circumstances by equitable relief . . ."

QUESTIONS

1. Was specific performance being employed to protect the interest of a stranger to the contract?

2. Is *Beswick* an unjust enrichment case?

12.1.3 Unreasonable expense

Specific performance may be refused in situations where it would operate in an economically inefficient manner.

Co-operative Insurance Society Ltd v Argyll Stores Ltd [1998] A.C. 1, HL

Lord Hoffmann: "My Lords . . . In this case . . . The appellant defendants, Argyll Stores (Holdings) Ltd ('Argyll'), decided in May 1995 to close their Safeway supermarket in the Hillsborough Shopping Centre in Sheffield because it was losing money. This was a breach of a covenant in their lease, which contained in clause 4(19) a positive obligation to keep the premises open for retail trade during the usual hours of business. Argyll admitted the breach and, in an action by the landlord, Co-operative Insurance Society Ltd ('CIS') consented to an order for damages to be assessed. But the Court of Appeal [1996] Ch 286, reversing the trial judge, ordered that the covenant be specifically performed. It made a final injunction ordering Argyll to trade on the premises during the remainder of the term (which will expire on 3 August 2014) or until an earlier subletting or assignment. The Court of Appeal suspended its order for three months to allow time for Argyll to complete an assignment which by that time had been agreed. After a short agreed extension, the lease was assigned with the landlord's consent. In fact, therefore, the injunction never took effect. The appeal to your Lordships is substantially about costs. But the issue remains of great importance to landlords and tenants under other commercial leases.

Specific performance is traditionally regarded in English law as an exceptional remedy, as opposed to the common law damages to which a successful plaintiff is entitled as of right. There may have been some element of later rationalisation of an untidier history, but by the 19th century it was orthodox doctrine that the power to decree specific performance was part of the discretionary jurisdiction of the Court of Chancery to do justice in cases in which the remedies available at common law were inadequate. This is the basis of the general principle that specific performance will not be ordered when damages are an adequate remedy. By contrast, in countries with legal systems based on civil law, such as France, Germany and Scotland, the plaintiff is prima facie entitled to specific performance. The cases in which he is confined to a claim for damages are regarded as the exceptions. In practice, however, there is less difference between common law and civilian systems than these general statements might lead one to suppose. The principles upon which English judges exercise the discretion to grant specific performance are reasonably well settled and depend upon a number of considerations, mostly of a practical nature, which are of very general application. I have made no investigation of civilian systems, but a priori I would expect that judges take much the same matters into account in deciding whether specific performance would be inappropriate in a particular case. . . .

. . . A principal reason [for regarding constant supervision as undesirable] is that . . . the only means available to the court to enforce its order is the quasi-criminal procedure of punishment for contempt. This is a powerful weapon; so powerful, in fact, as often to be unsuitable as an instrument for adjudicating upon the disputes which may arise over whether a business is being run in accordance with the terms of the court's order. The heavy-handed nature of the enforcement mechanism is a consideration which may go to the exercise of the court's discretion in other cases as well, but its use to compel the running of a business is perhaps the paradigm case of its disadvantages and it is in this context that I shall discuss them.

The prospect of committal or even a fine, with the damage to commercial reputation which will be caused by a finding of contempt of court, is likely to have at least two undesirable consequences. First, the defendant, who ex hypothesi did not think that it was in his economic interest to run the business at all, now has to make decisions under a sword of Damocles which may descend if the way the business is run does not conform to the terms of the order. This is, as one might say, no way to run a business. In this case the Court of Appeal made light of the point because it assumed that, once the defendant had been ordered to run the business, self-interest and compliance with the order would thereafter go hand in hand. But, as I shall explain, this is not necessarily true.

Secondly, the seriousness of a finding of contempt for the defendant means that any application to enforce the order is likely to be a heavy and expensive piece of litigation. The possibility of repeated applications over a period of time means that, in comparison with a once-and-for-all inquiry as to damages, the enforcement of the remedy is likely to be expensive in terms of cost to the parties and the resources of the judicial system.

This is a convenient point at which to distinguish between orders which require a defendant to carry on an activity, such as running a business over or more or less extended period of time, and orders which require him to achieve a result. The possibility of repeated applications for rulings on compliance with the order which arises in the former case does not exist to anything like the same extent in the latter. Even if the achievement of the result is a complicated matter which will take some time, the court, if called upon to rule, only has to examine the finished work and say whether it complies with the order. . . . This distinction between orders to carry on activities and to achieve results explains why the courts have in appropriate circumstances ordered specific performance of building contracts and repairing covenants. . . . It by no means follows, however, that even obligations to achieve a result will always be enforced by specific performance. . . .

There is a further objection to an order requiring the defendant to carry on a business, which was emphasised by Millett LJ in the Court of Appeal. This is that it may cause injustice by allowing the plaintiff to enrich himself at the defendant's expense. The loss which the defendant may suffer through having to comply with the order (for example, by running a business at a loss for an indefinite period) may be far greater than the plaintiff would suffer from the contract being broken. As Professor RJ Sharpe explains in 'Specific Relief for Contract Breach,' ch 5 of *Studies in Contract Law* (1980), edited by Reiter and Swan, p 129:

'In such circumstances, a specific decree in favour of the plaintiff will put him in a bargaining position vis-a-vis the defendant whereby the measure of what he will receive will be the value to the defendant of being released from performance. If the plaintiff bargains effectively, the amount he will set will exceed the value to him of performance and will approach the cost to the defendant to complete.'

This was the reason given by Lord Westbury LC in *Isenberg v East India House Estate Co Ltd* (1863) 3 De GJ S 263, 273 for refusing a mandatory injunction to compel the defendant to pull down part of a new building which interfered with the plaintiff's light and exercising instead the Court of Chancery's recently-acquired jurisdiction under Lord Cairns's Act 1858 (21 22 Vict. c 27) to order payment of damages. . . .

It is true that the defendant has, by his own breach of contract, put himself in such an unfortunate position. But the purpose of the law of contract is not to punish wrongdoing but to satisfy the expectations of the party entitled to performance. A remedy which enables him to secure, in money terms, more than the performance due to him is unjust. From a wider perspective, it cannot be in the public interest for the courts to require someone to carry on business at a loss if there is any plausible alternative by which the other party can be given compensation. It is not only a waste of resources but yokes the parties together in a continuing hostile relationship. The order for specific performance prolongs the battle. If the defendant is ordered to run a business, its conduct becomes the subject of a flow of complaints, solicitors' letters and affidavits. This is wasteful for both parties and the legal system. An award of damages, on the other hand, brings the litigation to an end. The defendant pays damages, the forensic link between them is severed, they go their separate ways and the wounds of conflict can heal.

The cumulative effect of these various reasons, none of which would necessarily be sufficient on its own, seems to me to show that the settled practice is based upon sound sense. Of course the grant or refusal of specific performance remains a matter for the judge's discretion. There are no binding rules, but this does not mean that there cannot be settled principles, founded upon practical considerations of the kind which I have discussed, which do not have to be re-examined in every case, but which the courts will apply in all but exceptional circumstances. . . .

CIS argued that the court should not be concerned about future difficulties which might arise in connection with the enforcement of the order. It should simply make the order and see what happened. . . . I think that it is normally undesirable for judges to make orders in terrorem, carrying a threat of imprisonment, which work only if no one inquires too closely into what they mean.

> ... Both landlord and tenant in this case are large sophisticated commercial organisations and I have no doubt that both were perfectly aware that the remedy for breach of the covenant was likely to be limited to an award of damages. The interests of both were purely financial: there was no element of personal breach of faith, as in the Victorian cases of railway companies which refused to honour obligations to build stations for landowners whose property they had taken: compare *Greene v West Cheshire Railway Co* (1871) LR 13 Eq 44. No doubt there was an effect on the businesses of other traders in the Centre, but Argyll had made no promises to them and it is not suggested that CIS warranted to other tenants that Argyll would remain. Their departure, with or without the consent of CIS, was a commercial risk which the tenants were able to deploy in negotiations for the next rent review. On the scale of broken promises, I can think of worse cases, but the language of the Court of Appeal left them with few adjectives to spare. . . .
>
> [Lords Browne-Wilkinson, Slynn, Hope and Clyde agreed with Lord Hoffmann that the appeal should be allowed.]"

QUESTIONS

1. Are there special rules for commercial contractors?

2. Did the defendants make a promise to the local community? Should they not have been estopped in equity from going back on this promise?

3. "When money talks people whisper" (graffiti in Swiss Cottage, London, 1970s). Discuss in relation to the law of remedies

4. Is *Argyle* an example of the theory of efficient breach of contract? (*Cf.* Cunnington (2006) 26 LS 369, at 384–9.)

12.1.4 Personal services

Equity will not grant specific performance to enforce a contract of personal services. Thus it will not normally specifically enforce a contract of employment: see e.g. *Page One Records Ltd v Britton* (1968); *Warren v Mendy* (1989).

12.1.5 Sale of land and other unique items

Equity normally will grant specific performance in all sale of land contracts, because land is regarded as a unique item. It is the availability of this remedy which creates, by ricochet, an equitable property right on behalf of the buyer of land after exchange of contracts but before conveyance of the title at common law. In fact it is not just land that attracts specific performance: a potential buyer who contracts to buy any unique item—say a rare *objet d'art*—may be granted specific performance if it can be shown that damages would be inadequate. See e.g. *Sky Petroleum Ltd v VIP Petroleum Ltd* (1974).

12.2 Injunction

Another key equitable remedy in contract is the injunction. This is in principle a negative remedy, in that it is an order forbidding a contractor from breaking his contract.

12.2.1 Nature of an injunction

Although an injunction is a court order, it remains nevertheless an independent remedy to be distinguished from, say, statutory orders.

Wookey v Wookey [1991] 3 W.L.R. 135, CA

Butler-Sloss L.J.: "... The grant of an injunction is a discretionary remedy derived from the equitable jurisdiction which acts *in personam* and only against those who are amenable to its jurisdiction; nor will it act in vain by granting an injunction which is idle and ineffectual. An injunction should not, therefore, be granted to impose an obligation to do something which is impossible or cannot be enforced. The injunction must serve a useful purpose for the person seeking the relief and there must be a real possibility that the order, if made, will be enforceable by the process *in personam*. However, the courts expect and assume that their orders will be obeyed and will not normally refuse an injunction because of the respondent's likely disobedience to the order."

NOTES

1. "It is obvious ... that there may be orders of the court which are not injunctions. The direction as to the removal of the children is such an order. It is neither an injunction nor in the nature of an injunction" (Lloyd L.J. in *In re P (Minors)* (1990), at 615).

2. "The High Court may by order (whether interlocutory or final) grant an injunction or appoint a receiver in all cases in which it appears to the court to be just and convenient to do so" (Supreme Court Act 1981, s.37(1)). This statutory rule does not allow a court to issue an injunction in every case where the court thinks it "just and convenient" to do so: see *Mercedes-Benz AG v Leiduck* (1996).

3. "If it appears that the debt is due and owing, and there is a danger that the debtor may dispose of his assets so as to defeat it before judgment, the court has jurisdiction in a proper case to grant an interlocutory judgment so as to prevent him disposing of those assets" (Lord Denning M.R. in *Mareva Compania Naviera v International Bulkcarriers* (1980), at 215).

12.2.2 Emergency (interlocutory) injunction

An interlocutory injunction is an emergency injunction obtained to preserve the status quo. The principles applicable to this type of injunction are set out in *American Cyanamid Co v Ethicon Ltd* (1975) (read in the law report).

12.2.3 Injunctions and contract

An injunction can be obtained in principle to prevent a party from breaching a contract.

Warner Brothers Pictures Inc v Nelson **[1937] 1 K.B. 209, KBD**

Branson J.: "The facts of this case are few and simple. The plaintiffs are a firm of film producers in the United States of America. In 1931 the defendant [Bette Davis] then not well known as a film actress, entered into a contract with the plaintiffs. Before the expiration of that contract the present contract was entered into between the parties. Under it the defendant received a considerably enhanced salary, the other conditions being substantially the same. This contract was for fifty-two weeks and contains options to the plaintiffs to extend it for further periods of fifty-two weeks at ever-increasing amounts of salary to the defendant . . . It is a stringent contract, under which the defendant agrees 'to render her exclusive services as a motion picture and/or legitimate stage actress' to the plaintiffs, and agrees to perform solely and exclusively for them. She also agrees, by way of negative stipulation, that 'she will not, during such time'—that is to say, during the term of the contract—'render any services for or in any other phonographic, stage or motion picture production . . . or engage in any other occupation without the written consent of the producer . . . '

In June of this year the defendant, for no discoverable reason except that she wanted more money, declined to be further bound by the agreement, left the United States and, in September, entered into an agreement in this country with a third person. This was a breach of contract on her part, and the plaintiffs . . . commenced this action claiming a declaration that the contract was valid and binding, an injunction to restrain the defendant from acting in breach of it, and damages . . .

I turn then to the consideration of the law applicable to this case on the basis that the contract is a valid and enforceable one. It is conceded that our courts will not enforce a positive covenant of personal service; and specific performance of the positive covenants by the defendant to serve the plaintiffs is not asked in the present case . . .

The defendant, having broken her positive undertakings in the contract without any cause or excuse which she was prepared to support in the witness box, contends that she cannot be enjoined from breaking the negative covenants also . . .

The conclusion to be drawn from the authorities is that, where a contract of personal service contains negative covenants the enforcement of which will not amount either to a decree of specific performance of the positive covenants of the contract or to the giving of a decree under which the defendant must either remain idle or perform those positive covenants, the court will enforce those negative covenants; but this is subject to a further consideration. An injunction is a discretionary remedy, and the court in granting it may limit it to what the court considers reasonable in all the circumstances of the case . . .

The case before me is, therefore, one in which it would be proper to grant an injunction unless to do so would in the circumstances be tantamount to ordering the defendant to perform her contract or remain idle or unless damages would be the more appropriate remedy.

With regard to the first of these considerations, it would, of course, be impossible to grant an injunction covering all the negative covenants in the contract. That would, indeed, force the defendant to perform her contract or remain idle; but this objection is removed by the restricted form in which the injunction is sought. It is confined to forbidding the defendant, without the consent of the plaintiffs, to render any services for or in any motion picture or stage production for any one other than the plaintiffs.

It was also urged that the difference between what the defendant can earn as a film artiste and what she might expect to earn by any other form of activity is so great that she will in effect be driven to perform her contract. That is not the criterion adopted in any of the decided cases. The defendant is stated to be a person of intelligence, capacity and means, and no evidence was adduced to show that, if enjoined from doing the specified acts otherwise than for the plaintiffs, she will not be able to employ herself both usefully and remuneratively in other spheres of activity, though not as remuneratively as in her special line. She will not be driven, although she may be tempted, to perform the contract, and the fact that she may be so tempted is no objection to the grant of an injunction . . .

I think . . . that an injunction should be granted . . .”

NOTES

1. Normally a court of equity will not enforce a contract of employment, but in *Warner v Nelson* the injunction was negative in its effect. It did not positively force the film star to work for the plaintiffs; she was just prohibited from working for anyone else in breach of her contract with the studio.

2. It is not just the parties to a contract who have the right to seek the remedy of an injunction: public interest bodies such as the Office of Fair Trading have statutory power to intervene to ensure compliance with regulatory texts. See

e.g. the Unfair Terms in Consumer Contracts Regulations 1999 (SI 1999/2083), reg.12; the Consumer Protection (Distance Selling) Regulations 2000 (SI 2000/2334), reg.27.

3. See also *Thomas Marshall Ltd v Guinle* (1979) (above, p.436).

QUESTION

Ought any private person or organisation to be given power to seek an injunction against a party abusing its contractual rights or power? (*Cf.* Unfair Terms in Consumer Contracts Regulations 1999, reg.12(2).)

12.3 Rescission

Another fundamental equitable remedy is rescission of a contract. This will normally be granted where a contract has been induced by misrepresentation, duress or undue influence. Rescission in equity was also available in cases of mistake, but this has now been suppressed (see *The Great Peace* (2003), above at p.259). Rescission is available as a result of statute: see e.g. the Electronic Commerce (EC Directive) Regulations 2002 (SI 2002/2013), reg.15. According to the modern case law rescission is also available at common law for fraud and duress (see *Halpern v Halpern (No.2)* (2006), at § 3). In addition to rescission, statute might also grant a right to terminate a contract: see e.g. the Consumer Credit Act 1974, ss.99 and 101. (See generally **10.3**.)

12.4 Rectification

See **5.3.4**.

12.5 Cancellation

Cancellation is probably an equitable remedy that exists in addition to rescission (see J. Tiley, *A Casebook on Equity and Succession* (Sweet & Maxwell, 1968), pp.140–2), but its importance today is as a statutory remedy. Some statutes give a contractor the right to cancel a contract during what is sometimes called a "cooling-off period" (see Consumer Credit Act 1974, s.68). Examples of such statutory cancellation rights are to be found in: Consumer Credit Act 1974, s.67; Timeshare Act 1992, s.5 (see also Timeshare (Cancellation Information) Order 2003 (SI 2003/2579), reg.3); Consumer Protection (Distance Selling) Regulations 2000 (SI 2000/2334), reg.10; Financial

Services (Distance Marketing) Regulations 2004 (SI 2004/2095), reg.9. One might care to reflect the extent to which this statutory remedy impacts upon the binding nature of contracts.

12.6 Self-help remedies

Self-help remedies require no intervention by the court. The aggrieved party is, in short, "taking justice into his own hands". Such remedies include rescission, termination, set-off and liens.

12.6.1 Rescission

See **12.3** above.

12.6.2 Refusal to pay

See *Vigers v Cook* (1919) (p.453); *Bolton v Mahadeva* (1972) (p.454). But *cf. Hoenig v Isaacs* (1952) (p.446); *Ruxley Electronics v Forsyth* (1996) (p.442).

12.6.3 Termination for breach

See **10.4**.

12.6.4 Set-off

Set-off is a remedy that applies mainly to debts. Where two contracting parties both owe each other money, one party can, if the two debts are connected, set off the other's debt against his own debt and pay over just the difference between the two. The history and general principles that apply to this remedy are discussed in *Eller v Grovecrest Investments Ltd* (1994). See also PECL, Ch.13 and UNIDROIT, Ch.8. Note that banking could not function without this device of set-off. For those interested in the civil law, Professor Pichonnaz, of Fribourg University, has written an exhaustive study of set-off (*compensatio*) in the civil law from Roman to modern times: *La compensation* (Éditions Universitaires Fribourg Suisse, 2001).

PROBLEM

Paula buys an expensive washing machine from Mitch's Machines Ltd using her credit card. The washing machine explodes after the third use and damages clothes and surrounding property. Can Paula set off the cost of all this against her credit card bill? What if the "Conditions of Use" in the credit card contract contains a clause denying the right of any credit card holder to use the remedy of set-off? (*Cf.* Consumer Credit Act 1974, s.75; *Stewart Gill Ltd v Horatio Myer Co Ltd* (1992).)

12.6.5 Lien

A lien is a possessory right attaching to another's property. It may arise as a result of certain types of contract. Full details of this self-help remedy can be found in Diplock L.J.'s judgment in *Tappenden v Artus* (1964).

12.7 Declaration

The remedy of declaration is one where a claimant asks the court simply to state the rights of the parties. It can sometimes be important in contract: see e.g. *Barton v Armstrong* (1975) (at p.281). For a discussion of the remedy of declaration, see *In re S (Hospital Patient: Court's Jurisdiction)* (1995). Note that statute may grant jurisdiction to a court to make declarations with regard to certain matters: see e.g. the Consumer Credit Act 1974, s.142.

12.8 Proprietary and similar remedies

Mention must briefly be made of some other remedies that can be relevant for contract lawyers. These are the remedies of tracing and the like, and subrogation. From a functional point of view these remedies can probably be seen as monetary, yet from a structural or conceptual point of view they are not actually orders by the court for one party to pay money to another. They are remedies that take as their object a "thing" (*res*), with the purpose of establishing a relationship between this thing and the claimant. The two remedies will be dealt with only in outline as they belong more to the law of restitution than to contract.

12.8.1 Tracing

Tracing was once thought to be a remedy, but recent dicta, following academic writing by restitution lawyers, have now demoted it to a "process" (see Millet L.J. in *Boscawen v Bajwa* (1995)). The term was once used as a name for an action that allowed a claimant to assert ownership in money or in some other object in another's patrimony. It was a money remedy *in rem*. The claimant was entitled to the money simply because he was owner either at common law or in equity (see F.H. Lawson, *Remedies of English Law*, 2nd edn (Butterworths, 1980), pp.147–60). The essence of tracing as a process is captured in s.305 of the Proceeds of Crime Act 2002 (research in the library).

What is confusing is that there are seemingly two such remedies—one at common law and the other in equity (see *Agip (Africa) Ltd v Jackson* (1990, Ch D); (1991, CA)). The common law version is confusing, because the actual cause of action is the quasi-contractual debt claim of an action for money had and received, and this of course is an *actio in personam*. Accordingly, the judges have rethought tracing as some kind of "process" so as to distinguish it from causes of action (see *Lipkin Gorman v Karpnale* (1991)). With the development of unjust enrichment as an independent normative principle in the common law, it may be that this is now the actual *cause of action*, leaving the action for money had and received as the debt *remedy*. Tracing in equity was more liberal in its scope (see Millet J. in *Agip v Jackson* (1990)), but normally had to be a fiduciary relationship between the claimant and the defendant. Again, the judges seem to be distinguishing between tracing as a process and the cause of action in equity underpinning the actual proprietary claim. This cause of action is a constructive trust and the proprietary claim that arises from it (*Foskett v McKeown* (2001)). Statute, as we have mentioned, also makes use of the tracing remedy or process: see Proceeds of Crime Act 2002, s.305.

12.8.2 Admiralty action *in rem*

In admiralty law there exists an actual *actio in rem* which can be brought against a ship. Details of this remedy can be found in Lord Steyn's judgement in *Republic of India v India Steamship Co (No.2)* (1998). The original Roman *actio in rem* was an action against the thing itself; consequently the thing, or some representative part of it, had to be in court (G.4.16–17). Later Roman thinking saw these actions as being against the possessor of the thing. Equity has recently developed a kind of *in rem* injunction that is analogous to the admiralty *in rem* remedy.

Allen v Jambo Holdings Ltd [1980] 2 All E.R. 502, CA

Lord Denning M.R.: ". . . It is a new case altogether. In the past *Mareva* injunctions have been confined to the commercial court. The judges of that court have granted injunctions to restrain foreign companies from removing moneys so as to defeat their creditors . . . But this is new. Not because it concerns an aircraft. There was one case where an aircraft ran up a bill for fuel. Its bill was not paid. The aircraft was restrained from moving until it was paid. But this is the first case we have had of a personal injury (this is a fatal accident case) where a *Mareva* injunction has been sought. The nearest parallel is a ship in an English port where there is an accident causing personal injuries or death. It has been settled for centuries that the claimant can bring an action *in rem* and arrest the ship. She is not allowed to leave the port until security is provided so as to ensure that any proper claim will be duly met. The question in this case is whether a similar jurisdiction can be exercised in regard to an aircraft. In principle I see no reason why it should not, except that it is to be done by a *Mareva* injunction instead of an action *in rem* . . ."

NOTE

Mareva injunctions are now called freezing injunctions. See above, **12.1.2**.

12.8.3 Subrogation

Subrogation is a remedy by which one person comes to "stand in the shoes" of another person. It is of particular importance in cases where insurance companies are parties to an action in the law of obligations (see *Orakpo v Manson Investments Ltd* (1978)). It is best understood as an institutional structure rather than as a remedy defined and governed by rules. It concerns the relationship between *persona* (legal subject) and *res* (legal object), and it is a means by which one legal object (*res*) is substituted for another legal object (real subrogation) or one legal subject (*persona*) is substituted for another legal subject (personal subrogation). It was probably imported into the common law from the civil law, the notion having been perfected by the Post-Glossators in the 14th century. Today subrogation is now regarded as an unjust enrichment remedy.

Boscawen v Bajwa **[1995] 4 All E.R. 769, CA**

Millett L.J.: "... Subrogation ... is a remedy, not a cause of action (see Goff and Jones *Law of Restitution* (4th edn, 1993 pp 589ff, *Orakpo v Manson Investments Ltd* [1978] AC 95 at 104 per Lord Diplock and *Re TH Knitwear (Wholesale) Ltd* [1988] Ch 275 at 284 per Slade LJ). It is available in a wide variety of different factual situations in which it is required in order to reverse the defendant's unjust enrichment. Equity lawyers speak of a right of subrogation, or of an equity of subrogation, but this merely reflects the fact that it is not a remedy which the court has a general discretion to impose whenever it thinks it just to do so. The equity arises from the conduct of the parties on well-settled principles and in defined circumstances which make it unconscionable for the defendant to deny the proprietary interest claimed by the plaintiff. A constructive trust arises in the same way. Once the equity is established the court satisfies it by declaring that the property in question is subject to a charge by way of subrogation in the one case or a constructive trust in the other. . . ."

12.9 Orders

Statutory orders must be distinguished from injunctions: Lloyd L.J. in *In re P (Minors)* (1990), at 615 (above, p.570). Statute may empower a court to make, for example, a restitution order: see e.g. the Financial Services and Markets Act 2000, s.382; Pensions Act 2004, s.16. And these orders are clearly different from injunctions: see s.380 of the 2000 Act. In the field of credit and security the powers of the court to make orders are quite extensive.

Consumer Credit Act 1974 (c.39)

"127. Enforcement orders in cases of infringement
(2) If it appears to the court just to do so, it may in an enforcement order reduce or discharge any sum payable by the debtor or hirer, or any surety, so as to compensate him for prejudice suffered as a result of the contravention in question. . . .

137. Extortionate credit bargains
(1) If the court finds a credit bargain extortionate it may reopen the credit agreement so as to do justice between the parties."

FINAL NOTES

1. The extract above is given simply as an example of the flavour of a statutory power granted to a court to make orders in respect of certain types of contract (and see further Lord Nicholls in *Wilson v First County Trust Ltd (No.2)* (2004) (above, at p.114). However, there is a more substantial point that might be made as a final observation to this collection of edited materials on contract. An increasing number of contracts are no longer governed just by the concepts, principles, rules and remedies developed by the judges; they are *regulated* by ever-more detailed legislative texts, such as the Consumer Credit Act 1974 and the Consumer Protection (Distance Selling) Regulations 2000, both of which, one might note, allow consumers to escape from the binding effect of the contract (*cf.* **8.1**) within a "cooling-off" period (and thus functionally modifying the whole concept of contract formation). The consumer can treat the contract "as if it had not been made" (Consumer Protection (Distance Selling) Regulations 2000, reg.10(2)). This may be a good thing or a bad thing, depending upon one's ideological point of view, but what needs to be emphasised here is that the common law general theory of contract is being modified to a considerable extent by such regulatory texts. The result is that contract as a classic area of private law is itself being transformed by public interest directives, often themselves provoked by EU Directives (the "constitutionalisation" of private law: see C. Joerges (1998) 18 LS 146). There are, accordingly, two levels of operation with respect to contract in the context of economic law: there are the classic general principles which find expression in, for example, textbooks on contract, the PECL and UNIDROIT; and there are the detailed regulations to be found in EU Directives and in UK Acts and statutory instruments.

2. This duality within contract as a body of knowledge is important in that the application of principles and concepts, on the one hand, and detailed regulatory texts, on the other hand, often requires different methodologies. It would be tempting to say that the application of regulatory texts is more formal in a logical sense (*cf.* **2.5.2**), and to an extent this can be true where the

rule uses clear-cut concepts based on mathematical calculations (see e.g. Consumer Protection (Distance Selling) Regulations 2000, reg.19) or technical language, the interpretation of which is either open to little doubt or is very tightly controlled by legislative "dictionaries" (see e.g. Consumer Credit Act 1974, s.189). However, such regulatory texts can equally grant quite wide discretionary powers with respect to certain defined matters such as extortionate credit bargains (see extract above). Nevertheless, regulatory texts are intended to impose themselves on tightly described factual situations in a way that general propositions, such as those found in precedents and codes, are not. Precedents and codes are models intended to provide a relatively secure foundation for arriving at solutions through *judgment*, in respect of factual situations that can be wide and varied in their possibilities (see extract from Dworkin, above p.101). Regulation, in contrast, is about the imposition of a defined economic or social policy on factual matters that are, normally, more constrained in their possibilities (e.g. certain specific types of transaction). When precedent and principle apply it is the judges who are speaking, but when regulation imposes itself it is the legislature which commands.

3. One effect of intermixing wide discretion with defined and limited types of transaction is that methodical concepts and notions need to be rethought. Perhaps one concept that becomes central in this dichotomy between private agreement and public regulation is that of an "interest". Thus, for example, individual interests need to be played off against the more general interests of consumers (*cf.* Treaty of Rome 1957 (revised), art.153), although the two interests can easily become confused within the notion of "commercial interest" (see e.g. *Director General of Fair Trading v First National Bank plc* (2002), above at p.131). Contract, in other words, needs now to be viewed from several interest positions: there are the private interests of each party; the institutional interests of status groups (e.g. consumers) and large institutions (e.g. banks); and there are the public interest perspectives attaching to public bodies like the Office of Fair Trading. On this private and public interest question, see S. Waddams, *Dimensions of Private Law* (CUP, 2003), pp.191–221.

SOME FINAL QUESTIONS (GENERAL REFLECTIONS ON CONTRACT)

1. Which interests were favoured by the law of contract in the following cases: *Director General of Fair Trading v First National Bank plc* (2002) (p.131); *Bolton v Mahadeva* (1972) (p.454); *Ruxley Electronics v Forsyth* (1996) (p.442); *Blackpool & Fylde Aero Club v Blackpool BC* (1990) (p.177); *Barclays Bank v O'Brien* (1994) (p.297); *Co-operative Insurance Society Ltd v Argyll Stores Ltd* (1998) (p.566). Imagine that in each of these cases the court wished to promote a different interest: using the law of contract, can you formulate a different judgment giving expression to this different interest?

2. The medieval civilian jurists came to distinguish two ideas within the Roman law materials devoted to contractual performance, namely, *impossibilia* and

579

difficultas. Are these two different ideas still to be found in the modern English law of contract? Are they to be found in the PECL and in UNIDROIT as well? If so, is the distinction still of value, or should it be abandoned?

3. What role does causation play in the law of contract as a whole?

4. Are parties to a contract under a duty to behave reasonably with respect to the formation, contents, performance and the use of remedies of contract?

5. Are consumers regarded as contractual parties lacking full capacity?

6. In tort cases an appeal to policy is quite common. Is this less true of contract cases; and, if so, why?

INDEX

LEGAL TAXONOMY
FROM SWEET & MAXWELL

This index has been prepared using Sweet and Maxwell's Legal Taxonomy. Main index entries conform to keywords provided by the Legal Taxonomy except where references to specific documents or non-standard terms (denoted by quotation marks) have been included. These keywords provide a means of identifying similar concepts in other Sweet & Maxwell publications and online services to which keywords from the Legal Taxonomy have been applied. Readers may find some minor differences between terms used in the text and those which appear in the index. Suggestions to *taxonomy@sweetandmaxwell.co.uk*.

(All references are to paragraph number)